The Major Nation-States in the European Union

The Major Nation-States in the European Union

J. Richard Piper
University of Tampa

New York   San Francisco   Boston
London   Toronto   Sydney   Tokyo   Singapore   Madrid
Mexico City   Munich   Paris   Cape Town   Hong Kong   Montreal

Executive Editor: Eric Stano
Acquisitions Editor: Edward Costello
Senior Marketing Manager: Elizabeth Fogarty
Supplements Editor: Kristi Olson
Managing Editor: Bob Ginsberg
Production Manager: Joseph Vella
Project Coordination, Text Design, and Electronic Page Makeup: Electronic Publishing
    Services Inc., NYC
Cover Design Manager: John Callahan
Cover Designer: Kay Petronio
Cover Illustration: PictureQuest
Senior Manufacturing Buyer: Dennis J. Para
Printer and Binder: Phoenix Color Corp.
Cover Printer: Phoenix Color Corp.

Photo Credits: **Page 44** Getty Images, Inc./Hulton∣Archive Photos; **107** AP/Wide World
Photos; **121** Getty Images, Inc./Hulton∣Archive Photos; **154** Markus Matzel/Das
fotoarchiv/Peter Arnold, Inc.; **169** David Gadd/Sportsphoto Agency/Getty Images,
Inc./Hulton∣Archive Photos; **199** AP/Wide World Photos; **218** AFP/Getty Images,
Inc./Agence France Presse; **241** AP/Wide World Photos; **262** Homer Sykes/Woodfin Camp
& Associates; **290** Getty Images, Inc./Hulton∣Archive Photos; **307** AP/Wide World Photos.

Library of Congress Cataloging-in-Publication Data

Piper, J. Richard, 1946-
  The major nation-states of the European Union / J. Richard Piper.
    p. cm.
  Includes bibliographical references and index.
  ISBN 0-321-10642-3
  1. European Union—Politics and government. 2. European Union countries—
Relations. 3. European Union countries—Politics and government—20th century. 4.
European Union countries—Politics and government—21st century. I. Title.
  D1060.P517 2005
  341.242'2'09—dc22
                                      2004021997

Please visit us at http://www.ablongman.com

ISBN 0-321-10642-3

1 2 3 4 5 6 7 8 9 10—PBT—08 07 06 05 04

CONTENTS

7 GERMANY   139

8 GERMANY AND THE EUROPEAN UNION   163

13   SPAIN   281

14   SPAIN AND THE EUROPEAN UNION   302

ABBREVIATIONS AND ACRONYMS

AP	Popular Alliance (Spain)
AWS	Solidarity Electoral Action (Poland)
BDA	Federation of German Employer Associations
BDI	Federation of German Industry
CAP	Common Agricultural Policy
CBI	Confederation of British Industry
CCOO	Workers' Commissions (Spain)
CDU/CSU	Christian Democratic Union/ Christian Social Union (Germany)
CEOE	Spanish Confederation of Employers' Organizations
CESDP	Common European Security and Defense Policy
CFI	Court of First Instance (European Union)
CFSP	Common Foreign and Security Policy
CGIL	Italian General Confederation of Labor
CISL	Italian Confederation of Workers' Unions
CiU	Convergence and Union (Catalonia/Spain)
CNAG	National Agricultural and Livestock Farmers Federation (Spain)
COPA	Confederation of Professional Agricultural Organizations (EU)
COREPER	Committee of Permanent Representatives (EU, in French)
DBV	League of German Farmers
DGB	German Confederation of Labor
DIHT	German Industrial and Trade Conference
EC	European Community (or Communities)
ECB	European Central Bank
ECJ	European Court of Justice
ECOFIN	Economic and Financial Council (European Union)
ECSC	European Coal and Steel Community
EDC	European Defense Community
EEC	European Economic Community
EFTA	European Free Trade Association
EH	Euskal Herritarrok (Basque Country/Spain, in Basque language)
ELDR	European Liberal Democratic Reform party
EMS	European Monetary System
EMU	Economic and Monetary Union
ENA	National School of Administration (France)
ENI	National Hydrocarbons Agency (Italy)
EPC	European Political Community (proposed in 1950s)
EPC	European Political Cooperation (1970s to early 1990s)
EPP	European People's party

ERDF	European Regional Development Fund	OECD	Organization for Economic Cooperation and Development
ERM	Exchange Rate Mechanism	OPZZ	National Trade Union Accord (Poland)
ERT	European Roundtable of Industrialists	PC	Popular Coalition (Spain)
ESCB	European System of Central Banks	PCE	Spanish Communist party
		PCF	French Communist party
ESDI	European Security and Defense Identity	PDS	Party of Democratic Socialism (Germany)
ETA	Basque Homeland and Liberty (Basque Country/Spain)	PES	Party of European Socialists
ETUC	European Trade Union Confederation	PHARE	Poland, Hungary: Assistance for Economic Reconstruction
EU	European Union	PNV	Basque Nationalist party
Euratom	European Atomic Energy Community	PP	Popular party (Spain)
		PR	proportional representation
FDP	Free Democratic party (Germany)	PR	Republican Pole (France)
		PRG	Left Radical party (France)
FI	Forza Italia! (Italy)	PS	Socialist party (France)
FN	National Front (France)	PSOE	Spanish Socialist Workers' party
FNSEA	National Federation of Agricultural Unions (France)	QMV	qualified majority voting
		RPF	Rally for France
GATT	General Agreement on Tariffs and Trade	RPR	Rally for the Republic (France)
		SEA	Single European Act
GDP	gross domestic product	SLD	Democratic Left Alliance (Poland)
INI	National Institute of Industry (Spain)	SPD	Social Democratic party (Germany)
IRI	Institute for Industrial Reconstruction (Italy)	TUC	Trades Union Congress (United Kingdom)
IU	United Left (Spain)	UCD	Union of the Democratic Center (Spain)
JHA	Justice and Home Affairs	UDF	Union for French Democracy
KGB	Committee for State Security (Soviet Union)	UGT	General Union of Workers (Spain)
LO	Workers' Struggle (France)	UIL	Italian Union of Labor
MDC	Movement of Citizens (France)	UMP	Union for a Presidential Majority (France)
MEDEF	Movement of French Enterprises	UNICE	Union of Industrial and Employers' Confederations of Europe
MEP	Member of the European Parliament		
NAFTA	North American Free Trade Agreement	WEU	Western European Union
NATO	North Atlantic Treaty Organization	WTO	World Trade Organization

LIST OF FIGURES, MAPS, AND TABLES

PREFACE

The Major Nation-States in the European Union is a text designed primarily for American students in political science, history, economics, or general social science courses who are eager to learn about the European Union (EU) and the major nation-states that are its members: France, Germany, Italy, Poland, the United Kingdom, and Spain. Unlike most other texts on contemporary Europe, it aims to integrate fully analyses of the European Union with those of its major component states rather than focusing primarily either on the EU or on the nation-states.

This book comes into print at a time when the European Union is undergoing major transformations, with a newly proposed constitution under debate and ten new member states having just joined the EU on May 1, 2004, bringing its membership overnight to 25 states from 15. It also comes into print at a time when the transatlantic partnership between Europe and the United States is undergoing new strains, reflected in the recent Iraq War but also present on a variety of worldwide issues including global warming, the International Criminal Court, and trade.

Against the backdrop of these exciting developments, this book aims to provide students with an understanding of the historical background, institutions, leaders, and participatory structures and processes that shape contemporary Europe and its relations with the United States and the rest of the world. The text is organized into three parts and 16 chapters, with an appendix that highlights active learning possibilities through a European Union simulation. The first part of the book, focused on the European Union, provides an introductory overview (Chapter One), followed by chapters on the historical development (Chapter Two), current institutions and leaders (Chapter Three), and public policies (Chapter Four) of the EU. The second part of the book emphasizes the five major nation-states of the pre-2004 European Union: France, Germany, Italy, the United Kingdom, and Spain. For each of these nation-states, an initial chapter discusses the development, governmental institutions, and participatory structures and processes of the country in question; a second chapter on each nation-state emphasizes the relationship between that country and the European Union. The third and final part of the book provides in Chapter Fifteen a comparative overview of all 15 states that were members of the EU before 2004, placing the five major states in a broad comparative context and enabling readers to gain an understanding of the importance of the smaller member states of the EU also. Chapter Sixteen emphasizes Poland as the newest major nation-state in the European Union, in the context of discussing the dramatic eastward expansion of the EU and the possible future roles of Turkey and Russia vis-à-vis the EU. Finally, the appendix offers suggestions concerning active learning through a simulation of the European Union and its major nation-states.

Among the unique features of this book are its readability, its frequent highlighting of quotations to humanize the text, and its "People in the EU" boxes on prominent Europeans and their contributions. To enhance accessibility for students who may be unfamiliar with certain European or social-science terms, key concepts appear in **bold print** on first usage and are defined clearly in the Glossary beginning on page 384. Each chapter begins with a quotation pertaining to its main themes, and several key quotations are highlighted to add a human dimension. The "People in the EU" boxes, accompanied in most cases by pictures, bring home to students the special impact of such European leaders as Margaret Thatcher, the British prime minister who presaged a movement toward free markets in both Europe and the United States; Jean-Marie Le Pen, the French nationalist who shook up French and European politics by coming in second in the French presidential election of 2003; and Romano Prodi, the former Italian prime minister who became president of the European Commission during a time of unusual turbulence.

This volume is dedicated to my wife and daughter, who have tolerated my long hours in the library and at the computer during the research and writing processes; to Katherine Bishop, who helped with the research in the early stages; and to my students, who have provided many useful suggestions when I have given them drafts of this text to read as class assignments. I would also like to thank the following reviewers and editors for their feedback and other assistance as this book took shape— Michael Baun, Valdosta State University; Williams Downs, Georgia State University; Erich Frankland, Casper College; Margaret Gonzalez-Perez, Southeastern Louisiana University; Kerstin Hamann, University of Central Florida; Gunther M. Hega, Western Michigan University; Reinhard Heinisch, University of Pittsburgh; William Kubik, Hanover College; Myron A. Levine, Albion College; Layna Mosley, University of Notre Dame; Steven D. Roper, Eastern Illinois University; James Walsh, UNC-Charlotte; and Chris Van Aller, Winthrop University. Last, I would like to thank the University of Tampa, which granted me a sabbatical leave to complete much of the research and writing of this book.

J. RICHARD PIPER

Chapter 1

THE MAJOR NATION-STATES IN THE EUROPEAN UNION: AN INTRODUCTION

"We need to build a union of hearts and minds, a shared sense of common destiny, of European citizenship."
—Romano Prodi, President of the Commission of the European Union, 2000,
New York Times, January 29, 2000, A17.

Despite some superficial resemblance to the United States of America (USA), the European Union (EU) is not a United States of Europe equivalent to the USA. It is also unlikely to become such an entity in the near future. The European Union is unique in its combination of features that enable it to make some decisions at an institutional level "above" its member states **(supranational)** while at the same time operating in many respects as an **intergovernmental** organization of highly distinctive nation-states that retain their own national identity and supreme power (known as **sovereignty**) over a particular territory and population in many domains. The futile efforts by European Union leaders to forge a common EU response to the United States of America's policies on Iraq in 2002–2003 illustrate clearly the distinction between the EU and the United States. While the Bush administration prepared to attack the regime of Saddam Hussein, the United Kingdom (Britain) provided staunch support and urged similar backing from the European Union, of which Britain is a prominent member. Spain and Italy, also EU members, eventu-

ally joined the United States and Britain but offered only qualified support. At the same time, France and Germany, long the leading nation-states in the EU, vehemently opposed American-British plans and actions and sought to rally both European and world opinion against them. Because the European nation-states possess distinctive cultures, languages, and histories that make them much more different from one another than are the fifty states of the United States of America, it is not surprising to find that these nation-states have often proved reluctant to surrender some of their sovereignty and have often found it impossible to develop common policies, as the Iraq case demonstrates.

However, a common desire to achieve peace among nation-states that had formerly fought increasingly terrible wars with one another and to achieve prosperity comparable to that in the United States of America have spawned the numerous supranational, and partially supranational, features of the contemporary EU. These features are quite evident even in the face of the policy divergences within the EU over the Iraq War. The member states of the EU have ceded far more authority to EU

1

institutions than the United States, Canada, and Mexico have ever considered giving up to such institutions through the North American Free Trade Agreement (NAFTA). As a result, Europe has moved much further toward supranational institutions than any other region of the world, whether it be North America, South America, Africa, or Asia. The European Parliament, for example, stands as the globe's only supranational representative body to which citizens of the member nation-states elect representatives through competitive elections and direct popular vote. On many public policy matters, including agricultural, trade, business competition, and environmental policies, the European Union has demonstrated impressive unity and a consistent ability to develop coherent common actions that are often quite distinctive from those of the United States.

The EU is important due to its size and impact on global politics and economics, as well as because of its unique combination of supranational and intergovernmental features. For example, multinational business corporations based in the United States have sometimes found their planned activities thwarted by the European Union if they wish to operate within its borders (as almost all do, because of the size and wealth of the EU). In July 2001, the EU blocked a proposed merger between General Electric and Honeywell corporations on grounds that it violated EU competition rules, even though the United States Department of Justice had approved the merger of these two American-based corporations. Increasingly, American business executives must be closely attuned to the European Union, because in many ways it can affect their operations. With the establishment of a European Central Bank (ECB) and the adoption of the euro as the common currency of twelve EU members, the European Union's collective impact on the global political economy is almost certain to rise above its already significant level. Already, the euro is beginning to challenge the supremacy of the American dollar as the prime currency of international exchange. Moreover, there are signs that the European Union is about to enhance its global political-military influence, too, as it moves toward developing a European Security and Defense Identity (ESDI).

During their rich histories, the major component nation-states of the contemporary EU have shaped many features of our modern world; and they continue to exert significant independent influence. For example, English conceptions of liberty grounded in such historic documents as the Magna Carta of 1215, in which the English nobles compelled King John to give formal recognition to a number of individual rights, have profoundly shaped American and global political thought. French Revolutionary ideas about national citizenship from the late 1780s and the 1790s have significantly changed global conceptions of nationalism and the nation-state. A resurgence of ideas stressing free-market economics became evident in Margaret Thatcher's Britain in the late 1970s, presaging an ideological wave that would sweep across most of the world in the next two decades. As a negative model, Adolf Hitler's Nazi regime in Germany has left an indelible record of gruesome inhumanity, from which most people around the world continue to recoil in horror. Therefore, not only the European Union but also its major nation-states merit the attention of every serious student of politics and economics.

INTERGOVERNMENTAL AND SUPRANATIONAL ASPECTS OF THE EUROPEAN UNION

"Europe will be stronger precisely because it has France in as France, Spain in as Spain, Britain in as Britain, each with its own customs, traditions, and identity," British Prime Minister

Margaret Thatcher declared in 1988 as she fiercely resisted what she feared were trends toward too much supranationalism in Europe.[1] Previously, in 1962, then President Charles de Gaulle of France had phrased his intergovernmental vision in even stronger terms: "There is and can be no Europe other than a Europe of the States—except, of course, for myths, fictions, and pageants."[2] Despite the strong views and strenuous efforts of such leaders as President Charles de Gaulle of France and Prime Minister Margaret Thatcher of Britain, both of whom strongly favored an intergovernmental approach that would leave almost all power in the hands of such member state governments as France and Britain, the European Union has become in some respects a supranational organization (often described as **federal,** though the latter term indicates a sharing of powers between at least two levels of government, in this case the EU and the nation-state and perhaps the states within the nation-state) that often impinges on its member states' policy preferences and institutions. However, the EU remains far from the "union of hearts and minds" aspired to by Romano Prodi, the current President of the European Commission. A Eurobarometer public-opinion survey conducted in October and November 2002 in all member countries of the EU found that 90 percent of the respondents felt very attached to their own country, while only 45 percent expressed a similar attachment to the European Union.[3]

"Europe will be stronger precisely because it has France in as France, Spain in as Spain, Britain in as Britain, each with its own customs, traditions, and identity."

British Prime Minister Margaret Thatcher, 1988, *cited by Timothy Bainbridge, The Penguin Companion to European Union, 1998, 27.*

". . . there is and can be no Europe other than a Europe of the States—except, of course, for myths, fictions, and pageants."

French President Charles de Gaulle, 1962, *cited by John Pinder, The European Union, 2001, 13-14.*

The reasons for the unique mixture in the EU lie in the differing perceptions and mixed motives of Europeans themselves concerning European integration. Obviously, many have perceived potential benefits, such as peace, trade expansion, and an enhanced environment, that may result from pooling sovereignty in European institutions instead of attempting to tackle all global problems primarily at the level of medium-sized and small nation-states, as in the past. The advent of the global preeminence of the United States of America (and for a time, the Soviet Union) and the spread of multinational corporations, often based outside of Europe, have been among the factors fostering such thinking. Reflection on World Wars I and II, which devastated Europe but grew out of the preexisting nation-state system, also has contributed, as have memories of the nationalistic excesses of Hitler in Germany and Mussolini in Italy.

However, many European governmental leaders, groups, and individual citizens feel a deep attachment to their nation-states and/or advantages that they derive from their nation-states. They may be willing to pool sovereignty on a limited basis but desire to maintain their nation-state as an important arena for decision-making. President Charles de Gaulle, Prime Minister Margaret Thatcher, and others of similar inclination have voiced this intergovernmental approach to European integration. The Eurobarometer survey of European public opinion cited previously indicates that national attachments remain much stronger than European attachments among most contemporary Europeans.

On the other hand, many other European officials, groups, and individuals have perceived that extensive pooling of sovereignty, perhaps a United States of Europe on a federal model similar to the United States of America, is desirable. Romano Prodi and many EU officials take this perspective, as do many leaders, groups, and citizens, particularly in nation-states that are seeking to escape their recent pasts (such as the Nazi experience in Germany under Adolf Hitler or the Fascist experience in Italy under Benito Mussolini) or that are too small to achieve many objectives on their own in the contemporary global environment (Luxembourg, for example). They advance the supranational approach or a modified federal version of it.

Then there are many Europeans who mix the supranational and intergovernmental approaches, depending upon the particular issue at hand and how they believe that pooling sovereignty or leaving it at the nation-state level will affect their own interests. For example, even Margaret Thatcher, a committed devotee of intergovernmental approaches, was willing to accept some supranationalism (generally in a federal framework) in order to achieve a European single market that accorded well with her free-market ideology and that she perceived to be in the interests of Britain and especially British business. In practice, such mixes have been widespread. One EU commissioner recently summed up the views of many of his colleagues: "I have never thought of Europe as an end in itself. I have always considered Europe to be a means to achieve certain political ends. . . . Europe is like a playground of Lego blocks where one stacks pieces upon one another, and that makes it possible to build a nice house."[4] The result has been the complex combination of supranational and intergovernmental elements that is evident in the contemporary European Union.

> "I have never thought of Europe as an end in itself. I have always considered Europe to be a means to achieve certain political ends. . . . Europe is like a playground of Lego blocks where one stacks pieces upon one another, and that makes it possible to build a nice house."
>
> EU Commissioner quoted by Liesbet Hooghe, *The European Commission and the Integration of Europe*, 2001, 215.

One prominent comparative politics analyst has aptly described the European Union as "a political system but not a state."[5] By this statement, he and similar commentators have meant that the European Union possesses a stable set of institutions for collective decision-making. Moreover, there exists a pattern of inputs, policy outputs, and feedback that Gabriel Almond, David Easton, and other political scientists have identified as characteristic of a political system.[6] However, they have also meant to indicate that the European Union's central institutions for transforming inputs into outputs lack the monopoly on the legitimate use of coercion that has usually been seen as the essential feature of a state, such as the United States of America, France, or Germany. There, military and police powers, backed by a wide sense of belonging to a "nation" deserving of loyalty and support as well as acceptance of the constitutional **democratic** procedures employed to channel inputs and produce outputs, combine the force and legitimacy largely absent in the EU. Despite proposals to grant such a monopoly in some spheres to the EU, such a development is occurring only on a very limited basis, in the case of the EU rapid reaction force. Because most member state leaders remain jealous of their prerogatives over military and police powers, and because public opinion in Europe does not now sufficiently embrace a union of hearts and minds (or even accept EU procedures as democratic), a monopoly for EU governance institutions on the legitimate use of coercion remains unlikely in the foreseeable future.

In its contemporary form, the European Union makes many common public policies for 470 million people (380 million before May 1, 2004), compared with 293 million people in the United States, and generates a **gross domestic product** (GDP)—the total value of the goods and services produced by the economy of an entity in a year, excluding the income of the residents that is derived from investment abroad—slightly smaller than the GDP of the United States. Even in policy domains where the national governments retain most of the authority, such as social welfare, actions by the EU often constrain national independence. Italy, for example, has recently slashed welfare spending to reduce its governmental debt and deficits enough to qualify for inclusion in the common euro currency.

At the same time, however, the European Union is an intergovernmental organization retaining the features highlighted by de Gaulle and Thatcher or evident on the Iraq issue in 2002–2003. The member state governments retain the legal monopoly on the use of legitimate force with the exception of the 60,000-member EU rapid reaction force that is just taking shape. The nations also possess distinctive political traditions and senses of history, national political parties and interest groups, and publics that are generally far more attached to their national identities and more attentive to national issues than they are to the EU and European issues.

THE MAJOR NATION-STATES IN THE EUROPEAN UNION

Of the 15 member states in the pre-2004 European Union, 5—Germany, France, the United Kingdom, Italy, and Spain—are significantly larger than the others in population and gross domestic product. Three—Germany, France, and the United Kingdom—have far outweighed the others in power on the global scene and within Europe. Each of the "big three" has made unique contributions to the development of the European Union, and Italy and Spain also have been significant shapers of the EU of today. Poland, the largest of the 2004 entrants (similar to Spain in population but much smaller in gross domestic product), will bring some distinctive new contributions into the process. Table 1.1 indicates the contemporary populations of the 15 member states of the pre-2004 European Union. Table 1.2 compares the populations, gross domestic products, and per capita gross domestic products of the five major member states in the pre-2004 European Union with those of Poland, Turkey, and Russia, and

TABLE 1.1   The Nation-States of the European Union, 2003

Nation-state	Population estimate (2003)
Germany	83,251,851
United Kingdom	59,778,002
France	59,765,983
Italy	57,715,625
Spain	40,077,100
Netherlands	16,067,754
Greece	10,645,343
Belgium	10,274,595
Portugal	10,084,245
Sweden	8,876,744
Austria	8,169,929
Denmark	5,368,854
Finland	5,183,545
Ireland	3,883,159
Luxembourg	448,569
EU TOTAL	379,591,298

Source: World Almanac, 2003.

TABLE 1.2   GDP and Per Capita GDP of the Major Pre-2004 EU Member States in Comparative Perspective

Major pre-2004 EU nation-states, Poland, Russia, Turkey, the United States, and the EU

Nation-state/EU	Population (million)	GDP (trillion)*	Per capita GDP*
France	60	$1,654	$27,500
Germany	83	2,271	27,600
Italy	58	1,552	26,800
Spain	40	886	22,000
United Kingdom	60	1,664	27,700
Poland	39	427	11,000
Russia	144	1,287	8,900
Turkey	69	455	6,700
United States	293	10,980	37,800
European Union	380	9,916	26,100

The smaller 10 EU nation-states

Nation-state/EU	Population (million)	GDP (trillion)*	Per capita GDP*
Austria	8	246	30,000
Belgium	10	298	29,000
Denmark	5	168	31,200
Finland	5	142	27,300
Greece	11	212	19,900
Ireland	4	117	29,800
Luxembourg	0.4	25	55,100
Netherlands	16	461	28,600
Portugal	10	182	18,000
Sweden	9	238	26,800

Source: *CIA World Fact Book,* 2003. EU totals tabulated by author.

*GDP and GDP figures are calculated using the purchasing power parity method, which takes into account the differences in what a dollar will actually purchase in each country.

those of the United States. Map 1.1 shows the locations of the pre-2004 EU states, the 2004 entrants, and the four additional states accepted by the EU as candidates for accession.

France played the biggest role in shaping the initial proposals for the European Coal and Steel Community (predecessor of the current EU), largely because its leaders wished to contain and channel a resurgent Germany that they had come to believe was inevitably going to emerge and wanted to use European integration as a means for Franco-German reconciliation. Moreover, France, long a major agricultural exporter but also facing high domestic political and economic costs in trying to modernize and bolster its relatively large agricultural sector on

MAP 1.1 Europe, the European Union Nation-States, and Nation-States Named as Accession Candidates indefinite

its own, has heavily influenced and protected the most expensive public policy of the EU, the Common Agricultural Policy (CAP). Farming has been more than an economic pursuit for France, however. It has been an integral part of a French heritage that emphasizes distinctive wines and cheeses and well-preserved medieval farming villages. Proud of its status for centuries as a global Great Power and facing a world in which factors beyond its leaders' control were operating to diminish that status, France has often viewed European integration as a vehicle for the French to provide political leadership, increasingly in conjunction with Germany.

Germany has usually served as the primary economic motor for the EU, reflecting the fact that it has had the largest gross domestic product of any member state since it underwent an economic miracle in the 1950s and 1960s. Because it has had economic clout and has also adhered to a long-term policy of low inflation that others have increasingly sought to emulate, Germany has played a particularly large role in influencing first the European Monetary System (EMS) and then the Economic and Monetary Union (EMU). Germany has also led or at least supported most of the drives toward European supranational or federal development. Initially hesitant to assert political leadership due to concerns that such assertion would revive its neighbors' bitter memories of past German aggression, German leaders have seen supranational development of European institutions as a means of "escaping into Europe" while obtaining many German goals through collective action.

The United Kingdom has proved more aloof than France or Germany, largely because of its island location off the shores of the continent of Europe; its economic, cultural, and political ties to the United States and its Commonwealth (former Empire); and its long history of independence from long-term alliances. However, global trader Britain, which reembraced its own traditions of free markets and

private enterprise with particular vigor after 1979, has successfully pushed the EU in the direction of freer trade and more business competition, albeit aided by United States encouragement and economic globalization pressures.

Despite its equivalence in size to France and the United Kingdom, Italy has generally enjoyed less influence in the EU than has Germany, France, or Britain. However, at least in the rhetoric of its leaders, it has been unusually consistent in pushing for further European integration since the early 1950s, even if it has often lagged in implementing supranational endeavors.

As for Spain, a relative latecomer to the EU (in 1986), it has played a leading role in shaping European regional and cohesion policies and has often forcefully spoken on behalf of other member states having lower per capita wealth than the founders of the European Communities. It has also proved a useful bridge between the European Union and Latin America.

Among the new entrants, Poland dwarfs all of the others in population and gross domestic product, though in the latter respect it remains far behind the five largest countries of the pre-2004 EU. While its impact on the EU remains to be seen, it is likely to bolster British efforts to promote transatlantic ties to the United States; and its large agricultural sector is likely to be a factor nudging the EU toward further modifications of its Common Agricultural Policy, if only to keep expenditures from soaring.

While each major member state has influenced the contemporary European Union, each also has found its own governmental institutions and political processes increasingly altered by the Europe beyond its own national boundaries—sometimes in unforeseen ways. For example, the European Court of Justice has not only impacted national laws and legal processes. It has also encouraged the development of **judicial review** (the power of courts to overrule or uphold the constitutionality of legislation or executive actions) in member states previously lacking such a tradition, including the United Kingdom, which has a largely unwritten constitution that assigned very limited political roles to its courts prior to British entry into the European Community.

National chief executives and cabinet ministers have become mediators between European Union institutions and various national political actors, sometimes enhancing the executives' powers (especially at the expense of national parliaments) but at other times causing them massive political headaches, as British prime ministers Margaret Thatcher and John Major (see Chapter Twelve) discovered. In Thatcher's case, her alienation of European leaders became an issue that her rivals inside her party employed to remove her as prime minister. In Major's case, European issues virtually destroyed his ability to govern by dividing his party between supporters and opponents of the treaty establishing the European Union.

Political issues pertaining to the EU have often been at the center of national partisan conflicts and have sometimes split major national parties. The British Conservative party of Major and Thatcher, referred to above, is but one example of a split within a major national party over European issues. The French Gaullist party has in recent years suffered a somewhat similar division, as has the British Labour party in the past. As for splits between parties or clusters of parties, Italy was one of several countries that witnessed a sharp division in the late 1940s and the 1950s between the parties of the government and the opposition Socialist and Communist parties over European integration issues.

EU initiatives have spawned new interest groups. For instance, a variety of new anti-integration groups emerged in both France and Britain in the early 1990s to mobilize popular opposition to the treaty establishing the EU. Moreover, because multinational corporations are by their very nature better positioned than labor unions or most voluntary citizen interest groups to operate on a transnational basis, and because they also possess vast economic resources and the talented lawyers and other advisers to master the intricacies of European Union decision-making processes, many analysts believe that European integration has often benefited large corporate interests over those of other groups.

THE AIMS AND STRUCTURE OF THIS BOOK

This book is about the European Union and its five major member nation-states. It aims to be concise but clear enough to introduce the subject to an American student audience. Key terms with which many students may be unfamiliar are highlighted in bold print and are defined in a glossary at the end of the text. This book will consider the European Union as the supranational organization that it has partially become, albeit one with multiple tiers of government and one less closely knit than a federal nation-state, such as the United States or Canada. However, this book will also consider the EU in terms of the intergovernmental organization composed of separate nation-states that it partially remains and is likely to be for some time to come.

Chapters Two through Four offer an overview of the European Union, examining its development in the broad context of modern European history, its major institutions, and its major public policies. Drawing upon theoretical frameworks widely employed in political science and related disciplines, Chapter Two sets the stage for examination of contemporary institutions in Chapter Three and public policies in Chapter Four.

Chapters Five through Fourteen examine each of the five major nation-states in the current European Union. The lead chapter on France, Germany, Italy, the United Kingdom, and Spain in each pair of two chapters features discussion of the political development of the nation-state in question, its governmental institutions, and its political processes. In analyzing political development, it focuses on the historical "crises" of development outlined by Gabriel Almond and G. Bingham Powell: nation-building and state building, participation (development of modern constitutional democratic processes), and distribution (evolution of modern economies and responses to globalization).[7] Each lead chapter also analyzes contemporary governmental institutions (executive leaders and bureaucracies, legislatures, judiciaries, and subnational governments) and the political processes involving political parties, interest groups, and elections that at least purport to link a democratic citizenry to their governments.

The second chapter on each major nation-state emphasizes that country's relations with the European Union. In each case, it examines the historical development of the relationship, assesses the most distinctive long-term features of that nation-state's approaches to the Union (as well as features that have shifted significantly), evaluates the impact of that country on the European Union, and draws conclusions about the effects of EU membership on the government and politics of the nation-state.

Following a chapter that compares and contrasts the other ten pre-2004 nation-states of the EU with the five major members and illustrates general patterns, the final chapter of the book deals with the issues raised by the expansion of the EU, focuses on Poland as the major nation-state that has just joined the EU, discusses why Turkey (despite being officially accepted in 1999 by the EU as an "accession candidate") and Russia are unlikely to join Poland in the near future, and suggests general conclusions about the European Union and its major nation-states.

Taken as a whole, this book provides a solid foundation of knowledge for students who wish to understand the significance of the forces that have been reshaping Europe for the past one-half century and that promise to continue building a "new Europe" in the years to come. Far more than most texts on the subject, it integrates analysis of the European Union with a focus on the major nation-state components of the EU, in the belief that one cannot really understand contemporary Europe without considering it as a whole. Supranational development in Europe has been remarkable but remains constrained by deep-rooted national differences. Through its emphasis on both the European Union and the major nation-states that comprise it, this text highlights the continuing intergovernmental aspects of the EU while also demonstrating how the Europeanizing forces generated by the supranational institutions and public policies of the EU have substantially affected its member states. The overriding aim of this text is to equip its readers to be effective citizens of the world in the twenty-first century. The European Union and its major member states are simply too important to ignore.

SUMMARY

- The European Union is unique among international organizations in its mixture of supranational and intergovernmental features.

- Widespread European desires to achieve prosperity and peace after the Great Depression of the 1930s and World War II (1939–1945) stimulated the movement toward European integration that has led to the European Union of today.

- European nation-states in the EU retain many distinctive political and cultural characteristics and continue to make unique contributions.

- Such national leaders as Charles de Gaulle of France and Margaret Thatcher of the United Kingdom have represented important voices in defense of national sovereignty in Europe.

- France has usually viewed European integration as a vehicle for France to provide leadership (often in conjunction with Germany), and it has played the largest role in shaping and maintaining the EC/EU's Common Agricultural Policy.

- Germany has sought to "escape into Europe" after a nineteenth- and twentieth-century history of assertive German nationalism and has spurred most drives toward further European supranational development.

- The United Kingdom initially resisted European integration and has remained the most aloof member of the EU and the member most closely associated with the United States.

- Italy has generally enjoyed less influence in the EU than member states of similar size; although it has usually urged supranational development, its record of implementing EC/EU actions has been spotty.

- Spain, which joined the EC only in 1986, has played a leading role in shaping European regional and cohesion policies and relations with Latin America.

- Poland, by far the largest of the 2004 EU entrants, poses special challenges to the EU because of its large agricultural sector, rel-

atively undeveloped economy, fears of Russia, and close ties to the United States.

- The European Union influences the internal political institutions, processes, and policies of its member states and at the same time is shaped by the distinctive inputs of its member states.

ENDNOTES

1. Cited by Timothy Bainbridge, *The Penguin Companion to European Union*, 2nd ed. (London: Penguin, 1998), 27.
2. Cited by John Pinder, *The European Union: A Very Short Introduction* (Oxford: Oxford University Press, 2001), 13–14.
3. Eurobarometer, field work conducted Oct.–Nov. 2002.
4. Quoted by Liesbet Hooghe, *The European Commission and the Integration of Europe: Images of Governance* (Cambridge: Cambridge University Press, 2001), 215.
5. Simon Hix, *The Political System of the European Union* (New York: St. Martin's, 1999), 2.
6. Gabriel A. Almond, "Comparing Political Systems," *Journal of Politics* 18, 2 (1956), 391–409; David Easton, "An Approach to the Study of Political Systems," *World Politics* 9, 5 (1957), 383–400, and *A Framework for Political Analysis* (Englewood Cliffs, NJ: Prentice-Hall, 1965).
7. Gabriel A. Almond and G. Bingham Powell, *Comparative Politics: A Developmental Approach* (Boston: Little, Brown, 1966), 34–41.

Chapter 2

THE DEVELOPMENT OF THE EUROPEAN UNION

"Europe has never existed. It is not the addition of national sovereignties in a conclave that creates an entity. One must genuinely *create* Europe."
—Jean Monnet, often described as the "father" of the modern European Union, 1952, *cited by Elizabeth Knowles, Twentieth Century Quotations (1998), 270.*

This chapter is about the efforts to create Europe, a process that continues today as the European Union drafts a new constitutional treaty as its governing document and undertakes a dramatic eastward enlargement, adding ten new members in 2004. The story is truly a momentous one, representing perhaps the most dramatic large-scale transformation of the past half-century in international politics; but it remains an unfinished story.

Europe gave birth to most of our contemporary conceptions of what it means to be "modern" or "developed": the nation-state, democracy, and both capitalistic and socialistic versions of economic modernity. However, it also gave rise to aggressive nationalism and genocide, leading noted author Mark Mazower to term it the "dark continent" (with a touch of irony in that Europeans have traditionally assigned that label to Africa). Since World War II, the continent that first spawned the nation-state has moved further than any other area of the world to develop a Union that entails substantial pooling of sovereignty among its nation-states and has sought to adapt the institutions of that Union to evolving modern con-

ceptions of democracy and an increasingly global, market-oriented, economy. Why and how the European Union has developed as it has are the prime topics of this chapter. However, the first step is to place the emergence of the European Union in its appropriate context by discussing briefly the historical backdrop: the emergence of European nation-states, democracy, and capitalistic and socialistic versions of modernity.

THE EMERGENCE OF EUROPEAN NATION-STATES, DEMOCRACY, CAPITALISM, AND SOCIALISM

Europe was the birthplace of the concept of state sovereignty and nation-states. Jean Bodin, a French political philosopher of the sixteenth century, is usually credited as the father of the modern notion of sovereignty, or supreme authority vested in the state.[1] Even before Bodin, however, a number of European monarchs had succeeded in asserting authority over territories roughly comparable to those of modern nation-states, amid the tangled web of political jurisdictions (often overlapping) that prevailed in Europe after the fall of the Roman Empire (476). Sizeable monarch-dominated territorial states had emerged gradually during the Middle Ages, often in tandem with developing broad popular senses of shared history and culture and eventually "national" languages. Between about 1000 and 1600, England and France became preeminent examples of such development. Yet even there, the type of national identity and citizenship associated with modern nation-states did not flourish until the era of the French Revolution and Napoleon I (1789–1815), with pockets of resistance even after that time. The process occurred even later in Southern, Central, and Eastern Europe. Therefore, the modern nation-states have been a relatively recent phenomenon, even in Europe, where they first appeared. The incompleteness is due not only to resistance by minority "nations" to assimilation into a dominant national identity but also to immigration into European nation-states of new groups possessing distinctive national-ethnic identities and revival of once latent national-ethnic feelings among some groups.[2]

Democracy possesses much earlier origins in European history than does the nation-state, because democracy in the sense of "rule by the people" (its literal meaning in ancient Greek), through direct participation of citizens in town meetings, dates back to ancient Athens in the fifth century before the Christian era. However, **authoritarian** governments, dominated by unelected executives subject to few constraints but lacking the nearly total control over society claimed by modern **totalitarian** governments, prevailed in European political life in most locales most of the time until the twentieth century. Moreover, the ancient Greek form of democracy had not assigned priority to protecting individual rights, had made no provisions for representation, and had

established no "constitutional" checks and balances among governmental institutions, all key elements of most modern conceptions of constitutional democracy.[3]

The English Magna Carta (1215) and Parliament (late thirteenth century) provided early but limited models for modern constitutional democratic concepts of guaranteed rights and political representation. The Levellers of the English Civil War (1642–1649) revived and modernized a participatory version of democracy, while the Diggers of the same period advanced an early version of socialistic democracy. However, both groups were unsuccessful in their own time, succumbing to the superior power of parliamentary and military elites led by Oliver Cromwell.[4] Even the French Revolution of 1789–1799, despite its importance in the development of modern democracy, gave rise in the short term to a new form of authoritarian government under Napoleon I.[5] Modern **constitutional democracies**, possessing universal suffrage, competitive elections, and extensive protections of individual rights, were to take shape on a wide basis in Europe only in the early twentieth century, within the framework of emergent nation-states. Moreover, they developed in a long "wave" that swept from northwestern Europe across the Continent in the nineteenth and early twentieth centuries and then receded after World War I, only to advance again in a "second wave" after World War II and then a "third wave" after 1974.[6]

Capitalism, a set of ideas and an economic system based on private ownership of property, pursuit of material gain, and market exchanges of goods and services, emerged gradually out of the European feudal system that prevailed in most of Europe during the Middle Ages. **Feudalism** lacked the capitalistic idea of material gain as a normal pursuit of daily life and operated primarily through agricultural manors, where most of the population lived and worked as serfs to the lords of the manors. In the towns and the few existing cities, guilds tightly organized the daily lives of artisans. As Robert Heilbroner has emphasized, "society ran by custom and tradition. The lords gave orders, and production waxed and waned accordingly."[7]

[Before the capitalist revolution] "society ran by custom and tradition. The lords gave orders, and production waxed and waned accordingly."

Economist Robert Heilbroner,
The Worldly Philosophers (1972), 27.

The capitalist "revolution" began transforming the basic feudal patterns in Europe long before it came to be conceptualized clearly. It did not crystallize into a clear model until Adam Smith, a Scottish philosopher, articulated it as such in his *Wealth of Nations*, originally published in 1776. Yet in its various forms, capitalism was to reshape Europe and the world during the nineteenth and twentieth centuries.[8]

In the political field, **classical liberal** ideologies, advocating free-market capitalism under the slogan of laissez-faire (leave us alone), served as the foundation of some of the new political parties and interest groups developing in a democratizing Europe. Particularly in northwestern Europe, classical liberal parties and interest groups enjoyed wide support from the rising business and professional classes in society. However, traditional aristocrats and established church leaders (especially Roman Catholic Church leaders) advanced a **traditional conservative** ideology, usually suggesting the need for some governmental and religious constraints on capitalist development to curb excessive materialism and sustain those who were left behind by free-market competition. Meanwhile, Karl Marx, Pierre-Joseph Proudhon, Beatrice and Sidney Webb, and others spawned a powerful European **socialist** movement in the nineteenth century that envisioned a modernity based on common ownership of property and social and economic equality, rather than the capitalism of Adam Smith or the classical liberal parties and interest groups. Socialists nearly always drew strong support from the labor union movement that was emerging in Europe. "The **proletarians** [members of the working class] have nothing to lose but their chains. They have a world to win. Working men of all countries, unite!" proclaimed Karl Marx and Friedrich Engels; and many workers in Europe responded to their call and similar calls from other socialist leaders. From the mid-nineteenth century onward, struggles over distribution and the nature of economic modernity in the democratizing nation-states of Europe came commonly to take the form of a partisan and interest group struggle in which the **"left"** (socialist and later communist parties and allied labor unions) pressed for some form of socialistic modernity, the **classical liberals** in the "center" or "center-right" advocated capitalistic modernity, and the **traditional conservatives** of the **"right"** invoked traditionalism (usually including religion) to restrain capitalism and avoid socialism. Though capitalistic patterns of private ownership, markets, and pursuit of profits came to predominate in modern Western Europe, these were substantially modified after the 1880s by expanding social welfare programs that provided a social safety net of unemployment compensation, pensions, and health care for much of the population, often reflecting compromises among socialists, liberals, and conservatives. Eventually, considerable consensus developed in support of a European version of economic modernity that also involved considerable regulation and steering of national economies by national governments. The result has been what many observers have termed **"mixed economies"** that blend elements of classical liberal capitalism with governmental social welfare programs and regulations.[9]

"The proletarians [members of the working class] have nothing to lose but their chains. They have a world to win. Working men of all countries, unite!"

Karl Marx and Friedrich Engels,
Communist Manifesto (1848).

Amid pressures of nation-building, democratization, and economic modernization, intense political-economic-military rivalries among the major European states (mostly nation-states by the late 1800s, though Austria and Russia remained multi-ethnic empires into the twentieth century) led to periodic wars that proved increasingly disruptive of political, economic, and social life. Although a **multipolar balance of power** system (multiple power centers checking and balancing one another's power) among major European states came to structure global politics from the Peace of Westphalia in 1648 into the twentieth century, World War I (1914–1918) and World War II (1939–1945) illustrated the sometimes devastating consequences of organizing European life around a nation-state system in which governmental leaders regularly sought to mobilize their national citizens for the use of force to redress grievances emergent from developmental crises and/or past wars.

After World War I, a few European leaders, such as Aristide Briand of France, sought to move Europe beyond nationalism to a United States of Europe. Briand called for "a system of federal union fully compatible with respect for traditions and for the characteristics peculiar to each people," but to little effect. The Great Depression of 1929–1939 sparked intensifying nationalism and sharp nation-state political, military, and economic conflicts on the road to World War II. After 1945, as West Europeans surveyed the massive destruction and loss of lives from the two world wars, pondered the political and economic successes of the United States of America, and faced diminishment of their influence in a **bipolar** world of two superpowers (the United States and the Soviet Union) confronting each other globally in a Cold War, an increasing number of their leaders began to consider seriously ideas of pooling sovereignty and downplaying at least some aspects of nationalism. Some proffered visions of a United States of Europe, either established on a **federal** basis with central institutions sharing powers with states (roughly on the American model) from the outset or brought about by a **functionalist** approach in which member states would pool sovereignty in only a few select sectors, with cooperation "spilling over" gradually into others, creating "ever closer union."[10]

". . . the understanding between European nations must be brought about . . . under a system of federal union fully compatible with respect for traditions and for the characteristics peculiar to each people."

French Foreign Minister Aristide Briand, 1932, *cited in Timothy Bainbridge, The Penguin Companion to European Union (1998), 23.*

EARLY STEPS TOWARD WEST EUROPEAN INTEGRATION, 1945–1958

A widespread desire to avoid future world wars spawned by European nation-state conflicts played a major part in stimulating increased interest in European integration after World War II. Such feeling was particularly strong in France and Germany, which had fought each other in the Franco-Prussian War of 1870, World War I, and World War II. The new chancellor of West Germany emphasized in a speech to his parliament in November 1949, "The Franco-German question is truly the keystone in the development of Europe." Desire to avoid another European war was also very strong in Italy, which had gained little from being on the winning side in World War I and had lost in World War II under Mussolini before abandoning its alliance with Nazi Germany. Belgium, the Netherlands, and Luxembourg, small nation-states that had been major World War II battlegrounds, were, of course, looking for means to avoid future Franco-German battles on their territory.

"The Franco-German question is truly the keystone in the development of Europe."

West German Chancellor Konrad Adenauer, November 15, 1949, *cited by F. Roy Willis, France, Germany, and the New Europe (1971), 66.*

However, other geopolitical considerations, stressed especially by **realist** analysts (who focus on nation-states and their geopolitical "national interests"), also came into play in Western Europe. These included a French wish to contain West German power, a West German goal of escaping its Nazi past and finding reliable European allies, and an Italian desire to regain respectability. The common perceived threat to West European governments posed by the Soviet bloc and the domestic Communist (and at times, as in Italy, Socialist) parties aligned with it further encouraged increased cooperation among the West European leaders. Moreover, the United States—now the superpower of the West in the confrontation with the Soviet Union and Communism—was nudging Western Europe toward integration by making European Recovery Program (Marshall Plan) assistance contingent on cross-national cooperation and by bringing many West European nation-states (but not initially West Germany) into the North Atlantic Treaty Organization (NATO), a collective security organization in which all members pledged to come to the defense of one another if threatened by external Communist attack. Therefore, West European integration ideas came to be linked to a high degree with notions of "the West" versus "the East" in an increasingly bipolar world, as well as with desires to enhance national security, resuscitate national reputations, and avoid repetition of wars among West European nation-states.[11]

Political-economic concerns, of the type emphasized by **liberal intergovernmental** theorists (who, like the realists, focus on nation-state leaders' motivations but assign highest priority to political-economic objectives and their bases in the major economic interest groups within nation-states) also exerted great influence propelling West European leaders toward integration after World War II. There was growing agreement among national political and business leaders in Western Europe that freer trade among them would lead to economies of scale and allow each country to specialize in the production of goods and services for which it was best equipped (what economists term **comparative advantage**). As the wealthiest country in the postwar world, the United States offered a model for economic success; and many West Europeans sought to emulate its large market with unrestricted trade inside its boundaries. Moreover, the power of the United States and its clear preference for freer trade and West European (and American) memories of the trade wars of the 1930s and their role in sparking World War II came into play in creating a political-economic environment conducive to West European economic integration efforts. As opportunities for industrial trade expanded in the early 1950s, increased numbers of West European leaders saw potential benefits in trade liberalization. However, as liberal intergovernmental analysts have correctly emphasized, each West European nation-state assigned high priority to its own industrial, commercial, and agricultural interests, backed by strong producer interest groups. Meshing these in a common European community would prove difficult and would shape the distinctive forms that integration would take in Western Europe, though environmental political-economic incentives to cooperate eased the path to integration.[12]

The European Coal and Steel Community (ECSC), founded in 1951 by France, West Germany, Italy, Belgium, the Netherlands, and Luxembourg (the latter three commonly referred to as the Benelux countries), and going into effect in 1952, represented the first major step toward the establishment of what has become the European Union. Jean Monnet, a French planning official, was the chief "father" of the proposal for the ECSC. Though Monnet promulgated a vision of a United States of Europe based upon **functionalism,** the chief immediate precipitator of his specific ECSC proposal was a Franco–West German crisis over the lifting of Allied restrictions on West German industrial recovery. Sparked by Cold War fears, Britain and the United States had overcome French objections and insisted on reviving West German industrial might. Seeing the likely resulting destruction of his Modernization Plan for the French economy, Monnet sought to cope with the new situation by proposing a supranational coal and steel organization that would foster the prosperity of these heavy industries in both major European countries. Robert Schuman, France's foreign minister at the time, took the lead in putting the proposal into action, in the form of the "Schuman Plan," publicly unveiled in a speech on May 9, 1950, after gaining the approval of both West German Chancellor Konrad Adenauer and the United States government. Italy and the Benelux countries soon joined with France and West Germany in negotiations to establish the European Coal and Steel Community.[13]

However, the British government, headed by Prime Minister Clement Attlee at the time—more interested in its economic ties to its former empire (now the British Commonwealth), its "special relationship" with the United States, and its internal political-economic projects than

in new European ties—showed no interest in joining the newly proposed Community. Neither did the Nordic countries of Denmark, Norway, Iceland, and Sweden, though they formed a loose cooperative Nordic Council among themselves in 1952, with Finland joining in 1955. Spain remained ostracized by West European governments for its dictatorship under Francisco Franco (1939–1975) and its Nazi-Fascist sympathies during World War II. It pursued for a time a policy of economic self-sufficiency, or **autarky,** without notable success. Thus, the movement toward the eventual European Union began with a core of six nation-states. Jean Monnet became the first chairperson of the **High Authority** (the leading executive body) of the new European Coal and Steel Community, responsible for formulating and overseeing the common market in coal and steel. The Council of Ministers, representing the six member nation-states' separate interests, was to act as a brake on supranationalism within the ECSC, beginning what would prove to be a long-term pattern in the European Community/European Union.[14]

On October 24, 1950, influenced again by Monnet, the French government proposed that the six move toward further cooperation by establishing a European Defense Community (EDC), which would develop a common defense policy. Anglo-American pressure for West German rearmament in the struggle against Soviet bloc Communism and West German Chancellor Adenauer's suggestion of shared sovereignty in the defense realm lay behind this French initiative. Subsequently, at the suggestion of Italy, the EDC proposal came to incorporate a proposed European Political Community (EPC) also.

However, this European Defense Community idea aroused considerable opposition, especially inside France itself. The EDC treaty was eventually killed in 1954 by a vote in the French National Assembly to postpone consideration of it indefinitely, in the midst of widespread

French concerns over West German remilitarization and strong Soviet opposition to the EDC. As the European Defense Community proposal died, the efforts to establish a supranational political authority (EPC), which would encompass the EDC and the ECSC and move into other policy areas as well, also collapsed. The Western European Union (WEU) took shape as a loose, intergovernmental organization including Britain and detached from the ECSC and supranational aspirations. However, the North Atlantic Treaty Organization, dominated by the United States and also intergovernmental in structure, was to play the leading role through the Cold War in coordinating West European and North American defense efforts. At this point, the movement toward European integration shifted back to the political-economic sphere and away from the military-political sphere that had proved highly contentious.[15]

At a meeting in Messina, Italy, in June 1955, the foreign ministers of the six ECSC member states adopted a proposal for the further integration of the members' economies. Belgium, the Netherlands, and Luxembourg, the three smallest member states of the ECSC, played the largest roles in initiating the groundwork and leading the preparations for the Messina Conference. Paul-Henri Spaak of Belgium, J.W. Beyen of the Netherlands, and Joseph Beck of Luxembourg (the latter of whom chaired the conference) played particularly prominent parts. At the Messina Conference, Italy, the host country, gave strong support to the new economic-integration efforts proposed by the Benelux countries. West Germany went along rather reluctantly at first, and France was initially the least enthusiastic of the six ECSC member states about proposals for a broad common market. However, France liked the idea of a European Community for Atomic Energy more than it liked that for a European Economic Community and pushed successfully for its inclusion

on the agenda. Though invited to participate, Britain again declined the opportunity to be involved in the "European project." Its political and business leaders remained focused on the British Commonwealth and ties to the United States and strongly preferred a loose, **intergovernmental** free-trade association to the kind of integration proposed at the Messina Conference.

The new efforts at Messina and subsequent negotiations resulted in the Treaties of Rome in March 1957, which established the European Economic Community (EEC) and the European Community for Atomic Energy (Euratom) alongside the European Coal and Steel Community. The three communities as a whole came increasingly to be referred to as the European Communities, or simply European Community (EC); in 1967 their structures were merged to a considerable extent. The EEC became the heart of the EC. Despite the economic focus of the Rome Treaty establishing the EEC, Paul Henri Spaak, who led the committee that prepared the Treaty, emphasized the long-term goals: "Those who drew up the Rome Treaty . . . did not think of it as essentially economic; they thought of it as a stage on the road to political union." Walter Hallstein, the West German representative at the Messina Conference and the first President of the EEC Commission, concurred: "We are not integrating economies; we are integrating politics." Only three years after the collapse of the proposals for the European Defense Community and the related European Political Community, European integration was moving forward in striking ways that few would have predicted in 1954.[16]

Neo-functionalist analysts of the movement from the ECSC to the EC described, in a manner somewhat similar to such **functionalist** advocates of European integration by increments as Jean Monnet, the extent to which the limited cooperation in the coal and steel sphere had now "spilled over" to the much broader cooperative endeavors established and planned for the European Community (including development of a **customs union** (ending all tariffs among the six members and adopting a common external tariff) and a Common Agricultural Policy (CAP), with the assistance of supranational actors such as Jean Monnet, who had resigned from the High Authority to lead the European Movement, a broad array of political activists from all six member states. They also stressed the leadership for further integration that would emanate from the Commission, the Court of Justice, and the Parliamentary Assembly (later Parliament) of the European Community. However, it was soon to be evident that the nation-state leaders, still in most cases wedded to concepts of national interest and concerns about their own domestic powers and power bases, and possessing strong executive and legislative roles in the European Community through the Council of Ministers, were not about to lose control over the European integration process to supranational elites or technocratic mechanisms. Business, agricultural, and labor interest groups within the member states reinforced the political leaders' inclinations. Charles de Gaulle, the new chief executive of France, was a leader who was intent on his pressing own nation-state's political-economic and geopolitical interests, as he understood them, with special vigor.[17]

"Those who drew up the Rome Treaty . . . did not think of it as essentially economic; they thought of it as a stage on the road to political union."

Paul Henri Spaak, leader of the committee that drew up the EEC Rome Treaty, 1957.

"We are not integrating economies; we are integrating politics."

Walter Hallstein, first President of the EEC Commission, 1957.

Both quotations cited by Derek Urwin, The Community of Europe (1991), 76.

EUROPEAN COMMUNITY DEVELOPMENT AND GAULLIST ASSERTIONS, 1958–1969

The European Communities (EC) began with a highly complex structure that gained some streamlining with the merging of executive structures in 1967 but remained quite complicated. Walter Hallstein, the first President of the Commission of the EEC, and some of his associates sought to play the leading supranational roles in guiding European integration that were prescribed by functionalist advocates such as Monnet and emphasized in analyses by such neofunctionalist scholars as Ernst Haas. However, the "high politics" of making major changes in the European Communities generally moved at a pace and in a direction dictated largely by the nation-state leaders of the members, particularly the leaders of France and West Germany. From the outset, the concerns of nation-state executives had made the European Economic Community (EEC) less supranational and more intergovernmental than the European Coal and Steel Community (ECSC). As the Communities merged, intergovernmentalism continued to predominate.[18]

Moreover, French President Charles de Gaulle (1958–1969) was to prove an unusually assertive national leader, motivated in part by a geopolitical vision of a "Europe of nation-states," guided by the executives of its major states (especially France!) to exercise a major role as a "third force" between the United States and the Soviet Union in global affairs. De Gaulle was also determined to employ the EC to protect French national economic interests, most notably by forging the nascent Common Agricultural Policy (CAP) in a fashion that would both protect and modernize French agriculture. Summing up the French approach, which de Gaulle often carried to extreme lengths, one leading analyst has written, "In essence, France wanted to retain its role as a great power and to harness the resources of the Community to this effect." While Chancellor Konrad Adenauer of West Germany and the leaders of the other four member states of the EC were less assertive than de Gaulle in their national demands than de Gaulle was, they, too, sought distinct national advantages (especially economic ones) through the EC, as liberal intergovernmentalism suggests and later chapters on individual member states and the EC/EU will detail.[19]

"In essence, France wanted to retain its role as a great power and to harness the resources of the Community to this effect."

Alistair Cole, *"National and Partisan Contexts of Europeanization"* (2001), 18.

A considerable convergence of the trade goals of the six member states of the EC in a global environment of expanding trade and economic growth led to a rapid movement to achieve a customs union among the six by 1968, eighteen months ahead of the original schedule. British efforts to displace the European Economic Community with a completely intergovernmental free-trade association focused on trade ended up as only a loose European Free Trade Association of Britain and six smaller European nation-states (Austria, Denmark, Norway, Portugal, Sweden, and Switzerland). By 1961, the British government had decided to seek the membership in the EC that it had previously shunned. The relatively weak performance of the British economy vis-à-vis the EC six, waning British trade with the Commonwealth, and American encouragement for Britain to join the EC all played important parts in this shift. Meanwhile, inside the EC, national bargaining over the shape of the Common Agricultural Policy (CAP), the foundations of which were laid in 1958, proved more difficult than other trade agreements in light of divergent national objectives among

the members, though it, too, ended with a broad agreement.[20]

Discord among the member states and between the Commission and national leaders was so sharp during the 1960s in some other areas that it threatened to paralyze the new EC, despite progress toward the integration of trade and agricultural policies. One issue of contention was the British application for membership, which was twice vetoed by de Gaulle's France despite support for the British from other member states. Another source of tension were the French drives to turn European integration in a decisively intergovernmental direction in line with the Gaullist conception of a "Europe of nation-states" and to weaken **Atlanticist** ties with the United States in accord with the Gaullist vision of a European "third force" in global politics. De Gaulle's efforts led to the first summit meetings of the chief executives of the six member states and the unveiling of the Fouchet Plan, which would have substantially restructured European integration on an intergovernmental basis. However, the summit meetings did not become fully institutionalized at this time (doing so later, in 1974); and the Fouchet Plan encountered strong opposition from Belgium, the Netherlands, and Luxembourg (which saw diminishment of supranationalism as likely to result in French or Franco-German domination) and lack of enthusiasm from West Germany and Italy (which feared that it might weaken NATO and disrupt the EEC). Meanwhile, EEC Commission President Hallstein and the Commission sought to gain a source of revenue independent of the member state contributions that had been funding the EEC, expansion of powers for the European Parliament (which parliamentary members and the Netherlands had been advocating with increasing vigor), and closure on the Common Agricultural Policy (CAP). When Hallstein took the lead in proposing a "package" to combine these three issues and move integration forward, he encountered intense opposition from de Gaulle's France. Furthermore, de Gaulle was concerned about a fourth issue, a long-scheduled change called for in the EEC's Rome Treaty to reduce national veto powers in the Council of Ministers in favor of majority voting on an array of issues. The result was the "empty chair" crisis of 1965, in which France boycotted the Council of Ministers meetings for a seven-month period. The outcome of the crisis was the Luxembourg Compromise agreed to in January 1966, which retained the practice of unanimity in Council of Ministers meetings on all major matters, informally accepted limitations on activism by the Commission and its president, and left the other issues to be resolved separately. In effect, the Luxembourg Compromise resolved the ambiguity in the EEC's Rome Treaty between supranationalism and intergovernmentalism in favor of the latter. The 1958–1969 patterns concerning European integration indicated the limitations of the neofunctionalist analysis and pointed to the importance of both political-economic (liberal intergovernmental) and geopolitical (realist) calculations by nation-state leaders as forces shaping the contours of European integration.[21]

De Gaulle left office in 1969, easing the way for the entry of Britain (and Ireland and Denmark) to the EC, though there is some evidence that de Gaulle himself was shifting his views on EC expansion before his retirement, once he had secured the type of Common Agricultural Policy that his government and French agricultural interests demanded (and that Britain strongly opposed). In general, de Gaulle's departure appeared to offer the prospects of reduced national tensions within the EC on a number of fronts. In particular, the Franco–West German collaboration that had characterized de Gaulle's relationship with West German Chancellor Adenauer, which had eroded badly under new West German leadership and the pressures of the crisis of 1965, seemed to be reviving under the leadership of the new French president, Georges Pompidou

(1969–1974), and the new West German chancellor, Willy Brandt (also 1969–1974), even though the two men were not personally close, as their successors, Valéry Giscard d'Estaing (1974–1981) and Helmut Schmidt (1974–1982) would be. The EC's Hague Summit of chief executives in December 1969 provided an arena for the member state leaders to "relaunch" European integration.

However, the increasing instability of international currency markets, the slowing of global and European economic growth, and the global oil embargo and price increases of 1973 created an environment that spurred divergent national responses by member states and was not conducive to bold new steps toward integration. Perhaps the most critical development was the collapse of a key part of the Bretton Woods monetary system that had been adopted back in 1944 and that had since then underpinned the currency exchanges of the non-Communist world. Under the Bretton Woods Agreement, the United States was bound to buy and sell unlimited amounts of gold at the official price of $35 an ounce. A major problem was that global confidence in the dollar plummeted in the 1968–1971 period due to large American balance of payments deficits as a result of spending on the Vietnam War and a simultaneous domestic war on poverty. Abruptly, in 1971, the Nixon administration in the United States terminated the American obligation to maintain the Bretton Woods exchange rate. Because the currencies of the EC member states had been denominated in dollars, the end of stable exchange rates with the dollar meant instability in the EC members' exchange rates with each other also.[22]

WIDENING, LIMITED REFORMS, AND "EUROSCLEROSIS," 1969–1984

The years between 1969 and 1984 were marked by two enlargements, widening the EC to include Britain, Ireland, and Denmark in 1973 (while at the same time Norwegian voters in a referendum rejected EC entry) and Greece in 1981. Negotiations for a third enlargement, to include Spain and Portugal, also neared conclusion and were to culminate in their entry in 1986. However, a side effect of the widening of the European Community was increased diversity of nation-state positions on major issues.

Britain as a new member of the EC nearly always adopted an intergovernmentalist stance, fiercely resisting most supranational proposals and defending its leaders' conceptions of the British national interest. Though French leaders also tended toward intergovernmentalism and an emphasis on the need to preserve national sovereignty, the British and French preferences rarely jibed with one another. On matters of agricultural policy, relations with the United States, and business competition, for example, the British and French governments engaged in often-bitter conflicts. Therefore, British entry markedly increased the difficulties of finding common ground among EC member states. Denmark was to prove almost as staunch a defender of intergovernmental approaches as the United Kingdom. Despite its small size, it, too, demonstrated considerable ability to confound the supranational goals of some European integration advocates. Ireland, the third new member in 1973, proved somewhat more eager to promote EC consensus and advance supranational development of the EC than Britain or Denmark, and Ireland soon began to utilize EC financial assistance quite successfully to boost its previously backward economy. Greece, Spain, and Portugal, like Ireland, lagged behind the rest of the EC in per capita wealth. Together, they constituted what many observers termed the "poor four." Their entry brought heightened emphasis on the need to address the large economic gap between wealthier and poorer areas of the EC if integration were to proceed successfully.

Even apart from the increasing diversity of national goals that expansion of membership injected into the EC, the global economic environment of the period seriously complicated efforts at European integration during this period. As noted previously, the Bretton Woods system underwent major modification in 1971, causing national currencies to fluctuate markedly. Economic growth slowed, too, particularly as enormous oil price increases at the time of the Middle Eastern war of 1973 put major new pressures on most European economies. The result was an atmosphere of economic upheaval and distress that often evoked conflicting national responses. Therefore, integration proceeded at a rather uneven pace, with a number of false starts despite some achievements.

One of the largely unsuccessful endeavors was the European Exchange Rate Agreement, popularly referred to as the **"snake-in-the-tunnel"** arrangement, based on the 1970 Werner Report (drafted by Luxembourg Prime Minister Pierre Werner with the backing of the French and West German governments) and launched in 1972, which sought to stabilize exchange rates among the members' currencies in a time of global economic turbulence. Instead of leading to monetary integration, as was hoped and anticipated at its establishment, the snake-in-the-tunnel approach largely disintegrated as all EC participants except West Germany and the Benelux countries abandoned it by 1976. Relatively high-inflation states, such as Italy, Britain, and France, pursued monetary policies that made it extremely difficult to keep their currencies pegged at relatively consistent ratios to the deutsche mark of the low-inflation economic leader of Europe, West Germany. Replacing the snake arrangement in 1979 was the somewhat similar European Monetary System (EMS), with an Exchange Rate Mechanism (ERM), which in effect again made the strong West German currency the benchmark for the other participants. It proved somewhat more durable than its predecessor, due largely to more serious Europe-wide efforts to curb inflation in the 1980s than in the 1970s. However, the system with its Exchange Rate Mechanism still created much dissatisfaction outside of West Germany, lost several of its key participants in 1992, and eventually gave way to the Economic and Monetary Union founded under the terms of the Maastricht Treaty of 1992.

If the monetary integration efforts of the 1970s illustrated some of the problems that came to be described as "Eurosclerosis" by many observers, so, too, did a prolonged battle over the EC budget precipitated largely by British complaints that they were being compelled to pay more than their fair share of the budget and growing conflicts among the members states over the burgeoning costs of the Common Agricultural Policy (CAP), which many felt imposed unfair burdens on certain states (such as Britain and Italy) and on consumers generally. The conflicts over the British budgetary contributions festered into the 1980s, as did those over the CAP, creating a climate of distrust and anger among member states as attention focused increasingly in many states on their individual costs and benefits stemming from EC membership.

Also creating national obstacles to European integration in ways that neofunctionalists had failed to predict were the nontariff barriers to trade that emerged increasingly in state after member state during the 1970s. As noted previously, the EC had succeeded in removing internal industrial tariff barriers by 1968, well ahead of schedule. However, as business corporations possessing close ties to national governments faced new problems in the 1970s, including often the threat of bankruptcies, the governments of the EC member states moved frequently to assist them through both direct financial aid and national specifications and regulations designed to keep out products of other member states. The European Court of Justice intervened to overrule some of these, most

notably in the landmark *Cassis de Dijon* case in 1979 (discussed further in Chapter Four), in which it ruled against West German regulations that kept a French liqueur out of West Germany. Nevertheless, nontariff barriers erected by member states to protect favored firms continued to constrain trade within the EC during this period—a problem that would be addressed more fully than ever before as part of an effort to revitalize the EC in the 1980s.

Despite a widespread European pessimism that stressed the conflicts, paralysis, and failures in the EC, some reforms of the period proved durable contributions to long-term European integration. The introduction in 1970 of EC revenue sources independent of the nation-state governments (previously blocked by France), the development of an intergovernmental European Political Cooperation (EPC) after 1970, the institutionalization of summits among national chief executives in the form of the European Council in 1974, the establishment of the European Regional Development Fund (ERDF) in 1974, and the institution of direct elections to the European Parliament in 1979 (previously blocked by France and Britain) were among important reforms of the era.

The independent revenue sources that the EC received from 1970 onward consisted of tariffs on agricultural and industrial goods imported into the European Communities from the outside world. In addition, the agreement of 1970 gave the EC a portion (initially limited to no more than 1 percent) of national revenues from the value added tax, a form of hidden sales tax employed by all member states. Though the EC/EU budget would remain small in comparison with the budgets of its member states (never to the present constituting as much as 4 percent of the total of the members' national budgets), the 1970 reform was an important step toward supranational development.

European Political Cooperation (EPC), also established in 1970, was explicitly intergovernmental in structure and purpose. Aimed at improving coordination of member states' foreign policies, it provided for state foreign ministers to meet twice per year and their subordinates to meet on a more frequent basis to try to hammer out compatible approaches. EPC was to be the forerunner of later efforts at further coordination. Nevertheless, many member states have remained jealous of their prerogatives on foreign and defense matters; and policies have often diverged significantly.

The European Council was an important institutional development of the period. The heads of the member state governments had met in their first "summit" back in February 1961. While such meetings had occurred from time to time since then, an agreement in 1974 institutionalized summits and officially termed them meetings of the European Council. The European Council has since then been a permanent component of the EC/EU institutional structure. Intergovernmental in nature and operating primarily on the basis of consensus, European Council meetings have often proved important means of calling attention to major issues and resolving difficult impasses.

Though developed originally in large part due to British (and Irish and Italian) demands for reallocation of the EC budget in a manner that would benefit their own nation-states, the European Regional Development Fund (ERDF) created in 1974 would eventually prove one of several developments that would encourage decentralization within the member states, because it stimulated many subnational units to press for European assistance. It also spawned other regional or structural expenditures, making this category of spending second only to agriculture in the long term as a claimant on a significant share of the EC/EU budget.

The innovation of direct popular elections to the previously appointive European Parliament was perhaps just as striking in its long-term effects as ERDF. Strongly resisted in the 1970s by many intergovernmentalists, particularly in Britain and France, who saw it as a step toward strengthening of a supranational institution, this innovation did generate pressures in the 1980s and beyond for granting additional powers to the Parliament. It also made the Parliament the only popularly elected body above the nation-state level anywhere in the world.[23]

Despite some EC reforms in the 1970s, as the United States and Japan gave evidence of vaulting ahead of Europe in the global economy of the 1980s, particularly in the realm of modern technology, there was a growing sense in European political and business circles that additional reform of the EC was in order. One proposal to revive European integration was the Genscher-Colombo Plan, put forward in 1981 by the foreign ministers of West Germany (Hans-Dietrich Genscher) and of Italy (Emilio Colombo). It called for adoption of additional common policies, strengthening of the European Parliament, extension of majority voting in the Council of Ministers, and an increase in the EC budget. Though this plan had little immediate impact, largely because it did not enjoy the full endorsement of the chief executives of the major member states, it contributed to an upsurge of discussions about renewing the drive for European integration in an environment in which many participants and observers saw reform as essential to compete effectively with the United States and Japan. In the meantime, however, the French government pursued economic strategies in 1981 and 1982 that were sharply at odds with those of both Britain and West Germany.[24]

INTEGRATION REVITALIZED, 1984–2000

Despite the long era seen by many as one of "Eurosclerosis," there were signs in 1983–1984 of a renewed drive to advance European integration. A major spur for change was an emergent consensus on the need for the EC to advance toward a single market economy in order to spur modernization through competition and cope with the globalized economy and the roles in it of American- and Japanese-based multinational corporations. In the environment of the era, an ideology that Europeans generally termed **neoliberalism** but that was commonly described in the United States as "Reaganite conservatism" (or, in somewhat more extreme form, **economic libertarianism**) was gaining support among political and business elites around the world. Though socialism and highly regulated versions of capitalism were deeply entrenched in most of Western Europe, the failure of François Mitterrand's Socialist effort to revitalize the French economy by state efforts to increase consumer demand and take ownership of key industries brought the Socialist-led government of France to a point of accepting the single-market preferences already evident in the governments of Britain and West Germany as well as in the top circles of European business. When Jacques Delors became president of the European Commission in 1985, he found that the greatest degree of consensus among the major nation-state governments of the EC centered on establishment of a single market. The result of collaboration among the nation-state leaders and Delors and the Commission was the Single European Act of 1986 (SEA), including both institutional changes and single-market reforms that would go far by 1992 to create a free-trade area within the EC/EU.[25]

The SEA represented the first major revision of the treaties establishing the European Communities. It formally recognized the European Council and European Political Cooperation, expanded the use of non-unanimous voting in the Council of Ministers (finally moving beyond the Luxembourg Compromise of 1966 that had preserved the national veto power largely intact), added to the powers of the European Parliament, and added new treaty articles on environmental, cohesion, and research and technology policies. Britain, long resistant to the degree of **supranational** development

inherent in the SEA, was willing to accept (reluctantly) the institutional reforms of the SEA only because of their linkage in a package with a strict timetable leading to the 1992 establishment of a single market, removing most significant national trade barriers within the EC—a cherished goal of British Prime Minister Margaret Thatcher. Although tariffs had been removed within the EC by 1968, many national trade barriers remained and had even proliferated during the 1970s. As noted previously the neoliberal consensus emergent at the top levels of most European governments and large business corporations in the mid-1980s in response to globalization pressures was a major contributor to the single-market reforms. Despite the growth of this consensus, most European socialist leaders saw the need to balance the single-market reforms with a Social Charter and an enhanced social dimension to the EC, though these proved rather vague and ambiguous in practice. Nonetheless, Thatcher opposed them with vehemence. Therefore, Britain refused on political-economic and ideological grounds to endorse even a watered-down Social Charter.[26]

The next major change in the European Community, including the establishment of the European Union, came with the Treaty on European Union, popularly known as the Maastricht Treaty, signed in Maastricht, the Netherlands, in February 1992. The end of the Cold War and the reunification of Germany provided important backdrops to this Treaty. However, liberal intergovernmental analyses highlighting political-economic calculations have provided more insights into the processes of the negotiations than realist analyses focused on geopolitical considerations. Many of the critical decisions took place before German reunification and were not profoundly affected by it. The Maastricht Treaty, like the previous major steps toward European integration, reflected intense nation-state bargaining and complex compromises among the major member states that were highly focused on economic concerns.[27]

The Maastricht Treaty laid the foundation and provided a schedule for an Economic and Monetary Union (EMU) to replace the EMS and its separate national banks and national currencies with a European Central Bank (ECB) and a common currency before the end of the decade. France, Italy, and other member states were able to persuade a reluctant Germany to give up the preeminence long enjoyed by its own central bank in favor of the new European Central Bank (ECB). However, in return, Germany shaped the structures and powers of the Economic and Monetary Union and gained the location of the ECB in Frankfurt, Germany. Meanwhile, Britain was able to opt out of the common currency project in light of its government's assurances that it could not obtain parliamentary ratification of the Maastricht Treaty at home without such an opt-out.

The Treaty also established three distinct structures of policy-making, termed **"pillars"**: 1) the European Community and the policies associated with it; 2) the Common Foreign and Security Policy (CFSP), the renamed and reorganized European Political Cooperation; and 3) most aspects of Justice and Home Affairs (JHA) policies. The latter two were to be largely intergovernmental, while the first would have a significant supranational character and encompass a widening range of public policies. Again the result represented a compromise among the leaders of the major member states. In this instance, the chief division was between German, Italian, and Spanish orientations toward enhanced **supranationalism** and British and French insistence on extensive **intergovernmentalism.**

As for the social dimension favored by most socialist governments and labor-union leaders, it was relegated to a Social **Protocol** to the Maastricht Treaty, endorsed by all member states except Britain but (as with the previous Social Charter) fairly vague and ambiguous regarding promotion and protection of workers' rights. Because on the common currency plans,

Britain and Denmark both opted out of participation in the project, and because Britain opted out of the Social Protocol, the early 1990s witnessed a two-track system in which some European Union members agreed to integrate more fully than others. This outcome was a compromise reflecting the differing orientations of member state governments and what they would agree to undertake. Eventually, Britain would agree to the incorporation of the Social Protocol into the Amsterdam Treaty of 1997, following the election of a new Labour government headed by Tony Blair. However, the idea of allowing different members of the European Union to integrate to varying degrees (what some have termed **differentiated integration**) became increasingly widespread, as enlargement and prospects of further widening to encompass Central and Eastern European states advanced.

The Maastricht Treaty generated considerable public controversy in Europe—more than any European integration moves that had been made since the European Defense Community of the 1950s. Margaret Thatcher, now Baroness Thatcher of Kesteven, serving in the House of Lords, denounced Maastricht as "a treaty too far," and did her best to arouse opposition in Britain. Denmark's voters rejected the Treaty in a 1992 referendum, accepting it only later, with revisions. The French electorate endorsed it by a very narrow margin, following a highly divisive referendum campaign there. The Treaty also generated considerable parliamentary opposition in a number of national parliaments among the member states, as well as challenges to its constitutionality in judicial proceedings. Furthermore, the ongoing project to institute a common European euro currency proved controversial. The sluggishness of economic growth in Europe and the relatively high unemployment rates of the 1990s led to widespread discontent, especially among Socialists, Communists, and labor unions, with the strict criteria that the EU national leaders mandated for participation of states in the EMU, because these emphasized control of inflation, often at the cost of growth and jobs, and were often used to justify cuts in social spending by national governments. In spite of wide concerns and common predictions that many prospective adherents to the common currency would be unable to meet the established criteria, 11 member states adopted the common currency on schedule in 1999, with Greece joining soon thereafter (leaving Britain, Denmark, and EU newcomer Sweden as the three nonparticipating EU members). However, a major struggle continued over the extent to which national governments could and should impose constraints on the European Central Bank and orient it in a direction favorable to socialist and labor union concerns.[28]

[Maastricht is] "a treaty too far."

Former Prime Minister Margaret Thatcher,
June 28, 1992, *cited in Stephen George,
An Awkward Partner (1998), 248.*

Therefore, the 1984–2000 era witnessed the development of both the single market and the single currency and considerable revamping of EC/EU structures (as well as further widening, with the addition of Portugal and Spain in 1986 and of Austria, Finland, and Sweden in 1995). In contrast to Portugal and Spain, the last three entrants were all relatively wealthy and immediately became net contributors to the EU budget. Of the three, Sweden proved the most resistant to further European integration, joining Britain and Denmark in rejecting membership in the Economic and Monetary Union, for example. On the other hand, Austria and Finland generally favored further integration and adopted the common currency as soon as it took effect. Despite the formation of the European Union and fairly dramatic movement toward supranational development in a number of fields during the 1984–2000 years, the period was also one of rising criticism of the path taken

by European integration and of democratic and social deficits in what many citizens viewed as an overly elitist and overly capitalistic European Union. Nationalistic concerns also remained alive and well in many member states, particularly in Britain, Denmark, and France, but also elsewhere. In fact, even supranational Germany, now that it had achieved reunification, showed some signs of placing increased emphasis on its national interest as something separate from supranational development.

TOWARD EASTWARD EXPANSION AND A EUROPEAN UNION CONSTITUTION, 2000–

Although the future of the EMU and the euro currency remain subjects of intense debate, two other issues have come to the forefront of discussions concerning the European Union since 2000. One major issue, percolating since the end of the Cold War and the collapse of Communist regimes throughout Central and Eastern Europe in the 1989–1991 period, has focused on the timing, means, and implications of eastward widening of the European Union. By 2002, 13 Central and Eastern European nation-states, including Turkey (which is mostly in Asia and considered by most observers unlikely to be admitted to the EU in the near future) had gained official recognition by the European Union as prospective entrants. The Amsterdam Intergovernmental Conference of 1997 had been expected to address the institutional and policy implications of eastward expansion with some specificity, but member-state conflicts were too severe to fulfill these expectations in the Amsterdam Treaty that emerged. Therefore, the subject had to be revisited at the 2000 Intergovernmental Conference and revisited again at the Nice Summit of December 2000. Although this summit proved unusually rancorous and fed speculation of a possible breakdown of the long pattern of

Franco-German cooperation in the EC/EU, it did manage in the Nice Treaty to address major issues of restructuring the European Commission to accommodate new members, reweighting the votes in the Council of Ministers, revamping national seat allocations in the European Parliament, and making other structural changes to cope with enlargement. It also made some clarification of processes allowing different states to pursue European integration at different rates, an important method of reconciling the wish to widen to include diverse new members and at the same time allow further deepening among existent members that wished to proceed in that direction. Annexed to the Treaty of Nice, signed by member state governments in February 2001, was a Declaration on the Future of the Union. Left to be clarified in the future were the legal status of a Charter of Fundamental Rights (a bill of rights) approved by the Nice Summit but not made legally binding on member states and the possibility of a constitution for the European Union.[29]

The negotiations over eastward expansion of the EU proved arduous; but by 2003, it was evident that ten of the accession nation-states would join the European Union in 2004: Poland, Hungary, Estonia, Latvia, Lithuania, the Czech Republic, Slovakia, and Slovenia from the former Communist bloc, plus Cyprus and Malta. Bulgaria and Romania were slated for likely entry to the EU in 2007. In June 2004, Croatia moved onto a fast track toward likely EU entry by 2009. Such a major widening of the European Union brought further discussion of how to restructure EU institutions and adjust policies and policy-making processes to avoid stalemate and increased costs. Because previous expansions had never involved entry by more than three new member states at a time, the scheduled addition of ten new members in one year in 2004, with two additional entrants likely in 2007, and still another entrant likely by 2009, represented a major new challenge to the European Union. Beyond the sheer numbers of new

states to fit into the EU structures, the new member states were significantly poorer than the EU average in terms of per capita gross domestic product, and most of their economies were much more heavily agricultural than the EU average. One result was increased impetus for a constitution that it was hoped would streamline EU institutions and clarify lines of accountability.

At the urging of the German government, with the support of many others who saw the need for an EU constitution or constitutional treaty, the EU agreed to hold a constitutional convention to be followed by an Intergovernmental Conference to review its internal constitutional arrangements. German Chancellor Gerhard Schröder and Foreign Minister Joschka Fischer brought forth proposals for a new constitution for the EU, evoking both support and criticisms from other member state leaders in 2001–2002. Early in 2002, a constitutional convention, headed by former French President Valery Giscard d'Estaing, met to develop constitutional recommendations and continued its work until June 2003, when it presented the draft of a constitution. Some political leaders and analysts preferred to call the proposed new constitution a "constitutional treaty," since it could take effect only when ratified by all of the 25 member states that would constitute the EU in 2004.

Romano Prodi, the president of the European Commission, hailed the draft as a "huge leap forward" for the European Union. A senior member of the convention emphasized, "What we are doing is moving off a treaty track and on to a constitutional track, and we will now roll forward on that track." While less enthusiastic than Prodi or the unidentified convention member, the heads of state and government at the Porto Carras, Greece, meeting of the European Council in June 2003 gave the draft their broad endorsement. However, other observers, such as Quentin Peel of the *Financial Times*, have criticized it as "depressingly long and wordy." Some, especially in Poland, Spain, and Italy, have been miffed by its failure to emphasize the role of Christianity in European history. While some European federalists have suggested that it does not move the EU far enough toward supranational development, many intergovernmentalists fear that it goes too far in a supranational direction. Seeking to reassure the numerous British **Euroskeptics,** who continually perceive EU threats to British sovereignty, Prime Minister Tony Blair declared, "There is no way Britain is going to give up our independent sovereign right to determine our tax policy, our foreign policy, our defense policy and our own borders."[30]

"What we are doing is moving off a treaty track and on to a constitutional track, and we will now roll forward on that track."

Senior constitutional convention member, *quoted in The Economist (June 21, 2003), 51.*

"There is no way Britain is going to give up our independent sovereign right to determine our tax policy, our foreign policy, our defense policy and our own borders."

British Prime Minister Tony Blair, *quoted in the New York Times (June 21, 2003), A2, on the powers that he would not permit a new EU constitution to take from Britain.*

The new constitution, or constitutional treaty, as presented by the constitutional convention (subject to amendment or rejection) consolidated the provisions of all previous treaties into a single document. However, it went well beyond mere synthesis and summation to make a number of substantive changes in the European Union. One notable innovation was that it proposed to incorporate the Charter of Fundamental Rights into European law (as the Nice Treaty stopped short of doing), in effect providing a European bill of rights that would apply to all EU laws, though not to national ones, in deference to concerns (such as Blair's) over national sovereignty. One unidentified senior figure in the convention stressed the importance of this change in developing a European identity: "It was the Bill of Rights that created American identity. They were Americans and so they had rights. It will be the same with Europeans." The new constitutional draft also proposed to revise a number of major aspects of the central institutions of the EU. Among the most important of these were the creation of a president of the European Council (now rotated every six months among member states) and a foreign minister/vice president and vesting them with significant new powers. The hope of the framers was to enhance the potential for strong, coherent leadership and accountability. However, some critics feared possible conflict between the president of the Commission and the president of the European Council. The convention rejected proposals to create a single president of the EU as too radical a change. The new draft also provided for no more than 15 voting members of the Commission, so that its size would not become too large to be manageable and so that the president would possess greater control over those primarily responsible for proposing and executing EU laws. However, this proposal encountered forceful criticism from leaders of many small member states, who expressed fears of losing their countries' votes on the Commission, and was eventually abandoned in favor of a system allocating each member state one Commission seat until 2009 and providing for a reduction of the Commission at that time to two-thirds the number of the member states. The new constitutional draft also proposed to expand the lawmaking powers of the European Parliament and to alter procedures for qualified majority voting in the Council of Ministers, as well as to move the EU in the direction of supranationalism or federalism in some policy domains (particularly justice and home affairs). Still other new features were provisions by which a member state could withdraw from the European Union and by which the EU could suspend a member state's voting rights. Neither of these matters has been the subject of previous treaties, though they are obviously matters of great importance. Table 2.1 summarizes major changes called for by the proposed new constitution.[31]

An Intergovernmental Conference of the governments of all 25 states that would be EU members in 2004 began meeting in October 2003 to consider the constitutional proposals. However, sharp conflicts soon emerged. In December 2003, a summit of EU national heads of government and state failed to reach agreement on the constitution. Among various controversial issues, the most contentious proved to be the proposal to alter qualified majority voting rules in the Council of Ministers, the chief legislative body of the EU and a primary center for the expression of distinctive member state interests. Spain and Poland, which had won 27 Council votes apiece (compared with 29 each for France, Germany, Italy, and the United Kingdom) flatly refused to accept the proposed shift to a system that would reduce their influence by requiring only a majority of member states representing at least

---

TABLE 2.1   Major Provisions of the Proposed EU Constitution

Charter of Fundamental Rights. This is a "bill of rights" for EU citizens that includes not just the freedoms from government (freedom of speech, freedom of the press) of the U.S. Constitutional Bill of Rights but also such "positive freedoms" as the right to strike, the right of workers to be informed and consulted, and the right to a free job placement service. The Charter's provisions are to apply only to European law, not to the laws of the individual member states. This Charter was previously approved as part of the Nice Treaty in 2001 but was not made legally binding at that time.

New Institutional Leadership Positions. The two major ones are to be the President of the European Council (previously rotated every six months among the member states, now to be held by a single individual chosen by the European Council for a term of two and one-half years, with election for a second term permissible) and the EU Foreign Minister (replacing two separate positions of Commissioner for Foreign Affairs and EU Foreign Policy Representative).

Revised Institutional Structures. The most important revisions are to be the changes in the membership of the European Commission, the major executive body of the EU, to one per member state until 2009 (with a reduction to a number of members corresponding to two-thirds of the number of member states subsequently), whereas the five largest states previously each had two members while each other state had one; the expansion of the powers of the European Parliament, the elected legislative body of the EU that shares lawmaking powers with the appointive Council of the EU/Council of Ministers; the altering of the qualified majority voting requirements in the Council of Ministers (to a requirement for a majority vote representing at least 55 percent of the member states representing at least 65 percent of the EU population, from the previous requirement for a qualified majority vote of 71 percent using a weighted voting system); and abolition of the "three pillar" structure of EU decision-making that had been established by the Maastricht Treaty of 1991.

Provision for Leaving the EU and for Suspension of EU Membership Rights. The constitutional draft provides for the first time that a member state can leave the European Union by giving a notice two years in advance, subject to negotiations with the Commission and Council and approval by a qualified majority vote of the European Council, with the consent of a majority of the European Parliament. It also provides for suspension of voting rights of a member state for "serious persistent violation of fundamental principles," by a reinforced qualified majority vote of the Council, disregarding the vote of the relevant member state for which suspension is being considered.

60 percent of the EU population to approve most Council decisions. In the wake of the December 2003 failure to gain the requisite member state support for the planned EU constitution, Irish Prime Minister Bertie Ahearn (because Ireland was serving as European Council president in the first half of 2004) took a leading role in bringing European leaders to a compromise that brought enough consensus to win the leaders' tentative approval of a somewhat revised constitutional draft in June 2004. However, many remained dissatisfied with the constitutional compromise; and the need to win ratification in all 25 member states posed a daunting challenge. Clearly, the European Union has remained a work in progress as the new millennium has begun.[32]

"It was the Bill of Rights that created American identity. They were Americans and so they had rights. It will be the same with Europeans."

EU Constitutional Convention Delegate, *quoted in The Economist (June 21, 2003), 52.*

In considering constitutional development, of course, the European Union is likely to focus renewed attention on popular concerns about its development up to the present day. These concerns are rooted in the European historical experience discussed at the beginning of this chapter: the development of democracy, the capitalistic and socialistic versions of economic modernity, and the modern nation-state. Well-entrenched European conceptions of democracy have suggested to many that there are serious deficiencies in the European Union. Most of the time, EC/EU "high politics" have been largely the preserve of nation-state leaders who often have shrouded their actions in the secrecy of European Council and Council of Ministers negotiations and worked closely with corporate moguls and central bankers. Meanwhile, EC/EU "low politics" have often operated in even greater secrecy and by complex means that often baffle even the best-informed observers and that vary from one policy domain to another. The "democratic deficit" in the contemporary European Union is a widespread concern. The continuing strength of European socialist values in the midst of the revival of free-market capitalism globally and within the EC/EU since the mid-1980s has also mobilized many Europeans in opposition to the trends evident in the single market, the Economic and Monetary Union (EMU), and a variety of other EU public policies. Moreover, nation-state identities have remained strong; and these have spawned continuing resistance to European supranationalism. Therefore, a democratic-socialist-nationalist combination of concerns, rooted in the historical developments discussed at the beginning of this chapter, may yet affect the course of European integration. However, unless there are dramatic changes in the evident patterns of major EU initiatives being driven largely by major nation-state leaders attentive primarily to the concerns of the executives of large business corporations, such a turn of events appears unlikely.

TABLE 2.2	The Widening Process, 1951–2004
The Original Six (1951 ECSC, 1957 EC)	Belgium, France, Germany (West)*, Italy, Luxembourg, Netherlands
1973	Denmark, Ireland, United Kingdom
1981	Greece
1986	Portugal, Spain
1995	Austria, Finland, Sweden
2004	Czech Republic, Cyprus, Estonia, Hungary, Latvia, Lithuania, Malta, Poland, Slovenia, Slovakia

* East Germany became a part of the German Federal Republic and the European Community in 1990.

TABLE 2.3	Major Steps in the Deepening Process, 1951–2003
1951	Treaty of Paris establishing European Coal and Steel Community.
1957	Treaties of Rome establishing European Economic Community (EEC) and European Atomic Energy Community (Euratom).
1958	Foundation for the Common Agricultural Policy (CAP).
1968	Completion of the customs union.
1979	Agreement on the European Monetary System (EMS).
1986	Agreement on the Single European Act with single market target and expansion of Community powers in various policy domains.
1992	Treaty on European Union (Maastricht Treaty) establishing European Union with three pillars.
1999	Implementation of the common monetary policy and single currency for 11 EU member states (12 with addition of Greece).
2001	Nice Treaty providing for the eastward expansion and further deepening of the EU.
2002	Convening of the constitutional convention to develop a constitution for the EU.
2003	Draft constitution; convening of Intergovernmental Conference on the constitution.

THEORETICAL PERSPECTIVES ON HOW AND WHY THE EUROPEAN UNION HAS DEVELOPED AS IT HAS

Theoretical models in political science and related disciplines seek to enable us to understand the forces that have guided political behavior. Thus, theories of European integration direct our attention to forces that have shaped the development of the European Union over the past five decades. Throughout the above account, there have been references to neofunctionalist, realist, and liberal intergovernmental theoretical approaches in particular.

Neofunctionalist Theory

Neofunctionalist theory has assigned an important role to supranational leaders (such as those often found in the European Commission and its bureaucracy) as important actors spurring integration and have argued that economic cooperation in limited arenas has led to **"spillover"** to other economic and political cooperative ventures, which have in turn fostered further supranational development. For example, it portrays the ending of tariffs (import taxes) among the six EC members in the 1960s as generating pressures to create a more genuine common market by linking the currencies of member states in the 1970s and 1980s, ending many other barriers to trade in the late 1980s and early 1990s, and then moving on to a common currency in the 1990s. Underlying most neofunctionalist theories has been the notion that national economies have become increasingly interdependent in a globalization process that has enhanced prospects in the last five decades for supranational cooperation.

The overview in this chapter has suggested the utility of considering the global economic environment's effects on European integration. However, it has indicated that some environmental effects, such as the turbulence of the 1970s, evoked European nation-state responses that stalled and even partially reversed integration. Furthermore, it has suggested that nation-state leaders have remained far more important actors shaping the "high politics" of major steps toward (or away from) European integration than neofunctionalist theory indicates. In the example cited above, national governmental responses to global economic turbulence in the 1970s actually increased national barriers to trade (contrary to the neofunctionalist model). Furthermore, German,

French, Italian, and other national leaders shaped the Economic and Monetary Union to reflect their own goals and domestic political-economic interests, while British, Swedish, and Danish national leaders have so far resisted adoption of the common currency. Despite the apparent limitations of neofunctionalism as an explanatory model, the cumulative effects of multiple "low politics" decisions by a mixture of supranational, national, and subnational officials have unquestionably shaped important aspects of EC/EU development. Moreover, there have been some spillover effects, albeit usually channeled and sometimes blocked by national governments.[33]

Realist Theories

The realist theories and their variants have stressed the importance of nation-state actors who compete for power and pursue distinctive national geopolitical interests. It downplays supranational actors, broad global patterns except for the power struggle among nation-states, and diverse domestic influences on national leaders. Though realism helpfully places European integration in the context of the bipolar balance of power that emerged during the Cold War and calls attention to the effects of the end of the Cold War and the reunification of Germany, its ability to explain most of the specific patterns emergent in Europe since the 1950s appears somewhat limited.[34]

Liberal Intergovernmental Theory

The overview presented here has relied more heavily on liberal intergovernmental theoretical perspectives than on either neofunctionalism or realism. Liberal intergovernmental approaches, most notably Andrew Moravcsik's, have, like those of the realists, emphasized nation-states as the major political units and rational calculations by national governmental executives as the key ingredients in the major bargaining processes that have shaped EC/EU

integration at most critical junctures. However, they have also focused on the major roles of economic interest groups in influencing national governmental bargaining objectives, thus establishing links to comparative politics analyses of domestic influences on governmental decision-makers in a fashion that finds considerable support in the later chapters of this text on individual states and their approaches to the EC/EU.[35]

Despite drawing fairly heavily upon liberal intergovernmental theory, the account in this text remains eclectic. More than most liberal intergovernmental theorists, it stresses the importance of both the global political economy and the global distribution of power among nation-states as important contextual variables influencing European integration. It also stresses the importance of ideas that sometimes transcend nation-states. The Cold War and the predominance of the United States in "the West" shaped the early efforts at integration and kept them focused on *West* European pooling of sovereignty. The end of the Cold War and the reunification of Germany altered the distribution of power (markedly increasing that of Germany) and some political behavior patterns (increasing the concerns of other member states to contain Germany) within the EC/EU, and also created pressures for eastward enlargement. Patterns in the global economy have sometimes encouraged, sometimes limited or even reversed, European integration. Growing global free trade and obvious benefits from it after World War II conditioned West European political and business elites to accept pooling of sovereignty in the ECSC and then the EEC. The turbulence of the early 1970s revived considerable economic nationalism in Europe and contributed to "Eurosclerosis." The rise of neoliberal or economic libertarian ideas and competitive pressures from external forces in the 1980s and 1990s spurred the single-market and many subsequent new dimensions of European integration.

Other Theoretical Approaches

Some recent approaches that fall short of being full theories shed light on some of these points. Those loosely grouped as **constructivist** approaches have stressed the importance of socially constructed shared understandings among actors about their environment and roles, cautioning against overemphasis on the nation-states and their leaders' supposed rationality. For example, concepts of "the West" and of "Europe" have conditioned actors' behavior. The nation-state is itself a rather ambiguous concept constructed by human beings and given somewhat different meanings in different locales at various points in time.[36]

Furthermore, as will become evident in some later chapters of this text, there is evidence in some instances to support a recent **historical institutionalist** critique of liberal intergovernmental theory for overestimating the extent to which national executives have been able to control the processes of European integration. Briefly, Paul Pierson, the leading proponent of historical institutionalist analysis, has concluded, "When European integration is examined over time, the gaps in member-state control appear far more prominent than they do in intergovernmentalist accounts."[37] Pierson calls attention to the somewhat autonomous actions of some EU institutional actors (as suggested also by neofunctionalists), to the likelihood of unintended consequences of national actors' decisions pertaining to integration, and to the possibility of changes in national leaders' preferences over time—all points that will be encountered later in some of the nation-state chapters of this study.

Two illustrations of the types of gaps in member state control described by historical institutionalism may be helpful. One example concerns the European Court of Justice (ECJ) and the member states. The activist decisions of the ECJ in many major cases have enabled it to affect the EC/EU and the member states far more profoundly than the nation-state governments that established it ever foresaw. Because of the great difficulty of formally reducing its powers through new treaty provisions, the European Court of Justice has enjoyed considerable leverage vis-à-vis the member states. However, as the liberal intergovernmental model suggests, pressures from member state governments have led the ECJ to exercise growing caution since the 1980s in challenging their interests. (See the discussion of the European Court of Justice in Chapter Three for elaboration on these points.)

Another illustration, covered in more depth in Chapter Eight, concerns the EU and the government of Germany, generally judged as the most powerful member state of the EU in recent years. At the insistence of German Christian Democratic Chancellor Helmut Kohl, who was heavily influenced by the German central bank, the Economic and Monetary Union (EMU) established in the 1990s was accompanied by strict criteria requiring that member state governments keep their public debt and annual deficits to specific low levels or suffer penalties. However, Kohl himself later found it very difficult to stay within the prescribed limits. Moreover, the succeeding German Social Democratic–Green coalition government chafed at the "straightjacket" in which a previous German government had helped to place it through the EMU provisions. Therefore, over time, German governmental control over the Economic and Monetary Union process was less complete than liberal intergovernmental theory seemed to suggest. Again, however, as liberal intergovernmental theory suggests, the German government (supported by the French government) proved strong enough to resist at least the initial efforts by the European Commission to discipline it for violating the EMU deficit limits.[38]

One other limitation on the liberal intergovernmental theoretical model is that it understates the diversity of EU policy-making patterns. Chapter Four illustrates some of the differences in policy-making processes across policy domains in the EU. Furthermore, recent emphases on "multi-level governance" call attention to the involvement of various levels of government in such policy domains as environmental and regional policies, particularly in the most decentralized EU nation-states, such as Germany and Spain.[39] Again, this point will emerge with increased clarity once this text addresses Germany and Spain in particular in later chapters.

Despite the amendments to liberal intergovernmental theory that have been suggested above, liberal intergovernmentalism provides a useful model that guides much of the analysis in this text. To summarize its main points, the major nation-states have been the primary engines of European integration and have shaped the major decisions affecting how it has occurred (and failed to occur). Within the nation-states, executive leaders (presidents, prime ministers, and major cabinet ministers) have played the largest roles in defining national interests and determining national approaches to the European integration processes. Economic interests, particularly those articulated by the executives of large business corporations (and by some agricultural interests), have played bigger roles than any others in influencing the behavior of national executive leaders in key European negotiations. Nevertheless, understanding of how and why European integration has developed as it has is often furthered by drawing appropriately on pertinent points raised by other theoretical frameworks and approaches.

* * *

Against the backdrop of this overview of the development of the European Union, it is time to turn our attention next to the central institutions of the contemporary European Union and how they operate. Chapter Two has alluded briefly to many of these institutions, such as the European Commission, the European Council, the Council of Ministers, the European Parliament, the European Court of Justice, and the European Central Bank. Chapter Three will examine their roles, powers, and interactions in contemporary Europe, as well as the changes in them that are likely to occur in the near future.

SUMMARY

- Europe, the continent that spawned the nation-state, has now moved further than any other area of the world to create a union that entails substantial pooling of sovereignty.

- Modern nation-states have been relatively recent and incomplete phenomena even in Europe; many contain minority ethnic regions due to history, and many have new ethnic minorities due to immigration.

- Constitutional democracy now prevails in all of the states in the European Union, but authoritarianism and totalitarianism are still recent memories in some; many critics perceive a "democratic deficit" in the European Union institutions.

- Contemporary Europe emphasizes mixed economies, possessing "capitalistic" markets and private ownership and "socialistic" provision of social services and governmental regulation of business; the social dimension is generally more extensive than in the United States' version of a mixed economy.

- Neofunctionalist theory concerning European integration, associated with scholars such as Ernst Haas, stresses the roles of supranational leaders and views economic cooperation among nation-states in limited areas as likely to spill over to encourage further supranational development.

- Realist theory, associated with scholars such as Hans Morgenthau, emphasizes intergovernmental features of the EU and the primacy of nation-state leaders who rationally pursue distinctive national geopolitical interests.

- Liberal intergovernmental theory, associated in particular with the scholar Andrew Moravcsik, stresses bargaining among national leaders in the EU (much as realist theory does) but also emphasizes the economic context of this bargaining and the large roles of major economic interest groups in influencing national leaders' bargaining objectives.

- This text draws upon these and other theoretical perspectives while giving particular emphasis to liberal intergovernmental theory.

- The creation of the European Coal and Steel Community (ECSC) in 1952 by France, West Germany, Italy, and the Benelux countries marked the first major step toward European integration.

- Spillover occurred to some extent in the creation of the European Economic Community and the European Community of Atomic Energy through the Treaties of Rome in 1957, but efforts to establish a European Defense Community failed due to French opposition.

- The 1960s saw the European Communities' creation of a customs union and a Common Agricultural Policy but also saw national assertiveness, particularly in the actions of French President Charles de Gaulle, who blocked much proposed supranational development and blocked British EC entry.

- The European Community widened significantly in 1973 (Britain, Denmark, and Ireland) and 1981 (Greece) and adopted some supranational reforms; however, the 1970s was a period of much national infighting within the EC and of considerable economic stagnation.

- European integration accelerated after 1984, with the Single European Act of 1986 and the Maastricht Treaty of 1992; further widening occurred with the admission of Spain and Portugal in 1986 and Austria, Finland, and Sweden in 1995.

- The European Union has sought to consolidate its treaty provisions and alter some of its key institutions in a constitution through a process that included a constitutional convention in 2002–2003 and that continues through 2004; national differences have complicated the constitutional development process.

- The European Union undertook its most ambitious widening ever, with ten new member states admitted in May 2004; Bulgaria and Romania have been scheduled for EU entry in 2007; Croatia has been recognized as an accession candidate with a likely entry date in the 2007–2009 period; Turkey has been recognized as an accession candidate but without a date for entry as of mid-2004.

ENDNOTES

1. Jean Bodin, *Six Books of the Commonwealth*, Abridged and translated by M.J. Tooley (New York: Barnes and Noble, 1967); George H. Sabine, *A History of Political Theory*, 4th ed. (Hinsdale, IL: Dryden, 1973), 372–385.

2. Linda Colley, *Britons: Forging the Nation 1707–1837* (New Haven, CT: Yale University Press, 1992); Rogers Brubaker, *Citizenship and Nationhood in France and Germany* (Cambridge, MA: Harvard University Press, 1992); David A. Bell, *The Cult of the Nation in France: Inventing Nationalism, 1680–1800* (Cambridge, MA: Harvard University Press, 2001); Stephen Wood, *Germany, Europe and the Persistence of Nations* (Aldershot: Ashgate, 1998), Ch. 1.

3. Richard Wollheim, "Democracy: Its History," in James A. Gould and Willis H. Truitt, eds., *Political Ideologies* (New York: Macmillan, 1973), 30–37; Terence Ball and Richard Dagger, *Political Ideologies and the Democratic Ideal*, 3rd ed. (New York: Longman, 1999), 20–24.

4. George P. Gooch, *English Democratic Ideas in the Seventeenth Century*, 2nd ed. (New York: Harper, 1959); Sabine, *A History of Political Theory*, 441–458.

5. Susan Dunn, *Sister Revolutions: French Lightning, American Light* (New York: Faber and Faber, 1999); Theda Skocpol, *States and Social Revolutions* (Cambridge: Cambridge University Press, 1979), 174–205.

6. Samuel P. Huntington, *The Third Wave: Democratization in the Late Twentieth Century* (Norman, OK: University of Oklahoma Press, 1991).

7. Robert Heilbroner, *The Worldly Philosophers: The Lives, Times, and Ideas of the Great Economic Thinkers*, 4th ed. (New York: Simon and Schuster, 1972), 27.

8. Adam Smith, *The Wealth of Nations* (New York: Dutton, 1957); Heilbroner, *The Worldly Philosophers*, 16–72.

9. Andrew Heywood, *Political Ideologies: An Introduction* (New York: St. Martin's, 1992), Chs. 2–4; Ball and Dagger, *Political Ideologies and the Democratic Ideal*, Chs. 3, 4, 5.

10. European federalism was strongly advocated after World War II by Altiero Spinelli of Italy, among others. See Spinelli, *Towards the European Union* (Florence: European University Institute, 1983). Jean Monnet of France was a leading proponent of functionalism. See Monnet, *Memoirs*, translated by Richard Mayne (Garden City, NY: Doubleday, 1978).

11. The leading realist scholar of the postwar era was Hans Morgenthau. See Morgenthau, *Politics Among Nations: The Struggle for Power and Peace*, 3rd ed. (New York: Alfred A. Knopf, 1964). A more recent realist analysis of global politics is Richard Crockatt, *The Fifty Years War* (New York: Routledge, 1996). For a realist analysis of nation-states' motivations and behavior vis-à-vis European integration specifically, see Thomas Pederson, *Germany, France, and the Integration of Europe: A Realist Interpretation* (London: Pinter, 1998).

12. Andrew Moravcsik is the founder of liberal intergovernmental theory. See Moravcsik, *The Choice for Europe: Social Purpose and State Power from Messina to Maastricht* (Ithaca, NY: Cornell University Press, 1998).

13. François Duchêne, *Jean Monnet: The First Statesman of Interdependence* (New York: Norton, 1994); Charles Williams, *Adenauer: The Father of the New Germany* (New York: Wiley, 2000), esp. 357–61.

14. David Gowland and Arthur Turner, *Reluctant Europeans: Britain and European Integration, 1945–1998* (Harlow: Longman, Pearson Education, 2000), 9–39; Stephen George, *An Awkward Partner: Britain in the European Community*, 3rd ed. (Oxford: Oxford University Press, 1998), 12–22; John W. Young, *Britain and European Unity, 1945–1992* (New York: Longman, 1997), 1–19.

15. Edward Fursdon, *The European Defense Community: A History* (New York: St. Martin's, 1980); F. Roy Willis, *France, Germany, and the New Europe*, Revised ed. (Stanford: Stanford University Press, 1968), 130–84; F. Roy Willis, *Italy Chooses Europe* (New York: Oxford University Press, 1971), 41–53.

16. Derek Urwin, *The Community of Europe: A History of European Integration since 1945* (New York: Longman, 1991), 71–84. The quotations are on p. 76.

17. Neofunctionalist analyses in political science have included Ernst Haas, *The Uniting of Europe: Political, Social, and Economic Forces 1950–57* (Stanford: Stanford University Press, 1958); Leon Lindberg, *The Political Dynamics of European Integration* (Stanford: Stanford University Press, 1963); and Leon Lindberg and Stuart Scheingold, *Europe's Would-Be Polity* (Englewood Cliffs, NJ: Prentice-Hall, 1970). Haas subsequently modified his analysis in "Turbulent Fields and the Theory of Regional Integration," *International Organization* 30 (Spring 1976), 173–212.

18. Moravcsik, *The Choice for Europe*, esp. Ch. 2; Urwin, *The Community of Europe*, 78–84.

19. The quotation is from Alistair Cole, "National and Partisan Contexts of Europeanization," 18; Edward Kolodziej, *French International Policy Under de Gaulle and Pompidou: The Politics of Grandeur* (Ithaca, NY: Cornell University Press, 1974); Willis, *France, Germany, and the New Europe*, 273–365; Moravcsik, *The Choice for Europe*, Ch. 3.

20. Rosemary Fennell, *The Common Agricultural Policy: Continuity and Change* (Oxford: Clarendon Press, 1997), Chs. 1 and 2; Moravcsik, *The Choice for Europe*, Ch. 3; Urwin, *The Community of Europe*, Ch. 7.

21. Urwin, *The Community of Europe*, Ch. 8; Moravcsik, *The Choice for Europe*, Ch. 3; Kolodziej, *French International Policy Under de Gaulle and Pompidou*.

22. Haig Simonian, *The Privileged Partnership: Franco-German Relationships in the European Community, 1969–1984* (Oxford: Oxford University Press, 1985); Urwin, *The Community of Europe*, 139–54.

23. Moravcsik, *The Choice for Europe*, Ch. 4; Urwin, *The Community of Europe*, 154–228.

24. Urwin, *The Community of Europe*, 221–228; Moravcsik, *The Choice for Europe*, 331–333.

25. Charles Grant, *Delors: Inside the House that Jacques Built* (London: Nicholas Brealey, 1994) assigns a major role to Delors. Moravcsik, *The Choice for Europe*, Ch. 5, builds a convincing case for the primacy of French, West German, and British chief executives in the process.

26. Gowland and Turner, *Reluctant Europeans*, Ch. 18; George, *An Awkward Partner*, Chs. 6, 7.

27. Moravcsik, *The Choice for Europe*, Ch. 6; Michael Baun, *An Imperfect Union: The Maastricht Treaty and the New Politics of European Integration* (Boulder, CO: Westview, 1996); J. M. Grieco, "The Maastricht Treaty, Economic and Monetary Union and the Neo-realist Research Programme," *Review of International Studies* 21, 1 (January 1995), 21–40.

28. James Walsh, *European Monetary Integration & Domestic Politics: Britain, France, and Italy* (Boulder, CO: Lynne Rienner, 2000); Bernard Benoit, *Social-Nationalism: An Anatomy of French Euroskepticism* (Aldershot: Ashgate, 1997); Alistair Cole, *Franco-German Relations* (Harlow: Longman, 2001), 128–144.

29. Hugh Schofield, "Key Points of the EU's Historic Agreement at Nice," Agence France Presse, December 11, 2000; Stephen Castle, "The Deal—Big Four Emerge Triumphant after Diplomatic 'Coup'," *The Independent*, December 12, 2000; Peter Ludlow, "The Treaty of Nice: Neither Triumph nor Disaster," *ECSA Review* 14, 2 (Spring 2001), 1–4; Gráinne de Búrca, "The EU Charter of Fundamental Rights," *ECSA Review* 14, 2 (Spring 2001), 9–10.

30. The senior convention member's quotation is from "Special Report: Europe's Constitution," *The Economist* (June 21, 2003), 51. The Peel quotation is from Quentin Peel, "Europe's Constitution Misses Its Moment," *Financial Times*, June 17, 2003, 15. The Prodi and Blair quotations are from Frank Bruni, "Leaders Broadly Back a Draft Charter for the European Union," *New York Times*, June 21, 2003, A2.

31. The quotation is from "Special Report: Europe's Constitution," *The Economist* (June 21, 2003), 52. Bruno de Witte, "Après Nice: Time for a European Constitution?" *ECSA Review* 14, 2 (Spring 2001), 10–11; William Pfaff, "Europe's Unification Debate Needs the Sound of Fresh Voices," *International Herald Tribune*, January 11, 2001, 6; Edmund Andrews, "Germans Offer Plan to Remake Europe Union," *New York Times*, March 1, 2001, A1, A3; Suzanne Daley, "French Premier Opposes German Plan for Europe," *New York Times*, May 29, 2001, A6; "Nice Uncle Gerhard and the Little'Uns," *The Economist* 358 (February 3, 2001), 50; George Parker and Daniel Dombey, "'Not Perfect but More than We Could Have Hoped for': Europe's Draft Constitution," *Financial Times*, June 20, 2003, 13; Richard Baldwin and Mika Widgren, "Europe's Voting Reform Will Shift Power Balance," *Financial Times*, June 23, 2003, 13; "Special Report: Europe's Constitution," *The Economist* (June 21, 2003), 51–54.

32. "A Difficult Birth," *The Economist*, 371 (June 26, 2004), 53–54; Gaby Hinsliff and Ian Traynor, "Europe's Grand Folly," *The Observer*, December 14, 2003; "Proving the Case for a Constitution," *Financial Times*, December 15, 2003, 14; George Parker, "Atmosphere of Resignation as Leaders Walk Away," *Financial Times*, December 15, 2003, 4; Stefan Wagstyl, "Failure May Have Impact on EU's Long-Term Future," *Financial Times*, December 15, 2003, 4; John Tagliabue, "Draft Charter Slips Away; Europe Asks, Now What?" *New York Times*, December 15, 2003, A9.

33. Haas, *The Uniting of Europe*; Lindberg, *The Political Dynamics of European Integration*; Lindberg and Scheingold, *Europe's Would-Be Polity*. See

note 17 for full citations of these and Haas's later modification.

34. Pederson, *Germany, France, and the Integration of Europe.*

35. Moravcsik, *The Choice for Europe.*

36. See, for example, Rey Koslowski, "A Constructivist Approach to Understanding the European Union as a Federal Polity," *Journal of European Public Policy* 6, 4 (1999), 561–578. Ben Rosamond, *Theories of European Integration* (New York: St. Martin's, 2000), 171–174, discusses a variety of constructivist approaches and their common themes.

37. Paul Pierson, "The Path to European Integration: A Historical Institutionalist Analysis," *Comparative Political Studies* 29 (April 1996), 126.

38. Bernard Benoit, "Surprise at Eichel's 'Emotional Response,'" *Financial Times*, November 26, 2004, 4; Ed Crooks, "EU May Yet Pay the Price of Not Playing by the Rules," *Financial Times*, November 26, 2003, 4; George Parker, "Ministers Conduct Late-Night Burial for EU Fiscal Framework," *Financial Times*, November 26, 2003, 4.

39. There is a growing number of studies emphasizing "multi-level governance" patterns in the European Union. See, for example, Gary Marks, Liesbet Hooge, and Karen Blank, "European Integration from the 1980s: State-Centric v. Multi-Level Governance," *Journal of Common Market Studies* 34, 3 (1996), 341–378 and Liesbet Hooghe and Gary Marks, *Multi-Level Governance and European Integration* (Lanham, MD: Rowman and Littlefield, 2001). Most would not classify these studies as constituting a full theory, and this author has not done so.

Chapter 3

THE EUROPEAN UNION: MAJOR INSTITUTIONS

"Mr. Delors said at a press conference the other day that he wanted the European Parliament to be the democratic body of the Community, the Commission to be the executive and the Council of Ministers to be the Senate. No! No! No!"

—Margaret Thatcher, *cited in Charles Grant,*
The House that Jacques Built (1994), 149.

A s noted in Chapter One, many analysts have identified the contemporary European Union as a political system but not a state. In doing so, they are emphasizing that the central institutions of the European Union lack the monopoly on the legitimate use of coercion that Max Weber and other social scientists have conventionally described as the essential feature of the state. Such a monopoly continues to reside in the hands of the national governments of the member nation-states in most respects. These observers also often note the relatively small budget of the EU, which totals less than 4 percent of the total budgets of its member states, and the widespread evidence that European citizens identify far more with their nation-states than with the EU. Margaret Thatcher's resounding "No! No! No!" in the quotation in the heading of this chapter expresses well the obstacles from intergovernmentalists to strengthening the central institutions of the European Union. While lacking certain critical features of a state as commonly defined, the European Union does possess the

stable set of institutions for collective decision-making, as well as the pattern of inputs, policy outputs, and feedback, that Gabriel Almond, David Easton, and others have identified as characteristic of a political system. Moreover, its public policies have had profound effects on the actions of its member states in almost all spheres. Indeed, most estimates are that at least two-thirds of the laws made within its boundaries in recent years have emanated directly or indirectly from EU institutions.[1]

The European Union has not operated under a formal constitution, as most European nation-states have. Instead, it has been governed by a series of treaties, commencing with the Treaty of Paris that established the European Coal and Steel Community in 1951, continuing with the Rome Treaties of 1957 that amended the Treaty of Paris and added the European Economic Community and the European Atomic Energy Community, and progressing through a variety of additional treaties to the Nice Treaty of 2001. However, the EU is now taking steps, through a constitutional convention that commenced in March 2002 and presented its proposals in June 2003, toward developing a constitution, though many term it a "constitutional treaty" (because, like a treaty, it will require the approval of all member states). "The fact that the EU is adopting a constitutional treaty underlines its hybrid nature, half-way between an international organization and a state," has noted the British weekly, *The Economist*, in a widely echoed assessment. The Constitutional Convention was chaired by former French President Valery Giscard d'Estaing and consisted of 105 delegates from the member states (including the 13 new accession states officially recognized as such in 2002). The breakdown of the December 2003 European Summit on the constitution showed the deep divisions in Europe over constitutional issues. Though the national leaders hammered out a compromise that brought a surface consensus on the constitution at the European Summit in June 2004, there remains the formidable task of gaining ratification in all 25 member states, at least 11 of which are pledged to hold popular referendums. While some analysts have compared the European Constitutional Convention to the American Constitutional Convention of 1787, it will not create a United States of Europe comparable to the United States of America. The EU's mixture of supranational (or federal) elements with intergovernmental elements will continue to distinguish the mixed "system" of the European Union from the federal state of the United States of America, though the new constitution will move the EU closer to a federal model than ever before.[2]

The most important central institutions of the EU political system are as follows:

- the European Commission
- the European Council
- the Council of the European Union (Council of Ministers)
- the European Parliament
- the European Court of Justice
- the European Central Bank.

Since the formation of the European Union by the Maastricht Treaty that took effect in 1993, the central institutions have primarily affected who gets what, when, and how on European Community matters within Pillar One, a set of fairly supranational procedures governing how the EU budget and a wide variety of legislative policies are to be made. Policy-making within the other two pillars, Common Foreign and Security Policy (Pillar Two) and much of Justice and Home Affairs (Pillar Three), has been largely structured around intergovernmental procedures and has required unanimous agreement among member national governments. The new constitutional text provides for abolition of the three pillar system, makes justice and home affairs policy-making considerably more supranational than before, but continues the national veto over foreign and security policy.

As the EU institutional structure has evolved, it has been the target of inputs from individual Europeans, interest groups, business corporations, national political parties, and the governments of member nation-states. Transnational party groups have become a major factor shaping behavior in the European Parliament but not to a very great extent in other EU institutions. By most accounts, the national governments remain the most important sources of political inputs. They are also important in the implementation of the public-policy outputs of EU institutions. In such policy domains as education, health care, and social welfare, the nation-state governments have taken care to maintain their own dominance while keeping the EU roles fairly minimal. These are, of course, the policy areas in which credit for effective delivery is widely perceived to be most critical to attaining reelection!

THE EUROPEAN COMMISSION

The Commission, sited in Brussels, consists of a College of Commissioners and a permanent civil service (bureaucracy) of about 20,000 staff members. Composed in late 2004 of 25 Commissioners (1 from each of the member states), the College of Commissioners provides leadership to the Commission. Prior to 2004, each of the five major member states had had two commissioners each, while other member states had been able to name one apiece. Under the Treaty of Nice, effective in 2005, each member state was be limited to 1 commissioner, with a ceiling on the size of the Commission that was to be set at or below 27. The decision on the nationalities of the commissioners was to be determined by a system of rotation if and when the number of member states exceeded the number of commissioners. The proposed new constitution would make some significant changes, providing initially for one commissioner from each member state, until 2009, when the number of commissioners would be reduced to a number representing two-thirds of the number of member states, with membership rotating among the member states. The president would be nominated by a qualified majority of the European Council, subject to an election by a majority of the European Parliament. The vice president/union minister of foreign affairs would be appointed by a qualified majority of the European Council, with the agreement of the Commission president and the approval of Parliament. The idea behind the new constitutional provisions was to reduce complexity and enhance accountability, since many believed that a Commission of 30 or more voting members would be unwieldy.

At present, the members of the Commission are all appointed by their governments for five-year renewable terms (though they may be removed as a collective body by a two-thirds no-confidence vote in the European Parliament). The president of the Commission is selected by the European Council, subject to approval by a majority of the European Parliament, in advance of member state governments' nominations of the other commissioners and is consulted by the governments about the other nominees. Under the Treaty of Nice, the president gained enhanced powers over assigning commissioners' duties and was authorized to demand the resignation of a commissioner, subject to Commission approval. The proposed new constitution would strengthen these powers further by granting the president the power to compel on his own authority the resignation of any commissioner.[3]

A few presidents of the Commission, particularly Jacques Delors (1985–1995), Walter Hallstein (1958–1967), and Roy Jenkins (1977–1981), have enjoyed substantial influence during at least a portion of their tenures in office. Others, such as Jacques Santer (1995–1999) and Franco Maria Malfatti (1970–1972), have proved unable to leave much of a mark. It should be stressed that even the most skillful president of the Commission is unlikely to be able to assume as forceful a leadership role as a French president or prime minister, a German chancellor, a British prime minister, or a Spanish prime minister is often able to do within his or her country. Even most Italian prime ministers have played larger leadership roles in Italy than most European Commission presidents have in the EU. Certainly, the EU Commission president enjoys far fewer powers than the president of the United States.

The Commission is structured much like a cabinet within a national government, in that each commissioner heads one or two Directorates General (DGs), which are roughly similar to civil service departments in national administrations (list in Table 3.1). However, the president of the Commission, unlike most national prime ministers, has had little control over the membership or tenure in office of his fellow commissioners. The Treaty of Nice and the draft of the new constitution suggest the

TABLE 3.1   Commissioners and DG Responsibilities, August, 2004

President	José Manuel Barroso (Portugal)
Administrative Affairs, Audit, & Anti-Fraud	Siim Kallas (Estonia)
Agriculture & Rural Development	Mariann Fischer Boel (Denmark)
Competition	Neelie Kroes-Smit (Netherlands)
Development & Humanitarian Aid	Louis Michel (Belgium)
Economic & Monetary Affairs	Joaquìn Almunia (Spain)
Education & Culture	Ján Figel (Slovakia)
Employment & Social Affairs	Vladimír Spidla (Czech Republic)
Energy	László Kovács (Hungary)
Enlargement	Olli Rehn (Finland)
Enterprise & Industry	Günter Verheugen (Germany)
Environment	Stavros Dimas (Greece)
External Relations & European Neighborhood Policy	Benita Ferrero-Waldner (Austria)
Financial Programming & Budget	Dalia Grybauskaite (Lithuania)
Fisheries & Maritime Affairs	Joe Borg (Malta)
Health & Consumer Protection	Markos Kyprianou (Cyprus)
Information Society & Media	Viviane Reding (Luxembourg)
Institutional Relations & Communication Strategy	Margot Wallström (Sweden)
Internal Market & Services	Charlie McCreevy (Ireland)
Justice, Freedom, & Security	Rocco Buttiglione (Italy)
Regional Policy	Danuta Hübner (Poland)
Science & Research	Janez Potocnik (Slovenia)
Taxation and Customs Union	Ingrida Udre (Latvia)
Trade	Peter Mandelson (United Kingdom)
Transport	Jacques Barrot (France)

Source: Financial Times, August 13, 2004, 2.

likelihood that presidential powers will be enhanced in the near future. Romano Prodi (1999–2004) has sought to strengthen the Commission presidency, to establish a leadership team of the most important commissioners after the enlargement of the Commission due to eastward expansion of the EU, and to fend off efforts emanating from the British and French governments in particular to shift power away from the Commission to the European Council and the Council of Ministers. (The box on pages 218–219 offers further discussion of Commission President Prodi and his contributions.) Some analysts believe that the European Union may ultimately merge the positions of president of the Commission and president of the European Council, centering executive authority in the hands of a single leader to an extent that has not been possible and remains too controversial to be attempted in the near future.

The primary responsibilities of the Commission are to initiate proposals for Community

PEOPLE IN THE EU

Jacques Delors and the Commission Presidency

 More than any of his predecessors or successors as president of the European Commission, Jacques Delors utilized the position to provide strong leadership that moved the EC/EU toward further integration. His leadership roles were particularly notable concerning the single-market reforms of the mid-1980s, the "social" policy initiatives of the late 1980s, German reunification in 1990, and the Maastricht Treaty of 1992. Although analysts disagree about the importance of Delors's leadership, even Andrew Moravcsik, who argues that the "entrepreneurship of supranational officials…tends to be futile and redundant,"[4] concludes that Delors showed unusual capacity to make "statesmanlike judgments" about the proper time to compromise.[5] Much more positively, George Ross has stressed Delors's "presidentializing" of the Commission and has suggested that "the Delors strategy for Europe may be the most elaborate proposal for a new left-of-center vision we have yet seen," while Timothy Bainbridge has concluded, "Delors was by far the most influential President of the Commission since Walter Hallstein…. Delors brought to the Presidency a broad strategic vision, a clear model of the society and of the Union he wanted to create, and an inexhaustible appetite for detail."[6] Close ties to the major national leaders, previous governing experience in a major nation-state (France), the prestige that resulted from these, and a good sense of political timing all contributed to Delors's relative success as Commission president. Of all of the major national leaders, only British Prime Minister Margaret Thatcher consistently challenged him, as in her famous response to his proposals to strengthen EC institutions: "Mr. Delors said at a press conference the other day that he wanted the European Parliament to be the democratic body of the Community, the Commission to be the executive and the Council of Ministers to be the Senate. No! No! No!"

Born in Paris in 1925, Delors took an unusual path to political power for a French Socialist politician. His first political engagements were with a Catholic youth movement. He did not attend a *grande ecole* but instead moved straight from secondary school to employment at the Bank of France. "At heart a moderate,"[7] he participated in several different parties before becoming a Socialist in the 1970s. Delors's first and only elective post was as a Socialist Member of the European Parliament in 1979. In 1981, French Socialist President Mitterrand appointed him as Minister of Finance in the French government. Delors's advice helped persuade Mitterrand in 1983 to shift away from a failing French policy that emphasized a "socialist" effort to use Keynesian methods to stimulate the French economy toward a policy of embracing European integration and combining new EC social commitments with development of the single market.

When in 1984 President Mitterrand floated Delors's name as a possible nominee for the European Commission presidency,

Delors was already well-known by most European national leaders. Both Chancellor Kohl of West Germany and Prime Minister Thatcher of the United Kingdom gave their support to his appointment, although Thatcher would later turn sharply against Delors, considering him too "socialistic" for her tastes.

Prior to taking office as Commission president in January 1985, Delors toured the capitals of all of the member states, searching for a "big idea" to rejuvenate the European Community. Based on the input he received, he settled on the single-market project but tried to combine it with social protections of European workers and strengthening of European Community institutions. Though less than fully successful in achieving his social and institution-strengthening objectives, he did move the EC toward some of them. During the upheavals leading to German reunification, Delors threw his support behind German Chancellor Kohl's rush toward quick merger of East and West Germany on Western terms (in contrast to the reluctance shown by Thatcher and Mitterrand) and helped to move Europe in the direction of adaptation to it. On the Maastricht Treaty, Delors was an active player; but clearly Chancellor Kohl and President Mitterrand played more important leading roles than he.

Though the constraints on leadership from the European Commission presidency are manifold (among them, a large group of commissioners over whom the president has little control, national leaders jealous of their prerogatives, and European publics unaccustomed to looking to the Commission presidency for leadership), Delors made the most of his position. The respect for him and his popularity in his native country made him a prospective candidate for the presidency of France in 1995; but he decided not to make the race. Since stepping down as president of the Commission in 1995, Delors has become an "elder statesman." The difficulties faced by Jacques Santer, his successor as Commission president, only served to highlight Delors's unique contributions. Romano Prodi, the subsequent president of the Commission (see box on pages 218–219), soon found his own leadership skills compared unfavorably with those of Delors after he assumed the position in 1999.

Despite inherent limitations on his role, Delors illustrated that a Commission president can provide effective leadership. Probably his greatest legacies will be his linking of the single market, the institutional reforms of the Single European Act, and the enhanced "social" dimension to European integration. His quick support for German reunification and his mediation roles among national leaders during the end of the Cold War and the drafting of the Maastricht Treaty also left an important mark on modern European history.[8]

legislation and for the budget (policy initiation or formulation) and to oversee implementation of Community public policies once they have been formally adopted. In the formulation process, the Commission has been formally designated as the sole initiator of most economic and social policies. However, in practice national governments often battle it (and one another) to initiate such policies; there is much debate among analysts over the extent to which the Commission is an independent actor capable of effective initiation. Most evidence suggests that on matters of "high politics," effective initiation lies more in the hands of executives of the major member states than in the hands of the Commission, largely in accord with what liberal intergovernmental and realist theories indicate. Interest groups, business corporations, and political parties also often play parts in the initiation process. In the implementation process, the small size of the Commission staff (20,000, in contrast to 500,000 or more in each of the major member states' bureaucracies) means that the Commission must rely heavily on member states for assistance. One result is often uneven and incomplete implementation of European Community legislation. In some policy domains, such as competition, the Commission enjoys direct implementation powers through its regulations; but in most policy sectors its reliance on national bureaucracies for assistance is extensive.[9]

Differing Perspectives on the Impact of Jacques Delors as Commission President

"Entrepreneurship of supranational officials... tends to be futile and redundant."

Andrew Moravcsik, *The Choice for Europe* (1998), 372.

"Delors was by far the most influential President of the Commission since Walter Hallstein.... Delors brought to the presidency a broad strategic vision, a clear model of the society and of the Union he wanted to create, and an inexhaustible appetite for detail."

Timothy Bainbridge, *The Penguin Companion to European Union (1998), 117.*

"Mr. Delors said at a press conference the other day that he wanted the European Parliament to be the democratic body of the Community, the Commission to be the executive and the Council of Ministers to be the Senate. No! No! No!"

Margaret Thatcher, *cited in Charles Grant, The House that Jacques Built (1994), 149.*

THE EUROPEAN COUNCIL

The European Council usually meets four times a year in what are often referred to as European Summit meetings and generally addresses major issues that have not been resolved elsewhere. Its members are the heads of government of the member states and the French president, as well as the president of the European Commission, assisted by the member state foreign ministers and the vice president of the Commission. It has been in existence on a regular basis only since 1975, following its establishment by an agreement reached in 1974. It was not given a legal foundation until it was recognized in Article Two of the 1986 Single European Act. However, "summits" were held from time to time from 1959 onward, initially at the suggestion of French President de Gaulle, who accurately foresaw that they would allow national chief executives to assert executive leadership in the EC.

Every six months, a different member nation-state takes the presidency of the European Council and the Council of Ministers. During its tenure of office, this state has responsibility for organizing and chairing Council and Council of Ministers meetings. The presidency also speaks for the Council and Council of Ministers in dealing with other EU institutions and with external actors. Because of the frequency of presidential changes and the ensuing discontinuity, the Council introduced the Troika system in 1983. Under this system, the current presidency works closely with the past and future presidential states. Though each member nation-state holds the presidency for just a six-month period at a time, most seek to use this period to pursue national policy objectives. However, small member states are sometimes nearly overwhelmed by the tasks of the presidency. Regardless of the size of the member state, some presidencies have been markedly more successful than others at steering the EU in desired directions. The new EU constitution drafted by the constitutional convention in 2003 proposes to replace the rotating presidency of the European Council with an individual president, to be elected by the membership for a two and one-half year term of office (with a second term permissible). This proposal originally encountered considerable opposition from many of the small member states of the EU, though their fears that it would strengthen the domination of large member states from which elected presidents might be most likely to be drawn appear to have been overcome.

European Summits nearly always attract a great deal more mass media attention than do the day-to-day operations of other EU institutions. Though the Commission must formally initiate legislative proposals, and normal EU lawmaking procedures must be followed to enact them into law, the European Council often shapes the direction of initiatives in significant ways. Increasingly, it has become the chief forum for determining treaty reforms and major public-policy shifts. Therefore, in practice, it allows the chief executives to give new directions to European integration when they can reach accords with one another. The European Council commonly operates on the basis of unanimous agreement, and formal votes are rarely taken.[10]

The Nice Summit of December 2000 illustrates some of the main points about the European Council, though it was unique in some respects also. The Summit was in Nice, France, because France held the presidency of the Council and Council of Ministers during the second half of 2000. As usual, the European Council meeting attracted wide mass media attention and fostered a great deal of speculation

Box 3.1

WHO'S COMING TO DINNER?

The chief executives of the EU member states (especially the major member states) often get together informally to discuss common concerns and prepare joint approaches, outside the formal meetings at the European Summits. Therefore, it was not unusual when Prime Minister Tony Blair of Britain invited the leaders of France and Germany to a dinner at his Downing Street residence in London on November 4, 2001, to discuss the war in Afghanistan and their roles in it. However, when Prime Minister Berlusconi of Italy learned of the planned dinner, he demanded an invitation, too, having been embarrassed at home by his exclusion from a similar informal session at the time of the Ghent Summit the previous month. After an invitation was duly issued to Berlusconi, Blair felt that he had better also invite Spanish Prime Minister Aznar and EU high representative for foreign policy, Javier Solana. Because Belgium held the rotating presidency of the EU in the second half of 2001, its prime minister was invited, too. When the Dutch prime minister learned of these developments, he also asked to receive a last-minute invitation and actually arrived after dinner was already in progress. Even the greatly expanded dinner list failed to satisfy demands for inclusion, however. A representative of one of the small member states that went unrepresented at Tony Blair's dinner complained: "Decisions are made and then we are just informed." Clearly, coordination among EU member states is often a difficult task, particularly given the considerable egos of most nation-state leaders.[11]

about national and personality conflicts and power plays. The chief subject of this meeting of the European Council was to hammer out the details of the Nice Treaty, which had not been completed at an earlier special Intergovernmental Conference of the EU. Though agreements on the disputed key points were reached by the Nice Summit, and the Nice Treaty could thus move on toward ratification by the member states, many analysts commented on the high level of conflicts evident among the national leaders present. One scholarly observer commented, "Recriminations were hurled about like shares on a falling market. Recollected in tranquility, however, the meeting and the Treaty that it produced do not seem to have been so bad after all."[12] The main focus of the Nice Treaty was on altering EU institutions and their procedures to accommodate a near-doubling of the membership due to anticipated eastward expansion. However, the temporary nature of many such agreements in the EU is evident in the fact that the draft constitution presented by the constitutional convention in June 2003 has proposed altering some of the "reforms" of the Nice Treaty before they have even been put into effect.

"Decisions are made and then we are just informed."

Leader of a small European state, complaining about frequent dominance of the EU by leaders of large European states, *cited in The Economist 361 (November 10, 2001), 47.*

THE COUNCIL OF MINISTERS (COUNCIL OF THE EU)

Closely related to the European Council but unlike it possessing a basis in the original Rome Treaty, the Council of the European Union, still commonly termed the Council of Ministers, its original title (and the title employed in the proposed new constitution), actually encompasses a complex of institutions that afford the most direct, regular expression of distinctive national interests in the European Union of today. Each member state sends a minister to represent it at each meeting of the Council of the EU, but the ministers vary according to the issue under discussion (i.e., foreign ministers meet as the General Affairs Council [GAC], economics and finance ministers meet as the Council of Economics and Finance Ministers [ECOFIN], agriculture ministers meet as the Council of Agriculture Ministers, etc.). Though the Council of Ministers is the voice of the nation-state governments, the agendas are set by the somewhat supranational Committee of Permanent Representatives (COREPER), including ambassadors from all of the member states, who both represent their own nation-states and develop ties to other national representatives that often lead them to try to find solutions that may transcend national differences. In addition, numerous technical committees provide service to the Council and also possess some supranational characteristics. One major recent study has concluded that approximately 85 percent of the decisions of the Council of Ministers have been effectively resolved at the level of COREPER or the technical committees.[13]

The Council of Ministers, as noted previously, consists of different sets of ministers on different policy matters. The General Affairs Council, Economic and Financial Council, and Agricultural Council meet about once per month—more frequently than most of the other Councils. They also tend to be the most influential sessions of the Council of Ministers.

The Council of Ministers is often described as the chief legislative body of the European Union, sharing lawmaking powers in many realms with the less powerful, popularly elected European Parliament. Because Council meetings are shrouded in considerable secrecy, unlike European Parliament sessions, many critics have portrayed them as less "democratic" than the

European Parliament. Especially now that **qualified majority voting** has been introduced into the Council of Ministers' decision-making processes on a wide array of issues, national governments sometimes are outvoted in secret sessions; and neither their national parliament at home nor their national voting public at home can determine how the national minister in question voted or hold her or him accountable. Under the qualified majority rules, each national representative has had a vote weighted roughly in proportion to his or her state's population and a majority of 62 of 87 votes has been required. Under the proposed new constitution, the qualified majority vote is to be adjusted so that approval will require a 55 percent majority of the member states representing at least 65 percent of the EU population. This revision, if adopted, aims to make passage of legislation in the Council easier than in the past. In practice, there has always been a strong preference for consensus on the Council; and a recent analysis found that 86 percent of the votes during a recent one-year period were by unanimous vote or by unanimity with one or more member states abstaining.[14]

The Council of Ministers possesses executive as well as legislative powers, sharing executive leadership with the Commission and the European Council. Its executive roles include setting guidelines for the Commission on Community legislation, monitoring the implementation of Community policies by the Commission, and taking the initiative within the European Union's Common Foreign and Security Policy (CFSP) and most aspects of Justice and Home Affairs (JHA) policy domains.

Though the Council of the EU is usually portrayed as a largely intergovernmental institution that represents the distinctive interests of the member nation-states, and is in fact such a body on major matters of controversy, it does possess some supranational features, particularly in its COREPER and committee structure, because these involve networks among bureaucrats who often have developed strong supranational ties among themselves.[15]

TABLE 3.2	Weighting of National Votes in Qualified Majority Voting, 2003
France	10
Germany	10
Italy	10
United Kingdom	10
Spain	8
Netherlands	5
Belgium	5
Greece	5
Portugal	5
Austria	4
Sweden	4
Denmark	3
Finland	3
Ireland	3
Luxembourg	2
Total	87

*Adoption of new constitution as drafted by the constitutional convention would replace this system with a requirement for a majority of at least 55 percent of the member states representing at least 65 percent of the EU population.

THE EUROPEAN PARLIAMENT

The European Parliament, which is housed in palatial buildings in both Brussels and Strasbourg, France, is the only popularly elected institution in the European Union. Despite its name, it is not the chief lawmaking body of the EU, though in a number of spheres it plays a significant lawmaking role; and the draft of the new constitution proposes to increase its lawmaking role significantly. It is presently composed of 732 members elected from each of the 25 member states on political party tickets. The introduction of direct elections since 1979 has enhanced the democratic legitimacy of the

Parliament and has indirectly contributed to strengthening its powers in the Community's legislative process. However, its elections draw a lower turnout than national elections and often center on national issues and approval or disapproval of national political leaders more than they do on European Union issues. Moreover, the European Parliament remains generally weaker than the Council of Ministers in the lawmaking sphere, though the Parliament's powers will be expanded substantially if the draft of the new constitution is adopted. Table 3.3 indicates the different types of lawmaking procedures and the roles of the European Parliament and the Council of Ministers in each. The section of this chapter summarizing the stages of the EU legislative processes will illustrate these points in the broad context of the major stages of these processes.

The major formal powers of the European Parliament include the following:

- Approves the appointment of the Commission president (election of the president by majority vote according to the draft of the new constitution)
- Approves the appointment of the entire Commission following public hearings
- Has the power to censure and remove the entire Commission by a two-thirds vote
- Questions the Council and the Commission
- Shares lawmaking powers with the Council in many policy domains (Table 3.3)
- Approves all enlargements of the EU and agreements with external countries
- Approves the annual budget
- Can amend some proposed expenditures.

On the surface, these resemble the powers of most national legislatures.

However, the European Parliament is even more a reactive legislature than most national parliaments in Europe are; it has been subordi-

TABLE 3.3 Legislative Procedures and Parliamentary Roles

Consultation: The Council is the chief lawmaker on matters covered by this procedure. Commission proposals to the Council are sent to the Parliament for an opinion. Has covered agriculture and the justice and home affairs topics falling under the Community rubric.

Cooperation: Commission proposals are sent to the Council for a "common position" and to the Parliament for a first reading, during which it may offer amendments. The Parliament may at its second reading amend the Council's common position or, by an absolute majority, reject it. Council can override a Parliamentary rejection only by a unanimous vote. A conciliation procedure may negotiate an agreement between Council and Parliament. Covers aspects of economic and monetary policy.

Co-decision: Both the Council and the Parliament must approve matters covered by this procedure. There are two readings in each body, followed by a conciliation procedure if the two institutions fail to agree. The results of conciliation must be approved by both the Council (in a qualified majority vote) and the Parliament (in a simple majority vote). Covers most areas of legislation since 1997 and will cover even more areas if the new constitution is adopted.

Assent: Both the Council and the Parliament must approve matters covered by this procedure. In a single vote, the Parliament must give its assent to a Council action by an absolute majority. Covers enlargement treaties, some international agreements, and a few other legislative areas.

nate in many policy domains to the Council of Ministers, in which national interests generally assume a preeminent role. It is also quite restricted in its ability to check the powers of either the Commission or the European Council/Council of Ministers. Nevertheless, when the Commission under the leadership of President Jacques Santer was accused of inefficiency and several of its members became embroiled in scandal, the Parliament employed its powers to investigate and virtually forced the resignation of Santer and the entire Commission in 1999 even though it had previously failed to pass a motion of no confidence in the Commission. Despite this example of assertiveness by the European Parliament and the significant growth in its powers over the past 25 years, it remains a relatively weak legislative institution in many respects. The new constitution, if ratified, will substantially increase the powers of the Parliament.

The seats in the European Parliament have been allocated among the member nation-states roughly proportionate to their populations, though the smaller states are somewhat over-represented (Table 3.4). The Treaty of Nice placed a limit of 732 (subsequently raised to 750 under the proposed new constitution) on the future size of the European Parliament and reallocated the number of seats per member state in anticipation of eastward enlargement of the EU. Voting behavior in the European Parliament generally reflects partisan attachments more than national allegiances, in considerable contrast to patterns on the Council.

More than any other European Union institution, the Parliament is influenced by transnational party groups. The largest of these are the European People's Party (composed of Christian Democrats and some conservatives) and the Party of European Socialists (mostly social democratic parties), though the European Liberal Democratic and Reformist Group, the Greens/European Free Alliance, and the European United Left/Nordic Green Left are also significant party groups with influence in the European Parliament (Table 3.5). Analysts have repeatedly found that Members of the European Parliament (MEPs) vote fairly consistently with their parties (but less so than in most lower chambers of European national parliaments), that the parties sometimes line up on issues in a

TABLE 3.4 Distribution of European Parliamentary Seats by State, 2002 and 2004

Nation	2002	2004
Germany	99	99
France	87	78
Italy	87	78
United Kingdom	87	78
Spain	64	54
Netherlands	31	27
Belgium	25	24
Greece	25	24
Portugal	25	24
Sweden	22	19
Austria	21	18
Denmark	16	14
Finland	16	14
Ireland	15	13
Luxembourg	6	6
Poland		54
Czech Republic		24
Hungary		24
Slovakia		14
Lithuania		13
Latvia		9
Slovenia		7
Cyprus		6
Estonia		6
Malta		55
Total	626	732

left-right pattern common to most European national parliaments, but that the most common coalition in voting in the European Parliament is a grand coalition of the European People's Party, the Party of European Socialists, and the European Liberal Democratic and Reformist Group. Since 1997, when employment issues

TABLE 3.5   Distribution of European Parliamentary Seats by Party (2004–2009 Parliament, as of 6/30/04)

European People's Party & European Democrats	279
The Party of European Socialists	199
European Liberal Democrats and Reformers	67
Greens/European Free Alliance	40
European United Left/Nordic Green Left	39
Union for a Europe of Nations	27
Europe of Democracies and Diversities	15
Independents	66
Total	732

and conflicts over the stability and growth pact have come to be major issues in the Parliament, the left-right cleavage in parliamentary voting has sharpened somewhat, with the Party of European Socialists often in opposition to the European Peoples party and Liberal Democratic Reformists on these issues.[16]

Although the European Parliament aspires to be a democratic and central institution of the European Union, most observers conclude that the low turnout in its elections, the lack of most voters' information and attention concerning European Parliament issues, and the lack of European Parliament powers vis-à-vis other central EU institutions mean that the reality falls somewhat short of these aspirations.[17]

THE EUROPEAN COURT OF JUSTICE

The European Court of Justice (ECJ), located in Luxembourg, is the major arbiter of legal disputes relating to the Community treaties and the legislation based upon them. As the highest court of the European Community, it has operated as an effective supranational institution, sometimes offending national governments, business corporations, and interest groups in the process. However, in recent years it has shown some inclination to restrain its challenges to member state governments in the wake of indications of growing discontent in some member states over some of its rulings.

The Court of Justice is composed of 25 judges, as well as 8 advocates-general who deliver preliminary opinions on cases. The judges are appointed by consensus of the governments of the member states (one judge from each) and occupy their positions for renewable terms of six years. These are staggered so that appointments are made every three years. Many ECJ judges are academics who possess legal expertise but have not previously served as judges. The judges select one member as President of the Court for a renewable term of three years. The president then directs the work of the Court and presides at hearings. Since 1989, a Court of First Instance (CFI), termed the High Court in the new constitution, has helped to relieve the burdens on the ECJ by handling certain cases, the decisions in which can be appealed, on points of law only, to the ECJ. In contrast to procedures on the United States Supreme Court, ECJ judgments are always announced in the name of the Court, with no recording of any dissenting opinions.

The main areas of jurisdiction of the European Court of Justice are the following:

- Failure of a member state to fulfill a treaty obligation or obligation under Community legislation. Such an action may be brought to court either by the Commission or by another member state. If the Court finds against the state, the state must comply or, at the initiative of the Commission, face a fine that the ECJ may impose.

- Judicial review of the legality of legal instruments adopted by the Commission, Council, or Parliament. Actions in this area may be brought to court by the Council, Commission, a member state, or Parliament (the latter only to protect its own prerogatives). Individuals or entities with legal personality may also bring such actions in relation to regulations or decisions concerning them, but these are heard in the Court of First Instance.

- Failure to act. The Court may require an offending EC institution to take "necessary measures" if it finds that the institution failed to act when it was legally required to do so. Actions in this domain may be brought to court by the same procedures as in the judicial review category.

- Preliminary rulings. If a question of Community treaties or laws is raised before a national court, the national court may request the Court of Justice to make a preliminary ruling. This procedure is used to resolve questions of incompatibility between Community laws and national laws. More than one-half the total cases coming before the ECJ are requests for preliminary rulings.

The European Court of Justice has often been an "activist" judicial body, interpreting treaties and legislation broadly to advance European integration and arousing considerable criticism in the process. Some cases, such as its overturning of the British Merchant Shipping Act in the *Factortame* cases in 1990, have aroused a storm of political controversy within some of the major European nation-states. Nevertheless, the Court has enjoyed good cooperation most of the time from national courts, which have found their own powers enhanced within their respective national political systems, and has played a major role in shaping the European Union and many of its public policies. Its impact has been particularly great in shaping the single market, competition policy, social policy, and the common fisheries policy. A good example is the *Cassis de Dijon* case (120/78,

1979), which played a major role in the movement toward a single market, highlighted in the box on this page.

The *Cassis de Dijon* Case (120/78, 1979)

This case, which came before the European Court of Justice at a time (1979) when member states of the European Community were imposing various non-tariff barriers on one another's products, was a landmark in the movement toward a single European market. In this case, the Court ruled that the German government had violated European law by preventing the sale in Germany of Cassis de Dijon, a liqueur produced in France. The Court went on to declare that any product legally sold in one member state should be permitted to be sold in any other member state. The only exceptions were to be on grounds of health and safety—grounds not demonstrated by the German government in this case. This decision spurred the European Community to adopt new health and safety standards on products and moved the EC significantly toward a single market.

Some analysts have concluded that the relatively great importance of the European Court of Justice in promoting European integration, sometimes over the opposition of important member state governments, has been a clear example of the historical institutionalist pattern (Chapter Two) of nation-state governments' inabilities to control the direction or pace of European integration. In this view, an activist Court has moved far beyond the original intentions of the member states by broadly interpreting EC/EU treaties and legislation in ways that have constrained the states. This interpretation is partially correct. However, after the early 1990s, there were signs that the European Court of Justice was exercising greater caution than previously in challenging the interests of member states.

As previously noted, the ECJ rulings in the *Factortame* cases in 1990 aroused great controversy in the United Kingdom. At the behest of such major member states as France and Britain, the Maastricht Treaty of 1992 excluded EU foreign and security policies (Pillar Two) and most justice and home affairs policies (Pillar Three) from the jurisdiction of the European Court of Justice, though the pillar structure is to be abandoned if the constitutional convention's draft of the new constitutional treaty is adopted, with a consequent broadening of ECJ jurisdiction. Some of the protocols of the Maastricht Treaty limited the effects of ECJ rulings. For example, one protocol permitted the Danish government to retain national legislation prohibiting foreigners from acquiring second homes in Denmark, contrary to an ECJ ruling a few years previously in *Commission v. Greece*. Although several Maastricht Treaty provisions supported the ECJ by incorporating some of its decisions and by granting it powers to impose financial sanctions, many observers believed that the general message to the Court was that it should restrain its activism. A similar message was conveyed by the ruling of the German Constitutional Court in 1993 in a case involving a German constitutional challenge to the Maastricht Treaty, in which the German Constitutional Court gave a clear indication that it would closely monitor future ECJ rulings on the scope of European supranationalism in light of the requirements of the German Basic Law (constitution). According to the leading scholarly analysis of the European Court of Justice, the effects of these and other signals from member states have been that "the ECJ has exercised ever greater caution in challenging member states' interests."[18]

The European Court of Justice has unquestionably emerged as a powerful shaper of the European Union, almost certainly far beyond the original expectations of the founding member states of the EC/EU. However, like the other institutions of the EC/EU, it operates in a political environment in which the member state governments remain significant actors.

THE EUROPEAN CENTRAL BANK

The European Central Bank (ECB) is by far the newest and least tested of the major European Union institutions, dating only from 1998. Sited in Frankfurt, Germany, the Central Bank works through the European System of Central Banks (ESCB) to provide overall direction to the Economic and Monetary Union, presently involving 12 of the 25 EU member states (all of the pre-2004 members except the United Kingdom, Sweden, and Denmark). With a legal mandate to "maintain price stability," the ECB and ESCB "define and implement" EMU monetary policy, conduct foreign exchange operations, "hold and manage" the foreign reserves of the participating member states, and "promote the smooth operation of payment systems."[19]

The European Central Bank is managed by a Governing Council and an Executive Board. The Governing Council, composed of the six Board members and the governors of the national central banks of the EMU member states, makes most decisions by a simple majority, though certain decisions are made by votes weighted according to the states' shares of the ECB's capital. The Executive Board is composed of the president, vice president, and four other members. Each has one vote, and decisions are made by a simple majority. The six members of the Executive Board are appointed by the participating member states after consultation with the European Parliament and the Governing Council for nonrenewable eight-year terms. However, the first president, Wim Duisenberg, let it be known that he would "not want" to serve his full eight-year term in order to ease the pressure from the French government, which was disappointed that its choice for the presidency (Jean-Claude Trichet) had not been selected. Moreover, Duisenberg did, in fact, step down in 2003, to allow French banker Trichet to replace him. Although the French Socialist government leaders, joined for a time by German finance minister Oskar Lafontaine (1998–1999) and some other Socialist participants from other member states, have expressed concern that there are insufficient political controls over the European Central Bank and have sought to employ the ECOFIN ministers of the 12 members of the EMU for that purpose, other observers point to the compromise over the Duisenberg appointment as evidence that politics have intruded on its operations from its very beginnings.[20]

STAGES IN THE LEGISLATIVE PROCESSES OF THE EU: AN OVERVIEW

Because different rules and procedures govern the legislative processes in different policy domains (and have frequently changed over time), it is impossible to describe "the" decision-making pattern as it relates to European Union institutions. In fact, the complexity is one of the factors that often leads frustrated Europeans to complain that the EU is unfathomable and undemocratic.

In terms of the formal rules, there is one set of procedures governing adoption of the EU budget, and there are four main sets of rules for regular lawmaking: consultation, cooperation, co-decision, and assent procedures (each defined in Table 3.3).

Initiation of Legislation

Formal powers of initiation lie in the hands of the Commission. However, the Commission does not operate in a vacuum. Member state governments, interest groups, business corporations, subnational governments, and others influence its agenda. Certainly careful consid-

eration of the orientations of the member state governments affects what the Commission will in fact seek to initiate. In contrast, on matters encompassed in Pillars Two and Three, the Commission may formally initiate; but it shares this right with the member state governments. The new constitution, if adopted, would end the three-pillar structure.

Lawmaking

After initiation come the lawmaking stages, heavily involving the Council of Ministers in all instances. The European Parliament, its behavior shaped to a considerable degree by national and transnational party politics and ideologies (and its members accountable for their behavior to the voting public in competitive elections), has gained formally a co-equal status with the Council of the EU in areas covered by co-decision rules, which since 1997 have included the majority of the Pillar One legislative measures. As one moves to assent, cooperation, and consultation rules, the roles of the Parliament lessen vis-à-vis the Council, with the smallest roles for Parliament being those in the consultation category (mainly agriculture and some justice and home affairs policies, the latter mostly transferred from Pillar Three). Under procedural rules in Pillar Two (foreign and defense matters) and Pillar Three (most justice and home affairs matters), the Parliament's role is mainly that of a debating society, while the Council of the EU is in these clearly the chief lawmaker. Therefore, despite its name, it should be reiterated that the European Parliament is not as powerful a lawmaking body as is the Council of the EU/Council of Ministers.

Implementation

Implementation follows the adoption of legislation in order to apply the law in the daily lives of people living in the European Union. Formally the Commission is responsible for the implementation of legislation. If the law in question is a **regulation,** it takes effect in all member states without having to be incorporated into the 25 sets of national laws. If it is instead a **directive,** then member states must adopt appropriate national legislation. In both instances, day-to-day implementation is heavily dependent on the administrative bureaucracies of the member states. When the Commission concludes that a member state has not complied satisfactorily with a European legal requirement, it must issue an opinion to that effect, allow the member state or states to respond, and may then opt to bring the case before the European Court of Justice (ECJ) if the matter falls within Pillar One (since the ECJ lacks jurisdiction in the other two pillars). The ECJ decision on the matter is final. If a member state fails to comply with the decision of the European Court of Justice, in the opinion of the Commission, the Commission may then choose to ask the Court to impose a financial penalty on the state.

THE POLITICAL CONTEXT OF EU INSTITUTIONAL OPERATIONS

The major institutions of the European Union that have been described are supplemented by a variety of others, some of which have been noted at least briefly above. While the institutions possess some autonomy, their actual operations have been significantly influenced by transnational organized interests (and, especially in the European Parliament, transnational political party federations) as well as by the member nation-states and their distinctive national arrays of political parties, interest groups, and individual political actors.

Interest Groups

Without question, the nongovernmental organized interests that have generally proved most capable of influencing the central European Union institutions have been multinational business corporations and interest groups in which they dominate, such as the Union of Industrial and Employers' Confederations of Europe (UNICE) and the European Round-table of Industrialists (ERT). Though many observers have termed the representational style in the EU institutions more **pluralist** than **corporatist,** the pluralism in question has been a distinctly "elite pluralism," in which major businesses are better represented than labor unions, consumer groups, or other types of organized interests.[21] Despite a distinct tilt favorable to large business corporations, some non-business interest groups, especially environmental ones, have at times been able to win victories at the EU level above and beyond what they have been able to achieve within some of the nation-states. While noting the limited resources (and successes) of the interest groups compared with those of big business, several analysts have described the impact of the "Gang of Seven" major EU environmental interest groups in Brussels, operating often in tandem with the most pro-environmental protection national governments, such as Germany, the Netherlands, Sweden, and Denmark, to set EU standards at high levels that compel such laggards as Spain and Italy to move their standards up to the EU level.[22]

Political Parties

Transnational political party federations have had their greatest influence in the European Parliament. As issues of stability, growth, and employment have come before the Parliament increasingly since 1997, "left-right" divisions between the Party of European Socialists on the one hand and the European People's party and the Liberal Democrats and Reformers on the other have become more pronounced than in the past. However, even in the Parliament, distinctive national political parties have often taken precedence in influencing the votes of members. Certainly the national parties remain the major factors in the elections to the European Parliament. In the European Council and the Council of Ministers, transnational party ties are of less significance than in the Parliament. At least part of the time, chief executives and ministers of the same party grouping have shown some limited tendencies to cooperate more than those of opposing party groupings. For example, Prime Minister Tony Blair of the United Kingdom and Chancellor Gerhard Schröder have sought to coordinate their social democratic "third way" approaches. For a time in 1998 and 1999, the French Socialist government of Prime Minister Lionel Jospin and his Finance Minister Dominique Strauss-Kahn worked in coordination with German finance minister and Social Democratic party leader, Oskar Lafontaine, to advance a more traditionally socialistic agenda in the European Union, though this effort did not survive the departures from office of Strauss-Kahn and Lafontaine. There is some general evidence that Socialist ministers have given somewhat higher priority in recent years to combating unemployment and promoting social welfare through EU efforts than their Christian Democratic or conservative colleagues.[23]

However, the closest long-term partnership on the European Council and the Council of Ministers has linked French and German chief executives and ministers even when they have been of different party groups: France's conservative President Giscard d'Estaing often worked in close harmony with West Germany's Social Democratic Chancellor Helmut Schmidt between 1974 and 1981, and France's Socialist President François Mitterrand worked in tandem much of the time (after abandoning his initial socialist moves of 1981–1982) with Germany's Christian Democratic Chancellor Helmut Kohl between 1983 and 1995.

Because of lack of transparency in Council of Ministers voting, and the resulting paucity of systematic studies, only a little can be said at this time about behavioral patterns there. On the Commission, the European Court of Justice, and the European Central Bank, the same problems exist. However, Liesbet Hooghe's recent empirical study, incorporating extensive interviews with Commission officials, has shown party to be one of several important variables (along with country and prior work environment) shaping the preferences of Commission officialdom. Partisanship may play a larger role within other major EU institutions, too, than most previous analyses have estimated.[24]

THE "DEMOCRATIC DEFICIT" IN THE EUROPEAN UNION

The previous chapter, reinforced by much of the evidence in this chapter, has presented a picture of the "high politics" of EU decision-making dominated by the executives of the major member states, often negotiating behind closed doors with one another and a cluster of big-business representatives and central bankers. It has also presented a picture of the "low politics" of daily decision-making (sometimes having significant cumulative effects) made in even greater secrecy and through even more complex negotiations by European, national, and sometimes subnational officials and interest groups. Furthermore, the very complexity of the procedures governing lawmaking in the European Union, and the differences between them and most national governments' procedures, has served to confuse and anger many Europeans and arouse their complaints that the EU "system" is fundamentally undemocratic.

This chapter has noted the weakness of "party government" mechanisms of accountability in the EU; the lack of transparency (or openness) in the operations of most key EU institutions; the use of qualified majority voting (and occasionally majority voting) in combination with secrecy on many issues in the Council of Ministers (making it difficult for national parliaments or voters to hold a minister accountable); the relative lack of power of the most popularly accountable and most transparent EU institution, the European Parliament (despite new powers granted to it in recent years); and the pattern in which the European Parliamentary elections usually reflect national issues or political personalities rather than European issues. These patterns have all fed a chorus of criticism to the effect that the European Union suffers from a "democratic deficit." "Until the EU is as democratic as national political systems," Simon Hix, a leading British political scientist has written, in words that are widely echoed in Europe, "it is rational for Europe's citizens to be skeptical of the European integration process."[25]

How, if at all, to address the widely perceived lack of sufficient democracy remains a matter of major controversy in Europe. Reform proposals include further strengthening the European Parliament, popular election of the Commission president, European-wide referendums, and greater accountability of EU institutions to national parliaments. However, each proposal faces its own set of critics. Many of the advocates of increased democracy have expressed disappointment in the limited "democratization" evident in the proposals of the European constitutional convention that met during 2002–2003, despite the ringing introduction of the preamble of the new constitution with the quotation from Thucydides: "Our Constitution...is called a democracy because power is in the hands not of a minority but of the greatest number."[26]

To a great extent, the European Union today is less a constitutional democracy than it is a reflection of the governments of the member nation-states, which are in turn more responsive, especially on European matters, to their own leaders' power drives and to the needs and desires of multinational corporations and central bankers than to a general public that displays low levels of awareness and understanding of the European Union, how it operates, and what it does. Although these governments are all themselves constitutional democracies in form, the elections through which they are held accountable to the voters are fought on national issues by national parties and/or on the basis of personalities as conveyed through the mass media. Europe-wide issues are rarely a central focus of these elections despite the primary importance of such issues. In sharp contrast to the assertion in the preamble of the proposed new EU constitution, political scientist Loukas Tsoukalis has concluded, "Integration has been mostly the product of an elite conspiracy, with good intentions and pretty remarkable results.... The elitist character of European integration has been rapidly reaching its limits."[27]

> "Integration has been mostly the product of an elite conspiracy, with good intentions and pretty remarkable results....The elitist character of European integration has been rapidly reaching its limits."
>
> Loukas Tsoukalis, *What Kind of Europe? (2003), 219.*

Enhancing democracy in the institutions of the European Union so that it comes close to matching the aspirations of the proposed constitutional preamble will require not only substantial revamping of those institutions but also the heightening of awareness and interest in EU institutions, policy-making processes, and issues among the members of the European electorate. Whether this challenge can be met successfully is still in doubt. Certainly, the path will not be an easy one, particularly given the varying diagnoses of the problems.

* * *

Most analysts agree that the governments of the member nation-states and the institutions, organized interests, and parties within these states have been major sources of political inputs to the EU institutions. Their impact has been particularly evident in the European Council and the Council of the EU (Council of Ministers), but it pervades the entire institutional complex of the EU. The member state governments determine the membership of the Commission, the Court of Justice, and the presidency and the governing bodies of the European Central Bank. Furthermore, the national governments, courts, and bureaucracies (and the array of organized interests and parties that are an important part of their national political systems) are of enormous importance in the implementation of EU public policies. The next chapter, on public policies, and later chapters, on the individual major member states of the EU and their relations with the EU, will address these points further.

SUMMARY

- The proposed new European Union Constitution must gain ratification in all 25 member states before it can take effect; its future remains uncertain in mid-2004.

- The most important central institutions of the EU are the European Commission, the European Council, the Council of the EU (often referred to as the Council of Ministers), the European Parliament, the European Court of Justice, and the European Central Bank.

- The European Commission, sited in Brussels, Belgium, and headed by a president who serves for a five-year term, consists of a College of Commissioners and a permanent civil service of about 20,000 employees; its functions are primarily executive.

- Jacques Delors, president of the Commission during 1985–1995, utilized the presidency to provide leadership furthering European integration more effectively than his predecessors or successors, by most accounts.

- The European Council, composed of the heads of governments of member states and the French president and the European Commission president, usually meets four times per year in European Summits to address major issues that have not been resolved elsewhere.

- The Council of the European Union (Council of Ministers), composed of different ministers of the member state governments on different issues, is often described as the chief legislative body of the EU, though it also exercises some executive functions.

- The European Parliament, sited in both Brussels and Strasbourg, France, and elected by direct popular vote, shares legislative powers with the Council of the EU; its powers have increased in recent years but remain somewhat less significant than those of the Council of the EU.

- The European Court of Justice, located in Luxembourg and composed of one judge from each member state, is the highest court and major arbiter of legal disputes relating to EU treaties and the legislation based upon them.

- The European Central Bank, sited in Frankfurt, Germany, works through the European System of Central Banks to provide direction to the Economic and Monetary Union, composed of 12 EU member states.

- The European Union institutions operate in a political context in which they are influenced by interest groups and political parties, as well as by member state governments.

- Weak accountability mechanisms, general lack of transparency, frequent use of qualified majority voting in combination with secrecy in the Council of the EU, and relative lack of power for the relatively accountable and transparent European Parliament are among the factors that have fed a chorus of European criticisms to the effect that the EU suffers from a "democratic deficit"; proposed remedies to the deficit vary widely.

- The general publics in Europe display low levels of awareness and understanding of the European Union, how its institutions operate, and what they do.

ENDNOTES

1. Simon Hix, *The Political System of the European Union* (New York: St. Martin's, 1999), 2; Gabriel A. Almond, "Comparing Political Systems," *Journal of Politics*, 18, 2 (1956), 391–409; David Easton, "An Approach to the Study of Political Systems," *World Politics* 9, 5 (1957), 383–400, and *A Framework for Political Analysis* (Englewood Cliffs, NJ: Prentice Hall, 1965).

2. George Parker and Daniel Dombey, "'Not Perfect but More than We Could Have Hoped For," *Financial Times*, June 20, 2003, 13; "Special Report: Europe's Constitution," *The Economist* (June 21, 2003), 51–54; George Parker, "Leaders to Insist on EU Treaty Deadline," *Financial Times*, March 25, 2003; Charlemagne, "Philadelphia or Frankfurt?" *The Economist* 366 (March 8, 2003), 52; "Ever Closer in All But Name," *The Economist* 363 (February 15, 2003), 47–48; "The Latest Battle for the Continent's New Shape," *The Economist* 361 (December 8, 2001), 47–48; Suzanne Daley, "Europe Agrees to a Review of Changes for Its Union," *New York Times*, December 16, 2001, A4.

3. The European Convention, *Draft Treaty Establishing a Constitution for Europe* (Brussels: June 2003), Articles I-25, I-26, I-27. Though there has never been a removal of the College of Commissioners by a two-thirds no-confidence vote, the College headed by Jacques Santer resigned in March 1999 after a parliamentary confidence vote of only 293–237.

4. Andrew Moravcsik, *The Choice for Europe: Social Purpose & State Power from Messina to Maastricht* (Ithaca, NY: Cornell University Press, 1998), 8.

5. Moravcsik, *The Choice for Europe*, 372.

6. George Ross, *Jacques Delors and European Integration* (Oxford: Oxford University Press, 1995), 4.

7. Ross, *Jacques Delors*, 231, 243.

8. Charles Grant, *Delors: Inside the House that Jacques Built* (London: Nicholas Brealey, 1994), and Ross, *Jacques Delors and European Integration* are major sources for the above analysis.

9. Liesbet Hooghe, *The European Commission and the Integration of Europe: Images of Governance* (Cambridge: Cambridge University Press, 2001), 209; European Commission, *Who's Who in the European Union? What Differences Will the Treaty of Nice Make?* (Luxembourg: European Communities Official Publications, 2001), at http://europa.eu.int/comm/igc/2000; Neill Nugent, *The European Commission* (Basingstoke: Palgrave, 2001); Neill Nugent, ed., *At the Heart of the Union: Studies of the European Commission* (Basingstoke and London: Macmillan, 2000); Michelle Cini, *The European Commission: Leadership, Organisation, and Culture in the EU Administration* (Manchester: Manchester University Press, 1996).

10. Timothy Bainbridge, *The Penguin Companion to European Union*, 2nd ed. (London: Penguin, 1998), 191–197; Simon Bulmer and Wolfgang Wessels, *The European Council: Decision-Making in European Politics* (London: Macmillan, 1987); Wolfgang Wessels, "The EC Council: The Community's Decision-Making Center," in Robert Keohane and Stanley Hoffman, eds., *The New European Community: Decisionmaking and Institutional Change* (Boulder, CO: Westview, 1991), 133–154.

11. Europe's Foreign Policy: Guess Who Wasn't Coming to Dinner?" *The Economist* 361 (November 10, 2001), 47–48.

12. Peter Ludlow, "The Treaty of Nice: Neither Triumph nor Disaster," *ECSA Review* 14, 2 (Spring 2001),1–4.

13. Fiona Hayes-Renshaw and Helen Wallace, *The Council of Ministers* (London: Macmillan, 1997), 78.

14. Richard Baldwin and Mika Widgren, "Europe's Voting Reform Will Shift Power Balance," *Financial Times*, June 23, 2003; Hayes-Renshaw

and Wallace, *The Council of Ministers*, 78; Ludlow, "The Treaty of Nice," 1–4.

15. The overall account here relies primarily on Hayes-Renshaw and Wallace, *The Council of Ministers*, and Philippa Sherrington, *The Council of Ministers: Political Authority in the European Union* (London: Pinter, 2000). On COREPER, see Jeffrey Lewis, "National Interests: Coreper," in John Peterson and Michael Shackleton, eds., *The Institutions of the European Union* (Oxford: Oxford University Press, 2002), 277–298.

16. Hix, *The Political System of the European Union*, 168–178; Tapio Raunio, "Political Interests: The EP's Party Groups," in Peterson and Shackleton, eds., *The Institutions of the European Union*, 257–276.

17. A thorough, but a bit dated, overview of the European Parliament is Francis Jacobs, Richard Corbett, and Michael Shackleton, *The European Parliament*, 3rd ed. (London: Cartermill, 1995). For a briefer, but more recent, account, see Michael Shackleton, "The European Parliament," in Peterson and Shackleton, eds., *The Institutions of the EU*, 95–117.

18. Renaud Dehousse, *The European Court of Justice: The Politics of Judicial Integration* (Basingstoke and London: Macmillan, 1998), 148, is the source of the quotation. Kieran St. Clair Bradley, "The European Court of Justice," in Peterson and Shackleton, eds., *The Institutions of the EU*, 118–138.

19. Article 3a EEC, cited by Bainbridge, *The Penguin Companion to European Union*, 175.

20. Alistair Cole, *Franco-German Relations* (Harlow: Longman, 2001), 128–144; Ben Clift, "The Jospin Way," *The Political Quarterly* 72, 2 (April–June 2001), 170–179; Bainbridge, 176.

21. Justin Greenwood, *Representing Interests in the European Union* (Basingstoke and London: Macmillan, 1997); David Coen, "The Evolution of the Large Firm as a Political Actor," *Journal of European Public Policy* 4, 1 (1997), 91–108; Franz Traxler and Philippe G. Schmitter, "The Emerging Euro-Polity and Organized Interests," *European Journal of International Relations*

1 (June 1995), 191–218; Wyn Grant, *Pressure Groups and British Politics* (New York: St. Martin's, 2000), 80–124; Michael Nollert in collaboration with Nicola Fielder, "Lobbying for a Europe of Big Business: The European Roundtable of Industrialists," in Volker Bornschier, ed., *State-Building in Europe: The Revitalization of Western European Integration* (Cambridge: Cambridge University Press, 2000), 187–209; Andrew W. McLaughlin, Grant Jordan, and William A. Maloney, "Corporate Lobbying in the European Community," *Journal of Common Market Studies* 31, 2 (June 1993), 191–212.

22. Alberta Sbragia, "Environmental Policy: Economic Constraints and External Pressures," in Helen Wallace and William Wallace, eds., *Policy-Making in the European Union*, 4th ed. (Oxford: Oxford University Press, 2000), 304. Also see Grant, *Pressure Groups*, 101–104.

23. Cole, *Franco-German Relations*, 128–144; Oskar Lafontaine, *The Heart Beats on the Left*, translated by Ronald Taylor (Malden, MA: Blackwell, 2000).

24. Haig Simonian, *The Privileged Partnership: Franco-German Relationships in the European Community, 1969–1984* (Oxford: Oxford University Press, 1985); Hooghe, *The European Commission and the Integration of Europe*, 209.

25. Hix, *The Political System of the European Union*, 187.

26. Erik Oddvar Eriksen and John Erik Fossum, eds., *Democracy in the European Union: Integration through Deliberation?* (London: Routledge, 2000); Catherine Hoskyns and Michael Newman, eds., *Democratizing the European Union: Issues for the Twenty-First Century* (Manchester: Manchester University Press, 2000); Andreas Følledal and Peter Koslowski, eds., *Democracy and the European Union* (Berlin: Springer, 1998); Dimitris N. Chryssochoou, *Democracy in the European Union* (New York: St. Martin's, 1998; Desmond Dinan, *Ever Closer Union*, 2nd ed. (Boulder, CO: Lynne Rienner, 1999), 295–299.

27. Loukas Tsoukalis, *What Kind of Europe?* (Oxford: Oxford University Press, 2003), 219.

THE EUROPEAN UNION AND ITS MEMBER STATES: PUBLIC POLICIES

Chapter 4

"The text [of the new EU constitutional treaty] could sow the seeds of a much more federal Europe, where issues such as foreign affairs and law and order are decided on a European rather than a domestic basis...."
—George Parker and Daniel Dombey, in the *Financial Times (June 20, 2003)*.

Public policies in the contemporary European Union emerge from a complex array of arenas that vary considerably from one policy domain to another and over time. Most analysts now agree that no single "European Union model" of policy-making predominates or is likely to do so in the future, though there has unquestionably been a long-term trend toward increased supranational policy-making patterns and, even more so, toward multilevel patterns that entail shared powers at EU, national, and sometimes subnational levels.[1] In some policy domains, such as single-market policies, competition policies, monetary policies, and the Common Agricultural Policy, the central European Union institutions have become the critical decisional centers, though the member states (especially the major ones) still heavily influence the central institutional actions and play important parts in implementation in a manner usually described as federal. Yet the policy-making patterns differ even among these policy domains and from one time period to another. Other policy domains, such as social-welfare policies and educational policies, continue to center on the national governments (and the state governments in Germany). Despite major efforts to forge common EU foreign and security policies, these, too, remain centered on the national governments, as the conflicts over the Iraq War of 2003 again illustrated. Most taxing and spending powers also remain lodged with the national governments, though the Economic and Monetary Union imposes important constraints. Still other policy domains, such as environmental policies, involve a complex mix of global, EU, national, and subnational actors. This chapter addresses some of the major public policies of contemporary Western Europe and illustrates the policy-making patterns that typify each, also noting the points on which major analysts disagree as to the dominant pattern. It also directs attention to the major policy challenges facing the contemporary European Union and its member states.

SINGLE-MARKET POLICIES

From the founding of the European Economic Community (EEC) in 1957, the goal of devel-

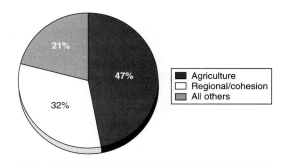

FIGURE 4.1   European Union Budget Expenditures, 2003, by Major Categories

oping a single market in Western Europe has been a high priority, both to avoid the national protectionist policies that many blamed for the Great Depression and World War II and to promote economic growth by emulating the large free market within the United States. The EEC Treaty of Rome set targets for establishment of a customs union, combining removal of tariffs among the original six member states with a common external tariff. There were to be steps toward increasingly free movement of goods, services, capital, and labor among the six. At first, progress toward these goals was more rapid than originally anticipated. However, after the elimination of all customs duties among the member states in 1968, the pattern shifted. Particularly during the economic difficulties of the 1970s, when currencies fluctuated widely and the postwar economic boom in Europe gave way to stagnation, governments of the member states increasingly erected nontariff barriers to protect their own industries (both state-owned and private firms). Particular national government regulations, subsidies, and requirements for procurement of national products proliferated. Intra-EC imports declined relative to total imports during this period. Complaints of Eurosclerosis became widespread as concerns about falling behind the United States and Japan grew. Moreover, in the late 1970s and

early 1980s, the British and French governments adopted highly divergent economic policies, with Britain under Margaret Thatcher stressing economic liberties and tight money and France under François Mitterrand for a time pursuing an effort at nationalizing major industries and seeking Keynesian economic expansion. Only later in the 1980s was there a convergence in the approaches of the major member nation-states and consensus on reviving the movement toward a single market.

Andrew Moravcsik, David Cameron, and some other major analysts have emphasized the roles of the British, French, and German national governmental leaders and the bargaining among them in the development of the Single European Act of 1985 and related public policies of the single-market project. However, Wayne Sandholtz and John Zysman have stressed the leadership of the European Commission, while Maria Green Cowles has discerned the primacy of multinational business interests. Thus, there is considerable debate over the nature of the single-market policy-making pattern in this critical period. However, most agree that the big three member nation-state governments heavily shaped the outcomes; that European Commission President Jacques Delors and Lord Cockfield, the commissioner in charge of the Commission single-market White Paper, demonstrated considerable leadership; and that big business roles were substantially greater than those of other organized interests. There is also wide consensus that the European Court of Justice accelerated movement toward the single market through such key rulings as that in the *Cassis de Dijon* case in 1979, featured in the Chapter Three discussion of the Court.[2]

Regardless of one's conclusions about the single-market project launched in 1985, it is clear that the single-market policies became central to defining the European Union in the 1990s and had an impact on a variety of other West European public policies. Their underlying free-market, neoliberal assumptions and the regulatory approach that the EU has adopted to move Western Europe further toward a full single market have increasingly affected the telecommunications and energy sectors that were not originally included in the single-market project. Even national welfare-state policies and national tax policies have bent to pressures generated by the single-market policies. For example, European Court of Justice decisions have made it clear that single-market requirements for free movement of labor mean that national welfare states must extend social benefits to resident noncitizens who are citizens of other EU member states. More indirectly, the single market has prodded member nation-states toward bringing their value added tax rates closer to those of other member states, though there remains strong resistance, particularly in relatively low tax countries such as Britain and Ireland, to overt steps toward tax harmonization in the EU.

Despite the dramatic movement toward a single market in Europe, challenges to completion of that task remain evident. Among these are various nontariff barriers, most notably in telecommunications and energy. Many national governments maintain close business corporate ties, through ownership of shares in firms, corporate campaign contributions to politicians and lobbying activities, and interchanges of key personnel between government and corporations, which sometimes stimulate actions that make markets less than wholly free in various other economic sectors, too. Quite a few communists, some socialists, and various other leftists in parties and labor unions continue to question the neoliberal ideology that underpins the single-market policies. Though these challenges from the left are relatively weak at present, they may revive in the future.[3]

COMPETITION POLICIES

West European competition policies bear more resemblance to the single-market policies than do most other European public policies. The **anti-trust** ideas (of breaking up business combinations that restrain free trade) inherent in competition policy rest on similar kinds of neoliberal or economic libertarian assumptions, and the policy-making style in the competition domain has followed a similar regulatory approach. However, by most accounts, the roles of the European Commission and the European Court of Justice have been more prominent in this domain than in single-market policy-making.

Although the West European traditions have been far less procompetition than those of the United States, Jean Monnet and other founders of the European Coal and Steel Community heeded American advice and included strong competition provisions in the 1951 Treaty of Paris. When the EEC Treaty of Rome was adopted in 1957, it, too, contained competition articles (though less supranational in character and narrower in scope than those in the Treaty of Paris). These provided a solid legal basis for subsequent competition policy initiatives by the European Commission and rulings by the European Court of Justice.

EC/EU competition policies have targeted anticompetitive practices of business corporations, governmental aids to businesses, and state-owned monopolies—the latter two mainly since the 1980s. In addition, the European Council of Ministers agreed in 1989 to a merger regulation that gave the Commission new authority over business mergers, taking effect in 1990.[4] Paradoxically, the European Commission has incurred the wrath of the United States government (which pressed the anti-trust approach on Europe in the 1950s) by occasionally blocking mergers of giant American-based corporations that operate in Europe after they had won the approval of the Anti-Trust Division of the U.S. Department of Justice. The Commission's overruling of the General Electric–Honeywell merger in July 2001 is a recent example. See Box 4.1.[5]

Box 4.1

MARIO MONTI, COMPETITION POLICY, AND THE GENERAL ELECTRIC–HONEYWELL MERGER CASE

"Globalization, world-wide cartels, and cross-border mergers present major challenges for competition authorities around the world," Mario Monti, the European Union Commissioner for Competition, declared. "They have highlighted the importance of seeking to ensure a degree of convergence and coordination between the world's competition law enforcement systems." Nicknamed "Super Mario," Monti, a commissioner from Italy, became one of the most powerful figures in Europe and on the global economic scene. Though his competition policy initiatives often evoked both denunciation and applause in Europe, his most controversial action from the American perspective—and one that has riveted attention on the growing impact of European Union public policies on the United States—was his successful move to persuade the European Commission in July 2001 to block a proposed $45 billion merger between two giant United States–based business corporations, General Electric and Honeywell. In this case, the United States Justice Department approval of the merger was negated by

Monti's convincing the European Commission that the combination of Honeywell's avionics and General Electric's strength in jet engines would lead to market domination that would restrain free trade. "Such integration, unless corrected, could have resulted in the foreclosure of the market for competitors," argued Monti.

The decision brought an immediate expression of concern from President George Bush and an angry denunciation from General Electric, which insisted that the Commission "took a fundamentally different approach" from that of the United States, thus in effect failing to achieve the "convergence and coordination" among competition authorities that Monti had previously described as a desirable goal. Of course, it should be emphasized that this case of conflict over competition policy between the European Commission and the United States government captured widespread attention because, so far at least, it has been the major exception to the common pattern of transatlantic agreement in this policy domain.

Although the member national governments have played smaller roles and the European Commission and Court of Justice, larger roles than in most policy domains, the major member state governments have exerted considerable influence over the basic direction of competition policies. Resistance from national governments hampered EC competition policy severely in the 1970s, while the growing national governmental convergence around market-oriented ideas during the 1980s enabled the Commission to assume an increasingly

assertive posture and led the Council to grant merger control authority to the Commission in 1989. During the 1990s, many member national governments opted to modify their own competition policies to align them closely with those of the EU. In member states, such as France, Italy, and Spain, in which the state has traditionally played a major role in owning national monopolies and running them as (often subsidized) public corporations and in assisting "national champions" in the private sector and a mixed public-private sector, the EC/EU competition policies since the late 1980s have brought major transformations, albeit not without some strong member state resistance, particularly in France.

Continuing French efforts to aid particular French-based firms clearly illustrate the nature of the continuing challenges to a fully market-oriented competition policy in the European Union. In 2002, the French government gave the French firm Groupe Bull a loan of 450 million euros to keep it functioning. Though the European Commission insisted that the loan be paid back by Groupe Bull within a year, the repayment did not occur on schedule. Meanwhile, in 2003, the French government again intervened to provide economic assistance, this time acting to buy many shares of the heavy-engineering corporation Alstom in order to stave off its likely bankruptcy. Old habits die hard, and the European Commission continues to face enforcement difficulties concerning business competition policy, not only in France but also in other member states.[6]

"Globalization, world-wide cartels and cross-border mergers present major challenges for competition authorities around the world."

Mario Monti, EU Commissioner for Competition.

MONETARY POLICIES

Active roles for central institutions of the European Union in monetary policy-making represent a more recent development than in the preceding two public policy domains. Moreover, the new pattern is quite distinctive in that it centers very much on the European Central Bank and the European System of Central Banks (ESCB).

The original ECSC and EEC provided for no supranational roles in monetary affairs, leaving these for the national governments and national central banks. Only in the late 1960s,

as currency stability in Western Europe was threatened by the growing instability of the U.S. dollar and by internal European social and political pressures, did West European national leaders make a serious effort to form an economic and monetary union in order to stabilize their currencies. Their initial endeavor proved unsuccessful, as the economies of the major European Community states diverged in an atmosphere of global economic and monetary turbulence. By the late 1970s, all that remained of West European monetary integration was a German deutsche mark zone that extended to smaller states in northwestern Europe (in which their currencies shadowed the deutsche mark). Britain, France, and Italy had all opted to go their separate ways on economic and monetary policy.

European Commission President Roy Jenkins (of the United Kingdom), together with French President Giscard d'Estaing and West German Chancellor Schmidt, played leading roles in establishing the European Monetary System in 1979. However, the British government under both prime ministers Callaghan and Thatcher refused to join the Exchange Rate Mechanism (ERM) that lay at its core and linked member state currencies to one another. Ultimately, Britain did join the ERM in 1990, only to leave it again (soon followed by Italy) during a currency crisis that swept Western Europe in September 1992.

Long before 1992, the European Community had begun moving toward an Economic and Monetary Union. A common currency and monetary policy and increased coordination of national **fiscal** (taxing and spending) policies through convergence criteria and a stability pact seemed to many Europeans to promise a solid underpinning for the single market and to be a logical complement to it. It appeared to them a means of avoiding the national currency instabilities vis-à-vis one another still evident in the EMS (most notably in September 1992, when both Britain and Italy devalued their currencies and left the EMS). It also held the promise of facilitating consumers' price comparisons across national borders in Europe and ending the transaction costs and inconveniences to businesses and tourists of cross-border currency exchanges in Europe.

The French government had initiated this effort, with strong backing from Italy and Belgium. When Jacques Delors of France became European Commission President in 1985, he gave this goal high priority. Although the German Bundesbank (Central Bank) resisted these moves, preferring the 1980s pattern, which in effect made their monetary policies the benchmark for all members of the ERM, the German government headed by Chancellor Kohl endorsed the Economic and Monetary Union (EMU) and played a major role in shaping the new institutional structures, the economic convergence criteria that states would have to meet to join the EMU (public debt of no more that 60 percent of gross domestic product, annual budget deficits of no more than three percent of GDP), and the ultimate monetary policies pursued by the European Central Bank (ECB) and the European System of Central Banks (ESCB). Adoption of the German approach was the price that Germany was able to demand in return for German agreement to give up its proud deutsche mark for the new European common currency, the euro.

Member states, such as France and Italy, were willing to accept the German demands in order to replace their previous dependence on monetary policies set by the German Bundesbank with a system that pooled sovereignty and gave them a role in shaping future policies through the ECB/ESCB system. Particularly in the case of Italy, there was also a desire by some leaders to use the new system to enforce budgetary discipline in the Italian national budgetary process (thanks to the convergence criteria insisted on by Germany but backed by Italy). Britain (along with Denmark and eventually Sweden) gained an exemption from adopting the euro when it became the common

TABLE 4.1	Major Landmarks in the Development of the Economic and Monetary Union (EMU)
1972	European Community leaders call for Economic and Monetary Union by 1980 (not achieved).
1979	Exchange Rate Mechanism established.
1990	Delors Report proposes three-stage approach to Economic and Monetary Union.
1992	Treaty on European Union (Maastricht Treaty) adopts three-stage process to create Economic and Monetary Union.
1995	Decisions made on name "euro" for new currency and transition timetable for currency changes.
1997	Agreement on Stability and Growth Pact.
1997	European Central Bank established in Frankfurt, Germany.
1997	Exchange rates set for all national currencies participating in EMU.
2002	Euro banknotes and coins replace national currencies in EMU member states.

currency in 1999. In Britain, the resistance reflected longtime concerns about maintaining British autonomy. However, it also was a response to the events of September 1992, when there was widespread British feeling that the Germans and their Bundesbank had created the situation that led to the British devaluation and departure from the EMS, which Britain had joined late and reluctantly. Greece was excluded until it met the economic convergence criteria, because it had accumulated huge public debt and had difficulty reducing its annual deficits. Therefore, the launching of the euro and common monetary policies began with only 11 of the 15 EU member states aboard. Greece joined subsequently. Others, including some of the 2004 EU entrants, will probably join the EMU in the future.

The economic aspects of the Economic and Monetary Union entail coordination of member state economic policies mainly through the ECOFIN of the Council of Ministers. The European Commission provides a draft of economic guidelines, which is reviewed and modified as desired by the Council of Ministers meeting as ECOFIN. They must then be approved by the European Council, and the Commission monitors implementation by the national governments. Although the Maastricht Treaty that created the Economic and Monetary Union assigned highest priority to fighting inflation and achieving low deficit and debt levels, the Council of Ministers/European Council possess considerable discretion to pursue other goals if members wish. Most taxing and spending (fiscal policy) continues to be under the direct control of the national governments, but the EMU framework imposes major constraints on their freedom of action.

The monetary policies of the EMU are determined by the European Central Bank and the European System of Central Banks but apply only to the member states that have adopted the euro as their common currency and participate in the ESCB. Therefore, for example, the Bank of England retains legal autonomy in making British monetary policies.

Some of the most penetrating challenges to EMU monetary policy-making have focused on the relative lack of transparency and political accountability in EMU processes, adding to concerns about the EU's alleged "democratic deficit." Certainly, most of the internal debates in the European Central Bank and the European System of Central Banks have been shrouded in secrecy, perhaps even more so than in the American Federal Reserve System, which carries out similar monetary policy functions in the United States. Others, however, see the process as too politicized, citing for example the deal under which Wim Duisenberg of the Netherlands agreed to yield his leadership of the European Central Bank to Jean-Claude

Trichet of France part way through his term of office in order to gain French support. Economic concerns focus particularly on the possibilities of economic divergence among member states, because taxing and spending policies remain mostly at the national level and because low labor mobility across national borders means that unemployment may be much higher in some nation-states than in others. Should such divergence occur, the EMU would face the same sorts of pressures that undermined previous efforts at European monetary integration. The new pattern of monetary policy-making through the ECB and ESCB has not yet stood the test of time, although the leaders of most member states have shown a strong commitment to make it successful.

Nevertheless, quite a few Socialist governmental leaders, especially in France but also in Germany and elsewhere, have sought to impose greater political control on the ECB and the ECSB, primarily from ECOFIN. Their primary goals have been not just democratic accountability but also the fostering of monetary policies that would stimulate consumer demand, which they and many labor union leaders believe to be essential to lowering the relatively high levels of unemployment in Europe. By 2003, the conservative French government, as well as the Social Democratic–Green German government, were calling for new monetary policies by the ECB and a loosening of the EMU's stability and growth pact in order to stimulate economic growth and reduce the relatively high levels of unemployment. Differences over central bank autonomy versus political accountability and over neoliberal versus socialist ideologies have been evident in this domain in recent years, as have national governments' inclinations to try to have their own way despite EU rules to which they have previously agreed. In fall 2003, both the French and German governments refused to lower their national budget deficits to the 3 percent of GDP limits mandated by the stability and growth pact, calling the future of the pact itself into question. All of these differences continue to challenge the European Union in the monetary policy domain.[7]

THE COMMON AGRICULTURAL POLICY

The Common Agricultural Policy (CAP) was one of the earliest EEC public policies. Aimed originally at increasing agricultural productivity, insuring a fair standard of living for farmers, stabilizing agricultural markets, providing regular supplies of food (in a postwar Europe that had often suffered shortages), and insuring reasonable consumer prices, it has since its inception involved the largest expenditures in the EC/EU budget (at times accounting for more than three-fourths of that budget, though that figure has dropped below 50 percent in the past decade). Not surprisingly, the CAP usually has been among the most controversial EC/EU policies. In sharp contrast to the market-oriented single-market and competition policies, it has been described by one major analyst as an example of "politics against markets,"[8] meaning that it has sought to employ political means to counteract the effects of global market pressures in the agricultural field. Among the stated objectives, much emphasis has continued to center on insuring a "fair" standard of living for farmers, even as the percentage of farmers in member states declined from 20 percent in the 1950s to 4 percent today and even as former food shortages turned into persistent surpluses. Its proponents have portrayed it as more than just an economic aid to farmers, however. They have commonly described it as preserving a way of life that maintains distinct cultural values and argue for its continuation without substantial changes.

Largely reflecting heavy pressure from the French government at the outset, the EEC Treaty of Rome in 1957 assigned agriculture a high priority. In the following decade, the Common Agricultural Policy took shape, again with major French contributions. The major features of the CAP that emerged in the 1960s were setting of "target" prices that farmers were to receive for farm products, generally above world market prices; "intervention" prices for each commodity at which the EC/EU would buy products to make sure that prices on the market did not fall below the target prices; and "entry" prices representing the minimum price at which farm products from outside the EC/EU could be imported. Expenditures grew rapidly in the 1960s and 1970s.

Critics of the CAP noted its high cost to the EC/EU budget, its additional costs to European consumers in the form of artificially high prices for agricultural products (undermining the stated goal of reasonable consumer prices), and its encouragement of overproduction and waste, in the form of surplus mountains of wheat and lakes of wine. The purchase of surplus products and subsequent sales of them at low prices on world markets also drew wide criticism for damaging agriculture in developing nations of Africa, Asia, and Latin America. Many Italian farmers felt that the CAP that took shape gave unfair advantages to agricultural interests in France and Germany but mostly demanded more benefits for themselves. Defenders portrayed the CAP as a means to good living standards in European farming communities, modernization of European agriculture, transformation of the EC/EU from a net importer to a net exporter of farm products, and protection against threatening global trade competition. They conjured up images of distinctive local cheeses, fine wines, and picturesque medieval farming villages preserved against heartless competition from giant global or American agribusiness corporate farming. Central to the agricultural policy-making process were the member state governments (especially their agricultural ministers) in the

Council of Ministers, and the Commission, with significant input from the Confederation of Professional Agricultural Organizations (COPA), which became the major organization of European farmers. The European Parliament's role was almost nonexistent, in contrast to most other public policy domains.

By the early 1980s, the CAP had come to consume over 70 percent of the European Community budget, even as the agricultural population of the EC declined, undermining the political base of support for the CAP. Moreover, pressures for reform of the Common Agricultural Policy grew, both from internal sources such as the environmental movement and various governments (especially the British government) and from external forces such as the General Agreement on Tariffs and Trade (GATT) negotiations with the United States and other countries that attacked the trade barriers imposed by the CAP against foreign agricultural commodities. The EC adopted limited reforms of the CAP in the 1980s, followed by rather extensive changes in 1992—the latter pushed forward by EU Agriculture Commissioner Ray MacSharry with the support of Commission President Jacques Delors. The so-called MacSharry reforms cut some prices substantially, shifted somewhat from supporting farmers through subsidies of production to providing direct support for their incomes, promoted early retirement of farmers, and encouraged environmentally sound agricultural practices. The CAP proportion of the EU budget dropped substantially as a result to below the 50 percent mark. However, the British government, the United States government, and others have continued to press for further adjustments in a market-oriented direction. The United States government has also been vehement in its opposition to various European agricultural regulations, such as bans on genetically modified food, that it believes to be antithetical to free trade and discriminatory in effect but which many Europeans see as protective of their health. The prospect of

enlargement of the EU to include Central and East European member states with large agricultural sectors has added to the pressures to introduce additional reforms of the CAP, because without these the costs of the policies and the size of EU agricultural surpluses would be likely to soar following enlargement. However, efforts to scale back the CAP and make it more compatible with world markets continue to be limited by strong resistance from some member states, especially France. (See Table 4.2, below, which illustrates the expenditures in euros and relative proportions of the CAP budget going to various member states.)

After a lengthy battle, and under intense pressure from international forces in the World Trade Organization, the European Commission, under the leadership of Agriculture Commissioner Franz Fischler, achieved

TABLE 4.2   Common Agricultural Policy Spending, as Distributed Among Member States, 2001

Member state	Billions of euros	% of total
France	9.23	22.2
Spain	6.18	14.9
Germany	5.86	14.1
Italy	5.34	12.9
Britain	4.00	9.6
Greece	2.61	6.3
Ireland	1.58	3.8
Netherlands	1.11	2.7
Denmark	1.11	2.7
Austria	1.05	2.5
Belgium	0.94	2.3
Portugal	0.88	2.1
Finland	0.82	2.0
Sweden	0.78	1.9
Luxembourg	0.03	0.1
Total	41.52	100.1

Source: The Economist, October 5, 2002, 47.

an EU "compromise" agreement in 2003 to keep subsidies at current levels but to break many of the continuing links between subsidies and production. The hope was that this compromise would reduce European overproduction and the dumping of European surpluses on world markets and, in doing so, make possible agreements with the United States and other countries in the Doha Round of World Trade Organization talks and ease criticisms from developing countries. However, many critics argue that the original proposals by Fischler have been watered down too much in response to pressures from France and some of the other member state governments.

Two Conflicting Assessments of the EU Common Agricultural Policy Reforms Agreed to in June 2003

"This decision marks the beginning of a new era. This reform sends out a strong message to the world. We are saying goodbye to the old subsidy system, which significantly distorts international trade and harms developing countries."

Franz Fischler, EU Agriculture Commission, *Financial Times (June 27, 2003), 1.*

"Farmers will continue to produce more than we need and will continue to dump it on the developing world."

Sam Barratt, Researcher at Oxfam, a British charity, *New York Times (June 27, 2003), A9.*

Everyone agrees that the reforms will not reduce EU budgetary expenditures on agriculture, as many Europeans would prefer. Many analysts believe that the reforms also inadequately address the ill effects of the CAP on third-world agriculturalists, but this point is a matter of sharp dispute, as the quotations above indicate. The charges of excessive costs and impoverishment of poor farmers in the devel-

oping world continue to pose challenges to EU agricultural policy-makers.

Another important challenge facing European agricultural policy-makers is that posed by the eastward expansion of the EU. Most of the 10 new members that entered the EU in 2004 possess large agricultural sectors, with Poland and Lithuania topping the list at 18.8 percent and 19.6 percent of their workforces in farming, compared with an average in the pre-2004 EU of 4.3 percent. Romania, scheduled for entry in 2007, still has 42.8 percent of its workforce in agriculture. In fact, there are more agricultural employees in Poland and Romania alone than in the entire pre-2004 European Union! Table 4.3 provides the figures for the pre-2004 EU and the 13 Central and Eastern European accession states. In

TABLE 4.3   Agricultural Employment in Pre-2004 EU and Applicant Countries, 2002

Nation	Agricultural Employment	
	(000)	As % of total employment
Pre-2004 EU	6,767	4.3
Cyprus	14	9.2
Czech Republic	193	7.4
Estonia	32	7.4
Hungary	227	4.8
Latvia	118	13.5
Lithuania	262	19.6
Malta	3	1.9
Poland	2,698	18.8
Slovakia	119	6.7
Slovenia	81	9.9
Bulgaria	342	11.3
Romania	4,861	42.8
Turkey	9,149	34.9

Sources: DG Agriculture; Eurostat.

order to restrain the likely costs of extending agricultural subsidies eastward, the EU has adopted a policy of providing a phase-in of these aids for farmers in the new member states, granting these agriculturalists only 25 percent of the Western subsidies at the outset, with gradual movement toward harmonization over a nine-year period of time, to 2013. Needless to say, this arrangement has aroused considerable opposition among many farmers in the entrant states. Moreover, while the phase-in will limit the initial additional costs to about seven billion euros in the 2004–2006 period, many analysts predict that expenditures will explode subsequently, as Eastern farmers become eligible for full subsidies and heavily agricultural Romania joins the EU.[9]

ENVIRONMENTAL POLICIES

In recent years, European Union environmental policies have been among the important forces (though not the most important ones) stimulating reforms of the Common Agricultural Policy, as seen in the previous section. Unlike the CAP, however, environmental policies received no clear legal foundation in the EEC Rome Treaty of 1957. Not until the early 1970s did the European Community central institutions become actively involved in this domain. At that time, spurred by the 1972 United Nations Conference on the Human Environment and a growing domestic environmental movement of groups and parties, the member state governments in the Council called upon the Commission to produce the first in what has been a series of Environmental Action Programs. Directives on clean swimming water and drinking water and air pollution standards soon followed, with resultant upgrading of many member states' environmental efforts. Germany, where new social movements stressing environmental protection and a Green party were particularly strong, often prodded the European Community to advance the environmental protection agenda. Since the 1970s, the EU central institutions have taken action on matters including waste disposal, chemical products, nature protection, environmental impact assessments, and labeling of environmentally friendly products. The general pattern has been for the EC/EU to adopt the more rigorous standards of the most environmentally conscious member states (usually Germany, the Netherlands, Sweden, Denmark, Finland, and Austria) and to prod the laggards to achieve these standards. The rising EU environmental standards have reflected a combination of 1) concerns by the advanced states that they will lose business to environmental laggards unless high and sometimes costly standards are enforced throughout the EU and 2) willingness of the laggards to raise their standards under EU prodding (probably due to awareness of popular environmental sympathies and the need to meet high environmental standards in many foreign markets).

The European Commission has usually assumed a leadership role in formulating EC/EU environmental policies. The Council of Ministers has been more important in legislating than the European Parliament, though the latter has gained influence over time and has been a force pushing for "greener" policies than the Commission or Council has often preferred. Implementation has occurred primarily at the nation-state level, with the European Commission monitoring and sometimes relying on the European Court of Justice to aid in enforcement through its rulings.

Perhaps more than most public policies, environmental policies in Europe have represented a mix of global actors such as the United Nations (as seen in 1972 and in the Rio and Kyoto summits in the 1990s), the EU central institutions, the member state governments (with the "greener" governments taking the lead), and (especially in Germany) the subnational governments. Environmental nongovernmental organizations have also been important. Economic considerations (i.e., the concerns of "greener" member states that they not lose business to members with lower environmental regulations and costs), in conjunction with awareness that air and water pollution problems usually cross national boundaries in Europe and cannot be dealt with effectively except at EU and global levels, have increasingly prompted EU nation-states to shift responsibilities for environmental policies to EU and global bodies. Particularly since the Bush Administration has come to office in the United States, the EU has increasingly taken positions on the global environment that go well beyond what the United States government has been willing to endorse. Disagreements over the Kyoto Agreement to combat global warming by reducing the emission of greenhouse gases in advanced industrial societies, which the European Union states endorse and which the Bush Administration opposes, have been a particular source of conflict. The search for effective means to engage the United States in advancing the global environmental agenda, particularly on global warming, is proving to be a significant challenge for EU environmental policy-makers.

Probably the greatest problems within the European Union in the environmental domain lie at the implementation stages. Environmental policy relies largely on EU directives, which must be transposed into national legal systems and then administered by nation-state bureaucracies. The European Commission, charged with monitoring transposition and enforcement, has often had to take member states before the European Court of Justice for their failures. Because the Commission lacks its own inspectors at ground level to gather data about enforcement, it is fairly dependent on complaints sent to it by environmental interest groups and individual citizens. Even Germany, long a leader in initiating high environmental standards, has had difficulties with implementation of EU directives, in part because Germany

decentralizes environmental policy in its internal federal system to its 16 state governments. In December 2003, EU Environment Commissioner Margot Wallström, felt compelled to warn that even on the Kyoto Protocol so strongly advocated by the European Union (in opposition to the United States), only Britain and Sweden had achieved the targets for reductions of greenhouse gas admissions. Her implicit threat of punitive actions against 13 of the 15 member states for less than full compliance with this hallmark protocol illustrates the dimensions of the implementation problems in the EU. Therefore, although the EU has in many respects been a global leader on environmental protection policies, a major internal challenge remains the gap between legal pronouncements and actual implementation.[10]

REGIONAL/COHESION POLICIES

Marked regional inequalities of wealth have posed social and economic difficulties for the EC/EU from the beginning, and the challenges have increased over time due to the inclusion of additional poor regions (and nation-states) with expansion to the South and to the East. One recent analyst has concluded that regional disparities in per capita income within the current boundaries of the EU are at least twice as great as in the United States.[11]

Although the preamble of the EEC Rome Treaty of 1957 recognized the need to reduce the wide differences in the economic levels of various regions within the European Economic Community, little action was taken in this regard until the creation of the European Regional Development Fund (ERDF) in the mid-1970s, mainly as a part of deals involving both enlargement and efforts at monetary union. The stated goal was to reduce regional disparities, but the original fund was too small to have a significant effect on them. Moreover, the processes involved at the outset seemed to reflect "pork barrel politics" among the governments of the member states, with Britain, Ireland, and Italy treating the ERDF as a means to gain greater shares than before of EC budgetary allocations. Later, Spain, Portugal, and Greece—all with relatively low per capita gross domestic products and with economically backward regions—were to add to the "pork barrel" demands.

The European Commission and the Directorate General responsible for regional policies sought to shape broad policies and to insist on the principle of "additionality," meaning that member states should pursue additional spending beyond preexisting national programs and not just substitute EC funds for national funds. Pursuit of the additionality principle has sometimes brought the European Commission into conflict with member state governments. These patterns have continued. However, major changes over time have included the adoption of increased social and economic "cohesion" among European regions as a formal goal in the Single European Act of 1986, the considerable expansion of funding for this purpose in the 1980s and early 1990s (with regional and other "cohesion" funds coming to rank as the second-largest expenditure in the EU budget, behind only the CAP), the subsequent slowing of growth in the later 1990s, and the extensive discussions at the turn of the millennium of the implications of EU expansion for regional/cohesion policies and funding.

In addition, the basic policy-making processes in this domain have altered over time. Originally established through intergovernmental bargaining, the regional/cohesion policies came to be shaped increasingly by the European Commission in the 1980s. However, there has been a shift toward member state reassertion in the process in recent years. Another development over time has been the increasing assertiveness of subna-

tional governments in the processes of shaping regional/cohesion policies. Once again, we see evidence of variability over time in EU policy-making processes, even within a particular policy domain.

Even though the European Union's regional and cohesion funds grew into the early 1990s to reach about one-third of the total EU budget, it should be stressed that the EU budget remains quite small relative to the budgets of the larger member states, constituting less than 4 percent of the collective total of the national budgets of member states. Because of the relatively small magnitude of the funding involved and the political deal-making that has often characterized the allocation and administration of funds, the redistributive effects have been limited. The EU regional and cohesion policies have served to narrow some of the gaps among countries and regions in the EU. However, they have fallen far short of equalizing the wide disparities that continue to exist. Expansion of the EU to include a number of poor regions and nation-states in Central and Eastern Europe will, for a time at least, create even greater challenges to social and economic cohesion within the European Union than have existed previously. The "poor four" of the pre-2004 European Union (Spain, Portugal, Greece, and Ireland) have insisted on protecting their EU assistance, which they have rightly perceived to be potentially threatened by the admission of 10 (and perhaps soon 13 or even 14) new members that are all poorer than they. This issue of revamping regional and cohesion policies to meet the needs of the new entrant states while retaining political support from current recipients and keeping costs from exploding in ways that outrage major donor states (led by Germany) poses a major challenge to European Union policy-makers in this domain. This issue will be explored further in Chapters Fourteen and Sixteen.[12]

SOCIAL POLICIES

European nation-states gave birth to modern welfare-state policies and continue to guard jealously their extensive national policies aimed at coping with poverty, unemployment, illness, and old age. National politicians usually rise or fall based in large part on public perceptions of their handling of these key issues of social citizenship. Although welfare states have traditionally been national states in Europe, and remain so in many key respects, the processes of European integration have transformed the distinctive European national welfare states into what two recent analysts have termed "semisovereign welfare states."[13]

The impact of the European Union on national social-welfare policies has been three-pronged, as Stephan Leibfried and Paul Pierson have stressed: 1) "positive" social policy initiatives to develop uniform standards at the EU level, with the European Commission, Council of Ministers, and Parliament shaping these and the European Court of Justice interpreting them through its rulings; 2) "negative" policy reform mostly through European Court of Justice imposition of single-market and related requirements; and 3) indirect pressures of European integration that encourage (but do not legally require) member states to modify their social-welfare policies. Examples of each should clarify the picture.[14]

The Social Chapter that began as a Social Charter signed by all member states except Britain in 1989, adopted as a Protocol to the Maastricht Treaty in 1992, and finally was incorporated in revised form into the Amsterdam Treaty of 1997, has generated a great deal of mass media and scholarly attention. However, like most EU initiatives in this domain, it is fairly vague and limited in its impact. Moreover, it deals with employment policies, rather than with social welfare generally. Nonetheless, it has generated some substantive policy changes from the EU central institutions, such as the European Works Council directive. This directive has required new consultative procedures between employers and employees in several hundred transnational business corporations having at least one thousand employees and operating in at least two member states, at the request of 100 or more employees in two or more facilities in different member states.

More extensive and significant than the "positive" social-welfare policy initiatives from the EU have been the cases of "negative" EU constraints on member state social-welfare policies, usually as a result of single-market requirements as interpreted by the European Court of Justice. For example, member states are no longer permitted to limit most social benefits to their own citizens and cannot apply benefits only within their own territories.

In the third category of "indirect" effects on national social-welfare policies of European integration have been the pressures generated by the criteria for inclusion in the Economic and Monetary Union. By requiring reduced budget deficits (to no more than 3 percent of **gross domestic product, GDP**) and overall public debt (to no more than 60 percent of GDP), for example, they generated pressures in a number of member states to trim social-welfare spending, though they did not require such actions because tax increases were another possible option to meet the criteria. Italy, for instance, sharply cut its welfare spending and revamped its system of pensions as a result. At the same time, efforts by the conservative French government to introduce major spending cuts generated massive strikes and demonstrations. The French government felt compelled to make a partial retreat from its initial social-welfare policy response (and soon lost its bid for reelection).

In general, the nation-states within the EU remain primarily responsible for most social-welfare policies and their funding, albeit now influenced by EU developments. As a result, considerable variation continues to exist among the member states' policies. The United Kingdom and the poorer member states generally have less extensive (and expensive) social-welfare policies than the richer Continental member states do. Nevertheless, through positive initiation of EU standards, negative restrictions on member state policies, and indirect pressures on member state policies, the processes of European integration have had considerable impact even on the welfare-state policy domain.

Challenges to the European welfare states have become increasingly evident. Demographics are the most obvious problem. Most EU member states have low birth rates and lengthening life spans, a combination that is creating fewer and fewer employee contributors to social insurance that must cover more and more retired persons. As the ratio of contributors to recipients declines, funding will become increasingly problematic. One possible solution, already begun in some European countries, is to raise the retirement age. This approach has encountered considerable resistance from employees and their unions; some estimate that raising the age of eligibility for pensions to 70 years or above may be required if present demographic trends continue. Another possible solution, which could be combined with modest increases in retirement ages, is to increase the immigration of young workers into Europe. However, there is strong resistance to this approach from cultural nationalists, the unemployed, and those who fear possible unemployment. In addition to the problems of funding social benefits for retirees, the current relatively high unemployment in much of the European Union since the 1990s has created increased demand for social benefits even as the work force has shrunk. Moreover, some analysts and many business leaders attribute the high unemployment and sluggish growth prevalent in much of the EU to the high costs to business of supporting extensive social-welfare benefits of employees.

Under the array of circumstances just described, there is rising pressure from neoliberal and conservative parties, backed by much of the business community, to trim social-welfare benefits, primarily at the national governmental level but also through indirect pressures generated at the level of the European Central Bank, ECOFIN, and other EU institutions. At the same time, communist and socialist parties, pushed by many labor unions, are fighting to preserve hard-won social benefits and sometimes seeking to reorient EU institutions to encourage such preservation. Therefore, social-welfare issues are likely to pose significant challenges to the skills of European policy-makers in the years to come.

FOREIGN AND DEFENSE POLICIES

Since the Maastricht Treaty on European Union of 1992, Pillars Two and Three have provided distinctive, largely intergovernmental, procedures for making common foreign and defense policies and most policies in the field termed Justice and Home Affairs (JHA). Though the draft of the new constitution proposes to abolish the pillar structure established by the Maastricht Treaty, it promises, at least in the short term, only a modest shift away from nation-state–centered foreign and defense policies. Member state governments guard their foreign and defense policy prerogatives carefully and continue to pursue often divergent policies of their own despite areas of common action, as became evident once again during the debates over appropriate actions concerning Iraq, which found Britain, Spain, and Italy seriously at odds with France and Germany.

In the foreign and defense policy realm, a major vehicle for coordinating European and North American policies has long been the North Atlantic Treaty Organization, founded in 1949 and including most but not all current EU members as well as the United States, Canada, Iceland, Norway, and Turkey from outside the EU. Its widely perceived effectiveness at providing mutual defense and addressing particular national security concerns over much of the past half-century, the existence of several other potential coordinating bodies outside the EC/EU framework (such as the Western European Union), and the national sovereignty concerns of many EC/EU member states have combined to minimize the EC/EU roles in foreign and defense policies most of the time since 1957.

However, the end of the Cold War and the inability of Europeans to address on their own the crises stemming from the breakup of Yugoslavia in the 1990s have pushed the major EU nation-states, led in this instance by Britain and France, toward acceptance of the need for an enhanced EU military role and enhanced cooperation throughout the foreign and defense policy domain.

The emergent cooperation in this sphere in the late 1990s surprised many longtime observers of the European Union. For decades, Britain gave prime emphasis to maintaining a strong link between the Western European Union (a loose, highly intergovernmental body outside the EC/EU) and the North Atlantic Treaty Organization and rejected efforts to enlarge the EC/EU functions in the foreign and defense area. At the same time, France favored a European foreign and defense policy quite independent of the United States and NATO, making it and Britain frequent adversaries on the subject. However, the 1990s witnessed a convergence between Britain and France around a position long advocated by Germany— one that endorsed considerable American engagement in Europe while simultaneously seeking a distinctive European effort and approach. Nevertheless, differences in 2002–2003 over U.S. policies concerning Iraq created serious divisions among the major nation-states in the EU, pitting Britain, Spain, and Italy (supportive of the United States' government) against France and Germany (highly critical of the United States government) and raising serious questions about the prospects for agreement on EU foreign policies, at least in the near future.

The recent movement toward creation of an EU Military Security Pool, or Rapid Reaction Force, designed to take collective action on behalf of the EU in cases when the United States is not militarily engaged, signals the likelihood of an expanding EU presence in this domain. Other such indicators were the appointment in 1999 of the prestigious Javier Solana, previously secretary-general of NATO, as the first EU high representative for Common Foreign and Security Policy and provisions in the draft constitution for merger of his position with that of the EU Commissioner for Foreign Affairs. There is at present a great deal of discussion about a European Strategic Defense Identity (ESDI) and about increasing defense spending by member states to support upgrading of military forces, which have fallen far behind those of the United States. However, there remain many pressures within the member states to constrain such increased military spending, which, as Table 4.4 below illustrates,

TABLE 4.4   Military Spending in the United States and Major EU States

Country	As % of GDP (2000)	In billions of dollars (2002)
United States	3.0	$300.0
United Kingdom	2.5	23.9
France	2.4	26.9
Italy	2.1	17.9
Germany	1.5	20.1
Spain	1.3	5.9
Total of EU NATO Members	n.a.	108.8

Sources: NATO (spending as % of GDP); Stockholm International Peace Research Institute (projects.sipri.se/milex/mex_data_index.html) is the source of the 2002 spending figures, calculated in U.S. dollars in 2000 prices.

is markedly lower in major EU states and in the EU as a whole than it is in the United States. Given the divisions among its member states on important foreign and defense matters (especially relations with the United States), the relatively low defense effort that most of its members are willing to make, and the deeply entrenched concerns about national sovereignty in a number of European defense ministries, the European Union is unlikely to develop as a global superpower in the military and foreign policy realm in the near future. Three major analysts of European affairs (one British, one German, and one French) have recently summed up the picture aptly: "Europe will never be a serious political actor as long as its national leaders keep using foreign policy as a vehicle for their imaginary greatness and as long as they decline to give Europe the means to realize its goals." It is also possible, as the quotation at the heading of this chapter indicated, that the new constitutional treaty drafted in 2003 "could sow the seeds of a much more federal Europe, where issues such as foreign affairs and law and order are decided on a European rather than a domestic basis...." However, the future of the constitutional treaty itself remains in doubt in 2004.[15]

JUSTICE AND HOME AFFAIRS POLICIES

In the Justice and Home Affairs field, most common EU policy efforts have occurred within Pillar Three (compared with Pillar Two for foreign and defense policies), again on an intergovernmental basis. If the new constitution is adopted, however, Justice and Home Affairs policies will shift markedly in a supranational or federal direction as the "pillar" system is abandoned.

In the early days of European integration, member state governments jealously guarded their sovereignty concerning border controls, police powers, and individual rights. Justice and home affairs ministries have long been among the most powerful in most states' national cabinets. Over time, however, pressures for enhanced cooperation in this field have come from increasing flows of immigrants into the EC/EU from outside Europe at a time when high unemployment since the 1970s has built strong resistance to their arrival by many citizens of EC/EU member states. Growing concerns about cross-border drug-trafficking and terrorism have also generated pressures for cooperative ventures. Another motivation for cooperation came from the effects of the growth of trade and travel among member states as European integration progressed. National border controls proved increasingly time-consuming and disruptive as traffic across these borders increased, generating pressures that led five European states (France, Germany, and the three Benelux countries) to sign in 1985 the Schengen Agreement, which went far toward removing frontier controls among its signatory states, in addition to providing standardized rules for entry to each signatory from outside the Schengen group of states. Later, other states joined the Schengen Agreement.

Fairly recent changes in the justice and home affairs field have been potentially significant. Perhaps most notably, the 1997 Treaty of Amsterdam moved migration and related policies from Pillar Three to Pillar One of the EU policy-making process (where most economically oriented EU public policies are made). The Amsterdam Treaty also incorporated the Schengen conventions on cross-border movement, including standards for controls over external movement of people into the European Union, while allowing Britain and Ireland, which have asserted special national needs because of their island locations, to opt out of the common agreement. Europol, a fledgling European police force headquartered in the Hague in the Netherlands since its establishment in 1995, has been primarily a data-gathering and analyzing body, not a European version of the American Federal Bureau of

Investigation, as some member states hoped and others feared.

Also in the area of Justice and Home Affairs, there have been ongoing efforts to institute a legally binding EU Charter of Fundamental Rights. In 1999, Germany took the lead in calling for the drafting of a bill of rights for the European Union. For years, there had been debate within the EC/EU over whether it should adopt the Convention of Human Rights of the Council of Europe as its own. However, the idea of a separate rights charter for the EU was a relatively new one. Because some member states, notably Britain, long a bastion of concerns about national sovereignty, have resisted the creation of a legally binding document, the Nice Treaty adopted a Charter of Fundamental Rights but left the issue of its binding legal status to be determined in the future. The constitutional convention of 2002–2003 has strongly endorsed the charter, making it the second part of the constitutional document or treaty that it has recommended, but has provided that the charter would be binding only on European law, rather than the laws of the individual nation-state members.

The terrorist attacks on the New York World Trade Center and the Pentagon in Washington, D.C., on September 11, 2001, aroused heightened concerns in Europe about terrorism and have spurred new cooperative efforts to address cross-border criminal matters collectively. A special meeting of the European Council convened to address such issues on September 21, 2001; the October meeting of the Justice and Home Affairs Council followed up with policy proposals. Among these have been upgraded airport security measures, a common EU definition of terrorism, a common list of trans-border crimes, and a European search and arrest warrant to facilitate the apprehension of suspects involved in such crimes. Despite wide consensus among EU member states on the need to address terrorist threats, differences of opinion have complicated some of

these efforts. For example, the Italian government blocked agreement on the EU arrest warrant at the JHA ministerial meeting in December 2001, perhaps reflecting fears that Prime Minister Berlusconi might himself be charged with some of the designated European crimes. Subsequently, under heavy criticism, Italy yielded; the initiative was adopted with an implementation date of 2004. Moreover, while France, Spain, and Britain have been highly concerned about terrorist threats and have pushed for EU-wide antiterrorism initiatives, the Scandinavian countries have demonstrated strong concerns that such measures not threaten civil liberties. Therefore, differing national perspectives continue to slow EU ventures in the JHA domain, even in the midst of heightened concerns about international terrorism and a trend toward making justice and home affairs policy-making much more supranational or federal than in the past.

One other important issue concerning terrorism has been that of cooperation with U.S. authorities. Here, a major concern shared by all of the EU states is the wide use of the death penalty in the United States and a shared EU view that no criminal suspect should be extradited to the United States unless the Americans agree that the death penalty will not be carried out in any cases resulting from extradition. Most Europeans also perceive that the American criminal justice system incarcerates far too many prisoners and is far too punitive in its approach to most of them.

Challenges to the European Union in the justice and home affairs field in the near future are likely to include efforts to devise means of applying the new Charter of Fundamental Rights, incorporated into the constitutional treaty proposed in 2003, to European law in the midst of national laws and procedures that continue to vary rather widely. Pressures to find common policies to address immigration into the EU also pose significant challenges to JHA policy-makers, given the widespread concerns over national sovereignty and the divergent laws of member states in this area. Still another challenge will be addressing international terrorism effectively, in the face of differences with the United States over criminal justice and foreign policy and problems of identifying potential terrorists residing within the EU itself while preserving civil liberties.[16]

EU PUBLIC POLICIES AND EUROPEAN-AMERICAN RELATIONS

As has been indicated in most of the preceding policy sections, almost all public policies adopted by the European Union carry potential consequences for European-American relations. Although this pattern has been the case since the foundation of the European Communities in the 1950s, it has become increasingly true in light of the growing policy roles of EC/EU institutions vis-à-vis the member states, the increasing numbers of member states, and the globalization patterns that have progressively made the world more interdependent than ever.

In the initial stages of European integration after World War II, the United States provided support and encouragement for moves toward enhanced West European unity, perceiving that such unity would strengthen the Western side in the Cold War with the Soviet Union and make Western Europe a prosperous trading partner for the United States. Despite some transatlantic conflicts over trade, monetary policy, agriculture, and other economic matters during the Cold War era, the initial American perception seemed largely justified. As Western Europe unified, there was also movement toward lower transatlantic tariffs and other trade barriers. Trade and investment between the United States and the European Community soared. Both sides prospered, despite the slowing of economic growth after 1973. Though occasionally ruffled by American uni-

lateral actions that upset Europeans, such as the abrupt devaluation of the dollar in 1971 and abandonment of key Bretton Woods agreements, economic relations remained generally positive. Agriculture proved a perennial sticking point, as both the EC and the United States charged the other side (accurately) with discrimination in favor of its own agricultural producers. On foreign and defense matters, the European Community appeared far less important to the United States than NATO was. The United States dealt primarily with the individual governments of the major European nation-states on issues of NATO coordination and defense efforts. Despite challenges from France to U.S. leadership, most other major European governments for the most part accepted U.S. primacy. The United States, in turn, nearly always consulted European governments on matters of common concern. The end of the Cold War in 1991 and the launching of the European Union the following year led some observers to predict heightened tension between the United States and the European Union. At first, these predictions seemed unfulfilled; but by 2001 and 2002, the transatlantic gap did indeed appear to be widening in an array of policy domains. One leading European analyst in 2002 described European-American relations as "descending to a nadir not seen in more than half a century." Even Christopher Patten, the normally pro-American Foreign Affairs Commissioner of the European Union, lambasted President Bush as "simplistic" and asserted that he had gone into "unilateralist overdrive" in relation to his policies on Iraq.[17]

With regard to single market, competition, and agricultural policy, the last of these has continued to be the biggest source of conflict between the European Union and the United States in the post–Cold War era. The 1990s witnessed a lengthy "banana war" in which the United States challenged the EU's protection of banana growers in countries that were former European colonies, arguing that the EU quotas violated international rules and obtaining a World Trade Organization ruling against the EU's banana quota system. In the realm of genetically modified crops, used extensively in the United States but not in Europe, the United States has continued to object strenuously to EU regulations of these and EU requirements for labeling of foods that involve genetic modification. EU–U.S. charges and countercharges over agricultural subsidy policies during the Doha Round of the World Trade Organization talks at times have reached a pitch that has threatened to cause a breakdown of the talks. Beyond agriculture, Europeans have denounced American unilateral economic sanctions against such countries as Cuba, Libya, and Iran and particularly U.S. efforts to punish European-based corporations that invest there. In such cases, EU leaders have insisted that these are extraterritorial measures that aim to impose American policies on Europeans, against their will. In the competition sphere, EU and U.S. policies have generally complemented one another, despite the exceptional case of the EU rejection of the General Electric–Honeywell merger that had been approved in the United States.[18]

As the Economic and Monetary Union (EMU) has taken shape, some in the United States have expressed fears that the euro may become a major challenger to the American dollar as the prime currency of international exchange, a development that could decrease United States power in the world. Another American concern, more widely shared, has been that the stability and growth pact underlying the EMU has slowed European growth, threatened deflation, and threatened to hold back growth in the United States and the rest of the world. Voiced initially by Treasury officials in the Clinton administration, this concern has also troubled leaders of the Bush administration.[19]

Social policy differences between the EU and United States have been highlighted by the growing importance of social policy (primarily on labor relations) at the EC/EU level since the social emphasis began in the late 1980s. Requirements for consultation of employees by employers are still far less extensive at the EU level than in some member states, but they go beyond the requirements of American social policy. The social rights to be guaranteed by the new European Union constitution have also provoked considerable commentary in the United States because such rights are unmentioned in the U.S. Constitution and Bill of Rights. Furthermore, the social-welfare policies of all EU member states are considerably more extensive (and expensive) than those found in the United States. Robert Hencke, a Belgian-born lecturer in political economy at the London School of Economics, sums up the feelings of many Europeans on the subject: "The idea that economic institutions must converge at some American model is ridiculous. It is neither inevitable nor desirable."[20]

"The idea that economic institutions must converge at some American model is ridiculous. It is neither inevitable nor desirable."

Robert Hencke, *quoted in the Washington Post (June 4, 2002), E1.*

Two notable recent conflicts between EU and U.S. policies have centered on global warming and the International Criminal Court. In both cases, the Bush administration has adopted policy stances strongly at odds with those of the European Union, heightening tensions that had already been evident during the Clinton administration. As noted previously, the European Union and all of its member states have endorsed the Kyoto Accords on global warming and have taken steps toward meeting the goals for reductions of greenhouse gas emissions. In contrast, the Bush administration has rejected the Accords as unfair to developed countries and has even refused to acknowledge that global warming poses a serious problem. On the matter of the International Criminal Court (ICC), the Bush administration has challenged EU policy in an even more confrontational manner. While the EU member states have all endorsed the ICC, the Bush administration has withdrawn the United States' signature on the Rome Statute providing for the ICC, has shown little inclination to discuss how the ICC could be made acceptable to the United States, and has pressured the new states scheduled to join the EU to try to force them to sign bilateral agreements with the United States to the effect that they will not refer any cases involving Americans to the International Criminal Court. With regard to both global warming and the ICC, perceptions in the EU have been that the United States has been working actively to thwart European Union policy objectives on the international scene.[21]

If global warming and the International Criminal Court have brought conflicts between the EU and the United States, the foreign and defense policy domain has produced clashes within the EU as well as between much of the EU leadership and the United States government. Part of the pattern evident here stems from the different structures and practices of the European Union and the United States in foreign and defense policy-making. In contrast to the intergovernmental approach in the EU, which still centers most power at the nation-state level and requires lengthy discussion and debate to achieve consensus, the United States is a federal system that vests enormous power over foreign and defense policy in the hands of the president and his closest advisers. Partly as a result of these structural differences, and partly as a result of differing values, there is also an enormous gap in military power between the European Union and the United States. Relatively free of checks on their foreign and military initiatives, and possessing vast military resources that dwarf those of their European counterparts, American governmental executives have displayed tendencies toward military

unilateralism and wariness of international legal constraints. The Bush administration has accelerated these tendencies. Europeans, on the other hand, lacking similar military resources and accustomed to cooperation within the EU framework, have generally advocated multilateralism and respect for international law. These differing inclinations have underlain much of the growing transatlantic conflict.

The United States has shown little enthusiasm for, and some outright opposition to, efforts to build a European Security and Defense Policy (ESDP), even though ESDP aims to enable the EU to take quicker and more decisive foreign and military actions than have been possible to this point. These American attitudes stand in contrast to strong American support for most previous efforts at European integration and reflect concerns that ESDP might undermine United States leadership through NATO. At the same time, American policy-makers have continually prodded Europeans to increase their defense spending and increase their military effort. The result has been considerable transatlantic misunderstanding and bickering.

The United States has stirred the greatest anger among the European Union leadership (including both Foreign Affairs Commissioner Christopher Patten and High Representative Javier Solana) by adopting what many have viewed as a divide and conquer strategy over Iraq policy in 2002 and 2003. As indicated previously, the Iraq controversies of 2002–2003 deeply divided the EU, mocking the dreams of those who had hoped for swift movement toward a European Security and Defense Policy. Though the divisions were perhaps inevitable, given the differing perspectives on Iraq (and the United States) among member state governments, American efforts to drum up support for their position, and American leaders' references to France, Germany, and their supporters as "old Europe," have aroused deep antipathy in many quarters. The effects of the policy divisions within Europe and between Europe and the United States over the Iraq issue will likely linger for some time to come.[22]

On justice and home affairs policies, as on foreign and defense policies, much European policy-making remains at the member state level rather than at the level of the European Union. Nonetheless, the EU has become an increasingly important policy-making center in this domain, more so than in the foreign and defense policy realm. The greatest differences between the EU and the United States in this arena have concerned the death penalty and general approaches to incarceration. While the EU mandates that no member state may employ capital punishment, most American states and the federal government impose the death penalty. As noted previously, disputes arise when the United States seeks to extradite prisoners from Europe to be tried in the United States, and Europeans resist the idea of sending prisoners to face possible death sentences in the United States. More incarceration, and harsher incarceration, in the United States than in EU member states is another source of transatlantic policy disagreements. Nevertheless, common fear of international terrorism has produced considerable policy cooperation between the European Union and the United States, particularly in the wake of the terrorist attacks on the World Trade Center and the Pentagon on September 11, 2001.[23]

Despite considerable evidence that American and European Union policies have diverged since the end of the Cold War and the formation of the EU at the beginning of the 1990s, the United States and Europe continue to share many basic values that underlie public policy: support for constitutional democracy and human rights, mixed economies with a market orientation, and tolerance for cultural diversity, among the most important ones. Moreover, given the relative power of the United States and the European Union in global affairs, most leaders on both sides of the Atlantic perceive the need to keep their policies broadly in harmony with one another. Karsten Voigt, the Coordinator of German-American Cooperation in the German Foreign Office, has aptly concluded, "Not a single problem in the world can be solved if Europe and the United States are at odds."[24] Undoubtedly, a major challenge for both the European Union and the United States in the years ahead will be to attain a level of cooperation that will enable them to tackle together the array of problems that confront the human race.

"Not a single problem in the world can be solved if Europe and the United States are at odds."

Karsten D. Voigt, Coordinator of German-American Cooperation in the German Foreign Office, 2003

---

* * *

As noted at the outset of this chapter, public policies in contemporary Western Europe emanate from a multiplicity of arenas that is often confusing not only to American observers but also to European Union citizens themselves. In fact, part of the "democratic deficit" about which many Europeans complain when discussing their institutions and public policies is rooted in the complexity of the processes and the difficulties of establishing clear responsibility and accountability. However, there is little evidence that the policy-making patterns will be simplified or clarified significantly any time soon. They have emerged over time and usually reflect the interests of important political actors.

The member state governments play particularly large roles in the largely intergovernmental realm of foreign and defense policies, where they control much of the initiation, shape the lawmaking processes, and are responsible for implementation. However, their roles are quite substantial in other EU policy domains also, despite a trend toward supranationalism and an increasingly federal style of shared policy-making that involves EU, nation-state, and often subnational levels of government within a policy domain. Even the supranational European Central Bank has seen its presidency influenced by tough bargaining between France and Germany and has been subject to pressures from nation-state economics and finance ministers. The supranational European Court of Justice has apparently restrained its tendency to challenge member state governments when faced with signs of their displeasure in the early 1990s. Major initiatives in all policy domains are unlikely to advance without the backing of most member states, especially the largest ones. The member state governments' direct representation in the Council of Ministers gives them enormous influence over formal lawmaking. Finally, the implementation stage is largely in the hands of the member state administrative bureaucracies, though the Commission and the Court of Justice may impose sanctions. Therefore, it is important now to shift the focus of this text to the major nation-states in the European Union. The next two chapters will examine the French nation-state and its relationships with the European Union. The following eight chapters will employ comparable methods to address Germany, Italy, the United Kingdom, and Spain.

SUMMARY

- Public policies in the European Union emerge from a complex array of arenas that vary considerably among policy domains and over time.

- Single-market policies based on neoliberal assumptions about the benefits of free-market competition have transformed the EU since the mid-1980s, though some barriers to free trade within the EU remain.

- Leadership by British, French, and German governments and by the European Commission, decisions by the European Court of Justice, and pressures from multinational business interests have decisively shaped EU single-market policies.

- Competition policies in the EU have reflected similar assumptions to those in the single-market domain; they, too, have encountered some resistance, particularly in France.

- The European Commission and the European Court of Justice have been major actors shaping EU competition policies.

- Common currency and monetary policies and increased coordination of national fiscal (taxing and spending) policies through convergence criteria and a stability and growth pact have characterized the Economic and Monetary Union, though high unemployment, slow growth, and German and French noncompliance with stability pact guidelines have presented challenges.

- The European Central Bank, the European System of Central Banks, and the national governments have been the major actors shaping monetary policies.

- The Common Agricultural Policy has reflected regulatory demands far more than neoliberal assumptions; it remains the largest source of EU spending, though it consumes less of the EU budget than it did in the past.

- Agricultural policies have reflected national demands by member state governments (particularly France's) but also Commission leadership and pressures from international actors.

- Environmental policies have grown dramatically in significance since the 1970s, with the EU assuming a leading international role in environmental protection, though implementation problems are evident in many member states.

- National governments (and sometimes subnational ones), the European Commission, the Council of Ministers, the European Parliament, and business and environmental groups have been active participants in shaping EU environmental policies; global actors have also often proved significant.

- Policies aimed at increasing social and economic cohesion within the EU have grown in importance over time and now constitute the second-largest set of expenditures in the EU budget.

- National and subnational governments on their own and through the Council of Ministers have been major forces shaping regional and cohesion policies, with the Commission sometimes able to play a leading role also.

- EU "social" policies have centered largely on employment practices, while welfare policies continue to be largely under the control of national governments.

- The European Commission, Council of Ministers, Parliament, and Court of Justice have played significant roles in shaping social policies; but national variations in welfare policies remain significant; left-right partisan differences are also evident in social and welfare policies.

- Foreign and defense policies remain nation-state–centered, with notable national differences evident on such matters as the 2003 Iraq War, though there is movement toward an EU Rapid Reaction Force.

- Justice and home affairs policies also remain largely nation-state–centered, though the proposed new EU constitution points toward a shift in a supranational direction in this domain.

- EU public policies carry significant potential consequences for the United States, as has been evident in the EU's blocking of the General Electric–Honeywell merger, EU-U.S. differences over the Kyoto Accords and the International Criminal Court, and a variety of EU-U.S. disagreements over agricultural and other trade matters.

ENDNOTES

1. Helen Wallace, "The Institutional Setting," in Helen Wallace and William Wallace, eds., *Policy-Making in the European Union*, 4th ed. (Oxford: Oxford University Press, 2000), 28–35.

2. Andrew Moravcsik, *The Choice for Europe* (Ithaca, NY: Cornell University Press, 1998), 314–378; David R. Cameron, "The 1992 Initiative: Causes and Consequences," in Albert Sbragia, ed., *Euro-Politics: Institutions and Policymaking in the "New" European Community* (Washington: Brookings, 1992), 23–74; Wayne Sandholtz and John Zysman, "1992: Recasting the European Bargain," *World Politics* 42, 1 (1992), 95–128; Maria Green Cowles, "The Politics of Big Business in the European Community: Setting the Agenda for a New Europe." American University Ph.D. dissertation (1994); Alasdair R. Young and Helen Wallace, "The Single Market: A New Approach to Policy," in Helen Wallace and William Wallace, eds., *Policy-Making*, 85–114.

3. Stephan Leibfried and Paul Pierson, "Social Policy: Left to Courts and Markets?" in Helen Wallace and William Wallace, eds., *Policy-Making*, esp. 278–279 and 285.

4. Michelle Cini and Lee McGowan, *Competition Policy in the European Union* (London: Macmillan, 1998); Leon Brittan, *European Competition Policy: Keeping the Playing Field Level* (London: Brassey, 1992); Francis McGowan, "Competition Policy: The Limits of the European Regulatory State," in Wallace and Wallace, eds., *Policy-Making*, 115–147.

5. Andrew Ross Sorkin, "Failure to Acquire Honeywell Is Sour Finish for G.E. Chief," *New York Times*, July 3, 2001, A1 and C4; "Merger Muddle," *The Economist*, 359 (June 23, 2001), 22–23; "GE/Honeywell: Welch Squelched," *The Economist*, 359 (June 23, 2001), 61; "GE/Honeywell: Engine Failure," *The Economist*, 360 (July 7, 2001), 58–59; "EU Blocks GE/Honeywell Deal," BBC News, July 3, 2001.

6. McGowan, "Competition Policy," 120–121, 129–131, 139–140; Paul Meller, "France Confirms Plan to Help Rescue Alstom," *New York Times*, August 7, 2003, W1 and W7.

7. George Parker, "Ministers Conduct Late-Night Burial for EU Fiscal Framework," *Financial*

Times, November 26, 2003, 4; Ed Crooks, "EU May Yet Pay the Price of Not Playing by the Rules," *Financial Times,* November 26, 2003, 4; Arthur I. Cyr, "The Euro: Faith, Hope, and Parity," *International Affairs* 79, 5 (October 2003), 979–992; James Walsh, *European Monetary Integration & Domestic Politics: Britain, France, and Italy* (Boulder, CO: Lynne Rienner, 2000); Amy Verdun, "Monetary Integration in Europe: Ideas and Evolution," in Maria Green Cowles and Michael Smith, eds., *The State of the European Union,* Vol. 5 (Oxford: Oxford University Press, 2000), 91–109; Daniel Gros and Niels Thygesen, *European Monetary Integration: From the European Monetary System to European Monetary Union,* 2nd ed. (London: Longman, 1997); Loukas Tsoukalis, "Economic and Monetary Union: Political Conviction and Economic Uncertainty," in Wallace and Wallace, eds., *Policy-Making,* 149–178; Kenneth Dyson, "EMU as Europeanization: Convergence, Diversity, and Contingency," *Journal of Common Market Studies,* 38 (November 2000), 645–666.

8. Elmar Rieger, "The Common Agricultural Policy: Politics Against Markets," in Wallace and Wallace, eds., *Policy-Making,* 179–210.

9. Robert Ackrell, *The Common Agricultural Policy* (Sheffield: Sheffield Academic Press, 2000); Wyn Grant, *The Common Agricultural Policy* (Basingstoke and London: Macmillan, 1997); Rosemary Fennell, *The Common Agricultural Policy: Continuity and Change* (Oxford: Clarendon Press, 1997; W. D. Coleman, "From Protected Development to Market Liberalism: Paradigm Change in Agriculture," *Journal of European Public Policy,* 5 (1998), 632–651; Michael Mann, "EU Farm Policy: France to Voice Protests Against Reforms," *Financial Times,* June 27, 2002, 7; Tobias Buck, "Fischler to Stand Firm on Proposals for Overhaul of EU Farm Subsidies," *Financial Times,* June 3, 2003, 6; Tobias Buck, "Patience Runs Low as Farm Talks Resume," *Financial Times,* June 26, 2003, 4; European Commission, "EU Fundamentally Reforms its Farm Policy to Accomplish Sustainable Farming in Europe," IP/03/898, Luxembourg, June 26, 2003; Tobias Buck, Guy de Jonquières, and Francis Williams, "Fischler's Surprise for Europe's Farmers: Now the Argument over Agriculture Moves to the WTO," *Financial Times,* June 27, 2003, 11; Brian Gardner, "Enlargement Farm Costs—Risks for the EU Budget," European Policy Centre, November 6, 2002.

10. Alberta Sbragia, "Environmental Policy: Economic Constraints and External Pressures," in Wallace and Wallace, eds., *Policy-Making,* 293–316; Hubert Heinelt, et al., *European Union Environmental Policy and New Forms of Governance* (Aldershot: Ashgate, 2001); Ariane Sains, "Seeing Green: Forecasting Europe's Environmental Future," in E. Gene Frankland, ed., *Global Studies: Europe,* 7th ed. (Guilford, CT: McGraw-Hill/Dushkin, 2001), 204–210; Andrew Jordan, "EU Environmental Policy at 25," in Henri Warmenhoven, ed., *Global Studies: Western Europe,* 6th ed. (Guilford, CT: Dushkin/McGraw-Hill, 1999), 195–207.

11. Jeffrey J. Anderson, "Structural Funds and the Social Dimension of EU Policy: Springboard or Stumbling Block?" in Stephan Leibfried and Paul Pierson, eds., *European Social Policy: Between Fragmentation and Integration* (Washington: Brookings, 1995), 123.

12. Ian Bache, *The Politics of European Union Regional Policy: Multi-Level Governance or Flexible Gatekeeping?* (Sheffield: Sheffield Academic Press/University Association for Contemporary European Studies, 1998); David Allen, "Cohesion and the Structural Funds: Transfers and Trade-Offs," in Wallace and Wallace, eds., *Policy-Making,* 243–265.

13. Stephan Leibfried and Paul Pierson, "Semisovereign Welfare States: Social Policy in a Multitiered Europe," in Leibfried and Pierson, eds., *European Social Policy,* 43–77.

14. Stephan Leibfried and Paul Pierson, "Social Policy: Left to Courts and Markets?" in Wallace and Wallace, eds., *Policy-Making,* 267–292.

15. The quotation is from Timothy Garton Ash, Michael Mertes, and Dominique Moïsi, "Only a Club of Three Can Bring European Unity," *Financial Times,* July 11, 2003, 8; Adrian Hyde-Price, *Germany and European Order: Enlarging NATO and the EU* (Manchester: Manchester University Press, 2000); Anthony Forster and William Wallace, "Common Foreign and Security Policy: From Shadow to Substance?" in

Wallace and Wallace, eds., *Policy-Making*, 461–491; John Van Oudenaren, *Uniting Europe: European Integration and the Post-Cold War World* (Lanham, MD: Rowman & Littlefield, 2000), 273–312; Anne Deighton, "The Military Security Pool: Towards a New Security Regime for Europe?" *The International Spectator*, 35, 4 (October–December 2000), 19–32; Paul Cornish and Geoffrey Edwards, "Beyond the EU/NATO Dichotomy: The Beginnings of a European Strategic Culture," *International Affairs* 77, 3 (July 2001), 587–603; Ian Traynor and Martin Walker, "Solana to Run Joint Security Policy for Bickering EU," *The Guardian*, June 5, 1999; Ian Black, "Two Men, One Goal, and Lots of Bickering," *The Guardian*, April 19, 2001; Steven Erlanger, "Europe's Military Gap," *New York Times*, March 16, 2002, A1 and A4; "Europe's Torment," *Financial Times*, March 20, 2003, 14.

16. Van Oudenaren, *Uniting Europe*, 205–228; Monica den Boer and William Wallace, "Justice and Home Affairs: Integration through Incrementalism?" in Wallace and Wallace, eds., *Policy-Making*, 493–519; David Lister, "Europol Prepares to Enter a Wider Arena," *The Times*, January 19, 2001; Gráinne de Búrca, "The EU Charter of Fundamental Rights," *ECSA Review* 14, 2 (Spring 2001), 9–10; Emek M. Uçarer, "Justice and Home Affairs in the Aftermath of September 11: Opportunities and Challenges," *EUSA Review* 15, 2 (Spring 2002), 1–4.

17. The quotations are from Andrew Rawnsley, "How to Deal with the American Goliath," *Observer*, February 24, 2002; and Ian Black, "EU Calls Truce in 'Axis of Evil' Row," *The Guardian*, February 20, 2002. Robert Kagan, *Of Paradise and Power: America and Europe in the New World Order* (New York: Knopf, 2003), provides an interesting, if exaggerated, overview of emerging American-European differences. John Newhouse, *Imperial America: The Bush Assault on the World Order* (New York: Knopf, 2003), Laurent Cohen-Tanugi, *Alliance at Risk: The United States and Europe Since 9/11* (Baltimore, MD: Johns Hopkins University Press, 2003) and Elizabeth Pond, *Friendly Fire: The Near-Death of the Transatlantic Alliance* (Pittsburgh, PA: EUSA, 2003) provide per-

spectives less sympathetic to the Bush administration than Kagan's. Joseph S. Nye, *The Paradox of American Power* (Oxford: Oxford University Press, 2002), esp. 29–35 offers a nuanced and carefully balanced perspective.

18. Christopher Stevens, "EU Policy for the Banana Market," in Helen Wallace and William Wallace, eds., *Policy-Making in the European Union*, 3rd ed. (Oxford: Oxford University Press, 1996), 325–352; Philip Crane and Charles Rangel, "Unity Against Sanctions," *Financial Times*, September 16, 2002, 10; Loch K. Johnson and Kiki Caruson, "The Seven Sins of American Foreign Policy," *PS: Political Science and Politics* 36, 1 (January, 2003), 5–10; Jeffrey Garten, "The Global Economy Is in Harm's Way," *Financial Times*, April 14, 2003.

19. C. Randall Henning and Pier Carlo Padoan, *Transatlantic Perspectives on the Euro* (Washington, D.C.: Brookings, 2000); Kevin Featherstone and Roy H. Ginsberg, *The United States and the European Union in the 1990s*, 2nd ed. (New York: St. Martin's, 1996), 161–163.

20. Edward Rothstein, "Europe's Constitution: All Hail the Bureaucracy," *New York Times*, July 5, 2003, A17, reflects a widespread American view of European social-rights guarantees. Gösta Esping-Anderson, *The Three Worlds of Welfare Capitalism* (Cambridge: Polity Press, 1990) is one of the best overviews of different types of welfare capitalism in Europe and America.

21. Ralph Carter, "Leadership at Risk: The Perils of Unilateralism," *PS: Political Science and Politics* 36, 1 (January, 2003), 17–22; Nye, *The Paradox of American Power*, 155–157; Elizabeth Becker, "U.S. Presses for Total Exemption from War Crimes Court," *New York Times*, October 9, 2002, A6; Quentin Peel, "An Empire in Denial Opts Out," *Financial Times*, August 19, 2002, 11; Christopher Marquis, "U.N. Begins Choosing the Judges for New Court," *New York Times*, February 6, 2003, A5.

22. Kagan, *Of Paradise and Power*; Judy Dempsey, "Europe's Divided Self," *Financial Times*, July 10, 2002; Ash, Mertes, and Moïsi, "Only a Club of Three Can Bring European Unity," *Financial Times*, July 11, 2003, 8; George Parker and Judy Dempsey, "After Iraq," *Financial Times*, April 16, 2003, 13.

23. Andrew Moravcsik, "The Death Penalty: Getting Beyond 'Exceptionalism'," *European Studies Newsletter* (January 2002); Stephen J. Slivia and Aaron Beers Sampson, "The New Abolitionism: American or European Exceptionalism Regarding the Death Penalty," *European Studies Newsletter* (January 2002); Uçarer, "Justice and Home Affairs in the Aftermath of September 11."

24. Karsten D. Voigt, "Common Roots—a Common Future? Transatlantic Partnership in the Twenty-first Century," Address at the University of Tampa, March 24, 2003.

Chapter 5

FRANCE

"France is central to the future of Europe, and, it sincerely believes, to the globe as a whole. With the fourth biggest economy, nuclear weapons and a permanent seat on the United Nations Security Council, it can claim to rank behind only Washington in international reach and ambition."

—Jonathan Fenby, *France on the Brink (1998), 1.*

Geographically, France lies at the heart of Western Europe and the European Union. It is one of the oldest European nation-states. Moreover, it has traditionally been a **unitary** system in which supreme constitutional power is vested in the national government (rather than being divided between the national government and state or regional governments, as in a **federal** system, such as the United States). In contrast to some European countries, such as Sweden and the United Kingdom, which have gradually and generally evolved peacefully into modern constitutional democracies, its history has been marked by intermittent constitutional democratic and authoritarian governments and frequent political upheavals, often accompanied by extensive violence. The current French constitutional structure dates back only to 1958, when the Constitution of the French Fifth Republic was ratified by the French voters in a popular vote; and it has gained widespread legitimacy only in the past three decades. In the two centuries that the United States has had just one constitution, France has had sixteen constitutions, with the current one being the fifth republican constitution.

France enjoyed "great power" status comparable to that of the United Kingdom over most of the past three centuries and was, prior to the twentieth century, usually the great continental rival to the United Kingdom in global politics. During World War I and World War II, France was an ally of the United Kingdom. However, in contrast to Britain, it suffered German invasion in World War I and German invasion and defeat in World War II. The history of rivalry with the United Kingdom and of terrible modern wars with Germany (the two world wars and the Franco-Prussian War of 1870–1871) has created an important backdrop to the outlooks and attitudes of the French since 1945. France remains a nation-state proud of its great-power heritage and convinced of its central importance in Europe (and the world). However, French political leaders have been far more willing than their British counterparts to accept a fairly high level of European integration and to seek to accomplish French national goals through the European Communities/European Union rather than unilaterally. For most French leaders, the EC/EU has represented a means of

MAP 5.1   France

asserting French influence in an era in which the United States (and for a time, the Soviet Union) have dominated global politics, protecting France from Germany, and promoting economic modernization.

France's population today is just under 60 million—slightly smaller than the United Kingdom's population and more than 20 million less than Germany's. Its gross domestic product has in recent years usually been second only to Germany's in the European Union, though Britain's GDP surpassed it narrowly in 2003. A long-dominant feature of the French political economy has been the strength of its centralized state administration vis-à-vis the private business sector—historically more pronounced than in any other major West European constitutional democracy and still a notable characteristic, though yielding somewhat to privatization and market influences in recent years.

POLITICAL DEVELOPMENT

Early Development

French national identity and state structures developed gradually and in a reciprocal relationship with one another over many centuries. Unlike the pattern in Germany, France evolved a state-anchored national consciousness, somewhat similar to the English experience but with greater emphasis on the role of the state in nation-building than was the case in England. Landmarks in the long development that extended over nearly a millennium were the separation of the West Frankish kingdom in 843 from what had been Charlemagne's empire; the growing authority of the Capetian kings from the tenth century to the fourteenth century despite feudal obstacles; the eventual expulsion of the English monarchs (who had controlled large portions of what is now France) in the fifteenth century; further monarchical centralization of state authority and wars with other emerging nation-

states (especially England); and, most notably of all, the centralizing and nationalizing effects of the French Revolution (1789–1799) and Napoleon I (1799–1815). The Jacobins of the French Revolution placed particular emphasis on the need for strong central institutions to build national identity, promote equality, and prevent counterrevolution. Napoleon I reinforced their centralization of authority. As Napoleon I illustrated clearly with his international empire-building, there was a global dimension to the French glorification of the nation-state also. Hubert Védrine, a recent French foreign minister, notes the long-term significance of the French fascination with the state:

> Historically, French identity has been defined by and built upon a strong central State, first monarchical and then republican. It was painstakingly built by jurists and based on the idea that France had a specific political, legal, and cultural role to play in the world.

Many analysts have portrayed the Revolutionary-Napoleonic era as critical in forging "modern" notions of national citizenship, based on the French model. Certainly, by the early nineteenth century, most of the French population had embraced a proud nationalism (though some regional languages, dialects, and identities lingered, notably in Brittany, Provence, and Corsica), French central state institutions had attained primacy and developed many of their distinctive modern features, and French territorial boundaries had come to approximate those of the contemporary era.[1] However, alongside these developments, France encountered great difficulty in creating governmental institutions that would enjoy widespread legitimacy and permanence. Furthermore, it faced major "modernizing" conflicts over participation and distribution simultaneously with sharp disputes over governmental institutions.

"Historically, French identity has been defined by and built upon a strong central state, first monarchical and then republican. It was painstakingly built by jurists and based on the idea that France had a specific political, legal, and cultural role to play in the world."

French Foreign Minister Hubert Védrine, *France in an Age of Globalization* (2001), 16.

The processes of mingled modernizing conflicts became evident during the French Revolution of 1789–1799. The storming of the Bastille and the seizure of power by the middle classes led at first to a limited monarchy under a constitution that expanded voting rights, then to a series of constitutions and to several unsuccessful efforts at equalizing wealth, before culminating in a dictatorship (and then an Empire) under Napoleon Bonaparte (1799–1815) in which middle-class elements dominated society under a system of considerable central-state influence. Democracy expanded drastically early in the Revolution, only to suffer later cutbacks and then distortions through Napoleon's staged **referendums** or **plebiscites,** in which voters were presented with simple yes/no choices in an atmosphere carefully managed by the state. In the end, the regime of Napoleon I fell due to its expansionistic efforts that brought France to defeat at the hands of most of the other European powers in 1814–1815.

From 1848 to the Fall of the Third Republic

Simultaneous conflicts of modernization continued to characterize French historical development through most of the nineteenth century and early twentieth century. From 1848 onward, French males all possessed voting rights; French women received them in 1944. However, most working-class voters felt excluded and undermined by the techniques employed to minimize their influence and by the overt repression of

their occasional armed rebellions (most notably in the Revolution of 1848 and the Paris Commune of 1870–1871). Only the French Third Republic (1875–1940) was able to achieve long-term stability in governmental institutions. Even it enjoyed only limited legitimacy, having alienated most of the Roman Catholic hierarchy and most devout Roman Catholics by its secularism and strict separation of church and state and having alienated most of the working class by its repression of some of their political activities and usual lack of attention to their key demands. It also faced difficulties in maintaining civilian control over the military. The Dreyfus Affair that raged from 1894 to 1906 illustrated many of the tensions that roiled the politics of the Third Republic. Alfred Dreyfus, a Jewish army captain, was convicted in a secret court martial of selling secrets to Germany and was sentenced to imprisonment on Devil's Island, the notorious French prison off the coast of South America. The military hierarchy and other antirepublican forces insisted upon Dreyfus's guilt, stirring up anti-Semitic mass prejudices in their campaign against him, despite growing evidence of his innocence. Eventually, after a long investigation spurred by intellectuals and prorepublican forces, Dreyfus was exonerated and promoted. For 12 years, however, the republic had been in a state of almost constant turmoil. Most of the time, the institutions of the Third Republic were stalemated by multiparty and legislative-executive conflicts. Even before the German invasion of 1940 brought the defeat and collapse of the Third Republic, there was considerable evidence that its governmental institutions rested on an unstable base.[2]

The Vichy Regime and the Fourth Republic

From July 1940 to August 1944, Hitler's Nazi Germany occupied northern France (including Paris) directly. In southern France, the so-called Vichy Regime (governed from the city of Vichy) was an authoritarian dictatorship headed by Marshall Philippe Petain and aligned with Germany. Therefore, France—long a system proud of its democratic heritage and practices—became distinctly undemocratic. This era has left many bitter conflicts concerning responsibility for collaboration with the German Nazis that have lingered to the present day. Although constitutional democracy was restored after the Anglo-American liberation of France in alliance with French General Charles de Gaulle and his forces, and de Gaulle became for a time head of the Provisional Government, France failed to establish stable and legitimate governmental institutions once again. The French Fourth Republic (1946–1958) was a parliamentary constitutional democracy (in contrast to the presidential type advocated by de Gaulle) but its institutions were strongly challenged both by de Gaulle and his political allies and by the French Communist party. The latter had played a major role in the French Resistance to Vichy and the Nazis and emerged from World War II with strong support from the long-alienated working class as one of the two largest Communist parties (with Italy's) in Western Europe. De Gaulle retired from politics in 1946, only to return in 1958 to replace the Fourth Republic with the Fifth Republic under a constitution of his own design.

Precipitating the return of de Gaulle and the creation of the Fifth Republic were events in Algeria, which France had colonized in 1830 and which the French government and many French citizens viewed as an integral part of France. The largely Arab and Berber Muslim population of Algeria had rebelled against French colonialism in the post–World War II era; and the governments of the Fourth Republic found themselves in the late 1950s immersed in trying to repress revolutionary forces demanding independence. In the wake of the loss of French Indochina (Vietnam, Laos, and Cambodia) in 1954, the French military and

the one and one-half million French and other European settlers in Algeria came increasingly to believe that the governments of the Fourth Republic were too weak to achieve victory in Algeria. The threat of a military coup, backed by the European settlers in Algeria, convinced the leaders of the Fourth Republic to invite de Gaulle to return to power as prime minister. His conditions were that he be allowed to rule by decree for six months and to develop a new constitution, under which he became the first president of the Fifth Republic.

The Fifth Republic

At first the Fifth Republic was clearly dominated by President de Gaulle and evoked some strong criticism from French political leaders who viewed it as overly executive-centered, even authoritarian. Over time, however, its hybrid institutional model blending an American-style presidency with a British-style parliamentary system (with a prime minister and cabinet accountable to the National Assembly) and providing for referendums, has apparently developed the stability and eventually the legitimacy that its predecessors lacked. In contrast to the past, alternations in government have given all of the major parties except the far right-wing National Front at least a share of governmental power at one time or another in the past several decades. Constitutional democracy has become so well established that its overthrow in France now seems inconceivable to most observers. Transfers of power from center-right to center-left presidents and governments and back again have occurred peacefully. Women, who gained the right to vote in France only in 1944 (considerably later than in the United States and Britain), have become increasingly active democratic participants, with Edith Cresson serving as Prime Minister in 1991–1992 and many other women occupying important political roles. In the realm of distribution, France has continued economic growth begun during the Fourth Republic, though the pace slowed after 1973. The once-large agricultural sector has shrunk markedly. Under the joint pressures of globalization and European Union "reforms," the traditionally state-oriented French capitalist economy has come since the 1980s to resemble the market-oriented economies of the United States and Britain more closely than in the past, though the French continue to embrace a political-economic model that places greater emphasis on the state and on equality than the Anglo-Americans prefer.

TABLE 5.1	Major Landmarks in French Political History
843	West Frankish kingdom separates from Charlemagne's former empire.
987	Hugh Capet establishes Capetian dynasty, beginning era of gradual nation-state development.
1789	"Great" French Revolution begins.
1799	Napoleon becomes ruler of France.
1815	Battle of Waterloo ends Napoleonic Era.
1830	Revolution establishes Orleanist Monarchy.
1848	Revolution establishes the Second Republic.
1852	Napoleon III becomes Emperor of France.
1875	The Third Republic is established.
1940	France suffers defeat by Germany in WWII and establishes the Vichy Regime.
1944	Anglo-American liberation of France; end of the Vichy Regime.
1946	The Fourth Republic is established.
1950	Robert Schuman unveils the Schuman Plan for the European Coal and Steel Community.
1952	France becomes a founding member of the European Coal and Steel Community.
1958	France becomes a founding member of the European Communities and establishes its Fifth Republic.

Four Modernization Crises: The French Patterns

Most overviews of French political development in terms of Gabriel Almond and G. Bingham Powell's four "crises" of nation-building, state-building, participation, and distribution have emphasized the extent to which the French have often had to grapple with the latter three crises simultaneously (far more so than the British, for example).[3] Even nation-building, which the French accomplished relatively early and relatively successfully (more so than the British in some respects), has been a subject of some disputes. In recent years, the most notable "nation-building" challenges have concerned sometimes violent separatist efforts on the island of Corsica (Napoleon's birthplace) and struggles over how to handle the waves of non-European immigrants to France in the post–World War II era. The immigration issue has become a highly divisive one in French politics in recent years. Non-European immigrants from the Arab world, Asia, and Africa south of the Sahara have come in large numbers to France in search of a better life. However, they have had difficulty in finding good jobs in a period of prolonged high unemployment and have tended to be concentrated in dilapidated high-rise suburbs around Paris and other major French cities (a contrast to American suburban-urban patterns), where their living conditions often contribute to high crime rates. Some politicians, most notably Jean-Marie Le Pen and his National Front, have sought to build political careers by denouncing these immigrants and even suggesting massive deportations as a means of "restoring" the French "nation." Other politicians, however, have sympathized with the plight of the immigrants, stressed the benefits of immigration and France's long tradition of offering citizenship to immigrants who assimilate, or even suggested the need for civil-rights legislation of the type enacted in the United States or Britain to protect the rights of ethnic minorities (rarely discussed in France until recently). Despite these challenges, France has long demonstrated a higher degree of national identity and national pride than most nation-states, in Europe or elsewhere.[4]

A Dispute over Headscarves in the French Public Schools

In October 1987, the principal of the public school in Creil, France, set off a national debate by expelling three Muslim girls who had refused his order to remove their headscarves in school. The principal argued that the scarves symbolized submission to religious authority and were disruptive of the public school classroom. The Socialist Minister of Education, Lionel Jospin, subsequently to be prime minister (1997–2002), sided with the girls, arguing, "The purpose of French schools is to educate and integrate, not to reject."

In 1989, France banned headscarves in public schools if the scarves were found by teachers to be worn "provocatively," saddling teachers with a new responsibility.

In 2003, President Jacques Chirac established a new commission to study the matter. Its report, which he endorsed, called for banning all "conspicuous" religious symbols in French public schools, including head scarves, Jewish skullcaps, and large crosses, in the name of "separation of church and state." Amid great controversy, the French government proceeded to push for new legislation to ban head scarves. "Religion," declared French Prime Minister Jean-Pierre Raffarin, "cannot be a political project."

Anne Sa'adah, *Contemporary France: A Democratic Education*, 220–221; *"Not All Are Gauls," Financial Times (July 9, 2003)*, 12; Elaine Sciolino, *"Ban Religious Attire in Schools, French Panel Says," New York Times (December 12, 2003)*, A1 and A12; Elaine Sciolino, *"Debate Begins in France on Religion in the Schools," New York Times (February 4, 2004)*, A8.

State-building in France has been more problematic than nation-building. The patterns are somewhat paradoxical. On the one hand, France has maintained a strong centralized state structure since the time of Napoleon, only partially modified by decentralizing reforms in the 1980s. On the other hand, it has had sixteen different written constitutions since the Revolution of 1789—some based on monarchy, some on authoritarian dictatorship, some on parliamentary democracy, and some on a style of democracy often referred to as **presidential/plebiscitary** (which has sometimes been transformed into authoritarian dictatorship). In the late 1940s, as France began its Fourth Republic, soon to give way to its Fifth Republic, huge advertising posters in the Paris metro stations captured the prevailing French attitude: "Republics pass; Soudée paint lasts."[5] However, the current mix of parliamentary and presidential/plebiscitary democracy in the Fifth Republic now appears to have generated widespread legitimacy, perhaps resolving (at least for the foreseeable future) the historical French conflict over state-building.

"Republics pass; Soudée paint lasts."

Post–World War II French advertisement

France was among the pioneers of democracy, but its development has followed a zigzag pattern of expansions and contractions of voting rights and democratic and authoritarian governments. Furthermore, French democrats have tended to divide between proponents of representative parliamentary democracy, who have sought to center authority in parliament and have distrusted the executive, and advocates of a more direct, or **plebiscitary democracy,** who have usually sought to bypass or minimize parliament and rely on a charismatic chief executive and popular referendums. The Fifth Republic initially veered toward the plebiscitary/presidential democratic version. However, the decreased use of referendums in the past several decades, the frequent need for presidents to share powers with prime ministers of different party affiliations, and the decentralization of some authority have led over time to a model that appears to have generated considerable consensus. The French generally have conceptualized participation less in terms of local autonomy and grassroots groups than Americans do.[6]

In the realm of extending democratic practices to the workplace, France has not gone as far as Germany, despite considerable rhetoric by French Socialists, especially during the early 1980s. In 1982, the French Socialist government did gain adoption of the Auroux laws mandating employees' consultation and rights guarantees at the level of the individual business enterprise. However, the applications of these laws have not consistently benefited workers or their unions.[7]

Like the other West European nation-states, France evolved from feudalism to a modern "mixed" economy. The most notable features of the French approaches to distribution over time have been the usually prominent roles of the centralized state and the relatively weak support for **laissez-faire capitalism** (even though French economic philosophers originally coined the term). France was slower to industrialize than either Britain or Germany. When it did industrialize on a massive scale, beginning after World War II, planning by government played a much larger role than in most of Western Europe (and certainly the United States). France also developed an extensive social-welfare state, particularly in the post–World War II period. In 1999, the percentage of its gross domestic product dedicated to government expenditure was 48.5 percent, a figure more than four points above the average of EU member states and more than 18 percent above the level in the United States (see Figure 5.1).[8] Because of its strong statist traditions, the prominence of

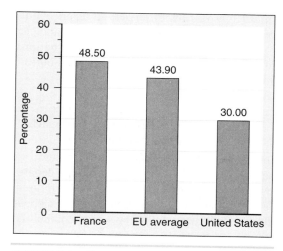

FIGURE 5.1   Governmental Expenditures as a Percentage of GDP, 1999
OECD National Accounts, 2001

the French state in generating modern economic development (often referred to as *dirigisme* or *etatism*), and the magnitude and popularity of its welfare state, France has only reluctantly and partially moved toward a privatized economy shaped primarily by market forces since the mid-1980s. The pressures to do so have been strong, stemming from the European Union as well as from the forces of the global economy; but resistant forces among French civil servants, trade unionists, intellectuals, and public opinion have also proved significant. Strikes and street demonstrations have long been part of the French political scene and have often been employed by workers, students, and farmers to protest against benefit cuts and other free-market "reforms." For example, in 1995, efforts by President Chirac and Prime Minister Juppé to reduce pensions as part of a cost-cutting drive to enable France to meet the criteria for inclusion in the European common currency provoked strikes and public protests that forced the government into a partial retreat.[9]

GOVERNMENTAL INSTITUTIONS

The Executive

The Constitution of the French Fifth Republic provides for a "dual executive" that combines elements of the American and British models. In contrast to the Third and Fourth Republics, which were parliamentary democracies, the Fifth Republic has usually featured a strong presidency. The president is the formal head of state but is also granted powers as commander in chief of the armed forces, emergency powers, powers to submit issues (with the agreement of the government or parliament) to the public in a referendum, powers to dissolve the National Assembly and call for new elections (but not more than once per year), and powers to preside over the council of ministers (cabinet). In addition, the president names the prime minister, with whom he shares executive powers, though the National Assembly can oust the prime minister by a vote of no confidence, in which a majority of those present and voting cast their ballots against the government, forcing the prime minister and cabinet ministers to resign. The prime minister ordinarily heads the government on a day-to-day basis, though if she or he shares the political affiliation of the president, he or she serves at the president's pleasure and as a result is often subordinated to the president. Thanks to a constitutional amendment adopted in a popular referendum in 1962 at President de Gaulle's initiative, the president is elected by direct popular vote and can thus claim a mandate from "the people." A recent constitutional amendment has set the term of office at five years for the future (the previous provision having been a seven-year term).

The ability of the National Assembly to oust the prime minister has meant that presidents have had to defer to the wishes of the Assembly or dissolve it and call for new Assembly elections when it has insisted upon a prime minister not of his choosing. The result has been a set of two very different patterns of executive power and decision-making: 1) a presidential dominance model (1958–1986, 1988–1993, 1995–1997, 2002–) when the president has enjoyed the support of a National Assembly majority, has been able to pick a politically compatible prime minister, and has been able to dominate the government most of the time; and 2) a "cohabitation" model (1986–1988, 1993–1995, and 1997–2002) when the president has been compelled by an unsympathetic National Assembly majority to appoint a prime minister who then has become the effective head of government, albeit one who has been somewhat checked by the president.

A single president may experience both patterns. For example, during 1981–1986 and 1988–1993, President Mitterrand was able to hire and fire prime ministers of his Socialist party largely to suit his own needs as he perceived them because he commanded strong parliamentary support in the National Assembly. Thus, he replaced Michel Rocard with Edith Cresson in 1991, when he concluded that she might improve the image of a government that had become tarnished by high unemployment, riots, and scandals, particularly since he had never cared much for Rocard's personality or style but had picked him to satisfy centrists in the Socialist party. When the Socialists fared poorly in local and regional elections in 1992, Mitterrand decided it was time to make another change; and he abruptly replaced Cresson with Pierre Bérégovoy. In contrast, when the parties of the Right controlled the National Assembly, as in 1986–1988 and again in 1993–1995, they were able to dictate to Mitterrand the appointment of prime ministers of their choosing (Jacques Chirac and Edouard Balladur, respectively). While Mitterrand was able to maintain considerable control over foreign policy, these periods of cohabitation required that he cede most domestic powers to the prime ministers and their governments.

After the National Assembly elections of 1997, occurring earlier than required due to conservative President Jacques Chirac's dissolution of the Assembly and calling of elections in the misplaced hope of winning a renewed majority, a coalition of Socialists, Communists, and Greens gained an Assembly majority and insisted upon having Socialist leader Lionel Jospin (whom Chirac had narrowly defeated for the presidency in 1995) named prime minister. From 1997 to 2002, Jospin headed a Socialist-Communist-Green cabinet and took the lead on most domestic policy matters, while Chirac continued to exercise his lessened presidential powers. In contrast, Chirac enjoyed dominance over a conservative coalition cabinet from 1995 to 1997, with the support of the National Assembly, and again did so following the presidential and legislative elections of 2002. Thus, the basic features of the French executive vary depending upon the partisan balance at different points in time.[10]

France possesses a more distinctive executive "elite" than most European states do. Two presidents of the Fifth Republic (Chirac and Giscard d'Estaing), five prime ministers, and numerous ministers and their immediate advisers have graduated from a single institution of higher learning, the National School of Administration, *Ecole Nationale d'Administration* (ENA), leading to numerous jokes to the effect that France is run by "Enarchy." Beyond the ENA is an array of other great schools (*grandes écoles*) that graduate an elite who staff the upper levels of the French civil service (especially the *grands corps*) and big business corporations.

TABLE 5.2   French Presidents and Prime Ministers Since 1958

Presidents (party affiliations)		Prime ministers	
Charles de Gaulle (Gaullist) (a)	1958–1969	Michel Debré	1958–1962
		Georges Pompidou	1962–1968
		Maurice Couve de Murville	1968–1969
Georges Pompidou (Gaullist)	1969–1974	Jacques Chaban-Delmas	1969–1972
		Pierre Messmer	1972–1974
Valéry Giscard d'Estaing (UDF with Gaullist support)	1974–1981	Jacques Chirac	1974–1976
		Raymond Barre	1976–1981
François Mitterrand (Socialist)	1981–1995	Pierre Mauroy	1981–1984
		Laurent Fabius	1984–1986
		Jacques Chirac (Gaullist)	1986–1988 *
		Michel Rocard	1988–1991
		Edith Cresson	1991–1992
		Pierre Bérégovoy	1992–1993
		Edouard Balladur (Gaullist)	1993–1995*
Jacques Chirac (Gaullist)	1995–	Alain Juppé	1995–1997
		Lionel Jospin (Socialist)	1997–2002*
		Jean-Pierre Raffarin	2002–

* Cohabitation

(a) Though de Gaulle considered himself above parties, the Gaullist party under its various acronyms was founded to support him and his legacy. Alain Poher served briefly as interim president in 1969 after de Gaulle's resignation and in 1974 after Pompidou's death in office.

Within each ministry (Education, Finance, Interior, etc.), the politically appointed minister is able to assemble a *cabinet* of his or her appointees, mostly from the upper civil service but selected also on the basis of presumed partisan/ideological sympathies, to mediate between the minister on the one hand and parliament, interest groups, and the regular civil servants on the other hand.[11]

The Parliament

During the Third Republic (1875–1940) and Fourth Republic (1946–1958), the national parliament played central roles in French government, ousting prime ministers and cabinets frequently and shaping most public policies, often by blocking executive initiatives. The framers of the 1958 Constitution consciously restricted parliamentary powers, reflecting General de Gaulle's low opinion of the national legislature. Among the Constitutional provisions weakening the parliament were 1) requirements that a no-confidence motion receive an absolute majority (not just a majority of those present and voting) in the National Assembly in order to replace a prime minister and cabinet, 2) reduction of the scope of parliamentary legislation and expansion of executive prerogatives, 3) limits on the time period for parliamentary consideration of the government's budgetary proposals, 4) procedures enabling the government to move its own bills to the top of the legislative agenda and obtain up-or-down votes on them, 5) unique provisions that a government bill given special designation by the prime minister be considered to be adopted without a parliamentary vote unless the National Assembly passed a no-confidence motion, and 6) reduction in the number of standing committees from 19 to 6 in each legislative chamber. In recent years, the French parliament has developed a fairly effective question period to hold ministers accountable, has utilized amendments to shape legislation more than early in the Fifth Republic, has developed small working groups to exercise more effective checks on the executive than the six large committees in each chamber could, and has persuaded governments not to use all of their constitutionally granted lawmaking powers. Nevertheless, the national legislature has not regained the central position that it occupied prior to the Fifth Republic.

French members of parliament cannot serve simultaneously in the cabinet or in any ministerial position, as legislators can and do in Germany and the United Kingdom and most cabinet-parliamentary systems that stress a **"fusion of powers"** between the executive and legislature. Instead, a French legislator who is appointed to an executive position must resign her/his parliamentary post. The goal of this constitutional requirement in the Fifth Republic has been to establish a **"separation of powers"** somewhat resembling that in the United States.

The French national legislature is composed of two chambers, the National Assembly, elected by direct popular vote for five years (unless the president dissolves it prior to that time), and the Senate, elected for nine years, one-third of the members every three years, by an electoral college of local and regional representatives. Only the National Assembly possesses the authority to remove the prime minister and cabinet. If the government wishes, the National Assembly can override the Senate on legislation. Therefore, the National Assembly is clearly the more powerful of the two legislative chambers.[12]

The Constitutional Council, Judiciary, and Legal System

Although France lacks the American tradition of judicial review, the Constitutional Council created by the Constitution of 1958 has come to assume the constitutional review functions of many supreme courts. Composed of three members appointed by the president of the republic and three each selected by the presidents of the two parliamentary chambers, the nine-member Constitutional Council received the authority to determine the constitutionality of legislation and resolve electoral disputes. Its chief differences from the United States Supreme Court are that it is not a part of the regular judiciary, that it can consider the validity of laws only when requested to do so by the government or at least 60 members of the National Assembly or Senate, that it makes its rulings immediately after the approval of a bill by parliament, and that its decisions are announced without the presentation of minority dissents.

Although at first the Constitutional Council rendered only occasional rulings on the constitutionality of law (nine times in its first 15 years) and usually sided with the president and his governments, it began to assert its independence and made key rulings with increasing frequency from the 1970s onward. Among its most important and controversial actions have been its decisions overturning a law authorizing prefects to refuse authorization to associations thought likely to undertake illegal activities (1971), portions of the nationalization legislation pushed through the National Assembly by President Mitterrand and his government in 1982, and parts of a 1993 statute requiring use of the French language. One leading analyst has recently concluded, "Today, all major controversial laws and all annual budgets end up in the Council." Moreover, during the 1990s, the Council found in nearly one-half of the cases brought before it that the law at issue was invalid.[13]

The French legal system resembles the German one in that both derive from the **Roman law** (or code law) tradition, rather than from the common law approach in England and the United States. The Napoleonic Code instituted by Napoleon I at the beginning of the nineteenth century remains the foundation of the French legal system. In accord with the code law tradition, the French place more emphasis than Anglo-Americans do on detailed legal codes (rather than precedents from previous cases) and tend to allow judges less discretion in their rulings than the Anglo-American system does. Nevertheless, in recent years, there has been a significant expansion of judicial roles and influence in France, extending well beyond the Constitutional Council discussed previously. Like most other Roman law countries, France has administrative courts separate from the rest of the judicial system, which deal with claims of individual citizens against the public administration. The judicial section of the Council of State, a venerable French institution dating back to the 1790s, rather than the Constitutional Court, serves as the highest of the administrative courts.[14]

Subnational Governments

The French bureaucratic state traditionally has been known for its hierarchical structure that has extended out into regional and local governments across France. Though France remains a unitary state, in which the national government enjoys legal sovereignty, it has become markedly less centralized and hierarchical since the 1980s than it was previously. Below the national level, France has 26 regions, 100 departments (geographic divisions about the size of most American counties but the major units of subnational government since the French Revolution), and more than 36,000 communes or local governmental units. Since 1986, each region and department has had a popularly elected council and council-appointed president as well as a prefect, an executive official appointed by the central government. Each commune has a popularly elected council and council-appointed mayor. The legal roles of the centrally appointed prefects have been reduced substantially from what existed prior to the 1980s. Under the system that prevailed from the French Revolution until the reforms of the 1980s, the prefects were national agents at the level of the geographic departments who in formal terms at least had enormous power in the form of "tutelage" or supervisory authority over local mayors and councils. In practice, because local mayors often held departmental, regional, and national offices simultaneously (under the *cumul de mandats* system that permitted multiple office-holding), politics were often not quite so centralized in the hands of the prefects as organizational charts suggested. Today, a mayor may hold only one other elective post, but mayors of large cities have become even more likely than in the past to serve simultaneously as members of the National Assembly or Senate. Overall, both formal and informal authority has been decentralized (and some say, democratized) since the reforms of the 1980s.[15]

Summary

French governmental institutions are a unique blend of modified presidentialism juxtaposed with British-style parliamentarism, a recently decentralized unitary structure of national-regional-local relations, a Constitutional Council with significant powers of constitutional review, and a long-entrenched Roman-based system of law. In contrast to the history of the past two centuries, the French governmental institutions appear to have attained at last a considerable degree of legitimacy in the eyes of French citizens. The recent pattern has been for the French public to respect their institutions while scorning their politicians—a stance that should be familiar to most Americans.

ELECTIONS, POLITICAL PARTIES, AND INTEREST GROUPS

Elections, political parties, and interest groups are major linkage mechanisms in France, as in other constitutional democracies, between the public and the governmental institutions. As the marked differences in presidential-prime min-

isterial relationships between presidential dominance and cohabitation have already illustrated, the outcomes of elections and other political processes in France can have a profound impact on how government functions.

The Electoral Process

France holds separate elections for president and National Assembly and also makes provisions for national referendums. Voter turnouts have been high by international standards, especially in presidential elections, where they have averaged well above the 80 percent mark. National Assembly elections have drawn voter participation in the 61–85 percent range, with the 61 percent turnout in the second round of the 2002 legislative elections being the lowest since World War II. Referendums have attracted turnouts ranging from a low of only 30 percent to a high of 85 percent, depending on the timing and the issue. The president is elected by direct popular vote under a system in which many candidates run in a first round (since nomination is relatively easy and France has many political parties) and then the top two candidates oppose each other in a second round two weeks later if no one wins a clear majority in the initial competition. Since the first popular presidential elections in 1965, no candidate has ever won the requisite majority on the first round; therefore, a second ballot has always been required. In the 1995 presidential election, Jacques Chirac of the conservative Rally for the Republic put together a conservative (Right) coalition on the second ballot to defeat his Socialist rival, Lionel Jospin, backed on the second round by a Left coalition, by 52.6 percent to 47.4 percent. Two years later, however, Jospin came to power as prime minister as a result of the National Assembly elections of 1997, which gave an Assembly majority to the Left coalition of Socialist, Communist, and Green parties. In 2002, Chirac gained reelection as president, winning only 19.9 percent on the first round in a race that astonished most observers by giving second place to Jean-Marie Le Pen of the far-right National Front (FN). Chirac went on to a landslide 82.2 percent to 17.8 percent victory in the second round, since all major parties save the National Front backed his candidacy in an effort to smother Le Pen's extremism. (See the box on page 107.) Socialist Prime Minister Jospin, humiliated by his third-place finish in the April 2002 first round, resigned in early May. Chirac then appointed fellow conservative and little-known Senator Jean-Pierre Raffarin as prime minister. Chirac and Raffarin assembled a new electoral alliance termed the Union for a Presidential Majority (UMP), renamed the Union for a Popular Movement (also UMP) following the elections. Stressing the need for a clear presidential majority to replace the cohabitation arrangement of the previous five years, this alliance won a solid majority in the June 2002 legislative elections. (See Table 5.4 for the 2002 and 1997 elections. Popular voting patterns during 1918–2002 appear in Table 5.5.)

President Chirac remains the dominant leader of the Union for a Popular Movement. He is not a lame duck president, because the French constitution places no American-style limits on presidential reelections; his popularity remained fairly high in early 2004, with three years still remaining until the next presidential election. Nonetheless, another UMP figure, notoriously ambitious Interior Minister Nicolas Sarkozy, widely known as "Sarko," was already laying the groundwork to succeed Chirac as president and leader of the center-right in France. Asked while he was shaving if he dreamed of being president, Sarko quickly shot back, "Yes, and not only when shaving."[16]

In response to a question asked while he shaved of whether he dreamed of being president: "Yes, and not only when shaving."

French Interior Minister Nicolas Sarkozy, *quoted by David Lawday in New Statesman (January 5, 2004).*

France originated the concept of the Left-Right spectrum during the French Revolution, and French politics has continued to be organized along Left-Right lines to a high degree, with the Left expressing longtime socialist goals

TABLE 5.3 The French Presidential Elections of 1995 and 2002

	1995	
Candidate (party)	Second round %	First round %
Jacques Chirac (RPR)*	20.7	52.6
Lionel Jospin (PS)	23.3	47.4
Edouard Balladur (RPR)	18.5	
Jean-Marie Le Pen (FN)	15.7	
Robert Hue (PCF)	8.7	
Arlette Laguiller (LO)	5.3	
Others	8.8	
Total	100.0	100.0

	2002	
Candidate (party)	Second round %	First round %
Jacques Chirac (RPR/UMP)	19.9	82.2
Jean-Marie Le Pen (FN)	16.9	17.8
Lionel Jospin (PS)	16.2	
François Bayrou (UDF)	6.8	
Arlette Laguiller (LO)	5.7	
Jean-Pierre Chevènement (PR)	5.3	
Noël Mamère (Greens)	5.2	
Others		24.0
Total	100.0	100.0

*Party/electoral alliance titles are as follows:
FN   National Front
LO   Workers' Struggle
PCF   French Communist Party
PR   Republican Pole
PS   Socialist Party
RPR   Rally for the Republic
UDF   Union for French Democracy
UMP   Union for a Presidential Majority

TABLE 5.4   The French National Assembly Elections of 1997 and 2002

Party	1997		2002	
	Popular vote %*	Seats	Popular vote %*	Seats
Socialist	24	241	24	140
Communist	10	38	5	21
Left Radical	1	12	2	7
Green	7	7	5	3
Diverse Left	3	21	1	6
Left Alliance	46	319	37	177
Union for a Presidential Majority (a)	16	134	34	357
Union of French Democrats	14	108	5	29
Diverse Right	7	14	5	12
Center-Right Alliance	37	256	44	398
National Front	15	1	11	0
Others	3	11	8	2
Total	100	577	100	577

*First-round popular vote percentages.
(a) Rally for the Republic in 1997; renamed Union for a Popular Movement after the 2002 elections.

TABLE 5.5   Party Percentages of the First-Round Popular Vote in French National Assembly Elections, 1978–2002

Party	1978	1981	1986	1988	1993	1997	2002
RPR/UMP	23%	21%	*42%	19%	20%	16%	34%
UDF	21	19	*	19	19	14	5
PS	23	38(a)	32	35	19(a)	24	24
Left Radical	2	(a)	3	1	(a)	1	2
PCF	21	16	10	11	9	10	5
FN			10	10	13	15	11
Others	10	6	3	5	20	10	19
Total	100	100	100	100	100	100	100

*RPR and UDF counted together in 1986.
(a) PS and Left Radicals counted together in 1981 and 1993.

Party titles are as follows:
RPR   Rally for the Republic (Gaullist)
UMP   Union for a Presidential Majority in 2002, later Union for a Popular Movement
UDF   Union of French Democrats
PS   Socialist party
PCF   French Communist party
FN   National Front

of social and economic equality and including the Communist (far left) and Socialist (center-left) parties and their allies, and the Right combining neoliberal and traditional conservative outlooks and including in recent years the Rally for the Republic/Union for a Presidential Majority, the Union for French Democracy, and their allies.

The National Assembly elections in France must be held at least once every five years, but the president may dissolve the Assembly and call for new elections prior to the expiration of a full five-year term. President Chirac did so in 1997 (four years after the previous elections) and soon came to rue his decision. The current system for Assembly elections divides the country into 577 districts, each of which elects one member. If a candidate wins a majority on the first round, he or she is elected. If no candidate wins a majority, a second round occurs one week later, in which only candidates whose vote exceeded 12.5 percent of the registered voters in the first round may compete. Often, candidates eligible to compete in the second round withdraw in favor of one of the top two candidates, based upon alliances between or among parties. In any event, in the second round, the candidate winning the most votes (not necessarily a majority) is elected. For a time in the 1980s, France used a **proportional representation** electoral system that encouraged a multiplicity of parties by awarding each a percentage of the seats roughly based upon its proportion of the popular vote. Since 1988, the current system has allowed many parties to persist but has made it difficult for parties that have not made coalition arrangements with others to win many National Assembly seats. For example, the far-right National Front, a nationalistic party that opposes non-European immigration into France, was able to win 37 seats with 10 percent of the popular vote in the 1986 legislative elections but only 1 seat with 15 percent of the popular vote in the 1997 legislative elections and no seats with 11 percent of the popular vote in the 2002 legislative elec-

tions. The reason for its poor showing has been that its candidates can rarely win enough votes in a single-member district on the second round to come first in competition with candidates who formed Left or Right alliances with other parties on the second round. Thus, the Socialist candidates would normally gain the support of Communist voters on the second round (if the Communist candidates were eliminated), or vice versa, while conservative candidates would enjoy the support of voters for other conservative candidates (if their first-choice candidates were eliminated). Lacking partners, because all of the other parties have considered them unacceptably racist, the National Front candidates have not drawn many voters from other parties even if the National Front candidates make it into the second round. Obviously, the electoral rules have had an important bearing on the composition of the National Assembly.

Table 5.6 (next page), showing the 2002 legislative election results in four districts illustrates how the French electoral system commonly operates. In particular, it demonstrates why the National Front (FN) has rarely been able to win seats despite often attracting about 10–15 percent of the national popular vote, while the Communists (PCF), lacking the ostracism facing the FN on the second round, have picked up far more parliamentary seats with a smaller national popular vote. In the Var 3 district, the FN candidate, Beauregard de David, came a fairly close second in round one but lost overwhelmingly to Giran of the Union for a Presidential Majority (UMP) one week later in a two-candidate race. In the Var 6 district, a slightly different pattern appeared. Tudury, the FN candidate, scored a strong second place finish in the first round but ended up a distant third in a three-candidate race in round two. The third example, in the Bouche du Rhone 4 district, shows the Communist (PCF) advantage over the National Front (FN) when the candidates of these two parties face one another in the second round. In this case, Bauman (FN) placed a very strong second in the first round

TABLE 5.6   2002 National Assembly Election Results in Four Districts

Var 3 District	First round	Percentage	Second round	Percentage
Giran (UMP) **Elected**	19,128	30.4	33,453	67.9
Beauregard de David (FN)	13,021	20.7	15,817	32.1
Masson (UDF)	10,434	16.6		
Joffre (Left Radical)	7,198	11.4		
Albergo (Green)	4,451	7.1		
Canapa (Communist)	4,103	6.5		
Others	4,670	7.3		
Total	63,015	100.0	49,270	100.0
Var 6 District				
Pons (UMP) **Elected**	27,554	31.3	38,743	46.4
Tudury (FN)	18,131	20.6	16,302	19.5
Menut (Socialist)	17,959	20.4	28,433	34.1
Gilardo (Communist)	5,724	6.5		
Bovis (UDF)	4,576	5.2		
Others	14,015	16.0		
Total	87,959	100.0	83,478	100.0
Bouche du Rhone 4 District				
Dutoit (Communist) **Elected**	6,163	25.9	13,272	64.8
Baumann (FN)	5,824	24.4	7,208	35.2
Mennucci (Socialist)	4,280	18.0		
Franceschi (RPR)	3,956	16.6		
Others	3,610	15.1		
Total	25,491	100.0	20,480	100.0
Albertville District				
Gaymard (UMP/UDF) **Elected**	24,323	50.9		
Vairetto (Socialist)	11,749	24.7		
Sondaz (FN)	4,651	9.8		
Others	6,958	14.6		
Total	47,590	100.0		

(just 339 votes behind Dutoit, the Communist) but then lost badly (64.8 percent to 35.2 percent) to Dutoit in round two. The kinds of results typified by these districts have repeated in election after election and constituency after constituency across France, though overall the FN has done less well in the popular vote than in these examples. The fourth district, Albertville, offers an example of a candidate who was able to win a majority on the first round.

Referendums have at times played an important role in determining key constitutional and policy outcomes in France—far more so than in the United Kingdom or the Federal Republic of Germany, the latter of which has made no use of them at the national level, though less so than in Italy and some of the smaller European countries. Two of the last three referendums have drawn low turnouts of less than 40 percent, but public opinion surveys continue to show strong public support for the use of referendums.

Political Parties

In sharp contrast to the American and British political party systems, which have tended toward competition between two major parties, the French have commonly had six or more significant political parties at a time. In recent years, the waning of some traditional ideological differences, combined with the pressures of the two-round system in both presidential and National Assembly elections, has nudged France toward two broad alliances of parties: a conservative **(Right)** coalition of the Rally for the Republic (commonly termed the Gaullists as the party that traces its origins to de Gaulle and his closest allies), the Union for French Democracy, the recently formed Liberal Democracy, and some smaller parties; and a **Left** coalition of the Socialist, party, the Communist party, and some smaller parties such as the Left Radicals and the Greens. However, the ultraconservative National Front, which has recently split into two competing parties, has stood outside both broad alliances in national politics.

The largest of the Right parties in recent years has been the Rally for the Republic (RPR), which originated as a political movement designed to support General (later President) Charles de Gaulle and is the party of the current President Jacques Chirac. Divided over leadership issues (with two competing presidential candidates in the first round of the 1995 presidential election, for example) and European policy, the RPR has generally united around pro-business ideas and policies and has a fairly strong base of support among upper-middle-class and devout Catholic voters. It constitutes the core of the pro-Chirac Union for a Popular Movement (UMP) now.

The Union for French Democracy has been the second major component of the mainstream Right alliance. Not really a party but a rather loose federation of parties, it was long identified with Valery Giscard d'Estaing, the president of France from 1974 to 1981 and a major force in French politics over several decades. In general, it has been more centrist in orientation and more supportive of European integration efforts than the RPR. In 1998, it suffered the defection of its longtime member, the Republican party, which was renamed Liberal Democracy and adopted a highly **libertarian** ideology.

Sometimes associated with the mainstream Right in regional and local politics but isolated from it in national politics (and recently at all levels) is the National Front (FN), usually described as a far-right party that has stressed intense nationalism, populism, and hostility to recent non-European immigrants. Some observers see it as **fascistic.** Its longtime charismatic leader, Jean-Marie Le Pen, quarreled bitterly with his former associate, Bruno Mégret, in the late 1990s, resulting in a party split that temporarily weakened the influence of both men and their followers. As noted previously, the abandonment of proportional representation in National Assembly elections and the lack of National Front allies on second ballots have diminished the National Front's presence in national politics. Nevertheless, Le Pen and the National Front surged to prominence again in 2002, buoyed by Le Pen's second-place showing in the presidential election.[17]

"France for the French"
    Slogan of Jean-Marie Le Pen's National Front

PEOPLE IN THE EU

Jean-Marie Le Pen as a French Political Phenomenon

Although Jean-Marie Le Pen organized the National Front (FN) in 1972, he captured little attention and his party fared poorly until 1983, when Le Pen ran for the city council in a district of Paris and won 11.5 percent of the vote on an anti-immigrant platform. Suddenly, he and his party captured national and even international mass media attention. From that point onward, he became a significant political figure on the French national political scene and has remained one. Concentrations of non-European immigrants in industrial suburbs, rising crime rates, and persistently high unemployment have created unease among many French citizens, and Le Pen and his allies have skillfully exploited this unease to build political support.

Le Pen has projected an image of a tough-talking populist who says what others think but are afraid to say. He has emphasized anti-immigrant rhetoric that most analysts and most other parties have branded as racist. To this rhetoric, he has added "law and order" appeals and nationalistic attacks on the European Union, for example, denouncing the euro as "the currency of occupation" and proclaiming that "France is in danger of death" at the hands of the EU. Despite his undeniable personal appeal to many of his followers, a recent survey of his voters found that agreement with the party's policies was stressed by nearly two-thirds of them.

In 1998, a major power struggle developed within the National Front between Le Pen and his chief deputy, Bruno Mégret, twenty-one years his junior and clearly eager to seize the leadership of the anti-immigrant crusade. When Mégret sought to lead the party into the 1999 European Parliament elections (after Le Pen was convicted of assault!), Le Pen had him and his allies expelled from the National Front, whereupon they promptly launched their own political party in competition with the FN. Though this split temporarily weakened the National Front, Le Pen has continued to mobilize considerable support and, at the age of 73, won second place in the 2002 French presidential election, confounding pollsters' predictions and shocking international opinion.

Le Pen has had considerable impact on French politics and society, despite the fact that he is unlikely ever to win high office and despite his party's inability to be a major force in the National Assembly in recent years due to the single-member plurality electoral system and the lack of allies for the second round. By drawing votes disproportionately from the mainstream parties of the Right (though he has also attracted some working-class support away from the Communists and Socialists) and by causing internal disputes within the mainstream Right parties over whether they should accept the National Front as an ally, Le Pen and his movement were particularly disruptive of attempts to create unity on the French Right in the 1990s. However, ironically, Le Pen's second-place finish in the first round of the 2002 presidential election united the major parties of both the center-right and the Left behind Le Pen's arch-enemy Jacques Chirac, enabling Chirac to win a landslide reelection victory in the second round in May 2002. Riding that

(continued on next page)

(continued from previous page)

momentum, Chirac's center-right political coalition went on to win a strong legislative majority in the June 2002 elections. As for the Left, Le Pen's second-place finish, ahead of Socialist Prime Minister Lionel Jospin in the first round of the presidential election of 2002, led Jospin to announce his retirement from politics. In the realm of public policy, the mainstream Right has sought to appeal to potential voters for Le Pen by backing tough legislation on nation-ality and immigration; and both the main-stream Right and Left have increasingly emphasized law and order themes similar to his. Beyond France, Le Pen's strong show-ing has helped to push immigration control to the top of the agenda of the European Union, as was evident at the Seville Euro-pean Summit in June 2002. Therefore, although Le Pen is unlikely to ever rise to the top of French politics, he has certainly left his mark.[18]

The Socialist party (PS) has dominated the French Left since the early 1980s, but it has usually had to form alliances with the Commu-nist party, small leftist parties, and recently the Greens in order to win the presidency and National Assembly victories during second rounds. A recent analysis of the "plural left" coalition that supported Prime Minister Lionel Jospin's government in the National Assembly concluded that it was held together by "mutual dependence born of political necessity."[19] Its members also achieved considerable inter-party consensus on expanding public health care, increasing economic equality, reducing the standard work week in an effort to counter unemployment, and seeking to equalize rights between men and women.

The Socialist party gained ascendancy on the French Left largely through the leadership of François Mitterrand, who spurred its reorga-nization in the early 1970s, led it to victory in the presidential elections of 1981 and 1988, and helped to achieve a Socialist National Assembly majority in 1981–1986 and a near-majority in 1988–1993. Mitterrand proved particularly adept at forming an alliance with the Commu-nists and then outmaneuvering them and dimin-ishing their influence. Since Mitterrand's death in 1995, Lionel Jospin has emerged as the chief Socialist spokesman. Although the French Socialist party is a partner of the German Social Democratic party and the British Labour party in both the EU Party of European Socialists and the Socialist International, and has in practice shown a willingness to adapt to global and EU market trends, it maintains more socialistic rhetoric than either of these other major West European parties of the democratic Left. Jospin's third-place finish in the 2002 presiden-tial election, his subsequent resignation as prime minister, and a major loss of National Assembly seats in the 2002 legislative elections have left the Socialist party in considerable disarray.

Positioning itself to the left of the Socialist party on most issues is the Communist party (PCF). Until the 1970s the largest party on the French Left, the Communists have seen their popular support drop from about 25 percent in most elections to less than 5 percent in 2002. Today, the PCF distinguishes itself from the Socialist party chiefly by its insistence on gov-ernment ownership of major business corpora-tions and distinctive **Keynesian** economic policies that reflect the ideas of John Maynard Keynes (himself a non-Communist British economist who advocated national government steering of the economy) in defiance of EU and global trends toward free-market capitalism.

Other components of the Left alliance are the pro-environment, antinuclear power

Greens; the rather fragmented Left Radicals (PRG); and the Movement of Citizens (MDC), later Republican Pole (PR), led by former Socialist Jean-Pierre Chevènement, who served as Interior Minister in the Jospin government until his angry resignation in August 2000 over Jospin's offer of **devolution** to Corsica. Despite repeated conflicts and tensions among the diverse parties of the "plural left" coalition, its components generally worked together more effectively in the 1990s than did the parties of the Right. However, the center-right made a major comeback in 2002, riding a tide of conservative sentiment that swept across most of Europe amid rising concerns over crime, immigration, and slow economic growth. French party politics are considerably more dualistic (divided into two major alliances) and less ideologically intense than they once were, but they are still far from the Anglo-American pattern of competition between two large, **pragmatic** parties of the center-right and center-left.[20]

Interest Groups

French interest groups have shared many of the same ideological roots and conflict patterns as the parties. However, they have usually lacked direct ties to the parties of the type prevalent in Britain, Germany, and many other European countries. Moreover, they have generally found it difficult to recruit a mass membership because a broad section of French public opinion has persistently seen them as detrimental to the kind of public interest exalted by Jean-Jacques Rousseau and many other French thinkers. The result has been a relatively weak and ineffectual array of organized interest groups, combined with periodic massive protest movements (sometimes violent ones) that have forced governments to retreat from major policy initiatives from time to time.

The Movement of French Enterprises (MEDEF) is the primary "peak" association of the business community. Organized as a federation, it tends to be dominated by big business interests. Trade associations and individual large corporations often make their own approaches to the French government and EU institutions and appear to have gained substantial power as European integration and globalization have diminished the former prominence of French governmental actors in economic affairs and weakened the clout of labor unions. Small businessmen have often felt the need to join protest movements to make their voices heard.

Also relatively well-organized among French interest groups has been the National Federation of Agricultural Unions (FNSEA), though the steady decline of the French farming population and the growing pressures to reduce European Union farm budgets (Chapter Four) have diminished its influence in recent years.

French labor unions have historically been ideologically divided along Communist-Socialist-Catholic lines and have never been as successful at organizing the workforce as have their counterparts in Germany, the United Kingdom, or most of the rest of Western Europe. Today, only about 10 percent of French employees are members of labor unions—a figure far below most of the rest of Europe and even below the United States.

Because labor unions have been particularly weak and fragmented, state institutions have been relatively strong, and interest groups in general have enjoyed only limited public support, France has never implemented a full-blown **corporatist** or **neo-corporatist** pattern of governmental consultation with major economic interests of the type often found in Germany, Sweden, Austria, and some other West European countries. This type of consultation is dependent upon a high degree of organization and central leadership in major economic groups, so that leaders can make agreements that will be binding upon their members. Such organization and leadership has generally been lacking in French groups, particularly in the case of organized labor. Although some analysts have described French agricultural policy-making patterns as neo-corporatist, most have ranked French government-group relations as among the least neo-corporatist in Western Europe, even when neo-corporatism was more widespread in the 1960s and 1970s than it is at present.[21]

If organized labor and many other economic interest groups beyond MEDEF and FNSEA have usually enjoyed less influence than most of their West European counterparts in other countries, France has long been noted for its explosive and often violent protest movements—some of which have been able to achieve their policy goals. A new element since the 1960s has been the rise of the "new social movements" in France, roughly paralleling developments elsewhere in Western Europe. Based largely on **post-material** and/or libertarian values in contrast to the previously prevalent material interests, these movements have included those among feminists, gays, students, and environmentalists. Although the level of new social movement activity in France appears to be lower than in Germany (and comparable to that in Britain), the new movements have added their protest activity to that of dissident French workers, farmers, small businessmen, and other traditional economic forces, often creating an atmosphere of considerable turmoil in modern France.[22]

Summary

Most analysts find much of the distinctiveness of French party and interest-group politics to be rooted in a unique political culture, shaped by French history in ways differentiating it from Britain, Germany, or the United States. For example, a French fascination with abstract symbols more than concrete problem-solving, and a tendency to contest these symbols vehemently, became apparent as early as the Age of Enlightenment in the eighteenth century, when authoritarian monarchs permitted the rising middle classes to debate intellectual abstractions but to exercise very little real political power.

The habits of treating politics in terms of abstract symbols and contesting them bitterly continued through the French Revolution of 1789–1799 and on through most of the two centuries that followed, affecting the distinctive style of modern French politics.[23]

Another example was the persistence until recently of a strong but distant centralized French state, which bred distrust of the state but at the same time encouraged high popular expectations of what it might deliver.[24] As noted previously in this chapter, simultaneous crises of state-building, participation, and distribution—and failures to resolve them to the satisfaction of many—often created cross-cutting cleavages of opinion that contributed to the fragmentation of the French political party and interest group systems. Some have perceived the French divisiveness to be rooted in the culture beyond politics. Only half in jest, President Charles de Gaulle once remarked, "How can you govern a country which has 246 varieties of cheese?"

"How can you govern a country which has 246 varieties of cheese?"

President Charles de Gaulle, *quoted by Mignon, Le Mots du General (1962).*

Of course, the impact of political culture should not be exaggerated. Constitutional provisions (i.e., creation of a strong presidency and a runoff system for electing the president) and electoral laws (i.e., the adoption and then abolition of proportional representation in National Assembly elections) have also helped to shape the French participatory process and its intermediaries, the parties and groups.

CONCLUSIONS

The French have long prided themselves on the "exceptional" traits of their system. These have included a strong central state, ***dirigiste*** approaches to economic management, the pursuit of grandeur in foreign relations, and the preservation of an agricultural society long known for its fine wines, unique cheeses, and quaint medieval villages. However, recent years have prompted heated debate among French intellectuals over the alleged "end of French exceptionalism" in an era marked by both globalization and Europeanization.[25] The following chapter focuses in part on the issues raised in this debate as it examines France's position in the European Union. Despite pressures toward conformity with European and global norms, France maintains and is likely to sustain many features that make it politically distinctive, even "something special" (as Jonathan Fenby has phrased it), though perhaps not quite "exceptional."[26]

SUMMARY

- France began to develop national consciousness relatively early, largely through central state efforts, though the centralizing and nationalizing effects of the French Revolution (1789–1799) and Napoleon I (1799–1815) were particularly important in building the modern French nation-state.

- The French state has been highly centralized since the 1790s and has played extensive roles in society. Despite continuity in the Napoleonic Code and many central bureaucratic institutions since the early nineteenth century, France has experienced far more different constitutional regimes than most European countries have.

- France possesses a strong democratic heritage that extends back to the eighteenth century, but its democratic participation has advanced and retreated over time, with authoritarian eras recurring until the 1940s.

- The French economy developed historically from feudalism to a modern mixed economy, with state roles prominent in its creation of a distinctive French modernity of *dirigisme* and social welfare.

- Simultaneous conflicts of modernization characterized French historical development through most of the nineteenth and early twentieth centuries, contributing to political instability.

- The Fifth Republic (1958–) has apparently developed the stability and legitimacy that it predecessors lacked, but modernization problems continue to challenge France.

- The French president and prime minister share executive powers; when they are of different political parties, the relationship is termed cohabitation; when they share a party affiliation, the president is in most respects the more powerful of the two executives.

- The current French president is Jacques Chirac, and the current prime minister is Jean-Pierre Raffarin (both of the Gaullist party currently termed the Union for a Popular Movement, UMP).

- France possesses a more distinctive bureaucratic elite than most European states or the United States.

- The French pattern of executive-legislative relations is a hybrid of the U.S. presidential system and the British cabinet-parliamentary system.

- The French parliament consists of the National Assembly and the Senate, of which the National Assembly possesses the superior powers.

- The French Constitutional Council has exercised constitutional review functions broadly similar to those of constitutional or supreme courts in many other countries, though it is not part of the French judiciary.

- The French legal system derives from the Roman law tradition; the Napoleonic Code instituted by Napoleon I at the beginning of the nineteenth century is its primary foundation.

- France is a unitary (rather than a federal) state, but it has become less centralized and hierarchical since the 1980s than it was previously.

- France holds separate elections for president and National Assembly and also holds national referendums from time to time.

- France has traditionally had multiparty politics and still tends in that direction, though it has moved toward two broad alliances (Right and Left) of parties in recent years. The largest parties are the Socialist party and the Rally for the Republic (which is the largest component of the pro-Chirac Union for a Popular Movement).

- Jean-Marie Le Pen has gained particular notoriety in recent years as the racist, anti-immigrant leader of the National Front and stunned much of the world by placing second in the 2002 presidential election.

- French interest groups suffer from widespread popular distrust, and French labor unions have been particularly weak and fragmented; though interest groups are relatively lacking in influence, mass protest movements are a common feature of French politics.

ENDNOTES

1. Rogers Brubaker, *Citizenship and Nationhood in France and Germany* (Cambridge: Harvard University Press, 1992); David A. Bell, *The Cult of the Nation in France: Inventing Nationalism, 1680–1800* (Cambridge: Harvard University Press, 2001); W. Scott Haine, *The History of France* (Westport, CT: Greenwood Press, 2000), Chs. 3–6.

2. On Catholicism, see Francois Goguel, "Six Authors in Search of a National Character," in Stanley Hoffman, ed., *In Search of France* (New York: Harper and Row, 1963), 391–392, and Suzanne Berger, "The French Political System," in Samuel H. Beer, et al., eds. *Patterns of Government*, 3rd ed. (New York: Random House, 1973), 348–353. On the working-class alienation, see Stanley Hoffman, "The French Political Community," in Hoffman, ed., *In Search of France*, 6–8. David Thomson, *Democracy in France Since 1870* (New York: Oxford University Press, 1964) provides an excellent overview of both the Third and Fourth Republics.

3. Gabriel A. Almond and G. Bingham Powell, *Comparative Politics: A Developmental Approach* (Boston: Little, Brown, 1966), 34–41; Philip M. Williams, *Crisis and Compromise: Politics in the Fourth Republic* (Garden City, NY: Doubleday, 1966), 3–6.

4. Brubaker, *Citizenship and Nationhood in France and Germany*; Anne Sa'adah, *Contemporary France: A Democratic Education* (Lanham, MD: Rowman and Littlefield, 2003), esp. Ch. 1; and Henry W. Ehrmann and Martin A. Schain, *Politics in France*, 5th ed. (New York: Harper-Collins, 1992), 4–10 provide good analyses of French national identity. On recent immigration and national integration issues, also see Sa'adah, *Contemporary France*, Ch. 7; James F. Hollifield, "The Migration Challenge: Europe's Crisis in Historical Perspective," in Henri Warmenhoven, ed., *Global Studies: Western Europe*, 6th ed. (Guilford, CT: Dushkin/McGraw-Hill, 1999), 185–191; and Sami Nair, "France: A Crisis of Integration," in Henri Warmenhoven, ed., *Global Studies: Western Europe*, 5th ed. (Guilford, CT: Dushkin/McGraw-Hill, 1997), 219–221. On Corsica, see Charles Bremner, "Jospin Offers Devolution Plan to Corsicans," *The Times*, July 11, 2000; Adam Sage, "Bombing Follows Corsica Initiative," *The Times*, August 18, 2000; Bronwen Maddox, "Jospin Is Not Rewarding Terrorism," *The Times*, August 30, 2000.

5. Williams, *Crisis and Compromise*, 2.

6. Sa'adah, *Contemporary France*, 200–201; Ehrmann and Schain, *Politics in France*, 11–15; Berger, "The French Political System," 356–367.

7. Ehrmann and Schain, *Politics in France*, 186–187; Vivien A. Schmidt, "The Changing Dynamics of

State-Society Relations in the Fifth Republic," in Robert Elgie, ed., *The Changing French Political System* (London: Frank Cass, 2000), 154–155.

8. "France Survey," *The Economist*, June 5, 1999, 6; Organization for Economic Cooperation and Development, National Accounts, 2001.

9. Schmidt, "The Changing Dynamics of State-Society Relations in the Fifth Republic," 141–165; Alistair Cole, "The *Service Public* Under Stress," in Elgie, ed., *The Changing French Political System*, 166–184; "France Survey," *The Economist*, June 5, 1999.

10. Jonathan Fenby, *France on the Brink* (New York: Arcade, 1999), 385–419, provides one of many good accounts of the transformations at the executive level and in French politics from 1995–1997. Also see William Safran, *The French Polity*, 5th ed. (New York: Longman, 1998), 177–220, for an extended overview of the French executive.

11. On the ENA, the Great Schools, and French executive elites, see Fenby, *France on the Brink*, 71–80, Safran, *The French Polity*, 265–302; and Ehrmann and Schain, *Politics in France*, 144–155. On the *cabinets* in comparative perspective, see Yves Mény and Andrew Knapp, *Government and Politics in Western Europe* (Oxford: Oxford University Press, 1998), 268–269.

12. Philip E. Converse and Roy Pierce, *Political Representation in France* (Cambridge: Harvard University Press, 1986); Ehrmann and Schain, *Politics in France*, Ch. 9; Safran, *The French Polity*, Ch. 7; John Huber, "Restrictive Legislative Procedures in France and the United States," *American Political Science Review* 86, 3 (September 1992), 675–687; Franco Rizzuto, "France: Something of a Rehabilitation," *Parliamentary Affairs* 50, 3 (July 1997), 373–379.

13. The quotation is from Vincent Wright, "The Fifth Republic: From the *Droit de l'État* to the *État de droit?*" in Elgie, ed., *The Changing French Political System*, 99. Also see Alec Stone, *The Birth of Judicial Politics in France: The Constitutional Council in Comparative Perspective* (Oxford: Oxford University Press, 1992).

14. Wright, "The Fifth Republic," 92–119.

15. John Ardagh, *France Today* (London: Penguin, 1988), 181–199; Emmanuel Negriér, "The Changing Role of French Local Government," in Elgie, ed., *The Changing French Political System*, 120–140; Ehrmann and Schain, *Politics in France*, 370–391; and Vivien A. Schmidt, *Democratizing France: The Political and Administrative History of Decentralization* (Cambridge: Cambridge University Press, 1991).

16. David Lawday, "Nicolas Sarkhozy," *New Statesman*, January 5, 2004.

17. Paul Hainsworth, "The Right: Divisions and Cleavages in *fin de siècle* France," in Elgie, ed., *The Changing French Political System*, 38–56; Fenby, *France on the Brink*, 209–242 and 409–419; Peter Davies, *The National Front in France: Ideology, Discourse, and Power* (London: Routledge, 1999); and Robert D. Zaretsky, "Neither Left nor Right, nor Straight Ahead: Recent Books on Fascism in France," *The Journal of Modern History* 73, 1 (March 2001), 118–132; Donald McNeil, Jr., "French Never-Say-Die Rightist Grasps at Top Spot a 5th Time," *New York Times*, April 19, 2002, A10.

18. Fenby, *France on the Brink*, 209–242; Davies, *The National Front in France*; McNeil, "French Never-Say-Die Rightist Grasps at Top Spot a 5th Time," *New York Times*, April 19, 2002, A10; Suzanne Daley, "Extreme Rightist Eclipses Socialist to Qualify for Runoff in France," *New York Times*, April 22, 2002, A1, A6; Alan Riding, "Jospin's Loss Reveals a Left That Is Losing Its Platform," *New York Times*, April 22, 2002, A6; Donald McNeil, Jr., "At Least for a Moment, Euphoria on the Right," *New York Times*, April 22, 2002, A6; Charles Fleming and Marina Rozenman, "Victory by Far-Right Candidate Shocks France," *Wall Street Journal*, April 22, 2002, A14; Gwladys Fouche and Simon Jeffery, "Le Pen's Policies," *The Guardian*, April 22, 2002; Steven Erlanger, "European Summit Talks Open Today; Focus Is Immigration Control," *New York Times*, June 21, 2002, A8.

19. Joseph Szarka, "The Parties of the French 'Plural Left': An Uneasy Complementarity," in Elgie, ed., *The Changing French Political System*, 31.

20. On Chevènement's resignation, see Maddox, "Jospin Is not Rewarding Terrorism," *The Times*, August 30, 2000. A good recent overview of the "plural left" is Szarka, "The Parties of the French

'Plural Left'," 20–37. Also see William Safran, "The Socialists, Jospin, and the Mitterrand Legacy," in Michael S. Lewis-Beck, ed., *How France Votes* (New York: Chatham House, 2000), 14–41, and Ben Clift, "The Jospin Way," *The Political Quarterly* 72, 2 (April–June 2001), 170–179.

21. Maria Green Cowles, "The Transatlantic Business Dialogue and Domestic Business-Government Relations," in Cowles, et al., *Transforming Europe: Europeanization and Domestic Change* (Ithaca, NY: Cornell University Press, 2001), 159–179; Ardagh, *France Today*, esp. Ch. 2 and 225–230; Jürg Steiner, *European Democracies*, 3rd ed. (New York: Longman, 1995), 155–156; Alain Guyomarch, Howard Machin, and Ella Ritchie, *France in the European Union* (New York: St. Martin's, 1998), 145–146.

22. Andrew Appleton, "The New Social Movement Phenomenon: Placing France in Comparative Perspective," in Elgie, ed., *The Changing French Political System*, 57–75; Charles Tilly, *The Contentious French: Four Centuries of Popular Struggle* (Cambridge: Cambridge University Press, 1986); and Sidney Tarrow, *Power in Movement: Social Movements and Contentious Politics* (Cambridge: Cambridge University Press, 1994).

23. Susan Dunn, draws insightful contrasts between France and the United States in *Sister Revolutions: French Lightning, American Light* (New York: Faber and Faber, 1999). Also see Ehrmann and Schain, *Politics in France*, 20.

24. Ehrmann and Schain, *Politics in France*, 15–18.

25. Jill Lovecy, "The End of French Exceptionalism?" in Elgie, ed., *The Changing French Political System*, 205–224.

26. Fenby, *France on the Brink*, Ch. 1.

Chapter 6

FRANCE AND THE EUROPEAN UNION

"France is our homeland, but Europe is our future."
—President François Mitterrand, 1988, *cited by Guyomarch, et al.,*
France in the European Union, 1998.

President Mitterrand's simple but ambiguous statement on France and Europe captures some of the complexity of relations between France and the European Union. The Schuman Declaration on May 9, 1950, by French Foreign Minister Robert Schuman (heavily influenced by French planner Jean Monnet) launched the effort that set Europe on a course eventually leading to the contemporary European Union. Although France has been at the center of the processes of European integration since the creation of the original European Coal and Steel Community, its relationships with the ECSC, EC, and EU have sometimes proved turbulent and have usually entailed complexity. Such forceful French leaders as Jean Monnet, Charles de Gaulle, and François Mitterrand have at times been able to leave their own distinctive imprints on both France and Europe. This chapter begins with a historical overview of France's evolving relationship with the European Communities/European Union, summarizes the most distinctive features of the relationship, and analyzes the primary influences of France on the EU and of the EU on France.

THE DEVELOPMENT OF THE FRENCH RELATIONSHIP WITH THE EC/EU

Post–World War II French Initiatives

As France emerged from World War II, its governments—both the provisional government of General Charles de Gaulle and the early governments of the Fourth Republic—initially emphasized French nationalism and the perceived need to punish and dismember Germany, rather than a drive toward European integration that would include Germany. Bitterness over France's humiliating defeat and occupation by Germany in World War II (as well as memories of the Franco-Prussian War and World War I) shaped this French postwar approach. However, American and British insistence on a revitalized West Germany, inspired largely by the developing Cold War with the Soviet Union, blocked French efforts. Eventually, Anglo-American pressures, and the Cold War concerns of the French governments themselves, led to the French rethinking that gave rise to the Schuman Declaration of 1950.[1]

There had been a strand in French governmental outlooks dating back to the 1920s and then-Foreign Minister Aristide Briand that had long promoted a vision of European integration.[2] Drawing upon this strand in an atmosphere of French reassessment of the European scene at the end of the 1940s, Jean Monnet, head of French national modernization planning after 1945, perceived distinct economic advantages not just for France but for Western Europe as a whole in European integration. He was also seeking means for successful implementation of his economic plan for France in the wake of Anglo-American insistence on rejuvenating West German economic might. Though Monnet's prime responsibilities were economic, his vision of a United States of Europe had political dimensions, too. For him, the United States of America was a desirable model for Western Europe. Robert Schuman, like Monnet a Christian Democrat but holding even more powerful posts than he, as prime minister 1947–1948 and foreign minister 1948–1952, assigned highest priority to the political goal of Franco-German reconciliation. When Monnet suggested that he take the lead in creating a European Coal and Steel Community (ECSC) that would include West Germany, Schuman readily agreed.

Both the coal and steel focus of the ECSC and its institutional structures reflected Monnet's ideas and efforts to a high degree. Monnet chose the coal and steel industries primarily for their psychological importance, because they were widely viewed as the chief bases for war production. He believed that their internationalization would encourage "spillover" to other sectors and promote political unification. As for the institutions of the new ECSC, Monnet succeeded in gaining establishment of a supranational High Authority (of which he became the first president) and Court of Justice, though he was compelled to compromise by conceding powers to the intergovernmental Council that represented member nation-states.[3]

While France (and especially Schuman and Monnet) played leading roles in founding the European Coal and Steel Community, there was considerable French ambivalence about the ECSC and the European integration model that Schuman and Monnet had shaped. A particularly prominent skeptic was Charles de Gaulle, prime minister of France from 1944 until his 1946 resignation, hero of the Gaullist political movement (then called the RPF), future prime minister of the Fourth Republic (1958), and founder and first president of the Fifth Republic. De Gaulle rejected supranational goals and argued for a loosely organized Europe of nation-states, in which France would retain full sovereignty. Much of the business community was also unsupportive of the ECSC, fearing that the outlined path toward European economic and political integration would threaten their protections by the French state and allow West German economic dominance. Still another major source of criticism of the ECSC within France emanated from the large Communist party, which denounced it as an anti-Soviet capitalist plot. Despite these sentiments among Gaullists, business interests, and Communists, the French parliament ratified the Paris Treaty establishing the ECSC in December 1951 by a vote of 376–240. Most of the French public displayed little interest or awareness of the whole matter.[4]

Beyond the European Coal and Steel Community

As France played a leading role in the creation of the ECSC, it also was responsible for killing the proposed European Defense Community (EDC) that would have established an integrated European army among the six member states. The paradox was that the EDC had been proposed by none other than French Prime Minister René Pleven at the urging of Monnet. Pleven and his allies viewed the EDC as a means both to avoid a separate German national military force, which the United States (and some German political leaders) favored, and to promote further European integration. However, the Pleven Plan, as it was called, incurred the wrath of the Gaullists and the Communists, as well as of many Socialists. It represented a far more direct challenge to French national sovereignty than did the ECSC, involved the sensitive issue of West German rearmament (as part of the proposed European armed forces), and aroused loud attacks from the Soviet Union. As a result, French opposition to the European Defense Community expanded far beyond that to the ECSC. The parliamentary battle in France raged during 1950–1954. In a highly melodramatic scene, the French parliament effectively killed the EDC Treaty in a key procedural vote on August 30, 1954, while its opponents shouted *Vive la France!* and sang the *Marseillaise*, the French national anthem.[5]

For a time, the French defeat of the EDC appeared to have derailed European integration for the long term. The EDC was dead, as was the idea for a supranational political community that had been associated with it. To replace the rejected EDC and still contain West Germany, France agreed to join with the other ECSC member states and Britain in a treaty creating the Western European Union (WEU), a loose intergovernmental body that preserved national sovereignty.

In the economic realm, however, there remained some French advocates of moving European integration beyond the realm of coal and steel. Monnet and his allies pushed for a European Atomic Energy Community, which enjoyed wide French support. French governmental leaders in general perceived a need to maintain momentum for integration, at least as a means of containing West Germany and strengthening its ties to France. However, most of the initiative for what was to become the European Economic Community came from Belgium, the Netherlands, and Luxembourg. In France, their ideas for a broadened "common market" aroused little enthusiasm at the outset. Even such pro-European French leaders as Socialist Prime Minister Guy Mollet (1956–1957) moved cautiously.

As the negotiations on the Rome Treaties for the European Economic Community and Euratom proceeded, the French negotiators favored a customs union of the six ECSC members rather than a free-trade area encompassing additional members, a common agricultural policy that would favor French farmers, Euratom, and strict limits on supranational institutions. Despite some compromises, they attained most of their objectives. Furthermore, the Suez Crisis of fall 1956, in which Britain abandoned its joint military venture with France against Egypt under American pressure, increased already strong French distrust of the "Anglo-Americans." In doing so, and in illustrating French weakness in an increasingly bipolar world, it convinced much of the French elite that France's destiny lay in the direction of the EC. Economics, negotiating success, and geopolitical considerations led to a fairly sizeable, but not overwhelming, parliamentary majority (342–239) for French ratification of the Rome Treaties.[6]

The Gaullist Era and the European Community

However, the French political scene was about to be transformed, with important consequences for French-EC relations. De Gaulle returned to power in June 1958 as the last prime minister of the Fourth Republic and then the founder of the Fifth Republic and occupant of its vastly strengthened presidency. He was willing to accept French membership in the European Communities, but he insisted that the EC take an intergovernmental direction and boldly asserted what he perceived to be French national interests. De Gaulle also deeply distrusted the Anglo-Americans and looked forward to building a "third force" on the continent of Europe that would operate independently of both the United States and its British ally and of the Soviet Union.

In quest of his vision, de Gaulle led France to 1) push aggressively (and successfully) for national advantage in the EEC's Common Agricultural Policy, 2) veto on two occasions British entry into the EC, 3) forge (fairly successfully, despite the German Bundestag's addition of a pro-American preamble that he found distasteful) a bilateral treaty formalizing a special French relationship with West Germany, and 4) advance (unsuccessfully) the Fouchet Plan to reorganize the EC around a state-centered structure. De Gaulle lost a key ally on many issues within the EC when West German Chancellor Adenauer in 1963 was forced by internal German political pressures to give way to Ludwig Erhard, a leader much less attuned than Adenauer to de Gaulle's wishes. By the 1965–1966 period, de Gaulle's France was seriously at odds with the other five EC members and the EC Commission and its president, Walter Hallstein of West Germany. In response to Hallstein's bid to enhance supranational powers in the EC, de Gaulle's France provoked the "empty chair" crisis, boycotting EC meetings and bringing stalemate to the organization. The result was the Luxembourg Compromise of 1966, largely a victory for de Gaulle, which permitted extensive national veto powers to persist on almost all matters within the EC into the 1980s. Furthermore, beyond the EC, but affecting French relations with their generally Atlanticist EC partners, de Gaulle withdrew France from the military command of NATO in 1966.

De Gaulle's approaches to the European Communities (and NATO) were partly a product of his own distinctive outlook. His ability to shape and direct the approaches taken by France reflected the strengthened French presidency, centralized coordination of French policies, and his own charisma. Nevertheless, it is important to stress that they resonated with many currents in French thinking and with a wide swath of parties, interest groups, and voters. Only rarely did they encounter really significant domestic opposition. Among the most notable dissenters from many of the Gaullists' positions vis-à-vis Europe were the main opposition presidential candidates in 1965, François Mitterrand (later to be the Socialist president of France, 1981–1995) and Jean Lecanuet (a Christian Democrat). These two men unexpectedly denied de Gaulle a first-round electoral majority, though in the second round de Gaulle handily defeated Mitterrand, 55–45 percent, indicating strong popular support for his leadership. Parliamentary opposition to de Gaulle's European policies was weak and ineffectual.[7]

When de Gaulle resigned the presidency in 1969, the Gaullists and their allies were able to elect Georges Pompidou to succeed him. France's stance toward Europe during Pompidou's presidency (1969–1974) underwent some changes, though there were also notable continuities. Under Pompidou, France agreed to expansion of the EC to include Britain, Ireland, and Denmark; but de Gaulle himself was probably moving in this direction at the time of his resignation. France had already achieved most of its goals concerning the Common Agricultural Policy (objectives strongly opposed by Britain) and had lodged them firmly within EC institutions. Therefore, Britain no longer posed a major threat to these. Furthermore, growing West German power meant that Britain might be useful to France as a counterweight to West Germany within the EC. The Franco-German "alliance within an alliance" persisted under Pompidou, and French-West German relations improved somewhat, though Pompidou and West German Chancellor Willy Brandt did not have a close personal relationship. In an overall sense, the French negotiating style vis-à-vis their European partners became more cooperative; the distrust of Britain and the United States, more muted, than under de Gaulle.[8]

Continuity and Change after de Gaulle

Valéry Giscard d'Estaing, Pompidou's successor (1974–1981), was an Independent Republican and founder of the center-right Union of French Democrats, but he was dependent on Gaullist political support. Despite his own inclinations to support European integration with a larger supranational component than de Gaulle or Pompidou had favored, he did not break sharply with his predecessors' approaches. Giscard placed great emphasis on Franco-German cooperation and forged a relationship with West German Chancellor Helmut Schmidt that made this "privileged partnership" more central than ever in EC affairs. With Franco-German backing, the EC moved toward further enlargement, created the European Monetary System, established biennial European Council meetings of heads of national governments (and the French president), and instituted in 1979 direct popular elections of a strengthened European Parliament. The European parliamentary reforms represented the clearest break with Gaullism. Most Gaullists viewed them as a major step toward supranationalism and an infringement of French national sovereignty. Not surprisingly, they provoked much criticism of Giscard from his Gaullist allies, including Jacques Chirac, the man who had been his prime minister during 1974–1976. For the last two years of his presidency, Giscard suffered a drumbeat of attacks on his EC approaches from Chirac and the Gaullists, contributing to his defeat in the 1981 presidential elections.[9]

France and the EC/EU in the Mitterrand Era

The new president, Socialist François Mitterrand, was to lead France for the next 14 years, though constrained by the need for domestic cohabitation with center-right prime ministers and governments during 1986–1988 and again in 1993–1995. Mitterrand possessed a reputation for favoring European integration, but his actions as president were at first ambiguous. Elected by an uneasy alliance of his own Socialists and anti-EC Communists and governing at the outset with a Socialist-Communist coalition government, he initially exhorted the European Community to adopt a "socialist" approach of Keynesian reflation, expanded social programs, and state-run or state-directed major business enterprises in order to combat rising unemployment and to jump-start the European economies. When Britain, West Germany, and most of the rest of the EC displayed no interest in this approach, he proceeded to seek to implement it unilaterally in France. The effort failed. Most analysts have concluded that a medium-sized nation-state such as France simply lacked the power by the 1980s to chart its own economic course.[10]

Confronted by widespread selling of the French franc, fleeing investment, rising unemployment, and lack of external support for his policies, Mitterrand began a tentative and partial retreat in 1982 and then made a dramatic "U-turn" in 1983, in which he abandoned most of what had been distinctive in his approach and adopted austerity. Mitterrand's reversal brought France into line with her major EC trading partners and was to create conditions for Franco-German-British cooperation in rejuvenating the European Communities. Mitterrand decided to take the lead in "relaunching" the drive toward further European integration. (See the box on page 121.)

The ultimate results of French policy convergence with her EC partners, Mitterrand's initiatives, and European Commission leadership came to include the Single European Act of 1986 and the Treaty on European Union (TEU, or the Maastricht Treaty) of 1992. Mitterrand and France achieved some key objectives while compromising on others. Without question, France under Mitterrand came to accept more European supranational authority than ever before and found many of its traditional institutions and public policies under pressures from the EC/EU level as never before. Mitterrand's 14-year tenure in office marked a significant turning point for France and Europe. Nevertheless, there were some marked continuities with the past. As Alistair Cole has emphasized, Mitterrand, like his predecessors, saw the EC/EU "as a surrogate nation-state through which the French genius could manifest itself, for the benefit of the other peoples of Europe. To this extent at least, de Gaulle's and Mitterrand's views of Europe were shaped by a common patrimony."[11]

> Mitterrand perceived Europe "... as a surrogate nation-state through which the French genius could manifest itself, for the benefit of the other peoples of Europe. To this extent at least, de Gaulle's and Mitterrand's views of Europe were shaped by a common patrimony."
>
> Alistair Cole, *François Mitterrand* (1994), 150.

There were two periods of cohabitation during Mitterrand's presidency, when the long-standing patterns of presidential dominance over French European policies were modified by political pressures for the president to share powers with a prime minister and government representing parties in opposition to the president. From 1986 to 1988, the Gaullist Jacques Chirac served as prime minister heading a center-right government. Tensions between Mitterrand and Chirac were evident during this time (particularly since Chirac ran against Mitterrand in the 1988 presidential election), but they generally centered more on power disputes than on policies toward Europe. A French elite consensus in support of the Single European Act and the desirability of a Treaty on European Union had developed and included both men and their leadership teams. From 1993 to 1995, Mitterrand again had to share power with a cen-

ter-right prime minister (Edouard Balladur) and government. This time, Balladur and Mitterrand proved to be more in agreement with each another than Balladur was with many of his parliamentary supporters.[12]

As the leaders of the three major parties (the Socialists, Gaullists, and Union of French Democrats) increasingly adopted converging views in support of enhanced European integration after 1983, the Communist party and the National Front (representing the far Left and far Right, respectively) for a time became the chief dissenters, joined by some disgruntled Gaullists, especially in parliament. However, a rising chorus of **Euroskepticism** rose across France in the early 1990s. Offered a chance to approve the Maastricht Treaty in a 1992 referendum, the French voting public endorsed it by a narrow 51–49 percent vote that proved highly divisive and sent shock waves through the French establishment.

Opposition to the Maastricht Treaty came from farmers' movements, two of the three largest labor union federations, small business groups, and a few prominent business executives and intellectuals. Jean-Pierre Chevènement left the Socialist party to found the Citizens' Movement on a Euroskeptical platform. Charles Pasqua of the Gaullist (RPR) party and Philippe de Villiers of Liberal Democracy (a part of the Union of French Democrats) led a growing Euroskeptical movement from within the ranks of the center-right alliance. Criticisms of the French government's embrace of further European integration lacked a single focus: some stressed the loss of French national sovereignty, others complained of the "democratic deficit" in the European Union, and quite a few emphasized economic concerns over loss of protection or high unemployment rates due to EU policies. Fragmentation, and lack of a clear alternative to French immersion in the emerging European Union, weakened French Euroskepticism and caused it to lose some of its momentum in the following

PEOPLE IN THE EU

François Mitterrand's U-Turn and the Course of European Integration

President François Mitterrand's decision to abandon his distinctive "socialist" French economic policies and his subsequent, and related, decision to emphasize a relaunching of the drive for further European integration illustrate the intertwining of French domestic politics and the politics of European integration.

The critical March 1983 decision by Mitterrand to make a U-turn almost took a different direction. If it had done so, the course of European integration and Mitterrand's legacy might well have been rather different.

As Mitterrand and his Socialist-Communist coalition government faced mounting trade and budget deficits, massive selling of the French franc in international financial markets, rising unemployment, and declining popularity in early 1983, they knew that they faced difficult choices. Mitterrand considered two very different options: 1) leave the European Monetary System (EMS), an arrangement among most EC member states to stabilize their currencies and prevent wide currency fluctuations; allow the franc to float; and try to restart French economic growth behind protectionist barriers; or 2) stay in the EMS; abandon his distinctive "socialist" approach in favor of a major dose of free-market capitalism; and adopt austerity in line with that of France's major trading partners. Mitterrand's advisers were divided between these options. After initially almost selecting the first approach, Mitterrand ultimately adopted

the second. He was heavily influenced in this direction by his finance minister, Jacques Delors. (See the box on page 44.)

Mitterrand's U-turn decision alienated his Communist allies, a large minority of his own Socialist party, and most labor unions and severely damaged his own popularity in the short term. These conditions, however, inspired him to seek a means of rejuvenating his presidency and his historical legacy: a major effort to spur further European integration, which had appeared stalled in many respects. This approach followed the advice of Delors, and it was realistic now that French economic policies were converging with—instead of challenging—those of its major EC partners. As France assumed the EC presidency in January–July 1984, Mitterrand used the occasion to announce a major diplomatic initiative to "relaunch Europe."

This relaunch effort proved unexpectedly productive. At the Fontainebleau Summit in June 1984, Mitterrand, Chancellor Helmut Kohl of Germany, and Prime Minister Margaret Thatcher of Britain found substantial common ground. With the assistance of Delors, when he became president of the European Commission, the three national political leaders would soon give European integration a mighty push forward. The results were the Single European Act of 1986 and the Maastricht Treaty of 1992. The U-turn and initiatives of 1983–1984 insured Mitterrand's place in French and European history. Mitterrand went on to win a triumphant reelection in 1988 and served as French President until 1995.[13]

decade, even though most of its major concerns have not yet been effectively addressed.[14]

France and the EU since 1995

Jacques Chirac won the French presidency in 1995 and for the next two years dominated the French government. During this period, France stayed on the same broad course vis-à-vis Europe that it had followed since 1984. Movement continued toward the completion of the Economic and Monetary Union with its euro currency to replace the franc, and the Amsterdam Treaty negotiations were nearly completed. However, the budget cuts that Chirac and his prime minister, Alain Juppé sought to institute in order to enable France to meet the convergence criteria for the EMU, aroused mass demonstrations and strikes and undercut popular support for the center-right parties. Seeing support for himself and his center-right coalition eroding badly and hoping to avert defeat that seemed likely if he waited until the scheduled 1998 elections, Chirac called for early elections to the National Assembly. His center-right alliance lost. As a result, Chirac found himself after June 1997 in a power-sharing cohabitation with a "plural left" coalition of Socialists, Communists, Greens, and others headed by his 1995 presidential election rival Lionel Jospin.

Jospin and his government began their term in office by proposing a "Stability, Growth, and Employment Pact" and seeking to move the European Union in a distinctly "social" direction. Their efforts to make last-minute revisions in the Amsterdam Treaty brought the new government into conflict with Chirac and won little support elsewhere in Europe. Subsequent Jospin government efforts to promote a "social" Europe enjoyed only limited success. Despite Jospin-Chirac differences over the prime minister's social agenda and some other matters, such as Chirac's call for a group of "advanced" EU member states to drive integration forward, the two men worked very closely together during the French presidency of the EU of July–December 2000 and in support of common French positions on agriculture, British beef, and world trade. A major analyst of the subject has concluded, "France still provides a model of tight policy co-ordination on European issues, even during cohabitation."[15]

Although Chirac and Jospin generally cooperated on EU affairs, including the French EU presidency, the Franco-German alliance during their cohabitation showed signs of strain once again. The tensions were particularly evident during and immediately after the rather fractious Nice Summit that France hosted in December 2000. On issues of EU reorganization to prepare for eastward expansion and German proposals for a federal EU constitution, the gap between French and German positions was especially evident. Predictions of the demise of the long-term Franco-German special relationship are likely to prove exaggerated, as they often have in the past. Close relations have been evident between France and Germany in 2002 and 2003, as cohabitation ended in France and Chirac reasserted his dominance over French EU policies. Coordination of efforts between Chirac and German Chancellor Shröder and their governments have been noteworthy on important issues ranging from agricultural policy reforms to the war in Iraq during 2003. Nevertheless, France will probably have to adjust to a situation in which its influence in the EU will diminish in the wake of growing German assertiveness and eastward expansion of the EU.

DISTINCTIVE FEATURES OF THE FRENCH APPROACHES TO THE EC/EU

Despite some notable shifts from the Fourth Republic to the Gaullist approach that endured in many respects far beyond de Gaulle's presidency, and then from Mitterrand's early initiatives to the post-1983 era, a number of patterns have recurred frequently in France's relationship with the EC/EU. These patterns are rooted in France's historical experience, geopolitical position, economic structures and concerns, and domestic political institutions, though these did not make them inevitable.

As the broad outlines of European integration began to take shape in the late 1940s and early 1950s, France remained, like Britain, proud of its long history as a nation-state and a global great power, even though its power had clearly waned vis-à-vis the two postwar giants, the United States and the Soviet Union. French cultural traditions and accomplishments also inspired a sense of French grandeur, extending beyond elites to the general public.[16]

France's geopolitical location, adjacent to Germany, with which it had fought three terrible wars in less than a century, further shaped a distinctive national outlook, albeit one that could and would be channeled in various directions. This proximity to Germany distinguished France from the United Kingdom in significant ways. Separating France from West Germany was its greater geographic distance from the front lines of the Cold War, a not insignificant factor in shaping French and German views of American roles in postwar Europe, all points stressed in realist theories.[17]

The centralized unitary state, another French inheritance, expanded its functions extensively after World War II. Historically, relative French self-sufficiency in food and a slowly developing private business sector that generally lacked dynamism had fostered state economic protectionism. The postwar expansion of a social-welfare state (typical also of most other West European nation-states) was accompanied in France by an emphasis on state involvement in economic "modernization" planning, widely referred to as *dirigisme*. Therefore, the economic roles of the French state extended well beyond West German or

British preferences and influenced French thinking about European political economy. Liberal intergovernmental theory stresses these points, as well as the importance of French business and agricultural groups (and to a lesser extent, labor unions) in shaping French approaches to the EC/EU.[18]

French statist conceptions extended beyond the political economy. French republican ideology, rooted in the political philosophy of Jean-Jacques Rousseau and developed by the Jacobins of the French Revolution of 1789, tended to emphasize representation of the French "general will" through the "One and Indivisible State."[19] Relatively high centralization and coordination characterized French approaches to European integration even under the Fourth Republic. The Fifth Republic, by fostering an unusually powerful presidency, was to make French styles of dealing with European integration issues even more distinctively centralized and coordinated. It also usually insulated them to a high degree from popular and group pressures.[20]

"French EU diplomacy has a bulldozerish quality that leaves lesser breeds both aggrieved and admiring."

Charlemagne, *"Valéry Giscard d'Estaing,"* The Economist 361 (December 22, 2001), 60.

On these foundations, the French built distinctive approaches to the EC/EU. As "Charlemagne," a columnist in the British newsweekly, *The Economist*, typifies many analysts in noting, "French EU diplomacy has a bulldozerish quality that leaves lesser breeds both aggrieved and admiring." Over time, the liberalizing of the globalized economy and the EC/EU and the growing engagement of France with the complex institutions of the EC/EU have shifted some French approaches from strong preferences to inclinations, as neofunctionalism predicts. There have also been some shorter-term variations, reflecting at times the proclivities of particular French public officials, most notably Fifth Republic presidents de Gaulle and Mitterrand. Over the years, however, the "bulldozerish" quality has remained evident. The most enduring distinctive French approaches to the EC/EU have been as follows:

A wariness of Atlanticism. Atlanticism emphasizes the need to keep the United States actively involved in European affairs and usually displays a willingness to defer to American priorities. French leaders have generally viewed deference to the United States with considerable distaste and have sought limits on American roles in Europe. In de Gaulle's case, the wariness of Atlanticism often became outright hostility to it. Even during the Fourth Republic, France tended to resent American leadership and to seek means of constraining it. Negative French attitudes toward Atlanticism have been most evident over the long term in the military defense realm: departure from the NATO military command and unwillingness to rejoin it even in recent years, maintenance of an independent French nuclear force, and repeated calls for an EU-focused defense effort are prominent examples. However, French resistance to American domination has extended to many fields beyond defense, including culture, language, and economics. As one analyst has put it, France has sought to become economically and socially modern "without such American sins as social conformity, economic savagery, and cultural sterility." Many analysts see France's intense wariness of Atlanticism as a problem for the European Union as a whole. Recently, for example, Timothy Garton Ash of Britain, Michael Mertes of Germany, and Dominique Moïsi of France argued, "Europe's French problem is twofold: the French political and administrative elites tend to think naturally that what is bad for the US is good for France and they tend to transfer their sense of frustration to their relations with their smaller European partners."[21]

> "Europe's French problem is twofold: the French political and administrative elites tend to think naturally that what is bad for the US is good for France and they tend to transfer their sense of frustration with Washington to their relations with their smaller European partners...."
>
> Timothy Garton Ash, Michael Mertes, and Dominique Moïsi

A wariness of global free-market capitalism. The French skepticism about global free-market capitalism (including but not confined to free trade) overlaps with their concerns about American domination. However, it is also rooted in long-term domestic economic practices and the preferences of major economically based interest groups, including most of agriculture and organized labor and much of the business community. What was once a strong protectionist and dirigiste preference in France has shifted since the 1980s to the wariness that remains evident today. Much of the French Left continues to hope to tame global free-market capitalism with European social constraints, as has been evident during the "plural left" government of Jospin. Well beyond the Left, however, is a widespread French inclination to try to sustain French state protections against globalization.[22]

An intergovernmentalist inclination. Though some French leaders of the 1950s (most notably Monnet and his closest allies) favored European supranational development, this view did not dominate French approaches, even during most of the Fourth Republic. Of course, de Gaulle's heavy emphasis on French national sovereignty was a distinct preference (not just an inclination). Recognizing the advantages of the EC for France (i.e., aiding French agriculture, providing France a vehicle for broadened political influence), de Gaulle accepted French membership. However, he was a vociferous advocate for intergovernmental decision-making (preserving the French veto) and strict curbs on such relatively supranational institutions as the Commission, Court of Justice, and Parliament. Giscard and Mitterrand accepted, and even initiated, some pooling of sovereignty in EC/EU central institutions. Even Mitterrand, who resorted to supranational rhetoric on occasion, usually pressed for intergovernmentalism in the EC/EU. France in recent decades has mostly shifted from an insistence on national sovereignty protections under de Gaulle to a stance that still usually displays an inclination toward intergovernmentalist approaches.[23]

An emphasis on Franco-German partnership to lead the EC/EU. One major analyst has described the Franco-German alliance within the EC/EU as the "linchpin" of French policies and of postwar European politics, and few if any have disagreed. Certainly, it was a major goal of Schuman and Monnet at the inception of the ECSC. De Gaulle pursued it avidly and secured the Elysée Treaty with West Germany in 1963. All French leaders since de Gaulle have sought (usually with considerable success) to sustain it. Though there have been several occasions (especially 1963–1969, the German reunification years of 1989–1990, and 2000–2001) when many observers have forecast the disintegration of the partnership, it has survived, albeit with a relative shift in influence from France to Germany over time. Containing a resurgent Germany and linking it economically and politically to France in a European framework has probably been the most consistently pursued French objective for half a century.[24]

A wariness of EC/EU enlargements. French governments have initially opposed each of the EU enlargements, eventually agreeing to each one under German influence. De Gaulle's vetoes of British entry have been widely discussed. However, French reluctance was evident again in the late 1970s and early 1980s concerning the southern enlargements (Greece in 1981, Spain and Portugal in 1986); the period

prior to the admission of Austria, Sweden, and Finland in 1995; and the early discussions of eastward expansion after the collapse of Communism. Rooted in a concern for maintaining French EC/EU leadership and EC/EU policies originally tailored to French preferences, this wariness has been a continuing thread in France's European policies, though some analysts believe that it has waned in recent years.[25]

A cohesive and centrally coordinated formulation of French EC/EU policies. This approach dates back to the Fourth Republic, when the General Secretariat for the Interministerial Committee on European Questions (SGCI), established in 1948, took responsibility for bringing coherence to French positions concerning European integration. The advent of the Fifth Republic added concentration of leadership authority in the presidency to the picture. Despite three cohabitations (1986–1988, 1993–1995, and 1997–), marked by presidential–prime ministerial power-sharing on European issues and the growing array and com- plexity of EU issues, France has maintained a relatively cohesive approach to EU issues, compared with most other member nation-states. On the other hand, its record on implementation of EU laws has been relatively weak, among the worst in the EU by some measures, particularly in recent years. This fact probably reflects French administrative reservations about European challenges to French preferences in a growing number of domains.[26]

An insulation of French EC/EU approaches from party, group, and popular pressures. This feature was not usually true during the Fourth Republic, when parliament played a central role in making and unmaking prime ministers and governments and played a significant role in shaping French policies toward Europe. However, the relative strength of the French executive and weakness of parliament since 1958, only partially modified in recent years, has usually insulated French executive

TABLE 6.1   Distinctive Features of French EC/EU Approaches

1. A wariness of Atlanticism.

2. A wariness of global free-market capitalism.

3. An intergovernmentalist inclination.

4. An emphasis on Franco-German partnership to lead the EC/EU.

5. A wariness of EC/EU enlargements.

6. A cohesive and centrally coordinated formulation of French EC/EU policies.

7. An insulation of French EC/EU approaches from party, group, and popular pressures.

decision-making from party, group, and popular pressures to a greater extent than in most EU member states. The inability of the anti-Maastricht movement to deflect French executive leaders from their chosen path is evidence of a continuing pattern.[27]

THE IMPACT OF FRANCE ON THE EC/EU

To an extent unmatched by any other member nation-state with the possible exception of Germany, France has played a leading role in shaping most major EC/EU institutions and public policies. However, it has often had to accept compromises. Moreover, as the historical institutionalist analysis suggests, the outcomes of policies have sometimes varied from the initial expectations of their framers.

In terms of shaping EC/EU institutions, French influence has usually operated to restrain supranational institutions and promote intergovernmentalism, though French opposition to supranational institutions reached its peak under de Gaulle. De Gaulle pushed unsuccessfully for the Fouchet Plan's confederal structure, provoked the "empty chair" crisis, and forced France's five EC partners to accept

the Luxembourg Compromise that entrenched nation-state vetoes for two decades to follow. Since the mid-1980s, France has shown some willingness to support supranational institutions when these have appeared likely to comport well with French policy objectives. For example, French concerns to constrain German dominance of monetary policies led France to play a leading role in the establishment of the European Central Bank. Even in the past two decades, however, France has frequently joined forces with Britain to maintain the powers of the Council of Ministers and to preserve extensive national veto powers within the Council. Most notably, France, backed by Britain and Denmark, fought hard and effectively to create the three-pillar design of the Maastricht Treaty, in which most foreign and justice and home affairs policies would continue to be made on an intergovernmental basis centered on the Council of Ministers.[28] It has also shown fairly consistent disdain for the European Parliament and little enthusiasm for German and other proposals for a federal constitution for the EU.[29] French political analyst Dominique Moïsi has captured the essence of the French approach to institutions in an apt assessment: "France wants a strong Europe, but with weak institutions that will not undermine its claim to continue to act as a *Grande Nation.*"[30]

"France wants a strong Europe, but with weak institutions that will not undermine its claim to continue to act as a *Grande Nation.*"

Dominique Moïsi, *"An Awkward Time for France to Take Over,"* Financial Times (November 20, 1995), 16.

French influence over the major public policies of the EC/EU have been highly evident in the early crafting of the Common Agricultural Policy (CAP) and the sustaining of many of its provisions in the face of strong opposition from other member states (especially Britain) and from global political-economic pressures.

Historically, French national policies toward agriculture had been protectionist, marked by high tariff barriers, import quotas, and price maintenance. France sought to continue protectionism and spread the cost to its EC partners, secure new markets for its farm produce, and encourage the modernization of French agriculture. It succeeded to a high degree in achieving most of its goals. However, the high cost of the CAP, growing demands for reform from other members, pressures from the General Agreement on Tariff and Trade (GATT) and then the World Trade Organization (WTO), and a widely perceived need for adjustment as eastward EU expansion approached have placed France on the defensive on agricultural issues in recent years. French resistance to freer agricultural trade has stressed the goals of European self-sufficiency in food and preservation of the traditional French (and European) countryside, while asserting also that the high quality of French (and other EU) produce justifies prices higher than those for mass-produced American or Australian alternatives. The struggle over EU agricultural policy continues. Unable to shape that policy to the extent that it once could, France continues to exert considerable influence.[31]

Another domain in which French influence has been especially pronounced has been that of EC/EU monetary policies. French President Giscard d'Estaing and West German Chancellor Schmidt launched the effort that led to the European Monetary System (EMS). Though the EMS failed to achieve the hopes of its initiators, and France pursued a unilateral monetary course in many respects during 1981–1983 early in the Mitterrand presidency, France shifted gears after 1983 and became an important influence on the new Economic and Monetary Union that emerged in the 1990s. Though French governmental leaders were compelled to compromise and accept convergence criteria and a Stability and Growth Pact that were too restrictive for their tastes, and to grant more independence to the European Central Bank than they preferred, they did achieve their goal of linking Germany to France within the EMU framework and in a manner that involved less overt German monetary dominance than the EMS method had. In addition, French leaders have viewed the new EMU and its euro currency as a means of expanding the influence of the EU (and France) in the world, challenging the United States dollar for supremacy, and lessening the threats to a stable currency from global financial markets.[32]

In the EC/EU social policy area, France has also sought to assert leadership. Yet here its success has thus far been considerably less evident than regarding agricultural or monetary policies. President Mitterrand, in an alliance with European Commission President Delors, pushed aggressively for the Social Charter in 1989 and its inclusion in the Maastricht Treaty. However, under pressures to compromise (and in the face of strong British opposition), Mitterrand and Delors had to content themselves with rather vague language and its incorporation in a separate protocol to the Treaty in 1992. Eventually all of the EU, including Britain, agreed to its terms; but it remained well short of French goals. The plural left government of Prime Minister Jospin made another concerted effort to assert French leadership on European social issues after 1997. Among the social policies that France has advocated, with only limited success, are tax harmonization (supported strongly by Germany also) and a coordinated employment program. Some analysts have discerned a Janus-like quality to French EU social policy in recent years, noting the resemblance of the French government to the ancient Roman god who faced two directions simultaneously. With one face, France calls for **subsidiarity** to the nation-state level to protect its own welfare state against EU market-oriented encroachments while the other face advocates new EU social actions to achieve egalitarian or protective goals that France cannot achieve on its own.[33]

With regard to European foreign and defense policies, France has long been assertive and influential. Back in the early 1950s, it both proposed and killed the European Defense Community project. France has often blocked Atlanticist approaches favored by many of its EC/EU partners. Though its hostility to Atlanticism abated somewhat in the 1990s, Bush Administration actions revived it. France has been at the forefront of efforts to develop improved defense capabilities through the EU, independent of the United States and NATO. Despite a long history of Anglo-French conflict over European relations with the United States, France joined with Britain to push successfully for an intergovernmental structure in the Maastricht Treaty for foreign and security policy and then, in the 1998 St. Malo Declaration, to urge movement toward an EU Rapid Reaction Force.[34]

In the Justice and Home Affairs (JHA) field, centered primarily on border controls and policing, France has generally displayed concerns for national sovereignty, though not to the extent that the United Kingdom has stressed these. In conjunction with Britain, France pushed for the Maastricht Treaty provisions that placed most JHA policy-making in an intergovernmental pillar. However, unlike Britain, France was an original signatory of the Schengen Agreement of 1985 laying out goals to abolish border controls among signatories and was a full participant in the "Schengen process" that hammered out provisions in this field. Again, unlike Britain, France did not opt out of the Amsterdam Treaty's incorporation of the border-control accords and made the requisite amendments to its national constitution.[35]

While France frequently has taken a positive role in actively shaping the EC/EU policies discussed previously, its policy-making roles in the single-market and competition domains have tended to be aimed at resisting and modifying the initiatives of others. This posture reflects continuing widespread French skepticism concerning the neoliberal ideology that underpins these policies to a high degree. It also reflects the extent of change that each has been forcing in traditional French political-economic practices.[36]

Finally, environmental and structural/cohesion/regional development have been policy domains in which France has usually been neither a major leader nor a tenacious resister. As a result, few studies have investigated closely the French roles in shaping them.

Over time, French influence on EU institutions and policy-making has diminished somewhat, as enlargement has increased the number of competing sources of influence, Germany has gained power, and global free-market pressures on the EU have generated pressures that have often operated against French preferences. Nevertheless, the Franco-German alliance within the EU and French assertiveness in many domains have enabled France to continue to be a key player.

THE IMPACT OF THE EC/EU ON FRENCH POLITICS

The impact of EC/EU institutional practices and public policies on France, as on other member states, has accelerated dramatically since the mid-1980s. Particularly since then, many analysts have focused attention on "Europeanization," defined by Robert Ladrech as "an incremental process reorienting the direction and shape of politics to the degree that EC political and economic dynamics become part of the organizational logic of national politics and policy-making."[37] This process has sometimes operated in France, as elsewhere, in the form of an independent EU variable producing changes that have gone against national traditions. At other times, it has been akin to what Alistair Cole has termed "a form of emulative policy transfer and policy learning."[38] At times, both aspects have been intertwined.

The Constitution

Since the early 1990s, the French have amended their national constitution on three major occasions to adjust it to new EU requirements: 1) to deal with the sovereignty-pooling aspects of the Maastricht Treaty (1992), 2) to bring it into accord with the Schengen Agreements (1993), and 3) to adjust to the Amsterdam Treaty (1999). The most controversial of these changes have been those granting voting rights and eligibility to run for office in French local governments to non-French citizens who are EU citizens and those reducing French national sovereignty with regard to border controls. Prior to these amendments, 60 French Senators who opposed the Treaty on European Union had unsuccessfully challenged the constitutionality of the Treaty in the French Constitutional Council.[39]

Governmental Institutions

The impact of Europeanization on French governmental institutions has been complex and at times ambiguous and difficult to measure. Some analysts have concluded that Europeanization has enhanced the roles of the French Constitutional Council and the judiciary. Both Giscard and Mitterrand asked for preliminary advice from the Constitutional Council on key EU issues; for Giscard, concerning the constitutionality of direct elections to the European Parliament; for Mitterrand, concerning the constitutionality of the Single European Act. The Council's affirmative response in these cases diminished domestic opposition to the changes. When in a similar situation, Mitterrand referred the Maastricht Treaty to the Council in advance of ratification, the Constitutional Council suggested necessary changes in the French Constitution. As noted previously, these were subsequently adopted by a joint session of parliament. Moreover, the expansion of EC/EU law, and of the role of the European Court of Justice, generated pressures that eventually, but rather gradually, increased the roles of the French Court of Cassation (the highest court for criminal and civil cases) and the Council of State (in its judicial role as the supreme court in administrative law cases and cases pertaining to state actions) in insuring compatibility between domestic French law and EC/EU law. In addition, some analysts such as French international legal scholar Laurent Cohen-Tanugi, have suggested that the EU has promoted a "return of law" and the development in France of a conception of democracy based more on legal rights and less on the French Jacobin tradition of centralized authority embodying the general will.[40]

The French president, the prime minister and the government, and the executive in general attained dominance over parliament at the advent of the Fifth Republic in 1958 for reasons that bore no relationship to the EC. Since then, the executive has maintained marked preeminence—both in formulating French positions vis-à-vis the EC/EU and in transposing European law into French law. In France, the latter has long been accomplished almost entirely by executive decrees, not by parliamentary statutes. Therefore, the growing importance of the EC/EU has probably served to enhance executive authority in relation to parliament. However, the effects of Europeanization have been complex. Some analysts, such as Ladrech, have argued that Europeanization generated concerns about the "democratic deficit" that in turn led to a 1992 French constitutional amendment mandating increased participation by the French parliament in French negotiations with the EU. The actual impact of this amendment, however, has been debatable. Further adding to the complexity of the picture, Europeanization since the mid-1980s has reduced the French state bureaucracy's powers vis-à-vis business corporations. Overall, the impact of Europeanization on French legislative and executive institutions has been rather ambiguous and subject to debate.[41]

A relatively direct and unambiguous example of EU impact on French institutions has concerned the Bank of France. Compared to other European central banks, it was long considered one of the most "dependent" on the executive, with real monetary policy-making power centered in the finance ministry, not the Bank. Once the EMU process began moving forward, however, a joint session of the French parliament was persuaded to adopt a constitutional amendment granting the Bank independence. The Bank is now a component of the European System of Central Banks, all of which are required to be relatively autonomous from political controls.[42]

Finally, the growing decentralization of the traditionally very centralized French unitary state illustrates some indirect effects of the EC/EU, though their extent remains a subject of some dispute. The French Defferre laws of 1982, which granted enhanced authority and financial autonomy to regions, departments, and communes while retaining a unitary framework, were primarily the result of a French Socialist party commitment made in the 1970s and fulfilled after its 1981 electoral triumphs. However, this decentralization, adopted largely independently of Europeanization, occurred at a time when the EC was increasingly emphasizing regional development funding and depriving the central state of some of its most important policy attributes. Two emerging patterns came to reinforce one another. 1) As a result of the Defferre reforms, French subnational governments possessed more resources than previously that they could channel into lobbying efforts in Brussels to gain further EC/EU aid. 2) The EC/EU was providing more resources than before to subnational units while at the same time reducing some key central state functions and promoting the single market. An indirect effect of the single market has been the growth of "transfrontier" alliances built on economic links between French border regions and subnational units within neighboring nation-states. In sum, French territorial decentralization since 1982 (within the limits of a still unitary structure) appears to have been significantly shaped by a combination of reinforcing domestic and EC/EU forces.[43]

Elections, Political Parties, and Interest Groups

The EC/EU has not altered basic French electoral and referendum procedures in any significant way. However, two major referendum campaigns (one in 1972 on EC enlargement, the other in 1992 on the Maastricht Treaty), especially the latter, affected the links between French voters and elites in some fairly important ways, diminishing some of the autonomy of political leaders on EC/EU matters. President Chirac has promised to hold another EU referendum, this one on the proposed EU constitution, with effects yet to be determined.[44]

EC/EU issues have also played central roles at times in defining French party ideologies and images. These roles have been clear-cut for the Christian Democratic MRP in the Fourth Republic, the Gaullists until the 1980s, the Communists most of the time, and the National Front since 1991. The Socialist party, which has taken rather different stances toward European integration at different points in time, has embraced Europe while downplaying socialism since Mitterrand's U-turn of 1983, despite some internal resistance to this shift in emphasis.

Of all of the French parties after World War II, the Christian Democrats were the most consistently dedicated to European integration as a matter of ideological principle. Often almost alone in France, they championed European supranational development. Their heirs have generally carried on their early traditions, but Christian Democracy has had limited influence during the Fifth Republic.

The Gaullist party, in contrast, favored a strong Europe with weak institutions and emphasized the desirability of an intergovernmental "Europe of nation-states." Under de Gaulle, this vision of Europe was central to Gaullist party ideology and imagery. Since then, however, the leaders of the Gaullist party (called the RPR and UMP in recent years) have made frequent pragmatic adjustments to this ideology, accepting in practice a degree of supranational development that de Gaulle would certainly have opposed. However, the previous Gaullist vision has continued to inspire many party activists and some leaders, sparking a significant split in 1999, when Charles Pasqua and his followers defected to form the Rally for France (RPF), the original name of the Gaullist party, based on an ideology of resisting further European federalism. The center-right parties usually aligned with the Gaullists have in recent years been somewhat more inclined to embrace European integration than the Gaullists.

Meanwhile, on the far left of the political spectrum, the Communists have maintained a fairly consistent position of hostility to the EC/EU, characterizing it as an agent of global capitalism. Since the 1991–1992 campaign against the Maastricht Treaty, the previously ambivalent National Front on the far right has also regularly denounced the EU, opposing free movement of workers, eastward enlargement, and other alleged threats to "the French nation," in particular.

Long lacking clear definition in terms of European issues, the Socialist party has become fairly supportive of European integration since the mid-1980s, though always emphasizing, at least in its imagery, the need for a more "social" Europe than the current model. Mitterrand and Jospin have enjoyed a high level of Socialist party backing for their European policies, though Chevènement split from the Socialists in the 1980s, partly over the displacement of socialist ideology by an emphasis on Europe, to form his own Movement of Citizens, which has expressed extensive Euroskepticism.

The "plural left" coalition of 1997–2002 included the Euroskeptical Communists and Movement of Citizens, as well as the Euroskeptical Greens. However, the desires of the leaders of these parties to share governmental power succeeded in overriding their concerns about the government's support for European integration. A general effect of Europeanization in France since the mid-1980s has been to drive the left parties, in practice if not fully in rhetoric and imagery, in a more market-oriented direction than ever before.

The general pattern since the mid-1980s has been for support for European integration to be strongest in the center-right and center-left portions of the French political spectrum and weakest on the far left and far right.[45] Despite the surge of Euroskepticism evident in the 1990s, the elites of the center-right and center-left have been able to keep their coalitions generally on a course supportive of European integration. No president or prime minister of the Fifth Republic has faced such daunting challenges from within his or her party or coalition as some British prime ministers have from within their parties.[46]

The upsurge of Euroskeptical interest groups and movements, particularly during and immediately after the Maastricht Treaty debates, appeared for a time to threaten the ability of centrist party elites and their interest group allies to continue to lead France further down the road to EU deepening and widening. However, that threat subsided in the wake of fragmentation and disarray among the French Euroskeptics.

European issues have split the mainstream business, labor, and agricultural interest groups in France. Many French small businessmen, two of the three major labor federations, and a large proportion of the organized farmers have been Euroskeptical in recent years. However, the Movement of French Enterprises (MEDEF) and the biggest and most powerful French businesses have been quite supportive of the course charted by the centrist party elites.[47]

Another effect of French participation in the EC/EU has been the drawing of French parties and interest groups increasingly into the transnational party federations and interest group federations that seek primarily to influence the EC/EU policy-making process. The extent of their engagement has been fairly modest, though it is growing. Some of the center-right parties have affiliated with the European People's Party (EPP), some with the European Liberal Democratic Reform group (ELDR), and some with neither; while the Socialists have been more fully engaged in the Party of European Socialists (PES). However, even the Socialists have pursued their own distinctively French approaches, often at odds with those of their British Labour party colleagues in the PES and sometimes at odds with their German Social Democratic colleagues.[48]

As for the French interest groups and Europe-wide federations, there has been some effort to coordinate with colleagues in other European states in common endeavors through such organizations as the Union of Industries of the European Community (UNICE). Almost certainly, large business corporations have proved most adept both at coordination across national boundaries and at obtaining direct access to EU central institutions. Europeanization has indirectly strengthened the hand of private business corporation executives in French internal politics, as well as cross-nationally, by reducing the economic roles of the French state in the past two decades.[49]

Public Policies

If the impact of Europeanization has been partial and uneven with regard to the Constitution, the major institutions of government, and the participatory processes of France, it has been profound and extensive on French public policies, particularly since the mid-1980s, when European integration accelerated in a number of policy domains and sometimes took a direction considerably at odds with long-standing French approaches. The single-market, monetary, and competition policies of the EC/EU in the past two decades have probably been the most dramatic in bringing French change. Traditionally pursuing much more state-oriented *(dirigiste)* economic policies than most West European nation-states, France has had to make more significant adjustments than they to the free-market thrust of EU single-market and competition policies and the anti-inflationary approaches favored by the European Central Bank and the convergence criteria and Stability Pact associated with the Economic and Monetary Union.

The changes in the French "national champions" policies offer a case in point. Building on a solid foundation of state-centered economic development, France after World War II expanded its public ownership of business corporations and increased the central state role in planning. A key part of this process entailed an array of state supports for French national champions in the global business environment: Elf Acquitaine in petroleum, Bull in computers, Thomson in electronics, France Télécom in communications, Renault in automobile manufacturing, Air France in air transport, among others. Some of these were or became publicly owned corporations; others were private but received state aids. Some were highly successful; others required continuing subsidies and ended up failing.

Although the Rome Treaty establishing the European Economic Community (EEC) in 1957 prohibited state aid to business that distorts competition, the EEC took few actions to interfere with French support for national champions until the 1980s. However, the adoption of the Single European Act of 1986, toughened European commission stances under the leadership of such competition commissioners as Leon Brittan and Karel van Miert, and European Court of Justice rulings have stimulated massive French privatizations (albeit partial ones in many cases) and have imposed increasingly strict limits on French state assistance to public or private business corporations and protection of monopolies.

The direct impact of the EC/EU on privatization has sometimes occurred through the Commission's making its acceptance of French corporate rescue plans contingent upon future privatization, as in the case of Crédit Lyonnais in 1998. Even when France has been able to persuade the European commission to accept French state aids to business, European Court of Justice rulings have sometimes imposed direct restraints, as in a 1998 Air France case.

At other times, Europeanization has operated indirectly. For example, the convergence criteria and the Stability Pact associated with the EMU have forced French governments to cut budgets; and sales of public corporations have been means of obtaining the funds to keep governmental budgets within the prescribed limits. In addition, the neoliberal ideas that have been ascendant in EU circles have been emulated by much of the French political elite, further fostering privatization and reduced state aids.

Although there have certainly been forces beyond the EU that have also encouraged French governments to shift away from their long-term national champions policies (i.e., globalization, high expenses of subsidies), there can be no doubt that Europeanization has been a major influence. The French government still fights to sustain aids to a variety of business corporations, retains partial ownership in many privatized firms, and steers procurement mainly to French businesses. However, it must now carefully consider the restraints imposed by the EU or face the possibility of embarrassing public reversals.

Beyond the issue of national champions, the general EC/EU impact on France since the mid-1980s has been to undermine, but not totally dismantle, the long tradition of French *dirigiste* policies aimed at steering the French economy in directions favored by nation-state leaders.[50]

CONCLUSIONS

Our overview of France's relationship with the EC/EU has illustrated important turning points in the early 1950s, the late 1950s, and the mid-1980s, as well as incremental changes over longer time spans. Despite undergoing more marked changes than the approaches of the other major nation-states in the EC/EU, French approaches to European integration have included a number of recurring themes that have been distinctive for the long term. France has had to accept some diminishment of its influence in the EU because of enlargement and growing German preeminence. Yet it remains a major EU leader.

The impact of the EC/EU has accelerated since the turning point following Mitterrand's shift of 1983–1984, particularly with regard to market-related public policies. Nevertheless, France has mostly maintained its major governmental institutions and political processes. Most major alterations in these have been in response to domestic as well as European factors. Even in such policy domains as competition, where the EC/EU influence has become quite pronounced, France has resisted Europeanization pressures in ways that are distinctively French.

Michel Gueldry has concluded that France has become a "transnational polity, which means that it operates in a European system of shared governance that is no longer entirely national nor fully federal."[51] In a broad sense, this assessment is true of all EU member states. Yet, as the previous chapter concluded, France, perhaps the prime early example of the nation-state, retains many features that make it politically distinctive. Moreover, given the French confidence in the superiority of their culture and institutions, France is likely to continue to try to shape the European Union in its own image to the greatest extent possible.

France has become a "transnational polity, which means that it operates in a European system of shared governance that is no longer entirely national nor fully federal."

Michel Gueldry, *France and European Integration* (2001), 191.

SUMMARY

- French political leaders Jean Monnet and Robert Schuman took the lead in the establishment of the European Coal and Steel Community (ECSC) in 1952.

- France played the leading role in killing the proposed European Defense Community (EDC) in 1954, even though French Prime Minister René Pleven had proposed the EDC.

- France endorsed the Rome Treaties of 1957 that created the European Economic Community (EEC) and Euratom.

- Charles de Gaulle, the dominant French leader during 1958–1969, shaped the Common Agricultural Policy, vetoed British EC entry, developed a special relationship with West Germany, withdrew French military forces from NATO, and provoked the "empty chair crisis" that led to the Luxembourg Compromise.

- Georges Pompidou permitted British EC entry while continuing the West German partnership.

- Valéry Giscard d'Estaing supported a somewhat more supranational EC while not breaking sharply with his predecessors' European policies; he strengthened the Franco-West German partnership, working very closely with West German Chancellor Helmut Schmidt.

- François Mitterrand accepted further supranational development of the EC/EU, seeking to assert French leadership through the EC/EU, sustaining the German alliance, aiming at a more socially oriented EC/EU, and winning narrow popular approval in a referendum for the Maastricht Treaty.

- Jacques Chirac sustained the German alliance, battled to maintain as much of the Common Agricultural Policy as possible in difficult circumstances, and led resistance in the EU (with German Chancellor Schröder) to American global domination and its conduct of the Iraq War.

- Major long-term features of French approaches to the EC/EU have been: a wariness of Atlanticism, a wariness of global free-market capitalism, an intergovernmental inclination, an emphasis on Franco-German partnership to lead the EC/EU, a wariness of EC/EU enlargements, a cohesive and centrally coordinated formulation of French EC/EU policies, and an insulation of French EC/EU approaches from popular pressures.

- France has traditionally sought to restrain supranational development of the EC/EU, though this pattern has lessened since the 1980s, when France has perceived supranational European development to serve its own national interests on some occasions.

- French influence over EC/EU public policies has been particularly evident on agriculture, the creation of the Economic and Monetary Union, and the three-pillar structure of policy-making under the Maastricht Treaty.

- EC/EU membership appears to have enhanced the powers of the Constitutional Council and the French judiciary, increased the independence of the Bank of France from the French executive, and reduced the powers of the French bureaucracy over French business.

- The Gaullists of the 1950s and 1960s strongly resisted European supranational development, but their successors proved more willing to accept some such development if it appeared to serve French national interests.

- Since the 1980s, the French center left (Socialists) and center right (Gaullists and allies) have generally supported major European integration efforts, while the Communist party on the far left and the National Front on the far right have opposed them.

- A major example of significant EC/EU impact on French public policies has been the restraint placed by the EC/EU since the 1980s on French *dirigisme* in general and French national champions policies in particular.

ENDNOTES

1. Alistair Cole, *Franco-German Relations* (Harlow: Longman, 2001), 4–6; F. Roy Willis, *France, Germany, and the New Europe*, Revised ed. (Stanford: Stanford University Press, 1968), 15–24; François Duchêne, "French Motives for European Integration," in Robert Bideleux and Richard Taylor, eds., *European Integration and Disintegration* (London: Routledge, 1996), 22–35.

2. Thomas Pederson, *Germany, France, and the Integration of Europe* (New York: Pinter, 1998), 70–71; Cole, *Franco-German Relations*, 4.

3. Willis, *France, Germany, and the New Europe*, 80–88; Jean Monnet, *Memoirs* (Garden City, NY: Doubleday, 1978); François Duchêne, *Jean Monnet: The First Statesman of Interdependence* (New York: Norton, 1994).

4. Willis, *France, Germany, and the New Europe*, 94–103; Alain Guyomarch, Howard Machin, and Ella Ritchie, *France in the European Union* (Basingstoke: Macmillan, 1998), 20–23.

5. Edward Fursdon, *The European Defense Community: A History* (New York: St. Martin's, 1980); Willis, *France, Germany, and the New Europe*, 130–184.

6. Andrew Moravcsik, *The Choice for Europe* (Ithaca, NY: Cornell University Press, 1998), 103–122; Willis, *France, Germany, and the New Europe*, 227–272.

7. Edward Kolodziej, *French International Policy Under de Gaulle and Pompidou: The Politics of Grandeur* (Ithaca, NY: Cornell University Press, 1974); Edward Morse, *Foreign Policy and Interdependence in Gaullist France* (Princeton: Princeton University Press, 1973); Willis, *France, Germany, and the New Europe*, 273–365; James Shields, "The French Gaullists," in John Gaffney, ed., *Political Parties and the European Union* (London: Routledge, 1996), 86–89.

8. Haig Simonian, *The Privileged Partnership: Franco-German Relationships in the European Community, 1969–1984* (Oxford: Oxford University Press, 1985), Chs. 4–8.

9. Simonian, *The Privileged Partnership*, Chs. 9 and 10; Guyomarch, et al., *France in the European Union*, 27–28; Shields, "The French Gaullists," 89–93.

10. Simonian, *The Privileged Partnership*, 324: "Firm lessons have been learned in Paris about the external constraints on national economic policy." Cole, "The French Socialists," in Gaffney, ed., *Political Parties and the EU*, 82: "French socialism was called to order by external constraints." However, David Cameron, "National Interest, the Dilemmas of European Integration, and Malaise," in John T. S. Keeler and Martin A. Schain, eds., *Chirac's Challenge: Liberalization, Europeanization, and Malaise in France* (New York: St. Martin's, 1996), esp. 331–33, suggests the viability of a French reflationary approach at this time, as do a number of French leftists.

11. Cole, "The French Socialists," 71–5; Gueldry, *France and European Integration*, esp. 34–35; Kevin Featherstone, *Socialist Parties and European Integration* (Manchester: Manchester University Press, 1988), Ch. 5; Wayne Northcutt, *Mitterrand: A Political Biography* (New York: Holmes&Meier, 1996).

12. Michel Gueldry, *France and European Integration: Toward a Transnational Polity?* (Westport, CT:

Praeger, 2001), 57–58; Guyomarch, et al., *France in the European Union*, 49–53.

13. Northcutt, *Mitterrand*, esp. Ch. 5; Alistair Cole, *François Mitterrand: A Study in Political Leadership* (London: Routledge, 1994), esp. 35–38, 150; Cameron, "National Interest, the Dilemmas of European Integration, and Malaise," esp. 331–33; Moravcsik, *The Choice for Europe*, esp. 332–47; Cole, "The French Socialists," 71-85.

14. Bertrand Benoit, *Social-Nationalism: An Anatomy of French Euroskepticism* (Aldershot: Ashgate, 1997); Gueldry, *France and European Integration*, 186–87; Guyomarch, et al., *France in the European Union*, Ch. 3.

15. The quotation is from Alistair Cole, "National and Partisan Contexts of Europeanization: The Case of the French Socialists," *Journal of Common Market Studies* 39, 1 (March 2001), 20. Also see Dominique Moïsi, "Jospin, Too, Wants to Lead Europe," *New Statesman* (January 2, 1998), 17; Cole, *Franco-German Relations*, 128–144; Ben Clift, "The Jospin Way," *The Political Quarterly* 72, 2 (April–June 2001), 170–79.

16. Simonian, *The Privileged Partnership*, 32–45; Cole, "National and Partisan Contexts of Europeanization," 18; Guyomarch, et al., *France in the European Union*, 113.

17. Simonian, *The Privileged Partnership*, 10–15.

18. Simonian, *The Privileged Partnership*, 16–32; Vivien Schmidt, *From State to Market? The Transformation of French Business and Government* (New York: Columbia University Press, 1996); Gueldry, *France and European Integration*, esp. Ch. 1.

19. Cole, *Franco-German Relations*, 42–43.

20. Gueldry, *France and European Integration*, 39–46; Guyomarch, et al., *France in the European Union*, Ch. 2.

21. The first quotation is from Richard Kuisel, *Seducing the French: The Dilemma of Americanization* (Berkeley: University of California Press, 1993), 3. The second is from Timothy Garton Ash, Michael Mertes, and Dominique Moïsi, "Only a Club of Three Can Bring European Unity," *Financial Times*, July 11, 2003, 8. Also see Cole, *Franco-German Relations*, 45, 108, 118; Gueldry, *France and European Integration*, 150–154 and 164–173; and Guyomarch, et al., *France in the European Union*, 112–145.

22. Gueldry, *France and European Integration*, 23–35; Cole, *Franco-German Relations*, 128–144.

23. François Duchêne, "French Motives for European Integration," in Robert Bideleux and Richard Taylor, eds., *European Integration and Disintegration* (London: Routledge, 1996), 32; Guyomarch, et al., *France in the European Union*, 28.

24. Julius W. Friend, *The Linchpin: French-German Relations 1950–1990* (New York: Praeger, 1991); Cole, *Franco-German Relations*; Pederson, *Germany, France, and the Integration of Europe*; Simonian, *The Privileged Partnership*.

25. Cole, *Franco-German Relations*, 77–79; Desmond Dinan, *Ever Closer Union*, 2nd ed. (Boulder, CO: Lynne Rienner, 1999), 189–190; Ronald Tiersky, "France, the CFSP, and NATO," in Pierre-Henri Laurent and Marc Maresceau, eds., *The State of the European Union: Deepening and Widening*, Vol. 4 (Boulder, CO: Lynne Rienner, 1998), 184.

26. Guyomarch, et al., *France in the European Union*, 45–60; Simonian, *The Privileged Partnership*, 34; Gueldry, *France and European Integration*, 57–58.

27. Benoit, *Social-Nationalism*; Gueldry, *France and European Integration*, 60–63; Guyomarch, et al., *France in the European Union*, 77.

28. Moravcsik, *The Choice for Europe*, 407, 450–452; Dinan, *Ever Closer Union*, 138.

29. Cole, "National and Partisan Contexts of Europeanization," 26–27.

30. Dominique Moïsi, "An Awkward Time for France to Take Over," *Financial Times*, November 20, 1995, 16. Also see Moïsi, "The Trouble with France," *Foreign Affairs* 77, 3 (May/June 1998), 94–104.

31. Guyomarch, et al., *France in the European Union*, Ch. 5; Moravcsik, *The Choice for Europe*, esp. 176–197; Michael Mann, "EU Farm Policy: France to Protest against Reforms," *Financial Times*, June 27, 2002, 7.

32. Jörg Bocher, "Franco-German Economic Relations," in Patrick McCarthy, ed., *France-Germany 1983–1993* (New York: St. Martin's, 1993), 73–92; Moravcsik, *The Choice for Europe*, 404–417; David Howarth, "The French State in the Euro Zone: Modernization and Legitimizing Dirigisme in the 'Semi-Sovereignty' Game," Paper Presented at the ECSA Conference,

Madison, Wisconsin, June 2001; Gueldry, *France and European Integration*, Ch. 5.

33. Moïsi, "Jospin, Too, Wants to Lead Europe," 17; Cole, *Franco-German Relations*, 128–144; Gueldry, *France and European Integration*, 113–118.

34. Guyomarch, et al., *France in the European Union*, Ch. 4; Gueldry, *France and European Integration*, Ch. 6.

35. Monica den Boer and William Wallace, "Justice and Home affairs: Integration through Incrementalism?" in Helen Wallace and William Wallace, eds., *Policy-Making in the European Union*, 4th ed. (Oxford: Oxford University Press, 2000), 494–496, 508, 511, 513–516; Guyomarch, et al., *France in the European Union*, 214–231.

36. Guyomarch, et al., *France in the European Union*, 158–160, 172–176; Moravcsik, *The Choice for Europe*, 318, 332–347.

37. Robert Ladrech, "Europeanization of Domestic Politics and Institutions: The Case of France," *Journal of Common Market Studies* 32, 1 (March 1994), 69.

38. Cole, "National and Partisan Contexts," 23.

39. Ladrech, "Europeanization of Domestic Politics and Institutions," 72–76; Gueldry, *France and European Integration*, 44–48.

40. Guyomarch, et al., *France in the European Union*, 65–71. Cohen-Tanugi is quoted and discussed by Ladrech, "Europeanization of Domestic Politics and Institutions," 76–78, and Christian Lequesne, "French Central Government and the European Political System," in Yves Mény, et al., eds., *Adjusting to Europe: The Impact of the European Union on National Institutions and Policies* (London: Routledge, 1996), 118.

41. On executive-legislative relations, see Ladrech, "Europeanization of Domestic Politics and Institutions," 76–79; Guyomarch, et al., *France in the European Union*, 63; Gueldry, *France and European Integration*, 60–62; and Franco Rizzuto, "The French Parliament and the EU: Loosening the Constitutional Straitjacket," in Philip Norton, ed., *National Parliaments and the European Union* (Portland, OR: Frank Cass, 1996), 46–59. On executive-business relations, see Maria Green Cowles, "The Transatlantic Business Dialogue and Domestic Business-Government Relations," in Maria Green Cowles, et al.,

eds., *Transforming Europe: Europeanization and Domestic Change* (Ithaca, NY: Cornell University Press, 2001), 159–79; Vivien Schmidt, "Loosening the Ties that Bind: The Impact of European Integration on French Government and Its Relationship to Business," *Journal of Common Market Studies* 34, 2 (June 1996), 223–252.

42. Howarth, "The French State in the Euro Zone," esp. 10–12; Martin Marcussen, "The Power of EMU-Ideas: Reforming Central Banks in Great Britain, France, and Sweden," Paper Given at the ECSA Conference, Pittsburgh, PA, June 1999.

43. Ladrech, "Europeanization of Domestic Politics and Institutions," 79–86; John Newhouse, *Europe Adrift* (New York: Pantheon, 1997), 56–66; Gueldry, *France and European Integration*, 176–185; Guyomarch, et al., *France in the European Union*, 297–313.

44. Andrew Gowers and Bertrand Benoit, "Chancellor Says Germany Will Attempt to Ratify the New EU Constitution This Year," *Financial Times*, July 16, 2004, 2; Benoit, *Social-Nationalism*; Guyomarch, et al., *France in the European Union*, 96–102.

45. Benoit, *Social-Nationalism*; Shields, "The French Gaullists," 86–109; Cole, "The French Socialists," 71–85; Cole, "National and Partisan Contexts of Europeanization," 15–36; Guyomarch, et al., *France in the Euroepan Union*, Ch. 3.

46. See Chapter Eleven on British prime ministers' frequent party management difficulties on EC/EU matters.

47. Benoit, *Social-Nationalism*; Moravcsik, *The Choice for Europe*, 108–110, 204–205, 336–337, 408–409.

48. Cole, *Franco-German Relations*, 128–144; Simon Hix, "The Transnational Party Federations," in Gaffney, ed., *Political Parties and the European Union*, 308–331.

49. Vivien Schmidt, "Loosening the Ties that Bind: The Impact of European Integration on French Government and Its Relationship to Business," *Journal of Common Market Studies* 34, 2 (June 1996), 223–252; Maria Green Cowles, "The Transatlantic Business Dialogue and Domestic Business-Government Relations," in Maria Green Cowles, et al., ed., *Transforming Europe: Europeanization and Domestic Change* (Ithaca, NY: Cornell University Press, 2001),

159–179; Gueldry, *France and European Integration*, esp. 85–88.

50. John S. Ambler and M. Shawn Reichert, "France: Europeanism, Nationalism, and the Planned Economy," in Eleanor E. Zeff and Ellen B. Pirro, eds., *The European Union and the Member States* (Boulder, CO: Lynne Rienner, 2001), 29–58; Vivien Schmidt, *From State to Market? The Transformation of French Business and Government* (New York: Columbia University Press, 1996); Schmidt, "The Changing Dynamics of State-Society Relations in the Fifth Republic," in Robert Elgie, ed., *The Changing French Political System* (London: Frank Cass, 2000), esp. 147–153. For contrasts with long-term patterns in Britain and Germany, see Geoffrey Shepherd, "A Comparison of the Three Economies," in Roger Morgan and Caroline Bray, eds., *Partners and Rivals in Western Europe: Britain, France and Germany* (Aldershot: Gower, 1986), esp. 48–50.

51. Gueldry, *France and European Integration*, 191.

Chapter 7

GERMANY

"...the German political experience, which once brought Germans the scorn and contempt of civilized societies, can also give us reason for optimism and faith in the ability of people to use democratic politics to better their lives and those of their neighbors."

—David P. Conradt, *The German Polity* (2001), 281.

Germany stands on the eastern flank of the pre-2004 European Union but near the center of Europe as a continent. In contrast to England and France, which are among the oldest European nation-states, Germany did not take shape as a modern nation-state until Kaiser Wilhelm I and Chancellor Otto von Bismarck forged it out of "blood and iron"[1] in the 1860s and early 1870s, just a little more than a century ago. Prior to that period, there had been considerable German consciousness of a common cultural identity but multiple competitive German kingdoms, duchies, city-states, and other political entities, divided by political loyalties and a Protestant-Catholic cleavage. Since that time, Germany has had a tumultuous history as a nation-state: the "Second Reich" (empire) created by Wilhelm I and Bismarck was defeated and reduced in size at the end of World War I in 1918; the democratic Weimar Republic that replaced it gave way after just 14 years (in 1933) to Adolf Hitler's totalitarian

"Third Reich," which aimed to conquer most of Europe and to exterminate the Jews but eventually faced defeat in 1945; the Cold War era saw the creation of a democratic German Federal Republic in the West and a Communist-controlled German Democratic Republic in the East; and then German reunification occurred under the auspices of the democratic German Federal Republic in 1990. Despite its turbulent history and continuing difficulties of East-West integration, Germany is today a stable, democratic nation-state, economically preeminent in Europe and poised to take a leading European political role.

Germany's population today is about 83 million, making it the most populous state in the European Union, though well short of the population of Russia (at 144 million). With a gross domestic product well over two trillion euros (and dollars), Germany is the economic giant of both the European Union and the European continent. Yet despite Germany's

MAP 7.1   Germany

population and economic power, German history (especially Hitler's conquest and Holocaust) and resultant reputation with European neighbors have oriented the leaders of the German Federal Republic toward emphasizing cooperation within the European Union rather than asserting German power independently. In this respect, Germany stands in sharp contrast to the United Kingdom in particular.

POLITICAL DEVELOPMENT

Early Development

Compared to France and England, the German nation-state developed late. Though the roots of German national identity may be traced back to the age of Charlemagne in the ninth century, that identity developed gradually and, in contrast to France and England, without much linkage to state structures. The Holy Roman Empire (800–1806) provided to some extent a statelike structure for a time, but it lost most features of statehood by the thirteenth century and also usually included many non-Germanic ethnic groups. Therefore, the German cultural identity developed amidst political fragmentation into numerous kingdoms, duchies, city-states, and other political jurisdictions. Prussia became the strongest of these states by the eighteenth century but lacked the power at that time to unify all Germans and failed to integrate its own large Polish minority into a Prussian "nation." The expansionistic French nationalism of the 1789–1815 era, however, began to push both the Prussian leaders and other Germans toward the building of a modern nation-state. Efforts to develop a German nation-state on a democratic basis in 1848–1849 foundered. Eventually, during the 1860s and 1870s, Prussia's military forces defeated Austria, Denmark, and France to forge considerable German political unity under the leadership of its chancellor, Otto von Bismarck, and its king, Wilhelm, who became the German chancellor and emperor, respectively, in 1871. The new regime, known as the Second Reich (Charlemagne's empire of the ninth century being conceived as the First Reich), had some superficially constitutional democratic and federal features establishing a constitution and a parliament and granting powers to the German states but was fairly authoritarian in that the chancellor (head of government) was responsible to the emperor rather than to parliament and in that Prussian aristocratic and military elites generally asserted dominance. Both Roman Catholics and Social Democrats suffered considerable repression in the early years of the German Second Reich. After some moves toward democratization, the system reverted toward authoritarianism during World War I before collapsing with the defeat of Germany by the United States, Britain, France, and Italy in 1918.[2]

The Weimar Republic and the Third Reich of Adolf Hitler

Issues of nation-building, state-building, participation, and distribution roiled German politics during the 14 years of the Weimar Republic, a democratic republic that emerged after the abdication of the emperor and the defeat in World War I. Political analyst Herbert J. Spiro has put the emergence of the Weimar Republic into a useful comparative perspective vis-à-vis France: "France had already had forty-seven years of her *Third* Republic, when the German nation-state was only forty-seven years old and the Germans were trying to build their *first* republic at Weimar." Of course, the Weimar Republic endured little longer than the first French republic had, and like the first French Republic gave way to a dictator (Napoleon in the French case, Hitler in the German one) in the midst of widespread turmoil.

"France had already had forty-seven years of her *Third* Republic, when the German nation-state was only forty-seven years old and the Germans were trying to build their *first* republic at Weimar."

Herbert J. Spiro, *"The German Political System"* *(1962), 469.*

German nationalism was offended by the harsh peace imposed by the victors in the Versailles Treaty, including the loss of German colonies and of German territory in both the East (to Poland) and the West (to France) as well as reparations payments for war damages inflicted by German military forces. Nationalists, including Adolf Hitler, propagated the myth that Germany had been "stabbed in the back" by unpatriotic Jews, liberals, and socialists, who had caused defeat in war and acceptance of a humiliating peace. Extreme nationalism became the basis in the 1930s and 1940s for much of Hitler's appeal to the German people and for his expansionistic drive to conquer Europe and his mass slaughter of Jews in the Holocaust.

The state institutions of the Weimar Republic included a directly elected president as chief of state, sharing powers with a chancellor as head of government who was appointed by the president but responsible to a majority in the popularly elected Reichstag (lower chamber of the national legislature). The system was federal in structure. However, its military establishment was unsympathetic to its democratic institutions, as were many of its judges and bureaucrats. Furthermore, its proportional representation electoral system combined with a voting population deeply divided by class, religion, and region to foster a multiparty system that was often stalemated. As Hitler's Nazis on the far right and the Communists on the far left gained increasing support, especially after the advent of the Great Depression, the Weimar Republic came to possess a parliament that was itself dominated by parties determined to overthrow the state structure. Unsurprisingly, the state gave way to the totalitarian Third Reich of Adolf Hitler in 1933.

The democratic political processes of the Weimar Republic were unfamiliar to most Germans and faced opposition from many sources, as noted above, including leaders of many of its own state institutions. A Communist uprising in 1918–1919, an attempted military coup in 1920, an attempted Communist revolution in Saxony in 1923, and Hitler's failed putsch in Bavaria in 1923 were all evidence of strong efforts by German parties and groups to effect change by undemocratic means. Although Hitler decided to pursue power through the democratic process after his unsuccessful effort to seize power by force in 1923, he and his National Socialist (Nazi) party were committed to the destruction of democracy. Having won more votes in the elections of 1932 and 1933 than any other party, the Nazis effectively dismantled the democratic process by seizing control over all of the state governments and then pushing through parliament (with the aid of their nationalist and conservative allies) the Enabling Act of 1933, which suspended the constitution. Before the end of the year, Hitler and his Nazis had eliminated all effective opposition. However, Hitler maintained a façade of pseudodemocratic participation by staging plebiscites and mass rallies to demonstrate his popular support. Undoubtedly, his popular support was extensive; but his regime was profoundly undemocratic in its use of extensive terror, imprisonment, and killing of political opponents and targeted groups (such as the Jews, gypsies, and gays) and its penetration of almost all areas of life in Germany.

Despite the severe challenges posed by outraged German nationalism, weak support for the legitimacy of Weimar Republican state institutions, and popular inexperience with democracy and considerable elite hostility to it, the Weimar Republic might have survived had it not also faced severe distribution crises. Runaway inflation undermined support for the existing mixed economy in the early 1920s. However, the severe unemployment and collapsing stock market of the depression that began in 1929 were critical factors feeding the rise of the antidemocratic National Socialist (Nazi) and Communist parties, whose support burgeoned in the early 1930s. The Third Reich retained considerable private ownership of property and preexisting social-welfare programs but moved toward a centralized economic mobilization that fostered employment and prepared for military expansion and war, significantly altering previous distribution structures in the process.

In the end, of course, Hitler's methods of national aggression by a totalitarian state failed to achieve long-term solutions to problems of nation-building, state-building, participation, and distribution, though Hitler apparently retained considerable German support for his regime until the collapse of the Third Reich in 1945. Of the several German plots to overthrow Hitler's regime, all were unsuccessful and none represented a popular uprising. Analysts disagree over the extent of German popular support for Hitler and his Holocaust, but it is undeniable that only military defeat by the combined forces of the U.S., Soviet, British, French, and other Allies brought the collapse of the Third Reich.[3]

The Development of the Federal Republic of Germany

Germany was occupied by the Allies, reduced in size (again) by ceding much of the Prussian heartland to Poland, and divided into four zones of military occupation at the end of World War II. Furthermore, many German refugees fled into West Germany from regions now in Poland, reassigned to Czechoslovakia (as in the case of the Sudetenland), or under other Communist control. In 1949, the three Western zones (American, British, and French) were merged to create the German Federal Republic, a Western-style constitutional democracy with a federal structure. The Basic Law, developed under close Allied supervision and supposedly a temporary document for West Germany pending reunification, provided what became the long-term framework for the federal constitutional democracy. In addition to enshrining a lengthy list of individual freedoms and establishing multiple checks and balances in the national government, it created a new system of states, termed *Länder*, which provided for more genuine decentralization of authority than in the German past. The Soviet zone became a Communist-controlled system, seen as authoritarian or even totalitarian by most analysts, but officially named the German Democratic Republic. Such developments might easily have created conditions for a continued lack of German success at coping with the key issues of nation-building, state-building, participation, and distribution. However, the German Federal Republic managed to deal with these effectively enough to achieve stability and legitimacy and eventually to absorb a collapsing East Germany after 1990. Already, by the end of Konrad Adenauer's 14-year tenure in office in 1963, the sharp differences from the German past were evident in the West. West German parliamentary leader Eugen Gerstenmaier aptly noted that Adenauer stood out as, "in a hundred years of eventful German history, the only one who, after a long period in government, is leaving office undefeated and in peace."

[Adenauer stands out as] "in a hundred years of eventful German history, the only one who, after a long period in government, is leaving office undefeated and in peace."

Eugen Gerstenmaier, *cited in Charles Williams, Adenauer (2000), 523.*

Modernization, the German Federal Republic, and Reunification

How was the success of the German Federal Republic possible? Perhaps the sharpest contrast to the past was the easing of the distribution crisis under the auspices of a "social market economy" that stimulated enterprise and economic growth while providing extensive social services and promoting labor-management cooperation. In contrast to the harsh Allied reparation policies after World War I or the initial Soviet plundering of East Germany after World War II, the United States in 1948 began to give Marshall Plan assistance to spur West German economic renewal. Moreover, with American encouragement, France, Italy, and the Benelux countries joined West Germany in beginning a process of enhanced economic integration that benefited all of their economies in the 1950s. Skilled political and economic leadership, especially by Chancellor Konrad Adenauer and Economics Minister Ludwig Erhard in the formative years, also contrasted with the Weimar past and the contemporary East German scene. By the mid-1950s, it was evident that West Germany was experiencing an "economic miracle."

"My people live in two states but continue to think of themselves as one nation."

West German Chancellor Willy Brandt, 1973,
*cited by Lewis Edinger and Brigitte Nacos,
From Bonn to Berlin (1998), 15.*

When West German Chancellor Willy Brandt declared in 1973 that "My people live in two states but continue to think of themselves as one nation,"[4] he pointed to a nation-building issue that could have provided a basis for explosive conflict but never did so. Despite sharp tensions between East and West Germany from the late 1940s into the 1960s, and periodic escalations of Cold War tensions thereafter, the two states recognized each other officially after 1972 as a result of Brandt's ***Ostpolitik*** policy of seeking compromise and open intercourse with the East. East German governmental leaders sought to develop a distinctive East German national identity; but the events of 1989–1990 showed how correct Brandt was and how ineffectual the East German efforts had been. West Germans' economic prosperity, ties to the Western Alliance and the European Communities, and memories of World War II effectively undermined the potential of any West German nationalistic movement that might have aimed at forcible reunification.

Back in 1961, the Soviets and East Germans had built the Berlin Wall separating West Berlin from East Berlin and the rest of East Germany in an effort to block the growing exodus of East Germans to West Germany via West Berlin. In 1989, after another growing mass exodus to the West from East Germany through a liberalizing but still Communist Hungary and spreading mass demonstrations for democracy in major East German cities, the East German regime agreed to allow free entry through the Wall to West Berlin. Shortly thereafter, the Communist German Democratic Republic collapsed, as did the Berlin Wall, symbolizing the beginning of a new era for Germany.

When the German nation came once again to live in a unified German state in 1990, the process was a peaceful one, achieved by negotiations and the democratically expressed will of the people. Nonetheless, nation-building conflicts were not fully resolved. While nearly two-thirds of the East Germans identified themselves as "Germans" rather than "East Germans" in 1990, only one-third did so in surveys a few years later.[5] Despite the creation of one Germany, two distinct communities (East and West) with differing outlooks and values remain evident today.

The other major nation-building issues to confront the German Federal Republic recently have concerned immigration and citizenship.

Due to a strong economy that attracted numerous foreign "guest workers" (many of whom stayed for the long term) and a liberal asylum policy embodied in Article 16 of its Basic Law, the German Federal Republic has attracted numerous immigrants—a process continuing into the 1990s even as Germany struggled with reunifying East and West Germany—with concomitant economic difficulties. By the 1990s, foreign residents came to constitute nearly 10 percent of the population. However, at the same time Germany continued until January 2000 its tradition (in contrast to French, British, and U.S. traditions) of determining citizenship "by blood," or proven ethnic heritage, rather than by place of birth. After mob violence against foreign residents in Germany escalated following reunification, the German government shifted its approaches to both immigration and citizenship. In 1992, it moved to a much more restrictive asylum policy than previously, reducing the influx of asylum-seekers from abroad. Then, in the late 1990s, Chancellor Schröder's government sought to grant automatic citizenship to children born in Germany of foreign residents (the American approach) and to ease some of the barriers to naturalized citizenship for their parents, though it had to compromise to gain enactment of its citizenship policy reforms. Further revisions occurred in 2001, as interparty consensus developed to tighten further the rules on asylum but grant permanent residency to highly qualified new migrants while mandating that new migrants enroll in national integration courses of study. This consensus broke down, however, as the 2002 federal election campaign began; and the Christian Democratic–Christian Social Union alliance in opposition to the government challenged the procedures used to pass the new legislation (but also suggested substantive criticisms of it). Just a few days before the election, conservative party leaders reemphasized their opposition to the government's efforts to make Germany, in the words of a government supporter, "a modern, multicultural land of immigration." However, business groups generally supportive of the conservative parties quickly voiced support for the new immigration policies and criticized the conservative leaders, illustrating how the immigration issue has tended to cut across traditional party lines in Germany.[6]

As far as state-building is concerned, at first the state institutions of the German Federal Republic evoked little loyalty or pride among West German citizens. Only 7 percent of West Germans in a 1959 survey expressed pride in their political system (compared with 46 percent in the United Kingdom and 85 percent in the United States in the same study). Surveys of the 1950s continued to show that significant minorities of West Germans preferred a return to monarchy (32 percent in 1951) and saw Hitler as one of Germany's greatest statesmen (48 percent in 1955). Over time, however, West Germans developed an increasing attachment to their state institutions. By 1988, 51 percent were expressing pride in their political system. By the 1990s, only one-tenth voiced support for monarchy and less than one-quarter saw Hitler as one of Germany's greatest statesmen.[7] Since reunification, however, East Germans have expressed markedly less trust for the institutions of the Federal Republic than have their West German neighbors.[8]

Participation in the German Federal Republic has usually been mediated through political parties, parliament, and interest groups rather than occurring through direct participation in referendums and plebiscites. Hitler's misuse of direct participatory methods discredited them in the eyes of many. However, some German states have used referendums; and the Social Democratic–Green coalition has suggested amending the Basic Law to permit them at the national level. Turnout in German Bundestag elections has averaged more than 80 percent (occasionally surpassing 90 percent), somewhat above the European norm and far above the 50 percent turnout recorded in recent

United States presidential elections. Women have come to play increasingly prominent roles in German politics, a sharp contrast to the past. One example has been the rise of Angela Merkel to become leader of the Christian Democratic Union. (See "People in the EU," page 154.) The percentage of parliamentary members who are women has also risen sharply. At 32.2 percent in the Bundestag and 24.6 percent in the Bundesrat, they are well above the United States' figures of 14.3 percent of the House of Representatives and 13.0 percent of the Senate, but are still well below the figures for the Scandinavian countries and the Netherlands.[9]

Beyond participation in elections, parties, and interest groups, Germans have greater participatory opportunities in the workplace than Americans or most other Europeans do. The German system of **"codetermination"** (established in 1951 and modified on several later occasions) grants employee representatives one-half of the positions on the supervisory boards of business corporations having more than 2000 employees and one-third of such positions in business corporations having 500 to 2000 employees. It also provides for the establishment of elected works councils when employees of companies with more than five employees so request. Advocates of German codetermination suggest that this form of workplace democracy has enhanced employee productivity and labor-management cooperation, though some business opponents argue that it hampers efficiency and unduly limits shareholders' property rights, and many Social Democrats argue that the codetermination principle has not been carried far enough to permit sufficient employee input.[10]

Although Germans still quarrel over the pace and progress of East-West integration and over immigration and citizenship policies, some aspects of their state institutions, the proper extent and nature of their constitutional democracy, and who should get what in their economic system, for the time being at least they have

TABLE 7.1	Major Landmarks in German Political History
800	Charlemagne establishes the First Reich.
843	Partition establishes East Frankish kingdom, later to become under Otto the Great the Holy Roman Empire.
1618	Thirty Years' War begins, further fragmenting already divided German states.
1744	Frederick the Great becomes Prussian monarch and builds strengthened Prussia.
1815	German Confederation of 39 states established after defeat of Napoleon.
1871	German Second Reich formed by Otto von Bismarck and Kaiser Wilhelm.
1918	Germany defeated in World War I.
1918	Weimar Republic established.
1933	Adolf Hitler becomes chancellor, establishes the Third Reich.
1945	Germany defeated in World War II.
1949	Federal Republic of Germany established.
1952	Federal Republic of Germany joins the European Coal and Steel Community as a founding member.
1958	Federal Republic of Germany joins the European Communities.
1989	Upheaval in East Germany; Berlin Wall falls.
1989	Reunification of Germany as the Federal Republic.

achieved a fairly high level of consensus on the critical issues of modernization delineated by Almond and Powell—one that stands in contrast to much of modern German history.

GOVERNMENTAL INSTITUTIONS

The Executive

The Basic Law of the German Federal Republic provides for a chancellor (prime minister) who is the head of government, chosen by and responsible to the popularly elected branch of the national legislature, the Bundestag. As in Britain, the Bundestag is organized along political party lines. Unlike Britain, however, there is rarely a majority party in the Bundestag. Therefore, it is usually necessary for a chancellor to put together a coalition of two or more parties to gain and maintain sufficient parliamentary support.

Upon election, the chancellor appoints the ministers to the cabinet, usually offering posts to key leaders of the parties that provide his base of parliamentary support. Thus, Social Democratic Chancellor Gerhard Schröder appointed to his cabinet Green parliamentary leader Joschka Fischer as deputy chancellor and foreign minister as well as such rival leaders of his own party as Rudolf Scharping as minister of defense and Oskar Lafontaine as finance minister to cement the Social Democratic–Green coalition. Lafontaine and Schröder, however, soon disagreed over basic policy; and Lafontaine abruptly left the cabinet in March 1999. Some analysts have referred to cabinet-parliamentary government in Germany as "chancellor democracy," suggesting the preeminence of the chancellor over the rest of the government.[11] Certainly, the first chancellor of the German Federal Republic, Konrad Adenauer, did assert his dominance over the policy-making process much of the time during his 14-year tenure in office (1949–1963, Table 7.2). However, most chancellors have encountered numerous checks on their authority from their coalitions in the Bundestag and their own cabinets, an upper legislative chamber (the Bundesrat) that has often been controlled by opposition parties, state governments, and the Constitutional Court. Most observers have concluded that the German chancellor is typically embedded in a system of **checks and balances,** albeit one that differs in some significant ways from American checks and balances.[12]

Though the German Basic Law also provides for a president as head of state (currently

Horst Koehler, a Christian Democrat), he is a largely ceremonial figure, unlike the French president. Elected for a five-year term, with the limit of two terms, by a Federal Assembly, composed of all Bundestag members plus an equal number of representatives from the state parliaments, the president formally proposes the chancellor and the cabinet to the Bundestag for their selection. However, he has never exercised any discretion in that process: There has always been a Bundestag majority (usually based on a coalition) that has determined the chancellor; and the chancellor has always taken the lead in determining the cabinet membership, based upon the governing coalition. Nevertheless, the president is regularly consulted and informed by the chancellor about proposed governmental actions. In general, Germans expect their president to be a ceremonial leader who can rise above ordinary partisan politics. Most presidents have sought to fulfill that expectation.

Below the level of the chancellor and the ministers stands a relatively small executive bureaucracy at the national level, because most administrative tasks are carried out (in contrast to both France and the United Kingdom) by state and local governments. The 16 national ministries typically have a few political officials

TABLE 7.2 Chancellors of the German Federal Republic Since 1949

Chancellor	Time in office	Coalitional support
Konrad Adenauer	1949–1963	CDU/CSU, FDP*
Ludwig Erhard	1963–1966	CDU/CSU, FDP
Kurt Kiesinger	1966–1969	CDU/CSU, SPD
Willy Brandt	1969–1974	SPD, FDP
Helmut Schmidt	1974–1982	SPD, FDP
Helmut Kohl	1982–1998	CDU/CSU, FDP
Gerhard Schröder	1998–	SPD, Green

*The Free Democratic party was a part of the coalition supporting Adenauer, except for the 1957–1961 period. Several smaller parties were coalition partners also in the early years.

at the top who are appointees of the ministers, followed by hierarchical levels of career personnel. The latter have traditionally enjoyed high prestige in Germany and have provided an important element of continuity in the execution of laws. Adding to their political influence is the distinctive German tradition of encouraging civil servants to seek and hold legislative offices (as many do) and subsequently to return to their administrative posts. East Germany possessed a much more centralized bureaucracy than the German Federal Republic, but its size and functions have been trimmed drastically since reunification. Alongside the public administration of Germany exist an array of semipublic agencies, such as those that administer the social security and health systems. In sum, the German executive bureaucracy enjoys considerable prestige and power but is more decentralized than most in Europe, both to state and local levels and to semipublic institutions.[13]

The Parliament

Germany possesses a **bicameral** legislature composed of the Bundestag and the Bundesrat. The Bundestag is composed of at least 598 (656 before 2002)[14] popularly elected members, who usually vote along party lines in a manner similar to that in the British House of Commons. The Bundestag alone elects the chancellor and may remove him by a "constructive vote of no confidence," in which the chamber gives a majority of its votes to elect a new chancellor. This provision differs from the Weimar Republic's procedure and from Britain's practice, in that a majority no-confidence vote alone is not sufficient to dismiss the chancellor. To date, only one chancellor has been replaced in the German Federal Republic by a constructive vote of no confidence. In 1982, the coalition between the Social Democrats and the Free Democrats that had supported Chancellor Helmut Schmidt (a Social Democrat) broke up, and the Free Democrats in the Bundestag joined with the

members of the Christian Democratic Union and the Christian Social Union to replace Schmidt in the chancellor's post with Helmut Kohl (a Christian Democrat). Another control mechanism that the Bundestag may employ vis-à-vis the chancellor and cabinet is the question hour, borrowed from the British parliamentary system and used increasingly by German parliamentarians to hold ministers and their representatives accountable. The Bundestag is central to the lawmaking process and must give its approval by majority vote before a proposal can be enacted. However, its dominance by a majority coalition that usually supports the cabinet has meant that it is primarily a "reactive" legislative body. Bundestag standing committees and special investigating committees are stronger than in either British or French parliaments but more dominated by political parties and less likely to challenge the executive than their U.S. Congressional counterparts.

The Bundesrat, the other chamber of the German parliament, is unique among major European national parliamentary bodies in that it directly represents state governments. State governments appoint and recall the 69 Bundesrat members, with each state receiving three to six votes, depending on its population. Each state must cast its vote as a block. Therefore, the membership and the overall partisan balance in the Bundesrat are subject to frequent changes, reflecting the outcomes of elections for state governments. Often the Bundesrat is dominated by parties different from those dominant in the Bundestag. Although party-line voting is less the norm in the Bundesrat than in the Bundestag, the Bundesrat (especially when dominated by opposition parties) often imposes significant checks on the ability of the chancellor and cabinet to obtain desired legislation because proposed laws that affect the states (about 60 percent of all federal legislation) must gain majority approval in the Bundesrat. The nine-month battle in 2003 between the Social Democratic-Green–dominated Bundestag and the Christian Democrat–dominated Bundesrat over the government's Agenda 2010 legislative program illustrated dynamics that have been fairly common in the German lawmaking process. Mediation committees, much like the conference committees in the United States Congress, often must iron out differences between the legislation passed by the two chambers. On non-state-related issues (such as defense and foreign policy), the Bundesrat has a voice; but a simple majority there can be overridden on such issues by a simple majority in the Bundestag, and a two-thirds majority there can be overridden by a two-thirds majority in the Bundestag. Certainly on state-related matters, the Bundesrat is far more powerful in the lawmaking process than the French Senate or the British House of Lords are in their countries' lawmaking processes.[15]

The Constitutional Court and the Legal System

The Constitutional Court has exercised judicial review over German legislation in a manner broadly similar to, yet different from, the review exercised by the United States Supreme Court. Like its American counterpart, the Constitutional Court has shaped significant public-policy outcomes. For example, it has overturned federal abortion legislation twice, struck down a Bavarian state requirement for crucifixes in all classrooms, and protected the states' constitutional powers against federal intrusions in the broadcasting field. It has also legitimized, by upholding their constitutionality, an even larger number of laws than it has overturned. Unlike the United States Supreme Court, the German Constitutional Court is divided into two separate chambers or senates of eight judges each— one having jurisdiction over cases concerning basic constitutional liberties, the other responsible for resolving other constitutional cases (which include federal-state relations, political parties and their activities, and international

issues). The procedures for bringing a case before the German Constitutional Court also differ from American practice. German citizens may take cases to the Court when they believe that the government has violated their rights under the Basic Law. The federal and state governments or one-third of the members of the Bundestag may also request that the Court review a law. In addition, lower court judges may refer cases to the Constitutional Court.

The German Constitutional Court and other German courts are embedded in a system of Roman or code law, similar to that found in France and distinct from the Anglo-American common law tradition. Germans are generally regarded as more legalistic than most Europeans in their approaches to resolving social problems, and this trait has shaped their legal system and enhanced its importance. Another factor unique to the contemporary German legal system has been the challenge since reunification of extending the West German system to East Germany, where the legal system had long been subordinated to Communist party domination.[16]

Federalism

Finally, German federal structures are among the most important features of the Republic. Unquestionably, they have shaped policy-making processes that are markedly more decentralized than those in France, the United Kingdom, or Italy. As with judicial review, there are some similarities between the American and German systems—a deliberate choice, since American advisers strongly suggested in the late 1940s the need for decentralization of authority to prevent a revival of German authoritarianism.

However, German federalism possesses a number of traits that distinguish it from the American pattern. The Federal Republic today includes 16 states (*Länder*) in a geographic area smaller than Texas, California, or Montana—11 from the original Federal Republic and 5 from

TABLE 7.3   States of the Federal Republic of Germany

State	Capital	Population
Baden-Württemberg	Stuttgart	10,400,000
Bavaria	Munich	12,000,000
Berlin	Berlin	3,400,000
Brandenburg	Potsdam	2,600,000
Bremen	Bremen	700,000
Hamburg	Hamburg	1,700,000
Hesse	Wiesbaden	6,000,000
Lower Saxony	Hanover	7,800,000
Mecklenburg–Western Pomerania	Schwerin	1,800,000
North Rhine–Westphalia	Dusseldorf	18,000,000
Rhineland-Palatinate	Mainz	4,000,000
Saarland	Saarbrücken	1,100,000
Saxony	Dresden	4,500,000
Saxony-Anhalt	Magdeburg	2,700,000
Schleswig-Holstein	Kiel	2,700,000
Thuringia	Erfurt	2,500,000

the former East Germany. Under the Basic Law, German state governments possess reserved powers in education, broadcasting regulation, cultural affairs, policing, and administration of justice. In addition, the state governments are responsible for administering most federal laws, to a much greater extent than is true in the United States. As noted previously, the state governments are also directly involved in the national policy-making process through their representatives in the Bundesrat (who unlike U.S. Senators are appointed directly by the state governments). The German national government exerts some leverage over the states through its regulations on the sharing of the 55 percent of total German tax revenues that it receives. However, the states are powerful and independent power centers in German government. Leading national politicians, such as Chan-

cellor Schröder and his major 2002 election rival Edmund Stoiber, have built their careers in the *Länder* (Lower Saxony and Bavaria, respectively) before bidding for the top national office.[17]

ELECTIONS, POLITICAL PARTIES, AND INTEREST GROUPS

Elections, political parties, and interest groups have been the major mediators in the German Federal Republic between governmental institutions and citizens. Election outcomes at both national and state levels, shifting party balances in the Bundestag, and changes among and within interest groups have had significant impacts on the operations of German government.

The Electoral Process

The only nationwide popular elections in Germany are for the Bundestag. The rules of the electoral game are a unique hybrid of **first-past-the-post** and proportional representation systems. On one part of their ballots, citizens vote for a candidate to represent their district in the Bundestag, with victory awarded to the candidate in each district who polls the largest number of votes (as in American elections to the House of Representatives). There are 299 districts (328 before 2002), and most of their seats have generally been won by the two largest political parties (a pattern found also in the first-past-the-post systems in the United Kingdom and the United States). However, on their ballots, German citizens also cast a separate party vote. All parties that receive at least 5 percent of the party votes nationwide, or win at least three district seats, are entitled to proportional representation in the Bundestag. The other half of the seats in the Bundestag are awarded from lists prepared by the state parties so as to give each party approximately the same overall proportion of the Bundestag membership as its share of the popular party votes.

This electoral process has fostered a party system of two large parties and several smaller parties in the Bundestag. It also usually has made government by one party at a time (the usual British practice) impossible. Because of the proportional element, it has enabled the small German Free Democratic party (FDP) to win enough seats with its usual 5–10 percent of the party votes to play a critical role in government by serving as a coalition partner with the Christian Democrats (1949–1957, 1961–1966, 1982–1998) and with the Social Democrats (1969–1982). At present, the Greens have been able to gain powerful positions in the Social Democratic–Green coalition government with their 7–9 percent of the party

votes (and Bundestag members) in the 1998 and 2002 Bundestag elections.

Advocates of the German electoral system claim that it is more representative of the voters' wishes than the Anglo-American first-past-the-post system, while it also provides a personal relationship between a constituency and "its" representative that is lacking in legislatures that rely entirely on proportional representation. Critics usually assert that the proportional aspects of the system often give too much power to small parties, as well as to party leaders of all parties who draw up the state party lists for the proportional awarding of party seats in the Bundestag.

TABLE 7.4   Results of the German Bundestag Elections

2002

Party	Popular vote percentages (District)	(Party)	Dist. seats	Party seats	Total seats
SPD	41.9%	38.5%	171	80	251
CDU/CSU	41.1	38.5	125	123	248
Greens	5.6	8.6	1	54	55
FDP	5.8	7.4	0	47	47
PDS	4.3	4.0	2	0	2
Others	1.3	3.0	0	0	0
Total	100.0	100.0	299	304	603

1998

Party	Popular vote percentages (District)	(Party)	Dist. seats	Party seats	Total seats
SPD	43.8%	40.9%	212	86	298
CDU/CSU	39.5	35.1	112	133	245
Greens	5.0	6.7	0	47	47
FDP	3.0	6.2	0	43	43
PDS	4.9	5.1	4	32	36
Others	3.8	6.0	0	0	0
Total	100.0	100.0	328	341	669

TABLE 7.5   Party Vote Percentages in Bundestag Elections, 1980–2002

Party	1980	1983	1987	1990	1994	1998	2002
SPD	43%	38%	37%	34%	36%	41%	39%
CDU/CSU	45	49	44	44	42	35	39
Greens		6	8	4	7	7	9
FDP	11	7	9	11	7	6	7
PDS				2	4	5	4
Other	1	1	1	5	4	6	3
Total	100	101	99	100	100	100	101

Bundestag elections must be held at least once every four years but may take place before four years have elapsed if the president agrees to the chancellor's request for dissolution of the Bundestag and calls for new elections. Early elections of this type have occurred twice: once in 1972, at the instigation of Chancellor Willy Brandt; and once in 1983, at the request of Chancellor Helmut Kohl. Both leaders achieved the electoral results that they desired—victory for the coalitions that they led (unlike French President Jacques Chirac, whose party allies lost their majority in the French National Assembly when he called early elections in 1997).

State elections are of considerable importance in Germany, not only because of the important powers of the states but also because they affect the composition of the Bundesrat, the upper chamber of the national parliament. State elections occur at various times in the calendar. As a result, the Bundesrat's membership shifts frequently to reflect the altered partisan control over the German state governments.[18]

Political Parties

The German Federal Republic has often been referred to as a "party state," reflecting the importance of the political parties in shaping German governmental institutions and public policies and also the large official subsidies that the parties receive from the government, far

beyond those found in most Western democracies. However, as we have seen, one-party dominance of the German executive and legislature at any point in time (in the manner found in Britain) has been almost impossible due to the multiparty effects of the Bundestag electoral system and the nature of the Bundesrat. Therefore, the German "party state" differs from British **"party government,"** though high levels of voting cohesion and party organization are typical of both the German Bundestag and the British House of Commons.[19]

The Christian Democratic Union (CDU), affiliated in the state of Bavaria with the more conservative and Catholic Christian Social Union (CSU), is a moderately conservative party that initially sought to reach out to both Catholics and Protestants and to organized labor as well as the business community in a fashion that led Otto Kirchheimer and others to term it a **"catchall"** party. While retaining a broad base, the CDU/CSU came over time to be a generally conservative, business-oriented party with more appeal to Catholics than to Protestants. Helmut Kohl, a Christian Democrat, held the German chancellorship from 1982 to 1998 and led the CDU/CSU to four consecutive electoral pluralities (not majorities) before losing first place to the Social Democratic party in 1998 and subsequently losing his reputation and party position due to his involvement in a party finance scandal. Though generally conservative, the CDU/CSU designed and has continued to support a "social market" policy including a sizeable welfare state, distinguishing the German Christian Democrats from such **neoliberal** approaches as those adopted by some European conservative parties and often by the German Free Democrats. The German Christian Democrats also have usually been in the vanguard of European Union/European Community integration efforts, in sharp contrast to some other European conservatives, such as the British Conservatives in recent years.[20]

In the 2002 election campaign, the Christian Democrats supported Edmund Stoiber of their Bavarian sister party, the Christian Social Union, for the Chancellorship of Germany, rather than their own party president, Angela Merkel. (See "People in the EU" on page 154.) In the end, the CDU/CSU fell just short of dislodging the governing coalition of Social Democrats and Greens, in the most closely fought election in modern German history.

"I have always said the chancellor candidate of the conservatives should be the person who has the greatest chance of victory."

Christian Democratic leader Angela Merkel as she yielded to Edmund Stoiber, *New York Times (January 12, 2002)*, A3.

The Social Democratic party (SPD), unlike the other contemporary German parties, dates back to the nineteenth century. Until the late 1950s, it adhered to an ideology that rested in large part on a Marxist critique of capitalism. In the post–World War II era, it was initially critical of NATO membership and European integration. However, it has become a moderately social democratic party, committed to codetermination instead of government ownership of business and supportive of NATO and European integration. The SPD is still based to a considerable extent in German organized labor, but increasingly it has sought and gained support from professional and business voters. Chancellor Gerhard Schröder, who led the Social Democrats into first place in the 1998 Bundestag elections and again (barely) in 2002, has emulated the British Labour party's Tony Blair in stressing a "Third Way" political-economic program quite close to the "social market" policies long advocated by most German Christian Democrats and positioned between socialism on the left and economic libertarianism on the right. Schröder developed close ties to the business community during his career in the state of Lower Saxony and has continued as chancellor business-friendly policies, including corporate tax cuts and business-favored immigration law changes to allow skilled foreigners to attain German citizenship. However, within the Social Democratic party are many who continue to advocate a "socialistic" emphasis on seeking more equality, extensive social benefits, full employment, and political resistance to global capitalism by the European Union. Oskar Lafontaine, generally recognized as the prime spokesman for such an emphasis, resigned from the cabinet and from his position as Social Democratic party leader in March 1999, ceding control of the party to the "Third Way" forces for the near future at least.[21]

During the 2002 election campaign, Chancellor Schröder emphasized the independence of his party and his coalition government from the United States, particularly over the Bush administration's policies concerning Iraq. This emphasis, combined with his quick and effective response to severe floods in eastern Germany just before the election, enabled him to lead his Social Democratic–Green coalition government to a narrow electoral victory, even after months of lagging behind the CDU/CSU in the public-opinion surveys. Because of the extremely close balance of power in the Bundestag, some analysts believe that the Schröder-led government may find it difficult to persist in office for a

PEOPLE IN THE EU

Angela Merkel Rises (Almost) to the Top as Christian Democratic Leader

Born in Hamburg, West Germany, in 1954 but raised in Communist East Germany from the time she was a few months old, Angela Merkel became the first woman to head a German political party when the Christian Democratic Union chose her as its leader in April 2000, after its long-time leader Helmut Kohl was forced to resign as a result of a campaign fundraising scandal. As the daughter of a Protestant pastor, Merkel was not pressured as a young person to join the Communist-run Socialist Unity party of East Germany; and she demonstrated little interest in politics until the final days of the Communist state, instead immersing herself in chemistry and physics.

Merkel was elected to the Bundestag of the reunited Germany in 1990, after which her rise to the top of her party was rapid. Though described by one observer as "a dowdy dresser with an unfashionable, pudding bowl hairstyle" and by another as "frumpy"[22] (descriptions unlikely to be applied to a male political leader), Merkel inspired growing respect in political circles. Her career moved upward through a succession of ministerial posts under Chancellor Helmut Kohl in the 1990s. Once the Christian Democrats lost office and scandal broke around Kohl, Merkel quickly abandoned her mentor and emerged as the Christian Democrats' choice as party president.

Though at first most analysts expected Merkel to be the joint candidate of the Christian Democratic Union and its conservative ally, the Christian Social Union, for the chancellorship of Germany in the 2002 elections, her generally centrist positions failed to inspire conservative activists. Worse from the point of view of her colleagues in the CDU leadership ranks, she fell far behind Social Democratic Chancellor Gerhard Schröder in public-opinion polls. When polls indicated that Christian Social Union leader Edmund Stoiber would stand a better chance than she of leading the conservative coalition of the CDU and the CSU to victory, party elites in her own CDU pressured her into withdrawing her candidacy in January 2002 in favor of Stoiber. Angela Merkel had appeared to be on a fast track to becoming Germany's first female chancellor. However, that prospect dimmed almost as quickly as it first emerged. "I have always said the chancellor candidate of the conservatives should be the person who has the greatest chance of victory," declared Merkel in January 2002 as she withdrew from the competition with her Christian Social Union rival for the joint party nomination. In September 2002, Edmund Stoiber led the two parties to a narrow defeat at the hands of Chancellor Schröder and his coalition of Social Democrats and Greens. Perhaps Angela Merkel will have her opportunity to be Germany's chancellor yet.[23]

normal four-year term. Continuing high unemployment and a stagnant economy have pushed the government to recommend labor market reforms that have caused considerable intraparty friction, particularly with organized labor, but have won grudging endorsement from the other parties. These reforms include reducing unemployment benefit payments from 32 to 12 months, providing financial aid to those taking low-paid jobs, and cutting benefits for those who refuse jobs or training. Though the business community has generally welcomed these proposals, the reforms have aroused concerns over loss of social benefits to employees—benefits that have become quite extensive in Germany in recent years and to which many Germans feel they are entitled. Largely as a result of high unemployment and an economic-reform package that many of their strongest supporters viewed as a betrayal of socialist traditions, both Schröder and the Social Democratic party suffered a sharp drop in popularity in 2003–2004.[24]

The Free Democratic party (FDP), the Greens, and the Party of Democratic Socialism (PDS) are the other three parties that have held seats in the Bundestag in recent years. Several far-right, racist parties have failed to pass the 5 percent barrier or win the three district seats requisite for Bundestag representation.

The Free Democratic party traditionally has taken a position in the middle of the road between the Christian Democratic Union and the Social Democratic party—less religious and more inclined to individual free choice on social issues than the CDU; less supportive of social-welfare programs, government regulation of business, and extended codetermination than the SPD. This position has enabled the Free Democratic party to occupy a key centrist position from which it could ally with either major party to form a coalition government and both gain power and modify public policies. In recent years, the party has moved toward a neoliberal ideology. However, it also lost its position in

government in 1998 and has fallen behind the Greens in public support.[25]

"To think Green is nothing less than to heal the human spirit and completely reallocate our resources and priorities," asserted Petra Kelly, one of the founders and most prominent leaders of the German Green party. The Greens emerged in the late 1970s from "new social movement" citizen-based interest groups seeking to promote environmental protection and block nuclear power plant development and placement of NATO missiles in Germany. They have also called for participatory democracy through referendums and workplace reforms. In the 1990s, the "realistic" faction in the party, headed by Joschka Fischer, gained the upper hand over the "fundamentalists" and led the Greens into a coalition government with the Social Democrats in a number of states and then in the national government. Fischer became the foreign minister in the Schröder Red-Green coalition government and a major figure in both German and European politics. The fundamentalists, with strong roots in the 1980s protest movements against nuclear energy development and nuclear weapons, have been extremely unhappy with Fischer and the compromises made in the context of the coalition government with Schröder's Social Democrats. Nevertheless, Fischer has maintained his dominance in the party and played a key role in improving its popular voting strength and number of seats in the Bundestag in the 2002 elections. As a result, he has made the Greens an even more important component of Germany's coalition government than they were between 1998 and 2002.[26]

"To think Green is nothing less than to heal the human spirit and completely reallocate our resources and priorities."

Petra Kelly, Green party founder, *"Thinking Green"* (1994), in Ball and Dagger, eds., *Ideals and Ideologies* (2002), 433.

The Party of Democratic Socialism (PDS) is the only one of the five parties in the Bundestag that has never held a cabinet post at the national level—perhaps unsurprisingly, since it is the successor to the Communist-controlled Socialist Unity party of East Germany. Its base of support lies almost entirely inside East Germany, where it serves primarily as a protest vehicle for those East Germans who are most dissatisfied with their lives since reunification. The PDS possesses some ties to the "socialistic" wing of the Social Democratic party, in 1998 formed a coalition with the SPD to govern the state of Mecklenburg–West Pomerania, and in 2001 joined the SPD to form a coalition government in Berlin. Conservatives of the CDU/CSU have seized upon these state coalitions to try to tar their Social Democratic rivals with the label of Communist sympathizers, still a label to be avoided in western Germany, where the PDS has little support.[27]

Interest Groups

Supplementing the party state (and, some say, partially displacing it) are the interest groups of the German Federal Republic. More so than in Britain or France (but less than in Austria or Sweden) neo-corporatist patterns of governmental consultation with highly organized major economic interest groups have characterized the German political economy, though these patterns appear to have weakened somewhat since the 1980s. Both business employers and industrial workers are highly organized in Germany, with government often mediating between them; and wage and benefits negotiations in particular have often centered on negotiations at the top levels that have been binding on both sides. German pensions and health care arrangements also reflect a neo-corporatist approach. Two recent analyses of neo-corporatism in Europe have independently ranked Germany well above all of the other major states in the EU in extent of corporatist patterns, though below Austria and the Scandinavian countries.[28]

In recent years, new social movements (environmental, feminist, and antinuclear ones in particular) have brought increased citizen involvement and new styles to German interest group politics. Ronald Inglehart and others have noted the rise of "post-materialist" values in Germany as in most other Western countries,

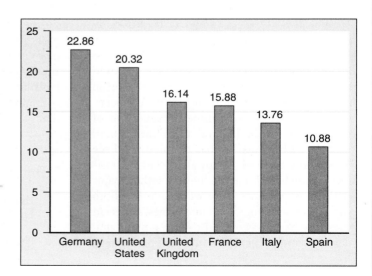

FIGURE 7.1 Hourly Compensation Costs for Production Workers in Manufacturing, 2001 (in U.S. Dollars)

U.S. Bureau of Labor Statistics

and these have clearly influenced German interest group patterns.[29] Another feature of German interest group politics has been the prominent role played by religious organizations, both Catholic and Protestant.

Business employers in Germany are highly organized and have always enjoyed excellent access to the government. Though the business community has generally favored the Christian Democrats or the Free Democrats over the Social Democrats or the other parties, Chancellor Schröder, a Social Democrat, has actively sought advice from business leaders. The Federation of German Industry (BDI) is a peak federation of trade associations that focuses on influencing governmental economic policies. Extensively overlapping its membership but focusing instead on labor-management negotiations is the Federation of German Employer Associations (BDA). A third business group, the German Industrial and Trade Conference (DIHT), primarily represents small business.

The German Confederation of Labor (DGB), composed of 17 separate **industrial unions**, is the peak association for organized labor in the German Federal Republic. Although labor unions have ties to both major parties, their links to the Social Democrats (such as through their campaign contributions and their members who sit as Social Democrats in the Bundestag) are far closer than those to the Christian Democrats. Organized labor has strongly supported expansion of codetermination, as well as a shortened workweek to 35 hours per week and increased job security. German union membership, standing at about 30 percent of the workforce, down slightly in recent years, is higher than in France or the United States, similar to the British figures, but substantially lower than the Swedish figures. The failure of a major strike called in summer 2003 by the large union of metalworkers (*IG Metall*), and the unions' difficulties in persuading the Social Democratic–led government to move slowly on labor market and other economic reforms are seen by many analysts as indicative of a decline in the strength of German organized labor.

The Green Front, an alliance of three agricultural interest groups, has enjoyed influence disproportionate to the relatively small and shrinking size of the German farm population. However, that influence, usually wielded in support of continuing the subsidies of the European Union Common Agricultural Policy, has waned somewhat in recent years.

The new social movements have created a more participatory style of democracy in recent decades than in the German past. Some of them helped to spawn the Greens as a party and have influenced Chancellor Schröder's Social Democratic–Green coalition government. Although the new social movements have gained broader support and been more active in Germany than in most Western European countries, their general impact remains lower than that of organized business and labor by most accounts.

Finally, the Roman Catholic and evangelical (Protestant, mostly Lutheran) churches, both of which (along with Jewish but not Muslim religious institutions) receive state subsidies and income from church taxes, continue to exercise considerable influence in German politics despite declining church attendance and religiosity in Germany to levels well below those in the United States but similar to most of Western Europe. The Catholic Church has long enjoyed considerable influence in the Christian Democratic Union (though the current CDU leader, Angela Merkel, is the daughter of a Protestant pastor) and even more so in the Christian Social Union in the heavily Catholic state of Bavaria. During the late 1980s, the Evangelical churches, relatively strong in the East as well as the North of Germany, played important roles in organizing mass demonstrations that helped to trigger the downfall of the Communist regime in the East.[30]

Political participation in the German Federal Republic has been channeled through peaceful elections, two major political parties, and established economic interest groups in ways that contrast with both the German past and the contemporary French political process. Of course, the rise of the new social movements, the emergence of the Greens as a party of government, the push for more active and direct participatory methods, and the new East German inputs into the processes of the German Federal Republic illustrate that the modification of participatory patterns is continuing.

CONCLUSIONS

Germany has experienced more dramatic transformations during the past century than either France or the United Kingdom—from Second Reich, to Weimar Republic, to Third Reich, to a split between a constitutional democratic West and a Communist authoritarian or totalitarian East, to reunification. Despite the upheavals, the German Federal Republic appears to have confronted the crises of modernization more successfully over the long term than any of its predecessors. Against the backdrop of the Weimar, Nazi, and Cold War legacies, Germany is now under considerable pressure to redefine its roles in Europe and in the world. How the Federal Republic has functioned and is likely to proceed within the framework of the European Union is the subject of the next chapter.

SUMMARY

- The German national identity developed amidst fragmentation into numerous kingdoms, duchies, city-states, and other political jurisdictions; only in 1871 did the German nation-state take shape— much later than French nation-state development.
- The German Second Reich lasted from 1871 to 1918; despite some democratic elements, it was generally authoritarian but took major steps toward building a modern mixed economy.
- The democratic Weimar Republic created after World War I collapsed under the pressures of crises of state legitimacy, national identity, and economic dislocation, giving way in 1933 to Adolf Hitler's Third Reich dictatorship (1933–1945).
- The Third Reich repressed all opposition, unleashed the Holocaust, and led Germany to disastrous defeat in World War II.
- Germany was divided between the Federal Republic of Germany in the West and the Soviet-dominated German Democratic Republic in the East after World War II; West Germany developed a strong and stable constitutional democracy and instituted a successful social market economy, while East Germany suffered under a Communist dictatorship and a sluggish state-dominated economy.
- East Germany collapsed in 1990; East and West were reunited in the Federal Republic of Germany under the West German Basic Law (constitution); East Germany lags significantly behind West Germany economically, making reunification a more difficult process than many had imagined.
- The Federal Republic of Germany appears to have addressed the modernization crises of nation-building, state-building, participation, and distribution more successfully than any of its predecessors or than the German Democratic Republic, though East-West differences, conflicts over new immigrant groups, and sluggish economic growth in the past decade pose some continuing problems.
- The chancellor (currently Gerhard Schröder) is the head of the German government, chosen by and responsible to the popularly elected branch of the national legislature, the

Bundestag, in a fairly typical cabinet-parliamentary arrangement.

- The German governments are nearly always composed of coalitions of two or more political parties (currently the Social Democratic and Green parties), with the parties generally dividing the cabinet ministries between or among them in rough proportion to the strength of the parties within the majority in the Bundestag.

- The president (currently Horst Koehler, a Christian Democrat) is a largely ceremonial head of state, unlike the French president.

- The German parliament is composed of the popularly elected Bundestag and the state-government–appointed Bundesrat; only the Bundestag may remove the chancellor (by a constructive vote of no confidence), but the Bundesrat has important lawmaking powers on state-related matters.

- The German Constitutional Court, divided into two chambers or senates, possesses significant powers of judicial review.

- The German legal system derives from Roman law; Germans are renowned for being highly legalistic.

- Germany possesses a federal system, in which the 16 states (*Länder*) possess significant reserved powers and are responsible for administering most national laws.

- The only nationwide popular elections in Germany are for the Bundestag; the election rules are a hybrid of first-past-the-post and proportional representation systems.

- Germany has two large political parties, the Social Democrats and the Christian Democrats, and several significant other parties (including the Greens, the Free Democrats, the Christian Social Union, and the Party of Democratic Socialism); the Social Democrats dominate the center-left and the Christian Democrats the center-right in Germany.

- Neo-corporatist patterns of government consultation with major economic interest groups have been more widespread than in most large European nation-states but have declined somewhat since the 1980s; employer organizations, such as the Federation of German Industry and the Federation of German Employer Associations, are powerful in Germany, as are labor unions, most of which are members of the German Confederation of Labor.

- New social movements (environmental, feminist, and antinuclear ones in particular) have brought increased citizen involvement and new styles to German interest-group politics.

- Roman Catholic and Lutheran churches receive state subsidies and income from church taxes and exert considerable influence, despite low and declining church attendance in Germany.

- Germany has experienced more dramatic transformations in the past century than France or the United Kingdom; but it has achieved stable and democratic institutions that appear capable of surmounting current problems.

ENDNOTES

1. The "blood and iron" phrase comes from Chancellor Bismarck's 1862 speech, "It is not through speeches and majority resolutions that the great questions of our time are decided...but through blood and iron." Quoted in Colin Campbell, Harvey Feigenbaum, Ronald Linden, and Helmut Norpoth, *Politics and Government in Europe Today*, 2nd ed. (Boston: Houghton Mifflin Company, 1995), 318. The phrase has been applied widely to German unification in the 1860s and early 1870s.

2. Rogers Brubacker, *Citizenship and Nationhood in France and Germany* (Cambridge: Harvard University Press, 1992); Michael Stürmer, *The German Empire, 1870–1918* (New York: Modern

Library, 2000); Wolfgang J. Mommsen, *Imperial Germany, 1867–1918: Politics, Culture, and Society in an Authoritarian State* (London: Edward Arnold, 1995).

3. On the Weimar era, see Eberhard Kolb, *The Weimar Republic* (London: Hutchinson, 1988). On Hitler, see John Toland, *Adolf Hitler* (New York: Doubleday, 1976) and Alan Bullock, *Hitler: A Study in Tyranny* (New York: Harper & Row, 1964). Karl Dietrich Bracher, *The German Dictatorship* (New York: Praeger, 1970), provides a good analysis of the Third Reich. Daniel J. Goldhagen, *Hitler's Willing Executioners* (New York: Alfred A. Knopf, 1996), offers a thought-provoking but controversial assessment of German responsibility for the Holocaust.

4. Lewis J. Edinger and Brigitte L. Nacos, *From Bonn to Berlin: German Politics in Transition* (New York: Columbia University Press, 1998), 15.

5. Edinger and Nacos, *From Bonn to Berlin*, 29.

6. Stevem Erlanger, "Bavarian, in Hard Race, Raises Specter of Immigrants," *New York Times*, September 17, 2002, A10; Hugh Williamson, "German Business Hits at Opposition over Immigration Stance," *Financial Times*, September 17, 2002, 4; Haig Simonian, "CDU Plays Immigration Card in Last Votes Gamble," *Financial Times*, September 19, 2002, 2; Panikos Panayi, "Racial Exclusionism in the New Germany," in Klaus Larres, ed., *Germany Since Reunification: The Development of the Berlin Republic*, 2nd ed. (Basingstoke: Palgrave, 2001), 129–148; David Bacon, "Germany's New Identity," in E. Gene Frankland, ed., *Global Studies: Europe*, 7th ed. (Guilford, CT: McGraw-Hill/Dushkin, 2002), 228–229; James F. Hollifield, "The Migration Challenge: Europe's Crisis in Historical Perspective," in Henri Warmenhoven, ed., *Global Studies: Western Europe*, 6th ed. (Guilford, CT: Dushkin/McGraw-Hill, 1999), 185–191; Simon Green, "Beyond Ethnoculturalism? German Citizenship in the New Millennium," *German Politics* 9, 3 (December 2000), 105–124; "German Immigration Law: Here Come the Lawyers," *The Economist* 362 (March 30, 2002), 43.

7. David P. Conradt, *The German Polity*, 7th ed. (New York: Longman, 2001), 74–80.

8. Robert Rohrschneider, *Learning Democracy: Democratic and Economic Values in Unified Germany* (Oxford: Oxford University Press, 1999), esp. 207–211; David P. Conradt, "Political Culture in Unified Germany: The First Ten Years," *German Politics and Society* 20, 2 (Summer 2002), 43–74.

9. Conradt, *The German Polity*, 82–88. The percentages of women in parliamentary bodies is from the Interparliamentary Union, "Women in Parliament," May 31, 2003.

10. Jürg Steiner, *European Democracies*, 3rd ed. (New York: Longman, 1995), 197–199; Gerard Braunthal, "Codetermination in West Germany," in James B. Christoph and Bernard E. Brown, eds., *Cases in Comparative Politics* (Boston: Little, Brown, 1976), 215–247; Shawn Donnelly, "Public Interest Politics, Corporate Governance and Company Regulation in Germany and Britain," *German Politics* 9, 2 (August 2000), 171–194.; Jutta Helm, "Co-Determination in West Germany: What Difference Does It Make?" *West European Politics* 9, 1 (January 1986), 32–53.

11. Conradt, *The German Polity*, 185; Alex N. Dragnich, Jorgen S. Rasmussen, and Joel C. Moses, *Major European Governments*, 8th ed. (Pacific Grove, CA: Brooks/Cole, 1991), 405–411.

12. Edinger and Nacos, *From Bonn to Berlin*, 50–54, discusses similarities and differences between German and American systems of checks and balances. Stephen Padgett, "Chancellors and the Chancellorship," in Padgett, ed., *Adenauer to Kohl: The Development of the German Chancellorship* (Washington, DC: Georgetown University Press, 1994), 1–19, portrays a shift from "Chancellor Democracy" to "Coordination Democracy."

13. Conradt, *The German Polity*, 209–228.

14. The number has usually exceeded 598 (previously 656) because, through the "excess mandate" provisions of the electoral law, parties are allowed to keep "extra" seats won in single-member plurality districts above what proportional representation entitles them to win. The number was 669 following the 1998 elections. The number was 603 after the 2002 elections.

15. For a discussion of "reactive" and "active" legislative bodies in comparative perspective, see Michael Mezey, *Comparative Legislatures*

(Durham, NC: Duke University Press, 1979), Ch. 2. Good recent treatments of the German parliament include Klaus von Beyme, *The Legislator: German Parliament as a Centre of Political Decision-Making* (Aldershot, England: Ashgate, 1998); Stephen J. Silvia, "Reform Gridlock and the Role of the Bundesrat in German Politics," *West European Politics* 22, 2 (April 1999), 62–81; Uwe Thaysen, *The Bundesrat, the Länder, and German Federalism* (Washington, DC: American Institute for Contemporary German Studies, Johns Hopkins, 1994).

16. Donald Kommers, *Constitutional Jurisprudence in the Federal Republic of Germany* (Durham, NC: Duke University Press, 1989); Edinger and Nacos, *From Bonn to Berlin*, 57–60; Conradt, *The German Polity*, 228–238; Von Beyme, *The Legislator*, 105–114.

17. Thaysen, *The Bundesrat, the Länder and German Federalism*; Conradt, *The German Polity*, 243–266.

18. See the collection of articles in David P. Conradt, Gerald R. Kleinfeld, and Christian Søe, eds., *Power Shift in Germany: The 1998 Election and the End of the Kohl Era* (New York: Berghahn, 2000).

19. Michaela W. Richter, "The German Party State: A Reassessment," in Christopher S. Allen, ed., *Transformation of the German Political Party System: Institutional Crisis or Democratic Renewal?* (New York: Berghahn, 1999), 62–98; Gerard Braunthal, *Parties and Politics in Modern Germany* (Boulder, CO: HarperCollins-Westview Press, 1996), 37–50; and Kurt Sontheimer, *The Government and Politics of West Germany* (New York: Praeger, 1973), 95, on the German "party state" and its contrast to the past. See the glossary and Ch. 10 on British "party government."

20. For the "catchall" conception, see Otto Kirchheimer, "Germany: The Vanishing Opposition," in Robert A. Dahl, ed., *Political Opposition in Western Democracies* (New Haven: Yale University Press, 1966), 245. On recent developments, see Clay Clemens, "The Last Hurrah: Helmut Kohl's CDU/CSU and the 1998 Election," in Conradt, Kleinfeld, and Søe, eds., *Power Shift in Germany*, 38–58, and Clay Clemens, "Crisis or Catharsis? Germany's CDU After the Party

Finance Affair," *German Politics and Society* 18, 2 (Summer 2000), 66–90. Mark Mazower, *Dark Continent: Europe's Twentieth Century* (New York: Random House, Vintage, 2000), 334–337, discusses British Conservative-German Christian Democratic similarities and differences.

21. Charles Lees, *The Red-Green Coalition in Germany: Politics, Personalities, and Power* (Manchester: Manchester University Press, 2000); Gerard Braunthal, "The SPD: From Opposition to Governing Party," in Conradt, Kleinfeld, and Søe, eds., *Power Shift in Germany*, 18–37; Herbert Kitschelt, "The German Political Economy and the 1998 Election," in Conradt, Kleinfeld, and Søe, eds., *Power Shift in Germany*, 200–220; Oskar Lafontaine, *The Heart Beats on the Left*, trans. by Ronald Taylor (Malden, MA: Blackwell, 2000).

22. Dennis Staunton, "The Mrs. Merkel Show," *The Observer*, April 30, 2000; "Germany's Centre-Right Opposition: Who Will Lead it into Battle?" *The Economist* 362 (January 12, 2002), 46.

23. This account of Merkel's career is based upon Staunton, "The Mrs. Merkel Show;" John Hooper, "New CDU Chief Takes Brussels by Surprise," *The Guardian*, April 11, 2000; Steven Erlanger, "Conservatives in Germany in Battle for Top Job," *New York Times*, January 10, 2002, A5; Steven Erlanger, "German Right Backs Bavarian to Run Against Schröder," *New York Times*, January 12, 2002, A3; and "Germany's Centre-Right Opposition," 46–47.

24. Roger Boyes, "Schröder Wins Razor-Thin Majority," *The Times*, September 23, 2002; "Slender Win for Schröder," *The Guardian*, September 23, 2002; Haig Simonian, "The Megaphone Diplomat," *Financial Times*, September 14–15, 2002, 7.

25. Christian Søe, "Neoliberal Stirrings: The 'New' FDP and Some Old Habits," in Conradt, Kleinfeld, and Søe, eds., *Power Shift in Germany*, 59–79.

26. E. Gene Frankland, "Bündnis '90/Die Grünen: From Opposition to Power," in Conradt, Kleinfeld, and Søe, eds., *Power Shift in Germany*, 80–97; Lees, *The Red-Green Coalition in Germany;* Tad Shull, *Redefining Red and Green: Ideology and Strategy in European Political Ecology* (Albany, NY: SUNY Press, 1999).

27. Gerald R. Kleinfeld, "The Party of Democratic Socialism: Victory Across the East and on to Berlin!" in Conradt, Kleinfeld, and Søe, eds., *Power Shift in Germany*, 98–113.

28. On previous West German patterns through the 1980s, see M. Donald Hancock, *West Germany: The Politics of Democratic Corporatism* (Chatham, NJ: Chatham House, 1989), esp. Ch. 6. The two recent studies are in Alan Siaroff, "Corporatism in 24 Industrial Democracies: Meaning and Measurement," *European Journal of Political Research* 36, 2 (October 1999), 175–205, and Steiner, *European Democracies*, Ch. 8.

29. On the new social movements, see Saral Sarkar, *Green-Alternative Politics in West Germany, Volume 1: The New Social Movements* (New York: United Nations University Press, 1993); Steiner, *European Democracies*, Ch. 9; and Andrew Apple- ton, "The New Social Movement Phenomenon: Placing France in Comparative Perspective," in Robert Elgie, ed., *The Changing French Political System* (London: Frank Cass, 2000), 57–75. Ronald Inglehart, *The Silent Revolution: Changing Values and Political Styles among Western Publics* (Princeton: Princeton University Press, 1977).

30. Bernhard Ebbinghaus, "Germany," in Bernhard Ebbinghaus and Jelle Visser, eds., *The Societies of Europe: Trade Unions in Western Europe Since 1945* (Basingstoke: Macmillan, 2000), 279–337; Conradt, *The German Polity*, 132–143; Hugh Williamson, "Big Unions Wade in with Warning on Stoiber win," *Financial Times*, September 19, 2002, 4; Mark Landler, "Schröder's Economic Plan Is Aided by a Union and His Party," *New York Times*, July 1, 2003, A4.

Chapter 8

GERMANY AND THE EUROPEAN UNION

"Germans aren't Europeans because they have to be, but because they want to be."

—German Chancellor Gerhard Schröder,
cited in Newsweek (December 7, 1998), 73.

From its inception in 1949, the Federal Republic of Germany has been in the forefront of the movement toward European integration. Article 24.1 of its constitution, the Basic Law, even provided for the transfer of sovereignty to "intergovernmental organizations." In part to sever links to the Nazi era of the past, the first West German chancellor, Konrad Adenauer, joined eagerly with French political leaders to found the European Coal and Steel Community in the 1950–1952 period and then worked with the leaders of West Germany's five ECSC partner states to establish the European Communities in 1957. As the Federal Republic grew and prospered, it gradually assumed enhanced power within the EC—a process that became even more evident after German reunification in 1990. As Chancellor Schröder's quotation above suggests, Germany remains committed to European integration, in terms of both increased unity and broadened membership.

Despite the growth of German influence over the past five decades, Germany has shown a considerably greater willingness than either France or Britain to pool sovereignty in the EC/EU and to compromise on controversial issues of national interest. As a result, some analysts have described Germany as a "gentle giant" or a "tamed power." One recent analyst has concluded that "…it is the integration and taming of Germany that is the great accomplishment of Europe—viewed historically, perhaps the greatest feat of international politics ever achieved."[1]

> "…it is the integration and taming of Germany that is the great accomplishment of Europe—viewed historically, perhaps the greatest feat of international politics ever achieved."
>
> Robert Kagan, *Of Power and Paradise* (2003), 56.

Nevertheless, Germany has taken distinctive positions vis-à-vis the EC/EU that have reflected its own history, geopolitical position, economic interests, and political institutions. This chapter examines the historical development of Germany's relations with the EC/EU, highlights the most distinctive long-term features of German approaches to the EC/EU, and considers the complex mutual influences of Germany on the EC/EU and the EC/EU on Germany.

THE DEVELOPMENT OF THE GERMAN RELATIONSHIP WITH THE EC/EU

An Escape into Europe?

At the end of World War II, Germany was defeated, devastated, and divided among the occupation forces of the United States, Britain, France, and the Soviet Union. As the Cold War split the Soviet Union from its three erstwhile allies, the groundwork was laid for the establishment of the Federal Republic of Germany (West Germany) in 1949 under the watchful gaze of the Western Allies.

The new "semi-sovereign" state of West Germany lacked full control over its foreign and defense policies or over its economy. Therefore, pooling sovereignty in a supranational Europe was far more attractive to its leaders than to most other Western European governments. Specifically, the European Coal and Steel Community (ECSC) proposed by the French would supersede the occupying powers' High Commission in control of the West German coal and steel industries.[2]

West Germany's new government, headed by Chancellor Adenauer, found the ECSC and European integration attractive for other reasons, too. In an environment in which most of West Germany's neighbors retained deep bitterness and distrust of German nationalism, stimulated by the recent Nazi era in particular, the ECSC and European integration offered a German "escape into Europe" and an opportunity to regain credibility and respect by stressing cooperation. A leading French analyst has concluded: "For the Germans, European unification has been, together with their participation in NATO, the way to sever their links with their Nazi past, to erase the grim legacy of that dark period."[3] Integration also held particular promise for building improved relations with France, a goal that Adenauer had articulated repeatedly even before becoming chancellor.

The United States, the critical source of military security for West Germany and the superpower of the West, was also a proponent of European integration. Even though the European Coal and Steel Community had no defense component, the proposed European Defense Community (EDC) did. The Adenauer government backed it, too, seeing in it a possible means of obtaining not just West German rearmament but also full sovereignty and entry into the North Atlantic Treaty Organization (NATO), which had been founded without West German membership in 1949.[4]

"For the Germans, European unification has been, together with their participation in NATO, the way to sever their links with their Nazi past, to erase the grim legacy of that dark period."

Dominique Moïsi, *Foreign Affairs (1998), 100.*

However, other West German objectives appeared to many Germans to clash with membership in the ECSC and EDC. Chief among these was reunification with Soviet-controlled East Germany, also enshrined as a goal in the Basic Law. Because the Soviet Union was hostile to West European economic and military integration, the likelihood that Soviet leaders would agree to reunification appeared to diminish as West Germany moved to integrate with the West. Many business interests questioned whether the ECSC had been established on a basis that would be economically beneficial to West Germany. Even within Adenauer's own cabinet, Minister of Economics Ludwig Erhard expressed concerns about the ECSC, praising the idea of free competition in a common market but warning of the danger of French-type *dirigisme* in the power of the ECSC High Authority. The leading opposition party to Adenauer's Christian Democratic–Christian Social–Free Democratic–German Party coalition government, the Social Democrats, opposed both the ECSC and the EDC, as did the small Communist party. Nevertheless, Adenauer was able to win parliamentary ratification of the ECSC Treaty and endorsement of the EDC, although the latter was hedged by the passage of additional parliamentary motions calling for various adjustments.[5]

When the French parliament blocked the creation of the European Defense Community, West Germany was accepted into the intergovernmental Western European Union that replaced it and achieved Adenauer's objectives of rearmament, regaining of sovereign rights, and entry into NATO. However, the dream of reunification appeared dead for the foreseeable future.[6]

As West Germany gained status and respect, the European Coal and Steel Community began to yield economic benefits for its members. Recovery from World War II, expanding global trade, and the "social market" economy of Economics Minister Erhard also fueled a general West German "economic miracle."

West Germany and the Progress of European Integration

The Federal Republic participated fully in the negotiations that led to the 1957 Rome Treaties creating the European Economic Community and the European Atomic Energy Community. Although the Social Democratic party under new leadership moved closer than previously to Adenauer's positions on European integration, conflict flared between Adenauer and Erhard over West German negotiating positions. Backed by much of the business community, which had also shared his previous reservations about the ECSC, Erhard especially objected to Adenauer's concessions to the French on the common external tariff that allowed it to be set above West German tariff levels. Erhard and West German organized business interests feared that the external tariff would damage Germany's position as the world's third-largest exporter and a heavy exporter (unlike France) to

advanced countries outside the EEC. In fact, Erhard, the Free Democratic party, and much of the West German business community showed sympathy for British proposals for a broadened free-trade area lacking the kind of supranational institutions envisioned for the EEC. However, these ideas were anathema to the French government. Emphasizing the importance of a Franco-German partnership and dismissing fears that the EEC would become the "economic burden" of which Erhard warned, Adenauer overrode the objections and gained overwhelming parliamentary ratification of the Rome Treaties in July 1957. Even Erhard reluctantly acquiesced, though the Free Democrats sustained their opposition to the EEC.[7]

Because Adenauer had placed Franco-German cooperation in the new European Communities high on his list of priorities, the return to power in June 1958 of the French nationalist Charles de Gaulle caused him considerable concern at first. However, the two leaders soon established strong rapport with each other. During the next five years, Adenauer and de Gaulle were able to achieve agreement between West Germany and France on acceleration of the original internal EEC tariff-reduction schedule, the basic features of the Common Agricultural Policy, and the Elysée Treaty formalizing the Franco-German "alliance within the alliance." However, de Gaulle's veto of British EEC entry, his continuing pressures on West Germany to side with France against the United States, and his Fouchet Plan to reorganize the six EC members on an almost entirely intergovernmental basis all aroused strong opposition in West Germany—opposition so intense that it weakened Adenauer's power and eventually played a major part in his replacement as chancellor by his longtime intraparty rival, Erhard.[8]

The Christian Democrats' selection of Erhard, long known as a global free-trade advocate, an Atlanticist, and a critic of Adenauer's compromises with de Gaulle, clearly signaled that West German approaches to the EC were diverging from those of France. The German Bundestag reinforced that signal by insisting upon the addition of an Atlanticist preamble to the Elysée Treaty with France before it would agree to ratification. The next five years were to be a time of conflict and stalemate within the EC. France was increasingly isolated, and West Germany under Erhard's weak and fragmented government (1963–1966) and then the Grand Coalition government of Christian Democrats and Social Democrats headed by Kurt Kiesinger (1966–1969) proved unable to provide leadership.[9]

Brandt, Schmidt, and the European Communities

The 1969 West German elections brought Willy Brandt to power as the first Social Democratic chancellor of the Federal Republic, heading a Social Democratic–Free Democratic coalition government. Brandt's *Ostpolitik* policy of reaching out to improve relations with East Germany, Eastern Europe, and the Soviet Union represented the sharpest break with the past and aroused strong Christian Democratic opposition at home and some concerns in Western capitals. However, Brandt sought simultaneously to build domestic consensus and reassure his EC partners, especially France, by stressing the need to revitalize the EC. He met frequently with French President Pompidou, and the two men (while not personally close) reached agreements on EC funding for the Common Agricultural Policy, enlargement to include Britain, and initial steps toward economic and monetary union (the latter soon to be derailed, however, by a resurgence of differing national responses to global monetary and oil crises). Brandt's compromises with France on economic and monetary issues caused conflicts inside his coalition cabinet, particularly with Finance Minister Karl Schiller, a staunch

Atlanticist, who eventually resigned in 1972. Brandt's coalition won the 1972 West German elections. However, in 1974, Brandt himself resigned, in the wake of a spy scandal involving one of his aides but also amid growing problems on a wide array of fronts, including the European Community.[10]

Helmut Schmidt, a fellow Social Democrat, succeeded Brandt in the chancellorship and continued the coalition government with the Free Democrats. His tenure in office (1974–1982) coincided almost perfectly with that of French President Giscard d'Estaing (1974–1981), and the two leaders developed the strongest personal relationship yet seen in the Franco-German partnership. However, the era was a difficult one economically, national differences often fragmented the EC, and the EC accomplishments of the partners were less than spectacular. In fact, their close ties often alienated other national leaders in the EC.

Schmidt's major contribution to the EC was the establishment of the European Monetary System (EMS), a project on which he played the leading role but collaborated actively with Giscard and Roy Jenkins of the United Kingdom, who served as president of the European Commission. An economist by training and a pragmatist by inclination, Schmidt apparently pushed hard for the EMS in an effort to lessen the appreciation of the West German mark by helping weak-currency EMS members impose economic discipline similar to West Germany's. His hope was that this approach would then allow West German economic growth.

However, the highly autonomous West German Bundesbank (central bank) resisted Schmidt's approach, raised interest rates, and triggered a recession. This economic downturn accelerated tensions that were already growing within Schmidt's coalition, particularly between the left wing of his own Social Democratic party and the increasingly conservative Free Democrats. In 1982, the Free Democrats withdrew from the coalition and, through a constructive vote of no confidence, joined with the Christian Democrats and their Bavarian Christian Social Union partners to place Christian Democrat Helmut Kohl in the chancellorship, at the head of a new coalition government.[11]

The Kohl Era, European Integration, and German Reunification

Kohl was to hold the chancellor's position for the next 16 years. His vision was, in the words of one analyst, "pure Adenauer," emphasizing further European integration in close cooperation with France, while maintaining strong transatlantic ties with the United States.[12] Unlike the Adenauer era, however, the unification of Germany emerged as a possibility that Kohl turned into a reality. Also in contrast to the Adenauer era, Germany had become the major political and economic power in the EC/EU—no longer what even Willy Brandt had described as "an economic giant but a political pygmy."[13]

[Germany is] "an economic giant but a political pygmy."

Chancellor Willy Brandt, *cited by Alistair Cole, Franco-German Relations (2001), 106.*

At first, Kohl was widely seen as a pragmatic political operator who lacked clear vision and was unlikely to survive the power struggles within his fractious government. His foreign minister, Free Democratic leader Hans-Dietrich Genscher, who had held the same post under Chancellor Schmidt from 1980 onward and had engineered his party's switch from Schmidt to Kohl, portrayed himself as the chief architect of Germany's external policies. In 1981, Genscher had launched, with support from the Italian foreign minister, the Genscher-Colombo proposal for enhanced EC power and decision-making in foreign relations and general movement toward greater European unity.

Although it had led in the short term only to a vague European Council "Solemn Declaration on European Union," it would play a part in the efforts of 1984 to revitalize the movement toward European integration.[14]

In the negotiations that led to the Single European Act of 1986, Kohl and Genscher welcomed internal market reform proposals, which enjoyed the backing of most German industrialists and financiers. The Federation of German Industry (BDI) had endorsed the opening of internal markets as well as global openness in 1982 and reiterated its support in 1985. Kohl and Genscher also pushed actively for supranational, or federal, development of EU institutions: strengthening of the European Parliament and adoption of qualified majority voting on some issues in the European Council of Ministers—in line with positions traditionally taken by West Germany. The resulting Single European Act won wide support from the West German parliament, parties, interest groups, and general public. However, its effects were to prove more extensive than most Germans anticipated.[15]

In contrast to the Single European Act, the Treaty on European Union (Maastricht Treaty), particularly its timetable for adopting the euro as a replacement for national currencies, encountered considerable German political resistance at the outset, particularly from the Bundesbank, the finance ministry, and agricultural interest groups. Responding to the numerous criticisms, Kohl sought and won concessions on the Economic and Monetary Union (EMU) that conformed to strong German internal political and economic pressures for location of the European Central Bank (ECB) in Frankfurt, autonomy for the ECB based on the German model, and convergence criteria fashioned to satisfy German preoccupation with keeping inflation low. (See "People in the EU" on page 169 for further discussion of the process.)[16]

Although Germany held no referendum on the Maastricht Treaty as France and some other member nation-states did—and avoided the upsurge of popular opposition to European integration in interest group and party politics that occurred in both France and Britain—German opponents challenged the constitutionality of the Treaty before the Constitutional Court. The Court upheld it but on a rather qualified basis and issued criticisms of the "democratic deficit" in European institutional structures. Ominously for Kohl, public-opinion polls indicated continuing and widespread unease about the single-currency project.[17]

Despite widespread predictions that the reunification of Germany would bring major shifts in German approaches to the European Union, continuity outweighed change. Kohl persisted in sustaining the Franco-German partnership, Atlanticism, further EU enlargement, and most other principles that German leaders had long embraced. Above all, Kohl viewed continued EU "deepening" and expansion eastward as means of insuring a peaceful future for Europe. "The policy of European integration is in reality a question of war and peace in the twenty-first century," he stressed. However, facing the higher-than-expected costs of reunification, Germany became increasingly insistent about setting strict limits on EU budgets and reducing Germany's large net contributions to those budgets (the largest of any member). It also became less reticent than previously about asserting German national interests.[18]

"The policy of European integration is in reality a question of war and peace in the twenty-first century."

Chancellor Helmut Kohl, February 22, 1996, *cited by Elizabeth Knowles, ed., Twentieth Century Quotations (1998).*

Germany and the EU in the Schröder Era

When Kohl and his party coalition suffered defeat in the 1998 elections, it was at the hands of a Red-Green coalition led by the young, dynamic Social Democrat Gerhard Schröder. Schröder's coalition government of Social Democrats and Greens got off to a shaky start in its relations with the European Union. Lack of coordination among ministries' negotiating positions in the EU was even more evident than usual in Germany, and Schröder's initially confrontational style offended many other European leaders. Most notably, Oskar Lafontaine, Social Democratic party leader and finance minister, in a sharp break with long-standing German positions, sought an alliance with French Socialists to challenge the European Central Bank's restrictive monetary policies and spur economic growth. He also joined the French Socialists in pressing for increased tax harmonization within the EU framework. These efforts outraged conservatives and big business interests at home and abroad and brought conflict between Lafontaine and Schröder, who as chancellor favored generally centrist policies. In March 1999, Lafontaine abruptly resigned as finance minister and party leader. Thereafter, the Schröder government's European policies generally adhered to fairly traditional German lines. Among the major initiatives advanced by the Schröder government in the next two years was a proposed federal constitution for the European Union, first advanced by Green Foreign Minister Joschka Fischer in May 2000 and subsequently endorsed by the Chancellor—a proposal received with little enthusiasm in either France or the United Kingdom. Many analysts detected a weakening in the long-term Franco-German partnership, particularly noting the lack of cooperation between the German and French leaders in the preparation and functioning of the EU Nice Summit of December 2000, as well as over the issue of the Fischer-Schröder EU constitutional proposals. Nonetheless, predictions of the demise of the Franco-German alliance within the EU are probably exaggerated, as they have often proved to be in the past. Germany and France have closely coordinated their policies

Helmut Kohl
and the European Economic and Monetary Union

Chancellor Helmut Kohl (1982–1998) found himself battling the finance ministry in his own government, as well as the German Bundesbank, even as he negotiated with Commission President Jacques Delors and the leaders of other European Community member states during the processes leading to the establishment of the Economic and Monetary Union in the early 1990s. This example illustrates the type of two-level "game" (one level among domestic economic interests; the other among member state leaders) that liberal intergovernmental theory posits as a major aspect of European integration processes.

Both the Bundesbank and the finance ministry were reluctant to give up the power that West Germany had long exercised in the monetary policy realm due to the strength of the West German economy and the deutsche mark. At the same time, most German export businesses and the labor unions favored the EMU. The Bundestag and German public opinion showed marked interest in increased powers for the European Parliament and cooperation on foreign policy. In addition to these domestic influences, Kohl was under intense pressure from France, Italy, and Delors to embrace a plan for a common currency and a monetary policy shaped by a supranational European Central Bank—seen by these key players as a logical extension of the single market that would enhance the benefits of that market (and also eliminate the need for other currencies to "shadow" the deutsche mark). Delors's active support of Kohl's goal of achieving German reunification likely increased Kohl's willingness to cooperate with Delors on the EMU project.

There was also likely a desire on Kohl's part to reassure his European allies that a unified Germany would continue to pursue European integration. However, Kohl's key commitment to the EMU occurred in 1989 prior to the fall of the Berlin Wall.

In the face of mixed pressures from within Germany, Kohl sought to satisfy the Bundestag and public opinion on political integration matters and went far during the Maastricht Treaty negotiations toward meeting the concerns of Delors and the leaders of France, Italy, and a number of the other member states on the EMU. However, to mollify his domestic critics, principally the Bundesbank, he also labored successfully to achieve the location of the European Central Bank in Frankfurt, Germany; the modeling of that Bank (including considerable autonomy for it) on the German Bundesbank; and the adoption of stringent convergence criteria (and a later stability pact) that required member states that wished to be eligible to join the "euro zone" to adopt anti-inflationary approaches similar to those of Kohl's Germany.

Although the Bundesbank continued to complain about Kohl's compromises, and many on the political Left throughout Europe criticized the EMU monetary approach as too restrictive and responsible for high unemployment, Kohl's ability to balance domestic demands with international pressures demonstrated considerable leadership skills. Kohl was later to lose the 1998 elections and then see his reputation badly tarnished by his refusal to reveal the names of illegal campaign contributors to his party. Nevertheless, his significant roles in establishing the European Economic and Monetary Union have left an important legacy.[19]

on Iraq and European agriculture during 2002 and 2003, suggesting a continuation of their past alliance. Germany's long inclination toward Atlanticism, however, waned noticeably under the Schröder government, most notably over the issue of the Iraq War, which pitted Germany against the United States to an extent never previously seen during the history of the German Federal Republic. German public opinion and electoral considerations played important parts in this shift away from Atlanticism, particularly because Chancellor Schröder appealed openly to antiwar sentiment in Germany to win a narrow reelection battle in September 2002, though it remains to be seen whether the rancor during 2002 and 2003 between Chancellor Schröder and President Bush over Iraq will translate into a long-term gap between German and American governmental definitions of their national interests.[20]

DISTINCTIVE FEATURES OF THE GERMAN APPROACHES TO THE EC/EU

A number of themes recur frequently in German approaches to the EC/EU. Despite variations over time that are evident from the preceding chronological narrative, German approaches have shown more long-term consistency than have the French approaches. The distinctive German outlooks and actions have been built on foundations laid in the post–World War II era.

In contrast to France and Britain, West Germany after World War II was seeking to escape its history, particularly that of the Third Reich. West Germany's military occupation by the Allies and lack of full sovereignty even after the establishment of the Federal Republic also conditioned its outlook on European integration in ways quite different from France or the United Kingdom. Furthermore, West Germany's geopolitical position on the front lines of

the Cold War, bordering Soviet-occupied East Germany, made it particularly dependent on the United States. Meanwhile, with France as its immediate Western neighbor—a country with which it had fought three wars in less than a century—there were considerable incentives to apply the lessons of the past and seek Franco-German rapprochement.

Reactions against Nazi totalitarianism and widespread desire to revive German federal traditions, as well as American pressures to establish a structure of checks and balances, molded West German state institutions that would continue to be far more decentralized than their French or British counterparts. In this respect, too, there would be continuing long-term consequences for German approaches to the EC/EU.

Economically devastated at the end of World War II, West Germany came to embrace a social market economy that won wide and enduring support across the domestic political spectrum as the economic miracle took shape. This free-market capitalism with a large welfare state stood between the usual American (and to some extent, British) brand of free-market capitalism and the French *dirigiste* approach. Furthermore, the booming West German economy developed distinctive trading patterns that linked it not just to the other five nation-states that were to be at the core of the EC/EU but also to advanced economies elsewhere in Europe and the world. Again, the pattern distinguished it somewhat from Britain (with its American and Commonwealth ties) and France (which possessed links to its former Empire but also displayed less engagement than Germany or Britain in general global trade).

All of these factors helped to shape distinctive German approaches to the EC/EU. Though memories of Hitler's Third Reich dimmed somewhat with the passage of time, and the dependence on the United States lessened markedly with the end of the Cold War and the reunification of Germany, there has been more continuity than change in basic German orientations toward the European Union.[21] Major features of German approaches to the EC/EU include the following:

An Atlanticist inclination, now waning. A near obsession with Atlanticism at the height of the Cold War, when West German governments assigned very high priority to maintaining American engagement in Europe, this approach gradually became over time an inclination, albeit a fairly pronounced one. At some points, most notably in the Adenauer-Erhard conflicts of the 1950s and 1960s, intense internal debates have erupted over the extent of German Atlanticism. In the long term, Germany has generally positioned itself between the French wariness of Atlanticism and the British embrace of a strong Atlanticist preference. Recently, however, the Red-Green German government headed by Chancellor Schröder has moved to a growing wariness of Atlanticism, most notably over issues related to Iraq.[22]

An emphasis on the "alliance within the alliance" with France. This emphasis, pursued most of the time since the days of Adenauer, has imposed limits on Germany's Atlanticist tendencies, most notably during the de Gaulle era but to a lesser degree at other times also. Balancing the two has preoccupied many German chancellors and foreign ministers. Over time, Germany has grown less inclined than in the 1950s to defer to French leadership. Some analysts detect in recent years a German distancing from France and a new German assertiveness. However, fears of arousing European memories of past German aggression continue to restrain German independence. A recent realist analysis has termed Germany's approach inside the EU "cooperative hegemony," operating in close coordination with France.[23]

A supranational inclination. Sometimes termed a European federalist approach, this supranational inclination has often appeared to be a distinct preference in German rhetoric. From the sovereignty-pooling provisions in its Basic Law of 1949 to the calls for a federal EU constitution emanating from Chancellor Schmidt and Foreign Minister Fischer at the dawn of the new millennium, Germany has usually been in the vanguard of the EC/EU member states urging increased European supranational development. Even though German actions have not always matched their words, partly due to frequent lack of coordination among German ministries and state governments, Germany has unquestionably demonstrated a more supranational and less intergovernmental approach than either France or Britain.[24]

An inclination toward global and EC/EU free trade. Reflecting its heavy reliance on industrial exports since the beginning of the postwar economic miracle, Germany has generally supported free trade both within the EC/EU and in EC/EU external trade policies. However, its free-trade preferences have been tempered by German agricultural interest groups' demands for protection and by German ties to France, which has been wary of free trade. As a result, Germany's approaches have been less consistently favorable to free trade than Britain's.[25]

A social market inclination. The German development of a domestic economy based on market-oriented but regulated capitalism, accompanied by codetermination and an extensive welfare state, has shaped German approaches to the EC/EU. Germans have usually been wary of French-style *dirigisme*, believing it too reliant on bureaucratic direction. However, they have also shown little inclination to embrace the American model of free-market capitalism lacking a significant social safety net or workplace democracy. Therefore, in their approaches to the EC/EU, the Germans generally have favored Europe-wide efforts to raise social standards and taxes to German levels.

This tendency has usually been accentuated by Social Democrat–led governments.[26]

A preference for EC/EU enlargement. In contrast to France, which has initially resisted most EC/EU enlargements, Germany has been a consistent advocate of widening and has often acted to convince France to acquiesce. This openness to new members has meshed well with Germany's broad trade ties and ambitions to broaden them further, as well as its sense of historical responsibility to overcome European divisions and foster stability. However, some analysts have suggested that broadening (especially the major eastward expansion) may conflict with Germany's efforts to promote EU deepening. One method to resolve such conflict is to support "differentiated integration" between a core of member states (including Germany) that proceed with deepening while other member states are permitted to integrate less fully than the core. Some German leaders have embraced the differentiated integration approach.[27]

A fragmented approach to formulation and implementation of EC/EU policies. As a result of both the numerous checks and balances embedded in its national governmental institutions and the decentralized federalism established by the Basic Law, Germany's approaches to the EC/EU have tended toward fragmentation. Further fostering this pattern have been the coalition governments and the usual division of partisan control between the Bundestag and Bundesrat and among the state governments. In addition, Germany has lacked the coordinating mechanisms at a high executive level that have characterized French approaches to the EC/EU. German "institutional pluralism," as several analysts have termed it, has contributed to Germany's often sending mixed messages to the EC/EU and accumulating a record of rather frequent noncompliance in the implementation of EC/EU law. However, German institutional pluralism bears some resemblance to that of the European Union itself.[28]

TABLE 8.1 Distinctive Features of German EC/EU Approaches: A Summary

1. An Atlanticist inclination, now waning.
2. An emphasis on the "alliance within the alliance" with France.
3. A supranational inclination.
4. An inclination toward global and EC/EU free trade.
5. A social market inclination.
6. A preference for EC/EU enlargement.
7. A fragmented approach to formulation and implementation of EC/EU policies.

THE IMPACT OF GERMANY ON THE EC/EU

Fragmentation in German formulation of EC/EU initiatives and reticence about appearing overly assertive have constrained the German impact on the EC/EU to some degree. Nevertheless, Germany has long exerted an influence second only to that of France and, since reunification and the end of the Cold War, has shown a growing inclination to take leadership roles, sometimes without coordinating them with France.

In reference to EC/EU institutions, Germany repeatedly has been in the vanguard of the member states that have advocated enhanced powers and direct elections for the European Parliament, enlisting reluctant French support and overcoming British opposition to achieve direct elections in 1979 and parliamentary power increases in increments over time. Germany has also usually taken the lead in winning approval for the increased reliance on qualified majority voting (QMV) in the Council of Ministers of the EC/EU, though its support has not been without exceptions. When distinct German national interests have appeared to be at stake, Germany has at times insisted upon retention of the nation-state veto power. Beyond the current institutions, Germany has also taken the lead in recent years in urging a federal constitution for the EU, as in the initiative of Foreign Minister Fischer and Chancellor Schröder.[29]

Probably the clearest German imprint on EU public policy in recent years has been in the economic and monetary policy realm, particularly concerning the form, location, orientation, and powers of the European Central Bank (ECB) and the convergence criteria and stability pact associated with the Economic and Monetary Union (EMU). The federal structure, Frankfurt location, emphasis on price stability, and autonomy of the ECB reflected heavy German influence during the critical formative stages of the EMU. The result has been a European Central Bank closely modeled on the German Bundesbank. Though the French government was in many respects more enthusiastic about the goal of Economic and Monetary Union than the German government was, the latter not only shaped the new Central Bank but also played the leading role in binding member state governments, through the convergence criteria and subsequent stability pact, to low public debt and deficit levels. An irony of this German accomplishment, however, has been that Germany itself has faced a difficult struggle to remain within the boundaries of the stability pact.[30]

Germany also has played an important role within the EC/EU in the drives for single-market reforms and low external tariffs. During the development and implementation of the Single European Act of 1986, Germany generally sided with Britain to push toward the completion of the single market. In the international trade negotiations of the early 1990s, Chancellor Kohl proved critical in crafting an acceptable compromise between the French and the American governments that fostered a lowering of external EU trade barriers. However, Germany has also sought to insure that free trade and regulatory harmonization do not occur at the expense of high standards or social and envi-

ronmental protections. Moreover, its agricultural policy approach has not reflected its general predilection for free trade.[31]

In the competition-policy sphere, Germany has long been a staunch supporter, at least in its rhetoric, of strict application of the competition provisions of the Rome Treaty and of their reinforcement in the mid-1980s. As the European Commission and European Court of Justice have become increasingly active in curbing state aids to industry, however, the German government has sometimes found itself at odds with these EU institutions. Much of the conflict has centered on the methods employed by the German government in the process of privatizing the formerly public business corporations in East Germany after reunification. Though German leaders have insisted that they continue to favor EU public policies that foster competition, a recent analysis has concluded, "German officials in practice adopted a visibly softer line in Brussels in order to secure favorable outcomes for the eastern region."[32]

The effects of German unification have also had some impact, though a subtle and indirect one, on German leadership in the domain of EC/EU environmental policies. Traditionally, Germany has been in the forefront of European countries that have adopted stringent environmental-protection regulations based upon a "command and control" philosophy and reliance on the "best available technology." Within the EC/EU, Germany usually has taken the lead in seeking to raise EC/EU standards to its own high levels. However, the German Federation of Industry (BDI) and other German business groups have long resisted Germany's moving out in the environmental field in advance of its economic competitors. The high costs of German reunification have combined with German business resistance and new approaches to environmental protection that de-emphasize command and control to weaken German leadership of EU environmental policy-making in recent years. Despite high hopes of environmental groups that the Social Democratic–Green government, in which Green leader Jürgen Trittin served as environment minister, would effectively reassert German leadership in this field, environmentalists have been rather disappointed by the actual record.[33]

In a pattern somewhat similar to that long evident in the environmental field, Germany has also frequently asserted a leadership role concerning EC/EU social policy. Here, however, Germany has often formed an alliance with France, as in the case of the Social Charter and the Social Protocol of the Maastricht Treaty and the Employment Pact of 1999. Moreover, it has been less successful, even with the frequent backing of France, in raising the EC/EU standards to German levels than it has been regarding environmental policies. For example, although Germany was instrumental in gaining EU acceptance of the European Works Council Directive in 1994, this legislation fell far short of providing for German-style codetermination and works councils. The well-organized German labor unions have played an important part in influencing even Christian Democrat–led governments to take the lead on EC/EU social policies. Nonetheless, the impact has been weakened due to strong counterpressures from international business, Britain, and the relatively poor member states of the EU that fear German standards would undermine employment in their countries.[34]

The Common Agricultural Policy (CAP) from its inception reflected the primacy of French influences. Yet Germany, too, played a significant role in shaping the original CAP and influencing its evolution over the years. That role, centered on goals of maintaining high prices for its relatively inefficient farmers and support for its predominantly small-scale agriculture, has been shaped primarily by the agriculture ministry and the League of German Farmers (DBV). Since unification added the substantial (and rather distinctive) agricultural interests of East Germany to the German mix,

the Eastern state governments have also played important parts in shaping German stances on EU agricultural matters. Not surprisingly, the fragmentation of German approaches to the EC/EU and the inefficiency of German agriculture have led to agricultural approaches at odds with the market-oriented German positions that have usually been evident on trade and competition matters and with German desires to keep EC/EU budgets under control (because Germany is the largest net contributor to these budgets). Chancellor Schröder's Socialist-Green government, less dependent on farmers' electoral support than any of its predecessors, has sought to reconcile German calls for EU budget retrenchment with German agricultural policies by proposing (with European Commission backing but without the support of its own agriculture minister) the adoption of a "co-financing" scheme. Under this proposal, national governments would be responsible for any additional farm support once a certain EU threshold has been reached. However, the French government has thus far fought a successful battle against this German/EU Commission effort.[35]

Perhaps the most notable negative influences by the German government on EC/EU public-policy initiatives by others has been in the area of the structural funds, of which the European Regional Development Fund (ERDF) has been the largest component. Back in the early 1970s, when the regional fund was first established, West Germany had blocked proposals for a large fund, in opposition to the strenuous efforts of Britain, Italy, and the European Commission. As the structural funds budget subsequently expanded, Germany's was a consistent voice for restraint. Since Germany was the largest net contributor to the EC/EU and the structural funds represented a growing proportion of that budget, the German position was clearly rooted in its perceived national economic interests. However, following reunification, the East German state governments pressed insistently for EU regional development aid on a scale equivalent to that given to Portugal and Greece, the poorest member states of the EU. Not only did German demands for such funding create considerable ill will among poor member states that had long suffered German lectures on the need to control structural fund expenditures, but the funding provided by the EU to East Germany also came at the expense of some EU aid to West German states and complicated the coordination of Germany's own regional-development plans. Although the long-term German influence in the EU regional-policy domain has long been primarily a restraining one, the picture has become increasingly complex in recent years.[36]

In the domain of justice and home affairs policies, Germany has been more supportive than France or Britain of Europe-wide approaches to border control and immigration issues. It was one of five signatories (with France) of the original Schengen Agreement on opening border crossings, an early proponent of Europol, and an advocate of full integration of justice and home affairs into the first pillar rather than separation of much of this policy domain into the intergovernmental third pillar.[37]

It has been in the area of foreign and defense policy that Germany has probably been most reticent about asserting leadership. Traditionally, it has sought to maintain its transatlantic ties to the United States and the North Atlantic Treaty Organization while at the same time sustaining its special relationship to France and its commitment to a European focus. The terms "European Security and Defense Identity" (ESDI) and "Common European Security and Defense Policy" (CESDP) have come into usage only since the late 1990s, but the concept behind them dates back at least to the abortive European Defense Community (EDC), which West Germany supported, albeit reluctantly, in the early 1950s. Though Germany has allowed Britain and France to take the lead since the late

1990s in laying plans for a Rapid Reaction Force and a broadened European security and defense policy, it has offered quick endorsement. In fact, recent progress toward common EU defense efforts has resulted from Britain's shifting away from its previous view that an EU approach would threaten NATO and France's movement away from its previous position that an ESDI could not be constructed within the Atlantic Alliance. Both countries for a time in the late 1990s came to occupy a position close to that long held by Germany: both European and Atlanticist simultaneously. Therefore, despite the lack of overt German leadership in this domain, Germany's basic position came to be emulated by the key players.

The conflict over Iraq in 2002 and 2003, and the emergence of what many Europeans viewed as a general stance of aggressive unilateralism in global affairs by the Bush administration, however, has disrupted the growing intra-EU harmony. Germany joined France in opposition to Britain and the United States over the initiation and conduct of the Iraq War. As noted previously, internal political considerations by Chancellor Schröder (particularly those related to his reelection effort) played a part in shaping the German position on Iraq. Nonetheless, the continuing popularity of that position inside Germany, the reinforcement from France, and the overt hostility of the Bush administration to the Schröder government have operated to weaken traditional German ties to the United States. A side effect has been that the dissension inside the European Union evident over the Iraq issue and Atlanticism in general (pitting Germany and France against Britain and Italy, with Spain shifting first toward the latter and then the former side) has made progress toward a coherent ESDI more difficult than it appeared to be in 2000 or 2001.[38]

For reasons noted previously, Germany has not exercised overt leadership in formulating EC/EU policies as often as has France. Nevertheless, its position over many years as the member state with the largest population and economy in the European Union (by a significant margin since reunification) has enabled it to exercise at least measurable influence in virtually all major European policy domains.

THE IMPACT OF THE EC/EU ON GERMAN POLITICS

Perhaps more than any other member nation-state, the Federal Republic of Germany has been shaped fundamentally by its membership in the organization now called the European Union. Joining the ECSC and then the EC solidified its links to the West and its commitment to constitutional democracy. Assurances in 1990 by Chancellor Kohl that a reunited Germany would be a Europeanized Germany were credible because of West Germany's long record within the European Community—and these credible assurances persuaded the Soviet Union (and Britain and France) to permit a reunification that otherwise would have been unlikely to take the form that it did.[39] Beyond these broad considerations, however, Europeanization has also shaped many of the particular features of contemporary German governmental institutions, participatory processes, and public policies.

The Constitution

As noted on the first page of this chapter, the Basic Law of 1949, the constitution of the Federal Republic of Germany, made a provision for the possible pooling of sovereignty at a supranational level. Nevertheless, there have been several major constitutional amendments required to adjust the German Basic Law to the European Union. For example, the revised Article 23 of the Basic Law permits the transfer of sovereignty specifically to the EU, but only with the agreement of the Bundesrat. Other amendments provide for a Bundestag committee for EU affairs, a European Chamber to be created

by the Bundesrat, and some of the powers of the German Bundesbank to be transferred to the European Central Bank.

Governmental Institutions

Significant roles for the German Constitutional Court and the judiciary in general predate German EC/EU membership. However, the Constitutional Court has become a major arena for resolving conflicting interpretations of the powers of the German states, the federal government, and European institutions. As early as 1952, West German opponents of the European Defense Community sought (unsuccessfully) to block it in the Constitutional Court. In 1974, the Constitutional Court held that, in cases where a conflict between German and EC law existed, the Constitutional Court would determine the limits on the supremacy of EC law. Against this backdrop came the landmark 1993 case involving a challenge to the constitutionality of the adoption of the Maastricht Treaty under the German Basic Law. In this case, the Court upheld the German agreement to the Treaty but ruled that future sovereignty transfers required specific Bundestag approval and must be in accord with the democratic rights and principles guaranteed by the German Basic Law. In 1998, the Constitutional Court rejected a case challenging German adoption of the euro currency.[40] Beyond the Constitutional Court, of course, the regular German judiciary has played an important role in adjudicating European Union laws in Germany—a pattern broadly similar to that of judges in other EU member states. However, recent analysis has shown that, compared with the judiciaries in France and Britain, "German courts are the most active participants in the European judicial dialogue.... German society has long been prepared to seize the opportunities of Europeanization through judicial forums."[41]

Virtually all analysts concur that the German parliamentary chambers, both the Bundestag and the Bundesrat, have come to play a larger role in EU policy formulation and implementation than any other legislative bodies in EU member states, except for Denmark's. However, exercising more powers on EU matters than most other national legislative bodies has not meant that European integration has enhanced their powers. Writing in 1987, Simon Bulmer and William Paterson concluded that EC membership "clearly involved a loss of powers for the legislature." That probably remains true, although reforms of 1991–1992 both codified in the Basic Law the two chambers' rights to information and created a new, potentially powerful, Bundestag Standing Committee on European Union Affairs.[42]

Within the German executive, some analysts have argued that the fragmented institutional pluralism characteristic of German policy-making vis-à-vis Europe may have given an advantage to the chancellor, "who alone can impose a sense of political direction on the myriad of conflicting bureaucratic and policy rivalries."[43] However, even Adenauer, the most powerful chancellor of the Federal Republic, found that European issues fractured his Christian Democratic Union and became entwined in power and policy struggles with such intraparty rivals as Erhard and his ministerial allies.[44] The extent to which the chancellor has been able to play a coordinating role has generally been quite limited. The chief constraints on chancellors have come from the agriculture, economics, finance, and foreign ministries, often complicated further by the usual need to hold together a coalition government and contend with intraparty ministerial rivals.[45]

The state governments have also placed major constraints on the chancellors' abilities to lead on European (as on other) issues. The Federal Republic's style of cooperative federalism dates from before the EC/EU and has constituted a much more decentralized system than in any of the other major nation-states in Western Europe. Over the first several decades of the EC, Europeanization appeared to erode the powers of the German states, as the German national government often transferred not only its own powers but also those of the state governments to the European level. However, in the wake of the acceleration of European integration after the mid-1980s, the German states asserted themselves effectively to obtain increases in their powers during both the formulation and implementation of EU policies.

The enhancement of the German state governments' powers in European policy-making has been most evident in the following areas: 1) Utilizing their roles institutionalized in the Bundesrat, the states have been able to convince the federal government to push for recognition of **subsidiarity** and the establishment of the Committee of the Regions by the EU. 2) The state governments have also gained a major revision of Article 23 of the Basic Law, including veto power for the Bundesrat over EU treaties and a prohibition on Basic Law amendments that would alter Germany's federal structure. 3) Furthermore, the German states have become active in lobbying in Brussels, often bypassing the German federal government, and have sought to mobilize regional governments in other member nation-states of the EU. Therefore, although the effects of European integration at first seemed to diminish the powers of the German states, they have since the early 1990s galvanized the states to revitalize German cooperative federalism and to utilize their powers more effectively than previously in the European arena.[46]

Elections, Political Parties, and Interest Groups

Germany has no provisions for national referendums, and its participation in European integration has had no noticeable effects on its domestic electoral laws or processes. As in other EC/EU member states, national issues have intruded upon elections to the European Parliament far more than European issues have shaped elections to the national legislature. Moreover, EC/EU issues have only occasionally since the mid-1950s been at the center of ideological or image differences between the two major German parties, the Social Democrats (SPD) and the Christian Democrats (CDU), both of which have been broadly committed to further European integration. Somewhat more frequently, European issues have played significant roles in intraparty conflicts within these parties. As in France in recent years, most Euroskepticism at leadership levels has emerged in small parties on the left and the right, rather than in the major parties at the center of the political spectrum. The far-right Republicans and others and the far-left former Communists of the Party of Democratic Socialism (PDS) have been most critical of the European Union in its present form but have also been completely excluded from positions of influence in the German federal government.[47]

Since its inception after World War II, the Christian Democratic Union (CDU), the dominant partner in most governments of the Federal Republic, has consistently played a leading role in promoting European integration. The distinctive features of the German approaches to the EC/EU were originally crafted primarily by CDU leaders, though often modified to reflect the wishes of their sister party, the Christian Social Union (CSU) of Bavaria, and their frequent liberal/libertarian coalition ally, the Free Democratic Party (FDP). The most serious internal CDU rift linked to European stances occurred in the late 1950s and early 1960s, when the Atlanticist faction led by Ludwig Erhard and Gerhard Schröder (no relation to the subsequent SPD chancellor) battled Konrad Adenauer's faction, which assigned priority to the Franco-German special relationship. The CSU leader of the time, Franz Josef Strauss, joined in the fray on Adenauer's side. After the 1960s, however, this intraparty CDU (and CSU) conflict subsided, though Strauss and the CSU sometimes staked out positions more critical of the central European institutions than the CDU would endorse.[48]

When Edmund Stoiber in 1992 became the CSU minister-president of Bavaria, he articulated positions that many observers have described as Euroskeptical. The CSU has usually been positioned toward the right of the German political spectrum, seeing itself and being portrayed as more conservative than the CDU. Thus, its relatively Euroskeptical stances since the early 1990s have comported well with the common European phenomenon of a rising Euroskeptical tendency as one moves from the center-right to the right of the spectrum. However, in the case of the Bavarian CSU, its positions have also been related to its reliance on the support of Bavarian agricultural interests that have been displeased over changes in the Common Agricultural Policy and to the efforts of Stoiber and Max Streibl, his predecessor, to use European issues as a lever for enhancing state powers in the German federal system.[49]

The small, centrist liberal/libertarian Free Democratic Party has generally been more free-trade-oriented than the CDU-CSU or the SPD. That outlook played a part in its preference in the 1950s for a broad free-trade area rather than the European Economic Community (EEC) and its votes in parliament against the EEC in 1957. However, in recent years, the party—an active participant in most CDU-led governments and in SPD-led governments during 1969–1982—has been a strong proponent of the mainstream German elite consensus on European integration.[50]

That consensus has also encompassed the leadership of the Social Democratic Party (SPD) since the mid-1950s. In the first years of the Federal Republic, the SPD opposed both the European Coal and Steel Community and the European Defense Community, clearly differentiating itself from its Christian Democratic rivals. A major part of its original objections, that West German integration with Western Europe would impede reunification, waned as reunification became only a distant goal. Perhaps more significantly, the SPD chose new moderate leaders, who wished to reposition the party closer than previously to the center of the German political spectrum. Taking pro-European integration stances almost indistinguishable from those of the Christian Democrats was a component of this repositioning endeavor, along with abandonment of Marxism, that eventually brought the Social Democrats into a Grand Coalition with the CDU-CSU in 1966. Since then, the two major parties have both championed similar approaches to European integration, though the Social Democrats have been more active than the CDU in promoting a "social" agenda.

Early in the Social Democratic–Green coalition government headed by Gerhard Schröder (1998–), European issues appeared to be about to lead to a major conflict within the SPD and to cause major internal problems for its Green coalition ally. As noted in the historical overview earlier in this chapter, the finance minister and SPD leader, Oskar Lafontaine, initially sought to pursue a European effort to provide economic stimulus that put him at odds with the chancellor (and most of the German financial and business community). However, Lafontaine abruptly resigned as both minister and party leader, avoiding what might have become a long-term intraparty rift. The Green party, on the other hand, has been fairly regularly divided since it entered the Red-Green coalition government between its pragmatic top leaders and their supporters and numerous party activists who have insisted upon a democratized, decentralized, and ecologically sensitive EU and who reject German military commitments abroad.[51]

As in France and the other EC/EU member states, the major German parties have joined transnational European party federations. However, as has generally been the case in most countries, they continue to define themselves primarily in national terms and to take distinctive national positions that differentiate them from compatriots in other nation-states.

A similar pattern has been evident for German interest groups. What has perhaps been most distinctive about German interest groups' involvement in European policy-making has been the extent to which groups beyond large business corporations, trade associations, and business peak associations have shaped German (and EU) positions on some matters. Agricultural groups, primarily the League of German Farmers, have long influenced the German government and the EC/EU on farming issues, though their influence appears to have declined recently. Trade unions have had some success in influencing German positions on EU social issues even under Christian Democrat–led governments (and somewhat less success in obtaining desired EC/EU outcomes). German environmental groups, too, have enjoyed some successes on environmental policy matters. Nevertheless, the recent changes in the Common Agricultural Policy, the vagueness of most EU social standards, and the frustrations of German environmental groups over the record of even the Red-Green coalition government indicate the limits on the effectiveness of nonbusiness groups when they challenge positions backed by large business corporations and their interest groups. There seems little reason to question Peter Katzenstein's conclusions: "Business, not labor, has become the international actor par excellence."[52] However, the institutional pluralism of the German policy-making process vis-à-vis Europe has probably given not just organized labor but also agricultural and environmental groups, and certainly state governments, more opportunities to affect EU policies than has been true in France and many other member states.[53]

"Business, not labor, has become the international actor par excellence."

Peter Katzenstein, *Tamed Power (1997)*, 39.

Public Policies

German public-policy preferences have usually meshed fairly well with EC/EU public-policy outcomes (partly due to German influence but also partly due to German preferences that have generally been situated closer than French preferences to those of many other member states and of EU officials). As a result, Europeanization has probably had a less disruptive impact on German public policies and society than on their French counterparts. Nevertheless, the effects of EC/EU membership on German public policies have been significant.

Sometimes even European public policies shaped extensively by German influence have had impacts on German public policy that have subsequently caused domestic political difficulties and stimulated German governmental resistance and efforts to shift EU policies. A good illustration lies in the economic and monetary policy domain.

During the European negotiations both before and after the signing of the Maastricht Treaty, the government headed by Chancellor Kohl, under intense pressure from the Bundesbank and private German financial and business interests, insisted first upon strict **convergence criteria** (i.e., government deficits of less than 3 percentof GDP, debts of less than 60 percent of GDP, inflation rates within 1.5 percent of the figure for the least inflationary member) and next upon a long-term stability pact imposing a procedure for punishment of Economic and Monetary Union (EMU) members that ran up excessive deficits or debts. As noted previously, the Kohl government also sought and achieved a relatively autonomous European Central Bank, insulated to a considerable degree from political pressures by member state governments. It was ironic that Germany itself under Kohl experienced great difficulty in achieving the debt goal in the convergence criteria and sought to use "creative accounting" methods (revaluing the Bundesbank's gold reserves) in

order to do so. The Bundesbank successfully resisted the revaluation effort. Therefore, the Kohl government felt compelled to impose welfare cuts and defer promised tax reductions to achieve the debt target upon which it had insisted.

The Kohl government's unexpected policy difficulties gave way in 1998 to major resistance and challenge to the conservative stability pact and European Central Bank from the new German Social Democratic–Green government, and particularly from its finance minister, Osker Lafontaine. Lafontaine and his allies strongly believed that the German-crafted EMU policy instruments severely handicapped governmental efforts in Germany and elsewhere to reduce high unemployment. Though Lafontaine soon resigned in frustration, the Red-Green government continued to chafe in the "straitjacket" of the stability pact. By early 2002, the German government, feeling constrained in its ability to stimulate a still-sluggish economy and unable to restrain spending increases by the 16 German state governments, was approaching dangerously close to the 3 percent of GDP deficit limit; soon it surpassed it. Therefore, Germany faced the embarrassing possibility of being the recipient of a warning and perhaps ultimately even a fine from the European Commission under a system that Germany had designed. Defending his government's deficit spending of more than 3 percent of GDP in both 2003 and 2004, and urging modification of the pact upon which Germany had insisted, Chancellor Schröder declared in July 2003 that, "in some circumstances, such as now, it is necessary to take measures to stimulate growth…. We must pay attention to the stability and growth pact, but we must not dogmatize it"—to which Wim Duisenberg, president of the European Central Bank (originally selected with strong German backing), replied, "A strong commitment to the stability and growth pact would make a major contribution to improving confidence." This example appears to many to illustrate the points made by the historical institutionalist analyses discussed in Chapter One.[54]

> #### Schröder versus Duisenberg on Germany's Failure to Keep its Budget Deficit Less than 3 Percent of its GDP, as Required by the European Stability and Growth Pact:
>
> "...in some circumstances, such as now, it is necessary to take measures to stimulate growth.... We must pay attention to the stability and growth pact, but we must not dogmatize it."
>
> Chancellor Gerhard Schröder, *in the Financial Times (July 16, 2003), 2.*

> "A strong commitment to the stability and growth pact would make a major contribution to improving confidence."
>
> European Central Bank President Wim Duisenberg, *in the Financial Times (July 16, 2003), 2.*

CONCLUSIONS

European integration has profoundly influenced the nature and standing of the Federal Republic of Germany—linking it firmly to France, its erstwhile enemy, and to Western Europe in general and providing it with an arena within which it could reunite and flourish politically, economically, and socially. If a Europeanized Germany has been a tamed power, it has nonetheless been a democratic and prosperous one by comparison both with its own past and with other nation-states.

Despite Europeanization, Germany retains its own collective historical memories. Partly as a result, it has developed its institutions and participatory processes in ways that emphasize more fragmentation and decentralization of authority than in most European nation-states. These have in turn affected its approaches to the European Union.

Although Germany's influence on Europe has not drastically risen or taken new forms since

unification as some observers (especially realists) once predicted, it has extended to virtually all European institutions and policy domains. Moreover, Germany appears almost certain to play a decisive role in shaping the European Union's next great challenge: the expansion to the East, where Germans unquestionably exert more influence than any of their EU partners. The future of Germany in an expanding European Union promises to be an interesting one.

SUMMARY

- From its inception in 1949, the Federal Republic of Germany has been in the forefront of the movement toward European integration, generally demonstrating a greater willingness than France or the United Kingdom to pool sovereignty and to compromise on issues of national interest.

- Chancellor Konrad Adenauer (1949–1963) viewed the European Coal and Steel Community and European integration in general as a means of linking West Germany to France and the West and of "escaping into Europe."

- Ludwig Erhard as chancellor was more oriented toward free trade and the United States than Adenauer had been, and these orientations affected German policies toward the EC during his chancellorship (1963–1966); German governments were weak and fragmented under both Erhard and Kurt Kiesinger (1966–1969), providing little leadership in the EC.

- The EC partnership with France was revitalized under both Willy Brandt (1969–1974) and Helmut Schmidt (1974–1982); Brandt was best known for his efforts to improve relations with East Germany and the USSR, Schmidt for his close ties to French President Giscard d'Estaing.

- Chancellor Helmut Kohl (1982–1998) reunified Germany and took leading roles in shaping the Single European Act, the Maastricht Treaty, and the Economic and Monetary Union.

- Chancellor Gerhard Schröder shared leadership on EU issues with Foreign Minister Joschka Fischer, renewed ties with France that had appeared to be weakening, and shifted away from Atlanticism, most notably over issues concerning Iraq.

- Major long-term features of German approaches to the EC/EU have been: an Atlanticist inclination, now waning; an emphasis on close ties with France; a supranational inclination; an inclination toward global and EC/EU free trade; a social market inclination; a preference for EC/EU enlargement; and a fragmented approach to formulation and implementation of EC/EU policies.

- Fragmentation in German formulation of EC/EU initiatives and reticence about appearing overly assertive have somewhat constrained the German impact on the EC/EU.

- German impact on the EC/EU has usually been to promote supranational development, notably for strengthening the European Parliament and reducing the opportunities for national vetoes.

- Germany has heavily influenced EC/EU economic and monetary policies, single-market reforms and low external tariffs, and environmental policies.

- Germany has rarely taken the lead on EC/EU foreign and defense policies.

- The German Basic Law of 1949 made provision for possible pooling of sovereignty, but several constitutional amendments have been required to adjust the Basic Law to the European Union.

- German courts have been highly active participants in shaping European Union law.

- German parliamentary involvement in EU policy formulation and implementation has been greater than in most EU member states, but EC/EU membership has probably advantaged executive over parliamentary institutions in Germany, as in most of the EC/EU.

- State governments, parliament, and different ministries have generally constrained chancellors' abilities to dominate German policies concerning the EC/EU more so than comparable institutions have constrained French presidents' EC/EU policies.

- Both major political parties, the Social Democrats and the Christian Democrats, have in recent decades supported most European integration (though the Social Democrats initially opposed the ECSC and the EDC back in the 1950s); sharp criticism of the European Union has largely remained confined to isolated parties on the far right (Republicans) and the far left (Party of Democratic Socialism).

- Euroskepticism has been much less characteristic of German public opinion, parties, and interest groups than in France or Britain.

- One of the greatest embarrassments for the Schröder government has been its continuing inability to produce a German governmental budget that keeps the annual deficit below the 3 percent of GDP mandated by the stability and growth pact upon which the German government had previously insisted.

ENDNOTES

1. The quotation is from Robert Kagan, *Of Paradise and Power: America and Europe in the New World Order* (New York: Alfred A. Knopf, 2003), 56. Simon Bulmer and William Paterson, "Ger-

many in the European Union: Gentle Giant or Emergent Leader?" *International Affairs* 72, 1 (January 1996), 9–32; Peter Katzenstein, ed., *Tamed Power: Germany in Europe* (Ithaca, NY: Cornell University Press, 1997).

2. F. Roy Willis, *France, Germany, and the New Europe, 1945–1967*, revised ed. (Stanford, CA: Stanford University Press, 1968), 104–105; Simon Bulmer and William Paterson, *The Federal Republic of Germany and the European Community* (London: Allen & Unwin, 1987), 5–6.

3. Willis, *France, Germany, and the New Europe*, 104, employs the "escape into Europe" phrase.

4. Charles Williams, *Adenauer: The Father of the New Germany* (New York: Wiley, 2000), 372–374.

5. Bulmer and Paterson, *The FRG and the EC*, 6–7; Willis, *France, Germany, and the New Europe*, Chs. 5 and 6; Karl Deutsch and Lewis Edinger, *Germany Rejoins the Powers* (Stanford, CA: Stanford University Press, 1959), Chs. 11 and 12; Richard Moeller, "The German Social Democrats," in John Gaffney, ed., *Political Parties and the European Union* (London: Routledge, 1996), 34–36.

6. Williams, *Adenauer,* 418–423; Willis, *France, Germany, and the New Europe,* 185–197.

7. Willis, *France, Germany, and the New Europe,* 265–272; Andrew Moravcsik, *The Choice for Europe* (Ithaca, NY: Cornell University Press, 1998), 90–103; Moeller, "The German Social Democrats," 36–37; Paterson, "The Christian Democrats," 54.

8. Williams, *Adenauer,* 503–523; Willis, *France, Germany, and the New Europe,* 312–318; Bulmer and Paterson, *The FRG and the EC,* 225–226.

9. Willis, *France, Germany, and the New Europe,* 318–365; Paterson, "The German Christian Democrats," 55.

10. Simonian, *The Privileged Partnership,* Chs. 4–8.

11. Simonian, *The Privileged Partnership,* Ch. 10; Moravcsik, *The Choice for Europe,* 244–259; Bulmer and Paterson, *The FRG and the EC,* 226–228.

12. Cole, *Franco-German Relations,* 17.

13. Cole, *Franco-German Relations,* 106.

14. Clay Clemens, "Introduction: Assessing the Kohl Legacy," in Clay Clemens and William Paterson, eds., *The Kohl Chancellorship* (Portland, OR: Frank Cass, 1998), 1–5; Alistair Cole, "Political Leadership in Western Europe: Helmut Kohl in Comparative Context," Clemens and Paterson, eds., *The Kohl Chancellorship,* esp. 122–124; Moravcsik, *The Choice for Europe,* 348–349.

15. Moravcsik, *The Choice for Europe,* Ch. 15; Cole, *Franco-German Relations,* 62–64, 73–75.

16. Joseph Grieco, "The Maastricht Treaty, Economic and Monetary Union, and the Neo-Realist Research Programme," *Review of International Studies* 21 (1995), 21–40; Thomas Pederson, *Germany, France, and the Integration of Europe: A Realist Interpretation* (London: Pinter, 1998), Ch. 8; Moravcsik, *The Choice for Europe,* Ch. 6.

17. Pederson, *Germany, France, and the Integration of Europe,* 176–177 on the Constitutional Court challenge; Jeffrey Anderson, *German Unification and the Union of Europe* (Cambridge: Cambridge University Press, 1999), 46–50; "Back to Basics," *The Economist* 356 (July 22, 2000), 48–49.

18. Anderson, *German Unification and the Union of Europe,* esp. Ch. 2; William Paterson, "From the Bonn to the Berlin Republic," *German Politics* 9, 1 (January 2000), 32–33; Simon Bulmer, Charlie Jeffrey, and William Paterson, *Germany's European Diplomacy: Shaping the Regional Milieu* (Manchester: Manchester University Press, 1999), esp. 3.

19. Moravcsik, *The Choice for Europe,* Ch. 6; Lawrence B. Lindsey, *Economic Puppetmasters: Lessons from the Halls of Power* (Washington, DC: AEI Press, 1999), 97–130.

20. Cole, *Franco-German Relations,* 128–144; Oskar Lafontaine, *The Heart Beats on the Left,* trans. by Ronald Taylor (Malden, MA: Blackwell, 2000); "Divorce after All These Years?" *The Economist* 358 (January 27, 2001), 49–50; "Nice Uncle Gerhard and the Little 'Uns," *The Economist* 358 (February 3, 2001), 50; Edmund Andrews, "Germans Offer Plan to Remake Europe Union," *New York Times,* May 1, 2001, A1 and A3; Suzanne Daley, "French Premier Opposes German Plan for Europe," *New York Times,* May 29, 2001, A6; Rainer Baumann, "The Transformation of

German Multilateralism: Changes in the Foreign Policy Discourse Since Unification," *German Politics and Society* 20, 4 (Winter 2002), 1–26; James Sloam, "'Responsibility for Europe': The EU Policy of the German Social Democrats Since Unification," *German Politics* 12, 1 (April 2003), 59–78.

21. Bulmer and Paterson, "Germany in the EU," 9–32.

22. Cole, *Franco-German Relations*, 17–18, 45, 108, 116–120; Simonian, *The Privileged Partnership*, esp. 10–12, 363–364; Josef Joffe, "No Threats, No Temptations: German Grand Strategy after the Cold War," in Bertel Heurlin, ed., *Germany in Europe in the Nineties* (London: Macmillan,1996), 259–272.

23. Pederson, *Germany, France, and the Integration of Europe* offers the "cooperative hegemony" interpretation. Also see various perspectives in David P. Calleo and Eric Staal, eds., *Europe's Franco-German Engine* (Washington, DC: Brookings, 1998).

24. François Heisbourg, "French and German Approaches to Organizing Europe's Future Security and Defense: A French Perspective," in Calleo and Staal, eds., *Europe's Franco-German Engine*, 51; Cole, *Franco-German Relations*, 65; Simonian, *The Privileged Partnership*, 32–45; Bulmer and Paterson, *The FRG and the EC*, 79–83.

25. Cole, *Franco-German Relations*, 71–73; Bulmer and Paterson, *The FRG and the EC*, 44–53; Simonian, *The Privileged Partnership*, 16–32.

26. Cole, *Franco-German Relations*, 43, 45, 83–84, 128–144; Carl Lankowski, "Germany: A Major Player," in Eleanor Zeff and Ellen Pirro, eds., *The European Union and its Member States* (Boulder, CO: Lynne Rienner, 2001), 95–100; Jeffrey Anderson, *German Unification and the Union of Europe*, 8–15.

27. Adrian Hyde-Price, *Germany and European Order: Enlarging NATO and the EU* (Manchester: Manchester University Press, 2000), Ch. 7; Henning Tewes, "Between Deepening and Widening: Role Conflict in Germany's Enlargement Policy," *West European Politics* 21, 2 (April 1998), 117–133; Barbara Lippert, et al., *British and German Interests in EU Enlargement: Conflict and Cooperation* (London: Continuum, 2001).

28. Simon Bulmer, Andreas Maurer, and William Paterson, "The European Policy-Making Machinery in the Berlin Republic: Hindrance or Handmaiden?" *German Politics* 10, 1 (April 2001), 177–206; Charlie Jeffery, "Towards a 'Third Level' in Europe? The German Länder in the European Union," *Political Studies* 44, 2 (June 1996), 253–266; Cole, *Franco-German Relations*, 38-41; Simonian, *The Privileged Partnership*, Ch. 3.

29. "Nice Uncle Gerhard," *The Economist* 358 (February 3, 2001), 50; Andrew Moravcsik and Kalypso Nicolaïdis, "Explaining the Treaty of Amsterdam: Interests, Influence, Institutions," *Journal of Common Market Studies* 37, 1 (March 1999), 59–85; Moravcsik, *The Choice for Europe*, Ch. 5; Dinan, *Ever Closer Union*, 84–85.

30. Anderson, *German Unification and the Union of Europe*, 46–50; Moravcsik, *The Choice for Europe*, esp. 387–404, 461–467; Cole, *Franco-German Relations*, 133–135; "Could the Euro's Nuclear Option Ever Be Used?" *The Economist* 362 (February 2, 2002), 47–48.

31. Anderson, *German Unification and the Union of Europe*, Ch. 3; Moravcsik, *The Choice for Europe*, 329–332.

32. The quotation is from Anderson, *German Unification and the Union of Europe*, 151. Also see Carl Lankowski, "Germany: A Major Player," in Eleanor E. Zeff and Ellen B. Pirro, eds., *The EU and the Member States* (Boulder, CO: Lynne Rienner, 2001), 94–95, and Francis McGowan, "Competition Policy: The Limits of the European Regulatory State," in Helen Wallace and William Wallace, eds., *Policy-Making in the European Union*, 4th ed. (Oxford: Oxford University Press, 2000), 139–140.

33. Rüdiger Wurzel, "Flying into Unexpected Turbulence: The German EU Presidency in the Environmental Field," *German Politics* 9, 3 (December 2000), 23–42; Alberta Sbragia, "Environmental Policy: Economic Constraints and External Pressures," in Wallace and Wallace, eds., *Policy-Making in the European Union*, Ch. 11; Anderson, *German Unification and the Union of Europe*, 83–95.

34. Martin Rhodes, "An Awkward Alliance: France, Germany and Social Policy," in Douglas Webber, ed., *The Franco-German Relationship in the European Union* (London: Routledge, 1999), 130–147; Cole, *Franco-German Relations*, 136–138.

35. Anderson, *German Unification and the Union of Europe*, 172–189; Cole, *Franco-German Relations*, 139–143; Douglas Webber, "Agricultural Policy: The Hard Core," in Webber, ed., *The Franco-German Relationship in the European Union*, 111–129.

36. Anderson, *German Unification and the Union of Europe*, 152–172; Bulmer and Paterson, *The FRG and the EC*, 202–222.

37. Bulmer, et al., *Germany's European Diplomacy* (Manchester: Manchester University Press, 2000), 14; Den Boer and Wallace, "Justice and Home Affairs," 496, 499, 500–501, 508, 509, 511, 513–514, 517.

38. Elizabeth Pond, *Friendly Fire* (Washington, DC: Brookings, 2004), esp. Ch. 3; Hyde-Price, *Germany and European Order*, esp. 195–198; Cole, *Franco-German Relations*, Ch. 6.

39. Anderson, *German Unification and the Union of Europe*, 23–34.

40. J. H. H. Weiler, "Does Europe Need a Constitution? Reflections on Demos, Telos, and the German Maastricht Decision," *European Law Journal* (1995), 219–258; Karl Meesen, "Hedging European Integration: The Maastricht Judgment of the Federal Constitutional Court of Germany," *Fordham International Law Review* 17 (1994), 511–530; Jefferey, "Towards a 'Third Level' in Europe?" 259–260; Geoffrey K. Roberts, *German Politics Today* (Manchester: Manchester University Press, 2000), 171–172.

41. Lisa Conant, "Europeanization and the Courts: Variable Patterns of Adaptation among National Judiciaries," in Maria Green Cowles, et al., eds., *Transforming Europe: Europeanization and Domestic Change* (Ithaca, NY: Cornell University Press, 2001), 113.

42. Bulmer and Paterson, *The FRG and the EC*, 166; Thomas Saalfeld, "The German Houses of Parliament and European Legislation," in Philip Norton, ed., *National Parliaments and the European Union* (Portland, OR: Frank Cass, 1996), 12–34.

43. Cole, *Franco-German Relations*, 57.

44. Williams, *Adenauer*, 503–523; Bulmer and Paterson, *The FRG and the EC*, 127.

45. Bulmer, Maurer, and Paterson, "The European Policy-Making Machinery," 177–206; Rometsch, "The Federal Republic of Germany," 66; Bulmer and Paterson, *The FRG and the EC*, Ch. 3.

46. Klaus Goetz, "National Government and European Integration: Intergovernmental Relations in Germany," *Journal of Common Market Studies* 33, 1 (March 1995), 91–112; Jeffery, "Towards a 'Third Level' in Europe?" 253–266; Tanja Börzel, "Europeanization and Territorial Institutional Change: Toward Cooperative Regionalism?" in Cowles, et al., eds., *Transforming Europe*, 137–158.

47. Catherine Freschi, James Shields, and Roger Woods, "Extreme Right-Wing Parties and the European Union," in Gaffney, ed., *Political Parties and the European Union*, 235–253; Wolfgang Rüdig, "Green Parties and the European Union," in Gaffney, ed., *Political Parties and the European Union*, 264.

48. Bulmer and Paterson, *The FRG and the EC*, 122–128; Paterson, "The German Christian Democrats," 53–61, 68–69.

49. Jeffery, "Towards a 'Third Level' in Europe?" 258; Quentin Peel, "Bavaria's PM Exposes Split on European Union," *Financial Times*, November 3, 1993, 1; Paterson, "The Christian Democrats," 61–68.

50. Bulmer and Paterson, *The FRG and the EC*, 132–135; Julie Smith, "How European Are European Elections?" in Gaffney, ed., *Political Parties and the European Union*, 283.

51. Cole, *Franco-German Relations*, 131–137; Moeller, "The German Social Democrats," 33–52; Rüdig, "Green Parties and the European Union," esp. 260–266; Bulmer, et al., *Germany's European Diplomacy*, 28–30.

52. Peter Katzenstein, "United Germany in an Integrating Europe," in Katzenstein, ed., *Tamed Power*, 39.

53. Evidence and examples of German interest group influences on European matters are in Bulmer and Paterson, *The FRG and the EC*,

85–107; Lankowski, "Germany: A Major Player," esp. 98–105; Anderson, *German Unification and the Union of Europe*, 66–67, 74, 76, 78–80, 119, 148, 172, 176–177, 180, 183, 184, 186; Bulmer, et al., *Germany's European Diplomacy*, 26.

54. "Could the Euro's Nuclear Option Ever Be Used?" *The Economist* 362 (February 2, 2002), 47–48; Cole, *Franco-German Relations*, 95–103, 133–138; Anderson, *German Unification and the Union of Europe*, 46–50; Bulmer, et al., *Germany's European Diplomacy*, 92–103.

Chapter 9

ITALY

"…because of the weakness of the national state and of the ruling class [Italy] never succeeded in 'making the Italians' as, for instance, France succeeded in 'making the French' during the same period."

—Gian Enrico Rusconi, *"Will Italy Remain a Nation?" (1998), 481–482.*

Occupying a boot-shaped peninsula jutting into the Mediterranean Sea, as well as the two major Mediterranean islands of Sardinia and Sicily, Italy (like Germany) took the critical steps toward becoming a modern nation-state only in the second half of the nineteenth century. Prior to that time, foreign interventions, Italian rivalries, and the authority of the Vatican in the center of the Italian peninsula prevented Italian political unification. Distinct regional differences, most notably those between a relatively wealthy North and a relatively poor South, also blocked unity and continue to characterize contemporary Italy.

When the Italian state took shape between 1859 and 1870, it did so under the leadership of northern political and industrial elites based in Piedmont (eventually in alliance with southern landowners) over the opposition of the Roman Catholic Church, which was outraged by the new state's annexation of the Papal States, which had been under the authority of the Pope. Moreover, the methods and outcomes of unification alienated many republican revolutionaries. The result was a constitutional monarchy based on the upper classes that lacked legitimacy in the

eyes of the dominant church and among many Italian citizens. Modernizing pressures for democratization and economic change and dislocations generated by World War I led to the collapse of the democratizing Italian state after World War I and the rise of the Fascist authoritarian state of Benito Mussolini (1922–1943), albeit with the backing of the king as an element of continuity. Only after World War II did Italy become a relatively stable constitutional democracy that took a republican form (abolishing the monarchy) and moved to institute a modern mixed economy.

Yet even this modern Italian nation-state has continued to be marked by the historical north-south cleavage. Furthermore, its state institutions, like those of past regimes, have gained only limited legitimacy among most citizens, continuing the pattern noted by Gian Enrico Rusconi in the quote at the outset of this chapter. For some of the same reasons, Italy's state institutions, like those of past regimes, have gained only limited legitimacy among most citizens, continuing a pattern that noted analyst Luigi Barzini has seen as endemic in Italy: "Most of the national governments we

MAP 9.1   Italy

achieved at one time or another were…feeble, arbitrary, and inefficient…."[1] With Italy's parliament fractured by multiple conflicts along party and factional lines and forcing governmental resignations regularly, its parties intent on turning the state administration toward servicing their own clienteles and demanding payoffs from prospective clients, and a series of scandals culminating in a truly massive set of indictments and convictions of major politicians in the early 1990s, it is unsurprising that Italians have given little respect to their post–World War II political order.

> "Most of the national governments we achieved at one time or another were…feeble, arbitrary, and inefficient…."
>
> Luigi Barzini, *The Italians* (1964), xiv.

Today, with 58 million people, Italy is in a virtual tie with France and the United Kingdom for second, third, or fourth place in population in the European Union. In gross domestic product, it is close to the economic magnitude of the United Kingdom and France, though noticeably behind Germany. Despite Italy's economic growth, which was dramatic in the 1950s and 1960s, that growth has been very uneven between the prosperous North and the poor South. The obvious wealth of Milan and Turin continues to contrast with the poverty of Naples and, even more so, many rural areas of the South. Moreover, Italy's relatively large population and gross domestic product have not led to equivalent political power beyond its borders. Both in the European Union and in world affairs, Italy lacks the status of a major power. In part, this reflects its lack of a large empire, a feared military force, or great-power status at any time in modern European history—a sharp contrast to France and the United Kingdom. In part, it is due to the nature of the contemporary Italian political system, particularly to the numerous checks and balances that inhibit strong executive leadership. Nonetheless, Italy was a founding member of the European Coal and Steel Community and has usually been in the forefront (at least rhetorically) of efforts to move Europe toward greater unity.

POLITICAL DEVELOPMENT

Early Development

Following the decline of the Italian-based Roman Empire in the fifth century, political fragmentation prevailed in the territory that constitutes modern Italy. Foreign invasions contributed to the splintering of Italy. Goths, Lombards, and Franks invaded and settled the Italian peninsula, mainly in the North, in the fifth, sixth, and eighth centuries, respectively. North African Muslims invaded Sicily in 827 and occupied it and some other parts of southern Italy for the next two and one-half centuries.[2] Later, France, Spain, and Austria imposed foreign rule on various parts of Italy. However, the Italians themselves showed little inclination toward political unity. During most of the Middle Ages and the Renaissance, city-states prevailed, especially in northern Italy, with Genoa, Florence, Venice, and Milan among the major examples. The Papal States under the authority of the Pope took shape from the eighth century to the nineteenth century, adding still another political jurisdiction to the complex mix.

Although an Italian language began to emerge with the poetry of Dante Alighieri (1265–1321), and some degree of "Italian" cultural identity emerged slowly, widespread illiteracy, distinct local dialects, and the lack of a political focus for the development of Italian nationalism retarded the building of an Italian "nation" until the nineteenth century. Nevertheless, Italy made enormous contributions to the arts, sciences, economics, and political philosophy during the Italian Renaissance of the fifteenth century. However, the sixteenth century witnessed Italian political and cultural decline.[3]

The invasion and occupation of Italy by Napoleon of France at the end of the eighteenth century and the beginning of the nineteenth century helped to sow the seeds of Italian nationalism and provided a centralized administrative state model that Italy would eventually emulate. Although the Austrian Prince Metternich described Italy as no more than a "geographic expression" as late as 1847,[4] it was becoming considerably more than that. In the 1830s, Giuseppe Mazzini had founded "Young Italy" as a movement dedicated to the expulsion of foreign rulers and the creation of a unified, democratic Italian republic. The 1840s witnessed the emergence of additional Italian nationalists, including such relative moderates as Vincenzo Gioberti, Count Cesare Balbo, and Massimo d'Azeglio. A nationalistic movement against Austrian political domination erupted in many parts of Italy from multiple sources in 1848, a revolutionary year in much of Europe, though the Italian movement failed to achieve its goals. Among the revolutionary nationalists of 1848 was Giuseppe Garibaldi, who became the most heroic figure of the Italian *Risorgimento*.

Unification and the Constitutional Monarchy

Ultimately, however, it was Count Camillo Benso di Cavour, the prime minister of Piedmont in northwestern Italy, who played the largest role in the creation of what became the Kingdom of Italy in 1861—a constitutional monarchy, headed by King Vittorio Emanuele II of the Piedmontese House of Savoy, with Piedmontese Prime Minister Cavour as the first prime minister of Italy. Cavour achieved his goals through a combination of diplomacy and war with Austria. Garibaldi's army played an important part in uniting the South with the North, but the new regime was to bear the imprint of Cavour far more than that of Garibaldi.[5]

The sense of nationhood among the Italian citizens remained relatively weak despite the *Risorgimento*, the new Italian state institutions enjoyed little legitimacy, electoral and other forms of participation were restricted to a very narrow base, and northern businessmen and southern landowners were economically dominant in a still largely agricultural and poor society. Retarding national consciousness was the fact that literacy remained low, especially in the South, where the majority of citizens could neither read nor write. Throughout Italy, local loyalties remained stronger than national ones. The Roman Catholic Church condemned the new secular state and its conquest of the Papal States, with the Pope forbidding devout Catholics (in a country in which 99 percent of the population were at least nominally Catholic) to take part in Italian political activity. Meanwhile, Mazzini attacked the constitutional monarchy; while Garibaldi expressed considerable alienation from it. The new administrative state emulated the centralized French model even though Italy remained divided into distinct regions and localities. Thus, Italian state institutions lacked a firm foundation. As for participation, only literate males older than 25 years who paid a substantial property tax (about 2 percent of the population) were given the right to vote; and of these, only 57 percent voted in the first elections of the new regime, in 1861. Economically, Italy remained poor, largely agrarian, deeply divided between north and south, and dominated by the wealthy classes. In light of these difficulties, it is perhaps surprising that Italy dealt with the crises of modernization as well as it did in the era from 1861 to 1922.

During the decades after unification, the centralized but poorly funded educational system gradually spread Italian literacy and helped to inculcate some popular sense of patriotism, though neither should be exaggerated. Early in the twentieth century, the Vatican began to ease its antagonism toward the state institutions. Political leaders agreed to extend voting rights but did so in stages (as in Britain), granting suffrage in 1881 to most literate adult males (still a minority), in 1911 to illiterate males who had either completed military service or were at least 30 years old, and in 1919 to all adult males. The participatory expansions of 1911 and 1919 more than doubled the electorate and gave rise to a real upsurge of participation.[6] The Italian Socialist Party and the (Catholic) Popular Party were the chief beneficiaries, while the long-dominant Liberals lost strength. As Italy industrialized, largely in the northern regions, labor unions enhanced their influence, as did socialist and anarchist ideologies. Such developments led Liberal Prime Minister Giovanni Giolitti, who held this post on numerous occasions between 1892 and 1921, to embrace moderate social reforms that included limitations on child labor, public health legislation, and old age pensions.[7] Until the end of World War I in 1918, it appeared that the Italian nation-state might be able to modernize in a relatively stable and orderly manner. However, such was not to be the case.

The pressures for expanded participation and economic redistribution intensified as the war ended. The Socialist party, dissatisfied with the Liberals' modest reforms of the emerging capitalist order in Italy, sponsored factory seizures in 1919 and 1920. Following the lead of Lenin's new regime in Russia, the Italian Communist party split from the Socialists in 1921. Meanwhile, demands for redistribution also spread across the Italian countryside. The upper classes of Italy recoiled in horror. In the midst of this postwar turmoil, there also came an upsurge of nationalistic sentiment, fueled by a widespread perception that Italy had not gained sufficient benefits from being on the victorious side in World War I. Prepared to take advantage of both the fears of the upper classes and the rise of nationalism was Benito Mussolini, a former Socialist journalist who had broken with his party to support Italian entry into World War I and who was now making an appeal to the forces of order and nationalism. The Roman Catholic Church, only partially reconciled to the "liberal" Italian state, also proved willing to bargain with Mussolini.

The Mussolini Era

The result was that Mussolini came to power in 1922, appointed as prime minister of a coalition government of both Fascists and non-Fascists, by King Vittorio Emanuele III, with the backing of most Liberals and other leaders of the "liberal" Italian state. By 1926, Mussolini had consolidated power and established authoritarian rule, eliminating the non-Fascist parties and stifling free expression. Mussolini's approaches to the challenges of modernization were to prove disastrous for Italy over the long term.

Although he claimed to be a totalitarian leader, Mussolini was never able to establish total control. Italians in general showed little more inclination to obey the laws made by Mussolini's regime than those of its predecessors. In a popular saying quoted by Luigi Barzini, Mussolini's government was "a tyranny tempered by the complete disobedience of all laws." Moreover, Mussolini signed the Lateran Pacts with Pope Pius XI in 1929, recognizing the Vatican as an independent state and the Roman Catholic Church as the official Italian church and granting the Church considerable autonomy in return for the Pope's official recognition of the Italian state. The army and navy also retained some independence, as did major private industrialists and their *Confindustria* organization. The bureaucracy grew and proved generally corrupt and inefficient. For a time, Mussolini established a **corporatist** system to replace a geographically based parliament with economically based representation of employers, employees, and professional groups—in reality, mainly a mechanism for the Fascist state to control the workforce. Mussolini's approach to state institutions was to merge the Fascist party and a centralized state, while leaving (probably of necessity) some islands of relative autonomy. His approach to participation was profoundly undemocratic, but he showed a considerable flair for manipulating public opinion that helped sustain his popularity until the Italian military disasters of World War II.

[Mussolini's government was] "a tyranny tempered by the complete disobedience of all laws."

Luigi Barzini, *The Italians (1964), xiv.*

With regard to distribution issues, Mussolini's regime sided largely with the industrialists and landowners behind the façade of corporatism. The regime repressed the militant labor unions of the early 1920s and banned all strikes. Italian wages, already low by contemporary European standards, declined further. Despite the appearance of maintaining social services, expenditures on them constituted a smaller proportion of national income than in nearly all other European countries. During the Great Depression of the 1930s, Mussolini established the Institute for Industrial Reconstruction (IRI), a state-owned holding company that purchased shares in failing business corporations to keep them in operation. The IRI would be a major long-term legacy of the Mussolini regime.

Mussolini's "nation-building" entailed persecution of the German and Slavic minorities concentrated in northeastern Italy, the French minority in the northwest, and the Jews. During World War II, Italy shipped substantial numbers of its Jews to German-run death camps. Mussolini's chief nationalistic emphasis came to be on foreign imperialism, invading Ethiopia in 1935; forming an alliance with Hitler's Nazi Germany in 1938; attacking Albania in 1939; and invading Greece, British Somaliland, and Egypt in 1940. Efforts at imperialism in alliance with Hitler brought the downfall of Mussolini's regime. In 1943, as the United States and Britain mounted an invasion of Italy through Sicily, Mussolini's own Fascist Grand

Council voted to oust him. On July 25, 1943, Mussolini was arrested; and power shifted to the same king who had appointed him in 1922 and to Mussolini's erstwhile ally, Marshall Pietro Badoglio, the new prime minister. Although the German air force rescued Mussolini and Hitler restored him to office in a German puppet regime in northern Italy, Communist partisans of the Italian Resistance movement eventually captured him and executed him in 1945.[8]

The Post–World War II Republic

Since the monarchy was discredited in the eyes of many by its long association with Mussolini, and since the anti-Fascist and anti-Nazi Italian Resistance movement pushed strongly for a democratic republican regime, Italy became a republic by a popular referendum in 1946. However, the vote was a close one, with the North voting heavily for a republic and the South for continuation of the constitutional monarchy. At first, the new Roman Catholic–oriented Christian Democratic Party of Alcide de Gasperi worked closely in a coalition government with its two major Resistance partners, the Socialists and the Communists. However, in 1947, pressures from the increasingly anti-Communist United States and the Vatican pushed the Christian Democrats to break their alliance with the Socialists and Communists and seek partners instead among small parties on the moderate-to-conservative side of the political spectrum. Even so, the Communists and Socialists cooperated with the Christian Democrats to develop a constitution that took effect at the beginning of 1948. With assistance from the American Central Intelligence Agency, the Roman Catholic Church, and business interests, the Christian Democrats and their allies won a convincing victory in the critical first elections under this new constitution in 1948. The Christian Democrats were to dominate governments for more than four decades to follow, until their disintegration in the 1990s in the wake of major corruption scandals, huge budget deficits, the end of the Cold War and declining anti-Communism, and the cumulative effects of long-term secularization in Italian culture.[9]

The Italian political order taking shape in the late 1940s prepared to grapple with the problems of trying to build national pride and loyalty, governmental institutions that would enjoy widespread legitimacy, participatory processes that would fulfill popular hopes and expectations, and economic prosperity and distribution patterns that would be widely perceived as fair. Though Italy was to enjoy greater success in these endeavors after 1948 than after 1861 or 1922, the achievements were to remain somewhat limited.

The new constitution retained the unitary system of the Italian past but provided for some decentralization to the still-distinctive regions of the country. At first, only the five "special regions" that were considered culturally unique were able to gain substantial autonomy. However, considerable devolution (or decentralization of powers) was to take place on a broad scale after 1970. Nevertheless, the North-South gap remained a threat to Italian national unity, as seen in the surge of northern demands in the 1990s for further decentralization or even creation of a separate nation-state in the North, termed "Padania" by the Northern League. Furthermore, growing immigration into Italy of East Europeans and non-Europeans produced what Carl Levy has termed a "rising tide of intolerance" from the 1980s onward. The anti-immigrant backlash has been fanned by harsh rhetoric from many political leaders, particularly those of the Northern League, a political movement that emerged from various "leagues" in the North of Italy in the 1980s and has often, under the leadership of Umberto Bossi, employed attacks on new immigrants to Italy as well as on alleged southern Italian "exploitation" of the North. The center-right government headed by Silvio Berlusconi enacted toughened immigration legislation in 2002, despite opposition from the Catholic Church, *Confindustria* (the leading employers' association), and the parties of the left; and a written protest by the United Nations High Commissioner for Refugees of its restrictions on asylum seekers.[10]

As in the past, the major institutions of Italian government failed to generate strong popular confidence. Multiparty politics in the parliamentary republic weakened executive leadership and fostered cynical jokes about *partitocrazia* even as they reflected divisions in Italian society (and the use of proportional representation). The state administration continued its long traditions of inefficiency, **clientelism** (now centered around party and factional leaders), and outright corruption. Clientelism, a system of using the state administration to do favors for businesses, groups, and individuals in return for political support for a party or a particular politician, has occurred in many countries but has been especially prevalent in Europe in the Mediterranean region. In Italy, the Christian Democrats' heavy reliance on the system more than on political ideology to mobilize support and build their party organization after World War II made party and factional clientelism widespread throughout the country. Eventually, reliance on clientelism spread to the Italian Socialist party and some of the Christian Democrats' other allies. In fact, repeated corruption scandals eventually became so severe that they helped to spark a major party realignment (and some analysts have gone as far as to suggest "the collapse of the first republic") in the 1990s.[11]

Italian women gained the right to vote in 1946, but they have lagged behind women in much of Europe in winning parliamentary seats or top executive posts. No woman has become prime minister or even come close to achieving that post. Italy ranks 14th of the 15 pre-2004 EU member states (ahead only of Greece) in the percentage of parliamentary posts held by women. Figure 9.1 compares percentage of women members in the Italian Chamber of

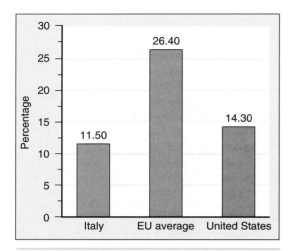

FIGURE 9.1   Women Members as a Percentage of Total Members of Lower Parliamentary Chambers, 2003

TABLE 9.1	Major Landmarks in Italian Political History
476	Roman Empire in the West falls to Germanic invaders.
1848	Revolutionary nationalism forges increased Italian national identity.
1861	Kingdom of Italy established by Cavour and Vittorio Emanuele II.
1922	Mussolini gains power.
1943	Mussolini overthrown, though subsequently restored to office in Northern Italy by the Germans.
1945	Mussolini executed; end of World War II.
1946	Republic of Italy established by referendum.
1952	Italy joins the European Coal and Steel Community as a founding member.
1958	Italy joins the European Communities as a founding member.
1992	*Tangentopoli* scandals spark upheaval in Italian politics.

Deputies with the average among EU member states' lower parliamentary chambers and with the United States House of Representatives.

General voting participation rates in Italy became among the highest in the world, often more than 90 percent of the citizens eligible to vote. Referendums became widespread from the 1970s onward. Local elections proliferated. Labor unions won many of their demands for workplace consultation for a time after the upheavals of the late 1960s. However, Italy has not mandated German-style codetermination; and employee influence waned by the 1980s. Certainly, in a general sense, political participation is broader in contemporary Italy than at any time in Italian history. But whether it is likely to result in either the perception or the reality of democratic accountability remains in doubt.[12]

In the realm of economic distribution, too, Italy has enjoyed some notable successes. As noted previously, it has now achieved a gross domestic product close to that of the United Kingdom and France. Moreover, post–World War II governments have built a substantial welfare state on the foundations laid back in the

early twentieth century by Giolitti's liberal reforms. A national health service modeled on the one established in Britain in the late 1940s took shape after 1978. Nonetheless, major problems remain. The Italian welfare state in general and the health service in particular have been plagued by inefficiencies and corruption, undermining support for them by the 1990s and generating pressures for reform and/or cutbacks. Moreover, the overall Italian GDP figures have masked the poverty that continues to prevail in much of southern Italy.[13]

GOVERNMENTAL INSTITUTIONS

The current Italian Constitution dates from 1948. However, as noted previously, the recent transformation of the Italian party and electoral system has been so substantial in its impact on constitutional processes that some analysts have suggested that a new constitutional order (a "Second Republic") has emerged since the early 1990s or is about to emerge.[14] However, Italy has formally amended its constitutional document only rarely and on relatively minor matters.

The Executive

Like Germany, Britain, and Spain, Italy places cabinet-parliamentary structures at the center of its constitutional system. In the absence of a monarch since 1946, a largely but not entirely ceremonial president serves as the head of state and appoints a prime minister (formally titled the President of the Council of Ministers) and the cabinet ministers recommended by the prime minister. The president of the Republic also nominates up to five senators and five Constitutional Court judges, heads the armed forces, and can dissolve parliament (after consultation) and call for new elections. The president of the Republic is elected by a joint session of the two chambers of parliament, supplemented by three representatives from each Italian region, and serves for a seven-year term. During the upheavals of the 1990s, President Oscar Scalfaro (1992–1999) was able to exercise considerable discretion in selecting prime ministers and influencing political outcomes. His successor, Carlo Ciampi (1999–), has had fewer such opportunities but did challenge Prime Minister Berlusconi's government over a mass media bill that President Ciampi refused to sign in December 2003 after parliament passed it. Though parliament possesses the constitutional power to override such an objection from the president by majority vote, it has usually sought to accommodate the president's concerns over legislation. At the very least, Ciampi's objections called attention to a matter that could potentially embarrass the Berlusconi government on a sensitive matter related to the prime minister's efforts to exert extensive influence over Italian broadcasting.

In contrast to his counterparts in the other major European Union nation-states, the prime minister of Italy must maintain the confidence of a majority in both parliamentary chambers or resign. This requirement, combined with widespread Italian distrust of authority and a multiparty system that has often been further fractured into quarreling intraparty factions, has usually undermined the prime minister's ability to dominate the council of ministers and provide strong executive leadership. Most prime ministers have experienced great difficulty even in maintaining their positions for long. (The average life of a government since 1945 has been eleven months.) Alcide de Gasperi (1945–1953) was the major exception to the prevailing pattern of highly constrained chief executives. Yet even he had to establish eight governments during his eight years in office.[15]

Silvio Berlusconi, the current prime minister, hopes to establish a new era of strong prime ministerial leadership, though his chances of long-term success in this endeavor appear only modest. He is a charismatic media mogul who has organized and clearly dominates his own party, Forza Italia (Let's go, Italy). Berlusconi has recently been described by Roberto Pazzi: "He's a rich man who derides professional politicians and who has made millions of Italians dream of emulating his luck by voting for him." Early in 2002, Berlusconi forced the resignation of his popular technocratic foreign minister and took the post for himself for a ten-month period. However, his party is far short of a majority on its own in either chamber of parliament. Moreover, two of his major allies, the National Alliance and the Northern League, are headed by strong-willed leaders, Gianfranco Fini (deputy prime minister) and Umberto Bossi (minister for reform until his resignation in July 2004), respectively, whose goals and bases of support diverge markedly from his own and from each other's, despite sharing a generally conservative orientation. In fact, Bossi's withdrawal of support back in 1994 brought the downfall of Berlusconi's previous effort to be a strong prime minister after just seven months in office. (See the box on pages 199–200.)[16]

TABLE 9.2   Italian Prime Ministers Since 1945

Prime minister	Period in office
Alcide Gasperi (8 consecutive governments)	Dec. 1945–Aug. 1953
Giuseppi Pella	Aug.1953–Jan. 1954
Amintore Fanfani	Jan. 1954–Feb. 1954
Mario Scelba	Feb. 1954–July 1955
Antonio Segni	July 1955–May 1957
Adone Zoli	May 1957–July 1958
Amintore Fanfani	July 1958–Feb. 1959
Antonio Segni	Feb. 1959–Mar. 1960
Fernando Tambroni	Mar. 1960–July 1960
Amintore Fanfani (2 consecutive governments)	July 1960–June 1963
Giovanni Leone	June 1963–Dec. 1963
Aldo Moro (3 consecutive governments)	Dec. 1963–June 1968
Giovanni Leone	June 1968–Dec. 1968
Mariano Rumor (3 consecutive governments)	Dec. 1968–Aug. 1970
Emilio Colombo	Aug. 1970–Feb. 1972
Giulio Andreotti (2 consecutive governments)	Feb. 1972–July 1973
Mariano Rumor (2 consecutive governments)	July 1973–Nov. 1974
Aldo Moro (2 consecutive governments)	Nov. 1974–July 1976
Giulio Andreotti (3 consecutive governments)	July 1976–Aug. 1979
Francesco Cossiga (2 consecutive governments)	Aug. 1979–Sept. 1980
Arnaldo Forlani	Sept. 1980–July 1981
Giovanni Spadolini (2 consecutive governments)	July 1981–Dec. 1982
Amintore Fanfani	Dec. 1982–Aug. 1983
Bettino Craxi (2 consecutive governments)	Aug. 1983–Apr. 1987
Amintore Fanfani	Apr. 1987–July 1987
Giovanni Goria	July 1987–Apr. 1988
Ciriaco De Mita	Apr. 1988–Aug. 1989
Giulio Andreotti (2 consecutive governments)	Aug. 1989–June 1992
Giulano Amato	June 1992–Apr. 1993
Carlo Ciampi	Apr. 1993–May 1994
Silvio Berlusconi	May 1994–Jan. 1995
Lamberto Dini	Jan. 1995–June 1996
Romano Prodi	June 1996–Oct. 1998
Massimo D'Alema	Oct. 1998–Apr. 2000
Giulano Amato	Apr. 2000–May 2001
Silvio Berlusconi	**May 2001–**

[Berlusconi is] "a rich man who derides professional politicians and who has made millions of Italians dream of emulating his luck by voting for him."

Roberto Pazzi, *New York Times* (July 13, 2003), IV, 13.

One new development in Italian government in the 1990s was the emergence for a time of technocrat-dominated cabinets, in which cabinet ministers were drawn increasingly from outside parliament, based upon their presumed expertise and lack of taint by the partisan "kickback" scandals. In fact, for the first time in the history of the Italian Republic, two prime ministers, Carlo Ciampi (now president of Italy) and Lamberto Dini, were themselves technocrats who did not serve in parliament. Though the technocratic trend has since subsided, even Berlusconi's cabinet of 2001 initially included five technocratic ministers.[17]

Below the council of ministers lies a large bureaucratic apparatus, consisting of departments but also public corporations and special agencies. For the most part, its reputation both at home and abroad has been negative. The upper levels of Italian public administration have long been permeated by party clientelism, in which the parties in coalition governments have turned departments, public corporations, and other agencies into fiefdoms for party loyalists. The loyalists in turn have been expected to provide services for their party's major clients. The Christian Democrats and their smaller-party allies proved masters at this game for more than four decades (1948–1992) before it exploded in their faces in the *Tangentopoli* (Kickback City) scandals. Career civil servants were generally induced to cooperate in the system by salary increases, promotions, and toleration of inefficient work habits. Within the civil service itself, legal requirements for examination-based merit appointments were often bypassed. While Italy made some effort to

emulate the French National School of Administration and create a professional bureaucratic elite by establishing the Superior School of Public Administration in 1957 to educate future administrative leaders, the plan fell far short of accomplishment. Another feature of the Italian civil service has been the disproportionate share of its positions held by southerners (while northerners have just as consistently dominated private business management). Although several governments of the 1990s undertook efforts to reorganize and improve the performance of Italian public administration, it is premature to assess the effectiveness and durability of their reforms.[18]

The Parliament

The Italian parliament, composed of the Chamber of Deputies (630 members) and the Senate (320 members), is the only national legislature among the major EU nation-states in which the two chambers have equal powers. To be enacted into law, bills must gain approval in both the Chamber of Deputies and the Senate, and (as noted previously) either house may remove a government by a majority no-confidence vote. In practice, Italian governments usually resign before the actual no-confidence vote, anticipating their ouster in advance. However, the government of Prime Minister Romano Prodi (later president of the European Union Commission, 1999–2004) was forced from office by a one-vote margin on a no-confidence vote in the Chamber of Deputies in 1998.

Among the major unique features of the Italian parliament, beyond its coequal chambers, has been its relatively great power in shaping legislative outcomes and making and unmaking governments. In addition, it was exceptional in its use of secret ballots until 1988 (a practice largely discontinued since then because it was widely perceived to shield representatives' actions from the view of their constituents and to weaken party discipline and thus executive leadership). Another distinctive feature of the Italian parliament—one that continues to exist—is its reliance on a strong system of specialized standing committees. In fact, much legislation that enjoys wide support is enacted by committees in each chamber without ever facing a vote by the full membership on the floor. If the government, 10 percent of the house members, or 20 percent of the committee members object, the bill must go to the floor for approval by a majority vote.

Although the Italian parliament has been more powerful than its counterparts in Western Europe, it has not won much praise or respect from the Italian public according to opinion surveys, which rate it far below EU institutions and similarly with the Italian public administration. The *Tangentopoli* scandal led to the investigation or indictment of nearly one-third of the members of the 1992–1994 parliament, fueling further public distrust and leading to a massive turnover in which only 11 percent of the 1994–1996 representatives were previous members of parliament. Despite this unprecedented influx of "new blood," a subsequent survey showed only one-third of Italians expressing confidence that the parliament could be relied on to make decisions in the public interest.[19]

The Constitutional Court, Judiciary, and Legal System

Like most of Europe beyond the British Isles, Italy has a legal system based on Roman law. It also has a Constitutional Court, composed of 15 judges (5 elected by parliament in joint session, 5 appointed by the president, and 5 elected by high court judges from the ranks of the judiciary), which possesses judicial review powers concerning matters of constitutionality. Though it did not become operational until eight years after the 1948 Constitution provided for its establishment, the Constitutional Court has become an important component of Italian national government. The growing powers and assertiveness of the regions and widespread use of referendums since the early 1970s have brought an increased number of important issues before it.

However, the most prominent and controversial judicial actors in Italian politics came in the early 1990s to be the local judges (magistrates), who played leading roles in unveiling the enormous *Tangentopoli* scandals that shook the Italian Republic to its very foundations. The truly extensive illegal financing of political parties and other corrupt bargains between politicians and businessmen revealed in court led to numerous convictions of prominent Italian leaders and brought major political changes. The 7000 Italian judges, recruited as in most Roman law countries by competitive examinations and increasingly insulated from the parties, have in turn become targets of attack by many politicians and businessmen. Prime Minister Berlusconi, himself caught up in the scandals in his roles as head of Fininvest before he ran for political office, has sought to turn public opinion against the judges. In June 2003, Berlusconi persuaded the parliament to pass a law granting immunity from prosecution to the prime minister and four other top officials in the Italian government, thus avoiding a possible conviction on corruption charges while he was in office. In January 2004, the Constitutional Court found this legislation to be unconstitutional and ruled it null and void. Summing up the enormous impact of the judiciary on recent Italian politics, Italian political scientists Patrizia Pederzoli and Carlo Guarnieri have concluded, "Many of the recent dramatic changes on the Italian political scene cannot be understood without considering the sudden escalation of judicial intervention in political, social and even economic life…. This phenomenon has acquired in Italy an intensity which is almost unique." Some analysts believe that the wave of judicial activism has begun to ebb in Italy, but the Constitutional Court's overruling of the immunity legislation pushed by Prime Minister Berlusconi suggests that court influence remains highly important in Italy.[20]

PEOPLE IN THE EU
The Rise and Fall of Silvio Berlusconi's First Government

Silvio Berlusconi, now generally believed to be the wealthiest man in Italy, had by the early 1990s built a business corporate empire (Fininvest) that included an array of broadcasting operations as well as a successful Milan soccer team. *Forza Italia!* (Let's Go, Italy!), the cry of his soccer team, became the name of Berlusconi's political party once he decided to enter politics as the Christian Democrat–dominated order began to collapse.

Launching his and his party's election campaign in January 1994, one that would lead to his becoming prime minister of Italy four months later, Berlusconi proclaimed his movement to be one of free-market reform that would institute a sharp break with "an Italy that is so politicized, statist, corrupt and hyper-regulated."[21] Relying heavily on television, of which he was a master, and such other mass-marketing techniques as a colorful brochure mailed to millions of Italian homes, Berlusconi portrayed himself as a populist who would promote free enterprise and defend the individual, the family, small businesses, and the nation. Some saw a resemblance to Ross Perot, the wealthy businessman who had stirred up American politics in an ultimately unsuccessful run for the presidency in 1992. However, Berlusconi was to prove far more skilled than Perot at advancing his political career.

Berlusconi's critics were unkind enough to suggest that there was considerable irony in a multimillionaire campaigning as a populist.

They also noted his close links to former Socialist prime minister Bettino Craxi and the special favors that Fininvest had obtained from Craxi and others by means that would later lead to bribery and fraud charges and convictions against Berlusconi (which he has appealed) and wondered how he could persuade the Italian public that he was a free-market reformer who would sweep away the clientelism in which he himself seemed to have been deeply immersed. Despite the critics, Berlusconi led Forza Italia (FI) to a stunning success in the March elections, with FI emerging as the largest party in terms of both parliamentary seats and popular vote and Berlusconi emerging as the obvious choice to be prime minister of Italy.

It took Berlusconi more than a month to assemble his first government, for reasons that suggested that his break with the past might not be as dramatic as he had promised: tough bargaining among the parties to constitute the Right coalition over the allocation of cabinet posts and other jobs among Forza Italia, the National Alliance, the Northern League, and other supplicants. Nor was the governing process to live up to Berlusconi's promises of an end to politics as usual. Quarrels continually wracked the coalition government, most notably a serious conflict between Berlusconi and Bossi that only worsened over time. By November, just six months after taking office, Berlusconi was clearly in danger of being ousted as prime minister. His plans to continue budget cuts that would enable Italy to stay on track to adopt the euro currency had gone off course. One and one-half million demonstrators marched through

(continued on next page)

(continued from previous page)

Rome on November 12 in opposition to his budget. His efforts to take over Italian state television, which he thought was slanting news broadcasts against him, aroused strong opposition. From within his own government, Bossi was denouncing him as "Emperor Berlusconi." Then on November 22 came a letter from the Milan magistrates to the prime minister, summoning him to appear before them to answer charges of bribery and fraud. On December 13, Berlusconi had to suffer the humiliation of appearing in person before the magistrates.

At this point, Bossi led his Northern League out of Berlusconi's coalition, depriving it of its parliamentary majority. Berlusconi lashed out at Bossi as a traitor, denounced the alleged Communists who were behind the magistrates' investigation of his Fininvest operations and the charges against him, and called for new elections to parliament. Angering Berlusconi further, President Scalfaro called upon Berlusconi to resign and refused his request to call new parliamentary elections. After two weeks of intense bargaining among prime minister, president, and other leading players, a compromise of sorts emerged, though not without further outbursts of indignation from Berlusconi. Berlusconi would be replaced as prime minister by Lamberto Dini, a nonpartisan technocrat who had served in Berlusconi's cabinet. With this appointment of Dini by President Scalfaro in January 1995, the first Berlusconi government came to an end. However, Berlusconi would be back in power as prime minister a little over six years later.[22]

"Many of the recent dramatic changes on the Italian political scene cannot be understood without considering the sudden escalation of judicial intervention in political, social and even economic life.... This phenomenon has acquired in Italy an intensity which is almost unique."

Patrizia Pederzoli and Carlo Guarnieri, *"Italy: A Case of Judicial Democracy?" (1997), 253.*

Subnational Governments

Beyond the national governmental institutions lie the 20 regions (including five with special autonomy because of their unique cultural features) and the provinces and communes. Italy has traditionally been a centralized unitary state since the *Risorgimento*, based on the French model. The Constitution of 1948 largely continued this tradition by referring to the republic as "one and indivisible" and creating no representation for the regions in the Senate. However, in response to considerable decentralizing sentiment in the wake of Mussolini's centralized Fascist dictatorship, the Constitution made provision for regional governments. Largely because the governing Christian Democrats and their allies in the years following 1948 were loath to share the power that they enjoyed at the national level with regional governments that would undoubtedly be Communist-dominated in the "red belt" of north-central Italy, the national parliament refused to enact the enabling legislation for the 15 non-"special" regions until 1970. Devolution to the regions has proceeded since then in stages. The national government nonetheless maintains significant influence through an appointed regional commissioner, who must approve regional laws. The national government also retains the power to dissolve regional councils. Therefore, Italy remains much more centralized than a federal system such as Germany or the United States. The current Berlusconi government continues to wrestle with the issue of decentralizing further powers to the regions, as the Northern League presses for devolution and such other coalition partners as the National Alliance resist. The performance of the regional governments has varied widely, according to Robert Putnam's widely cited analysis, with the most effective governments found generally in the northern areas with strong "civic" traditions.[23]

Summary

Italian governmental institutions—rarely, if ever, enjoying widespread legitimacy—have come under intense pressures for reform, especially since the early 1990s. Though their changes have so far been less dramatic than those of the Italian party and electoral systems, the institutions have shown some responsiveness to criticisms of their corruption, inefficiency, and overcentralization. Whether they can gain genuine and durable popular support remains in doubt.

ELECTIONS, POLITICAL PARTIES, AND INTEREST GROUPS

If Italian institutional patterns have recently shifted, the changes in the electoral and party systems since the early 1990s have constituted a "revolution" in the eyes of at least some analysts.[24] Despite major changes in election laws and the destruction of most of the parties that previously dominated Italian participatory processes for more than four decades, there nonetheless remain some elements of continuity.

The Electoral Process

From 1946 to 1993, proportional representation was employed in the elections to both chambers of parliament, though the methods used in Senate elections differed somewhat from those in Chamber of Deputies elections (the latter giving small parties more representation than the former and permitting voters up to four preference votes for individual candidates on their chosen party list in multimember districts). The preference voting system fostered personal rivalries and factionalism within the parties, particularly the dominant Christian Democratic party, because it compelled candidates of the same party in multimember districts to campaign against one another for the "preference" votes. Therefore, individual party candidates in one district needed their own sources of funds and other campaign support in addition to those provided for the party. Factional ties to party candidates and leaders in Rome were among the ways of gaining such support. The proportional representation system encouraged multiple parties, while preference voting factionalized them. Of course, underlying economic and cultural divisions in Italian society also contributed to the fractured party system that typified the First Republic.

By the early 1990s, popular discontent with the party system, which had come to be seen as the chief source of corruption and other ills of Italian politics, focused on the electoral laws. In a June 1991 referendum, 96 percent of the voters voted to reduce preference voting. In April 1993, 83 percent voted to abolish the Senate electoral law. These signs of popular displeasure convinced parliament to revamp the entire electoral system in August 1993.

The new laws resulted from compromises among various reform proponents. They provide that each Italian voter now has two votes to cast in every Chamber of Deputies and Senate election—one, a "candidate" vote, the other a "party list" vote. Three-fourths of the Deputies and Senators are elected by the candidate votes in single-member constituencies using a first-past-the-post system that gives victory to the plurality winner in each district, as in legislative elections in Britain and the United States. One-fourth of the Deputies and Senators are elected by proportional representation from the party list votes, in a manner designed to make the overall allocation of seats more proportional (for lists winning more than 4 percent of the national vote) than the first-past-the-post results alone would be.[25]

Many observers and participants in 1993 believed that the new electoral system would move Italy toward two-party politics or at least toward two-coalition politics, in which a stable governing party (or coalition) and a coherent opposition party (or coalition) would offer effective government and responsible alternatives. The results have so far fallen somewhat short of these expectations. Although the new electoral

procedures have pressured the evolving multiple parties to cluster into three major electoral coalitions in 1994, two major coalitions but with one major party (the Northern League) outside of them in 1996, and two major coalitions with several small parties and alliances of parties outside of them in 2001, the party system remains quite fragmented. The center-left (Olive Tree) coalition that won the 1996 election did govern Italy for the succeeding five years, but it proved rather fractious and went through three different prime ministers and governments. The center-right coalition (House of Freedom) defeated the Olive Tree coalition in the 2001 elections, but its components certainly have the potential to undermine stable government also.

TABLE 9.3   **Percentages of Vote Polled by Parties in Italian Chamber of Deputies Elections, 1983–2001**

Party	1983	1987	1992	1994	1996	2001
DC/PPI	32.9%	34.3%	29.7%	11.1%	5.8%	*3.2%
PCI/PDS	29.9	26.6	16.1	10.3	21.1	16.6
PSI/PSU	11.4	14.3	13.6	2.2	–	–
MSI/DN/AN	6.8	5.9	5.4	13.5	15.7	12.0
PRI	5.1	3.7	4.4	–	–	–
PLI	2.9	2.1	2.8	–	–	–
LN	–	–	8.7	8.4	10.1	3.9
FI	–	–	–	21.0	20.6	29.4
Prodi List	–	–	–	–	6.8	–
Dini List	–	–	–	–	4.3	–
PRC	–	–	5.6	6.1	8.6	5.0
Daisy All.	–	–	–	–	–	14.5
Others	11.0	13.1	14.7	27.4	7.0	15.4
TOTAL	100.0	100.0	100.0	100.0	100.0	100.0

*Biancofiore list

Party/electoral alliance titles are as follows:

DC/PPI	Christian Democratic Party/Popular Party of Italy	PLI	Italian Liberal Party
PCI/PDS	Italian Communist Party/Democratic Party of the Left	LN	Northern League
PSI/PSU	Italian Socialist Party/United Socialist Party	FI	Forza Italia
MSI/DN/AN	Italian Social Movement/National Right/National Alliance	Prodi List	Centrist alliance led by Romano Prodi
PRI	Italian Republican Party	Dini List	Centrist alliance led by Lamberto Dini
		PRC	Party of Communist Refoundation

Political Parties

During the years from 1947 to 1992, the Christian Democratic party, aligned with Roman Catholic interest groups and backed by the Church hierarchy but also enjoying substantial business support and reaching out to a broad cross-section of the public, dominated every Italian government and was the party of every prime minister but two. However, the Christian Democrats were divided into factions, in large part stimulated by the preference voting system that led to alliances and rivalries among its candidates. Moreover, the Christian Democrats shared governmental power in coalitions with an array of center-right and eventually center-left parties. The Communists on the left were consistently the second largest Italian party and formed the major opposition. However, they were never included in a government after a brief "grand coalition" in 1945–1947 fell apart, as pressures from the Vatican and the United States, and Christian Democratic desires to isolate their major rivals, kept them from national executive offices. For a short period in the 1970s, the Christian Democrat–led governments consulted regularly with the Communists and in return enjoyed their backing in parliament, but this pattern was atypical and ended in 1979. On the far right, the neo-Fascists and the monarchists were also perpetually kept out of government.

Much of the electorate felt frustrated by the nature of the party system and its effects. The Christian Democratic factionalism and the multiparty coalitions meant that prime ministers and governments frequently changed in between elections with outcomes over which the voters had no control. Furthermore, there was no alternation in power between major parties representing divergent viewpoints and sections of the population, as in all of the other major European democracies. The Communist voters and the neo-Fascist and monarchist voters never saw a government including the leaders for whom they had voted. Voters had many party choices at election time, and voter turnout was among the highest in Western Europe (often surpassing 90 percent). However, weak executive leadership, backroom deals over which the public had little or no influence, and exclusion of the Communists and the far right were other features of the system.[26]

The new and still evolving party system remains highly fragmented. However, it has proved more fluid since 1993 than the 1947–1992 party system and it has provided a basis for both center-left and center-right governments that have included between them most of the parties (unlike the 1947–1992 system).

The long-dominant Christian Democratic party has disintegrated into different parties and other electoral groupings, some aligned with the right, some with the left, and some seeking to rebuild the center of Italian politics. Its Communist rivals have reoriented themselves toward moderate social democracy, reorganized, and renamed themselves the Democrats of the Left. However, they have suffered the defection of traditional Communists, who have organized as Communist Refoundation (which has in turn lost some supporters to the recently formed Italian Communist party).

In terms of the left-right spectrum normally used to describe Italian politics (and European politics generally), the new party system finds Communist Refoundation on the far left, reasserting traditional Communist attacks on capitalism and the globalized market economy. It remained aloof from any electoral alliance in 2001. The center-left parties and party alliances composing the Olive Tree (*Ulivo*) electoral coalition include the Italian Communists, the Democrats of the Left, the Daisy (*Margherita*) alliance, and the Sunflower (*Girasole*) alliance. The Daisy alliance centers on Catholic social reformers, including 2001 Olive Tree prime ministerial candidate and later "leader of the opposition" Francesco Rutelli. The Sunflower alliance centers on the environmentalists of the Green party and some other secular reformists. From 1996 to 2001, the Olive Tree formed rather unstable coalition governments under three prime ministers: Romano Prodi (centrist, 1996–1998), Massimo D'Alema (Democrats of the Left, 1998–2000),

and Giulano Amato (centrist, 2000–2001). It fragmented considerably in the wake of its defeat in the 2001 elections.[27]

The center-right parties and party alliances composing the House of Freedom electoral coalition, which now forms the government of

TABLE 9.4   Results of the 2001 Italian Parliamentary Elections

Chamber of deputies			
Party or alliance	*PR%*	*PR seats*	*Total seats*
Communist Refoundation	5.0%	11	11
Left Democrats	16.6	32	137
Daisy Alliance	14.5	28	80
Sunflower Alliance	2.2	0	17
Italian Communist Party	1.7	0	10
Olive Tree Coalition	35.0	60	244
Bonino List	2.3	0	0
Italy of Values	3.9	0	0
European Democracy	2.4	0	0
Forza Italia	29.4	60	189
National Alliance	12.0	24	96
Northern League	3.9	0	30
Biancofiore List	3.2	0	40
Others	0.9	0	2
House of Freedom Coalition	49.4	84	357
Far Right	2.0	0	9
Others	4.0	0	9
Total	100.0	155	630
Senate			
Communist Refoundation	5.0	3	3
Olive Tree	39.2	51	128
Bonino List	2.0	0	0
Italy of Values	3.4	1	1
European Democracy	3.2	2	2
Home of Freedom	42.5	25	177
Far Right	1.0	0	0
Others	4.2	1	4
Total	100.5	83	315

Italy with majority backing in both chambers of parliament, include Forza Italia (Let's Go, Italy), the National Alliance, and the Northern League, as well as the Democratic Union of the Center drawn mainly from the old Christian Democrats. The components are broadly conservative in orientation, but their approaches are heavily influenced by three strong leaders—Prime Minister Silvio Berlusconi for Forza Italia, Gianfranco Fini for the National Alliance, and Umberto Bossi for the Northern League. Forza Italia is mostly neoliberal in its ideology and business-oriented in its basic posture. Berlusconi's own Fininvest conglomerate has been a key ingredient in its organization, and his wealth has been a major factor in its financing. The National Alliance has Fascist and neo-Fascist roots, but Fini has moved it away from extreme-right nationalism toward moderately conservative policies and away from its once-distinctive southern base to considerable national appeal. Bossi's Northern League, as its name suggests, has appeal only in the North of Italy, where it blends anti-southern and anti-immigrant rhetoric; demands for autonomy (and, at times, even independence) for Northern Italy, which it terms Padania; and anti-establishment populism.[28]

Referendums

Referendums are another important part of Italian participatory politics and have been since 1970. As noted previously, they played an important role in triggering election law changes in the 1991–1993 period. They have also been held on a wide variety of other issues, including divorce, abortion, wage indexation, nuclear energy, drug decriminalization, and public financing of political parties. Referendums can be called by petition of 500,000 voters or five regional councils, subject to review and approval by the Constitutional Court, and can be employed only for the purpose of repealing or amending an act of parliament (though by rejecting an act they may force fur-

ther legislative action, as in the case of electoral reform). Despite these restrictions, Italian referendums have become more numerous and politically significant than in any of the other major EU nation-states (yet less so than in Switzerland).[29]

Interest Groups

Italian interest groups, many of them linked for years to political parties, have generally gained some freedom to maneuver in the new political atmosphere since the early 1990s. As in most of Western Europe, business, labor, and agricultural interest groups based on economic concerns have increasingly been joined by more fluid and less materialistic "new politics" groups, though the economic groups continue to exert more influence than the newcomers. On the other hand, Catholic interest groups that once played important roles in Italian politics, as Catholic Action did for many years, have lost influence in the wake of the marked secularization of Italian society and now the demise of the Christian Democratic party with which most of them were allied. Even at the peak of its political powers, the Roman Catholic Church's real ability to shape Italian culture was questioned by some analysts. Roberto Pazzi, for example, has concluded, "Italians have always been incurable and marvelous individualists, resistant to any dream of the absolute, including the Christian one. Their Catholic faith is but a veil covering the pagan cult of beauty, imagination, youth, glory, etc."[30]

"Italians have always been incurable and marvelous individualists, resistant to any dream of the absolute, including the Christian one. Their Catholic faith is but a veil covering the pagan cult of beauty, imagination, youth, glory, etc."

Roberto Pazzi, *New York Times* (July 13, 2003), IV, 13.

Confindustria is the oldest and most powerful of the Italian business interest groups.

Though it has a large membership in which small, family-run businesses predominate, and though some large business corporations are unaffiliated and pursue their own routes to influence, its policy recommendations usually reflect the interests of big business when these interests are fairly uniform. *Confindustria* traditionally maintained strong links to the dominant Christian Democrats. Nevertheless, many big businessmen really preferred the small, secular Liberal and Republican parties and also gave them financial support. The presence of giant, state-owned holding companies, the Institute for Industrial Reconstruction (IRI) dating back to Mussolini and the National Hydrocarbons Agency (ENI) of the postwar era, outside the private sector has meant that these have often operated as institutional interest groups independent of *Confindustria*. Both were linked for years to the Christian Democrats, though ENI became part of the Socialist party's fiefdom in a deal struck among coalition partners in the late 1970s as part of the clientelist system. Privatization is now reducing the roles of these state giants in the Italian economy and political system.

Due to the relatively large role that organized crime has played in Italian interest group politics (compared to the rest of Western Europe), no discussion of groups should ignore the economic and political power of the Mafia, especially in its base in Sicily, and of three other "underworld" organizations on the mainland. The *Tangentopoli* scandals and the resulting upheavals appear to have reduced the influence of organized crime in Italy, though this development may prove temporary.

Organized labor has been split ideologically since the post–World War II period. The largest labor union federation, the Italian General Confederation of Labor (CGIL), became Communist-oriented in the late 1940s and remains strongly identified with the political left, though it has become increasingly independent of any party. The second-largest union federation, the Italian Confederation of Workers' Unions (CSIL), was an ally of the Christian Democratic party and in the "Second Republic" since the early 1990s generally represents more affluent workers. The third-largest union federation, the Italian Union of Labor (UIL), was long tied to the secular centrist Republican and Social Democratic parties. Although the Italian union movement has surged at times, particularly in the late 1960s and the 1970s, its membership and influence have generally declined since 1980. Most analysts estimate union membership to constitute between one-sixth and one-third of the Italian workforce today (just a little more than that in France, Spain, or the United States, well below the figures for Northern Europe), a fairly sharp drop from the 30–40 percent range estimated by most observers in the 1980s. The significant number of independent unions and the unreliability of their membership claims make estimates of overall union membership in Italy difficult to verify. Union leaders in Italy have often sought inclusion in tripartite neo-corporatist consultations with business and governmental leaders. There have been some significant agreements of a neo-corporatist nature in recent years, such as the workplace representation and contract negotiation system hammered out in 1990–1993. However, most assessments of the Italian patterns are that the unions have been too weak and fragmented to enable a full neo-corporatism to function effectively, as it has often done in such countries as Sweden and Austria.

In Italy, as in most of Western Europe, the agricultural sector is a declining force, though it remains a factor of some political and economic consequence. Like labor, agricultural interest groups have been fragmented. The most influential of these is the *Coldiretti*, or National Confederation of Direct Cultivators. It is composed primarily of small independent owners and tenant farmers. Long linked to the Christian Democratic party, the *Coldiretti* now operates independently of any parties.[31]

Summary

Overall, participatory processes in Italy have undergone more dramatic changes in the years since 1990 than those in any other nation-state in Western Europe. The end of the Cold War made the Christian Democratic party seem less necessary than before as a bulwark against Communism, and secularization of society has progressively weakened its base of support. Rising government debt fed growing concerns about the adequacy of long-prevalent party and governing processes. In this environment, the *Tangentopoli* scandals crystallized public discontent that had long been building and led to major changes. Voter turnout has declined slightly in Italy but remains higher than in most Western democracies. Although Italians continue to complain bitterly about their lack of effective political participation, there have been some recent reforms of a positive nature. Certainly, participatory opportunities exceed those available during most of Italian history.

CONCLUSIONS

Italy has undergone three significant transformations in the past century—from "liberal" constitutional monarchy to Fascist dictatorship in the 1920s, then to the post–World War II Republic, and now to what many analysts are terming the Second Republic. Throughout its modern history, it has often grappled less than satisfactorily with the crises of development. Despite some notable successes since World War II that contrast favorably with its past (particularly economic growth and effective adaptation to a globalizing economy), and the recent adjustments in its participatory processes that have just been discussed, Italy is in many respects a discontented democracy. Numerous surveys of Italian public opinion confirm widespread alienation. Among the effects of lack of confidence in their own governments has been a general willingness on the part of Italians to look to the European Union for leadership. The next chapter focuses on Italy's roles within the EU and the impact of the EU on Italian politics.

SUMMARY

- Foreign interventions, the authority of the Vatican over most of the central part of the Italian peninsula, and distinct regional differences prevented the development of an Italian nation-state until the second half of the nineteenth century—much later than in France or England but about the same time as in Germany.

- When the Italian nation-state took shape between 1859 and 1870, it did so under the leadership of northern political and industrial elites based in Piedmont (eventually in alliance with southern landowners), over the opposition of the Roman Catholic Church.

- The Italian state gradually expanded participation between 1861 and 1919, when all adult males gained voting rights, but it failed to deal effectively with economic distribution crises or to win the loyalty of the citizenry.

- Benito Mussolini became prime minister in 1922 by appointment by the constitutional monarch, King Vittorio Emanuele, and proceeded to transform Italy into an authoritarian state, with the acquiescence of Pope Pius XI, who signed the Lateran Pacts officially recognizing Mussolini's regime in 1929.

- Mussolini led Italy into alliance with Adolf Hitler of Germany but was overthrown by the Italians in 1943 as defeat in World War II loomed; the Germans restored Mussolini as a puppet leader in northern Italy, 1943–1945, after which Communist partisans of the Italian Resistance captured and executed him.

- Italy became a democratic republic by a popular referendum in 1946 that abolished the monarchy; it has remained a democratic republic since then.

- Though the democratic republic has presided over an era of long-term economic growth, it has failed to reduce significantly the North-South economic gap and has failed to generate strong popular confidence in its competence or fairness.

- The *Tangentopoli* scandal of the early 1990s destroyed the Christian Democratic party that had been at the center of Italian governments since 1946, shook up many governmental institutions, and fed continuing Italian distrust of their state; some analysts also have discerned a "second republic" emergent from the upheaval of the 1990s.

- The prime minister (currently Silvio Berlusconi) is the head of the Italian government and (unlike other prime ministers in major EU member states) must maintain the confidence of a majority in both the chambers of the parliament.

- The president (currently Carlo Ciampi) is the largely but not entirely ceremonial head of the Italian state.

- Coalition governments have long been the norm in Italy; the current center-right coalition is composed of Berlusconi's Forza Italia, the National Alliance, the Northern League, and the Democratic Union of the Center.

- The Italian parliament is composed of two popularly elected bodies of equal powers: the Chamber of Deputies and the Senate; the parliament has asserted more control over governments and legislation than most European legislatures have, but Italians do not hold it in high regard.

- Like most of Europe beyond the British Isles, Italy bases its legal system on the Roman law tradition.

- The Constitutional Court has become an important component of the Italian state, exercising constitutional judicial review functions; however, the most prominent and controversial judicial actors in Italy in recent years have been the local magistrates who unveiled the *Tangentopoli* scandal and have tangled with Prime Minister Berlusconi.

- Despite a traditionally unitary structure, Italy's regions have gained significant powers in stages since 1970; five of the twenty regions possess special autonomy because of their unique cultural features.

- The Italian electoral and party systems have changed dramatically since the early 1990s, with diminishing use of proportional representation, several major new parties, and a tendency toward center-left and center-right coalitions in competition with one another.

- The House of Freedom coalition has backed the Berlusconi government, but its component parties vary in their preferred versions of conservatism.

- The Olive Tree coalition backed the Italian governments of 1996–2001, but its components vary across the center and left of the Italian political spectrum.

- Referendums have become more numerous and significant in Italy than in any of the other major EU member states.

- Roman Catholic and agricultural interest groups have lost influence in Italy in recent years, labor unions have been relatively fragmented and weak, and *Confindustria* has long been the most powerful business group.

- Among the major EU nation-states, Italy continues to be the most discontented with its state institutions and the quality of its democracy.

ENDNOTES

1. Luigi Barzini, *The Italians* (New York: Bantam Books, 1964), xiv.

2. Harry Hearder, *Italy: A Short History* (Cambridge: Cambridge University Press, 1990), Chs. 2, 3, 4.

3. On the emergence of the Italian language, see Denis Mack Smith, *Italy: A Modern History* (Ann Arbor: University of Michigan Press, 1969), 5, and Hearder, *Italy*, 69.

4. Hearder, *Italy*, 164; Smith, *Italy*, 1.

5. See the collection of articles in Charles F. Delzell, *The Unification of Italy, 1859–1861: Cavour, Mazzini, or Garibaldi?* (New York: Holt, Rinehart, and Winston, 1965) for varied perspectives among historians on the unification process.

6. On the franchise, see Hearder, *Italy*, 205, 211–212; Hilary Partridge, *Italian Politics Today* (Manchester: Manchester University Press, 1998), 8; and Smith, *Italy*, 133–134, 257–258.

7. Smith, *Italy*, 211–262; Martin Clark, *Modern Italy, 1871–1995*, 2nd ed. (New York: Longman, 1996), Ch. 7.

8. On Mussolini and his regime, see John Whittam, *Fascist Italy* (Manchester: Manchester University Press, 1995); Clark, *Modern Italy*, 203–301; and Smith, *Italy*, 357–492.

9. Patrick McCarthy, *The Crisis of the Italian State: From the Origins of the Cold War to the Fall of Berlusconi* (New York: St. Martin's, 1995), esp. Ch. 2; Clark, *Modern Italy*, 302–326; Elisa A. Carrillo, *Alcide De Gasperi: The Long Apprenticeship* (Notre Dame, IN: University of Notre Dame Press, 1965), esp Ch. 8.

10. Levy's quote is from Carl Levy, "Introduction: Italian Regionalism in Context," in Levy, ed., *Italian Regionalism: History, Identity, and Politics* (Oxford: Berg, 1996), 21. Also see Damian Tambini, *Nationalism in Italian Politics* (London: Routledge, 2001); Gian Enrico Rusconi, "Will Italy Remain a Nation?" in Mark Donovan, ed., *Italy*, Vol. I (Dartmouth: Ashgate, 1998), 477–490; Anna Cento Bull, "Ethnicity, Racism, and the Northern League," in Levy, ed., *Italian Regionalism*, 171–188; Gavin Jones, "The Trouble with a Long Coastline," *Financial Times Survey: Italy*, July 22, 2002, 3, 4.

11. Gabriel Almond and Sidney Verba, *The Civic Culture: Political Attitudes and Democracy in Five Nations* (Boston: Little, Brown, 1965), esp. Chs. 3 and 8, emphasizes the extent to which Italians held negative views of their governmental institutions in their survey, contrasting Italy in this respect with Britain and the United States, in particular. On the "second" republic concept, see Sondra Z. Koff and Stephen P. Koff, *Italy: From the First to the Second Republic* (London: Routledge, 2000); Clark, *Modern Italy*, Ch. 20; and Mark Donovan, "A New Republic in Italy? The May 2001 Election," *West European Politics* 24, 4 (October 2001), 193–205. A useful recent collection of readings on clientelism that places the Italian patterns in a comparative perspective is Simona Piattoni, ed., *Clientelism, Interests, and Democratic Representation* (Cambridge: Cambridge University Press, 2001), particularly Jonathan Hopkin and Alfio Mastropaolo, "From Patronage to Clientelism: Comparing the Italian and Spanish Experiences," 152–171.

12. Partridge, *Italian Politics Today*, esp. 118–122; Mimmo Carrieri, "Industrial Relations and the Labour Movement," in Stephen Gundle and Simon Parker, eds., *The New Italian Republic: From the Fall of the Berlin Wall to Berlusconi* (London: Routledge, 1996), 294–307; Mario B. Mignone, *Italy Today: A Country in Transition* (New York: Peter Lang, 1995), 54–58; McCarthy, *The Crisis of the Italian State*, esp. 193–197, on "the elusive citizen." For a sophisticated analysis of regional variations in Italian civic participation, see Robert D. Putnam, with Robert Leonardi and Raffaella Y. Nanetti, *Making Democracy Work: Civic Traditions in Modern Italy* (Princeton: Princeton University Press, 1993).

13. Clark, *Modern Italy*, Ch. 19; Partridge, *Italian Politics Today*, 104–116; McCarthy, *The Crisis of the Italian State*, 114.

14. See the last three sources cited in note 11. Others, such as Filippo Sabetti, *The Search for Good Government: Understanding the Paradox of Italian Democracy* (Montreal and Kingston: McGill-Queen's University Press, 2000), 242, see the declaration of a "Second Republic" as "premature."

15. For recent presidential–prime ministerial relations, see Tony Barber, "Berlusconi May Launch

Emergency Decree to Save Media Legislation," *Financial Times*, December 17, 2003, 3, and Barber, "Italians Get a Reminder that Their President Is More than a Figurehead," *Financial Times*, December 18, 2003, 4. On the general powers of prime ministers, see Koff and Koff, *From the First to the Second Republic*, Ch. 7; Smith, *Italy*, esp. 494–509; Sassoon, *Contemporary Italy*, Ch. 10; Ciro D'Amore, "Studying Italian Politics Since the 1990s," *South European Society & Politics* 7, 1 (Summer 2002), 103–112.

16. Donovan, "A New Republic in Italy?" 193–205; Sergio Fabbrini and Mark Gilbert, "The Italian General Election of 13 May 2001: Democratic Alternation or False Step?" *Government and Opposition* 36, 4 (Autumn 2001), 519–536; Gianfranco Pasquino, "Berlusconi's Victory: The Italian General Elections of 2001," *South European Society & Politics* 6, 1 (Summer 2001), 125–137; "Berlusconi Strikes Out," and "A Foreign Minister Goes, but Does a Foreign Policy?" *The Economist* 362 (January 12, 2002), 14–15 and 45–46, respectively.

17. Donovan, "A New Republic in Italy?" 203; Koff and Koff, *From the First to the Second Republic*, 132.

18. Rodolfo Lewanski, "Italian Administration in Transition," *South European Society & Politics* 4, 1 (Summer 1999), 97–131; Koff and Koff, *From the First to the Second Republic*, 149–163; McCarthy, *The Crisis of the Italian State*, 61–101.

19. Vincent della Sala, "Italy: A Bridge Too Far?" *Parliamentary Affairs* 50, 3 (July 1997), 396–409.

20. Mary L. Volcansek, "Political Power and Judicial Review in Italy," *Comparative Political Studies* 26, 4 (January 1994), 492–509; David Nelkin, "A Legal Revolution? The Judges and *Tangentopoli*," in Gundle and Parker, *The New Italian Republic*, 191–205; Patrizia Pederzoli and Carlo Guarnieri, "Italy: A Case of Judicial Democracy?" *International Social Science Journal* 152 (June 1997), 253–270; "Parliament in Italy Passes Immunity Law for Berlusconi," *New York Times*, June 19, 2003, A11; Tony Barber, "Blow for Berlusconi as Court Rules Law Is Invalid," *Financial Times*, January 13, 2004, 2; "Back in the Dock," *Financial Times*, January 15, 2004, 12. James Newell and Hilary Partridge, "Conclu-

sion," in Newell, ed., *The Italian General Election of 2001*, 243, suggest the possible waning of Italian judicial activism since 2001.

21. McCarthy, *The Crisis of the Italian State*, 81.

22. McCarthy, *The Crisis of the Italian State*, 80–83 and Ch. 9; Mark Donovan, "The 1994 Election in Italy: Normalisation or Continuing Exceptionalism?" *West European Politics* 17, 4 (December 1994); Donovan, "A New Republic in Italy?" 193–205; Partridge, *Italian Politics Today*, 150–162.

23. Levy, "Introduction: Italian Regionalism in Context," 1–32; David Hine, "Federalism, Regionalism, and the Unitary State: Contemporary Regional Pressures in Historical Perspective," in Levy, ed., *Italian Regionalism*, 109–130; Donald Sassoon, *Contemporary Italy: Economy, Society and Politics Since 1945*, 2nd ed. (New York: Longman, 1997), Ch. 11; Barber, "Italian Coalition Seeks Accord on Reforms," *Financial Times*, August 15, 2003, 5; Putnam, et al., *Making Democracy Work*. Filippo Sabetti, *The Search for Good Government*, challenges Putnam's explanation of differing regional cultural traditions and blames an overly centralized "state based on law" (*stato di diritto*) for most Italian governmental problems.

24. See, for example, James L. Newell, *Parties and Democracy in Italy* (Aldershot: Ashgate, 2000), esp. Ch. 1, for a good survey of analysts' assessments.

25. In-depth analyses of Italian election laws may be found in Sassoon, *Contemporary Italy*, Ch. 9, and Newell, *Parties and Democracy in Italy*, 98–101. On the role of electoral reform in the upheaval of the 1990s, also see Simon Parker, "Electoral Reform and Political Change in Italy," in Gundle and Parker, *The New Italian Republic*, 40–56.

26. McCarthy, *The Crisis of the Italian State*, Ch. 2; Clark, *Modern Italy*, Ch. 16; Gundle and Parker, eds., *The New Italian Republic*, Part II. For a more positive assessment than most, see Joseph La Palombara, *Democracy, Italian Style* (New Haven: Yale University Press, 1987).

27. Fabbrini and Gilbert, "The Italian General Election of 13 May 2001," 519–536; Donovan, "A New Republic in Italy?" 193–205; Pasquine, "Berlusconi's Victory," 125–137; Martin J. Bull, "The Democratic Party of the Left in Italy's

Transition," in Gundle and Parker, *The New Italian Republic*, Ch. 10.

28. McCarthy, *The Crisis of the Italian State*, esp. Ch. 9; Tambini, *Nationalism in Italian Politics* (on the Northern League); Ilvo Diamanti, "The Northern League: From Regional Party to Party of Government;" Patrick McCarthy, "Forza Italia: The New Politics and Old Values of a Changing Italy;" and Carlo Ruzza and Oliver Schmidtke, "Toward a Modern Right," the last three of which appear in Gundle and Parker, eds., *The New Italian Republic*, Chs. 7, 8, and 9, respectively. Also see the sources in note 25 on the 2001 elections.

29. Sassoon, *Contemporary Italy*, 234–235; Newell, *Parties and Democracy in Italy*, 26–28.

30. The quotation is from Roberto Pazzi, "Germans Are from Mars, Italians Are from Venus," *New York Times*, July 13, 2003, IV, 13. Mignone, *Italy Today*, 189–203, thoroughly covers secularization and loss of power by Catholic groups.

31. Alan Friedman, "The Economic Elites and the Political System," and Carrieri, "Industrial Relations and the Labour Movement," both in Gundle and Parker, eds., *The New Italian Republic*, Chs. 17 and 18, respectively; Mignone, *Italy Today*, esp. Chs. 5 and 6. Koff and Koff, *From the First to the Second Republic*, Ch. 5, provides a good overview of current Italian interest groups. Joseph La Palombara, *Interest Groups in Italian Politics* (Princeton: Princeton University Press, 1964), is a classic on the postwar patterns. Jelle Visser, "Italy," in Bernhard Ebbinghaus and Jelle Visser, *The Societies of Europe: Trade Unions in Western Europe Since 1945* (Basingstoke: Macmillan, 2000), 371–428, covers labor unions thoroughly and provides some discussion of business groups also.

Chapter 10

ITALY AND THE EUROPEAN UNION

"In spite of being a founding member and one of the big four nations in the EU, Italy has felt like a poor relative."

—Sondra Z. and Stephen P. Koff, *Italy: From the First to the Second Republic (2000)*, 206.

An abstract commitment to European integration has long been an attribute of Italian political leaders and, to a considerable degree, the Italian general public—certainly to a greater degree than in France or Britain, and probably to a greater degree than in Germany. The Italians have liked to portray themselves as responsible for the only successful historical efforts to unite most of Europe: the Roman Empire and the Roman Catholic Church. In modern times, such Italian political leaders as Luigi Einaudi, Altiero Spinelli, Carlo Sforza, Alcide De Gasperi, and Romano Prodi have repeatedly articulated the vision of European integration. Writing back in 1918, for example, Einaudi, later to serve as finance minister and then president of post–World War II Italy, called for a United States of Europe, to be followed by a United States of the world: "Beside the United States of America, we ought to see, in close association, the United States of Europe, while waiting to see the birth at a later moment of human progress of the United States of the world."[1] In a fashion similar to that in the West German Basic Law, the 1948 Italian Constitution provided for the pooling of sovereignty in the cause of "peace and justice among nations" (Article 11).[2]

In accord with its embrace of an abstract vision of European integration, Italy was a founding member of the European Coal and Steel Community (ECSC) and the European Economic Community (EEC), and its leaders have almost continuously advocated an "ever closer union." However, practical calculations of how to utilize European institutions to enhance their own rather weak legitimacy at home, increase their international prestige, impose difficult decisions on an often-recalcitrant Italian society, isolate domestic Communists and their allies, and gain economic advantages have often guided Italian leaders' decisions vis-à-vis Europe. Major Italian contributions to shaping European institutions and public policies have been infrequent. The Italian public's superficial enthusiasm for a united Europe has been accompanied by a shockingly low awareness and understanding of how the European Union operates or what it does.[3] Furthermore, Italy possesses an undistinguished record as a persistent laggard in the implementation of EC/EU directives. More often than any other member state, it has been brought before the European Court of Justice (ECJ) in infringement proceedings. Italy also ranks first in the number of failures to execute European Court of Justice (ECJ) judgments.[4]

Paralleling the previous chapters on France and Germany and the European Union (Chapters Six and Eight, respectively), this chapter will elucidate the apparent paradox of Italy's enthusiasm for the ideals of European integration and its general record of few initiatives and frequent noncompliance with EC/EU laws. Like the previously noted chapters, it commences with a historical overview and proceeds to analyses of the most distinctive long-term features of Italian approaches toward the EC/EU and the mutual influences of Italy on the EC/EU and the EC/EU on Italy.

THE DEVELOPMENT OF THE ITALIAN RELATIONSHIP WITH THE EC/EU

Early Italian Moves Toward European Integration

Italy after World War II was a nation-state that retained few of its Mussolini-era pretensions to great-power status. The Mussolini regime had proved disastrous. Northern Italy remained under Anglo-American military control until December 1945. The peace treaty stripped Italy of its colonies, imposed reparations payments on Italy, made Trieste for a time a free territory, and was widely viewed by Italians as a humiliation. Already lagging far behind Britain, France, and Germany economically in the prewar era, Italy lost one-third of its wealth to destruction in World War II. Sharp ideological and regional cleavages marked Italian society and politics. In this environment, Prime Minister Alcide De Gasperi (1945–1953) and his close associates Carlo Sforza and Luigi Einaudi emphasized the rhetoric of West European

unity and interdependence while struggling for survival and respect.[5]

As the broad Italian postwar coalition governments that included Communists and Socialists as well as Christian Democrats and smaller parties gave way in 1947 to Christian Democrat–dominated governments, De Gasperi, Sforza, Einaudi, and their allies shaped Italy's embrace of West European integration and the Atlantic Alliance. Massive American economic assistance to Italy helped spur Italian economic growth and cemented strong ties to the United States that were reinforced by military, intelligence, and cultural links, fostering a long-term Atlanticist inclination among most Italian policy-makers. However, Italy's Atlanticism from the outset was linked to an emphasis on West European political and economic integration. "What other myth are we to offer to our young people, in terms of the relations between states, the future of our Europe, the future of the world, security, peace, if not this effort towards Union?" asked De Gasperi in 1950.[6] The "myth" was also to prove useful to De Gasperi, his allies, and his successors in bolstering the weak domestic legitimacy of their governments, isolating the domestic Communists and Socialists (who initially opposed West European integration), linking the Italian economy to stronger economies to the North, and giving Italy at least the appearance of equality with France and the Federal Republic of Germany.

"What other myth are we to offer to our young people, in terms of the relations between states, the future of our Europe, the future of the world, security, peace, if not this effort towards Union?"

Prime Minister Alcide De Gasperi, *cited by D. H. Ellwood, "Italy, Europe, and the Cold War: The Politics and Economics of Limited Sovereignty" (1995), 41.*

The De Gasperi government's early enthusiasm for West European political and economic integration was evident in its 1947 support for an American proposal for a customs union among Marshall Plan aid recipients and, failing that, a customs union with France (rejected in 1949 by the French National Assembly). Foreign Minister Sforza in 1948 proposed using the Organization for European Economic Cooperation (OEEC) as a means toward achieving West European political integration, but his proposals were largely ignored.

When France and West Germany unveiled the Schuman Plan for the European Coal and Steel Community (ECSC) in May 1950, Italy played no role in conceiving or preparing it but quickly endorsed the idea and joined the talks that opened in Paris in June. The Italians accepted the ECSC institutional structure proposed by the French, gained ECSC Assembly seats equal to the French and West German representation, and bargained with some success for safeguards for weak Italian sectors, such as the Sardinian coal mines. Although the ECSC was to prove of little economic significance to Italy, the Italian governmental leaders endorsed it on political grounds and as a first step toward European integration. Despite vehement opposition from the Communists and Socialists, who denounced it as another aspect of capitalist and American dominance, and a pessimistic assessment of its likely economic effects by *Confindustria*, the leading Italian employers' association, the Italian parliament approved the ECSC Treaty in June 1952.[7]

The Pleven Plan for the European Defense Community (EDC), put forward by France in October 1950, evoked less initial enthusiasm from the Italian government than had the Schuman Plan. Italy had supported American proposals for West German rearmament and feared that the Pleven proposal might be merely a means to delay such rearmament and might also bring a long-term lessening of the American role in West European military security, as well as increased military costs for Italy. On the other hand, De Gasperi's government wanted to maintain good relations with France and to promote further European integration. Therefore,

it joined the Paris negotiations on the European Defense Community but adopted a strategy of delay. Influenced by the independent European federalist Altiero Spinelli, De Gasperi in 1951 became a leading advocate of creating a European Political Community (EPC) along with the EDC. This was to be Italy's major contribution to the European discussions, and it resulted in the inclusion of an EPC article (Article 38) in the draft treaty for the EDC.

As in France, the European Defense Community Treaty became a major issue of political controversy in Italy, generating even stronger opposition from the Communists and Socialists than the European Coal and Steel Community had. De Gasperi hoped to convince Italians that the EDC was a minor component of a broad policy of achieving a European integration that would bring political and economic benefits to Italy. However, his Christian Democrats lost their parliamentary majority in the 1953 elections; and De Gasperi was forced to resign as prime minister. His replacement, fellow Christian Democrat Giuseppi Pella, showed little interest in European integration and was in any event soon also compelled to resign for lack of parliamentary support. The next prime minister, Mario Scelba, revived De Gasperi's European policy approach. However, the French National Assembly effectively killed the European Defense Community and European Political Community in August, before the Italian parliament took any action. The result was the creation of the Western European Union (WEU), with Italy as a charter member of this intergovernmental security organization that permitted West German rearmament. The WEU, however, was not the type of supranational organization that Italy favored. Italy's hopes for a European Political Community appeared moribund.[8]

From the Messina Conference to the Rome Treaties

Soon, however, the drive for European integration revived with the proposals and negotiations for the European Economic Community (EEC) and Euratom. Although the June 1955 Messina Conference of the six ECSC member states' foreign ministers in Messina, Italy, proved critical in launching the new integration efforts, and the EEC and Euratom Rome Treaties were signed in Rome in 1957, Italy's role in the process was relatively small. France, Belgium, the Netherlands, and Luxembourg offered most of the initiatives. Italian Prime Minister Antonio Segni gave little direction to the Italian negotiators. While they pursued the broad European aims laid down previously by De Gasperi, their primary emphases were on economic demands including a special "Protocol concerning Italy" that focused on the special needs of poverty-stricken southern Italy; a European Social Fund to aid depressed regions; and a European Investment Bank to spur economic development, modernize businesses, and fund major projects of community interest. As the poorest member of the EEC in terms of per capita gross domestic product, Italy sought economic benefits from its membership. On agriculture, the Italian delegation had difficulty formulating its position. However, most specific decisions concerning what would become the Common Agricultural Policy were postponed for later negotiations. Although the Italian Communist party opposed both of the Rome Treaties, the Socialists abstained on the EEC and endorsed Euratom, and the Communist-dominated CGIL union displayed some marked ambivalence before finally opposing the Treaties. The Italian Chamber of Deputies ratified the Treaties in July 1957 and the Senate did so the following October, though the members of parliament displayed fairly minimal interest in the debates.[9]

As the European Communities took shape, Italy underwent an economic boom that had begun before 1957 but was almost certainly spurred further by membership in the EEC. The Italian gross domestic product grew by 71 percent in the decade from 1958 to 1968, and the gap between Italy and the other members in per capita wealth narrowed appreciably, enhancing Italian popular support for European integration.[10]

Italy and the European Community in the 1960s and 1970s

Major European issues of the 1960s included the Common Agricultural Policy (CAP), the Gaullist resistance to supranational development, and the Gaullist vetoes of British EC entry. Italian negotiators failed to gain the benefits for producers of fruits, vegetables, and olive oil that were granted to grain, dairy, and livestock interests under the CAP. Despite Italian hopes, the European Agricultural Guidance and Guarantee Fund (FEOGA) did not prove advantageous to Italy. Italy supported the European Commission's efforts to advance supranational development of the EEC. However, when de Gaulle of France responded to these with his "empty chair" policy, the Italians sought to mediate between France and the other members and helped achieve the Luxembourg Compromise that gave de Gaulle most of what he had demanded. On the enlargement issue, Italy favored British EC entry and felt frustrated by de Gaulle's two vetoes. Also blocked were Italy's proposals to increase the powers of the European Parliament. Despite efforts to cooperate with France throughout this period, most Italian officials concerned with the EC welcomed de Gaulle's 1969 resignation and hoped for renewed progress toward European integration.[11]

"With the ouster of De Gasperi, Italian government policy lost its consistency.... While Europeanism remained the cardinal principle of the DC's [Christian Democrats'] foreign policy, it became a general belief rather than a practical program."

F. Roy Willis, *Italy Chooses Europe* (1971), 47.

Italian leadership in the drive for European integration was only sporadic at best after the end of the De Gasperi era in 1953. As F. Roy Willis has noted, "With the ouster of

De Gasperi, Italian government policy lost its consistency…. While Europeanism remained the cardinal principle of the DC's [Christian Democrats'] foreign policy, it became a general belief rather than a practical program."[12] Writing in 1992, another analyst has concluded, "The Italian political class is moved primarily by its fight for internal power, and daily foreign policy is subservient to the internal fight for power and influence."[13] Illustrative of the general pattern was the resignation of Franco Maria Malfatti, Italy's first (and until 1999, only) president of the European Commission, less than two years into his term of office because he felt that his political career was being ruined by his absence from Rome.[14]

"The Italian political class is moved primarily by its fight for internal power, and daily foreign policy is subservient to the internal fight for power and influence."

Luigi Vittorio Ferraris, *"Italian-European Foreign Policy," (1992), 136.*

If domestic political preoccupations and factional and party conflicts hampered Italian leadership in the EC, the inefficiency and corruption of its state bureaucracy created a record of non-compliance with Community laws that earned Italy a negative reputation in Brussels and other European capitals. This record had already become quite evident by the 1970s.[15]

In spite of its problems both in taking the initiative and in implementing EC policies, Italy during the 1970s played a part in finally securing direct elections and some power enhancement for the European Parliament (a longtime goal) and the establishment of the European Regional development Fund (ERDF) that would benefit southern Italy. However, new EC member Britain by most accounts played a larger role than Italy did in establishing the ERDF. Italy tried, unsuccessfully, to participate in the "snake in the tunnel" exchange-rate mechanism that grew out of the 1970 Werner Plan and then joined the European Monetary System set up in 1979 on the initiative of France and West Germany.[16]

Italy and EC/EU Transformation in the 1980s and 1990s

The next major effort at Italian leadership in the drive for European integration occurred in 1981, when Foreign Minister Emilio Colombo, long a major Italian player in EC politics in his multiple roles in various cabinet posts (and two years as prime minister), joined with West German Foreign Minister Hans-Dietrich Genscher to launch the Genscher-Colombo "Draft European Act," advocating an expanded EC foreign-policy role. Although this effort had few direct effects, it indirectly helped to stimulate the moves that revitalized the drive for European integration in the mid-1980s.[17]

Italian governments had shifted a little to the left after 1963, when the Socialist party (accepting West European integration and Atlanticism gradually over the 1957–1961 period) came to be regularly incorporated into Christian Democrat–dominated coalition governments. Though the Communists were to remain excluded from Italian governmental posts until after the end of the Cold War, even they cooperated with the governing coalitions for a time in the late 1970s. In August 1983, Bettino Craxi became the first Socialist prime minister of Italy, albeit in a government dominated by Christian Democrats. The slight tilt to the left of the Italian governments had little impact on Italy's positions vis-à-vis the EC, because the Socialists generally competed with the Christian Democrats in their pro-European federalism rhetoric. Even the Communists moved gradually toward acceptance, and eventually endorsement, of the EC. Nevertheless, the previous pattern of domestic political preoccupations and weak implementation of EC laws continued.[18]

Italy's roles in shaping the EC's Single European Act (SEA) of 1986 were smaller than those of France, West Germany, or Britain. However, Italy did assert leadership at one critical point. Christian Democratic Foreign Minister (and former Prime Minister) Giulio Andreotti, competing with Prime Minister Craxi to be seen as a premier pro-European leader, developed a plan with the European Commission to call for an unprecedented majority vote at the Milan Summit of 1985 for the convening of a formal Intergovernmental Conference (IGC). When Italy as president called for the vote, the motion passed 6–3, with Britain, Greece, and Denmark opposed. Margaret Thatcher of Britain was particularly infuriated. However, the subsequent IGC succeeded in drafting the Single European Act. Therefore, although the content of the SEA was largely of non-Italian origin, Italy had made a significant contribution. In substantive terms, Italy also gained agreement in the negotiations to increase the structural funds to aid poor EC regions, including its own South.[19]

Italy joined France in the late 1980s as a major proponent of an Economic and Monetary Union (EMU) with a single currency. Like France, Italy saw the EMU as a means of replacing the power of the German Bundesbank over their monetary policies (through the European Monetary System's operations) with that of a European Central Bank, over which the European national governments might collectively exercise some influence. More than the French, the Italian negotiators in the Maastricht Treaty deliberations saw EMU membership for their country as necessary both to counter their Europe-wide reputation for poor domestic fiscal performance and to impose genuine external discipline on a national budget widely viewed as out of control. Beyond the EMU issue, Italy favored German efforts in the Maastricht process to expand further the powers of the European Parliament, joined with France to push (unsuccessfully) for a common EC indus-

trial policy and an EC cultural policy, and reiterated its usual rhetoric about the desirability of European supranationalism.[20]

As the Maastricht Treaty took shape and began to be implemented, Italian politics were in turmoil, triggered especially by the *Tangentopoli* scandal (Chapter Nine) but also by the end of the Cold War and Italy's abrupt forced departure from the Economic and Monetary System (EMS) in September 1992 amid wild speculation that drove down the value of the Italian lira in global currency markets. By 1993, both of the major parties of government, the Christian Democrats and the Socialists, had collapsed. A major party realignment, and perhaps even the creation of a *de facto* Second Republic, were under way in Italy. The Maastricht Treaty won the approval of the Italian parliament despite opposition from the Refounded Communists, the neo-Fascists, and the populistic Northern League. However, a major question remained about the likely long-term impact of Italy's political upheaval on its approaches to European integration.

The Amato, Ciampi, Dini, Prodi, and D'Alema governments, backed by the center-left in parliament but often dominated by nonpartisan technocrats, generally continued Italy's past rhetorical emphasis on European supranational development while struggling with considerable success to impose sufficient austerity at home to gain Italian participation on schedule in the adoption of the euro currency.[21]

Berlusconi and the EU: A New Italian Approach?

On the other hand, the new center-right coalition governments dominated by Silvio Berlusconi (May 1994–January 1995 and May 2001–) gave mixed signals on European issues and indicated potential major departures from Italian traditional approaches to Europe. Berlusconi and his Forza Italia political movement have at times used semi-Gaullist and Thatcherite rhetoric emphasizing a Europe of nation-states

PEOPLE IN THE EU

Romano Prodi: From Bologna to Rome to Brussels

As discussed previously, Italian leadership in the EC/EU has been a relatively rare commodity. Before 1999, the only Italian to serve as President of the European Commission, Franco Maria Malfatti, proved a weak leader and resigned his presidency less than halfway through his term of office because he feared that his Italian political career was being undermined by his duties in Brussels. Furthermore, most Italian prime ministers have lacked both the will and the resources to shape European institutions or public policies significantly.

However, Roman Prodi has shown a marked commitment to European Union integration and expansion both before and after his elevation to the presidency of the European Commission in May 1999, following the ignominious forced resignation of the previous president, Jacques Santer of Luxembourg, and the entire Commission, amid scandal and criticism from the European Parliament.

Born in Scandiano, Italy, August 9, 1939, Romano Prodi embarked late in life, in 1995 and already in his mid-fifties, on a career in elective Italian politics. Prior to that time, he had been an economics professor at the University of Bologna and had served twice, once in the 1980s and again in 1993–1994, as head of the gigantic Italian state holding company, the Institute for Industrial Reconstruction (IRI). Widely seen as "above" conventional party politics, Prodi played a key role in organizing Italy's center-left Olive Tree alliance and leading it to victory in the 1996 Italian parliamentary elections. He became prime minister of Italy in June 1996 and served in that position for a little more than two years.

As prime minister, Prodi won plaudits from most other European leaders and from most of the Italian and international business and financial community for his central role, assisted by such leading technocrats as Lamberto Dini and Carlo Ciampi, in imposing the fiscal austerity on Italy that enabled it to join the common European currency on schedule—much to the surprise of many observers at home and abroad. At the same time, however, his actions angered many Italian labor union members and the Refounded Communists, who resented his government's major cuts in social-spending programs. As a result, Prodi was to suffer in October 1998 a 313–312 defeat on a vote of no confidence in the Italian Chamber of Deputies over his government's budget and was forced to resign as prime minister.

His successor as prime minister, Democrats of the Left leader Massimo D'Alema, put forward Prodi's name to fill the vacancy created early in 1999 by Santer's resignation from the European Commission presidency. The other major candidate was Wim Kok of the Netherlands. Solidly backed by Britain's Tony Blair, an admirer of his record in Italy and on European issues generally, Prodi soon gained the backing of the new German Chancellor, Gerhard Schröder, and went on to win the unanimous backing of the 15 chief executives of the EU member states, as well as a vote of 392 in favor, 72 against, and 41 abstentions in the European Parliament.

Early in his tenure as Commission president, Prodi aroused a storm of protest by describing the Commission as a "European government" and himself as the "European prime minister." His record overall proved solid, if unspectacular. Although some observers have compared him unfavorably with Jacques Delors (president 1985–1995) in terms of vision, leadership skills, and effective links to top national leaders, Prodi has restored respectability to a scandal-plagued Commission and obtained some new powers over its personnel and day-to-day operations. Probably more than any other Italian, Romano Prodi has established a solid record of achievement in both Rome and Brussels.[22]

at odds with long-term Italian support for European supranationalism. He and his party also have often employed free-market language different from that of most Italian prime ministers. Further complicating matters have been the inclusion of a number of nationalistic elements long unsympathetic to European integration in the National Alliance part of the coalition and the frequent outbursts from the Northern League critical of the "democratic deficit" of the EU and its "Brussels bureaucracy." Prime Minister Berlusconi's abrupt removal of his independent, pro-European foreign minister, Renato Ruggiero, in January 2002 spurred another flurry of speculation about the future course of his government's approaches to Europe, as did his often offensive and bizarre behavior during the July–December 2003 period, when Italy served as president of the European Council.[23]

DISTINCTIVE FEATURES OF THE ITALIAN APPROACHES TO THE EC/EU

As has been true of France and Germany, Italy has developed distinctive approaches to European integration that have been based on its own historical experience, geopolitical position, economic conditions, and national political institutions.

In the period after World War II, Italy lacked the pride in its national history so clearly demonstrated by France (and Britain). Like West Germany, it sought an "escape into Europe," partly to erase memories of the Mussolini regime and its record but partly also to gain an international prestige that it had consistently lacked in modern times.

The geopolitical location of Italy in the Mediterranean and relatively far from the front lines of the Cold War, as emphasized in realist theories, made Italy less concerned about military protection than West Germany was. However, its large domestic Communist party, aligned with the Socialist party after World War II, frightened its postwar centrists and conservatives into actively welcoming a large American role in Europe. Italy's relatively backward economy, especially in the South, also inclined Italian leaders to court the United States, as did the large number of Italian emigrants to America who retained close ties to their relatives still in Italy. Nonetheless, Italy's Mediterranean position and its ties to North Africa and the Arab Middle East often colored its approaches to European issues in ways that modified its general Atlanticism.

The Italian political economy, long marked by extensive protection and other forms of state involvement (such as the IRI state holding company), bore some resemblance to that of France. However, many globally competitive North Italian businessmen favored free-market capitalism. Meanwhile, the pronounced economic backwardness of the South distinguished the Italian economy from that of France, making Italian leaders particularly intent on seeking economic-development assistance from European institutions (as well as from the United States). Liberal intergovernmental theory highlights distinctive Italian political-economic interests.

The Italian state, modeled to some extent on the centralized French model, never developed the professional civil-service elite characteristic of France and certainly lacked the coordinating capabilities with regard to European approaches that the French governments normally displayed, particularly in the French Fifth Republic. Instead, the Italian governments, especially after 1953, lacked effective mechanisms for either leadership or implementation regarding European policies. The game of musical chairs in Italian cabinets and the clientelism that permeated Italian politics and public administration were traits that profoundly affected distinctive features of the Italian approaches to the EC/EU.

Historical, geographic, economic, and political factors have shaped a fairly consistent pattern of Italian approaches vis-à-vis European integration. Once established, these have usually persisted over time. Among the major patterns are the following:

An inclination to balance Atlanticism and a European focus. Like Germany, Italy has usually positioned itself between the French wariness of Atlanticism and the British embrace of the United States and support for its active involvement in European affairs. Also like West Germany, Italy demonstrated its greatest attachment to the United States in the early years of the Cold War, though less for military protection against external threats than for economic assistance and containment of the internal Italian Communist-Socialist threats. At times, Italian Atlanticism has been a subject of internal

debate, challenged not only by the left opposition for many years but also by certain elements within the Italian government that have favored what some have termed **neo-Atlanticism** (downplaying the military aspects of the American alliance in favor of economic and political cooperation while stressing Italy's Mediterranean/Arab ties).[24] Nevertheless, the Italian government's desire to maintain American engagement in Europe has been a fairly consistent and dominant element for more than five decades. Italian mild Atlanticism was evident again in the 2002–2003 European divisions over the Iraq War, when the Italian government positioned itself closer to the United States and Britain than to France and Germany but made no major commitment of troops or funds to the war itself, as Britain did.[25]

A supranational inclination. In their rhetoric, Italian leaders have demonstrated a dedication to European supranational development at least as evident as that of the Germans. From the sovereignty-pooling provisions of the Italian Constitution of 1948 to the strong Italian endorsement of, and great struggle to achieve, Economic and Monetary Union (EMU), Italy has inclined toward European federalism. Lack of a traditional role as a great power, desire to escape from the record of the Mussolini regime, hope for economic gains from association with wealthy North European states, and (in the 1990s) determination by key Italian elites to use European institutions to compel a revamping of the Italian budgetary process have all been factors shaping the Italian willingness to cede sovereignty to European institutions.[26]

A weak inclination and ability to lead on European issues. Although Italy has had a population and gross domestic product close to that of France or Britain in recent years, its governmental leaders have demonstrated little inclination or ability to take the initiative effectively and consistently on major matters of European concern. The usual lack of will since the demise of De Gasperi and Sforza has reflected most Italian leaders' preoccupation with maintaining their power in Italy's complex multiparty and factionalized domestic politics. Moreover, the resources for leadership have generally been lacking given the high turnover in key ministerial positions, partisan and personal battles among ministers, and the absence of an undisputed coordinating institution (since the Ministry for the Coordination of Community Policy lacks adequate staffing and status and often conflicts with the Foreign Ministry and the Interministerial Committee for Economic Planning).[27]

A weak inclination and ability to implement EC/EU policies. In addition to lack of initiative, Italy possesses a record of noncompliance with EC/EU laws that has damaged its reputation throughout Europe, though some analysts detect an improvement in Italy's record since the early 1990s. The low levels of professionalism, the clientelism, and the outright corruption characteristic of the Italian public administration have been major components of the implementation problem. Another contributor for many years was the Italian practice that the two independent chambers of the Italian parliament should transpose most EC/EU directives into Italian law in the midst of their already crowded legislative agenda. In 1989, Italy sought to address this problem by allowing the parliament to address in one Annual Community Law the unimplemented European directives and those that were about to expire. However, continuing parliamentary difficulties have been evident in the fact that the 1995 Annual Community Law was not finally approved until April 1998. Despite what some observers see as improvements in the Italian compliance record, problems in this area remain.[28]

A wariness of global free-market capitalism. This has been a frequent but not entirely consistent Italian approach to the EC/EU. A few Italian leaders, such as Luigi Einaudi and Silvio

---

TABLE 10.1 Distinctive Features of Italian Approaches to the EC/EU

1. An inclination to balance Atlanticism and a European focus.
2. A supranational inclination.
3. A weak inclination and ability to lead on European issues.
4. A weak inclination and ability to implement EC/EU policies.
5. A wariness of global free-market competition.

Berlusconi, have proved exceptions to this pattern. However, Italy has tended to side with France in expressing concerns about American-style free enterprise without a strong social safety net or extensive regulations. For example, Italy joined France in the Rome Treaty negotiations of the 1950s to favor a high external tariff and a *dirigiste* approach to competition policy. Through the 1970s and 1980s, Italy again joined France in urging (unsuccessfully) a common industrial policy for the EC. Italy has also generally supported France in advocating additions to EC/EU social policy. Though less clearly or consistently wary of free-market capitalism than France, Italy has often displayed inclinations in this direction.[29]

THE IMPACT OF ITALY ON THE EC/EU

Italian leaders' weak inclination and ability to lead on European issues have been reflected in an Italian impact on the EC/EU that has been relatively slight relative to Italy's size—far less than that of France or Germany and, in most respects, less than that of the United Kingdom, also.

With regard to EC/EU institutions, Italy has consistently expressed verbal support for European supranational development. Perhaps even more consistently and intensely than

Germany, Italy has advocated enhanced powers for the European Parliament. However, Italy's ability to come forward with practical and specific proposals to advance EC/EU supranational development has often been faulted. Only a few major successful supranational initiatives have borne a distinctive Italian imprint. Recently, Prime Minister Berlusconi, by stressing the merits of intergovernmentalism and removing his European federalist foreign minister, has appeared to depart from Italy's long advocacy of strengthened supranational institutions. However, it is premature to predict a major break with the past.[30]

Among the major policy domains of the EC/EU, Italian influence probably has been most pronounced in shaping the cluster of public policies associated with the structural funds, mostly for regional development. The relatively backward South of Italy has long been a major concern of Italian policy-makers, and European integration has afforded the opportunity to obtain external funding to promote development in southern Italy. However, even in this realm, Italian leaders were relatively unsuccessful at obtaining substantial European assistance until Britain and Ireland entered the European Communities in 1973 and made establishment of the European Regional Development Fund (ERDF) a high priority. Even though in the 1970s Italy was able to obtain the largest portion of the allocations from the ERDF, British leadership was more critical than the Italian role in shaping this policy initially. Since then, Italy has joined other recipients in pressing successfully for expansion of European funding of programs to assist the poor regions of the Union. Since the late 1980s, however, Spain has most frequently taken the lead in the drives for such assistance and has become the recipient of the largest share (though Italy was in second place in structural fund allocations between 1993 and 1999).[31]

The Common Agricultural Policy (CAP), which has constituted the biggest part of the budget of the EC and now the EU, has shown the limits of Italian influence perhaps as strikingly as any illustration can. Although the proportion of the Italian population engaged in agriculture was (at 40 percent) the highest in the European Community at the time that the CAP began to take shape,[32] Italy was unable to gain proportional benefits for its farmers. Such typical Italian products as fruits, vegetables, and olive oil did not gain the same levels of support as the grains predominant in France or the eggs, poultry, and dairy products predominant in Germany. Early patterns established in the CAP have generally persisted, despite recent agricultural policy reforms. Taking an overview, one leading analyst of the Common Agricultural Policy has concluded, "Italy has done remarkably badly."[33] Though some observers have credited an Italian willingness to sacrifice national gain for the progress of European integration, most have depicted a general absence of effective Italian leadership.[34]

"Italy has done remarkably badly [in obtaining a fair share of the EC/EU agricultural budget.]"

Rosemary Fennell, *The Common Agricultural Policy (1997), 43.*

Italy has more often been a mediator fostering European policy compromises than a leader seeking to mobilize support for bold initiatives. Such a mediating role was evident, for example, in the 1960s, when Italy sought reconciliation between the French Gaullists and the rest of the EC, and in the late 1980s, when Italy assisted French efforts to build support for the Economic and Monetary Union (EMU). Italy's five presidencies of the European Council have also generally exhibited successful efforts at mediation, though the most recent one (in the second half of 2003) appears to be the exception. Therefore, despite exerting an impact less evident than that of comparably sized EC/EU member states, Italy has left an imprint on the European Union.[35]

The Impact of the EC/EU on Italian Politics

Just as the Federal Republic of Germany solidified its links to the West and its commitment to constitutional democracy through membership in the ECSC, EC, and now EU, Italy has also done so. Although Italian leaders have not always bargained effectively for Italian economic interests on such matters as the Common Agricultural Policy (CAP), most analysts would stress that participation in European integration has also fostered Italian economic growth and convergence with successful economies to the North and West of Italy. Moreover, Italy's recent accession to the Economic and Monetary Union of the EU, amidst pressures to reduce its heavy public debt and a succession of large governmental budget deficits, has had profound effects (some more positive than others) on the Italian state and its economic and social policies.

The Constitution

In contrast to both France and the Federal Republic of Germany, where European integration has produced significant amendments to national constitutions, the Constitution of Italy has undergone no formal amendments as a direct result of EC/EU developments. As noted at the beginning of this chapter, the 1948 Italian Constitution, in Article 11, made provision for "constraints on national sovereignty rendered necessary, on the basis of reciprocity, by the creation of organizations that promote peace and justice among the nations."[36] Thanks to the interpretation of this article by the Italian Constitutional Court, European Union regulations take precedence over Italian national law, and no constitutional amendment or special law has been deemed necessary by the Court to bring this result. However, European Union directives require adaptation and implementation by the Italian executive and/or parliament. Only in a case involving a violation of fundamental rights guaranteed by the Italian Constitution does the Italian Constitutional Court review a regulation of the EU.[37]

Governmental Institutions

The Italian Constitutional Court, established only in 1956, one year before the European Economic Community (EEC), has played a critical role in interpreting the Italian Constitution so as to facilitate Europeanization, as noted above. It has also been called upon to resolve numerous issues concerning the powers of the Italian national state vis-à-vis the regional governments, including those that relate to European Union matters.

As indicated in the previous chapter, the Italian Chamber of Deputies and Senate possess equal lawmaking powers and checks on the executive and have been able to limit executive authority more fully and more of the time than have most European national parliamentary bodies. However, the powers of the two Italian parliamentary chambers have often been exercised in practice by party and factional leaders rather than by most legislators.

On EC/EU matters, the Italian executive has lacked an unchallenged coordinating institution; and high turnover in many ministries and partisan and factional conflicts within most coalition governments have hampered the ability to formulate clear and coherent policies vis-à-vis Europe. Despite its formidable lawmaking and checking powers, parliament has been virtually excluded from the process of formulating Italian positions on EC/EU issues, despite a 1987 law mandating its inclusion. Therefore, European initiatives, when they have occurred at all, have emanated from the executive, thus increasing its powers in relation to the legislature.

In the implementation stages of European policies, the Italian parliament sought until 1989 to assert itself by addressing EC directives on a piecemeal basis in the midst of its ordinary lawmaking processes. Even then, however, it often felt compelled by time constraints to delegate **transposition** powers to the executive. The confusion and delays stemming from parliamentary efforts to handle EC directives one at a time led the parliament in 1989 to adopt a new procedure whereby it could address in one Annual Community Law all appropriate European directives. Though this reform has improved the transposition procedure, the new system has worked imperfectly, since parliament has now delegated more extensive transposition powers than before to the executive and has still often been tardy in passing the Annual Community Law.

The Italian Senate has established a council for European affairs, and the Chamber of Deputies has a special committee for European policy. Nevertheless, these have had limited effectiveness in practice. Most Italian legislators continue to display low levels of information and interest in European matters, even though the impact of the European Union on Italian public policy and society has accelerated in recent years. Overall, the effects of Europeanization have almost certainly been to diminish the importance of parliament. However, it should be noted that the Italian parliament has played a larger role in transposition than most European national parliaments have and has generally exercised more powers over the national executive than most European national parliaments have.[38]

If Europeanization has lessened the importance of the Italian parliament, it has not necessarily or uniformly strengthened Italian governments or the executive as a whole. Vincent della Sala argues convincingly, for example, that technocratic elites in Italy used the Economic and Monetary Union and the related convergence criteria and stability and growth pact to "hollow out" Italian state authority while "hardening its shell." The "hollowing out" has entailed displacing traditional state authority by portraying Europe and international financial markets as external forces dictating major public policies (especially budgetary austerity) and reducing state involvement in many realms of social and economic life. Treasury and budget officials have unquestionably gained powers, while executives governing public corporations and social-service ministries have lost powers in the wake of privatization and social-service reductions. The "shell hardening" aspects have involved reducing the susceptibility of the Italian budgetary process to influence by labor unions and other groups seeking social benefits. Later in this chapter, analysis of the impact of the EMU on Italian public policies will return to this subject in depth from a policy rather than the executive power perspective emphasized here.[39]

Regional-national relations have constituted another area of EC/EU impact on governmental institutions in Italy, although the nature of the impact has been ambiguous and subject to some dispute. After reviewing cohesion policies in Italy, one analyst has concluded that the EU "has helped to move the Italian political system closer to an effectively functioning regional system" by empowering regional governments to design and execute their own development policies and reducing the control capacities of the central government.[40] Moreover, some observers believe that EC/EU-generated pressures may have helped to galvanize the Northern League in the 1980s and early 1990s, which in turn added to domestic pressures for decentralization. Others portray a rather different picture. The Italian national government has been reluctant to cede increased authority to the regions. Despite Constitutional Court decisions granting limited autonomy to the regions in their dealings with the EU, the Italian regions continue to be much more restricted (by the national government) in their abilities to contact EU officials than are their German or even French counterparts. Although the Community Law of 1989 requires sessions between the national and regional governments twice a year to discuss European matters, the regional governments have found it very difficult to use these sessions to play an effective role in shaping Italian positions on EU issues. Therefore, while some observers see the EU as a significant factor stimulating Italian regional power gains, the effectiveness of the regions should not be overstated. Italy remains a relatively centralized system, despite some recent reforms and continuing nudges toward decentralization from the EC/EU.[41]

Elections, Political Parties, and Interest Groups

The EC/EU has enjoyed broad but shallow popular support in Italy consistently over the past five decades. Though referendums have become more common in Italy than in any of the other major member states since 1970, they have only occasionally dealt directly with issues of European integration, as in the 1989 popular vote in which 88 percent of the Italian voters endorsed further European integration. Italy held no referendum on the Maastricht Treaty and avoided the divisiveness over that Treaty that characterized French politics in the early 1990s. The basic reforms of the Italian system of referendums and elections have been related not to European issues but rather to domestic considerations. As in most other member states, national issues have intruded more into Italian elections to the European Parliament than European issues have shaped the outcomes of national elections. However, as the linkage between the EMU and budgetary austerity illustrates, it is becoming increasingly difficult to differentiate between European and national issues.[42]

In the early years of Italy's First Republic, a cluster of European issues—including Italian membership in the European Coal and Steel Community (ECSC), the European Defense Community (EDC), and the North Atlantic Treaty Organization (NATO)—sharply defined the ideological differences between the two major opposition parties of the left, the Communists (PCI) and the Socialists (PSI), on the one hand, and on the other hand the Christian Democrats and their allies in a series of coalition governments. The Italian Socialists split in the late 1940s over issues of European integration and ties to the Communist party. The left faction led by Pietro Nenni became the PSI and joined the Communists over the next decade in opposition to NATO, the ECSC, and the EDC, all of which were seen as linking Italy to the capitalist world and the United States in a global struggle with Communism. Meanwhile, Giuseppe Saragat led a minority faction of the Socialists into what became the Italian Social Democratic Party (PSDI), which joined the Christian Democrats in support of West European integration and Atlanticism (and in a series of coalition governments).[43]

By 1957, this clear-cut partisan division over European integration issues was beginning to erode. Nenni's PSI endorsed Italian membership in Euratom and decided to abstain on the parliamentary vote concerning membership in the European Economic Community (EEC). The latter decision reflected internal Socialist party divisions over whether the EEC might become an instrument for laissez-faire economic policies (opposed by most Socialists) or whether it would prove to be what the Socialists desired, "a force for democratic and social progress, mediation, and peace."[44] By 1961, the PSI had embraced the view that the EEC could and should be reformed from within and thereafter pursued European policies almost indistinguishable from those of the Christian Democrats, who soon brought the Socialists into the government in an "opening to the left" (though some might argue that the PSI moved to the right). The impetus behind the PSI's move to endorse West European integration grew out of its break with the Italian Communist party but also related to its leaders' desires to join the Italian government and to reconcile with the

Social Democrats (PSDI), though the latter reconciliation was to prove short-lived.

Meanwhile, the Italian Communists began a reassessment of their European stance. However, their shift was a very gradual and prolonged one that retained a great deal of criticism of the pro-capitalist operations of the European Communities. Eventually, in the 1980s, the Italian Communists joined with their Spanish colleagues (in opposition to the French Communists) to endorse European integration in the EC framework. In the Italian party realignment of the early 1990s, most Communists joined the new Democrats of the Left, which affiliated itself with the Party of European Socialists in the EU (along with the French Socialists, German Social Democrats, British Labourites, and Spanish Socialists) and like them advocated further European integration with a pronounced social dimension. However, a minority of the Italian Communists joined the Refounded Communist party, which revived a long tradition of stinging criticisms of the capitalistic features of the EC/EU. The Refounded Communists voted in parliament against the Maastricht Treaty, unsuccessfully demanded a popular referendum on the Treaty, and denounced the convergence criteria and stability and growth pacts related to the Economic and Monetary Union (EMU) for eviscerating the Italian welfare state, undermining workers' rights, and creating high unemployment. Though relatively small and politically isolated, the Refounded Communist party succeeded in bringing the collapse of the center-left Prodi government in October 1998 (see box on pages 218–219), primarily over its EMU-related budgetary austerity policies.[45]

From the late 1940s to the early 1990s, the Italian center-right was dominated by the Christian Democrats, who began with a strong endorsement of European integration and generally sustained it in their rhetoric. However, as the Socialists came to embrace the European Communities from the early 1960s, the Christ-

ian Democratic commitment waned in intensity. Already before the 1960s, Christian Democratic factions had diverged somewhat from one another on such matters as Atlanticism and Mediterranean relations while maintaining a generally pro-integration stance. Most of the factionalism within the Christian Democratic party, however, had less to do with Europe than with power and patronage conflicts at home.[46]

While the Italian Left since the early 1990s, with the exception of the Refounded Communists on the far left, has adopted most of Italy's long-standing positions vis-à-vis Europe, the center-right has displayed marked divisions and some new patterns concerning the current and future European Union. The National Alliance, a major component of the center-right alliances and the Berlusconi-led coalition governments, has retained a nationalistic orientation rooted in its neo-Fascist past. The populistic, decentralist, and anti-immigrant Northern League has regularly denounced the "Brussels bureaucracy" of the EU as elitist and eager to burden businessmen with over-regulation. Forza Italia and Berlusconi himself have also shown some inclinations to detach themselves from the Italian center-right's long support for European supranational development. While the Democrats of the Left have integrated fairly well into the EU's Party of European Socialists (PES), both the Northern League and the National Alliance have not joined the European People's Party that was long the home of the Italian Christian Democrats; and Forza Italia did so only in 1998. Therefore, it is plausible to suggest that the Italian center-right may become a center of Euroskepticism in the years to come, while the center-left advocates further European integration.[47]

Beyond the political parties, European issues have spurred responses but only rarely initiatives among the major Italian interest groups. *Confindustria*, the largest and most influential Italian business group, has, since overcoming its initial reservations about the European Coal and Steel Community, consistently backed the Italian government's support for European integration, viewing it in the early years as a means to contain Communist power in Italy and almost always as a means to gain new markets and stabilize Italian capitalism. Large Italian firms, including the giant state holding companies, have developed their own networks of influence in the EU. Such well-known Italian magnates as Fiat's Giovanni Agnelli have at times played important Europe-wide roles, as Agnelli did in the drive for European supranational development. In contrast to business, labor unions in Italy initially split over European issues, with the largest union federation, the Communist-Socialist Italian General Confederation of Labor (CGIL), long skeptical of West European integration (though for a brief time in 1957 it supported the Treaties of Rome before returning to opposition) while the other major union federations showed considerable enthusiasm for European federalism with a social dimension. Agricultural groups have generally faulted Italian governments for failing to secure sufficient funding for Italian farmers vis-à-vis their Northern European counterparts but have not usually resorted to the aggressive measures to further their interests by which French farmers have regularly disrupted French politics.[48]

Public Policies

It is in the realm of public policies that the effects of EC/EU membership have probably had the most profound effects on Italy, at least in recent years. Though Italy's impact on EC/EU public policies has been relatively slight (scornfully likened by *The Economist* in a recent editorial to the impact of Portugal),[49] EC/EU changes have had marked effects on Italian public policies, albeit quite often with the active collaboration of Italian governmental leaders.

Nowhere has Europeanization backed by a national government to accomplish policy (and power) goals that it could not obtain on its own been more evident than with regard to Italian budgetary policies in the 1990s. Italian governmental deficits had soared to more than 10 percent of Italy's gross domestic product (GDP) every year but one (when it was a mere 9.9 percent of GDP) during the decade of the 1980s. The public debt had swollen to be more than Italy's gross domestic product by 1991. The clientelist system, pressures for social spending from labor unions and other interest groups, and fragmented coalition governments lacking strong executive leadership had come to mean that even those officials constituting a "public finance core executive" in the Italian government could not impose fiscal constraint. The key Italian officials who negotiated the Maastricht Treaty and the tough convergence criteria (budget deficits less than 3 percent of GDP; public sector debt less than 60 percent of GDP) of the Economic and Monetary Union (EMU) came largely from this public finance core executive. Only about 16 in number, and operating quite autonomously, they saw clearly that they might be able to use an external constraint—the EMU and its convergence criteria (and subsequent stability and growth pact)—to increase Italian taxes, reduce spending, and bring Italian budgetary policies into line with West European norms for the first time in years. The upheavals generated inside Italy by the *Tangentopoli* scandals and the shocks following the forced ouster of the Italian lira from the European Monetary System (EMS) in September 1992 created an atmosphere in which the Italian public finance core executive leaders were able to transform Italian budgetary policies.

The government of Giuliano Amato (June 1992–April 1993), a former treasury minister, gave key posts to nonpolitical technocrats, introduced substantial tax increases, and gained from parliament powers to institute even larger reductions in spending. Carlo Ciampi, longtime governor of the Bank of Italy, headed a cabinet of nonelected technocrats from April 1993 to May

1994. Lamberto Dini from the Bank of Italy served as treasury minister under Berlusconi in his brief first government (May 1994–January 1995) and then became prime minister by presidential appointment and headed another government of technocrats (January 1995–June 1996). This government was replaced in June 1996 by a center-left coalition government headed by former economics professor and IRI executive Romano Prodi, which created a super-ministry combining the treasury and budget ministries, headed by Ciampi. It also placed Dini in the foreign ministry. The Prodi government (see the box on pages 218–219) instituted further massive budget cuts. By the time it was ousted by a parliamentary vote of no confidence in October 1998, the Italian budget had been sufficiently transformed to permit Italy to embark on the euro currency on schedule.

Not only did a European external constraint "force" the Italian government to raise taxes and cut spending substantially, it also had the effect of reshaping Italian public policies regarding pensions, health care, and labor and industrial relations. Although Italy's own public-finance core executive of largely nonelected technocrats were highly complicit in the process (and almost certainly essential to its effectiveness), the impact on Italian public policies of the European Union, as mediated by these political actors, was almost revolutionary.[50]

CONCLUSIONS

The impact of the EC/EU on Italy has almost certainly outweighed the effects of Italy on European institutions or public policies. Europeanization has solidified Italy as an integral part of Western Europe, aided in propping up its still rather flawed constitutional democratic institutions while modifying them somewhat, fostered its economic growth to a level of well-being almost unimaginable five decades ago, pushed its economy toward free-market capitalism, and altered its internal budgetary and other public policies in some significant ways. In contrast, Italy's impact on the EC/EU has been rather slight, particularly in light of Italy's population and gross domestic product. Despite the frequency of its leaders' pronouncements of their commitment to European integration from the 1940s until quite recently, Italy has rarely asserted effective leadership in EC/EU forums. Furthermore, while its record of compliance with EC/EU laws has shown some signs of recent improvement, the broad picture remains one that calls into question the depth of Italy's commitment to European integration. The future course that Italy will take in the European Union remains a subject of debate, particularly given the nature of the Berlusconi-led center-right coalition government.

SUMMARY

- The Italian EU paradox is that Italy has combined a strong abstract commitment to European integration with a poor record of state implementation of EC/EU law and few examples of Italian leadership in the EC/EU.

- Prime Minister Alcide De Gasperi (1945–1953) used the European integration movement to bolster the weak legitimacy of his government, isolate the Italian Communists and Socialists, link the Italian economy to stronger economies to the north, and give Italy at least the appearance of equality with France and the Federal Republic of Germany.

- After De Gasperi, Italian governments continued to voice support for supranational development of the EC but focused more on domestic power struggles than on major European issues.

- Italian failures to comply with European Community laws earned Italy a negative reputation in Brussels and other European capitals.

- Italy joined France from the late 1980s onward as a major proponent of an Economic and Monetary Union (EMU); Italian leaders saw the EMU largely as a means to enhance Italy's prestige and to impose external discipline on an Italian national budget widely viewed as out of control.

- Prime Minister Silvio Berlusconi (1994–1995 and 2001–) frequently gave mixed signals on European issues (especially during the Italian EU presidency in the second half of 2003) and appeared to back away from Italian leaders' traditional rhetorical embrace of European supranational development.

- Romano Prodi, prime minister of Italy 1996–1998, served as president of the European Commission during 1999–2004, only the second Italian to hold that post; his record as Commission president earned mixed reviews, with many critics comparing his leadership unfavorably with that of Jacques Delors.

- Major long-term features of Italian approaches to the EC/EU have been an inclination to balance Atlanticism and a European focus, a supranational inclination, a weak inclination and ability to lead on European issues, a weak inclination and ability to implement EC/EU policies, and a wariness of global free-market capitalism.

- Among the major policy domains of the EC/EU, Italian influence has probably been most pronounced in shaping the structural funds, mostly for regional development (though Britain and Ireland initially and Spain eventually played larger roles than Italy).

- Italy has more often been a mediator fostering European policy compromises than a leader seeking to mobilize support for bold initiatives.

- EC/EU membership has fostered Italian economic development, weakened the influence of the Italian parliament vis-à-vis the Italian executive, and generated support for devolving powers to the Italian regions.

- Initially, the Socialists and Communists opposed West European integration, while the Christian Democrats and their allies supported it; but first the Socialists and then the Communists became supporters of supranational European development.

- Since the 1990s, Euroskepticism has been more widespread in the center-right House of Freedom coalition than in the center-left Olive Tree alliance.

- A major example of EU effects on Italian public policies is evident in the ways in which the Economic and Monetary Union and its related convergence criteria and Stability and Growth Pact served in the 1990s as a force to effect increased taxes, reduced spending, and enhanced Italian budgetary discipline.

- The impact of the EC/EU on Italy has almost certainly outweighed the influence of Italy on European institutions or public policies.

ENDNOTES

1. F. Roy Willis, *Italy Chooses Europe* (New York: Oxford University Press, 1971), 3.
2. Willis, *Italy Chooses Europe*, 11.
3. Martin Clark, *Modern Italy*, 2nd ed. (New York: Longman, 1996), 343; Sondra Z. Koff and Stephen P. Koff, *Italy: From the First to the Second Republic* (London: Routledge, 2000), 199.
4. Mario Giuliani and Simona Piattoni, "Italy: Both Leader and Laggard," in Eleanor Zeff and Ellen Pirro, eds., *The European Union and the Member States* (Boulder, CO: Lynne Rienner, 2001), 120–126; Timothy Bainbridge, *The Penguin Companion to European Union*, 2nd ed. (Harmondsworth: Penguin, 1998), 315; Koff and Koff, *From the First to the Second Republic*, 199, 206.

5. D. H. Ellwood, "Italy, Europe, and the Cold War: The Politics and Economics of Limited Sovereignty," in Christopher Duggan and Christopher Wagstaff, eds., *Italy in the Cold War: Politics, Culture, and Society, 1948–1958* (Oxford: Berg, 1995), 25–46; Antonio Varsori, "Italy's Policy Towards European Integration (1947–1958)," in Duggan and Wagstaff, eds., *Italy in the Cold War*, 47–48; Willis, *Italy Chooses Europe*, 3–29.

6. Ellwood, "Italy, Europe, and the Cold War," 41.

7. Willis, *Italy Chooses Europe*, 21–22, 30–41; Varsori, "Italy's Policy Towards European Integration," 50–56; H. Stuart Hughes, *The United States and Italy*, 3rd ed. (Cambridge, MA: Harvard University Press, 1979), 246–248.

8. Varsori, "Italy's Policy Towards European Integration," 57–64; Varsori, "Italy and the European Defense Community," in Peter Stirk and David Willis, eds., *Shaping Postwar Europe: European Unity and Disunity 1945–1957* (New York: St. Martin's, 1991), 100–111; Willis, *Italy Chooses Europe*, 41–53.

9. Willis, *Italy Chooses Europe*, 53–71; Varsori, "Italy's Policy Towards European Integration," 62–66.

10. Willis, *Italy Chooses Europe*, 72.

11. Willis, *Italy Chooses Europe*, 72–100; 219–220; Robert Ackrill, *The Common Agricultural Policy* (Sheffield: Sheffield Academic Press, 2000), 26–27, 31–32, 36; Rosemary Fennell, *The Common Agricultural Policy: Continuity and Change* (Oxford: Clarendon Press, 1997), 43.

12. Willis, *Italy Chooses Europe*, 47.

13. Luigi Vittorio Ferraris, "Italian-European Foreign Policy," in Francesco Francioni, ed., *Italy and EC Membership Evaluated* (New York: St. Martin's, 1992), 136.

14. Koff and Koff, *From the First to the Second Republic*, 203.

15. Primo Vannicelli, *Italy, NATO, and the European Community* (Cambridge, MA: Harvard University Center for International Affairs, 1974), 29–33.

16. Clark, *Modern Italy*, 343; Stephen George, *An Awkward Partner*, 3rd ed. (Oxford: Oxford University Press, 1998), 66–69; Giulani and Piattoni, "Italy: Both Leader and Laggard," 126–127.

17. Bainbridge, *The Penguin Companion to European Union*, 284.

18. Willis, *Italy Chooses Europe*, 274–285, 287–310; David Bell, "Western Communists and the European Union," in John Gaffney, ed., *Political Parties and the European Union* (London: Routledge, 1996), 223–226.

19. Andrew Moravcsik, *The Choice for Europe* (Ithaca, NY: Cornell University Press, 1998), 363–364, 367.

20. James Walsh, *European Monetary Integration & Domestic Politics: Britain, France, and Italy* (Boulder, CO: Lynne Rienner, 2000), Chs. 4, 5; Patrick McCarthy, *The Crisis of the Italian State* (New York: St. Martin's, 1995), 53–54; Moravcsik, *The Choice for Europe*, 454–456.

21. Walsh, *European Monetary Integration & Domestic Politics*, 134–137; Alberta Sbragia, "Italy Pays for Europe: Political Leadership, Political Choice, and Institutional Adaptation," in Maria Green Cowles, et al., eds., *Transforming Europe: Europeanization and Domestic Change* (Ithaca, NY: Cornell University Press, 2001), 79–96.

22. Sbragia, "Italy Pays for Europe," esp. 91–92; Martin Walker, "Rome-Bonn Deal Puts Prodi on Course for EC Presidency," *The Guardian*, March 23, 1999; Mike Bracken, "Who Is Romano Prodi?" *The Guardian*, March 24, 1999; Martin Walker and Ian Traynor, "Leaders Unite to Pick Italy's Prodi," *The Guardian*, March 25, 1999; "EU Parliament Gives Prodi Vote of Approval," *The Guardian*, May 5, 1999; Stephen Bates, "Signore Mortadella," *The Observer*, October 10, 1999; Peter Norman, "Defiant in Defending His Views on Europe," *Financial Times*, March 10, 2002; George Parker and Tony Barber, "Prodi Prepared to Stay as President if EU Leaders Ask," *Financial Times*, April 3, 2003, 6; "Don't Go There," *Financial Times*, April 3, 2003, 12.

23. Martin Bull, "The Italian Christian Democrats," in Gaffney, ed., *Political Parties in the European Union*, 151; McCarthy, *The Crisis of the Italian State*, 54; Catherine Fieschi, James Shields, and Roger Woods, "Extreme Right-wing Parties and the European Union," in Gaffney, ed., *Political Parties in the European Union*, 248–249; "Berlusconi Strikes Out," *The Economist* 362 (January 12, 2002), 14–15; "A Foreign Minister Goes, but Does a Foreign Policy?" *The Economist* 362 (January 12, 2002), 45–46; George Parker, "Atmosphere of Resignation as Leaders Walk Away," *Financial Times*, December 15, 2003, 4.

24. Willis, *Italy Chooses Europe*, 272–274, discusses neo-Atlanticism within the Christian Democratic party.

25. Ferraris, "Italian-European Foreign Policy," 134–135; Koff and Koff, *From the First to the Second Republic*, 200–201.

26. Moravcsik, *The Choice for Europe*, 376; Ferraris, "Italian-European Foreign Policy," 134; Koff and Koff, *From the First to the Second Republic*, 198, 205–206; Bull, "The Italian Christian Democrats," 147–150.

27. Middlemas, *Orchestrating Europe*, 315–316; Koff and Koff, *From the First to the Second Republic*, 201–203; Hilary Partridge, *Italian Politics Today* (Manchester: Manchester University Press, 1998), 184–185; Ferraris, "Italian-European Foreign Policy," 136.

28. Giulani and Piattoni, "Italy: Both Leader and Laggard," 117–119; Marco Giulani, "Italy," in Dietrich Rometsch and Wolfgang Wessels, eds., *The European Union and Member States: Towards Institutional Fusion?* (Manchester: Manchester University Press, 1996), 119–131; Grottanelli de Santi, "The Impact of EC Integration on the Italian Form of Government," in Francioni, ed., *Italy and EC Membership Evaluated*, 184–186.

29. Paolo Cesarini, "Competition Policy," in Francioni, ed., *Italy and EC Membership Evaluated*, 51–70; Ellwood, "Italy, Europe, and the Cold War," 42; Moravcsik, *The Choice for Europe*, 146, 149, 358, 454.

30. Bull, "The Italian Christian Democrats," 147; Moravcsik, *The Choice for Europe*, 366–338, 376; "Berlusconi Strikes Out," *The Economist* 362 (January 12, 2002), 14–15; "A Foreign Minister Goes, but Does a Foreign Policy?" *The Economist* 362 (January 12, 2002), 45–46.

31. Moravcsik, *The Choice for Europe*, 300, 303, 367, 446; George, *An Awkward Partner*, 66–69; Giulani and Piattoni, "Italy: Both Leader and Laggard," 126–140; figures on structural funds from Ian Bache, *The Politics of European Union Regional Policy: Multi-level Governance or Flexible Gatekeeping?* (Sheffield: Sheffield Academic Press, 1998), 85.

32. Leon Lindberg and Stuart Scheingold, *Europe's Would-Be Polity: Patterns of Change in the European Community* (Englewood Cliffs, NJ: Prentice-Hall, 1970), 144. The figures for France and Germany were 27 percent and 18 percent, respectively, in 1956.

33. Fennell, *The Common Agricultural Policy*, 43.

34. The positive assessment of Italy's sacrificing national gain is found in Ackrill, *The Common Agricultural Policy*, 36.

35. Koff and Koff, *From the First to the Second Republic*, 205; Willis, *Italy Chooses Europe*, 72–100.

36. Cited in Grottanelli de Santi, "The Impact of EC Integration on the Italian Form of Government," 183.

37. Grottanelli de Santi, "The Impact of EC Integration," 182–184.

38. Paul Furlong, "The Italian Parliament and European Integration—Responsibilities, Failures, and Successes," in Philip Norton, ed., *National Parliaments and the European Union* (Portland, OR: Frank Cass, 1996), 35–45; Grottanelli de Santi, "The Impact of EC Integration," 180–186; Koff and Koff, *From the First to the Second Republic*, 201–202; Giulani and Piattoni, "Italy: Both Leader and Laggard," 116–119.

39. Vincent della Sala, "Hollowing Out and Hardening the State: European Integration and the Italian Economy," *West European Politics* 20 (1997), 14–35. Also see Kenneth Dyson and Kevin Featherstone, "Italy and EMU as a '*Vincolo Esterno*': Empowering the Technocrats, Transforming the State," *South European Society & Politics* 1, 2 (Autumn 1996), 272–299, and Sbragia, "Italy Pays for Europe," 79–96.

40. Jürgen Grote, "Cohesion in Italy: A View on Non-Economic Disparities," in Liesbet Hooge, ed., *Cohesion Policy and European Integration* (Oxford: Oxford University Press, 1996), 287.

41. Koff and Koff, *From the First to the Second Republic*, 208–209; Giulani and Piattoni, "Italy: Both Leader and Laggard," 119; Middlemas, *Orchestrating Europe*, (London: Fontana, 1995), 316.

42. Koff and Koff, *From the First to the Second Republic*, 198.

43. Kevin Featherstone, *Socialist Parties and European Integration: A Comparative History* (Manchester: Manchester University Press, 1988), 214–240; Willis, *Italy Chooses Europe*, 287–293, 299–306.

44. Willis, *Italy Chooses Europe*, 306.

45. Willis, *Italy Chooses Europe*, 287–299; Bell, "Western Communist Parties and the EU," 220–234; Sbragia, "Italy Pays for Europe," 94.

46. Willis, *Italy Chooses Europe*, 252–285; Bull, "The Italian Christian Democrats," 139–154.

47. Fieschi, et al., "Extreme Right-Wing Parties and the EU," 246–249; Sergio Fabbrini and Mark Gilbert, "The Italian General Election of 13 May 2001," *Government and Opposition* 36, 4 (Autumn 2001), 534–535; Bull, "The Italian Christian Democrats," 150–151; Raunio, "Political Interests: The EP's Party Groups," in John Peterson and Michael Shackleton, eds., *The Institutions of the European Union* (Oxford: Oxford University Press, 2002), 259.

48. Middlemas, *Orchestrating Europe*, 316, 454–455; Willis, *Italy Chooses Europe*, Chs. 11, 12.

49. "Berlusconi Strikes Out," *The Economist* 362 (January 12, 2002), 15.

50. Sbragia, "Italy Pays for Europe," 79–96; Walsh, *European Monetary Integration & Domestic Politics*, 133–137; Dyson and Featherstone, "Italy and EMU as a '*Vincolo Esterno*,'" 272–299; Della Sala, "Hollowing Out and Hardening the State," 14–33; Maurizio Ferrera and Elizabetta Gualmini, "Reforms Guided by Consensus: The Welfare State in the Italian Transition," *West European Politics* 23, 2 (April 2000), 187–208.

Chapter 11

THE UNITED KINGDOM OF GREAT BRITAIN AND NORTHERN IRELAND

"What seems indisputable is that a substantial rethinking of what it means to be British can no longer be evaded."
—Linda Colley, British historian, *Britons: Forging the Nation (1992), 375.*

Located off the northwest coast of Europe on the island of Great Britain, a portion of Ireland, and smaller neighboring islands, the United Kingdom of Great Britain and Northern Ireland has maintained a distinctive insularity that has affected both its domestic institutions and political processes and its external relations with the rest of Europe and the world. Politically, the United Kingdom (or Britain, as it is commonly called) boasts a long tradition of constitutional government (but without a written constitution) and a shorter, but still relatively long, tradition of democratic practices. At the center have arisen the cabinet (and prime minister), representative of and accountable to the majority party in a predominantly two-party, elective House of Commons. Alongside these, however, exist the monarchy and the House of Lords, symbols of Britain's older institutional heritage, without counterparts in France, Germany, or Italy. Although the United Kingdom has traditionally possessed a centralized, unitary state structure (in contrast to the federalism of Germany or the United States), it is at the same time a multinational state composed of four parts: England (83 percent of the U.K. population), Scotland (9 percent), Wales (5 percent), and Northern Ireland (3 percent). Recently, the United Kingdom has taken steps to "devolve" some authority to Scotland and Wales and to try to renew decentralized authority in Northern Ireland.

From the seventeenth to twentieth centuries, Britain was a "great power" internationally, ruling over the largest empire on earth and exercising a unique role as the "keeper of the balance" in the global balance-of-power system prevailing most of the time between 1648 and 1914. During World War II, the United Kingdom escaped both invasion and defeat, unlike France, Germany, or Italy. The image of Britain's standing alone was never more vivid than in 1940 and 1941, as the United Kingdom stood as the sole major opponent of the Axis powers of Germany, Italy, and Japan. Memories of this heritage linger and continue to influence Britain's relations with Europe and the rest of the world. Also influencing those relations are the shared language and cultural heritage that Britain enjoys with some of its former colonies, including the United States and the English-speaking portions of the Commonwealth. However, Britain is now a second-level power, often described as the "awkward partner"[1] in the

MAP 11.1 The United Kingdom of Great Britain and Northern Ireland

European Union, which it joined with considerable misgivings in 1973. Its difficulties in finding an appropriate balance between national unity and devolution at home and between its overseas ties and its links to Europe are reflected in the quotation from British historian Linda Colley that opened this chapter, regarding the current "substantial rethinking of what it means to be British."

Having a population today of just under sixty million people, the United Kingdom is in a virtual tie with Italy and France for second place in population in the EU (behind Germany, with about eighty-three million people). Economically, after years of relative decline, it has enjoyed considerable growth since the 1990s and by 2004 surpassed (narrowly) the per capita gross domestic products of both Germany and France. Another economic feature of Britain that makes it distinctive in Europe is its relatively strong emphasis on free markets and private entrepreneurship, partly reflecting a long tradition of a minimal state (in contrast to most Continental European countries), nineteenth-century free-trade practices associated by many with British greatness, long-term global trading patterns, and recent developments, particularly the policies of Prime Minister Margaret Thatcher (1979–1990). However, despite Thatcher's free-market efforts, Britain remains a mixed economy with a substantial welfare state.[2]

POLITICAL DEVELOPMENT

Nation-Building

England (as opposed to the United Kingdom) emerged relatively early as a distinctive nation-state possessing sovereign state institutions capable of penetrating society, a well-defined territory over which sovereignty was exercised, and a widespread sense of national identity. English kings such as William I, "the Conqueror" (1066–1087), and Henry II (1154–1189) built central authority before comparable patterns took shape in most of the rest of Europe. French-speaking Normans merged gradually with the previous Anglo-Saxons, Scandinavians, and others to form an English language and nation. The island location combined with central authority and a growing sense of nationhood to protect against foreign invasions after 1066. On the so-called "Celtic fringe," populated extensively by earlier Celtic immigrants, Wales (joined with England in the fourteenth century) and Scotland (English and Scottish crowns united in 1603, parliaments united in 1707) appeared to integrate into Britain in the eighteenth and early nineteenth centuries, though as Linda Colley notes, "Welshness, Scottishness and Englishness also remained powerful divides."[3] Moreover, Scottish and Welsh national identities reasserted themselves and took modern "nationalist" forms to some extent in the twentieth century, as Protestantism, British imperial hegemony, and British global commercial supremacy declined as forces to unify the United Kingdom. Ireland (conquered repeatedly, most fully in the seventeenth century, formally joined to the United Kingdom in 1801) rejected a common nationhood with England much more vociferously than Wales or Scotland. The 26 counties of southern Ireland gained independence in 1922, while the six counties of Northern Ireland have been a source of continuing conflict, pitting mainly Catholic nationalists favoring union with Ireland against mainly Protestant loyalists who stress their ties to the United Kingdom. Just recently, in 1999, a Scottish Parliament in Edinburgh and a less powerful Welsh Assembly in Cardiff have taken shape in response to "national identity" pressures, following approval of devolution in Scottish and Welsh referenda. In Northern Ireland, efforts to find a solution to national identity conflicts remain elusive.

Another set of national identity issues that remains a source of some controversy in the United Kingdom concerns the integration of new immigrants (especially those who are non-white) into the British "nation." A wave of post–World War II immigration to Britain aided the rebuilding of a country devastated by war but also sparked anti-immigrant sentiments and even rioting by the late 1950s. Britain tightened immigration restrictions in the 1960s and has also adopted a restrictive approach to asylum-seekers. As a result, the United Kingdom has had many fewer new immigrants in recent decades than Germany and some other West European nation-states. Although Britain has enacted more race-relations-focused civil-rights legislation than any other EU member state, third-world immigrants and their children are not yet fully a part of the British national community. As evidence of continuing problems of national integration, urban riots with distinct racial overtones have exploded on a number of occasions.[4]

State-Building

More characteristic of the United Kingdom than popular consensus on a "national community" has been the continuity of basic British state institutions. England (and now the United Kingdom) is the only major European nation-state that has found it unnecessary to codify its "constitution" in a written document. Instead, the British constitution is a blend of 1) major parliamentary statutes and other great historic documents reaching back to the Magna Carta (1215); 2) basic principles of common law, composed of judicial decisions; 3) interpretations by such constitutional experts as A.V. Dicey and Walter Bagehot;[5] and 4) an array of "conventions" or unwritten rules and practices. Among the conventions are such critical rules as that requiring that a government resign or request the dissolution of the House of Commons if it loses a parliamentary **"vote of confidence."** In other major European states and in the United States, such important matters are clearly specified in the written constitution. Although the

monarchy and the House of Lords have lost most of their once-great medieval powers, and the prime minister, cabinet, executive departments, and House of Commons have become the central institutions of the state, the transformation has been mostly gradual and nonviolent. The most recent violent constitutional upheaval in Britain, apart from the situation in Ireland, occurred in the seventeenth century!

Participation

The democratization of British politics, like the alteration in its basic state institutions, has occurred gradually and nonviolently since the seventeenth century. Before most of the rest of Europe, England had a long tradition of constitutional checks on governmental authority, dating back to the Magna Carta's limits on the powers of King John (1215), the early establishment of the English parliament (late thirteenth century), and a series of parliamentary efforts to limit monarchial authority and protect at least the rights of its most influential constituents. Parliamentary struggles with King Charles I led to the Civil War of 1642–1649, sometimes referred to as the Puritan Revolution, because many of the parliamentary leaders adhered to Puritan religious doctrines as well as desires to enhance parliamentary authority. As a result of the Civil War, the monarchy was temporarily abolished, though it was restored with some limits on its powers in 1660 and further limits on its powers after 1688. During the Civil War, a group known as the Levellers emerged from the Puritan-parliamentary forces to demand extension of voting rights to the general male adult population. Another group, known as the Diggers, advocated a form of democratic socialism. However, their efforts proved unsuccessful in their own time because the parliamentary-military leadership was determined not to move in the democratic directions suggested by either of these groups. Modern democracy was not well-developed in

Britain until the nineteenth century. Even then, it remained quite limited. Because of property-ownership requirements, religious tests, lack of female voting rights, and other restrictions, less than 2 percent of the adult population could vote in the early 1800s. The Whig and Tory "parties" were really elite factions. The Reform Act of 1832 granted voting rights to most of the male middle class and did away with the old "rotten boroughs" where a few major landowners could dictate the "election" of two Members of Parliament for largely depopulated rural districts. However, the franchise expanded only gradually, with further extensions in 1867 (much of the male industrial working class), 1884 (most of the remainder of the male working class), 1918 (all males older than 21 and females older than 30), and 1928 (females older than 21). As voting rights expanded in the nineteenth century, the Whig and Tory factions became the Liberal and Conservative parties, party organizations strengthened, and "party government" became a characteristic feature of the new British democracy.

Under the norms of party government, two cohesive teams of party candidates would compete for public favor, each presenting a **manifesto** of public-policy proposals and running on its past record. The majority party would gain control of the House of Commons, name its leader as prime minister, and govern through the leadership of the party-backed prime minister and cabinet. At the next election the voting public could render its democratic verdict by either returning the same majority party to power or electing the opposition.[6] The emergence of a third major party, the Labour party, after 1900 complicated matters for a time. However, from the 1920s onward, Labour displaced the older Liberal party; and a general two-party pattern returned, encouraged and reinforced by the British electoral system. This system, often termed "first-past-the-post" or the "single-member plurality" system, provides for the election of one Member of Parliament from each district—the candidate winning more votes than anyone else, even if this vote falls short of a majority (50 percent plus one). It has usually had the effect of giving the victorious party a considerably higher percentage of the parliamentary seats than it has won in the popular vote and severely penalizing parties that come third (or fourth or fifth). Thus, for example, as Table 11.3 later in this chapter illustrates, the first-place Labour party in the 2001 election won 41 percent of the popular vote but gained 63 percent of the seats in the House of Commons, while the third-place Liberal Democratic party won 18 percent of the popular vote but only 8 percent of the seats. Therefore, the electoral system enabled the Labour party to win a large parliamentary majority and govern alone, even though a majority of the voting public did not vote for its candidates. Party government and the British electoral system have encountered considerable criticism. In recent European Parliament, Scottish Parliament, Welsh Assembly, and Northern Ireland elections, a form of proportional representation has been used instead, encouraging multiparty patterns. Whether proportional representation and multiparty patterns should come to characterize the British House of Commons also is a matter of keen debate.[7]

Other rising issues of British democracy in the twentieth century include the use of referendums and, to a lesser extent, various proposals for workplace democracy. Unlike France and Italy, where referendums have been fairly common, Britain never employed a popular "yes-no" vote on a public issue until 1975, when Prime Minister Harold Wilson's Labour government sponsored a referendum on whether Britain should remain in the European Union under terms that had just been renegotiated. Since that time, there have been referendums (twice) in Scotland and Wales on devolution and in London on a revamped governmental structure, as well as numerous calls for referendums on other matters. The traditional British view has been that parliamentary representation is preferable to the direct democracy of referendums. As one recent analyst described it, "The British see the ideal of democracy best fulfilled in government *of and for* the people. At the core of this notion is the belief that Parliament can better speak for the people than the people themselves."[8] This view appears to be eroding, though the shift should not be exaggerated.

"The British see the ideal of democracy best fulfilled in government *of and for* the people. At the core of this notion is the belief that Parliament can better speak for the people than the people themselves."

Jürg Steiner, *European Democracies* (1995), 135.

Calls for workplace democracy have traditionally been much weaker in Britain than in Continental European nation-states, especially Germany. Though G. D. H. Cole and his followers in the Labour party of the early twentieth century advocated a guild socialism with a form of workplace democracy at its core, this approach has never won wide support in the British Labour movement. The Conservative governments of Margaret Thatcher and John Major were so hostile to Continental European ideas of workplace democracy and workers' rights that they, alone of all of the European Union governments, refused to agree to the social chapter that was originally part of the Maastricht Treaty. Their objections focused primarily on perceived threats to the powers of business executives and British economic growth. Tony Blair reversed this position, and the chapter became a part of the European Union's Amsterdam Treaty in 1997, to which all 15 EU member governments gave approval. Moreover, Blair and "New Labour" generally have embraced the idea of a **"stakeholder economy"** in which there is a mutuality of rights and obligations among employees, shareholders, consumers, and communities. Whether this rather vague concept will entail meaningful workplace democracy remains in doubt.[9]

Even though Britain extended voting rights to women relatively early (1918, for women over 30) and has had a woman as prime minister (Margaret Thatcher, 1979–1990), women have not won parliamentary seats at a rate even close to that of their male counterparts. The percentage of women in the House of Commons at present (17.9 percent) is about at the European Union average and a little higher than the percentage of women in the United States House of Representatives. (See Table 15.7.) As for the impact of women on British government, a recent empirical study based on extensive interviews of male and female Members of Parliament (M.P.s) has found that women M.P.s have differed little from their male counterparts on issues concerning Europe, the economy, and moral traditionalism. On these matters, party differences far outweighed gender differences, as might be predicted given the nature of party government in Britain. However, the study also found that women M.P.s demonstrated attitudes far more supportive than those of the men toward gender equality policies.[10]

Placing British democracy in a comparative perspective, it is evident that, despite some recent modifications of party government and proposals for further reforms, Britain remains a system based mainly on conceptions of democracy as competition between two teams of major party leaders and representation through parliament. It remains distinctive from the referendum-oriented Swiss system and from the multiparty patterns characteristic of Italy, France, and Germany and has approached workplace democracy concepts with considerable skepticism. Nonetheless, its democracy is in a process of some flux.

TABLE 11.1   Major Landmarks in British Political History

1066	William the Conqueror leads the Norman Conquest of England.
1215	King John signs the Magna Carta.
1265	The English Parliament begins to meet.
1534	Henry VIII breaks with the Roman Catholic Church, establishes Church of England.
1649	Charles I is executed by Oliver Cromwell, leader of parliamentary forces in English Civil War.
1660	The monarchy is restored by Charles II.
1688	The Glorious Revolution establishes parliamentary supremacy, English Bill of Rights.
1776	The United States declares independence from Britain.
1832	The Reform Bill expands voter participation and links representation to population in House of Commons constituencies.
1867	The Second Reform Bill further expands voter participation, gives rise to mass-based political parties.
1911	The House of Lords recognizes the legislative supremacy of the House of Commons.
1922	Ireland separates from the United Kingdom, while Northern Ireland remains a part of the United Kingdom.
1973	The United Kingdom joins the European Communities.

Distribution

The final area of political development stressed by Almond and others concerns distribution. Like the rest of Western Europe, Britain has moved from feudalism to a modern "mixed" economy with a capitalist base in private property and a market mechanism but with extensive state regulation and provision of social welfare. As elsewhere in the West, economic globaliza-tion in recent decades has spurred privatization and renewed market emphases. The most distinctive aspects of British development in the distribution sphere have been the relative weakness of feudalism historically in Britain relative to much of Europe, the checks on state power that have usually prevailed throughout British history, and the relatively strong commitment to private property and markets apparent at least in recent centuries. Britain's experiences with laissez-faire capitalism went further and lasted longer than in most of Europe, and Britain has led the drive toward privatization and free markets since the late 1970s. Nevertheless, in the twentieth century, the welfare state emerged strongly in Britain. The National Health Service established by the postwar Labour government in 1948 is just the best-known example. As Figure 11.1 illustrates, British governmental spending as a percentage of gross domestic product is below the average of EU member states, though somewhat above the American figure. Recent studies have confirmed that on welfare-state issues British public opinion is closer to that of Continental

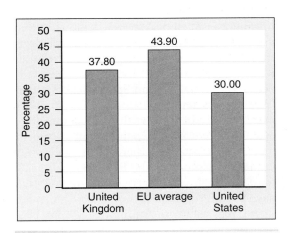

FIGURE 11.1   Governmental Expenditures as a Percentage of GDP, 1999
OECD National Accounts, 2001.

Europeans than to that of Americans. British public policies do not fully reflect this pattern. However, it is evident that the British mixed economy entails both a relatively strong commitment to private property and markets and a social-welfare component that is only somewhat smaller than that of most Continental European nation-states.[11]

GOVERNMENTAL INSTITUTIONS

The Executive

The greatest power to shape major public policies and assert leadership resides in the "government," referring in British terms to a collective body including the prime minister and a cabinet of about twenty members plus about eighty to ninety additional ministers and junior ministers. The government is accountable to the majority in the House of Commons through the vote-of-confidence procedure and almost always represents a Commons majority party that is highly cohesive on most parliamentary votes. The contrast is sharp with the United States's presidential system, in which the president is elected separately from the Congress and is often of a different political party from the congressional majority, and from the French hybrid system. It is closer in structure to the German, Italian, and Spanish cabinet-parliamentary systems, differing from the first two most notably in the fact that the British government is normally dependent on a majority parliamentary party, rather than a coalition of parties (due in part to the British electoral system). Though some participants and analysts have portrayed modern British government as increasingly **"prime ministerial"** or even **"presidential"** in nature, because of the great emphasis in modern campaigning on the personalities and styles of the candidates for prime minister and the roles of the prime minister in creating an image for the entire government, most conclude that the cabinet remains more

powerful vis-à-vis the chief executive than its counterpart in the United States, due to the fact that there are usually at least several British cabinet ministers who have major power bases in the governing party and are themselves likely future candidates for prime minister. There are, of course, variations over time, even during the tenure of a particular prime minister, depending on the individuals, issues, and power configurations. For example, Margaret Thatcher as prime minister first found herself checked by cabinet ministers less committed to free-market capitalism than she, later purged her cabinet of most opponents and asserted strong leadership, but was eventually ousted in large part due to challenges from present and former cabinet colleagues. Thatcher's "presidential" approach was evident in her oft-quoted comment, "I don't mind how much my Ministers talk, as long as they do what I say." Tony Blair as prime minister has had to share power with Gordon Brown, the chancellor of the exchequer (finance minister) and a major political force within the Labour party (discussed further in the box on page 241). He has also faced embarrassing resignations in protest, as when Robin Cook and Claire Short gave up their government posts to protest the Blair government's support for American policies in Iraq. However, many analysts have termed his leadership style, like Thatcher's, "presidential."[12]

"I don't mind how much my Ministers talk, as long as they do what I say."

Prime Minister Margaret Thatcher, *quoted by Elizabeth Knowles, ed., Twentieth Century Quotations (1998), 305.*

"The Blair administration is as badly disfigured by personal rivalries and jealousies as any of its predecessors and, at the heart of these quarrels, stands Gordon Brown."

Philip Stevens, *"The Treasury Under Blair" (2001), 206.*

PEOPLE IN THE EU

Tony Blair and Gordon Brown— Dual (and Sometimes Dueling) Architects of New Labour

Although charismatic prime minister Tony Blair is often portrayed as displaying "presidential" leadership akin to that of a U.S. president and has been widely credited as the leader who has revamped the Labour party into "New Labour" and carried it to victory in two general elections, he in fact has shared power to a marked degree with another architect of New Labour, his chancellor of the exchequer, Gordon Brown. The two men reside next door to one another on Downing Street in London and have generally divided the leadership of the Labour government between them. While Brown has focused on economic and welfare policies and kept the budget under control, Blair has emphasized foreign affairs, defense policy, Northern Ireland, health, and education. When John Smith, the leader of the Labour party, died in 1994, Blair and Brown were the leading candidates to succeed him. Most analysts believe that a bargain was struck between the two men at that time, with Brown standing aside for Blair in the leadership contest and Blair agreeing to share power with Brown and perhaps even at some point help him to become his successor as prime minister.

Although Blair and Brown have worked together to rid the Labour party of most of its socialist image and policies, loosen its traditional ties to the labor union movement, and transform it into centrist, pragmatic New Labour with an appeal across all social classes—and have agreed to a division of the chief tasks of governing between themselves—the two men sometimes find themselves in conflict. In part, this is due to personality differences. Many observers have described Brown's temperament as "brooding" or "Presbyterian," reflecting his Scottish upbringing, and have emphasized his apparent insecurity despite his power. Beyond these traits, he has also in policy terms been much more skeptical than Blair about adopting the euro currency. Thus, differing styles and differing policy preferences have at times led to duels between the top two leaders of the British government. One recent analysis has concluded that "the Blair administration is as badly disfigured by personal rivalries and jealousies as any of its predecessors and, at the heart of these quarrels, stands Gordon Brown." Nevertheless, the "partnership" between Blair and Brown has continued and has proved of considerable benefit to each.[13]

Below the "government" in the executive branch is a large civil service divided mainly into departments according to subject matter. Most departments have their headquarters in the vicinity of Whitehall in London and are often collectively referred to as "Whitehall" by British political commentators. The image that "Whitehall" conjures up for most Britons is somewhat inaccurate, for civil servants are now widely scattered around the country in various locations in the wake of considerable decentralization of administration in recent years.

Though the majority of the 500,000 civil servants carry out routine tasks, senior civil servants play significant policy-shaping roles by advising busy and often novice ministers and overseeing the implementation of policy decisions. In contrast to Germany and the United States, where a minister may make her or his own political appointments to major executive-branch posts, or to France and Italy, where a special office (the *cabinet*) assists the minister and mediates with the civil service, a British minister brings in just a few political assistants and these serve simultaneously as Members of Parliament. Upper-level British civil servants thus enjoy a high potential for political influence, though norms emphasize the need for their neutrality in advising and implementing cabinet/ministerial decisions.[14]

The monarchy today plays a largely ceremonial and symbolic role in the executive branch. This role is important to many Britons as an element of continuity (Queen Elizabeth II has occupied the throne since 1953!), a link to Britain's proud traditions, and a focus for national unity. Despite the extensive publicity surrounding the British royal family, especially in the tabloid newspapers, the monarch no longer is a major force in British politics. Nevertheless, the massive public outpouring of affection for Princess Diana after her untimely death provides evidence of the emotional attachment that many citizens still have to at least some members of the royal family. Probably the most notable potential power of the monarchy is that the queen or king can conceivably play a part in the selection of a prime minister in the event that there is no clear-cut majority in the House of Commons, though the likelihood of this power being exercised independently is quite remote.

The Parliament

According to the British constitution, parliament is sovereign, or supreme, in British politics and society. Britain has a bicameral legislature, composed of the House of Commons and the House of Lords. However, the House of Lords, recently reduced in size from substantially more than 1000 to less than 700 by eliminating most of its "hereditary peers" (who have inherited or been appointed to the peerage), has sat on the sidelines of political power on most matters since a major reform in 1911. It is now composed of a little more than 550 life peers (appointed for life), 26 dignitaries of the Church of England, and 12 Lords of Appeal in Ordinary who act as judges of Britain's highest court of appeals, in addition to 92 hereditary peers who for the time being continue to have voting rights. Though it provides a few of the members of the government, exercises a unique judicial function as the highest British court of appeal through the Lords of Appeal in Ordinary (a subgroup within the chamber appointed specifically to carry out this function and possessing legal expertise), and scrutinizes legislation, it can be overridden by a House of Commons majority in the lawmaking realm and has no power to oust the government. The House of Lords has in the past century usually served as a scrutinizing chamber to review and slow down the quick actions normally taken by a House of Commons very much dominated by the majority party of the day. What form it will take and what roles it will play in the future remain uncertain. The Blair government is in the process of instituting major changes. It has already greatly reduced the number of hereditary peers and is proposing that a new supreme court replace the Lords of Appeal in Ordinary.

The House of Commons, composed of 659 Members of Parliament (M.P.s) popularly elected in single-member districts, enjoys lawmaking powers superior to those of the House of Lords, the power to probe and challenge and perhaps embarrass the prime minister and cabinet ministers at **Question Time** weekly, and the sole ability to oust a government by a majority vote. It also provides most of the members of the government, always including in modern times the prime minister. The two major parties in the House of Commons usually confront each other directly in debates, votes (called **"divisions"** because members divide by going into "yes" and "no" lobbies to vote), and Question Time. However, because the House of Commons is nearly always dominated by a cohesive majority party led by the prime minister and major cabinet ministers, it usually accepts their leadership in enacting laws and supports them in votes of confidence. This pattern does not reflect blind obedience by party members. "The usual government tactic," wrote one recent analyst, "is to publish details of a proposed bill, test the reactions to it and, if necessary, make concessions."[15]

"The usual government tactic is to publish details of a proposed bill, test the reactions to it and, if necessary, make concessions."

Guardian analysis cited by Philip Cowley and Mark Stuart, "In Place of Strife?" June (2003), 325.

Prime Minister James Callaghan and his government were compelled to call upon the queen to dissolve the House of Commons and call new elections due to a House of Commons no-confidence vote of 311–310 in 1979, but this event occurred in the unusual situation in which the Labour government had lost its previous Commons majority due to deaths and defeats in **by-elections** (special votes scheduled to fill vacant seats caused by death or resignation). Conservative Prime Minister Margaret Thatcher was pressured into resignation in 1990, but her sudden departure was due to her assessment that she could not win a vote to be renamed as party leader within the Parliamentary Conservative party rather than to a no-confidence vote. In the latter case, certainly, the attitudes of the ordinary M.P.s (termed "backbenchers" if they do not hold government posts as the "frontbenchers" do) played a significant

part in Thatcher's political demise. Table 11.2 indicates the post–World War II prime ministers of Britain, their terms of office, and their party affiliations.

A feature of the British House of Commons that distinguishes it from most European parliaments is the extent to which it is organized around adversarial confrontations between the governing party and the official opposition (the second-largest party). The latter has a "shadow cabinet" on its front benches, with its backbenchers arrayed on the benches rising behind. Though the opposition can expect to lose quite consistently in House of Commons divisions (votes) over public policy, it devotes extensive energy to articulating critiques of the government and putting forth its own programs to woo the mass electorate with the goal of winning the next election and constituting the next government.

Because the House of Commons is usually dominated by the government, through its control of the majority party, the House more often legitimates government-developed public

TABLE 11.2 British Prime Ministers Since 1945

Prime minister	Time in office	Party affiliation
Clement Attlee	1945–1951	Labour
Winston Churchill	1951–1955	Conservative
Anthony Eden	1955–1957	Conservative
Harold Macmillan	1957–1963	Conservative
Alec Douglas-Home	1963–1964	Conservative
Harold Wilson	1964–1970	Labour
Edward Heath	1970–1974	Conservative
Harold Wilson	1974–1976	Labour
James Callaghan	1976–1979	Labour
Margaret Thatcher	1979–1990	Conservative
John Major	1990–1997	Conservative
Tony Blair	1997–	Labour

policies than it takes the initiative or shapes the laws directly. Therefore, it is much less an "active" lawmaking institution than the United States Congress and more a "reactive" body. It reacts to government initiatives by either legitimating them outright or by modifying them through amendments, and it only occasionally rejects them completely or substitutes a legislative initiative. In this respect, it resembles most national parliamentary bodies in Europe. Its committees play a much less active role in shaping legislation than those of the U.S. Congress, the German Bundestag, or the Italian Chamber of Deputies or Senate, and somewhat less than even the French parliamentary committees. Nonetheless, the House of Commons remains an important part of the British state structure, albeit a largely reactive one and one in which the adversarial confrontations between government and opposition capture the most public attention.

The Legal and Judicial System

Britain (except Scotland) shares with the United States (exept Louisiana) a **common law** tradition that emphasizes judicial interpretations, case law, precedents, and an adversarial style in court. The other major nation-states of the European Union, in contrast, have a Roman law tradition that emphasizes a detailed legal code, less leeway for judicial interpretation, and an inquisitorial style in court. However, unlike Germany, France, and Italy, which have all adopted forms of constitutional judicial review that at least partially resemble the United States's approach, British courts have lacked the authority to declare unconstitutional an act of parliament. This fact is due in part to the absence of a written constitutional document; it is due in part to the constitutional principle of parliamentary sovereignty. The new supreme court, as proposed by the Blair government, will still not have the authority to override parliament on British constitutional grounds. As will be discussed more fully in the next chapter, however, British membership in the European Union has had the effect of undermining parliamentary sovereignty and enhancing judicial powers on matters pertaining to EU law.[16]

Subnational Governments

Finally, despite Britain's unitary structure, which has centralized considerable authority in the institutions of the national government, subnational governments do exist and merit some discussion. Because the national government has enjoyed constitutional supremacy, it has at times used its powers to alter or even abolish regional and local governments to suit the interests of the national governing party. For example, Prime Minister Margaret Thatcher used her national parliamentary majority to abolish the Greater London Council regional government and five similar metropolitan area governments in the 1980s. Governments have often redrawn the boundaries of counties. In the federal system of the United States, in contrast, the national government has no authority to alter state or local governmental boundaries and certainly cannot abolish any of them!

The recent devolutions in Scotland and Wales, instigated by the Blair government as part of its efforts to decentralize authority, are particularly noteworthy. The Scottish parliament has gained powers over a wide range of policies, including health, education and training, housing, the law and home affairs, and the environment, as well as limited powers to raise its own revenue (though most of its spending will derive from grants from the national government). The Welsh assembly has a narrower range of powers and lacks any taxation authority. Whether a decentralized government for Northern Ireland will be able to take hold again (the previous one at Stormont having been disbanded by the British government due to political upheaval in 1972) remains to be seen. Another future issue is what to do about subnational government in England, where 83 percent of the population of the United Kingdom reside. One possibility is to create an English parliament alongside the others and replace the unitary structure with a federal or quasi-federal system, but a major objection is that the English Parliament might be so large and powerful that it would challenge the primacy of the national parliament. Another option is to establish a number of regional parliaments within England. However, objections focus on the difficulties in establishing the number and the boundaries for these, particularly because many areas of England lack a strong sense of regional identity.[17]

ELECTIONS, POLITICAL PARTIES, AND INTEREST GROUPS

As in the other West European nation-states, the actual operations of the governmental institutions in the United Kingdom reflect to a high degree the electoral process, the major political parties, and the leading interest groups. These provide important linkages between governmental institutions and the general public (or at least its more articulate and active segments). In addition, as previously noted in discussions of party government, the parties play a comparatively large role in Britain in organizing the cabinet-parliamentary institutions for policy-making and other purposes—certainly more so than in the United States and probably more so than in most Continental European nation-states.

The Electoral Process

In contrast to France and the United States, with their popular presidential elections held separately from legislative elections, the only national elections in the United Kingdom are for the House of Commons. These are run on a highly partisan basis. Voters may vote only for

a local House of Commons candidate in a single-member constituency. Victory goes to the candidate who wins the most votes, even if his or her total is less than a majority in the district. Candidates need not live in the district, and many do not. Most voters are less concerned about local residency than in the United States because they see Members of Parliament primarily as party representatives who will back a particular party leader for prime minister and support the program outlined in the party manifesto, usually a set of pledges both more specific and more likely to be fulfilled than American party platforms are. Therefore, in making their choices, voters usually give primacy to their assessment of the parties, evaluate the prime ministerial candidates of the parties as part of a retrospective and prospective performance consideration, and only to a much lesser degree take into account the individual parliamentary candidates. Despite the importance of the parties, British voters have loosened their partisan attachments and placed increasing emphasis on performance, in a **"dealignment"** pattern seen in many other Western countries.[18] Voter turnout has also declined, to 60 percent in the most recent general election (2001), the lowest figure in the United Kingdom since 1918, though still higher than the 50 percent turnout in the U.S. presidential election of 2000.[19] In every election but one since 1931, one party has won a majority of the seats in the House of Commons. The majority party then usually constitutes a one-party government and governs until the next election. In the most recent national elections, in 2001, the results were as indicated in Table 11.3.

Table 11.4 shows the popular vote percentages and the seat distribution among the parties in the elections from 1979 through 1992, all of which were won by the Conservative party by similar percentages of the vote, though the seat distribution varied rather widely. The 1983 election gave the Conservatives a huge majority of the seats with only 42 percent of the popular

TABLE 11.3 Results of the 2001 and 1997 British General Elections

Party	2001 Popular vote %	Seats	% of seats
Labour	41	413	63
Conservative	32	166	25
Liberal Democrat	18	52	8
Other	9	28	4
Total	100	659	100
	1997		
Labour	43	418	64
Conservative	31	165	25
Liberal Democrat	17	46	7
Other	9	30	4
Total	100	659	100

Source: Calculated by the author from "Elections around the World."

vote, largely because the votes won by the second-largest party (Labour, at 28 percent) fell far below the Conservatives' vote and the votes of the third-largest party (the Liberal-Social Democratic Alliance, at 25 percent) were rarely concentrated in a particular geographic area sufficiently to allow it to win many districts. Thus,

the Liberal-Social Democratic Alliance won only 23 seats (3.5 percent of the total) despite winning 25 percent of the popular vote. The contrast with the Labour party, which had concentrated strength in a number of working-class districts, was fairly dramatic. Both Table 11.3 and Table 11.4 illustrate the frequent gaps between popular voting patterns and distributions of parliamentary seats that result from the British first-past-the-post electoral system.

Political Parties

The Labour party is the current majority party in the House of Commons and supports the government headed by Prime Minister Tony Blair. Under Blair's leadership since 1994, the Labour party has continued a process begun by his predecessors, Neil Kinnock and John Smith, of recasting itself as a center-left political party with a loosened attachment to the trade unions. Committed at least symbolically to "socialism" as an ideology since 1918, the party has long struggled to define the meaning of that term. During most of the period from 1945 to the late 1970s, the party was dominated by pragmatic leaders of the center-left who often had to battle a succession of left socialist factions that wanted the state to take over major industries, redistribute wealth to create an egalitarian society, and create a socialist Britain distinct and

TABLE 11.4 Party Percentages of the Popular Vote and Seats Won in British General Elections, 1979–1992

Party	1979 %	Seats	1983 %	Seats	1987 %	Seats	1992 %	Seats
Conservative	44	339	42	397	42	376	42	336
Labour	37	269	28	209	31	292	34	271
Liberal Dem.*	14*	11*	25*	23*	23	22	18	20
Others	5	16	5	21	4	20	6	24
TOTAL	100	635	100	650	100	650	100	651

* The 1979 votes and seats are for the Liberal party. The 1983 votes are for the Liberal-Social Democratic Alliance.

separate from the rest of Europe and the United States. Labour governments (1945–1951, 1964–1970, and 1974–1979) nationalized a few industries but mainly expanded the British welfare state. In the late 1970s and the early 1980s, the leftists gained temporary dominance of the Labour party, provoking a party split (in which some prominent moderates departed to establish a Social Democratic party, most of which eventually merged with the Liberal party to form the Liberal Democrats). Labour also suffered a disastrous electoral defeat in 1983. Following that electoral catastrophe, in which Labour nearly fell to third place, the party began to moderate its positions. Eventually, at Blair's instigation, it abandoned state ownership of business corporations as a major goal, revising clause four of its party constitution on this subject, and distanced itself somewhat from the labor unions, which had given it its name and much of its original sense of purpose. Blair also proclaimed that "Labour is the party of law and order in Britain today. Tough on crime and tough on the causes of crime." With this slogan, he sought (rather successfully) to retain Labour's traditional emphasis on social programs to ameliorate the causes of crime with a "get-tough" approach to prosecuting criminals. Gradually, in a process beginning well before Blair became leader, Labour also adopted positions more supportive of both European integration and cooperation with the United States.

"Labour is the party of law and order in Britain today. Tough on crime and tough on the causes of crime."

Tony Blair (before he was prime minister), September 30, 1993, *cited by Elizabeth Knowles, Twentieth Century Quotations (1998), 3.*

New Labour, as it came to be called by Blair and his supporters, has succeeded in capturing much of the middle ground of British politics since the mid-1990s. For a time it stressed the theme of a "stakeholder" economy and society (entailing shared economic powers among corporate executives, consumers, employees, and other groups), rather than the socialism of the early 1980s, though this theme has diminished recently, giving way to high priority for improving public services (which deteriorated noticeably during the previous two decades and remain at low levels relative to much of Western Europe). Moreover, and more specifically, it has emphasized constitutional reforms to devolve powers in Scotland and Wales, abolish the right of hereditary peers to vote in the House of Lords, elect London mayors by direct popular vote, institute a Freedom of Information Act to limit governmental secrecy, enact a Human Rights Act to enhance civil liberties protection, and hold a referendum on the future of the British electoral system. These shifts have brought Labour much closer than before to the Liberal Democratic party and have created a sharper contrast with the Conservative party on constitutional matters than on the economic issues and ideologies traditionally separating the "Socialists" (Labourites) from the "Tories" (Conservatives).[20]

The Conservative party grew out of the old Tory faction in predemocratic British politics. Much older than the Labour party, it has also been much more inclined to see itself as the "natural" governing party of the United Kingdom. Shocked by the Labour victory near the end of World War II in 1945, the Conservative party quickly adjusted to the new postwar atmosphere, accepted most of Labour's welfare-state innovations, and came back to govern for 13 consecutive years (1951–1964) and then again for 4 years (1970–1974) with Edward Heath as prime minister. Margaret Thatcher led it back into government in 1979, and the Conservatives continued to govern for 18 consecutive years under the leadership of Thatcher and then John Major. Now the party finds itself again in the unaccustomed position of opposition to the government, having badly lost two successive general elections to Labour in 1997 and 2001.

Prime Minister Thatcher was much more inclined toward what most British call a "neoliberal" commitment to privatization and checks on labor union power than her immediate predecessors and reoriented the Conservative party in this direction, despite some opposition from so-called Tory "wets" who favored a more moderate approach. Often Thatcher went beyond most European neoliberalism in the direction of American-style Reaganite conservatism or even economic libertarianism, particularly in her rhetoric. "There is no such thing as Society," she famously proclaimed. "There are individual men and women, and there are families." Both her assertive style and her attachment to British state sovereignty led her into repeated conflicts with the European Commission, leaders of other major European Community nation-states, and leaders of her own party, eventually contributing to her downfall in 1990. Prime Minister Major tried to bridge a widening gap within the Conservative party over European issues but generally failed in this endeavor. By 1997, the Conservatives were badly divided over Europe, shaken by a wave of scandals and demoralized by their consistently low standing in the public-opinion polls. Since their electoral defeat, they have sought to regroup with limited success. Major Conservative party themes at the dawn of the new millennium have become a defense of constitutional traditions and the nation-state against allegedly "radical" Labour reforms or encroachments from the European Union. The party's 2001 campaign placed particular emphasis on the need to save the pound sterling by rejecting adoption of the euro as the British currency. Following the party's disastrous defeat in that election, it was further fractured by a bitter struggle over the party leadership, from which Iain Duncan Smith, a staunch Euroskeptic and devotee of Thatcherism, emerged on top. Soon, however, the Conservative party, dismayed by their new leader's apparent inability to triumph over Prime Minister Blair in either Question Time or parliamentary debate, and by his poor showings in public-opinion polls, replaced him with Michael Howard, another Euroskeptic, but one with a wide array of experience and political skills. The party has sought to maintain its traditionally close ties with the business and financial community, though a major segment of big business and most of the financial community have been less than pleased with the Euroskepticism that has swept over the Conservative party in recent years.[21]

> "There is no such thing as Society. There are individual men and women, and there are families."
>
> Prime Minister Margaret Thatcher, October 31, 1987, *cited by Elizabeth Knowles, ed., Twentieth Century Quotations (1998), 306.*

Beyond the two major parties, the Liberal Democrats have been the most competitive and possess the most potential to play a significant role in national government. Unless Britain shifts to a proportional representation electoral system—a major goal of the Liberal Democratic party, unsurprisingly—that potential is unlikely to be fulfilled. Long occupying a generally centrist position on the left-right political spectrum, the Liberal Democrats now share a number of ideological and policy positions with New Labour advocates but remain more committed to European integration than either of the two major parties.[22]

Other political parties of importance include the Scottish Nationalists, who may some day gain control of the Scottish parliament, with possibly dramatic impact on the future of the United Kingdom, and Plaid Cymru, the Welsh Nationalists. The Greens have done moderately well in some European parliamentary elections in Britain, in part because these elections do not determine who will constitute the British government (and thus voters feel freer than in national elections to vote for parties other than the top two) and in part because proportional representation is now used in the European parliamentary contests (and thus prevents third-party votes from being "wasted"). However, they hold no seats in the British House of Commons. Northern Ireland has its own distinctive party system, in which the moderate Social Democratic Labor party and the militant Irish nationalist Sinn Fein compete for the votes of (largely Catholic) nationalists who wish to unite Northern Ireland with the Republic of Ireland in the South; while the moderate Unionist and militant Democratic Unionist parties compete for the (largely Protestant) voters who wish to maintain Northern Ireland as a component of the United Kingdom.

In electoral terms, Britain has become a multiparty system since the early 1970s. However, the electoral system has continued to give a House of Commons majority, and thus the ability to support a one-party government, to one of the two major parties after every election except that of February 1974 (though Labour had to make concessions to the Liberals in the late 1970s to stay in office after loss of its very narrow postelection majority).

Interest Groups

Just as British political parties have played a larger role in shaping British politics than American political parties have done in the United States, British interest groups have generally had less room for maneuver and less influence than their American counterparts. The legislative process, including the committee system as well as the formal votes, is characterized by much more partisan behavior than in the United States. Because the parliamentary members of the majority party nearly always vote as a cohesive body, they are able to carry bills through the nonspecialized standing committees and pass them on the floor of parliament

without much opportunity for effective lobbying or consideration of major amendments. The result is diminished potential for interest group lobbyists to sway British M.P.s. Moreover, the relative centralization of authority and weakness of judicial power have meant that subnational and judicial arenas offer limited opportunities for interest-group influence. The result has been that traditionally British interest groups have especially targeted government ministers and junior ministers and civil servants.

Of course, a few major interest groups, such as the Confederation of British Industry or the Trades Union Congress, have often possessed sufficient clout to exercise significant influence on the prime minister and cabinet. The Confederation of British Industry, founded in 1965 by a merger of the Federation of British Industries, the British Employers' Confederation, and the National Association of British Manufacturers, has been the prime "peak" association for the business community. However, the business community is also represented by The Institute of Directors, in recent years less dominated than the CBI by large, multinational firms, and by an array of business trade associations. Moreover, "the City" (the term applied to the financial interests and institutions of the City of London) often expresses distinctive interests in various ways. Most of the business community has a long but not formal association with the Conservative party. The New Labour party of Tony Blair, however, has established close ties with many business and financial interests. On the other hand, a large number of the unions in the Trades Union Congress, founded back in 1868, have long possessed formal ties to the Labour party that go beyond the union-party links found in the United States or even most Continental European states. These have included payment of Labour party dues by their members, sponsorship of Labour M.P.s, and voting power at Labour party conferences. These ties have weakened somewhat since the early 1990s. By most measures, labor union power has declined in Britain in the past two decades. For example, union membership has declined from 53 percent of the civilian work force in 1978 to about 30 percent today, partially reflecting a general trend in Western societies and partially resulting from policies instituted by the Thatcher government in the 1980s.[23]

It is common in Britain to distinguish between "sectional" interest groups based primarily on shared economic functions (such as unions, business groups, agricultural groups, and professional groups) and "promotional" groups that primarily promote particular causes and draw supporters from differing occupations. The promotional groups have proliferated in recent years in Britain but generally lack the influence of some of the major sectional groups, particularly those representing business.

In comparing Britain with the other major nation-states of the European Union, at least two points about interest-group politics are noteworthy. First, corporatist or neo-corporatist patterns of governmental consultation with major business and labor interest groups have rarely been as common in the United Kingdom as in most Continental European states. Though the Conservative Macmillan government set up a neo-corporatist National Economic Development Council in the 1960s and there were further moves toward government-business-labor consultation in the 1970s, particularly under the Labour governments of Harold Wilson and James Callaghan, the Conservative Thatcher government was very hostile to this approach; and it has never been as widespread as in most of Western Europe. The Blair government has shown no inclination to revive it. Second, British interest groups have rarely employed the radical ideological rhetoric, suffered the ideological splits (in the labor movement, for example), or engaged in the massive, often violent, protests that frequently have characterized France and Italy. Most analysts see the roots of this difference in approach as embedded in a British political culture that takes an empirical rather than rational approach to problem-solving, stresses allegiance to the political system, is cooperative in making decisions, and emphasizes trust.[24]

CONCLUSIONS

The United Kingdom of Great Britain and Northern Ireland possesses a number of distinctive features that have conditioned and will continue to shape its relationships with the European Community/European Union. Among the most prominent are its island location; lengthy and proud historical experience as a nation-state; distinctive constitutional traditions and conceptions of democracy; unique World War II experiences; special ties of language and culture with the United States and the English-speaking Commonwealth; global economic ties; and (particularly again since the late 1970s) preferences for private property, entrepreneurship, and free-market mechanisms. Beyond these, other features of British politics provide the structures for decision-making that underlie significant decisions that the British nation-state has made and will make concerning Europe: the importance of the cabinet and prime minister in initiating major policy changes; the advice-giving and implementation roles of ostensibly neutral senior civil servants; the "party government" model, with a usual pattern of one-party government; and the influence of financial and business groups and to a lesser degree now, labor unions, mingled with the rising importance of promotional interest groups. At the same time, it is important to recognize that the European Union has had and will continue to have a significant impact not only on British public policies but also on the political processes, institutions, and constitution of the United Kingdom. British leaders have also sought to steer the European Union in directions that they prefer, sometimes successfully but often without the desired British outcomes. It is to these subjects that we turn in the next chapter.

SUMMARY

- English kings such as William the Conqueror (1066–1087) and Henry II (1154–1189) built central state authority in England before comparable patterns took shape in most of Europe; English national identity developed gradually as French-speaking Normans merged with Anglo-Saxons, Scandinavians, and others to form an English language and nation.

- The United Kingdom includes, in addition to England, Wales, Scotland, and Northern Ireland, each with its own distinctive cultural identity; in Northern Ireland, nationalists (mostly Catholics) who desire to be part of Ireland combat unionists (predominantly Protestants) who wish to remain in the United Kingdom, with the unionists maintaining a slim majority.

- Another set of identity issues in the United Kingdom today centers on the integration of new immigrants (especially those differentiated by skin color and/or religion) into the British "nation."

- British state institutions have demonstrated unusual continuity, evolving gradually under a largely unwritten constitution, unique in Europe.

- The democratization of British politics, like the alteration of its basic state institutions, has occurred gradually and mostly nonviolently since the seventeenth century, in contrast to patterns in most major European states.

- Like the rest of Western Europe, Britain has moved from feudalism in the middle ages to a modern mixed economy; the British mix is somewhat more oriented toward free markets and property rights than Europe as a whole, particularly since the era of Prime Minister Margaret Thatcher (1979–1990).

- The United Kingdom is the originator and a prime example today of cabinet-parliamentary government that fuses power between the executive and the legislature.

- Britain retains the monarchy (currently held by Queen Elizabeth II) and the House of Lords from the middle ages; however, the monarchy has become mostly ceremonial; and the House of Lords is far less powerful than the popularly elected House of Commons.

- The prime minister (now Tony Blair) is the head of the government; governing through a fairly cohesive majority party (presently Labour) in the House of Commons, the prime minister is usually less checked and balanced than most of his counterparts in Europe or than the U.S. president.

- Prime ministers may be removed by rebellions within the majority party (as Margaret Thatcher was in 1990) or by a vote of no confidence in the House of Commons; the latter is likely only when no party holds a majority, as in 1979, when James Callaghan was the last prime minister to lose office in this manner.

- A distinguishing feature of the House of Commons is the great extent to which it is organized on the basis of "party government," with adversarial confrontations occurring regularly between the governing party and the official opposition (the second-largest party, currently the Conservatives); it is also especially renowned for its active use of question tie vis-à-vis the prime minister and other government ministers.

- Britain (except Scotland) shares with the United States (except Louisiana) a common law tradition that emphasizes judicial interpretations, case law, precedents, and an adversarial style in court—in contrast to the Roman law tradition of most of Europe.

- The highest British court, the Law Lords (Lords of Appeal in Ordinary) in the House of Lords, lacks the power to declare parliamentary acts to be in violation of the British (largely unwritten) constitution; the Blair government has proposed a new supreme court that would also lack such power; however, judicial powers have grown concerning EU legal matters.

- Britain has traditionally been a unitary rather than a federal system, but recent devolutions in Scotland and Wales, instigated by the Blair government in response to demands, have entailed considerable decentralization from the highly centralized past pattern.

- The only British national elections are for the House of Commons; they employ the first-past-the-post system, are highly partisan, and nearly always result in a House of Commons majority for one party, which then names the prime minister; usually the prime minister then selects a government entirely from her or his parliamentary party.

- The center-right Conservative party and center-left Labour party have alternated in power for most of the past century; the centrist Liberal Democratic party is the largest of the minor parties in Britain but (unlike many minor parties in France, Germany, and Italy) has not held any cabinet posts in recent decades.

- Tony Blair has played the leading role in making "New Labour" a more centrist (and popular) party than the more socialistic Labour party of the 1970s and 1980s; however, he must share power with others in his cabinet, most notably Chancellor of the Exchequer Gordon Brown.

- Because of the strength of the two major parties in the United Kingdom, British interest groups have generally enjoyed less room for maneuver and less influence than their American counterparts.

- The Confederation of British Industry and the Trades Union Congress, organizing British business and labor respectively, have nonetheless often possessed sufficient clout to exercise influence on the prime minister and cabinet and over other components of the British state.

- Corporatist or neo-corporatist patterns of governmental consultation with major business and labor interest groups have been less common in the United Kingdom than in most Continental European states and have declined from their peak in Britain in the 1960s and 1970s.

ENDNOTES

1. Stephen George, *An Awkward Partner: Britain in the European Community*, 3rd ed. (Oxford: Oxford University Press, 1998).

2. Ian Adams, *Ideology and Politics in Britain Today* (Manchester: Manchester University Press, 1998), Ch. 7; Percy Allum, *State and Society in Western Europe* (Cambridge: Polity Press, 1995), esp. 46–47 and 97–101; Robert Skidelsky, ed., *Thatcherism* (Cambridge: Basil Blackwell, 1988).

3. Linda Colley, *Britons: Forging the Nation 1707–1837* (New Haven: Yale University Press, 1992), 373. Colley's book provides an excellent analysis of British nation-building in the eighteenth and nineteenth centuries. On recent "national" issues and problems, see Colin Pilkington, *Devolution in Britain Today* (Manchester: Manchester University Press, 2003); Andrew Sullivan, "There Will Always Be an England," *New York Times Magazine*, February 21, 1999, 38–45+; Sean Ferren and Robert Mulvihill, *Paths to a Settlement in Northern Ireland* (New York: Oxford University Press, 2000); Christopher T. Harvie and Peter Jones, *The Road to Home Rule:*

Images of Scotland's Cause (Edinburgh: Polygon, 2000).

4. Mark Mazower, *Dark Continent: Europe's Twentieth Century* (New York: Random House, Vintage, 2000), 346–347; Helen Seaford, "The Future of Multi-Ethnic Britain: An Opportunity Missed," *The Political Quarterly* 72, 1 (January–March 2001), 107–113; "Race and Poverty: Down and Out Up North," *The Economist* 361 (December 15, 2001), 47–48; Sarah Lyell, "Britain Raises Barriers High Against the Asylum Seekers," *New York Times*, April 3, 2000, A1 and A10; Warren Hoge, "Britain's Nonwhites Feel Un-British, Report Says," *New York Times*, April 4, 2002, A6.

5. Walter Bagehot, *The English Constitution* (Ithaca, NY: Cornell University Press, 1966), and A. V. Dicey, *An Introduction to the Study of the Law of the Constitution*, 10th ed. (London: Macmillan, 1959).

6. Richard Rose, *Do Parties Make a Difference?* 2nd ed. (Chatham, NJ: Chatham House, 1984), and Rose, *The Problem of Party Government* (London: Penguin, 1976) offer good analyses of British party government in action.

7. Janet Mather, *The European Union and British Democracy: Towards Convergence* (New York: St. Martin's, 2000), esp. Chs. 1, 2, and 9. Bill Jones, "Reforming the Electoral System," in Bill Jones, ed., *Political Issues in Britain Today*, 5th ed. (Manchester: Manchester University Press, 1999), 42–61.

8. Jürg Steiner, *European Democracies*, 3rd ed. (White Plains, NY: Longman, 1995), 135.

9. Will Hutton, *The State We're In* (London: Cape, 1994); David Coates, "Placing New Labour," in Jones, ed., *Political Issues*, 346–366; Steiner, *European Democracies*, Ch. 11; John Pinder, *The Building of the European Union*, 3rd ed. (Oxford: Oxford University Press, 1998), 134–136.

10. Joni Lovenduski and Pippa Norris, "Westminster Women: The Politics of Presence," *Political Studies* 51, 1 (March 2003), 84–102. Also see Joni Lovenduski, "Women and Politics: Minority Representation or Critical Mass?" in Pippa Norris, ed., *Britain Votes 2001* (Oxford: Oxford University Press, 2001), 179–194.

11. Geoffrey Evans, "Britain and Europe: Separate Worlds of Welfare?" *Government and Opposition* 33 (Spring 1998), 183–198; Gosta Esping-Anderson, *The Three Worlds of Welfare Capitalism* (Cambridge: Polity Press, 1990).

12. The Thatcher quote is from Elizabeth Knowles, ed., *Twentieth Century Quotations* (Oxford: Oxford University Press, 1998), 305. On prime ministerial government, see Richard Crossman, "Introduction," in Bagehot, *The English Constitution*, 51–53. On "presidentializing," see Sue Pryce, *Presidentializing the Premiership* (New York: St. Martin's, 1997), and Michael Foley, *The British Presidency: Tony Blair and the Politics of Public Leadership* (Manchester: Manchester University Press, 2000). On Thatcher, see Margaret Thatcher, *The Downing Street Years* (New York: HarperCollins, 1993); Dennis Kavanagh, *Thatcherism and British Politics: The End of Consensus?* (Oxford: Oxford University Press, 1990); Hugo Young, *One of Us* (London: Macmillan, 1989); Anthony King, "Margaret Thatcher as a Political Leader," in Skidelsky, *Thatcherism*, 51–64; Peter Jenkins, *Mrs. Thatcher's Revolution: The Ending of the Socialist Era* (Cambridge, MA: Harvard University Press, 1988). Examination of the "presidential" qualities of the Blair premiership are found in Dennis Kavanagh, "New Labour, New Millennium, New Premiership," in Anthony Seldon, ed., *The Blair Effect: The Blair Government 1997–2001* (London: Little, Brown, 2001), 3–20, and Peter Riddell, "Blair as Prime Minister," also in Seldon, ed., *The Blair Effect*, 21–42.

13. John Rentoul, *Tony Blair* (London: Warner Books, 1996), esp. Ch. 12; Philip Stevens, "The Treasury Under Labour," in Seldon, ed., *The Blair Effect*, 185–207. The quotation from the analyst is from Stevens, "The Treasury Under Labour," 206.

14. See the cross-national comparisons in Yves Mény and Andrew Knapp, *Government and Politics in Western Europe*, 3rd ed. (Oxford: Oxford University Press, 1998), 268–269. Also see Rod Rhodes, "The Civil Service," in Seldon, ed., *The Blair Effect*, 95–115; Kevin Theakston, *The Civil Service since 1945* (Oxford: Blackwell, 1995); Peter Barberis, *The Elite of the Elite: Permanent Secretaries in the British Higher Civil Service* (Aldershot: Dartmouth, 1996); and Colin Pilkington, *The Civil Service in Britain Today*

(Manchester: Manchester University Press, 1999).

15. *Guardian* analysis cited by Philip Cowley and Mark Stuart, "In Place of Strife? The PLP in Government, 1997–2001," *Political Studies* 1, 2 (June 2003), 325.

16. Patrick Wintour and Clare Dyer, "Cabinet Reshuffle; Ministers Shun US Model for Supreme Court," *The Guardian*, June 16, 2003, 4; Warren Hoge, "Blair Seeks a Supreme Court Modeled on the U.S. Version" *New York Times*, June 14, 2003, 11; Alan Davies, *British Politics and Europe* (London: Hodder & Stoughton, 1998), Ch. 4; Philip Norton, *The British Polity*, 3rd ed. (New York: Longman, 1994), 326–327.

17. Vernon Bogdanor, "Constitutional Reform," in Seldon, ed., *The Blair Effect*, 138–156; Nevil Johnson, "Taking Stock of Constitutional Reform," *Government and Opposition* 36, 3 (Summer 2001), 331–354; Robert Hazell, "Reforming the Constitution," *The Political Quarterly* 72, 1 (January–March 2001); James Mitchell, "Devolution," in Jones, ed., *Political Issues*, Ch. 7; Keith Robbins, "Britain and Europe: Devolution and Foreign Policy," *International Affairs* 74 (January 1998), 105–118. Also see sources in note 3.

18. Anthony King, "Why Labour Won—At Last," in Anthony King, ed., *New Labour Triumphs: Britain at the Polls* (Chatham, NJ: Chatham House, 1998), Ch. 7; D. M. Wood and Philip Norton, "Do Candidates Matter? Constituency-Specific Vote Changes for Incumbent MPs, 1983–1987," *Political Studies* 40 (May 1992), 227–238. Also see the analysis of performance evaluation by Paul Whiteley, cited by Norton, *The British Polity*, 97–98.

19. Tim Hames, "Election Round-Up," *The Times*, June 9, 2001, E10–E11; Martin Harrop, "An Apathetic Landslide: The British General Election of 2001," *Government and Opposition* 36, 3 (Summer 2001), 295–313; Anthony King, ed., *Britain at the Polls, 2001* (New York: Chatham House, 2002).

20. Stephen Driver and Luke Martell, *Blair's Britain* (London: Polity Press, 2002); Richard Heffernan, *New Labour and Thatcherism: Political Change in Britain* (New York: St. Martin's, 2000); Adams, *Ideology and Politics in Britain Today*, Ch. 9; Patrick Seyd, "Tony Blair and New Labour," in King, ed., *New Labour Triumphs*, 49–74; James Mitchell, "The Battle for Britain? Constitutional Reform and the Election," in Andrew Geddes and Jonathan Tonge, eds., *Labour's Landslide: The British General Election 1997* (Manchester: Manchester University Press, 1997), Ch. 9. The most recent of several good historical overviews of the Labour party is Andrew Thorpe, *A History of the British Labour Party*, 2nd ed. (Basingstoke: Palgrave, 2001).

21. The Thatcher quotation is cited in Knowles, ed., *Twentieth Century Quotations*, 306. Philip Lynch, *The Politics of Nationhood: Sovereignty, Britishness, and Conservative Politics* (New York: St. Martin's, 1999); Earl A. Reitan, *Tory Radicalism: Margaret Thatcher, John Major, and the Transformation of Modern Britain 1970–1997* (Lanham, MD: Rowman & Littlefield, 1997); Adams, *Ideology and Politics*, Chs. 6, 7; Philip Norton, "The Conservative Party: Is There Anyone Out There?" in King, ed., *Britain at the Polls*, 68–94; Warren Hoge, "British Conservatives Choose 'Euroskeptic' Leader," *New York Times*, September 14, 2001, B1.

22. Don MacIver, ed., *The Liberal Democrats* (Hemel Hempstead: Prentice Hall, 1996); Adams, *Ideology and Politics*, 64–67.

23. Union membership figures are from Mark Evans, "Political Participation," in Patrick Dunleavy, et al., eds., *Developments in British Politics*, Vol. 5, 111. On interest groups generally, see Wyn Grant, *Pressure Groups and British Politics* (New York: St. Martin's, 2000).

24. Steiner, *European Democracies*, Ch. 8; Allum, *State and Society*, 254–260 and 276–277; Norton, *The British Polity*, 23–35 on political culture and 163–170 on corporatism; Robert Taylor, "Employment Relations Policy," in Seldon, ed., *The Blair Effect*, 244–269, and Coates, "Placing New Labour," in Jones, ed., *Political Issues in Britain Today*, 5th ed., 554–555, on Blair's lack of enthusiasm for neo-corporatism.

THE UNITED KINGDOM AND THE EUROPEAN UNION

"Europe's British problem is that, after 30 years of membership, the British still cannot make up their minds whether they really want to be full participants in the European adventure."

—Timothy Garton Ash, Michael Mertes, and Dominique Moïsi,
Financial Times (July 11, 2003).

"Reluctant European" and "awkward partner" are two sobriquets that analysts have often used to describe the United Kingdom in its approaches to Europe.[1] On January 1, 1973, the United Kingdom formally joined the European Communities, an action that appeared to mark a decisive turning point in Britain's relationship with the rest of Europe. However, less has changed than many observers predicted. The British role in the European Communities/ European Union has been one marked by noteworthy conflicts: a renegotiation of entry terms followed by a referendum on remaining a member, a prolonged struggle over the budget, frequent opt-outs, adversarial confrontations between British prime ministers and other European leaders, and even a period in which Britain blocked EU Council of Ministers' actions on all matters requiring unanimity. Britain's continuing nonparticipation in the Economic and Monetary Union is just the most notable recent example of the country's distinctiveness from the other pre-2004 major member states of the EU. This chapter will offer a brief historical overview of Britain's relationship

with the European Communities/European Union, highlight the most distinctive features of that relationship and seek to explain them, and assess the impact of Britain on the EU and of the EU on Britain.

THE DEVELOPMENT OF THE BRITISH RELATIONSHIP WITH THE EC/EU

Early British Aloofness

Britain emerged victorious from World War II, with a proud record of resistance to the Axis powers—standing almost alone in 1940 and 1941, after the defeat of France and before Soviet and American entry into the War. Britain's island location and the absence of a successful invasion since 1066 also continued to condition British attitudes toward "the Continent." Moreover, Britain's relatively great distance from the Soviet Union and its new Central and East European "satellite" Communist states made the United Kingdom less inclined than West Germany or France to seek security through West European integration. Like France, but unlike Germany and Italy, Britain had enjoyed a long history as a great imperial power. Though the days of empire appeared limited already in 1946, most British leaders (far more than the French leaders vis-à-vis their empire) believed that ties to the Empire/Commonwealth offered a viable alternative to long-term economic and political integration with Europe. In contrast to the rest of Western Europe, Britain's trade remained heavily dependent on preferential access to colonial and Commonwealth markets. The British economy was showing severe strains, but Britain's gross domestic product in the late 1940s still occupied first place in Western Europe. Moreover, Britain possessed a "special relationship" with the United States, the "superpower" of the West, rooted in a common language and culture and fused by the experiences of World War II. Beyond these factors, the Labour party had won a House of Commons majority in 1945 for the first time in history and had embarked on a program of nationalizing some of Britain's major industries and expanding the British welfare state. With moderate-to-conservative Christian Democrats dominating most postwar European governments, many in the new Labour government perceived that integration with Europe might well block their road to democratic socialism. Still others in Labour feared that a focus on Europe would detract from Britain's commitment to a wider internationalism.[2]

Against the backdrop of these considerations, it is unsurprising that the postwar Attlee government (1945–1951) displayed a lack of enthusiasm for moves toward European integration. Britain would agree to join only those regional organizations, such as the Council of Europe and the North Atlantic Treaty Organization, that were intergovernmental, without powerful supranational institutions, so that the British government could safeguard its vaunted sovereignty. When others sought to nudge the Council of Europe in a supranational direction,

Britain resisted fiercely. The dramatic unveiling of the Schuman Plan in 1950, and the invitation to Britain to join in the formation of the European Coal and Steel Community (ECSC), elicited a quick negative response from the British government.

A Conservative government headed by Prime Minister Churchill (the World War II prime minister whose party had been defeated by Labour in 1945, much to the surprise of most Americans) replaced Attlee's Labour government in 1951. Although Churchill had spoken positively about a "united" Europe in a widely quoted 1946 speech in Zurich, and had approved his son-in-law's founding of the United Europe Movement shortly thereafter, his government and the subsequent Conservative government headed by Anthony Eden showed no more enthusiasm for European federal projects than Attlee's had. Britain remained aloof from the proposed European Defense Community and viewed its failure as an indication that European integration efforts were likely to make little progress. Britain did join the intergovernmental Western European Union (WEU) after the collapse of the effort to build the European Defense Community. However, the WEU did not play the large role that some of its founders had envisioned. When the ECSC members asked Britain to join in planning for a broad European Economic Community, the British government refused. Thus, the Treaties of Rome, founding the European Communities in 1957, took shape without British participation.[3]

As the European Economic Community (EEC) emerged as the central part of the European Communities, Britain reacted by proposing to create a European free-trade area broader than the EEC but including its members. Following French and then West German rejection of the British proposal, the Conservative Macmillan government took the lead in organizing the European Free Trade Association (EFTA) in 1959–1960 with six smaller European nation-states. It was an intergovernmental organization aimed at free trade, without the supranational institutions and political goals of the European Communities. The British government hoped (in vain) that it would absorb the six EEC member states and send the EEC into oblivion. Meanwhile, the European Economic Community proceeded to make progress toward its stated goals and showed no signs of the imminent collapse expected by many British observers. Its member states enjoyed economic growth rates exceeding Britain's. Britain watched from the sidelines with growing concern.

British Reassessment and Rejection

Prime Minister Macmillan and his government began to reassess Britain's approach to the European Communities as early as 1960 and announced in July 1961 their intention to apply for membership in the EC. In 1960, senior civil servants on an interdepartmental committee reported a strong political case for entry—probably an important factor in convincing the prime minister. Anticipating opposition from within the Conservative government and party and among some senior civil servants, especially in the Ministry for Commonwealth Relations and the Ministry of Agriculture, Macmillan proceeded cautiously and moved pro-entry leaders into key cabinet positions prior to the announced shift in the British position.[4]

Why did the shift occur when and as it did? Analysts have suggested a number of factors. Among the most significant international political reasons were 1) pressures from the United States for Britain to join, 2) growing British perceptions (reinforced by American advice) that British membership was needed to steer the EC in the "right direction" before it was too late, and 3) rising British disillusionment with the Commonwealth, especially after its expulsion of South Africa in 1961, despite British government opposition to that expulsion. Domestic

political factors included 1) growing pressures favoring entry from the City, the Federation of British Industries, the Institute of Directors, and other sectors of the business community and 2) a more general shift of elite opinion in favor of entry. Political-economic considerations included 1) fear of discrimination against British products in the rapidly growing EC markets and 2) declining British trade with the Commonwealth relative to that with the EC. Macmillan emphasized the international political considerations in his initial public statements, but Andrew Moravcsik and other liberal intergovernmentalists have built a persuasive case for the importance of commercial concerns that also shaped domestic political-economic pressures.[5]

After a year and a half of negotiations between Britain and the European Communities, the effort came to an abrupt end. In January 1963, President Charles de Gaulle of France announced his veto of British membership, citing what he viewed as the United Kingdom's lack of a sincere European orientation and its close ties to the United States. Many in Britain and elsewhere perceived that his greatest fear was of a British challenge to French leadership and designs for the EC, particularly regarding the Common Agricultural Policy. Although all of the other five EC member states favored British entry, unanimity was required. Therefore, de Gaulle's veto was decisive.[6]

The Labour party, which had continued its general hostility to EC entry well into the 1960s, came to power in the 1964 elections. The Labour left, in particular, saw the EC as an antisocialist organization; and some other elements of the party retained many of the other concerns noted previously. For example, Hugh Gaitskell, the moderate Labour party leader of the late 1950s and early 1960s, portrayed British membership as the betrayal of "a thousand years of history" and expressed concern that Britain might become a "province of Europe."[7] Nevertheless, the Trades Union Congress backed British entry; and the new

Labour prime minister, Harold Wilson, concluded that EC membership would benefit Britain. Despite considerable opposition within his own party, he was able to lead his government to renew the British application for EC membership in 1966–1967—only to face a second, humiliating veto from de Gaulle in 1967.

Referring to the prospect of British entry into the EEC: "It means the end of a thousand years of history."

Hugh Gaitskell, Labour Party Leader, 1963.

British Entry into the European Communities

Two years later, the abrupt resignation of President de Gaulle of France cleared the way for eventual British entry into the European Communities, though some analysts have concluded that de Gaulle himself might have permitted British entry once it was clear that the Common Agricultural Policy was entrenched and that British industrial competition appeared less threatening to French interests than in the past. In any event, de Gaulle's successor, Georges Pompidou, soon indicated his receptivity to a reconsideration of the British application; and Wilson's government moved forward into negotiations. These were not completed until a new Conservative government, headed by Edward Heath, came to office. Despite some intense resistance from a small cluster of Conservative backbenchers, and the criticism of most of the Labour opposition of the terms negotiated by the Heath government, parliament gave its assent to membership in 1971. Great controversy swirled through much of 1972, as a parliamentary struggle ensued over the legislation to give legal effect to U.K. membership. As noted previously, Britain officially joined the European Communities on January 1, 1973, along with Denmark and Ireland.

Despite Prime Minister Heath's reputation as a pro-European leader, he and his cabinet associates encountered a number of difficulties in their relations with other European leaders and the EC Commission in Brussels. Conflicts emerged over British assertiveness on such matters as the budget, the European Regional Development Fund (ERDF), monetary union, and energy policy.[8] However, the return to power in 1974 of a Labour government, headed by Harold Wilson and pledged to renegotiate the terms of British entry, was soon to make Britain an even more "awkward partner" than before.

British-EC Relations Under Wilson and Callaghan

Prime Minister Wilson's approach to the European Communities, like that of his foreign minister and successor (in 1976), James Callaghan, seemed dictated primarily by a desire to manage a highly fractious Labour party while maintaining British membership in the EC, if possible. To accomplish these aims, which were made increasingly difficult by the rising power of the anti-EC Labour left, the Wilson government pressed hard to gain some EC concessions to Britain on Commonwealth trade and budgetary issues. Though nearly one-third of the Labour cabinet, with leftist Tony Benn as their leading spokesman, and a plurality of the Parliamentary Labour party opposed the new terms, Wilson won enough Conservative and Liberal support to gain an easy victory in the House of Commons. Next came a referendum, in which the British people voted by a 2–1 margin to keep Britain in the EC under the renegotiated terms.

However, the opposition to the EC within the Labour party continued to plague Wilson and Callaghan. Both Labour prime ministers were constrained in their actions vis-à-vis the EC by major party-management problems. After Labour's loss of power in the 1979 elections, the Labour left attained the ascendancy in the party and led it to shift to a position demanding withdrawal from the European Communities in its 1983 election manifesto.[9]

Adding to the pressures that brought Britain into conflict with the EC supranational bodies and the other major nation-state leaders was a continuing and growing budgetary crisis. The terms renegotiated by the Wilson government proved insufficient to stem rising British net contributions to the EC budget, from about 60 million pounds per year in the 1973–1976 period, to 369 million in 1977, 822 million in 1978, and 947 million in 1979.[10] Though Britain had the third-lowest per capita gross domestic product in the EC, it had become the second-largest net contributor (behind only Germany) by 1978.[11] The EC's largest spending program, the Common Agricultural Policy, provided relatively small payments to Britain, with its small and efficient agricultural sector. Meanwhile, high and rising levels of British consumption and imports (fueled by North Sea oil revenues that kept personal taxation relatively low) meant that Britain's payments to the EC budget (based largely upon taxes on consumption) were higher than those of some wealthier countries. A majority of British opinion demanded a change in the budgetary situation.

The Thatcher-Major Era and British Relations with the EC/EU

After Margaret Thatcher took office as Conservative prime minister in 1979, this festering problem came to dominate British relations with the rest of the EC. Though most EC and nation-state leaders understood Britain's legitimate concerns, Prime Minister Thatcher's strident style antagonized them. Finally, after five years of extremely difficult bargaining, a compromise settlement on the budget emerged, with Britain receiving an annual rebate that has continued to the present. Nonetheless, Britain has remained a consistently high contributor to the EC/EU. For a short time, Britain appeared to be moving toward a cooperative relationship with the EC supranational bodies and the other major member states. Especially on the single-market project, aimed at eliminating the remaining nontariff trade barriers among the member states, Thatcherite free-trade ideas played a leading role. However, conflict pitting the British government against all or most of the other EC members soon erupted again. At heart, Thatcher was a committed British nationalist who deeply feared the loss of British control over British destinies to supranational institutions. As long as supranational development was in the cause of promoting free trade, Thatcher was willing to accept limited doses of it. However, any hint of socialism associated with supranational development was certain to arouse her hostility.[12]

The growing emphasis on a "social Europe" by the European Commission, headed by French Socialist Jacques Delors and backed by most Socialist and Christian Democratic nation-state leaders and Members of the European Parliament, stirred not just Thatcher but the neoliberal and economic libertarian forces dominant in the Conservative government and the broader Conservative party. Prime Minister Thatcher herself was outraged by the socialistic trends that she detected. "We haven't worked all these years to free Britain from the paralysis of socialism only to see it creep through the back door of central control and bureaucracy in Brussels," she proclaimed.[13] The Thatcher government stood alone among the 12 EC member governments in objecting to the Charter on the Fundamental Social Rights of Workers (Social Charter) in 1989, and the Major government again stood alone in refusing to endorse incorporation of it as the Social Chapter of the Maastricht Treaty in 1991.

"We haven't worked all these years to free Britain from the paralysis of socialism only to see it creep through the back door of central control and bureaucracy in Brussels."

Prime Minister Margaret Thatcher, October 15, 1988, *cited by Stephen George, The Awkward Partner (1998), 94.*

Although the British governments enthusiastically contributed to the single-market movement of the late 1980s and early 1990s, Prime Minister Thatcher feared the simultaneous growth in power of the supranational European Parliament and expansion of qualified majority voting (rather than one-state, one-vote procedures allowing a British veto) in the European Council of Ministers. In an oft-quoted address at the College of Europe in Bruges, Belgium, on September 20, 1988, she laid out her intergovernmental vision of the EC in terms reminiscent of Charles de Gaulle (but without his rejection of Atlanticism). Stressing national sovereignty and diversity within the EC, she insisted, "Europe will be stronger precisely because it has France in as France, Spain in as Spain, Britain in as Britain, each with its own customs, traditions and identity."[14]

Between 1988 and 1990, Prime Minister Thatcher's relations with the EC and other nation-state leaders in Europe deteriorated further. In November 1990, pro-European integration deputy prime minister, Sir Geoffrey Howe, resigned in protest of the prime minister's approach to Europe, triggering a quick challenge to her leadership by Michael Heseltine. Though a variety of domestic factors beyond the EC issues played a part in Thatcher's subsequent downfall, her relations with the EC and the other European national leaders were certainly at or near the top of the list.

Despite being forced from office as prime minister in December 1990, Thatcher was able to thwart Heseltine's bid for the top office and to gain the election of her Chancellor of the Exchequer, John Major, as the new prime minister. Major pledged to place Britain "at the heart of Europe"[15] and at first undertook a nonconfrontational approach vis-à-vis the EC. However, his predecessor's attacks on EC "socialism" and Brussels bureaucrats, along with her appeals to traditional national sovereignty, had struck a responsive chord among many British Conservative leaders and activists. And

Thatcher was far from silent after her ouster, speaking out on several occasions about her concerns regarding further European integration. Major would soon find himself in a delicate balancing act between the pressures to work cooperatively with the EC and other European national leaders on the one hand and the demands of party management at home on the other hand—a position reminiscent of the Wilson and Callaghan situations in the Labour party during the 1970s.[16]

Major proved unable to put Britain at the heart of Europe. His government signed the Maastricht Treaty and, after a great struggle, won parliamentary approval for the necessary supportive legislation, but only after making a critical division a vote of confidence. Britain stood alone in forcing the Social Chapter out of the treaty into a **protocol** endorsed by all of the other 11 members (and subsequently by the 3 new member states joining the EU in 1995). The Major government also insisted on opting out of the Maastricht plan for the Economic and Monetary Union.

However, Margaret Thatcher, sitting after 1991 in the House of Lords as Baroness Thatcher of Kesteven, was not satisfied. She denounced the Maastricht Treaty as "a treaty too far" and criticized Major for supporting it and for agreeing to the reappointment of Jacques Delors as head of the European Commission.[17] The "Euroskeptic" wing of the Conservative party, growing in size and vehemence and often urged on by ex-Prime Minister Thatcher, would continue to impose heavy pressures on Prime Minister Major until his resignation following the landslide electoral defeat by Labour in 1997. Often Major's efforts to placate his intraparty critics caused conflicts with other European leaders and damage to Britain's reputation in the European Union, without satisfying the Conservative Euroskeptics. A classic example came when his government chose to protest EU handling of an outbreak among British cattle herds of bovine spongiform encephalopathy ("mad cow disease") by refusing to vote for any measure requiring unanimity in the European Council of Ministers during much of May and June 1996. This action stalemated important EU decision-making and outraged most European leaders but only momentarily restored Major to the good graces of the Euroskeptics.[18]

Britain and the EU in the Blair Era

In 1997, most European Union leaders welcomed the new Labour government headed by Tony Blair, who began by proclaiming that "we must end the isolation of the last twenty years and be a leading partner in Europe."[19] Of course, some pointed out the resemblance between his opening declaration on Europe and his predecessor's unfulfilled pledge to put Britain at the heart of Europe. Nevertheless, Blair (unlike Major) headed a party with a huge parliamentary majority and that was no longer sharply divided over European issues. Since the Labour party's call in its 1983 manifesto for Britain to withdraw from the EC, the Labour had shifted, in two stages, to a position more supportive of integration than ever before (and certainly more supportive than the Conservatives' position). The first shift, 1983–1987, appeared motivated by electoral defeat and was ambiguous. The second shift began after a thorough policy review, instigated in 1987. A growing Labour party and trade union perception that a "social Europe" could improve working conditions and curb the powers of multinational business corporations more than could a British government alone influenced both the Labour party and the Trades Union Congress toward positive approaches to the EC/EU. Furthermore, visceral dislike of Margaret Thatcher and a desire to oppose her approach probably played some part.[20]

The Blair government moved swiftly to endorse the Social Chapter's inclusion in the Amsterdam Treaty of 1997, which subsequently

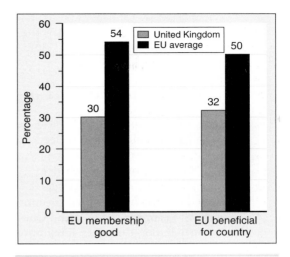

FIGURE 12.1   Popular Assessments of the EU, 2003

Eurobarometer, July 2003.

won overwhelming parliamentary approval in spite of nearly unanimous Conservative opposition. With a huge parliamentary majority and a party retaining only a small strongly anti-EU faction, Blair has been less constrained by party-management concerns in shaping his government's EU policies than either John Major or the earlier Labour governments were. However, the Blair government has retained much of the reticence about European integration that has long characterized British policies. Britain remains just one of three pre-2004 EU countries (and the only major one) outside the Economic and Monetary Union. The Labour government has not gone beyond a pledge to bring the matter of British entry into the EMU up for a referendum vote at some time after the 2001 general election. In such other important policy areas as border and immigration controls, Britain has also remained outside the EU consensus. In the debates over the proposed new EU constitution, the Blair government adamantly restated that it would not forfeit its "independent sovereign right" to make its own

PEOPLE IN THE EU
European Integration and the Fall of Margaret Thatcher

On November 22, 1990, having failed to win reelection as leader of her Conservative party on the first ballot, Prime Minister Margaret Thatcher resigned abruptly as prime minister and Conservative party leader. European integration issues played a major role in precipitating this stunning event.

Prior to 1990, Prime Minister Thatcher had led her party to three consecutive election victories and had triumphed over all of her intraparty rivals—for example, facing down Defense Minister Michael Heseltine and virtually compelling his resignation in 1986. However, by 1990, many of her cabinet and party colleagues were growing increasingly concerned about her ability to lead the party again to victory and progressively alienated by what many deemed her high-handed style. In the June 1989 European Parliament elections in Britain, the Labour party had trounced the Conservatives. Thatcher's staunch support for a **regressive** tax, taking a higher proportion of the incomes of the poor than of the rich, to fund local government, which was widely unpopular, also worried many Conservative leaders and caused a sharp decline in her standing in the public-opinion polls. Reviewing the evidence, David Gowland and Arthur Turner aptly stressed that Thatcher "had become an electoral liability rather than an asset. Her stance towards the EC was nevertheless a major reason for her loss of support within the Conservative Party and more generally."[21]

The immediate causes of Thatcher's demise centered on her continuing expressions of deep skepticism about British entry into the EC's Exchange Rate Mechanism (which her cabinet colleagues had compelled her to accept in October 1990) and her vehement hostility to the prospective monetary union toward which the EC was moving. When Thatcher returned from the Rome European Council (Summit) in October 1990 and defiantly rejected European Commission President Jacques Delors's plans for union, Deputy Prime Minister Geoffrey Howe had had enough. He resigned his post and publicly chastised Thatcher for her negative approach to the European Community. Michael Heseltine, still smarting from his 1986 showdown with Thatcher, now emerged to challenge her for the leadership of the Conservative party (and the office of prime minister).

On the first ballot for the Conservative party leadership, neither Thatcher nor Heseltine received sufficient support to win. When Thatcher's closest advisers indicated that she would likely lose on the next ballot, she chose instead to resign. One of the leading analysts of European integration has concluded, "This was the first time in the EC's history that 'Community affairs' had impinged so dramatically and so directly on domestic politics."[22] European issues had contributed directly to the downfall of a once-mighty prime minister of the United Kingdom.[23]

policies on taxes, foreign affairs, defense, and border controls, thus imposing strict limits on what European supranationalists could hope to accomplish. Hostile public opinion, concerns that the euro has been weaker than the British pound sterling, and Britain's continuing distinctive geopolitical and economic positions vis-à-vis the rest of Europe have all constrained Blair. Another constraint has been the second most powerful figure in his cabinet, Chancellor of the Exchequer Gordon Brown, a past and perhaps future rival who is known to view the common currency with a skeptical eye. Criticizing the Blair government for its internal divisions over European issues, Charles Kennedy, leader of the pro-euro Liberal Democratic party, has focused attention on the Blair-Brown divisions over the currency and general approaches to European integration, jibing, "The Prime Minister and his Chancellor have got to resolve their collective political position. Europe has become an unacceptable conspiracy of silence in British politics." Meanwhile, the Conservative opposition has moved markedly in a Euroskeptical direction, under the leadership of William Hague, Iain Duncan Smith, and Michael Howard, though not without considerable internal conflict.[24]

"The Prime Minister and his Chancellor have got to resolve their collective political position. Europe has become an unacceptable conspiracy of silence in British politics."

Charles Kennedy, Liberal Democratic Leader, *cited by David Baker, "Britain and Europe" (2003), 249.*

"She [Margaret Thatcher] has the mouth of Marilyn Monroe and the eyes of Caligula [a Roman emperor notorious for his cruelty]."

French President François Mitterrand, *cited in J. M. and M. J. Cohen, The Penguin Dictionary of 20th Century Quotations (1993), 266.*

DISTINCTIVE FEATURES OF THE BRITISH APPROACHES TO THE EC/EU

As has been previously suggested, reluctance and awkwardness have continued to mark British approaches to the EC/EU as distinctive, particularly in relation to those of the other major member nation-states. Some observers have seen this pattern as a result of Britain's late entry. Because many key European institutions (including supranational ones) and public policies (such as the expensive Common Agricultural Policy) were deeply entrenched before Britain joined the European Communities, so goes the argument, Britain has found it difficult to cope with these. Neofunctionalist theories suggest that, over time, cooperation will spill over from one domain to another. Along similar lines, some analysts have suggested what Helen Wallace has termed a "Europeanization trajectory" for late-joiners of the EC/EU, in which entrants progressively undergo "symbolic and substantive engagement" with Europe. While Ireland, Greece, Spain, Portugal, and (perhaps) Finland show evidence of such a trajectory, Britain clearly does not (and Denmark, too, calls the universality of the pattern into question).[25]

Other theoretical perspectives noted in Chapter One suggest some of the underlying reasons for Britain's continuing status as a reluctant European and the particular forms which that reluctance has taken. The liberal intergovernmental model calls attention to political economic motivations rooted in Britain's diversified trade and investment patterns and its small and efficient agricultural sector.[26] In contrast, realist perspectives assign highest priority to such geopolitical considerations as the long-term "special relationship" between Britain and the United States, Britain's history of Empire and Commonwealth, and its island location.[27] Comparative politics approaches focus on the distinctive ideological mix in British public opinion, interest groups, and political parties and on the ways in which British "party government" has shaped British approaches and constrained leaders' options on European issues.[28]

Against this backdrop, it is appropriate to summarize the most distinctive long-term aspects of Britain's approaches to the EC/EU and note some specific factors that appear to underlie each. Several themes have persisted over time—four of them, primarily substantive; two of them largely stylistic. Two others have recurred frequently enough to warrant discussion.

An Atlanticist preference. Although this approach has also characterized Denmark and Portugal to a considerable degree and has sometimes enlisted broad support in the EC/EU, Britain has been its strongest and most consistent proponent in Western Europe, both before and after its entry into the European Commu-

nities. Atlanticism assigns high priority to keeping the United States engaged in European affairs and has also often involved, in the British case, active Anglo-American cooperation on matters ranging from trade issues to intervention in the Persian Gulf. Although the "special relationship" between Britain and the United States has ebbed and flowed, and has probably undergone a long-term decline as the Americans have taken account of the growing powers of Germany and the EU as a whole, the Thatcher-Reagan, Blair-Clinton, and Blair-Bush ties have shown a distinctive closeness even in recent years. During the events surrounding the Iraq controversies of 2002–2003 and the war itself, the close British-American relationship once again stood out as unique. The Anglo-American economic ties also remained very close. Figure 12.2, for example, illustrates how much greater American investment is in Britain than in other major EU member states, and how British direct investment in the United States dwarfs that by Germany, France, Italy, or Spain. Shared language, culture, and economic interests have

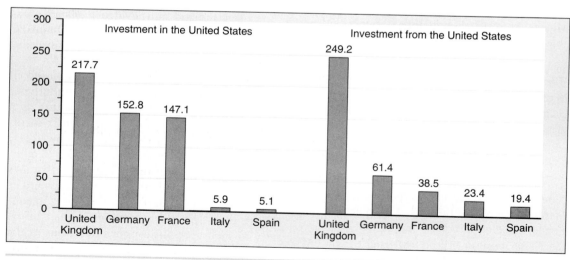

FIGURE 12.2 Foreign Direct Investment to and from the United States, 2001 (in Billions of Dollars)

World Almanac, 2003.

clearly tended to contribute to Britain's Atlanticist inclination.[29]

A global free-trade preference. Reflecting long-term and contemporary trading and investment patterns (i.e., of all EU member states, the highest percentage of its trade with non-EU members[30] and the highest overseas investment and receipt of overseas investment[31]), this British approach has reflected basic commercial calculations. Although British rhetorical commitment to free trade in the past was sometimes combined, especially in the 1930s and 1940s, with preferential trading arrangements within the Empire/Commonwealth, the declining importance of these since the 1950s has fostered a strengthened commitment by Britain to global free trade. Because this preference in recent years also has generally coincided with a U.S. interest, it has provided another basis for British Atlanticism. These two British approaches have tended to reinforce one another.

A national sovereignty preference. More than any other EC/EU member state, Britain has consistently stressed the need to preserve national sovereignty (often also stressing the tradition of "parliamentary sovereignty" as embodied in the British constitution). Every British government since entry has emphasized a Europe of nation-states, not a "federal" Europe of strong supranational institutions. Thatcher was the most outspoken on this subject, but all of the other prime ministers have shared her general outlook. Although national sovereignty was a primary emphasis of French President de Gaulle also, his French successors have shown less consistency and greater willingness to sacrifice this preference to achieve other goals than British leaders have.[32]

A preference for EC/EU enlargement. Since its entry in 1973, Britain has been in the forefront of all of the drives to enlarge EC/EU membership, though its partners have often suspected that its primary motivations have been to blunt the drives toward supranationalism and to destroy the Common Agricultural Policy. Broadening of free trade and a desire to promote European stability have been other likely British goals underlying this preference for widening.[33]

An adversarial style. Even the most pro-European prime minister, Edward Heath, adopted a confrontational approach with the other major European governments and the EC institutions. Thatcher carried such confrontation to new heights. Adversarial relations have characterized not only the styles of most British governmental leaders vis-à-vis Europe but also the styles of many British higher civil servants. In assessing why, Timothy Bainbridge has identified the major roots in the British practices of party government. As Bainbridge notes,

> The decision-making system within the European Union is oriented toward consensus, whereas the British political system is essentially adversarial. The British system delivers winners and losers, majorities and minorities, and governments accustomed to being able to carry out their legislative programmes with a minimum of compromise.[34]

Stephen George suggests that British higher civil servants may share this inclination toward an adversarial style in European forums.[35] It may be noteworthy that the English common law tradition also embodies an adversarial approach.

"The decision-making system within the European Union is oriented toward consensus, whereas the British political system is essentially adversarial."

Timothy Bainbridge, *The Penguin Companion to European Union* (1998), 502.

A legalistic approach to enforcement. Studies have shown that Britain has adopted a "legalistic" enforcement style leading to relatively high levels of effective implementation of

EC/EU legislation. Though this might seem incompatible with its usual adversarial stances during the legislative process, Stephen George has discerned a link between the two approaches. British commitment to strict enforcement may be a factor leading British negotiators to drive hard bargains in the legislative process, he suggests.[36] In any event, strong British norms emphasizing rule of law and "the Whitehall ethos itself, according to which ministers trust their civil servants to get it right once the initial policy framework is set," are probably underlying explanatory factors shaping the legalistic approach to enforcement. Evidence suggests that Italy offers the sharpest contrast to Britain within the EU on this dimension.[37]

Other significant traits. Two other themes, one stylistic and the other substantive, have also appeared fairly often in British behavior toward the EC/EU. One has been frequent *leadership preoccupation with intraparty management* in the shaping of British policies concerning Europe. Wilson, Callaghan, and Major all felt compelled to structure their European policies around party-management concerns; and Macmillan planned his policy shift to seek EC entry in 1960–1961 with a careful eye on his party. The British system of party government has often but not always meant that the prime minister must contend with a Euroskeptic or even Europhobic faction or tendency within the majority party. In contrast, European governments having coalition governments have usually governed from a pro-European center, with Euroskeptics relatively isolated on the left and right extremes.

A final frequent British theme, most characteristic of the Thatcher and Major governments, has been an *antibureaucracy, pro-free-market preference*. Hostilities to the Social Charter/Social Chapter by Conservative governments, to the Common Agricultural Policy by all British governments, and to the "Brussels bureaucracy" by a wide cross-section of British

TABLE 12.1 Distinctive Features of British EC/EU Approaches

1. An Atlanticist preference.
2. A global free-trade preference.
3. A national sovereignty preference.
4. A preference for EC/EU enlargement.
5. An adversarial style.
6. A legalistic approach to enforcement.
7. Frequent leadership preoccupation with intra-party management.
8. Frequent anti-bureaucracy, pro-free-market preference.

opinion provide evidence of this preference, though criticisms of CAP have mainly reflected cold economic calculations of costs and benefits. The underlying motivations of this tendency appear to be a mixture of ideological and economic considerations.

THE IMPACT OF BRITAIN ON THE EC/EU

Given Britain's late entry and frequently "awkward" status, it is not surprising that Britain's impact on European Communities/European Union institutions and public policies has been limited—certainly less substantial than the impact of France or Germany. Nevertheless, Britain has left its mark in several institutional areas and public-policy domains, often through its ability to block or delay the initiatives of others. Britain's efforts have been assisted by its effective coordination of its European policies through the Cabinet Office and by the high quality of its permanent representation in Brussels. "In terms of the smooth and consistent management of business, the efficient transmission of communications, and the preparedness for European meetings," Helen Wallace has accurately noted, "British administration is second to none."[38]

"In terms of the smooth and consistent management of business, the efficient transmission of communications, and the preparedness for European meetings, British administration is second to none."

Helen Wallace, *"Relations Between the EU and the British Administration" (1996), 64.*

Institutionally, the United Kingdom has gained some concessions on scaling back proposed new powers for the supranational European Parliament and restricting proposed extensions of qualified majority voting (QMV) in the European Council of Ministers. In both cases, the outcomes have involved more parliamentary powers and more QMV than British leaders have wished, but the British impact has been clear. Britain also advocated the creation of the three-pillar structure mandated by the Maastricht Treaty.[39]

The area of common EC/EU public policy in which Britain's impact has been most notable in the positive sense of offering initiatives and providing leadership has been in the development of the Single European Act of 1986, particularly its single-market aspect, and its implementation to remove internal nontariff barriers among the member states. Britain has also pushed in the 1990s for liberalized global trade agreements and has enjoyed some success in nudging EU public policy in this direction.[40]

Another policy domain in which Britain has sometimes exercised leadership and has generally aligned its own laws quickly with European Union rules is competition policy, which emphasizes establishing and maintaining competitive business practices. The free-market values underlying recent European competition policy have reflected long-standing British preferences more than those of the French or Germans. Though the United Kingdom in the early 1990s resisted efforts to lower the threshold above which the EU would review business mergers, British Commissioner Leon Brittan (supported by the British government) played a leading role during the late 1980s and early 1990s in tightening EC/EU restrictions on government subsidies to businesses. The Blair government has recently brought British competition law into almost full accord with EU provisions.[41]

On monetary policies, in contrast, the British impact has been generally minimal. In the late 1980s, as a French initiative soon turned into a Franco-German initiative and gained critical support from the European Commission and Italy, the British government and the Bank of England tried in vain to slow the momentum of the drive toward an Economic and Monetary Union (EMU) with a common currency. Because Britain has opted out of the EMU, it has been unable to affect public policies in this sphere to any significant degree. The Bank of England must now exert what limited influence it can from outside the structure of the European System of Central Banks and the European Central Bank.[42]

The Common Agricultural Policy has always been unpopular with British governments and the British public. Though the British impact in this domain has been relatively small, it has combined with a number of other forces in the past decade (international pressures from the United States and others, increasingly unacceptable costs, new members unsympathetic to the traditional CAP, likely prohibitive costs with eastern expansion of the EU) to bring limited reforms of agricultural policy.[43]

Britain in the 1970s and 1980s gained a well-deserved reputation for seeking to weaken or halt EC environmental-policy initiatives that were usually instigated by Germany. However, the pattern has shifted in recent years, in part due to the waning enthusiasm within the German government in the 1990s for enhanced environmental protection, in part because of the new Blair-led Labour government after 1997 and Britain's growing ability to bring the EU Commission toward its perspectives. These perspectives have emphasized environmental quality with member state latitude in the choice of methods to achieve it and consideration of the economic costs of proposed new environmental regulations. Compliance with environmental directives has been a widespread problem in Britain, but Britain is not unusual in the EU in this respect. In fact, the December 2003 report of the EU Environmental Commissioner found Britain to be one of only two EU member states (the other being Sweden) to have achieved the EU targets for reducing greenhouse-gas emissions in accord with the Kyoto Protocol, another positive indicator of Britain's new EU roles in the environmental policy domain.[44]

In the regional-policy domain, Britain played a major role (along with Italy and Ireland) in the establishment of the European Regional Development Fund as part of its negotiations for EC entry in 1973. At the time, this fund, which provided aid to economically backward regions, was viewed by the British government primarily as a means to compensate Britain for its large net contributions to the Common Agricultural Policy. In recent years, leadership in expanding this fund has passed to Spain and other Mediterranean countries, as the emphasis has come to be on overall "cohesion" to close the economic gaps within the EU and Britain has ceased to be a major recipient. Moreover, the United Kingdom has been the most resistant of the EU member states to the European Commission's efforts to insure that EU structural funds to subnational regions complement, rather than replace, national funding—yet another indicator of the British government's preoccupation with national sovereignty.[45]

Britain's contributions to common European social policy have been slight and largely negative. For example, Britain prevented the

Social Chapter from becoming a part of the Maastricht Treaty in 1991 but could not keep the other 11 (eventually 14) members from adopting it as a protocol. Another example of Britain's isolation on social policy came in November 1996, when the European Court of Justice ruled against Britain's challenge to the legal base upon which the European Council of Ministers had adopted a directive on working time by qualified majority vote. Eventually, in 1997, the new Labour government of Tony Blair accepted what the other EU countries had already adopted in the Social Chapter; and the Chapter was incorporated into the EU Amsterdam Treaty. However, even the Blair government has opposed most European efforts to adopt new regulations under the Social Chapter, arguing that these might undermine the competitiveness of British businesses, which generally offer fewer benefits and lower pay scales and rely more on part-time employees than many businesses operating in other European countries.[46]

In the Justice and Home Affairs (JHA) field, which mostly constitutes a separate and largely intergovernmental pillar since the Maastricht Treaty, Britain has shown its usual special concern for preserving national sovereignty. The fact that this "pillar" is designated as primarily intergovernmental owes a good deal to British efforts in the early 1990s, though there was a fairly widespread reluctance in many other states, too, to make Justice and Home Affairs supranational, as proposed by Germany. The "Schengen" process of seeking to achieve free movement across borders of EC/EU countries has been one of the most important in the JHA domain. While France and Germany were among the original five signatory states (along with the Benelux countries) of the Schengen Agreement in 1985, taking the first big step toward free movement across borders, the United Kingdom refused to go along. In 1995, the Schengen Convention on frontier controls took effect in France, Germany, and five other EU member states. The Amsterdam Treaty of 1997 incorporated the Schengen Convention, with opt-outs permitted for the United Kingdom (and Ireland). The British government has argued that Britain's island location requires that Britain pursue its own distinctive border controls. However, once again, Britain has appeared to assume a role as a "reluctant European."[47]

Finally, in the Common Foreign and Security Policy (CFSP) domain, the largely intergovernmental nature of the process has comported well with British preferences concerning national sovereignty. Although Britain has been far from alone in seeking to make and keep CFSP intergovernmental, it has played a leading role in that effort. Britain's strong Atlanticist inclinations and a history as a global power both have propelled it toward frequent attempts at foreign-policy leadership vis-à-vis other European nation-states. Britain has had some measurable influence on its EU partners in recent years, during the Kosovo crisis in 1999 and in efforts to build EU defense capabilities. The Anglo-French St. Malo Declaration (1998), calling for an EU Military Security Pool of up to 60,000 personnel, has certainly offered the most dramatic evidence of a new British effort to play a prominent role in shaping a European Union military security policy. Previously, British governments have taken the view that a distinctive EU policy might threaten NATO and ties to the United States and have strongly opposed French suggestions for an EC/EU-based approach. However, France appeared for a time to have abandoned some of its former hostility to Atlanticism, and the Blair government has felt comfortable working cooperatively with France. One leading analyst has concluded that "St. Malo is a leap in the dark for Britain and for the EU, and represents the greatest change that New Labour has made in EU policy."[48] The disparate responses of Britain and France to the American-led war in Iraq have, of course, raised questions about the future of British-French cooperation.

THE IMPACT OF THE EC/EU ON BRITISH POLITICS

Membership in the European Communities/European Union has reshaped the British constitution in significant ways that have provoked enormous domestic controversy in the United Kingdom. In addition, EC/EU issues have split both major British political parties severely at various times, served as the subject of the country's first and only national referendum, and will almost certainly be the subjects of other referendums in the future (on EMU and the proposed EU constitution). EC/EU practices and public policies have also had a number of indirect effects on British politics, though assessing their importance in relation to separate domestic influences is a complex and difficult task.

The Constitution

As noted previously, the United Kingdom is unusual in its lack of a codified constitution and in its constitutional doctrine of the sovereignty, or supreme legal authority, of parliament. According to this doctrine, there could be no legal limits to the powers of parliament; and no parliament could legally bind its successors. Parliament could delegate powers to the regional or local levels of government but reserved the right to reclaim them if it wished.

By approving the 1972 European Communities Act at the time of British entry into the EC, and subsequently the Single European Act, the Maastricht Treaty, and later treaties, the British parliament has ceded a portion of its sovereignty to the treaties and related documents that compose the written "constitution" of the European Union and to the European Court of Justice, which interprets and applies them in concrete cases. When the European Court of Justice ruled in *R. v. Secretary of State for Transport, ex parte Factortame Ltd.* (1990) and related cases that the British courts could suspend an act of the British parliament that appeared to violate EC law until a final determination could be made, and then found the British Merchant Shipping Act of 1988 in conflict with EC law, it aroused a storm of protest in Britain. The cases were particularly controversial because they highlighted the primacy of EC law over British parliamentary legislation.[49] Furthermore, the advent and expansion of qualified majority voting in the European Council of Ministers after adoption of the Single European Act of 1986 increased the likelihood that British governments could frequently be compelled to implement public policies that they had opposed in the EC/EU legislative process.

In the view of such critics as Lord Beloff, the legal developments noted above mean that "the British Constitution is no longer operative because Britain is already a unit within a federal system."[50] Although many observers find this view exaggerated, EC/EU membership has unquestionably eroded de jure (legal) national and parliamentary sovereignty in Britain. Whether it has eroded de facto (actual) parliamentary or national sovereignty and the extent to which such sovereignty can really exist in the contemporary global economy are matters of much debate. Some make the point that political supremacy within Britain has long resided more with the government than with parliament. Some suggest that the global marketplace has eroded nation-state power, especially in medium-size states such as Britain, and that British membership in the EC/EU has actually helped British governments to reclaim de facto sovereignty from the marketplace. Undoubtedly, these controversies will continue to shape assessments of the impact of the European Union on the British constitution and its major governmental institutions.[51]

Governmental Institutions

Indirect effects of EC/EU practices and public policies on British governmental institutions may be found in the enhancement of British judicial powers and the increased autonomy of the Bank of England. There is wide agreement that the EC/EU has also served to enhance British executive powers, often at the expense of parliament, but much ambiguity surrounds the effects on prime ministerial power. Some analysts have seen EU effects additionally with regard to the devolution of powers to Scotland and Wales and perhaps eventually to other regions. In each case, it is important to note, domestic political pressures independent of the European Union have also influenced these patterns.

The traditional absence of a codified constitution and the heritage of parliamentary legal sovereignty have long rendered the British courts less politically powerful than their counterparts in the United States, Germany, and (often) France and Italy as well. As noted earlier, the advent of Britain's EC membership brought to Britain a written (EC, now EU) "constitution" (of treaties and supportive documents) and a court, the European Court of Justice, to interpret and apply it, perhaps in ways that override British domestic law. Although enhanced British judicial activism in challenging governments and parliament appears to have begun to emerge in the 1960s, before British entry to the EC,[52] membership in the EC/EU has almost certainly furthered this development. Jonathan Levitsky has stressed that joining the EC meant that "British courts soon found themselves required to engage in judicial review to ensure the compatibility of domestic with Community law."[53] Moreover, Alan Davies has described "a new generation of judges increasingly influenced by European jurisprudence where judges are more politically exposed."[54] Lisa Conant has illustrated the growing tendency of British courts to refer cases to the EU judicial system and the enormous array of British court citations of the European Court of Justice rulings, though she notes that the United Kingdom continues to lag far behind Germany and France in this respect.[55]

"British courts soon found themselves required to engage in judicial review to ensure the compatibility of domestic with Community law."

Jonathan Levitsky, *cited by James Caporaso and Joseph Jupille, "The Europeanization of Gender Equality Policy" (2001), 41.*

The effects of British EC/EU membership on the executive and the legislature remain subject to considerable dispute. There is wide agreement that the British executives far more than Members of Parliament have acted as mediators between the EU and the domestic polity and that British parliamentary scrutiny of EU policies has shown marked weaknesses. The House of Commons' oversight processes of EU legislation have lagged behind those of the House of Lords and have done little to ease the British public's concerns about the "democratic deficit" stemming from the lack of clear accountability in the European Union. As for the effects of EC/EU membership on prime ministerial powers, the picture remains far from clear. Though some analysts have stressed enhanced prime ministerial powers stemming from prime ministers' prominence as representatives of the United Kingdom in the European Council in recent years, others have seen gains from their abilities to deflect blame for unpopular political-economic actions and results to the EU level and away from themselves, and still others have focused on the extent to which EC/EU issues have undermined the legitimacy of at least some prime ministers and complicated their tasks of party leadership.[56]

The increased autonomy of the Bank of England and devolution are other examples of likely indirect European Union influences on British governmental institutions, though domestic pressures have certainly outweighed EU influences in the case of devolution. Economic and Monetary Union requirements for central bank independence within the member states created an environment that probably increased the pressures on the new Labour government in 1997 to move toward granting enhanced autonomy to the Bank of England, even though the government was not seeking immediate EMU membership. Writing of Britain (as well as Sweden and France), Martin Marcussen has concluded his analysis of new central bank political independence by stating, "EMU ideas turned out to be so powerful that they managed to decisively transform the elite discourse within just a few years." British moves were congruent with those required of EU member states that adopted the euro currency.[57]

In the realm of decentralizing government, some authors have cited the EC/EU processes relating to regional funding of various types as spurring British domestic activities aimed at decentralizing government there. In addition, the increased EU emphasis on a "Europe of the regions" during the 1990s appears to have modestly supplemented strong pressures from Scotland and to a lesser degree from Wales to nudge the British central government toward devolution. Almost certainly, British subnational governments have increasingly questioned whether the British central government has taken full advantage of regional grants available from the EU. For example, in 2000, the Welsh assembly forced the Welsh first secretary (a close associate of Prime Minister Blair) from office in large part over his lack of success in obtaining British governmental matching funds for EU assistance. Furthermore, the European Union has indirectly created an environment in both the United Kingdom and Ireland in which there has emerged considerable consensus in both countries for a regional assembly combined with some type of "dual sovereignty" arrangement for Northern Ireland as a way toward peace in that long-troubled land. Nonetheless, the United Kingdom remains a highly centralized polity, and EU influences toward decentralization in Britain should not be exaggerated.[58]

Elections, Political Parties, and Interest Groups

European experiences with proportional representation and referendums have increasingly influenced British electoral processes since Britain's EC entry in 1973. Meanwhile, issues of Britain's relations with the EC/EU have provoked serious internal splits in both major British political parties and have played important roles in spawning several new (but so far relatively unsuccessful) parties. In addition, the shift of some major policy-making powers from Westminster to Brussels appears to have enhanced the influence of some British interest groups while diminishing that of others.

British electoral processes have traditionally been distinguished from those of much of Europe by their use of the first-past-the-post system in single-member districts and by their avoidance of referendums. In 1979, when direct elections to the European Parliament were introduced, Britain alone insisted upon using the first-past-the-post system to elect its Members of the European Parliament (MEPs). By the late 1990s, however, Britain had switched to proportional representation (PR) in its European parliamentary elections, as well as in elections to Northern Irish, Scottish, and Welsh parliaments. The British government was even considering some form of PR for its national parliamentary elections. Again, as in the cases of EC/EU influences on governmental institutions, there were independent domestic political pressures that also influenced the noted shifts. Most important were the Liberal Democrats' insistent demands for PR and the subsequent responses of Prime Minister Blair and other Labour party leaders. Nevertheless, the practices of the European Union and most of its member states were a part of the environment for electoral change inside Britain. This was also the case regarding referendums. Here, the issue of relations between Britain and the EC became the subject of the first (and so far only) national referendum in the United Kingdom, in 1975. Moreover, Prime Minister Blair has pledged to hold another national referendum on the subject of British entry into the Economic and Monetary Union (should the government decide that the timing for entry is right) as well as one on the new EU constitution.[59]

In the 1970s and early 1980s, issues concerning Britain's relationships to the European Communities badly split the Labour party, creating severe party management problems for the leaders and helping to precipitate the schism of 1980, in which four major moderate and pro-EC leaders left the Labour party and founded the new Social Democratic party. As Labour moved toward a position demanding British withdrawal from the EC in its 1983 electoral manifesto, the Social Democrats formed an electoral alliance with the pro-EC Liberals. By the 1990s, it was the Conservative party's turn to be sharply divided over British policies concerning the EC/EU. Though pro-European integration Tories ran a separate slate of candidates in the 1999 European parliamentary elections, to protest the Euroskeptical approach that had come to characterize the Conservative party leadership under Hague, the party has so far managed to avoid a schism comparable to that of the Labour party in 1980. However, the European issues played a major role in the downfall of one Conservative prime minister (Thatcher) and rendered another one (Major) virtually incapable of governing. They were also a major feature of the bitter contest between Kenneth Clarke and Iain Duncan Smith for the party leadership in 2001, with the Euroskeptic Smith triumphant over the pro-EU integration Clarke. Michael Howard, elected Conservative leader in November 2003, has continued Smith's Euroskeptical approach to the EU. Beyond the major parties and their internal rifts over Europe, two third parties have been founded in the 1990s entirely on the basis of hostility to European integration: the Referendum party and the U.K. Independence party.[60] The latter party scored a major breakthrough in the June 2004 European Parliament elections, when it won 12 of the 78 British seats and 16 percent of the British popular vote.

As far as British interest groups are concerned, the EC/EU has had a less evident impact than it has had on electoral processes and the party system. Probably its major effects have been to give added advantages to some groups at the expense of others. Such business groups as the Confederation of British Industry and major trade associations, together with individual multinational corporations, have been earlier and better positioned to focus their influence on EC/EU institutions and processes than the Trades Union Congress and individual trade unions. Multinational corporations, operating cross-nationally and possessing the wealth and expertise to gain easy access to the European Commission and member state executives, have been particularly successful in pushing their agenda of the single market, privatization, and deregulation of business. However, organized labor has enjoyed some successes in Brussels, especially in gaining extension of regulations on workplace health and safety and gender equality in pay, though its efforts to get the EU to promote full employment have yielded largely symbolic responses. The environmental groups, particularly those such as Greenpeace that operate on an international basis, appear to have been generally more successful in Brussels than inside Britain, particularly during the years of Conservative rule in Britain, when their appeals evoked few positive responses from the Thatcher or Major governments. Nevertheless, the business groups and multinational corporations appear to have gained the greatest advantage from Britain's EU membership.[61]

Public Policies

Not surprisingly, the impact of EC/EU membership on British public policies has proved greatest in policy domains in which supranationalism has been most evident, British efforts to shape EC/EU public policy have been ineffective, and the "fit" between traditional British policy approaches and those taken by the EC/EU has been poor. The Common Agricultural Policy (CAP) has offered a good illustration of such a policy domain. Its chief elements were in place prior to British entry into the Common Market, its supranational features have been prominent, and its approach from the 1960s to at least the early 1990s clashed sharply with traditional British agricultural policies. Its impact on British public policies well beyond the field of agriculture itself has been enormous and controversial.

The CAP got off the ground in 1962, 11 years before British membership in the European Community; and its funding process was established firmly in 1970. It was so deeply entrenched by the time of British entry that efforts to alter it significantly through entry negotiations were doomed to failure. Though some recent analysts have suggested that many observers have overstated the supranational characteristics of the agricultural policy-making process in the EC/EU, those characteristics have been far more in evidence than in most EU policy domains. Furthermore, the policy in effect at the time of British accession was very different from that previously followed in Britain.

British agricultural policy had been to let food prices find their own level in a competitive market and then to compensate British farmers through British governmental payments funded by British tax revenues for income shortfalls. This policy had kept British food prices relatively low by European standards, while stabilizing domestic farm income. It also encouraged heavy reliance on food imports.

In contrast, the Common Agricultural Policy was based on guaranteed prices, EC purchase and storage of ever-growing surpluses, and export subsidies. Under a 1970 agreement, its funding derived largely from taxes on imported food, a major portion of the external tariff on industrial goods, and up to 1 percent of national revenues from the Value Added Tax.

British entry meant not only a complete revamping of British agricultural policies, but it also led to sharp increases in British food prices and made Britain (long a major importer of food from outside the EC) fund a disproportionate share of the Common Agricultural Policy budget. Needless to say, the policy adjustments and their far-ranging ramifications fed Euroskepticism among much of the British population. *The Economist*, the leading British weekly news magazine, summed up much of the popular feeling in describing the CAP in 1990 as the "single most idiotic system of economic mismanagement that the rich western countries have ever devised."[62] Initially, however, most British farmers found that CAP increased their incomes; and they generally approved the policy changes.

Eventually, in the early 1990s, a combination of British governmental persistence, soaring costs of the Common Agricultural Policy, American and other international pressures, and prospects of EU enlargement into agrarian Eastern Europe caused modification of the CAP in directions long favored by the British government. However, the agricultural public-policy domain remains probably the clearest example of the impact of Europeanization on British public policy and British life.

For an example of a smaller but still significant impact on British public policy by the Europeanization process, the domain of gender-equality policy is illustrative. In this realm, European Community/European Union policy-making has been less supranational than in the agricultural-policy domain. In addition, EC/EU substantive policies and procedures at the time of British entry did not clash markedly with preexisting British legislation. Prior to its membership in the European Community, in 1970, Britain had passed the Equal Pay Act, providing for equal pay for equal work regardless of gender. At least in part, this act was designed to comply with Article 119 of the 1957 Rome EEC Treaty. Therefore, in contrast to the agricultural public-policy pattern, there was considerable harmony between British and EC public policies.

Nevertheless, over the succeeding years, EC/EU initiatives on gender-equality policy have had considerable impact on British public policies. The EC Equal Pay Directive, passed in 1975, provided additional specifics to the rather vague Article 119 (and preexisting British law). When the European Commission concluded that Britain had not properly implemented this directive, it instituted infringement proceedings, resulting in a decision by the European Court of Justice in 1982 that found the United Kingdom in violation of the directive. British women's interest groups and the British Equal Opportunities Commission generated pressures on the British government to amend British domestic law to bring it into compliance with EC requirements—a pattern that was to be repeated in a number of other instances. A recent analysis of British public policies in the gender-equality realm has concluded that "Europeanization has generated substantial changes in British legislation."[63] Thus, European Union influence has penetrated British public policy well beyond such well-publicized areas as agricultural policy.

"Europeanization has generated substantial changes in British legislation."

James Caporaso and Joseph Jupille, *"The Europeanization of Gender Equality Policy" (2001), 38.*

CONCLUSIONS

Membership in and interaction with the European Communities/ European Union has eroded some of the sovereignty claimed by the British government and parliament while altering political practices, causing intraparty conflicts and modifying the balance of interest-group power, and revamping some major public policies and affecting others. However, the impact should not be exaggerated. Britain's long-standing but evolving constitution, major governmental institutions, and political processes remain largely intact. Major British welfare-state and educational policies have resisted extensive EC/EU influence. Nevertheless, the effects of the EC/EU on Britain have probably been more extensive than British impact on the EC/EU has been. Britain's modest impact on the "European project," especially relative to that of either France or Germany, has certainly been a major factor underlying the reluctance of Britons to embrace the European Union.

As the EU moves toward further widening (and perhaps deepening, too), Britain remains what it has been: a reluctant European, an awkward partner. This stance is deeply rooted in both economics and geopolitics. In recent years, economic patterns have shifted considerably, bringing Britain closer to the rest of the EU than before. However, unless the shifts are more dramatic than they have been in both spheres, Britain's position on the edge of Europe is likely to continue in more than just a geographic sense.

SUMMARY

- "Reluctant European" and "awkward partner" are two sobriquets that analysts have often used to describe the United Kingdom in its approaches to Europe and the European Union.

- Victorious in World War II; proud of its long history as a great power; and closely tied by culture, economics, and politics to the United States and to its Commonwealth, Britain under both Labour and Conservative governments declined to become involved in 1950–1952 with the formation of the European Coal and Steel Community and rejected invitations to join the European Communities in 1957.

- Prodded by the United States and major sectors of its own business community to join the EC, disillusioned with the prospects of its Commonwealth, and worried by Britain's slower economic growth than the EC, the Macmillan government sought EC entry in 1961, only to face a veto from French President de Gaulle.

- An effort by Prime Minister Harold Wilson to gain British EC entry also met a similar rejection in 1967.

- Britain finally joined the EC in 1973, along with Ireland and Denmark, under the leadership of Prime Minister Edward Heath, who faced considerable opposition within his own Conservative party and even more opposition from the Labour party to the terms of entry that he negotiated.

- On his return to office in 1974, Harold Wilson renegotiated the terms of British EC entry and won approval of parliament and a public referendum for Britain's remaining in the EC; both Wilson and his successor, James Callaghan, encountered strong opposition to EC membership from within their own Labour party, especially from its left wing, which viewed the EC as too capitalistic.

- Britain's disproportionately large contribution to the EC budget fed widespread discontent with the EC in Britain, as did the EC Common Agricultural Policy, which received widespread blame for rising British food prices.

- Prime Minister Margaret Thatcher (1979–1990) won an annual budget rebate from the EC (still in effect in 2004 and still controversial) after prolonged negotiations; she also played important roles in shaping the single-market and competition policies of the EC; however, she strongly rejected EC social policies and repeatedly stressed the need to maintain Britain's national sovereignty.

- Deteriorating relations between Thatcher and other EC leaders played a part in stoking rebellion against her leadership within the Conservative party, which brought her downfall as prime minister in 1990.

- Despite pledging to place Britain "at the heart of Europe," John Major, Thatcher's successor as prime minister (1990–1997), rejected the Social Chapter, opted out of the Economic and Monetary Union, and even stalemated the EU Council of Ministers for a time to protest the EU's handling of Britain's "mad cow" crisis; his actions alienated other EU leaders but failed to placate Thatcher and other EU critics within his Conservative party.

- Tony Blair (1997–) endorsed the Social Chapter's inclusion in the EU's Amsterdam Treaty of 1997 but has not (as of 2004) taken Britain into the Economic and Monetary Union, adopted the Schengen border control agreements, or agreed to demands from many EU members for an end to national vetoes in such areas as taxation and foreign and defense policy; Blair's close alliance with the Bush administration on Iraq also distanced him from many EU colleagues.

- The most distinctive long-term aspects of Britain's approaches to the EC/EU have been: an Atlanticist preference, a global free-trade preference, a preference for EC/EU enlargement, an adversarial style, and a legalistic approach to enforcement. Two other fairly common themes have been its leaders' preoccupation with intraparty management on EC/EU matters and an anti-bureaucracy, pro-market preference.

- Britain's impact on the EC/EU has been evident in numerous restrictions on supranational development at Britain's behest;

single-market and competition and regional policies in a more positive sense; and reductions in the scale and cost of the Common Agricultural Policy.

- EC/EU membership has eroded British legal parliamentary and national sovereignty (amid much domestic controversy), enhanced British judicial powers, and increased the autonomy of the Bank of England; it has also led to Britain's acceptance of proportional representation in European Parliament elections (and, less directly, in some other elections also).

- EC/EU issues have nearly always split both major British political parties, creating major party-management problems for party leaders, though internal divisions over European issues have since the late 1980s split the Conservative party more deeply than the Labour party.

- EC/EU membership has altered many British public policies, most notably (and controversially) in agriculture, but also in such domains as gender equality policies.

- Britain's marked reluctance to embrace fully the European Union continues to distinguish it from the other major nation-states in the EU.

ENDNOTES

1. David Hale, "Great Britain: The Reluctant European," in Ronald Tiersky, ed., *Europe Today* (Lanham, MD: Rowman and Littlefield, 1999), 95–126; David Gowland and Arthur Turner, *Reluctant Europeans: Britain and European Integration, 1945–1998* (Harlow: Longman, Pearson Education, 2000); Stephen George, *An Awkward Partner*, 3rd ed. (Oxford: Oxford University Press, 1998). Andrew Geddes, "Europe: Major's Nemesis?" stresses the large number of "reluctant Europeans" in Britain in Andrew Geddes and Jonathan Tonge, eds., *Labour's Landslide* (Manchester: Manchester University Press, 1997), 85. Also see Jorgen Rasmussen, "Britain:

Aloof and Skeptical," in Eleanor E. Zeff and Ellen B. Pirro, eds., *The European Union and the Member States: Cooperation, Coordination, and Compromise* (Boulder: Lynne Rienner, 2001), 145–174.

2. The points concerning Britain generally are widely accepted, though emphases vary. See, for example, Gowland and Turner, *Reluctant Europeans*, 9–39; George, *An Awkward Partner*, 12–22; Alex May, *Britain and Europe since 1945* (New York: Longman, 1997), 1–19; John W. Young, *Britain and European Unity, 1945–1992* (New York: St. Martin's, 1993), 1–35. On Labour specifically, see May, 17–18, and C. M. Woodhouse, *British Foreign Policy Since the Second World War* (London: Hutchinson, 1961), 222–223.

3. Derek W. Urwin, *The Community of Europe* (London: Longman, 1991), 27–87; George, *An Awkward Partner*, 23–26. On Churchill in particular, see May, *Britain and Europe*, 15–16, 20–24, 99–100, and Urwin, 30–31.

4. Miriam Camps, *Britain and the European Community, 1955–1963* (Princeton: Princeton University Press, 1964), 314–315; Gowland and Turner, *Reluctant Europeans*, 110–124; George, *An Awkward Partner*, 29–30; Young, *Britain and European Unity*, 72.

5. Camps, *Britain and the European Community*, 274–366; Gowland and Turner, *Reluctant Europeans*, 110–135; George, *An Awkward Partner*, 28–34; Young, *Britain and European Unity*, 70–77. Andrew Moravcsik, *The Choice for Europe: Social Purpose and State Power from Messina to Maastricht* (Ithaca, NY: Cornell University Press, 1998), 164–176, makes the strongest case that commercial considerations were primary.

6. Moravcsik, *The Choice for Europe*, particularly stresses the CAP factor. Gowland and Turner, *Reluctant Europeans*, 141–151, and most sources emphasize multiple factors.

7. Stephen George and Deborah Haythorne, "The British Labour Party," in John Gaffney, ed., *Political Parties and the European Union* (London: Routledge, 1996), 110, 113.

8. On Heath's uniquely pro-European stance, see Young, *Britain and European Unity*, 107, 117; George, *The Awkward Partner*, 49. On assertiveness toward EC partners by Heath and his gov-

ernment, and by British higher civil servants, see George, *The Awkward Partner*, 61–70 and 105, and May, *Britain and Europe*, 54–55.

9. On the referendum, see Anthony King, *Britain Says Yes: The 1975 Referendum on the Common Market* (Washington, DC: American Enterprise Institute, 1977). The primacy of party management concerns is stressed by George, *The Awkward Partner*, 76–77, 92–93, 96–97, 114, and 124–126, and Young, *Britain and European Unity*, 119–135.

10. Desmond Dinan, *Ever Closer Union*, 2nd ed. (Boulder, CO: Lynne Rienner, 1999), 89.

11. George, *The Awkward Partner*, 131–134.

12. Virtually all analysts see truculence in Thatcher's style vis-à-vis the EC. May, *Britain and Europe*, 70–71, and George, *The Awkward Partner*, 162–163, see it as useful in courting domestic public opinion but counterproductive inside the EC.

13. George, *The Awkward Partner*, 194. Also see John Turner, *The Tories and Europe* (Manchester: Manchester University Press, 2000), 85–86.

14. Timothy Bainbridge, *The Penguin Companion to European Union*, 2nd ed. (London: Penguin, 1998), 27.

15. Helen Wallace, "At Odds with Europe," *Political Studies* 45 (September 1997), 677.

16. Martin Holmes, "The Conservative Party and Europe: From Major to Hague," *The Political Quarterly* 69 (April–June 1998), 134–135, develops the Major-Wilson comparison, as does Wallace, "At Odds," 682.

17. George, *The Awkward Partner*, 248.

18. George, *The Awkward Partner*, 271. However, Holmes, "The Conservative Party," 135, concludes that Major kept his party from splitting but missed the chance to lead it in a genuinely Euroskeptical direction.

19. Kirsty Hughes and Edward Smith, "New Labour—New Europe?" *International Affairs* 74 (January 1998), 93.

20. George and Haythorne, "The British Labour Party," 118.

21. Gowland and Turner, *Reluctant Europeans*, 270.

22. Desmond Dinan, *Ever Closer Union*, 2nd ed. (Boulder, CO: Lynne Rienner, 1999), 135.

23. For Thatcher's own account of the events leading to her resignation, see Margaret Thatcher,

Margaret Thatcher: The Downing Street Years (New York: HarperCollins, 1993), 829–862.

24. Hughes and Smith, "New Labour—New Europe?" 93–103; David Baker, "Britain and Europe: Treading Water or Slowly Drowning?" *Parliamentary Affairs* 56, 2 (April 2003), 237–254; Turner, *The Tories and Europe*, 220–265; Holmes, "The Conservative Party," 136–140; Nicholas Watt and Kevin Maguire, "A Leap in the Dark," *The Guardian*, September 14, 2001; Anne Perkins, "Eurosceptics Take Charge," *The Guardian*, September 15, 2001. The Kennedy quotation is from Baker, 249.

25. Wallace, "At Odds," 686.

26. Moravcsik, *The Choice for Europe*. For a critique, see Anthony Forster, "Britain and the Negotiation of the Maastricht Treaty: A Critique of Liberal Intergovernmentalism," *Journal of Common Market Studies* 36 (September 1998), 347–368.

27. Thomas Pederson, *Germany, France, and the Integration of Europe: A Realist Interpretation* (New York: Pinter, 1998).

28. George, *The Awkward Partner*, is one of a number of accounts that often employs this general approach, though not to the exclusion of others.

29. Stephanie B. Anderson, "Problems and Possibilities: The Development of the CFSP from Maastricht to the 1996 IGC," in Pierre-Henri Laurent and Marc Maresceau, eds., *The State of the European Union*, vol. 4 (Boulder, CO: Lynne Rienner, 1998), 134–135.

30. George, *The Awkward Partner*, 278; Turner, *The Tories and Europe*, 142–219.

31. Hale, "Great Britain: The Reluctant European," 121–122.

32. Bainbridge, *Penguin Companion*, 309; Lord Beloff, *Britain and European Union* (New York: St. Martin's, 1996), esp. 113–127.

33. Barbara Leppert, et al., *British and German Interests in EU Enlargement: Conflict and Cooperation* (London: Continuum, 2001); Anthony Forster and William Wallace, "The IGCs and the Renegotiation of European Order After the Cold War," in Laurent and Maresceau, eds., *The State of the European Union*, 347.

34. Bainbridge, *Penguin Companion*, 502.

35. George, *The Awkward Partner*, 278.

36. George, *The Awkward Partner*, 279.

37. Quote is from Keith Middlemas, *Orchestrating Europe* (London: Fontana, 1995), 300; the comparative statement, contrasting with Italy, is from Middlemas, 315–316.

38. Helen Wallace, "Relations Between the European Union and British Administration," in Yves Mény, Pier Muller, and Jean-Louis Quermonne, eds., *Adjusting to Europe: The Impact of the European Union on National Institutions and Policies* (London: Routledge, 1996), 64.

39. Moravcsik, *The Choice for Europe*, 417–419.

40. On U.K. leadership on the single market, see Moravcsik, *The Choice for Europe*, 319–326. Margaret Thatcher, *The Downing Street Years* (London: HarperCollins, 1993), 546, concurs. However, Thomas Pederson, *Germany, France, and the Integration of Europe* (London: Pinter, 1998), 101, emphasizes that Germany and Italy had already placed the single market on the EC agenda. On liberalized global trade, see George, *The Awkward Partner*, 252.

41. Francis McGowan, "Competition Policy: The Limits of the European Regulatory State," in Wallace and Wallace, eds., *Policy-Making in the European Union*, 4th ed. (Oxford: Oxford University Press, 2000), 131, 135, 138; George, *The Awkward Partner*, 247–248.

42. Loukas Tsoukalis, "Economic and Monetary Union: Political Conviction and Economic Uncertainty," in Wallace and Wallace, eds., *Policy-Making*, 149–178; Moravcsik, *The Choice for Europe*, Ch. 6; Bainbridge, *Penguin Companion*, 174; Gowland and Turner, *Reluctant Europeans*, 359–362.

43. Dinan, *Ever Closer Union*, 344–350.

44. Alberta Sbragia, "Environmental Policy: Economic Constraints and External Pressures," in Wallace and Wallace, *Policy-Making*, 293–316; Andrew Jordan, "EU Environmental Policy at 25," in Henri Warmenhoven, ed., *Global Issues: Western Europe*, 6th ed. (Guilford, CT: Dushkin-McGraw-Hill, 1999), 195–207; John Bradbier, "UK Environmental Policy under Blair," in Stephen P. Savage and Rob Adkinson, eds., *Public Policy under Blair* (Basingstoke and London: Palgrave, 2001), 86–109; Ralph Minder, "Most EU Members Failing to Meet Kyoto

Protocol Pledges," *Financial Times*, December 3, 2003, 3.

45. George, *The Awkward Partner*, 66–69; Gowland and Turner, *Reluctant Europeans*, 179–180, 195–196.

46. Gowland and Turner, *Reluctant Europeans*, 287–288, 327–328; Bainbridge, *Penguin Companion*, 450–452.

47. Monica den Boer and William Wallace, "Justice and Home Affairs," in Wallace and Wallace, *Policy-Making*, 493–519; Dinan, *Ever Closer Union*, 440–443; Bainbridge, *Penguin Companion*, 434.

48. The quotation is from Anne Deighton, "European Union Policy," in Seldon, ed., *The Blair Effect*, 323. Also see Anne Deighton, "The Military Security Pool: Towards a New Security Regime for Europe?" *The International Spectator* 35, 4 (October–Dec 2000), 19–32; Stephanie B. Anderson, "Problems and Possibilities: The Development of the CFSP from Maastricht to the 1996 IGC," in Laurent and Maresceau, eds., *The State of the European Union*, 133–147; Anthony Forster and William Wallace, "Common Foreign and Security Policy: From Shadow to Substance?" in Wallace and Wallace, eds., *Policy-Making*, 461–491.

49. Damian Chalmers, "The Positioning of EU Judicial Politics Within the United Kingdom," *West European Politics* 23, 4 (October 2000), 177; Stephen George and Ian Bache, *Politics in the European Union* (Oxford: Oxford University Press, 2001), 281; Philip Norton, *The British Polity*, 3rd ed. (New York: Longman, 1994), 326–327; Bainbridge, *Penguin Companion*, 257.

50. Lord Beloff, "Amery on the Constitution: Britain and the European Union," *Government and Opposition* 33 (Spring 1998), 170.

51. Davies, *British Politics and Europe*, 54–56; Alan S. Milward, *The European Rescue of the Nation-State* (Berkeley: University of California Press, 1992).

52. Nevil Johnson, "The Judicial Dimension in British Politics," *West European Politics* 21, 1 (January 1998), 148–166; Norton, *The British Polity*, 333.

53. Cited by James Caporaso and Joseph Jupille, "The Europeanization of Gender Equality Policy and Domestic Structural Change," in Maria Green Cowles, et al., eds., *Transforming Europe: Europeanization and Domestic Change* (Ithaca, NY: Cornell University Press, 2001), 41.

54. Quotation from Davies, *British Politics and Europe*, 57.

55. Lisa Conant, "Europeanization and the Courts: Variable Patterns of Adaptation among the National Judiciaries," in Cowles, et al., eds., *Transforming Europe*, 97–115.

56. On the effects of EC/EU membership on U.K. parliamentary and executive powers, see Philip Giddings and Gavin Drewry, eds., *Westminster and Europe: The Impact of the European Union on the Westminster Parliament* (New York: St. Martin's, 1996). For varied portrayals of the impact on prime ministers, see George, *The Awkward Partner*, and Jim Buller, *National Statecraft and European Integration: The Conservative Government and the European Union, 1979–1997* (London: Pinter, 2000).

57. Martin Marcussen, "The Power of EMU-Ideas: Reforming Central Banks in Great Britain, France, and Sweden," Paper Given at the European Community Studies Association Conference, Pittsburgh, PA, June 2–5, 1999; Hale, "Great Britain," 101. Also see Buller, *National Statecraft*, 171, who interprets the move primarily as a means for the Blair government to escape blame for economic problems that might arise.

58. On EU influence on Scottish and Welsh devolution, and possible foreign-policy implications, see Keith Robbins, "Britain and Europe: Devolution and Foreign Policy," *International Affairs* 74 (January 1998), 105–118; "Undoing Britain," *Economist*, November 6, 1999, 6–7; and Rasmussen, "Britain," 155–156. On EU influence concerning Northern Ireland, see Richard Kearney, *Postnationalist Ireland: Politics, Culture, Philosophy* (New York: Routledge, 1997), esp. Ch. 5. For doubts about EU decentralizing effects, see David Allen, "Cohesion and the Structural Funds: Transfers and Trade-Offs," in Wallace and Wallace, eds., *Policy-Making*, esp. 259–260. Ian Bache, Stephen George, and R. A. W. Rhodes, "The European Union, Cohesion Policy, and Subnational Authorities in the United Kingdom," in Liesbet Hooge, ed., *Cohesion Policy and European Integration* (Oxford: Oxford

University Press, 1996), 294–319, notes the limited effects in the United Kingdom under the Thatcher and Major governments.

59. On PR trends and arguments in the United Kingdom, see Norton, *The British Polity*, 98–104. On referendums, see King, *Britain Says Yes*, and Davies, *British Politics and Europe*, 57–61.

60. On the role of the EC issue in the Labour–Social Democratic split, see Young, *Britain and European Unity*, 143, 178; Davies, *British Politics and Europe*, 85. On the Referendum and U.K. Independence parties, see Justin Fisher, "Third and Minor Party Breakthrough?" in Andrew Geddes and Jonathan Tonge, eds., *Labour's Landslide* (Manchester: Manchester University Press, 1997), 63–64.

61. Janet Mather, *The European Union and British Democracy: Towards Convergence* (New York: St. Martin's, 2000), esp. 145–152; Mark Evans, "Political Participation," in Patrick Dunleavy, et al., eds., *Developments in British Politics*, vol. 5 (London: Macmillan, 1997), 114–115; Davies, *British Politics and Europe*, 94–101.

62. The quotation is cited by Elmar Rieger, "The Common Agricultural Policy: Politics Against Markets," in Wallace and Wallace, eds., *Policy-Making*, 192. Most of the analysis in this and the preceding paragraphs is based upon Rieger, 179–210; Priscilla Baines, "Parliament and the Common Agricultural Policy," in Giddings and Drewry, eds., *Westminster and Europe*, 191–222; George, *The Awkward Partner*, esp. 51–56 and 224–225; and Hix, *The Political System*, 250–256.

63. Caporaso and Jupille, "The Europeanization," 38.

Chapter 13   Spain

"Geography aside, Spain frequently has found itself isolated from the rest of Europe."

—Michael Marks, *The Formation of European Policy in Post-Franco Spain (1997), 13.*

Situated on the Iberian peninsula in the southwest of Europe, Spain was relatively isolated from some of the major developments of modern West European history—including the Reformation, the early phases of the commercial and industrial revolutions, and the early waves of democratization.[1] Although Spain emerged as a great power during the fifteenth and sixteenth centuries, it did not develop all of the features of a modern nation-state at that time. Ferdinand and Isabella completed the Roman Catholic "reconquest" of the Iberian peninsula from the Muslim Moors, instituted the Inquisition that linked Spain firmly to Roman Catholicism, brought the kingdoms of Castile and Aragon closer together than before, and laid the foundations for a great Spanish Empire. However, they did not create a modern nation-state. Their Spain and that of their Hapsburg successors was highly fragmented at home, and many of its governmental resources centered on building and maintaining a far-flung empire abroad. As Spain struggled over the succeeding centuries to become a modern nation-state, it experienced numerous conflicts between its center in Castile and parts of its periphery, particularly in Catalonia and the Basque Country. The coming of modernization brought new clashes between formerly dominant groups and would-be participants and over economic structures and distribution of wealth. From 1936 to 1939, Spain was torn by a violent civil war that brought death to about 600,000 of its citizens, drove nearly 300,000 of them into exile, and left the country with a long-term authoritarian regime headed by the dictator Francisco Franco from 1939 to 1975. Only since the mid-1970s has Spain established constitutional democracy and joined the mainstream of European politics and economics, entering the European Community (with its Iberian neighbor Portugal) in 1986.

Spain has a population today of just over forty million people. Its gross domestic product and its per capita gross domestic product are well below those of the other large nation-states that were pre-2004 members of the European Union, and its unemployment rate remains higher than the others, despite several decades of relatively strong economic growth. The legacies of long-term economic stagnation, authoritarian government, center-periphery conflict,

MAP 13.1   Spain

and isolation from the European mainstream have been difficult to overcome. Nonetheless, Spain has since 1975 achieved considerable economic growth, a stable constitutional democracy, a new sharing of powers between its regions and its central government, and a position of considerable importance within the European Union.

POLITICAL DEVELOPMENT

Early Development

A major difference between the development of Spain and that of most of Western Europe was the domination of Spain for centuries after 711 A.D. by the Muslim Moors who had invaded from North Africa. Christian kingdoms gradually regained much of northern Spain and fought their way southward. Not until 1492 was Spain united under Roman Catholic rule as a political system run by the "Catholic Kings," Ferdinand of Aragon and Isabella of Castile, who had married in 1469, established new links between their two kingdoms, and eliminated the last Moorish bastion of Granada. In the same year that Granada was incorporated into Spain (1492), Columbus made his first visit to America, laying the foundations for what became a large Spanish Empire across the seas. Roman Catholicism, the Spanish state religion, became a tool in Spanish nation-building, as church and state used the Spanish Inquisition to impose religious and cultural uniformity— forcing the conversion of tens of thousands of Spanish Jews and Muslims to Roman Catholicism, killing many who resisted, and forcing several hundred thousand into exile. Though primarily religious in inspiration, the Inquisition had its political effects. As one leading scholar phrased it, "Compensating in some respects for the absence of a Spanish nationhood, a common religious devotion had obvious political overtones, and consequently a practical value which Ferdinand and Isabella were quick to exploit."[2]

"Compensating in some respects for the absence of a Spanish nationhood, a common religious devotion had obvious political overtones, and consequently a practical value which Ferdinand and Isabella were quick to exploit."

John Huxtable Elliott, *Imperial Spain (1963),* 97.

From Great Power to European Backwater

Although Spain emerged as one of the early European global empire-builders under the Catholic Kings (1479–1516) and their Hapsburg successors (1516–1700), the years of Spanish glory were to prove short-lived. Gold and silver from Spanish America diminished the government's interest in developing Spanish commerce, and the entrepreneurial spirit was in any event relatively weak in Castile, the center of Spain and the Empire. Moreover, the Spanish Inquisition expelled many of the commercially oriented Jews and Moors and stifled intellectual life in Spain with its censorship, atmosphere of fear, and closure of Spain to external ideas. Political-military overcommitment abroad combined with commercial stagnation in the Castilian heartland to result in Spanish political and economic decline relative to England and France. Though this decline became evident after the 1640s, its root causes lay in preceding decades. Spain's decline relative to England and France would continue through the seventeenth and eighteenth centuries.[3]

Spain was a great power in the fifteenth and sixteenth centuries but lacked many of the features of a modern nation-state. As a state, it lacked even a capital until Philip II established his governmental and administrative center at Madrid in 1561. Castile became the "center" of the new Spain and itself had a Cortes composed of the three estates of church, nobility, and towns and a uniform legal and economic system. Castilians dominated imperial institutions but also paid most of the taxes to support the Spanish Empire. Within the Kingdom of Castile, the elites of the three Basque provinces, Galicia, and Asturias enjoyed considerable autonomy. Aragon was even more decentralized than Castile was, placing more checks on monarchial authority than existed in Castile. Within the loose federation that was Aragon, Catalonia possessed its own Catalan language; and its leaders often went their own way. During the era of the Catholic Kings and the Spanish Hapsburg dynasty, ordinary Spaniards had no sense of common nationhood and felt little loyalty even to their regions. Instead, as Henry Kamen has stressed, "loyalties were directed to the local township or seigneur rather than to the realm as a whole."[4]

"...loyalties were directed to the local township or seigneur rather than to the realm as a whole."

Henry Kamen, *Spain (1991), 246.*

The Spanish state became increasingly authoritarian and centralized under the Spanish Bourbon dynasty that took office in 1700 and solidified its position as a result of the War of the Spanish Succession (1702–1713). In effect, Castile gained dominance over Spain. Within Castile, the Cortes lost influence to the monarch and his ministers, assembling only four times during the eighteenth century and then only to grant the wishes of the king. The crown of Aragon ceased to exist, as did the traditional customs barriers between Castile and Aragon; Castilian became the official language of the Spanish state; and a French-style system of centralized administration became universal in Spain. However, the Basque provinces were able to retain their traditional laws (*fueros*).[5]

Bourbon absolutism came under challenge from the liberalizing ideas of the French Enlightenment that began to influence Spain in the late eighteenth century and had even more impact after the invasion of the armies of Napoleon I of France during the first decade of the nineteenth century. Napoleon imposed his brother Joseph on the Spaniards as their king in 1808. Although a revolt against him was successful only four years later and a new liberal constitution was adopted in 1812, Spain was to be torn by liberal versus conservative internal conflicts for more than a century thereafter and suffered from chronic governmental instability. Multiple constitutions, civil wars, and military coups and attempted coups roiled Spanish politics and society. Overseas, most of the Latin American Spanish Empire rebelled and gained independence between 1810 and 1825. At the end of the nineteenth century, Spain lost Cuba, Puerto Rico, and the Philippines as a result of its defeat in the Spanish-American War.

If Spanish state institutions lacked legitimacy and stability throughout most of the nineteenth century, consensus on the nature of the nation also came under renewed challenge. Basque and Catalan nationalism emerged vigorously in the nineteenth century, pressing for regional autonomy and defense of the distinctive Basque and Catalan languages. While early Basque nationalism was largely peasant-based and traditionalist in nature, nationalist movements in Catalonia displayed a mixture of rural and urban business bases. Both regions were more industrialized than the rest of Spain and resisted dictation from the capital at Madrid. Eventually, demands for regional autonomy were to spread to Galicia in the northwest and Andalusia in the south of Spain. Thus, the political-cultural conflict came in the twentieth century to be widely characterized as a **center-periphery** division.[6]

Spain was relatively unsuccessful at generating economic growth and had fallen far behind most of the rest of Western Europe in per capita wealth by the nineteenth century. The old nobility lost much of its political power but retained considerable wealth and social status; a wealthy urban bourgeoisie emerged, especially in Catalonia and the Basque Country; and lawyers dominated electoral office and public administration. Meanwhile socialist and **anarchist** ideologies won adherents among the usually poverty-stricken peasantry and in the new but relatively small urban industrial working class. Moreover, uneven regional economic development contributed to the conflicts that pitted the Basque Country and Catalonia against the Spanish national governments. When the Great Depression hit Spain after 1929, the distribution crisis worsened and was reflected in increasingly violent clashes between Spanish upper and lower classes.[7]

As Spain gradually industrialized and modernized, albeit well behind most of Western Europe, demands for democratic participation multiplied also. For a brief time after 1869 and again after 1890, Spain extended voting rights to all adult males. However, genuine democratic rule was usually thwarted by the dominance of patron-client networks of local bosses called *caciques,* who sometimes stole votes outright and engaged in bribery and intimidation but who also often did favors in exchange for votes. Behind the façade of Spanish democracy lay a hierarchical reality that rested on widespread ignorance and apathy concerning national issues.[8]

Civil War and the Franco Era

Demands for further democratization and efforts to destroy the *caciquismo* system occurred simultaneously in the early twentieth century with demands for regional autonomy and defense of regional languages, continuing disagreements over state institutions, and sharp economic cleavages. During most of the 1920s, Spain became an authoritarian dictatorship under General Miguel Primo de Rivera, who seized power in 1923. However, it lurched toward a democratic republic in 1930–1931, as Primo de Rivera fled into exile, soon followed by the abdication of the king. In the 1930s, the Republican supporters of the Spanish Republic (Communists, anarchists, socialists, Basque and Catalan nationalists, and some centrists) and the Nationalists (mostly conservatives from the Roman Catholic Church, the upper class, and the military) battled each other for control of Spain. While the former called for a more equal distribution of wealth and power within the framework of a republic, the latter sought to protect positions of relative wealth, status, and power and supported authoritarian government. Civil war erupted between the two sides and devastated Spain from 1936 to 1939. The Communist Soviet Union assisted the Republican side, as did quite a few volunteers from Western countries (especially France), while Nazi Germany and Fascist Italy supported the Nationalists, leading many observers to describe the Spanish Civil War as a training exercise for World War II. Indicating the major

significance of the Spanish Civil War, a leading historian has concluded, "Perhaps at no time in the history of any nation (including revolutionary France of 1789–99 and revolutionary Russia of 1917–28) has so large a proportion of the people acted out of intimate, conscious political conviction as did the Spanish people during the years of 1931–39."[9]

> "Perhaps at no time in the history of any nation (including revolutionary France of 1789–99 and revolutionary Russia of 1917–28) has so large a proportion of the people acted out of intimate, conscious political conviction as did the Spanish people during the years of 1931–39."
>
> Gabriel Jackson, *The Spanish Republic and the Civil War (1964), 493.*

In 1939, the Nationalist forces led by Francisco Franco triumphed. Franco became the dictator of Spain for the next 36 years. Despite the assistance that Hitler and Mussolini had provided to the Spanish Nationalists in the Spanish Civil War, Spain remained neutral in World War II. However, the dictatorial Franco government was a pariah in the eyes of most democratic West Europeans for decades to come. This status reflected not only its links to Nazism and Fascism but also its continuing authoritarian features. Only the death of Franco in 1975, and the building of a Spanish constitutional democracy in the years that followed, made it possible for Spain to gain entry to the European Community/European Union in 1986 and join the West European mainstream.

Much of modern Spanish development has been a story of unsuccessful coping with the modernization crises of nation-building, state-building, distribution, and participation. The Franco era was no exception. Franco's regime stressed the Spanish national identity but antagonized the adherents of Basque, Catalan, and other national identities by its repression of their efforts and aspirations. Franco and his closest associates subordinated executive, legislative, and judicial institutions to their commands. Participation during the Franco regime was tightly controlled and occurred primarily through authoritarian corporatist structures somewhat similar to those found in Mussolini's Italy. For the most part, the regime encouraged passivity among the Spanish populace, though it lessened its repression of participation in its final years. The Spanish economy was insulated, **autarkic** (aiming at self-sufficiency), and stagnant during the first years of the Franco regime. The state-run holding company, the National Institute of Industry (INI), coordinated most industrial development in a manner similar to that in Fascist Italy. Eventually, the Spanish government partially relaxed its economic controls and began to open up to global trade and investment. Spain underwent considerable growth in the 1960s, spurred by tourism and foreign investment. However, Spain remained quite poor by West European standards. Almost two million Spaniards moved outside the country to earn improved incomes during the 1960s alone.[10]

Spanish Modernization Since 1975

Following the death of Franco in November 1975, Spain underwent a relatively rapid transformation from authoritarian rule to constitutional democracy. The leadership of King Juan Carlos, whom Franco had designated in 1969 as his successor, and Adolfo Suárez, whom the new king picked in 1976 as his prime minister, contributed significantly to this process. Other factors facilitating democratization in Spain included the emergence of prodemocratic forces in the last years of Franco's regime as repression eased somewhat, the shift of the Catholic Church toward support for democracy, recent democratizing examples in Portugal and Greece, and international pressures from the European Community. Still another factor was the 1973 assassination by the Basque terrorist organization, Basque Homeland and Liberty (ETA), of Admiral Luis Carrero Blanco, Franco's prime minister and an authoritarian who would likely have been a major obstacle to democratization had he been in office at Franco's death.[11]

Spain adopted a new democratic Constitution in 1978, following its endorsement by both chambers of parliament and by 88 percent of the voters in a plebiscite. Though Prime Minister Suárez as a former official of the Franco regime and King Juan Carlos as Franco's designated successor were able to overcome most resistance from the old authoritarian elites, there was an attempted coup in February 1981. Lieutenant Colonel Antonio Tejero Molina and a group of civil guards seized control of parliament and held its members hostage in an effort to reverse the democratization process. However, King Juan Carlos quickly condemned this action and rallied most of the Spanish military and the population to quash the attempted coup. Appearing on national television in the wee hours of the morning while the attempted coup was in progress, Juan Carlos declared, "The Crown, the symbol of the permanence and unity of Spain, cannot tolerate any actions by people attempting to disrupt by force the democratic process."

"The Crown, the symbol of the permanence and unity of Spain, cannot tolerate any actions by people attempting to disrupt by force the democratic process."

King Juan Carlos, June 24, 1981, *cited by Elizabeth Knowles, Twentieth Century Quotations (1998), 165.*

From this point onward, the new constitutional democracy became firmly entrenched. When the Socialist Workers party of Spain (PSOE) won the 1982 elections and formed the new government, the transfer of power was a smooth and peaceful one, even though the Socialists had been a focal point of opposition to Franco's regime, along with the Basques.

Although Spain has continued to struggle with questions of nationhood and of economic growth and distribution, its new constitutional institutions have attained widespread legitimacy and its democratic practices have at least reduced the feelings of exclusion and the widespread passivity that characterized most of the population previously.

With regard to nation-building, the post-Franco Spanish government has moved toward a semi-federalism that has devolved considerable authority to 17 autonomous communities (regions). The Basque Country, in particular, remains a problem area, due to the continuing terrorist activities sponsored by ETA and the Spanish government's resort (in the 1980s) to extralegal methods to repress these. Recent banning of Basque political parties linked to ETA have failed to bring peace. However, moderate Basque nationalists have run the Basque Country government and have at times been an important part of coalition governments in Madrid—a far cry from the situation that prevailed under the centralized, authoritarian Franco regime. Catalonia, like the Basque Country one of the autonomous communities, has pursued a peaceful course under the leadership of moderate Catalan nationalists. Therefore, despite continuing ETA-sponsored violence and a number of examples of state-sponsored violence in the 1980s against ETA and its sympathizers, the fracas over the banning of Basque nationalist parties linked to the ETA, and the inclusion of more extreme Catalan nationalists late in 2003 in the government of Catalonia, Spain has addressed its most important long-term nation-building conflicts more successfully than in the past. Nevertheless, as Spain has become increasingly prosperous, it has drawn an increasing number of immigrants, particularly from North Africa and Latin America, and has attracted sharp criticism from Amnesty International in 2002 for "racism" and failure to integrate these newcomers into the Spanish nation. Gillian Fleming, author of the Amnesty International report, concluded, "The cases we have documented show a pattern of violation by law enforcement officers of the rights of members of ethnic minorities or persons of non-Spanish origin." The Basque Country and Catalonia also continue to pose problems for Spanish nation-building.[12]

"The cases we have documented show a pattern of violation by law enforcement officers of the rights of members of ethnic minorities or persons of non-Spanish origin."

Gillian Fleming's *Amnesty International Report*, cited in *New York Times* (April 19, 2002), A11.

The cabinet and parliament, the constitutional monarchy, the Constitutional Court, and an evolving semi-federal structure have come to enjoy legitimacy in the eyes of most Spaniards. Since the attempted coup of 1981, there has been no major threat to these institutions. The past three decades thus represent a significant shift to stable constitutional democracy—a sharp contrast to Spain's historical pattern of often-unstable and usually authoritarian state development.

Spain has, of course, been a late-developing democracy. The previous major effort to build Spanish democracy collapsed in the 1930s during the Spanish Civil War and gave way to Franco's long-term authoritarian rule. As Figure 13.1 illustrates, Spain stands out from other major West European states in the length of its periods of nondemocratic government in the twentieth century. The new, post-Franco participatory processes have included elections to the national parliament and to autonomous community parliaments, referendums, and competitive political parties and interest groups. Women's political roles have expanded substantially. Though no woman has yet become prime minister, Ana Palacio became a very prominent foreign

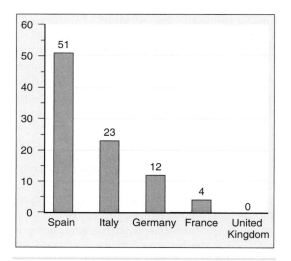

FIGURE 13.1   Years of Undemocratic Government Since 1918

TABLE 13.1   Major Landmarks in Spanish Political History

711	Moors complete their conquest of most of Iberian peninsula.
1469	Ferdinand of Aragon and Isabella of Castile marry, uniting their two Christian kingdoms.
1492	Christian reconquest of Spain completed with fall of Granada.
1516	Spanish Hapsburg rule begins.
1700	Spanish Bourbon rule begins.
1808	Napoleon conquers Spain, imposes his brother Joseph as Spanish king.
1810	Beginning of a series of Latin American revolutions against Spanish control.
1812	Joseph overthrown, new Spanish liberal constitution ushers in era of instability.
1936	Spanish Civil War between Republicans and Nationalists begins.
1939	Spanish Civil War ends with triumph of Francisco Franco.
1975	Francisco Franco dies.
1978	Democratic constitution ratified.
1986	Spain joins the European Communities.

minister; and more than one-fourth of the members of the Cortes are now women. Spain has in recent years been home to some workplace democracy in the private sector, such as the Mondragon cooperative network in the Basque Country, and has required works councils in all business corporations with 50 employees or more if at least 10 percent of the employees want them, but its government has not institutionalized codetermination methods of consulting employees on the scale employed in Germany or Sweden. Neo-corporatist arrangements among government, business, and labor, while employed in Spain on some occasions in recent years, have been less commonly used than in much of Northern Europe.[13]

No longer autarkic or predominantly agrarian, the Spanish economy has in recent years become an integral part of the European economy. The democratic Spanish government has fostered privatization of business enterprises while at the same time expanding educational opportunities, provision of health care, and social security. Public spending in Spain doubled during the 20 years between 1975 and 1995, largely due to the enormous growth of the Spanish welfare state. In sum, Spain has assumed most features of the modern European mixed economy. However, a persistent problem has been high unemployment, well above the European Union average for more than two decades, probably due to a combination of the legacy of the past autarkic policies of the Franco regime, continuing rigidities in Spanish labor markets, and EC/EU policies oriented more toward promoting low inflation than toward reducing unemployment.[14]

GOVERNMENTAL INSTITUTIONS

The Spanish Constitution of 1978 has established a cabinet-parliamentary form of government with a constitutional monarchy, modeled on the British system. However, despite his normally ceremonial functions, King Juan Carlos played a political role far beyond that of modern British monarchs during the critical transition to constitutional democracy, particularly in blocking the attempted antidemocratic coup of 1981. The Spanish Constitution emulates the German Basic Law in providing that the Congress of Deputies can remove the prime minister and government only through a "constructive vote of no confidence," in which the Congress elects a replacement by a majority vote. This provision has prolonged minority governments on three occasions. Spain has experienced a mixture between majority one-party governments (1982–1989 and 2000–2004) and minority governments kept in office by agreements with some smaller parties that have stopped short of full-scale coalitions.

The Executive

The formal constitutional title of the Spanish prime minister is "President of the Government." However, because the office is essentially prime ministerial rather than presidential in nature, this text will use the term "prime minister." At times since 1978, the prime minister has been the dominant leader in Spanish government to an extent comparable to the "Chancellor Democracy" in Germany under Adenauer. The Constitution fosters the centrality of the prime minister by its procedures for appointment of the prime minister and government. The Constitution provides for the king first to appoint the prime minister after consultation with the Congress of Deputies, subject to an absolute majority vote of the Congress on the first ballot (with only a simple majority required

on subsequent ballots). The prime minister then presents the government and its program to the Congress of Deputies for its approval. The Constitution also strengthens the prime minister by granting authority to appoint cabinet ministers from outside parliament (and outside the governing party) and to add and remove ministers. Perhaps more important than the constitutional provisions in influencing prime ministerial power has been the partisan balance in the Congress of Deputies. Felipe González, whose Socialist party held a Congress majority from 1982–1989, and José María Aznar, whose Popular party held a similar majority from 2000–2004, were able to dominate the policy-making process in ways that they could not as easily do when they lacked such a majority. In the absence of a majority, the prime minister must usually bargain with smaller parties to gain the support to be elected and to win passage of the government's programs. Prime ministers Adolfo Suárez and Leopoldo Calvo Sotelo never enjoyed legislative majorities, and González and Aznar lacked them during parts of their tenures in office.[15]

Most government ministers (except those "without portfolio") head departments of government (or ministries). Their upper-level associates in the administration are mostly

TABLE 13.2 Spanish Heads of Government Since 1976

Head of government	Time in office	Party affiliation
Adolfo Suárez	1976–1981	UCD
Leopoldo Calvo Sotelo	1981–1982	UCD
Felipe González	1982–1996	Socialist (PSOE)
José María Aznar	1996–2004	Popular (PP)
José Luis Rodríguez Zapatero	2004–	Socialist (PSOE)

The Rise and Fall of Prime Minister Adolfo Suárez

When King Juan Carlos named Adolfo Suárez as prime minister of Spain in July 1976, the appointment took many domestic and foreign observers by surprise because Suárez had been a relatively unknown official in the Franco regime and had demonstrated no pronounced leadership skills or commitment to democracy. However, the new prime minister was to lead Spain rapidly toward democratization and initiate negotiations that would eventually make possible its entry into the European Community in 1986. For a time, he was also able to head a new center-right political coalition, the Union of the Democratic Center (UCD), which won the first post-Franco democratic elections and provided parliamentary support for his government—until the UCD fragmented, leading to the downfall of Suárez and his government in 1981.

Suárez's most lasting contribution was almost certainly his prominent role in Spanish democratization. Whereas his predecessor, Carlos Arias Navarro, had proved incapable of moving the regime still populated largely by officials holding on to the Francoist past quickly toward democratic reforms, Suárez employed what Samuel Huntington has termed "Fabian strategy, blitzkrieg tactics" to accomplish democratization with lightning speed. By this, Huntington meant that the prime minister staggered the reforms sequentially, emphasizing one at a time (as British Fabian Socialists had suggested socialists should do in transforming capitalism into socialism) to avoid antagonizing too many defenders of the old regime simultaneously. The

blitzkrieg aspect (as practiced by Hitler's blitzkrieg tactics in World War II) involved compressing the sequential democratic reforms into a short period of time.[16]

Despite Suárez's successes in democratization and in impressing European Community and member state leaders sufficiently to launch Spain's bid for European Community membership, the prime minister encountered great difficulties in managing his coalition and in dealing with the demands of the Spanish regions for increasing powers at the expense of the central government. As the UCD that provided his base of support in parliament broke up into quarreling parties and factions, Suárez found himself unable to govern effectively and resigned after five years in office. A coup attempt, during which some members of the civil guard (still populated by many devotees of Franco's authoritarianism) seized the Cortes, nearly derailed constitutional democracy as Suárez stepped down. However, the king's timely intervention saved the democracy that Suárez had done so much to build.

The UCD disintegrated and was soon displaced as the major party of the center-right by the Popular Alliance, later renamed the Popular party. Suárez's efforts to revive his political fortunes through a new party were largely unsuccessful. The Socialists under Felipe González were to win the 1982 elections and govern Spain for the next 14 years. Despite his downfall and his inability to build a party that would be successful over the long term, Suárez was a key leader in the development of Spanish democracy. Even in this realm, however, his effort might not have proved successful in the long run without the assistance of the King.[17]

political appointees. Even though competitive examinations are required for entry into the civil service, political ties appear to influence many appointments. One recent analyst has noted that the system "is widely thought to be rife with abuse." Under the label of "clientelism," some scholars have discerned a pattern of links between influential patrons and societal clients permeating Spanish administration and society in a manner often associated with southern Europe and "less developed" countries. However, at least one recent study has questioned the extent of clientelism in Spain. Nonetheless, the Spanish mass media and judiciary have uncovered a sizeable number of scandals in recent years reaching into the Council of Ministers. Thus, the effectiveness, neutrality, and efficiency of Spanish administration have been called into serious question. Further complicating Spanish administration has been the growing assertiveness of many of the regional autonomous communities.[18]

The Parliament

By most accounts, the Spanish Cortes (parliament), composed of the Congress of Deputies and the Senate, has been relatively weak—largely reactive to the Council of Ministers even when the government has lacked a clear parliamentary majority, but especially docile when the government has possessed such a majority. The 350-member Congress of Deputies, elected by a modified proportional representation system for a four-year term of office (subject to earlier elections if called by the king upon the request of the prime minister), is the more powerful of the two chambers. It alone can replace the government by the constructive vote of no confidence, and it can override the Senate on legislative matters. The Senate, mostly elected by popular vote but partially appointed by the regional parliaments, possesses only slight delaying powers. Although a British-style question time is employed in both legislative chambers as a means of holding the government

accountable, it has proved fairly ineffective. Parliamentary committees have been generally weak vis-à-vis the government also.[19]

The Constitutional Court, Judiciary, and Legal System

Like France, Germany, and Italy, Spain possesses a legal system based on Roman law, rather than the Anglo-American common law system. The judicial system was subordinated to the executive during the authoritarian Franco regime but has become independent since the establishment of constitutional democracy in Spain. Separate from the regular Spanish judiciary, and exercising powers of judicial review on constitutional matters, is the Constitutional Court, a new institution created in 1978. The Constitutional Court is composed of 12 members, who are judges or lawyers. The government nominates two of these (subject to parliamentary approval), the Congress of Deputies names four by a three-fifths majority, the Senate names four by a three-fifths majority, and the General Council of the Judiciary names two. Each serves for a nine-year term, with one-third of the positions filled every three years. The Constitutional Court handles appeals concerning constitutionality on petition by the prime minister, 50 members of the Congress or the Senate, the head of government or parliament of an autonomous community, or the Defender of the People (the Spanish title of the ombudsperson, borrowed from Scandinavia, and responsible for protecting individual rights). Under a unique Spanish procedure, it may also protect individual rights by blocking the application of a law or executive order without ruling on the constitutionality of the law or order. Unquestionably, the Constitutional Court has become an important part of the Spanish state structure, often determining the boundaries (ill-defined in the Constitution) between the autonomous communities and the national government and handing down rulings in significant civil-liberties cases.[20]

The Autonomous Communities

As previously noted, national-regional relations have caused conflict during much of Spanish history. The Constitution of 1978 represented a compromise between the centralism of the Franco regime and the decentralized federalism favored by most of the political Left. Like most compromises, it was ambiguous and left many matters to be sorted out through political bargaining. The Constitution granted supreme authority to the national government but provided for the formation of autonomous communities that would allow particularly distinctive regions with their own "national" identities (such as the Basque Country, Catalonia, and Galicia) to gain various degrees of autonomy and home rule. What has evolved has been the establishment of 17 autonomous communities, including all of Spain, with each autonomous community possessing its own distinctive statute of autonomy negotiated with the central government. Most autonomous communities are further subdivided into provinces, though six are single-province autonomous communities. Some analysts have described the Spanish system of national-regional relations as "semi-federal" or "quasi-federal," reflecting the lack of a German- or American-type federal division of powers in the constitution but the considerable devolution of authority established by law.[21] Others have termed it "asymmetric federalism," calling attention to the variations in the powers possessed by the different autonomous communities, as opposed to the uniform powers assigned to the states in Germany and the United States.[22] Still other scholars have contrasted Spain's frequently "confrontational" national-regional relations to the "cooperative" German national-state patterns.[23]

Most of the continuing disputes between the Spanish national government and the autonomous communities have been handled peacefully as matters for political or legal resolution. The Constitutional Court has played an important part in determining issues of constitutionality. For example, it rejected as unconstitutional legislation by which the national Cortes sought to make regional authority uniform.

Despite the generally peaceful resolution of disputes between the Spanish national government and the regions, there has been one major exception. In the Basque Country, the Basque Homeland and Liberty (ETA) terrorist group, first organized in the 1960s against the centralist

TABLE 13.3 The Spanish Autonomous Communities

Autonomous community	Capital	Population
Andalucia	Sevilla	7,300,000
Aragòn	Zaragoza	1,200,000
Asturias	Oviedo	1,100,000
Balearic Islands	Palma de Mallorca	800,000
Canary Islands	Sta.Cruz de Tenerife/ Las Palmas de Gran Canaria	1,700,000
Cantabria	Santander	500,000
Castile and Leon	Valldolid	2,500,000
Castile-La Mancha	Toledo	1,700,000
Catalonia	Barcelona	6,300,000
Valencia (Community of)	Valencia	4,100,000
Extremadura	Merida	1,100,000
Galicia	Santiago de Compostela	2,700,000
Madrid	Madrid	5,200,000
Murcia	Murcia	1,100,000
Navarra	Pamplona	500,000
Pais Vasco (Basque Country)	Vitoria	2,100,000
Rioja (La)	Logroño	100,000

and authoritarian Franco regime, has continued its campaigns of violence during the constitutional democratic era. The Spanish government has responded, even after democratization, with examples of state-sponsored violence, notably in the 1980s. Recently it has banned pro-ETA parties and sanctioned prison terms for Basques as young as 14 if they engage in riots. Demanding an independent Basque nation-state of their own, the ETA members are linked to a political party that wins only 10–20 percent of the vote in Basque elections. Nonetheless, the terror campaign has been highly disruptive and has caused more than 800 deaths.[24]

ELECTIONS, POLITICAL PARTIES, AND INTEREST GROUPS

As the Spanish democratic system has developed since the 1970s, a new system of elections, political parties, and interest groups has emerged to replace the authoritarian political processes and intermediaries of the Franco era. After considerable flux in the early post-Franco years, particularly on the center-right side of the political spectrum, the electoral, party, and interest group patterns have become institutionalized in Spain.

The Electoral Process

The Spanish employ a modified system of proportional representation in elections to the Congress of Deputies, using the 50 provinces as multimember districts. Elections must be held at least once every four years, though the prime minister can call them before the full four-year term has expired. Because parties must win at least 3 percent of the popular vote in order to gain legislative representation, and only a few seats are available in most multimember districts, the largest parties receive more seats than their popular vote percentages would indicate.[25]

In four elections, one party has been able to win an outright majority in the Congress of Deputies while falling short of a popular majority. In 2000, for example, the Popular party of Prime Minister Aznar was able to win more than 52 percent of the Congress seats with just 44 percent of the popular vote. However, regional parties with geographically concentrated strength have consistently been able to win parliamentary seats, often in sufficient numbers to deny a clear majority to either major party. Voter turnout in Spain has ranged between 68 percent and 80 percent during the post-Franco era and has been relatively stable. Table 13.4 presents the results of the most

TABLE 13.4 Results of the Elections of 2000 and 2004 for the Congress of Deputies

Party	Popular vote %	Seats	% of seats
2004			
Socialist (PSOE)	43	164	47
Popular (PP)	38	148	42
Convergence & Union (CiU)	3	10	5
United Left (IU)	5	5	3
Other	12	23	13
Total	101	350	100
2000			
Popular (PP)	44	183	52
Socialist (PSOE)	34	125	36
Convergence & Union (CiU)	4	15	4
United Left (IU)	5	8	2
Other	13	19	6
Total	100	350	100

TABLE 13.5 Party Percentages of the Popular Vote in Congress of Deputies Elections, 1979–2004

Party	1979	1982	1986	1989	1993	1996	2000	2004
PSOE	30.5	48.2	44.1	39.6	38.8	37.5	34.0	42.6
AP/PP	6.0	26.0	26.0	25.8	34.8	38.9	44.0	37.6
PCE/IU	10.8	4.1	4.6	9.1	9.2	9.2	5.4	5.0
CiU	2.7	3.9	5.0	5.0	4.9	4.9	4.2	3.2
UCD	35.0	6.8						
CDS		2.8	9.2	7.2				
Others	15.0	8.2	11.1	13.3	12.3	9.5	12.5	11.6
Total	100.0	100.0	100.0	100.0	100.0	100.0	100.1	100.0

recent elections to the Congress of Deputies, while Table 13.5 illustrates the shifting partisan percentages of the popular vote in the Congress of Deputies elections since 1979.

Membership in the less-powerful Senate is determined in part by popular election using a plurality system in the provinces and in part by appointments by the governments of the autonomous communities. Reforms of the Senate and its selection process are likely in the near future.

In addition to elections to the two chambers of the Cortes and regional elections, referendums are a part of the Spanish political process. Spain falls in the middle range of European countries in frequency of referendums. Since Franco's death, there have been national referendums on political reform, the Constitution of 1978, and membership in NATO, as well as a number of regional referendums concerning grants of autonomy.

Political Parties

The Spanish political party system has evolved into one centered on competition between two major parties, the Popular party (PP) on the center-right and the Spanish Socialist Workers party (PSOE) on the center-left. Nevertheless, the Spanish Communist party (PCE) and its allies in the United Left (IU) also compete on a national basis; and regional parties consistently win seats in the Basque Country and Catalonia.

Moreover, in the early post-Franco era, a coalition of centrist parties called the Union of the Democratic Center (UCD) dominated Spanish politics for a few years, backing Prime Minister Adolfo Suárez and then Prime Minister Leopoldo Calvo Sotelo. However, this coalition fragmented; and the UCD suffered a severe defeat in the 1982 elections, from which it never recovered. The Socialists led by Prime Minister Felipe González governed Spain from 1982 to 1996, and returned to power in 2004 under Prime Minister José Luis Rodríguez Zapatero, while the Popular party led by Prime Minister José María Aznar governed from 1996 to 2004.

Founded in 1976 as the Popular Alliance (AP), the Popular party (PP) reorganized as the Popular Coalition (PC) and took its present name in 1988 as it sought to expand to include a number of former UCD leaders. Scoring poorly in the initial post-Franco elections, when it was tainted by the association of many of its leaders with Franco's authoritarianism, the Popular party has emerged as the chief voice of moderate conservatism. Under Aznar's leadership, it won the largest popular vote of any party in both the 1996 and 2000 elections. Ideologically, the party emphasizes tax reduction and privatization, resistance to further decentralization, a hard line on terrorism and law and order, and a moderate social conservatism, and draws its support particularly from the business community and practicing Roman Catholics. It also supported the Bush administration's policies in Iraq, defying Spanish public opinion to do so. However, ideology has been less important than personal appeals of the party leaders in recent Spanish elections. Under heavy influence from Prime Minister Aznar, the party endorsed First Deputy Prime Minister Mariano Rajoy as its leader for the 2004 elections. Rajoy, known as a skilled negotiator and a man with a good sense of humor, won the nod over the better-known economy minister Rodrigo Rato, in September 2003. Though most pre-election polls had given Rajoy and the Popular party the edge in the 2004 elections, the outcome returned the Socialist party to power.[26]

Much older than the Popular party is the Spanish Socialist Workers party (PSOE), with origins dating back to 1879. The Socialists long adhered to a Marxist ideology, even long after their split with the Communists in 1921. The Socialists' advocacy of social welfare, workers' rights, land reform, and secularism brought the party into sharp conflict with Spanish conservatives and contributed to the Spanish Civil War. During the Franco era, when all opposition parties were banned, the Socialists had to operate from exile or underground. Felipe González, who worked underground inside Spain and became party leader in 1974, led the party away from Marxism toward moderate social democratic positions in the post-Franco democratic era. As prime minister, González embraced a market economy with extensive privatizations while expanding the previously meager Spanish social programs into a sizeable welfare state. He also led the party to support membership in both the European Union and NATO, despite its previous opposition to the latter. Therefore, as in much of Western Europe, the ideological and policy distance between the two major par-

ties in Spain has narrowed markedly. After losing control of the government in the 1996 elections, the PSOE struggled to find an effective leader who could restore it to power. In July 2000, it named 39-year-old José Luis Rodríguez Zapatero as its new secretary-general, after a closely fought contest; and he has directed the party's programs, strategies, and tactics since then. Therefore, the 2004 elections featured a battle between the two major party leaders, Zapatero for the Socialists and Rajoy for the Popular party, for the post of prime minister, at the same time that they offered a contest between the parties for control of the Cortes. The devastating bombings in Madrid on the eve of the elections, at first attributed by the government to Basque terrorists despite evidence pointing to Islamic terrorists linked to Al-Qaeda, apparently led a significant number of Spaniards to vote against the Popular party due to its unpopular alliance with the Bush administration concerning Iraq and its apparent deception concerning the identities of the terrorists. Voter turnout rose markedly above expectations, to 77 percent. Zapatero, the new prime minister, had distanced himself and his party from the United States' policies in Iraq, in contrast to the Popular party. Because the PSOE lacks a majority in the Cortes, it needs to obtain support from some of the small parties in order to enact its programs.[27]

The third most important national party in democratic Spain has been the Spanish Communist party (PCE), which split from the PSOE in 1921. Dedicated originally to Marxism-Leninism and support for the Soviet Union, it was suppressed for decades under the Franco regime and reemerged as a legal party in 1977. Since then, it has advocated democracy while positioning itself to the left of the Socialists by criticizing their privatization and market-oriented policies, their shift to support for NATO, and the scandals of many of their officeholders. The Communist party fragmented in the 1980s, but its major component formed an alliance with some smaller leftist parties called the United Left (IU) and has competed electorally on this basis since the 1989 election. The 2000 elections saw a sharp decline in the United Left vote and its number of seats in the Congress of Deputies, followed by a further, but slight, decline in 2004.

Most of the other political parties in Spain are regionally based, indicating the continuing importance of the central-regional conflicts. The largest of these is Convergence and Union (CiU), an alliance of moderate Catalan nationalists that currently holds third place in the Cortes and plays a major role in politics in Catalonia. Founded and led for many years by Jordi Pujol, it dominated the government of Catalonia for more than two decades after 1980, though it lost control there in 2003 to a Socialist-led coalition. Between 1996 and 2000, the CiU bargained with Aznar and the Popular party to sustain their minority government in exchange for concessions on autonomy. Other regional parties include the moderate Basque Nationalist Party (PNV) and the radical, pro-ETA Batasuna, the latter of which has recently been outlawed by the Spanish Supreme Court and the Constitutional Court at the request of the Spanish government. Spanish Foreign Minister Ana Palacio defended the ban, arguing, "What has been outlawed is not a political ideology but a terrorist group that seeks to use the institutions for legitimacy…. A democracy must be equipped with the means to defend itself against those who seek to destroy it." Even many moderate Basques, however, have condemned the ban as undemocratic. Speaking for his own party, Batasuna, which has been banned, Joseba Azpeitia, mayor of the town of Zestoa in the Basque Country, has retorted to the Spanish government, "We are a people who are in favor of self-determination and who remain insubordinate in the face of injustices. We are a town that wants to welcome back its sons who have been deported or are in prison."[28]

> "What has been outlawed is not a political ideology but a terrorist group that seeks to use the institutions for legitimacy…. A democracy must be equipped with the means to defend itself against those who seek to destroy it."
>
> Foreign Minister Ana Palacio, *"Why Batasuna Must Be Banned," Financial Times (September 3, 2002), 15.*

> "We are a people who are in favor of self-determination and who remain insubordinate in the face of injustices. We are a town that wants to welcome back its sons who have been deported or are in prison."
>
> Batasuna Mayor Joseba Azpeitia of Zestoa, *quoted by Leslie Crawford, Financial Times (August 24, 2002), 8.*

Interest Groups

In contrast to the Franco era, when interest groups (except for the Roman Catholic Church) were controlled by the state, interest groups have become important democratic intermediaries that supplement and penetrate the party system. Nonetheless, most analysts judge their influence to be less than that of groups in most Northern European countries. Neo-corporatist consultations in which the government has brokered agreements between organized business and the trade unions have sometimes characterized Spanish economic decision-making, for example, the Interconfederal Framework Agreement of 1980, the National Agreement on Employment in 1981, and several agreements in the 1990s. However, this pattern has not been the norm in Spain. The majoritarian Socialist governments of the 1980s and early 1990s took the view that they possessed a "mandate" to govern in the public interest and foreswore most neo-corporatism, despite pressures from their erstwhile allies in the General Union of Workers (UGT).[29]

As in Western Europe generally, organized business has represented the most powerful part of Spanish interest group politics. Under Franco, business employers enjoyed significant influence, along with the Roman Catholic Church and the military, but had no independent interest group organization. Since Franco, the Spanish Confederation of Employers' Organizations (CEOE) has emerged as the primary peak association for business employers. Not affiliated with either major party, the CEOE has generally supported the Popular party but has enjoyed influence in Socialist-led governments also.

Organized labor enjoyed a brief spurt of growth in the 1970s after years of repression by Franco. However, the labor unions have been split between the General Union of Workers (UGT), long associated with the Socialists, and the Workers' Commissions (CCOO), traditionally affiliated with the Communists. Among West European states, Spain ranks below all except France in the percentage of its workforce in labor unions. Most estimates are that unions now likely represent 15–20 percent of the Spanish workforce, though a few put the figure even lower than that. Moreover, the General Union of Workers ended its affiliation with the Spanish Socialist Workers Party in 1990. The two major federations of unions have worked with one another more closely in recent years than in the past, but their influence is widely perceived to be less than that of business employers.

Agriculture remains an important, though declining, part of the Spanish economy; and agricultural interest groups exert influence on Spanish governmental stances concerning the European Union's Common Agricultural Policy. The National Agricultural and Livestock Farmers Federation (CNAG) represents large landowners who see themselves primarily as agribusinessmen. In fact, it is a member of the CEOE, the peak association for business. Agricultural groups representing small farmers and farm workers are relatively fragmented and weak.

The Roman Catholic Church and the armed forces, which enjoyed great influence during the Franco regime, have lost some of their clout in recent years. Like the rest of Western Europe, Spain has seen the spread of secularism and declining church attendance. Nonetheless, the Church itself and the Catholic lay organization, God's Work (*Opus Dei*), possess some continuing influence, especially when the Popular party controls the government. The military has been firmly under civilian control since the early 1980s, but it has been a factor influencing Spanish entry into NATO, firm antiterrorist approaches, and general conservatism.[30]

Although participation in interest groups and membership in political parties is lower in Spain than in most of the West European nation-states that have longer democratic histories than Spain has, Spanish voter turnout has been near the West European average and much higher than the American rate. The electoral, political party, and interest group systems of contemporary Spain clearly illustrate the dramatic shift that has been made from the authoritarian Franco period and from the turbulent and unsuccessful Spanish experiment with democracy in the 1930s.

CONCLUSIONS

Spain, like Germany and Italy, has undergone major transformations in the past century. Hobbled in the past by unsuccessful efforts to cope with the crises of modernization, Spain has addressed these with surprising success since 1975, though Basque terrorism and relatively high unemployment remain persistent problems. In addressing major modernization issues effectively, Spain has broken out of its past isolation from the mainstream of West European politics, economics, and society to become an important nation-state in the European Union. The next chapter will focus on how Spain came to join the European Community/European Union, the roles that it has played in the EC/EU, and the impact of the EC/EU on Spanish politics.

SUMMARY

- Ferdinand and Isabella, married in 1469, brought the kingdoms of Aragon and Castile together to form Spain, completed the Roman Catholic "reconquest" of the Iberian peninsula from the Muslim Moors, instituted the Inquisition that linked Spain firmly to Roman Catholicism, and laid the foundations for a great Spanish Empire; however, they and their Hapsburg successors failed to build a modern Spanish nation-state.

- Spain declined economically and politically as a great power after the 1640s—a decline relative to both England and France that would continue through the seventeenth and eighteenth centuries.

- The Spanish state became increasingly centralized and authoritarian under the Spanish Bourbon Dynasty that took office in 1700; in the nineteenth century, multiple constitutions, civil wars, and military coups and attempted coups roiled Spanish politics and society.

- Spain lost most of its overseas Latin American empire between 1810 and 1825 and lost Cuba, Puerto Rico, and the Philippines as a result of the Spanish-American War in 1898.

- Basque and Catalan nationalism surged in the nineteenth and twentieth centuries, resisting dictation from the capital at Madrid and creating a center-periphery division in Spain that continues to the present.

- After the overthrow of the dictatorship of Miguel Primo de Rivera in 1931, Spain briefly became a democratic republic; however, it was torn by conflict, and Francisco Franco's victory in the Spanish Civil War (1936–1939) instituted an authoritarian dictatorship that endured until Franco's death in 1975.

- Franco's authoritarian regime, like most of its predecessors, coped rather unsuccessfully with nation-building (due to antagonism of regional nationalism, especially in Basque Country and Catalonia), state building (due to repressive government), participation (due to mandated popular passivity), and distribution (due to economic stagnation and inequality in the early decades, though some growth occurred later).

- Under the leadership of Franco's designated successor, King Juan Carlos, and Prime Minister Adolfo Suárez, Spain underwent a rapid transition to constitutional democracy (1978 constitution) and achieved entry into the European Community (1986).

- Despite lingering problems of Basque terrorism and relative high unemployment, democratic Spain since 1978 has addressed the major crises of modernization more successfully than any of its predecessor regimes did.

- Spain has a cabinet-parliamentary form of government with a constitutional monarch, modeled generally on the British system.

- The Spanish prime minister, or "president of the government," (currently José Luis Rodríguez Zapatero) is the head of government, while the monarch (now King Juan Carlos) is the head of state.

- The prime minister is subject to removal only by a constructive vote of no confidence in the Congress of Deputies (emulating Germany); this provision has facilitated Spanish minority governments, in which the prime minister's party (as at present) lacks a majority in the Congress of Deputies but can keep him in office because the other parties are too fragmented to agree on an alternative prime minister.

- The Spanish Cortes (parliament) is composed of the Congress of Deputies and the

Senate; the Congress of Deputies is the more powerful of the two chambers.

- Like France, Germany, and Italy, Spain possesses a legal system based on Roman law.

- The Constitutional Court, enjoying substantial powers of constitutional judicial review, has resolved numerous legal disputes between autonomous communities and the central government and has made significant rulings concerning civil liberties.

- Spain encompasses 17 autonomous communities, the powers of which vary in a pattern that some analysts describe as "asymmetric federalism."

- The Basque Homeland and Liberty (ETA) terrorist group, first organized against the centralist and authoritarian Franco regime, has continued its violent campaigns.

- The most important Spanish elections are those for the Congress of Deputies, using a modified proportional representation system; Spain falls in the middle range of European countries in the frequency of popular referendums.

- The two major Spanish political parties are the Popular party (PP) on the center-right and the Spanish Socialist Workers Party (PSOE) on the center-left; the PP has roots in the Franco regime but is now moderately conservative, while the PSOE has Marxian socialist origins but is now moderately left reformist.

- Smaller parties, including the United Left and various regional parties, often hold the balance of power in parliament, though coalition governments are infrequent in Spain.

- The Spanish Confederation of Employers' Organizations is the primary peak business interest group, and the two major labor union groups have been the General Union of Workers and the Workers' Commissions; interest groups are generally less influential in Spain than in northern Europe.

- The Roman Catholic Church has lost much of its traditional influence in Spain, with Spanish society becoming increasingly secular since the 1970s.

- Spain, like Germany and Italy, has undergone major transformations in the past century; Spanish constitutional democracy and integration into the EU have become well-established.

ENDNOTES

1. For the three major "waves" of democratization and the role of Spain, see Samuel P. Huntington, *The Third Wave: Democratization in the Late Twentieth Century* (Norman, OK: University of Oklahoma Press, 1991), esp. Ch. 1.
2. Quotation is from John Huxtable Elliott, *Imperial Spain, 1469–1716* (New York: St. Martin's, 1963), 97. Also see John Edwards, *The Spain of the Catholic Monarchs, 1474–1520* (Malden, MA: Blackwell, 2000), and Henry Kamen, *Spain, 1469–1714: A Society of Conflict*, 2nd ed. (New York: Longman, 1991).
3. Paul Kennedy, *The Rise and Fall of the Great Powers* (New York: Random House, 1987), Ch. 2; Elliott, *Imperial Spain*, 373–378.
4. Kamen, *Spain, 1469–1714*, 236.
5. Rhea Marsh Smith, *Spain: A Modern History* (Ann Arbor, MI: University of Michigan Press, 1965), esp. 279–281; Kamen, *Spain, 1469–1714*, 264–269.
6. Marianne Beiberg, *The Making of the Basque Nation* (Cambridge: Cambridge University Press, 1989); Juan Díez Medrano, *Divided Nations: Class, Politics, and Nationalism in the Basque Country and Catalonia* (Ithaca, NY: Cornell University Press, 1995); Daniele Conversi, *The Basques, the Catalans, and Spain: Alternative Routes to Nationalist Mobilisation* (Reno, NV: University of Nevada Press, 1997); M. K. Flynn, *Ideology, Mobilization, and the Nation: The Rise of Irish, Basque, and Carlist Nationalist Movements in the Nineteenth and Early Twentieth Centuries* (New York: St. Martin's Press, 2000).

7. Raymond Carr, *Spain, 1808–1939* (Oxford: Oxford University Press, 1970), esp. 430–455.

8. Carr, *Spain, 1808–1939*, 366–379; Smith, *Spain: A Modern History*, 414–415.

9. The quotation is from Gabriel Jackson, *The Spanish Republic and the Civil War, 1931–1939* (Princeton: Princeton University Press, 1964), 493; George Esenwein and Adrian Shubert, *Spain at War: The Spanish Civil War in Context, 1931–1939* (New York: Longman, 1995); Hugh Thomas, *The Spanish Civil War*, rev. ed. (New York: Harper & Row, 1977); Raymond Carr, *The Spanish Tragedy: The Civil War in Perspective* (London: Weidenfeld and Nicolson, 1977).

10. Paul Preston, *Franco: A Biography* (New York: HarperCollins, 1994); Raymond Carr and Juan Pablo Fusi Aizpurua, *Spain: Dictatorship to Democracy*, 2nd ed. (London: George Allen & Unwin, 1981); David Gilmour, *The Transformation of Spain: From Franco to the Constitutional Monarchy* (New York: Quartet Books, 1985); Juan J. Linz, "An Authoritarian Regime: Spain," in Stanley G. Payne, ed., *Politics and Society in Twentieth-Century Spain* (New York: Franklin Watts, 1976), 160–207.

11. Huntington, *The Third Wave*, esp. Ch. 2; Gilmour, *The Transformation of Spain*; Paul Preston, *The Triumph of Democracy in Spain* (London: Routledge, 1986).

12. John Newhouse, *Europe Adrift* (New York: Pantheon Books, 1997), 23-56; Conversi, *The Basques, the Catalans, and Spain*, Ch. 6; Díez Medrano, *Divided Nations*, 144–151, 167–189; Albert Balcells, *Catalan Nationalism* (New York: St. Martin's, 1996), 169–201; "A Survey of Spain," *The Economist* 357 (November 25, 2000); Kenneth McRoberts, *Catalonia: Nation-Building Without a State* (Oxford: Oxford University Press, 2001); Emma Daly, "Amnesty Says Spain Is Racist in Its Treatment of Immigrants," *New York Times*, April 19, 2002, A11.

13. On Spanish workplace democracy, see Martin Carnoy and Derek Shearer, *Economic Democracy* (Armonk, NY: M. E. Sharpe, 1980), 149–152, 188; "A Survey of Spain," *The Economist* 14; and Marc van der Meer, "Spain," in Bernard Ebbinghaus and Jelle Visser, eds., *The Societies of Europe: Trade Unions in Western Europe Since 1945* (Basingstoke: Macmillan, 2000), 573–603.

14. Mary Farrell, *Spain in the EU: The Road to Economic Convergence* (Houndmills, Basingstoke: Palgrave, 2001), esp. 46–477 on unemployment and 97–108 on the welfare state.

15. Paul Heywood, "Governing a New Democracy: The Power of the Prime Minister in Spain," *West European Politics* 14, 2 (April 1991); John Gibbons, *Spanish Politics Today* (Manchester: Manchester University Press, 1999), 72–78.

16. Huntington, *The Third Wave*, 125–126.

17. Carr and Fusi, *Spain: Dictatorship to Democracy*, Chs. 10, 11; Preston, *The Triumph of Democracy in Spain*.

18. Gibbons, *Spanish Politics Today*, 123, is the source of the "rife with abuse" quotation. On clientelism and its limits in Spain, see Jonathan Hopkin, "A 'Southern' Model of Electoral Mobilization? Clientelism and Electoral Politics in Spain," *West European Politics* 24, 1 (January 2001), 115–136.

19. Juan L. Paniagua Soto, "Spain: A Fledgling Parliament, 1977–1997," *Parliamentary Affairs* 50, 3 (July 1997), 410–422.

20. Gibbons, *Spanish Politics Today*, 78–83; Thomas Lancaster and Michael Gates, "Spain," in Alan Katz, ed., *Legal Traditions and Systems* (New York: Greenwood Press, 1986), 360–380.

21. John Gibbons, "Spain: A Semi Federal State," in D. McIver, ed., *The Multinational State* (London: Macmillan, 1999); E. Rámon Arango, *Spain: Democracy Regained* (Boulder, CO: Westview, 1995), 175.

22. Donald Share, "Politics in Spain," in Gabriel A. Almond, Russell J. Dalton, and G. Bingham Powell, eds., *European Politics Today*, 2nd ed. (New York: Longman, 2001), 269.

23. Tanja Börzel, "Europeanization and Territorial Institutional Change: Toward Cooperative Regionalism," in Maria Green Cowles, James Caporaso, and Thomas Risse, eds., *Transforming Europe: Europeanization and Domestic Change* (Ithaca, NY: Cornell University Press, 2001), 137–158.

24. "A Survey of Spain," *The Economist*, esp. 11–13; "Aznar Hurt, ETA Clobbered," *The Economist* 359 (May 19, 2001). For a generally negative assessment of the overall impact of Spanish decentralization on democracy, see Alfred P. Montero, "Decentralizing Democracy: Spain and Brazil in Comparative Perspective,"

Comparative Politics 33, 2 (January 2001), 149–170.

25. Richard Gunther, "Electoral Laws, Party Systems, and Elites: The Case of Spain," *American Political Science Review* 83, 3 (September 1989), 835–858.

26. Joshua Levitt, "A Cigar, a Deck of Cards, and a Sense of Humour," *Financial Times*, September 1, 2003, 4; Levitt, "Spanish Premier to Anoint Rajoy as His Successor," *Financial Times*, September 1, 2003, 4; Levitt, "Party Confirms Rajoy as Candidate for PM," *Financial Times*, September 3, 2003, 6; Gibbons, *Spanish Politics Today*, 38–43; Charlemagne, "José Luis Rodríguez Zapatero, Spain's New Socialist," *The Economist* 359 (January 27, 2001), 54.

27. Elaine Sciolino, "Following Attacks, Spain's Governing Party Is Beaten," *New York Times*, March 15, 2004, A1 and A10; David E. Sanger, "Blow to Bush: Ally Rejected," *New York Times*, March 15, 2004, A1 and A11; "Zapatero Formará Gobierno en Solitario con Acuerdos Puntuales," *El Pais*, March 15, 2004; Gibbons, *Spanish Politics Today*, 44–48; Charlemagne, "José Luis Rodríguez Zapatero," 54.

28. Leslie Crawford, "Divided by Violence," *Financial Times*, August 24, 2002, 8; Crawford, "Spanish Court Bars Basque Coalition from Local Elections," *Financial Times*, May 10, 2003, 8; Emma Daly, "Spanish Court Outlaws a Basque Party, Seeing Terrorism Links," *New York Times*, March 18, 2003, A7; Ana Palacio, "Why Batasuna Must Be Banned," *Financial Times*, September 3, 2002, 15.

29. Arango, *Spain: Democracy Regained*, 246–250; Gibbons, *Spanish Politics Today*, 125–126.

30. J. M. Molins and A. Casademunt, "Pressure Groups and the Articulation of Interests," *West European Politics* 21, 4 (October 1998), 124–146; Gibbons, *Spanish Politics Today*, 124–129; Richard Gillespie, "The Break-Up of the 'Socialist Family': Party-Union Relations in Spain, 1982-89," *West European Politics* 13, 1 (January 1990), 47–62; "A Survey of Spain," *The Economist* 14, 18; Van der Meer, "Spain," 573–603.

Chapter 14

SPAIN AND THE EUROPEAN UNION

"Regeneration is the desire; Europeanization is the means to the desire. Truly one thinks clearly from the principle that Spain is the problem and Europe the solution."

—José Ortega y Gasset, Spanish philosopher, *cited by Michael Marks,*
The Formation of European Policy in Post-Franco Spain (1997), 15.

Until the end of its long authoritarian era under dictator Francisco Franco (1939–1975), Spain was ineligible to enter the European Communities or even attain associate status with them and therefore stood on the sidelines as the critical early stages of European integration occurred. Even after moving toward constitutional democracy and beginning accession negotiations with the EC, Spain was unable to gain formal EC entry until 1986, due largely to difficulties of meeting the requirements of the EC and overcoming French resistance. Thus, Spain is the newcomer among the five pre-2004 major nation-states in the European Union, though Poland joined as a still-newer major member in 2004. The long Spanish desire for regeneration through Europeanization, noted by Ortega y Gasset in the introductory quotation above, is closely related to the popularity of European integration that continues to characterize Spain to a high degree.

Despite its late entry and its economic backwardness relative to France, Germany, Italy, and Britain, Spain has become an important player in EU affairs, particularly in devel-

oping its cohesion policies and its relationships with Latin America and the Arab world. Because Spanish constitutional democracy has been shaped extensively first by the Spanish aspiration to be a part of European integration and then by actual membership in the EC/EU, the impact of Europeanization on Spain has been highly significant. The specific effects on Spain's evolving relations between its central government and its autonomous communities and on an array of Spanish public policies, such as environmental, competition, and fisheries policies that were at first markedly at odds with EC/EU patterns, have also been profound.

THE DEVELOPMENT OF THE SPANISH RELATIONSHIP WITH THE EC/EU

Spain as an Outsider: The Franco Era

As France, West Germany, Italy, and the Benelux countries began their moves toward economic and political integration in the years after World War II, Spain under the Franco regime stood in political isolation. Not only was the Spanish government authoritarian; it had come to power with the aid of Nazi Germany and Fascist Italy. Though a nonbelligerent, and at times a neutral, during World War II, Franco's Spanish government was widely viewed as sympathetic to Hitler and Mussolini. Especially on the Socialist and Communist left, but in other quarters also, there was a widespread determination among West European leaders after the war to ostracize Spain as long as it was ruled by Franco (who was to remain dictator of Spain until his death in 1975).

Spurred by a perception that the two political systems shared anti-Communist ideological goals, and desirous of enlisting Spain as a strategic ally in the Cold War, the United States partially ended Spain's isolation by resuming diplomatic relations with it in 1951 and in 1953 signing the Pact of Madrid, under which the Americans established military bases in Spain and granted the Franco regime a loan of $226 million. However, America's European partners in the North Atlantic Treaty Organization (NATO) would not permit Spain's entry into this key mutual security organization.[1]

Spain was less isolated from most of Western Europe economically than it was politically. However, the Franco regime pursued an economic policy emphasizing self-sufficiency (autarky) behind protective tariff barriers until 1957, when Franco instituted a governmental change that gave key economic posts to ministers who sought increased foreign trade and investment.

As both the European Economic Community (EEC) and the British-initiated European Free Trade Association (EFTA) took shape in the late 1950s, the Spanish government initially hoped that the loosely organized EFTA would absorb the EEC and that Spain might be able to develop some relationship with it. It was clear from the outset that the political goals of integration among the constitutional democracies of the EEC would be incompatible with the authoritarian government of Spain. In December 1961, the European Parliamentary Assembly of the EEC endorsed the Birkelbach report named after German Social Democrat, Willy Birkelbach, which stated that democratic government was a prerequisite not just for membership in the European Community (EC) but also for association status with it.[2]

Nevertheless, the economic successes of the EEC relative to EFTA, and Britain's 1961 decision to seek membership in the EEC, led Spain to make an application for association status in 1962, undeterred by the Birkelbach report. Although the conservative governments in France and West Germany gave Spain some encouragement, other member states were unenthusiastic. The European Parliament, which had endorsed the Birkelbach report, was firmly opposed to granting association status to Spain. Therefore, the most that Spain could achieve vis-à-vis the European Community as long as Franco was in power was a preferential trade agreement between Spain and the EC, signed in Luxembourg in June 1970. This agreement provided for a mutual reduction of tariffs and import quotas.[3]

Spain's Quest for Admission to the European Community

However, the opposition to Franco both internally and among exiles from Spain emphasized Spain's continuing exclusion from "Europe" and the need to democratize Spain in order to join the European integration project. The attraction of membership in the European Community (EC) was eventually to prove so compelling in Spain that it united all Spanish political parties (both pro- and anti-Franco) in support of seeking entry to the EC following Franco's death in 1975. Reasons for the attraction of "Europe" for Spaniards were varied. Most perceived economic benefits from linkage to economies that were more prosperous than Spain's (despite the dangers that integration posed to some obsolete Spanish economic sectors that had long been propped up by protection and subsidies). Symbolically, many saw EC membership as a means of promoting "progress" and ending Spanish isolation. All democratic parties certainly viewed EC membership as a guarantee for democratization and a means of consolidating democracy once it was established in Spain. Many analysts have concluded that European integration played an important role in fostering the rapid democratization that occurred in Spain after the demise of Franco, since the EC and its member state governments made it quite clear that Spanish entry was unthinkable without internal democratization.[4]

King Juan Carlos became the Spanish head of state following Franco's death, as had been established under Spanish law at Franco's bidding. In his first speech in this role to the Spanish parliament (Cortes), the king stressed the prime importance of Spanish integration into Europe:

> Europe must identify itself with Spain, and we the Spaniards are European. It is an urgent necessity that the two sides understand this and draw the appropriate consequences.[5]

Despite the king's enthusiasm for European integration and his endorsement of Spanish democratization, his first prime minister, Carlos Arias Navarro, a holdover from the Franco regime, proved inadequate to the task of building Spanish democracy and advancing quickly toward Spanish entry into the EC. The European Parliament, member state governments, and both cross-national and individual member state political parties sought to aid the democratic forces in Spain, both through direct assistance and through expressions of displeasure at the slow pace of democratic reform under Arias Navarro.

> "Europe must identify itself with Spain, and we the Spaniards are European. It is an urgent necessity that the two sides understand this and draw the appropriate consequences."
>
> King Juan Carlos, in his first speech to the Cortes as king, 1975, *cited by Julio Crespo MacLennan, Spain and the Process of European Integration (2000), 125.*

In July 1976, King Juan Carlos replaced Arias Navarro with Adolfo Suárez. Though Suárez was a relatively unknown official who had served under Franco, and his appointment initially aroused little enthusiasm in the EC, he proved surprisingly successful at moving Spain rapidly toward both constitutional democracy and a formal application to join the EC. Democratic elections, in which Suárez's Union of the Democratic Center (UCD) coalition won a parliamentary majority, took place on June 15, 1977. On July 6, the European Parliament congratulated Spain on its democratization and officially expressed "its political will to see Spain occupy a place in the European Community as soon as possible." On July 28, 1977, Spain officially applied for entry into the European Community.[6]

Although Spanish democratization removed the major political obstacle to Spain's integration into the EC, and the threat of a coup in 1981 heightened desires in the EC to admit Spain to help it consolidate its democracy, other obstacles to entry remained, many of them economic. Spain (and Portugal, which was seeking admission at the same time) possessed numerous economic features that made harmonization with EC practices and policies difficult and aroused misgivings among some EC member state governments, particularly the French government. Spain's per capita wealth was less than two-thirds of the EC average, its agricultural sector was large, its fishing fleets were larger than the EC total, and its industry still enjoyed considerable governmental protection and support. France was particularly concerned about the potential impact of Spanish entry on the operations of the EC's Common Agricultural Policy, from which French farmers had derived many benefits that they saw threatened by Spain. Therefore, the negotiations on Spanish entry proved long and arduous, stretching from 1979 until 1985, despite almost universal Spanish desires for a quick and positive resolution of the issues at hand.[7]

An additional complicating factor in the Spanish EC negotiations was the issue of Spanish membership in the North Atlantic Treaty Organization (NATO). Though all Spanish political parties and most interest groups agreed on EC membership, their views concerning NATO differed. While the center-right parties favored membership in NATO, the Socialists initially opposed it; and the Communists strongly opposed it and continued to do so. Spain joined NATO in 1982. However, the election of a Socialist government headed by Felipe González that same year was to lead to a 1986 referendum on whether Spain should remain in NATO. Though the EC did not make continued Spanish membership in NATO a condition for Spanish EC entry, the governments of both Britain and West Germany clearly signaled their preference that Spain remain a NATO member, which may have influenced González to endorse continued Spanish NATO membership despite his previous position on the issue. In any event, Spain gained EC entry prior to the 1986 referendum on NATO. In the referendum campaign, González's support and active campaigning for continued membership proved critical in gaining popular approval of that position with a 52.5 percent favorable vote. Therefore, Spain maintained its membership in NATO while gaining admission to the EC.[8]

The González Era and Spanish-EC/EU Relations

Once inside the European community, Spain under González's leadership asserted significant influence in a number of areas. González enjoyed close ties to a number of other European leaders, particularly those representing Socialist parties. Given Spain's long and continuing cultural, economic, and political ties to Latin America, the González government sought to forge new links between the EC/EU and that region. For example, it played a major role in moving the EU toward an Interregional Cooperation Agreement with Mercosur, composed of Argentina, Brazil, Paraguay, and Uruguay; and it fought to gain the inclusion of the Spanish-speaking Dominican Republic in the EU's Lomé Accords when France pushed for their extension to French-speaking Haiti, with which the Dominican Republic shares the island of Hispaniola. The González government also sought to strengthen ties between the EC/EU and the Arab world, particularly North Africa, though these efforts were modified by a desire to establish improved relations with Israel and to give precedence to the wishes of Spanish economic interests.

González also assumed leadership of the "poor four" of the EC/EU (Spain, Portugal, Greece, and Ireland) in bargaining effectively for expansion of the existing EC structural funds (to aid backward regions in pursuit of cohesion) and adoption of a new Cohesion Fund earmarked specifically to assist these four member states to rise to the economic level of the wealthier member states and thus promote harmony within the developing single market. (See the box on González later in this section.)[9]

During this period, Spain endorsed the major initiatives to deepen European integration, joining the European Monetary System (EMS) in 1989 and struggling to continue in its Exchange Rate Mechanism (ERM) despite the currency upheavals of the early 1990s, as well as favoring the Economic and Monetary Union (EMU) in the Maastricht Treaty negotiations and the convergence criteria and stability pact linked to the EMU. Even in such policy domains as environmental policy, where

Spanish policies lagged far behind the EC/EU norms, Spain accepted the higher EC/EU standards, though it did experience some implementation difficulties and resisted efforts to end member state veto power in most environmental fields. In general, the González government's record was one of support for supranational European development, despite a few notable exceptions.[10]

Spain under Aznar and the European Union

When the Popular party under José María Aznar as prime minister in 1996 replaced the Socialist government of González, some observers expected a shift in Spain's positions and roles within the EU. The Popular party, possessing roots that lay deep within the Franco regime, was markedly more conservative than the Socialist party and had traditionally been less enthusiastic about supranational development of the EC/EU than the Socialist party had. Furthermore, Aznar was widely viewed as a less charismatic leader than González.

Though Aznar adopted a somewhat lower profile in the EU than his predecessor, Spain's major positions on European issues did not shift dramatically. The Aznar government did make some changes that reflected its conservative orientation. For example, it encouraged the EU to take a more critical view of Castro's Cuba than previously and sided with the United States over the Iraq War of 2003 (over the opposition of the Spanish Socialists). However, Aznar continued to emphasize EU ties to Latin America and the Mediterranean; and he continued González's assertive leadership in support of continued cohesion funds, successfully battling efforts by Germany, Austria, and others to reduce them in the 2000–2006 EU budget. His government also showed its seriousness about the Economic and Monetary Union by imposing a pay freeze for Spanish public employees and other domestic budget cuts that enabled Spain to meet the requirements for adoption of the euro currency on schedule, thus placing Spain in the first group of members states to join the "euro zone." In the EU constitutional debates after 2001, the Aznar government tended to position itself with the British and French in favoring a strengthened Council of Ministers over a federal EU led by a powerful Commission, as the Commission president, Germany, and most smaller member states have proposed. It also refused to budge on the constitutional issue of Spain's voting power on the EU Council of Ministers, secured after much struggle at the Nice Summit in 2000. Spanish refusal to compromise on this matter (backed fully by Poland) proved critical in the inability of the Brussels Summit in December 2003 to move forward on the proposed new EU constitution. The Socialist government led by José Luis Rodríguez Zapatero (2004–) showed the flexibility required to achieve compromise at the June 2004 European Summit on the EU constitution and also moved Spain back toward positions taken under previous Socialist governments.[11]

Despite some clear differences between Socialist and Popular party governments, Spain's European policies have shown more continuity than change since Spanish EC entry in 1986. Also fairly continuous throughout this period has been an ongoing struggle between the central government and the autonomous communities, a subject that will be explored further in the section examining the impact of the EC/EU on Spanish institutions.[12]

"If some countries go through a tough, but necessary, exercise in order to converge their economic policies...others should, logically respond with a similar effort of solidarity by accepting decisions which imply a higher level of social and economic cohesion."

Spanish Prime Minister Felipe González, 1988, *cited by Rachel Jones, Beyond the Spanish State* (2000), 96.

PEOPLE IN THE EU
Felipe González and EU Cohesion Policies

Prime Minister Felipe González (1982–1996) often played a major role, sometimes described as "presidential," in the formulation of Spain's positions on important EC/EU issues and in negotiations with leaders of other member states in order to achieve them. A prime example was his role in articulating and pursuing Spain's goals concerning the broad set of EC/EU policies often referred to as aimed at "cohesion," or evening out intra-EC/EU disparities to make the single market operate more smoothly. "If some countries go through a tough, but necessary, exercise in order to converge their economic policies…others should, logically respond with a similar effort of solidarity by accepting decisions which imply a higher level of social and economic cohesion," proclaimed González, in a stirring speech in Brussels in 1988. Though the goal of cohesion had been stated in the EC previously, and the European Regional Development Fund (ERDF) had been established in part to foster cohesion back in the 1970s, "it took Spain to pitch it at the level it deserved," according to one of the top advisers to González.[13] At least, this was the view of González and his government.

Despite wide rhetorical support in the EC for the ideals of cohesion at the time of Spanish entry, the González government found itself a net contributor to the EC budget during Spain's first year of membership. Because Spain possessed per capita wealth at a level only about two-thirds that of the EC average, González was determined to alter Spain's position as a net contributor. Aggressively, he demanded a doubling of the budget for EC structural funds that would benefit Spain. At the Copenhagen Summit of the European Council in December 1987, he threatened to veto the entire EC budget unless his demands were met. However, the other member state governments among the "poor four" were less assertive than González; and the wealthier member state governments were opposed to his insistent demands. As a result, there was a stalemate that led to an emergency summit in Brussels the following February to try to hammer out a solution. Eventually, wealthy West Germany, the largest net contributor to the EC, agreed at the Brussels Summit to institute the doubling of the funding demanded by González over a six-year period, thus ending the summit on a relatively positive note with a considerable victory for the Spanish prime minister.

Recognizing the need for additional European allies on cohesion issues, González in the future made increasingly effective efforts to link Spain's goals to overall European single-market objectives that were widely shared and to demonstrate Spain's strong commitment to European supranational development. However, tough bargaining was still required to achieve the funding that González desired for Spain. Spanish negotiators implicitly threatened a Spanish parliamentary rejection of the Maastricht Treaty and overtly threatened to veto EC/EU enlargement to include Austria, Finland, and Sweden unless richer member states agreed to share additional resources with the "poor four" (Spain, Portugal, Greece, and Ireland). At the Edinburgh Summit of 1992,

(continued on next page)

(continued from previous page)

González enjoyed one of his greatest triumphs, securing a new Cohesion Fund, in addition to the previous structural funds, that earmarked aid just for the "poor four" member states (not for poor regions in many member states, as ERDF provided). Not surprisingly, Spain was to be the biggest beneficiary of the new Cohesion Fund, though González was shrewd enough to seek to conceal this fact by stressing that per capita aid was greater in the other three member states of the "poor four."

Although other Spanish participants certainly contributed to Spain's successes in shaping EC/EU cohesion policies, González's prominent leadership role is undeniable, most clearly evident in the European Summits of the member states' chief executives. His successor, Prime Minister Aznar, while less assertive than González, has continued to give high priority to guarding Spanish interests in European cohesion policy, even though when in opposition he had criticized González for acting more like a beggar than a statesman in his drives for cohesion aid at European Summits.[14]

DISTINCTIVE FEATURES OF THE SPANISH APPROACHES TO THE EC/EU

Since the late 1970s, Spanish political leaders of all ideological persuasions and party affiliations have demonstrated a high degree of consensus on the desirability of Spanish membership in the EC/EU. Although some disagreements erupted over the terms that were negotiated for Spanish entry, and though the González and Aznar governments have displayed some stylistic differences as well as substantive policy differences on such matters as EU-Cuban relations, the continuity in Spanish approaches to the EC/EU since the advent of constitutional democracy in Spain has been rather striking. Spanish public opinion has continued to view EU membership as good and the EU as good for Spain, at rates much higher than the average in EU member states, as Figure 14.1 illustrates. In this respect, Spain stands in particularly sharp contrast to the United Kingdom.

As was true of West Germany and Italy after World War II, Spain after Franco displayed a widespread yearning to "escape into Europe." In the case of post-Franco Spain, the desire was not just to erase memories of an unpleasant authoritarian past and to aid in consolidating a new constitutional democracy; it was also to overcome a long-term sense that Spain had been isolated from the European mainstream. These types of considerations, stressed by constructivist analysts who note how humanly constructed concepts, such as

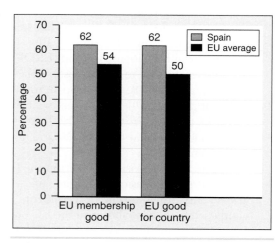

FIGURE 14.1   Popular Assessments of the EU, 2003

Eurobarometer, July 2003.

"Europe," can shape the behavior of human actors, have continued to make Spain a strong advocate of European supranationalism, though its own economic interests have certainly sometimes modified that advocacy.[15]

Realist theories, emphasizing geopolitical considerations, direct attention to Spain's proximity to North Africa (just across the narrow Straits of Gibraltar from Spain) and the strategic position that aroused the interest of the United States in developing military ties with Spain even under Franco and caused Britain and West Germany to exercise their influence to bring democratic Spain into NATO and keep it there.

Both neofunctional and liberal intergovernmental theories stress the economic factors that have drawn relatively poor Spain into progressive integration with the relatively wealthy EC/EU. While neofunctionalism aids understanding of why Spanish acceptance of the EC single market led also to its embrace of the Economic and Monetary Union and the single currency, liberal intergovernmental theories call attention to the economic interests inside Spain that have influenced the Spanish drives on cohesion policies, its defenses of its fishing industry vis-à-vis the EU Common Fisheries Policy, and its hesitant approach to expansions of the EC/EU that may pose threats to Spanish commercial and agricultural interests.

Against this backdrop, there are a number of noteworthy patterns in the approaches that Spain has generally adopted vis-à-vis the EC/EU.

An assertive approach to linking Spanish economic interests to broad European concerns. This feature has been repeatedly evident since Spanish entry into the EC in 1986. Backed by all major parties and interest groups in Spain, Spanish governments have fought aggressively for various "cohesion" aids that have benefited Spain economically. However, in part to win necessary support from wealthier member states, Spain has usually taken care to couch these in terms that portray them as beneficial to all of Europe and has lodged them within a framework of generally strong Spanish support for European supranational development. Its leaders' arguments have been that European and Spanish national interests largely coincide. Though there is evidence that this position genuinely reflects their own belief systems, it has also enhanced the effectiveness of Spanish efforts to build wide support in the EU and to put member state opponents on the defensive.[16]

A supranational inclination but with some growing intergovernmentalism. Spanish Socialist party elites demonstrated a strong proclivity for European supranational development even prior to Spanish EC entry, though the conservative parties (including the Popular party governments under Aznar during 1996–2004) have often shown a tendency to support an intergovernmental approach. In practice, Spanish approaches since attaining membership in 1986 have been somewhat mixed, depending on the issue at hand. For example, Spain has supported strengthening the European Parliament, has usually endorsed the increased use of qualified majority voting in the Council of the EU, and has joined in expansion of common EU policies in many domains, sometimes (as on some social and environmental policies) even when doing so posed genuine economic problems for Spain. However, Spain has shown a willingness on occasion to threaten (at least implicitly) to veto supranational development when its own major economic interests have appeared to be at stake, as it did during the Maastricht Treaty negotiations of the early 1990s when it was battling to gain the new Cohesion Fund. Moreover, in the 2002–2003 EU constitutional debates, the Aznar government joined the British and French governments in favoring a strengthened Council of Ministers (heavily influenced by member state governments) over a federal EU led by a powerful Commission, as Germany and most small member states advocated. It also played a key role in blocking European Summit endorsement of the compromise draft of the new EU constitution when it failed to get its way concerning national voting weights on the Council of Ministers.[17]

A wariness of EU expansion. Although Spain has not overtly opposed EU expansion, either to include Austria, Finland, and Sweden in 1995 or the Central and East European applicants, it proved a tough negotiator during the events leading up to the 1995 enlargement and displayed considerable concern about the terms of entry in the eastward widening. In 1994, for example, Spain insisted on an increase in cohesion funds using major contributions by the new member states before it would agree to support the admission of Austria, Finland, and Sweden. The poverty of the Central and East European applicants relative to Spain has aroused deep Spanish concerns that their entry (and eligibility for EU economic aid) will cause Spain to lose a share of its EU assistance in the future.[18]

A blending of Atlanticism with a European focus. Although Atlanticism (concerning the European roles of the United States and NATO) sharply divided the Spanish Left from the Right in the early post-Franco years, with the Socialists and Communists hostile to American ties and NATO (largely due to long U.S. links to the Franco regime) and the Spanish Right taking a pro-Atlanticist stance, a compromise blending of the two inclinations has characterized both Socialist and Popular party governments since 1986. Spain has been a strong supporter of developing a European common Foreign and Security Policy and a defense identity independent of the United States and NATO. However, it has also maintained its NATO membership (even joining more fully than before in the alliance's Military Committee after the mid-1990s) and favored continuing extensive American engagement in

Europe. The appointment of former Spanish Socialist Foreign Minister Javier Solana to be first secretary general of NATO and then high representative for the EU's Common Foreign and Security Policy (CFSP) illustrates Spanish leaders' abilities to blend Atlanticism with a European focus. During the Iraq crisis in 2003, Aznar's Popular party government veered toward Britain and the United States but committed only very limited troops to their effort in Iraq, while the Socialists (who returned to office in May 2004) lined up with France and Germany in opposition to the Anglo-American policies.[19]

An aspiration to be a bridge between Europe and Latin America. A consistent thread in Spanish approaches to the EC/EU has been an effort to draw upon Spain's historical ties to Latin America and to forge a close relationship, with Spain as the key mediator, between Europe and Latin America. This effort has yielded some successes, such as the EU-Mercosur Interregional Cooperation Agreement of 1995. Moreover, Spanish officials have dominated most key EU posts dealing with Latin America. To a lesser degree, and with less success, Spain has also sought to be a bridge between Europe and the Arab world.[20]

A fairly centralized and cohesive formulation of Spanish EC/EU policies. During the negotiations over accession to the EC and the early years of membership, the Spanish prime minister enjoyed a high degree of control and autonomy in formulating Spanish European policies. Reasons for this pattern included the prime minister's strong constitutional powers, the "presidential" styles of both Suárez and González, the broad consensus among Spanish political parties and interest groups concerning the advantages of EC/EU membership, and the relative weakness of Spanish interest groups in general compared to those in Northern European nation-states. However, prime ministerial capacities to dominate the formulation process

TABLE 14.1   Distinctive Features of Spanish EC/EU Approaches

1. An assertive approach to linking Spanish economic ends to broad European concerns.
2. A supranational inclination but with some growing intergovernmentalism.
3. A wariness of EU expansion.
4. A blending of Atlanticism with a European focus.
5. An aspiration to be a bridge between Europe and Latin America.
6. A fairly centralized and cohesive formulation of Spanish EC/EU policies.

have waned somewhat as some of the autonomous communities (especially Catalonia and the Basque Country), as well as other domestic actors, have increased their demands for involvement in the process. The current formulation process remains somewhat more centralized and cohesive (formally coordinated by the Secretariat of State for the European Union within the foreign ministry) than in Italy or Germany but involves more diverse and extensive inputs (and sometimes attempts at bypassing coordination) than was the case during the 1980s.[21]

THE IMPACT OF SPAIN ON THE EC/EU

Despite its late entry into the European Community, and a population and gross domestic product markedly lower than those of the other four major nation-states in the pre-2004 EC/EU, Spain has successfully exercised leadership that has affected European integration in a several areas.

As has previously been noted, Spain has generally favored supranational institutional development. This support has been evident in its backing for additional powers for the European Parliament, a number of new limits on the

veto powers by member states in the Council of Ministers, and the establishment of the Economic and Monetary Union and its structures. Its approach contrasts not only with Britain and France but also with neighboring Portugal, which entered the European Community at the same time as Spain but adopted a generally intergovernmental approach similar to that of Portugal's long-term ally, Britain, and to some other recent entrants, such as Sweden. At the same time, however, Spain has been willing to block supranational development when it perceives its own national interests to be threatened. For example, its assertive defense in 2003 of its voting power in the European Council of Ministers played a critical role in the breakdown of the European Summit on the proposed new EU constitution that would have furthered supranational development.[22]

Spanish influence over the major public policies of the EC/EU has been especially pronounced with regard to regional/cohesion policies, as has been noted previously. (See the box on González, in particular.) Other public-policy domains in which Spain has played significant leadership roles include the Common Foreign and Security Policy. In this domain, Spain initially worked closely with France in a joint effort to move the Western European Union closer to the EC/EU and to distance it from NATO. Spain has been supportive of the Anglo-French efforts to develop an EU Rapid Reaction Force and a European Strategic Defense Identity (ESDI). In the foreign and defense realm, Spain has been most distinctive in asserting leadership with regard to efforts to promote cooperation and security in the Mediterranean, drawing upon its long-term close relations with much of the Arab world. With regard to foreign trade, it has sought to foster close EU–Latin American relations.[23]

In other policy domains, Spain has usually not been a major leader, though its impact has still been felt. For example, in the environmental-policy realm, where Spain initially lagged far behind the EC/EU standards for environmental protection, Spain adopted a position at odds with its general supranationalism by blocking in the Maastricht Treaty negotiations the introduction of qualified majority voting for most Council of Ministers' environmental decisions. The Spanish government clearly wished to retain its veto power, though in practice it has been generally supportive of toughened environmental standards despite their costs to Spain.[24]

Stable governments and effective prime ministerial leadership, particularly by Felipe González, have given Spain a somewhat higher profile in the EC/EU than Italy has often enjoyed. Nevertheless, the impact of the EC/EU on Spain has almost certainly outweighed the effects of Spain on the EC/EU. As the European Union embarks on a major expansion to perhaps as many as 29 members in the next decade, that pattern will almost certainly become increasingly pronounced.

THE IMPACT OF THE EC/EU ON SPANISH POLITICS

Given Spain's late entry and its long-term isolation, authoritarianism, and economic underdevelopment, it is not surprising that Europeanization has had profound effects on Spanish politics and society. The aspiration of most Spaniards to "re-join Europe" was a major spur to democratization in the 1970s even before Spanish entry into the EC, because democratization was clearly a requirement for admission. The prospect of membership and actual membership itself have served to consolidate constitutional democracy in Spain. Furthermore, joining the EC/EU has forced economic deregulation and fostered competition and expanded trade with other member states. Though EU membership has harmed some Spanish industrial and agricultural sectors and done little to reduce the high unemploy-

ment that had already emerged as a major problem in post-Franco Spain, on balance most economists believe that it has been a major spur to Spanish economic growth. Spain's average growth rate has consistently been above the EU average, and its per capita gross domestic product has risen relative to that of the EU in general (jumping from 66 percent to 77 percent of the EC/EU average in the 1985–1994 period when the membership was 12 nations).[25]

The Constitution

As is true of the German Basic Law and the Italian Constitution, the Spanish Constitution of 1978 contains an article (Article 93) that provides for the transfer of sovereignty to supranational institutions. Because of this article, and prevailing interpretations of it, no constitutional amendments of the types seen in Germany and France have been added in Spain to accommodate European integration.[26]

Governmental Institutions

Because contemporary Spanish governmental institutions barely predate the negotiations to enter the EC/EU, it is almost impossible to assess their operations in terms of a "before EC/EU" and "after EC/EU" set of patterns. From the outset, the Spanish executive, and particularly the prime minister, have enjoyed predominance over parliament, due to a combination of constitutional provisions, the usual (but not unbroken) pattern of one-party dominance, and the weakness of interest groups. On European issues, the executive dominance has tended to be even more evident than on most ordinary domestic issues because of the high level of societal and elite consensus in Spain on the basic goals of Spain's European approaches and the low level of parliamentary knowledge about the EC/EU. The executive has established procedures vesting coordination powers in the Secretariat of State for Foreign Policy and the EU, located within the foreign affairs ministry. Prime ministers have tended to set the basic guidelines governing the formulation of Spain's major approaches to the EC/EU, as illustrated in the discussion of Prime Minister González in the box earlier in this chapter. The Cortes (parliament) possesses the sole authority to ratify EC/EU treaties, and it has established a Joint Committee for the EU, a nonlegislating committee composed of members of both the Congress of Deputies and the Senate, to monitor European policies. However, a recent analysis has described its impact on European affairs as "minimal" and has concluded that Spain's membership in the EC/EU has "distanced parliament from the decision-making process."[27]

The Spanish Constitutional Court has become actively involved in resolving numerous legal disputes between the Spanish central government and the autonomous communities concerning enforcement of EC/EU directives in domains shared between the central government and the autonomous communities according to the Spanish Constitution and the statutes of autonomy and the rights of regional governments to deal directly with the EU in policy formulation. For example, regarding formulation, the Constitutional Court in 1994 ruled that relations between the EU and the Basque regional government should not be regarded as within the area of international relations exclusively reserved to the national government by Article 149.1.3 of the Constitution. Therefore, EC/EU membership has generated a large number of cases drawing the Constitutional Court into major political/legal disputes.[28]

Probably the greatest impact of EC/EU membership on Spanish governmental institutions has been in the area of relations between the central government and the autonomous communities, primarily by creating controversy about the initially low level of regional involvement in formulating Spanish positions on EC/EU issues and about the responsibility (often unclear under the Constitution and in the various autonomy statutes) for implementing EC/EU directives. Over time, a combination of court rulings and political pressures has increased the roles of the autonomous communities in both implementation and formulation. Their roles have been more extensive in the former category than in the latter. Though some of the autonomous communities, particularly Catalonia and the Basque Country, have increasingly bypassed the central government to deal with Brussels directly, the Spanish central government continues to dominate the formulation of European public policies. Some of the Spanish autonomous communities and several cities have established cooperative arrangements with counterparts in other EU member states. The most widely noted has been the formation of the "Four Motors of Europe" linking Catalonia with Baden-Würtemburg in Germany, Rhône-Alpes in France, and Lombardy in Italy in lobbying activities and other joint endeavors. Joaquin Llimona, the director of external relations for the regional government of Catalonia, has emphasized the economic benefits of the EU to his autonomous community: "Now we think of the EU as our market. We are part of the European structure—with four hundred million consumers."[29]

"Now we think of the EU as our market. We are part of the European structure—with four hundred million consumers."

Catalonia's External Relations Director Joaquin Llimona, explaining his region's embrace of the EU, cited by John Newhouse, *Europe Adrift* (1997), 46.

Elections, Political Parties, and Interest Groups

EC/EU membership has had little effect on Spanish electoral and referendum procedures. However, it did generate a considerable controversy over the type of electoral process to be employed in Spanish elections to the European Parliament (proportional representation).[30]

Though only indirectly related to EC/EU issues, the question of Spanish membership in NATO was the subject of a referendum in 1986 that ended with a narrow majority voting in favor of retaining Spanish NATO membership.[31]

The EC/EU has consistently enjoyed strong support from all major Spanish political parties and interest groups; and issues pertaining to European integration have rarely caused major splits among or within the major parties and groups, as they have often done in all of the other major member states. Nevertheless, the impact of EC/EU membership (and prospective membership in the 1975–1985 period) on the major Spanish political parties has been significant, drawing the Socialist party (PSOE) away from the relatively radical anticapitalist and anti-NATO stances that it took while in opposition to Franco, and drawing Spanish conservatives toward an embrace of constitutional democracy. Support of the EC/EU also served to establish the legitimacy of the Socialist party as a party of government in the eyes of many non-socialists and the Popular party as a genuinely democratic alternative in the eyes of many nonconservatives.

As the Franco regime came to an end, the Spanish Socialists initially reasserted their Marxist heritage, their commitment to equality and criticism of capitalism for its inequalities, and their opposition to NATO. While expressing enthusiasm for integration of Spain into Europe, they remained hesitant about the capitalistic aspects of the existing European Economic Community. However, interactions with the German Social Democratic Party in particular and the other parties of the Socialist International in the 1976–1977 period turned the Spanish Socialists into strong advocates of Spanish membership in the EC, viewing it especially as a vehicle to advance and consolidate Spanish democratization, which was a highly important Socialist goal, and one that at first seemed threatened by pro-Franco forces within Spain.

The attraction of European integration, as well as their lack of electoral success in the first democratic Spanish elections, stimulated the Spanish Socialists under their dynamic new leader, Felipe González, to drop their Marxist label, accept a market-oriented economy, and emphasize the need to adapt Spain to West European norms in order to attain membership in the European Community. Eventually, after coming to power in 1982, the Socialists moved away from their anti-NATO stance. In 1986, González campaigned to achieve a popular majority in a national referendum to maintain Spanish NATO membership. As prime minister, he also led his government to support market-oriented economic policies that would enable Spain to enter the EC single market that was emerging, even as he also pushed vigorously for EC cohesion policies to aid the transition of poorer EC members such as Spain into the single market. Without question, Europeanization was a major factor that led the Spanish Socialist Party to moderate its previous leftist positions. At the same time, the party's embrace of Europe added to its legitimacy in the eyes of the Spanish electorate. The PSOE has long been active in the Party of European Socialists within the EC/EU framework.[32]

The parties on the right of the Spanish political spectrum underwent a major realignment in the early 1980s, as the Union of the Democratic Center coalition of Adolfo Suárez disintegrated and the Popular party (PP), originally the Popular Alliance (AP), emerged as the major voice of Spanish conservatism. This party possessed strong and obvious roots in the Franco regime. Therefore, support for the EC/EU proved a means by which it could demonstrate its democratic credentials and increase its legitimacy in the eyes of the Spanish electorate. Originally, the Popular party and its leaders took a less supranational approach to the EC/EU than their Socialist rivals; and they also criticized the Socialists for their heavy emphasis on European cohesion policies. They have also been somewhat more inclined than the Socialists to follow the lead of the United States. However, these distinctions between the two major Spanish parties on European issues have diminished, though the PP remains generally more pro-United States than the PSOE, as illustrated by their divisions over the Iraq conflict. The Popular party has joined the European People's party, an alliance of conservatives and Christian Democrats, in the European Parliament.[33]

To the left of the Socialist party, but also endorsing the EC/EU, stood the Communist party, which has been a part of a leftist alliance of parties known as the United Left (IU) since 1986. The United Left has maintained its opposition to NATO (unlike the Socialist party) and has criticized the Maastricht Treaty and the capitalist biases and democratic deficit of the EC/EU but has supported European integration in general.[34] The major regional parties, the Convergence and Union (CiU) of Catalonia and the Basque Nationalist party (PNV), have also been generally supportive of the EC/EU, particularly seeking to use it to enhance the autonomy of their regions within Spain and to make contacts with subnational governments elsewhere.[35] Therefore, in comparison with most European national party systems, the Spanish one has been relatively united on European matters.

Spanish interest groups have been weaker than those in most EU member states, though the solidification of constitutional democracy has led to some strengthening since the 1970s. Like the parties, they have been generally supportive of the Spanish government's efforts to integrate Spain into the EC/EU. The Confederation of Spanish Employers' Organizations (CEOE) has been a member of the Union of Industrial and Employers' Confederations of Europe (UNICE) ever since Spain entered the EC; and it has strongly supported further European integration as well as the free-market deregulating policies endorsed by the EC/EU and Spanish governments. The lack of large Spanish multinational corporations (MNCs) has weakened the influence of the CEOE in the EU according to some analysts, since the large MNCs based in other member states have tended to enjoy disproportionate influence in Brussels. As for the Spanish labor unions, both major Spanish union federations, the leftist Workers' Commissions (CCOO) and the more moderate General Workers' Union (UGT), have affiliated with the European Trade Union Confederation (ETUC). The UGT also maintains its own office in Brussels. Both unions have sought to democratize the European Union and orient it toward social issues and full employment policies. Membership in the EC/EU has brought somewhat greater consultation and cooperation between the Spanish government and the traditionally weak and fragmented array of agricultural interest groups in coping with the Common Agricultural Policy and its reforms.[36]

Public Policies

Even more notable than the effects of the EC/EU on Spanish governmental institutions and participatory processes and structures have been the effects on Spanish public policies. As in France and other systems in which the state has traditionally played a large economic role, the single market and competition policies of the EC/EU have brought a diminishment of the Spanish state's role in the economy. Even the Socialist government (1982–1996) saw the need to deregulate and reduce state assistance that had been used to maintain industries that could not compete effectively in the "new" Europe or amid the growing global competition. However, EC/EU pressures sometimes pressed the González government to withdraw assistance more rapidly than it wished. For example, conflicts were often sharp between Spain and the

European Commission over governmental aid to Seat, the major Spanish automobile manufacturer, until 1995, when it was purchased by Volkswagen. Even then, there were tensions over the terms for the restructuring of Seat that were imposed by the European Competition Commissioner.[37]

The Common Fisheries Policy of the EC/EU has also brought major Spanish policy changes. Since its entry to the EC, Spain consistently has had the largest fishing industry of any member state. Because previously Spanish fishermen were accustomed to fishing far from Spanish territorial waters with few restraints, membership in the EC/EU has meant various restrictions on Spanish fishing imposed by the Farm and Fisheries Commissioner under guidelines set by the Council of Farm and Fisheries Ministers, aimed at preserving stocks of fish and achieving compromises among member states' fleets. For example, a major struggle that lasted for several years in the 1990s concerned the number of Spanish vessels that would be allowed to fish in an area between Britain and Ireland known as the "Irish box." A well-known case of Spanish noncompliance with a judgment of the European Court of Justice also occurred in the fisheries policy realm. Because the Spanish fishing fleet is so large (presently about 30 percent of the total tonnage in the EU fleets), this policy domain has been one of particular importance to Spain. The 2002 proposals by the EU Farm and Fisheries Commissioner to cut the size of EU fishing fleets, end public subsidies for new fishing vessels, and boost aid to help fishermen retrain have won strong support from environmentalists and backing from the German and British governments but have aroused fierce opposition in Spain.[38]

Another especially clear example of major EC/EU impact on Spanish public policies has been in the environmental-policy domain. Prior to its entry to the EC, Spain had undertaken only a few isolated measures of environmental protection and lacked a ministry of the environment. What actions had been taken were largely symbolic rather than effective means of protection. When Spain entered the EC, it committed itself to incorporating all EC environmental legislation that had already been enacted, without asking for a transitional period or any special exemptions. Not only has the transposition of EC/EU environmental directives into Spanish law markedly upgraded Spanish environmental standards, but it has also led to a major restructuring of the domestic framework for environmental policy-making. The European Directive on Environmental Impact Assessment, for example, has opened up the authorization procedures of major projects to participation by environmental and other societal groups by providing them with the right to information and consultation. The need to meet European environmental standards and the encouragement of Spanish environmental groups by the Directive on Environmental Impact Assessment and other EU initiatives has spurred the upgrading of environmental agencies in both the Spanish central government and the autonomous communities. In 1996, Spain became the last member state of the EU to establish a ministry of the environment. The autonomous communities have become responsible for day-to-day environmental policy implementation, though the central state must develop the framework legislation and must accept the ultimate responsibility to the European Commission. Although environmental-policy implementation has at times proved problematic in Spain, in part due to tensions between the central state and the regions, the overall impact of EC/EU membership has been to enhance the protection of the environment in Spain and to shift the Spanish environmental-policy style in the direction of increased consultation and diversity of inputs. Without doubt, Europeanization has profoundly reshaped Spanish public policies in this domain, as in many others.[39]

CONCLUSIONS

Spain has experienced much greater consensus in support of European integration than has been true of most other nation-states in the European Union. Despite the pressures for major readjustments from isolation to integration, from authoritarianism to constitutional democracy, and from a state-protected economy to competition, Spain has made the transition with a minimum of dissent or upheaval. In many respects, its policies and policy-making processes have been transformed, as has been illustrated in the environmental-policy sphere. Spain has also become an important actor in European Union affairs, though certainly not to the degree that France or Germany has been. Its roles in shaping EU cohesion and Latin American policies have been prime examples of Spanish influence, as has been the elevation of Javier Solana to be the chief coordinator of the European Common Foreign and Security Policy. Above all, Spain has become "European" to an extent almost unimaginable just three decades ago.

SUMMARY

- Spain was a late entrant to the European Community (1986) compared to most West European nation-states but has been an enthusiastic and often important player in EC/EU affairs since its entry.

- The Birkelbach report (1961), making democratic government a prerequisite for EC membership or association status, prevented Francoist Spain from attaining even association status in the EC.

- The attraction of EC membership was so compelling in Spain that it united all significant Spanish political parties in support of seeking entry to the EC after Franco's death in 1975; most perceived economic benefits, a boost to Spanish governmental

legitimacy, and consolidation of democracy as likely results of Spanish EC membership.

- Spain's economic backwardness, large agricultural sector, and government-business ties made the negotiations for EC entry long and arduous; French resistance, in particular, was difficult to overcome.

- Prime Minister Felipe González (1982–1996) led Spain into the EC and seized leadership of the "poor four" states to expand regional/cohesion funding for Spain while endorsing supranational European development in general.

- Prime Minister José María Aznar (1996–2004) favored a somewhat more intergovernmental EU than González had and displayed a more Atlanticist inclination than González but maintained an emphasis on regional/cohesion funding for Spain.

- Prime Minister José Luis Rodríguez Zapatero appears likely to emphasize ties to Germany and France over those to the United States and to follow EU approaches similar to those of the previous Socialist governments of González.

- The most distinctive general Spanish approaches to the EC/EU have been an assertive approach to linking Spanish economic interests to broad European concerns, a supranational inclination (but with some intergovernmental aspects, particularly under Aznar), a wariness of EU expansion, a blending of Atlanticism with a European focus, an aspiration to be a bridge between Europe and Latin America, and a fairly centralized and cohesive formulation of Spanish EC/EU policies (albeit complicated by some autonomous community assertiveness).

- Spain's influence over the EC/EU has been most pronounced with regard to the expansion of regional/cohesion policies and expenditures.

- Membership in the EC/EU has promoted Spanish economic growth (while harming some industrial and agricultural sectors), consolidated constitutional democracy, increased the roles of the autonomous communities, and made Spaniards proud of their place in Europe; in sharp contrast to Britain and France, the EC/EU has enjoyed support from all major Spanish political parties and interest groups; EC/EU membership appears to have moderated both of the major Spanish parties' ideologies.

- EC/EU membership effects on Spanish public policies have been especially evident in the dismantling of state business controls and subsidies, enhancing of environmental protection efforts, and placing major new restrictions on the Spanish fishing industry.

ENDNOTES

1. Julio Crespo MacLennan, *Spain and the Process of European Integration, 1957–1985* (Houndsmills, Basingstoke: Palgrave, 2000), Ch. 1.

2. MacLennan, *Spain and the Process of European Integration*, Ch. 2; Paul Preston and Denis Smyth, *Spain, the EEC, and NATO* (London: Routledge, 1984), Ch. 3.

3. MacLennan, *Spain and the Process of European Integration*, Ch. 3; Rachel Jones, *Beyond the Spanish State: Central Government, Domestic Actors, and the EU* (Houndsmills, Basingstoke: Palgrave, 2000), 25–26.

4. Michael Marks, *The Formation of European Policy in Post-Franco Spain: The Role of Ideas, Interests, and Knowledge* (Avebury, VT: Ashgate, 1997), 76–79; MacLennan, *Spain and the Process of European Integration*, 1–8 and Chs. 4 and 5; Jones, *Beyond the Spanish State*, 39–42.

5. MacLennan, *Spain and the Process of European Integration*, 125.

6. MacLennan, *Spain and the Process of European Integration*, Ch. 5; Jones, *Beyond the Spanish State*, 26–27; Jonathan Story, "Spain's External Relations Redefined: 1975–89," in Richard Gillespie, Fernando Rodrigo, and Jonathan Story, eds., *Democratic Spain: Reshaping External Relations in a Changing World* (London: Routledge, 1993), 31–34.

7. MacLennan, *Spain and the Process of European Integration*, Ch. 6; Jones, *Beyond the Spanish State*, 27–46; Story, "Spain's External Realtions Redefined," 34–44; Marks, *The Formation of European Policy*, Ch. 5.

8. Fernando Rodrigo, "Western Alignment: Spain's Security Policy," in Gillespie, et al., *Democratic Spain*, Ch. 4; Marks, *The Formation of European Policy*, Ch. 4; MacLennan, *Spain and the Process of European Integration*.

9. Andrew Moravcsik, *The Choice for Europe* (Ithaca, NY: Cornell University Press, 1998), 446–448; Jones, *Beyond the Spanish State*, Ch. 4; Marks, *The Formation of European Policy*, Ch. 6.

10. Francesc Morata, "Spain," in Dietrich Rometsch and Wolfgang Wessels, eds., *The European Union and the Member States: Towards Institutional Fusion?* (Manchester: Manchester University Press, 1996), 138 and 140–141; Roy and Kanner, "Spain and Portugal," 243–246; Alfonso de Esteban Alonso and Alejandro López López, "Environmental Policy," in Amparo Almarcha Barbado, ed., *Spain and EC Membership Evaluated* (London: Pinter, 1993), 60–68.

11. John Gibbons, *Spanish Politics Today* (Manchester: Manchester University Press, 1999), 143, 157–158; Roy and Kanner, "Spain and Portugal," 250, 256–257; Marks, *The Formation of European Policy*, 119–121; Paul Betts, "Romano Prodi's Unlikely Allies," *Financial Times*, June 26, 2002, 10.

12. Caterina Garcia, "The Autonomous Communities and External Relations," in Gillespie, et al., *Democratic Spain*, 123–140; Jones, *Beyond the Spanish State*.

13. Jones, *Beyond the Spanish State*, 96 for González quotation, 74 for the second quotation.

14. George Parker, "Atmosphere of Resignation as Leaders Walk Away," *Financial Times*, December 15, 2003, 4; Jones, *Beyond the Spanish State*, esp. Ch. 4; Roy and Kanner, "Spain and Portugal," 256–257; Richard Gillespie, "The Spanish Socialists," in John Gaffney, ed., *Political Parties and the European Union* (London: Routledge, 1996), 155–169.

15. Marks, *The Formation of European Policy*, esp. in Ch. 8, makes explicit links to constructivist approaches

in explaining Spanish behavior vis-à-vis European integration and the concept of "Europe."

16. Jones, *Beyond the Spanish State*, 96–97; Marks, *The Formation of European Policy*, 118–119.

17. Jones, *Beyond the Spanish State*, 90–91, discusses the implicit veto threat. Parker, "Atmosphere of Resignation as Leaders Walk Away," *Financial Times* 4, covers the Spanish role in the collapse of the summit on the EU constitution. On Spain's generally supranational inclination, see Jones, 90; Roy and Kanner, "Spain and Portugal," 239–240; Marks, *The Formation of European Policy*, 119–121. On recent Spanish intergovernmentalism, see Betts, "Romano Prodi's Unlikely Allies," 10.

18. Jones, *Beyond the Spanish State*, 92–94.

19. Marks, *The Formation of European Policy*, 107–112.

20. Jean Grugel, "Spain and Latin America," in Gillespie, et al., *Democratic Spain*, 141–158; Roy and Kanner, "Spain and Portugal," 249–250.

21. Story, "Spain's External Relations Redefined," 37–38 on Suárez and González. Jones, *Beyond the Spanish State*, Chs. 4 and 5, and Morata, "Spain," 138–151, stress increasing diversity of inputs over time but also note key roles retained by the central government.

22. Marks, *The Formation of European Policy*, 119–121; Roy and Kanner, "Spain and Portugal," 239–240; Karen Anderson, "Sweden: Retreat from Exceptionalism," in Zeff and Pirro, eds., *The European Union and the Member States*, 285–304; George Parker, "Atmosphere of Resignation as Leaders Walk Away," *Financial Times*, December 15, 2003, 4.

23. Ana Palacio, "EU Divisions over Iraq Can Be Mended," *Financial Times*, February 17, 2003, 13; Marks, *The Formation of European Policy*, 43–75 and 107–112; Gibbons, *Spanish Politics Today*, 155–157.

24. Susana Borrás, et al., "The Europeanization of National Policies in Comparison: Spain as a Case Study," *South European Society & Politics* 3, 2 (Autumn 1998), 30–33.

25. Statistics from Roy and Kanner, "Spain and Portugal," 243.

26. Gibbons, *Spanish Politics Today*, 148; Roy and Kanner, "Spain and Portugal," 242; Manuel Sánchez de Dios, "Executive Parliamentary Control," in Almarcha Barbado, *Spain and EC Membership Evaluated*, 219.

27. The quotations are from Jones, *Beyond the Spanish State*, 67 and 69. Also see Sánchez de Dios, "Executive Parliamentary Control," 219–223; Carlos Closa, "Spain: The Cortes and the EU—A Growing Together," in Philip Norton, ed., *National Parliaments and the European Union;* and Morata, "Spain," 142.

28. Morata, "Spain," 146–147; Jones, *Beyond the Spanish State*, 75.

29. The quotation is from John Newhouse, *Europe Adrift* (New York: Pantheon, 1997), 46. Jones, *Beyond the Spanish State*, esp. 70–75.

30. Francisco J. Vanaclocha Bellver and Miguel Angel Ruiz de Azúaa Antón, "The Impact of the Electoral System of the European Parliament on Spain," in Almarcha Barbado, *Spain and EC Membership Evaluated* (London: Pinter, 1992), 233–245.

31. Marks, *The Formation of European Policy*, Ch. 4; Story, "Spain's External Relations Redefined," 44–45.

32. Gillespie, "The Spanish Socialists," 155–169; Kevin Featherstone, *Socialist Parties and European Integration* (Manchester: Manchester University Press, 1988), 286–293, 296–298.

33. Gibbons, *Spanish Politics Today*, 39–42, 148; Marks, *The Formation of European Policy*, 120–121.

34. David Bell, "Western Communist Parties and the European Union," in Gaffney, ed., *Political Parties and the European Union*, 220–234; Gibbons, *Spanish Politics Today*, 48–51.

35. Gibbons, *Spanish Politics Today*, 53.

36. Jones, *Beyond the Spanish State*, 75–79; Gibbons, *Spanish Politics Today*, 124–129.

37. Gibbons, *Spanish Politics Today*, 153–154.

38. "EU Fisheries Policy: Too Much Vigour in Vigo," *The Economist* 362 (March 30, 2002), 44; Jones, *Beyond the Spanish State*, 141; Gibbons, *Spanish Politics Today*, 146; "Anger at EU Fishing Plans," *Financial Times*, June 10, 2002, 3.

39. Tanja Börzel, "The Greening of a Polity? The Europeanization of Environmental Policy-Making in Spain," *South European Society & Politics* 3, 1 (Summer 1998), 65–92; Borrás, et al., "The Europeanization of National Policies in Comparison," 24–33.

Chapter 15

A COMPARATIVE OVERVIEW OF THE FIFTEEN CURRENT EU MEMBER STATES

"The great era of nation-state autonomy is past, and the globalization of capital (and labor) forces countries to give up exclusive control of some areas of policy; but this Europe of overlapping sovereignties should not be confused for one in which nation-states are vanishing and disappearing into larger and larger entities."

—Mark Mazower, *Dark Continent (1998), 402.*

The preceding ten chapters (Chapters Five through Fourteen) have analyzed the five major nation-states in the pre-2004 European Union: France, Germany, Italy, the United Kingdom, and Spain. This chapter will compare major features of these five nation-states with the other ten members of the pre-2004 European Union: Austria, Belgium, Denmark, Finland, Greece, Ireland, Luxembourg, the Netherlands, Portugal, and Sweden. It will focus first on their political development and then examine contemporary governmental institutions and participatory processes. The last part of this chapter will examine their relationships with the European Union. Where appropriate, the chapter will draw upon major theoretical perspectives to assist in explaining the observed patterns. In doing so, it aims to review and place in a broad comparative context the predominant patterns already observed in the major EU member states while at the same time providing explicit comparisons and contrasts with those in the smaller member states. While not the chief focus of this text, the smaller states often do play significant roles within the European Union. Moreover, they often illustrate unique patterns not found in the major member states but deserving of attention: more egalitarian welfare states in the Nordic countries and more complex ethnic-cooperation patterns in Belgium than in the major EU member states, for example.

COMPARATIVE POLITICAL DEVELOPMENT AMONG THE MEMBER STATES

Using the framework first advanced by Gabriel Almond and G. Bingham Powell for analyzing political development,[1] the preceding chapters have focused on similarities and differences among the "big five" with regard to timing and responses to the nation-building, state-building, participation, and distribution crises of modernization. The broad similarities among the 5 major EU member states, and indeed among all 15 pre-2004 EU member states, are fairly striking. All have become modern nation-states and have moved "beyond" the nation-state to pool considerable sovereignty in the institutions of the EC/EU. All have become constitutional democracies. Furthermore, all now rely heavily on free markets, private property, and profit motives but have mingled these with extensive social-welfare programs and governmental economic regulations, the latter increasingly being shifted to the EU level.

Nation-State Development Patterns

England and France developed as modern nation-states much earlier than Germany and Italy did. Spain became a "great power" internationally relatively early but lagged in developing such features of a modern nation-state as a centralized bureaucratic apparatus and national citizenship conceptions (and has continued to be marked by sharp language/cultural divisions). Broadening the analysis to include the other ten pre-2004 member states of the EU, Sweden, Denmark, and the Netherlands became modern nation-states relatively early. Greece achieved independence from the Ottoman Empire in the 1820s; Belgium gained independence from the Netherlands in 1830 but remained deeply fractured between Flemish (or Dutch) -speakers in the North and French-speakers concentrated in its South. Luxembourg, a "grand duchy," is in many respects a survivor of the medieval era; but it broke its ties to the Netherlands and its links to the German confederation in the late 1860s to assume roughly its modern state form. Portugal's pattern was somewhat similar to Spain's: early achievement as a significant power center but slow development of modern bureaucracy and citizenship norms. Austria was long the center of a multiethnic European empire and became a modern nation-state only after World War I (and then merged with Germany from 1938–1945 before regaining status as an independent

nation-state). Finland was under Swedish rule until 1809 and was part of the Russian Empire during 1809–1917 before attaining its independence at the end of World War I. Finally, Ireland, long under British rule, gained independent nation-state status only in 1922 following years of turmoil and armed struggle. Table 15.1 summarizes the broad patterns of nation-state development among the 15 pre-2004 EU nation-states, though precise dating of the achievement of nation-state status is a matter of some dispute, given varying assessments of what such status entails.[2]

As suggested in the previous references to regional language-based ethnic divisions that have led to conflict in Spain and Belgium in particular, it is of course important to recognize that these (and at times religious-based cultural divisions, as in Northern Ireland) have led many citizens of European nation-states to perceive themselves more as members of an embattled "ethno-national" minority than as members of the "community" of the nation-state of which they are formally citizens. Pronounced economic differences among regions within a nation-state often encourage or heighten ethno-national identity, and (as is evident in Northern Italy) may foster regional identity even in the absence of an ethno-national base.[3]

TABLE 15.1 Approximate Timing of Nation-State Development in EU Nation-States

Before 1820	1820–1900	Since 1900
United Kingdom	Greece	Austria
France	Belgium	Finland
Denmark	Portugal	Ireland
Netherlands	Spain	
Sweden	Italy	
	Luxembourg	
	Germany	

Further complicating issues of national identity have been the perceptions of many recent foreign immigrants to European nation-states that they are not really full members of the "nation" in which they reside. Often coming from Asia, Africa, Eastern Europe, or the Caribbean in search of jobs or to escape civil war and/or discrimination in their previous homes, these foreign immigrants frequently encounter difficulty finding good jobs and adjusting to a new cultural environment. They also often encounter hostility from the rest of the population. For example, a recent British government survey found that most nonwhite residents of the United Kingdom feel that they do not belong to the British nation.[4] Table 15.2 shows the percentage of the population in each of the EU member states who are foreign residents, which ranges from a high of 34 percent (but largely from neighboring EU states) in Luxembourg to a low of 1 percent in Greece. While these figures should be treated with caution because they reflect variations in citizenship requirements in different nation-states and make no distinctions concerning the origins of the foreign residents, they provide some information pertinent to discussions of national identity. Table 15.2 also indicates the number of asylum seekers in each member state between 1999 and 2001. Here, Germany and the United Kingdom have been the leaders in terms of absolute numbers.

Many leaders of the European Union, such as Commission President Romano Prodi, whose wish for a European "union of hearts and minds" opened Chapter One of this text, look forward to a day when European identities will assume an importance greater than, or at least fully compatible with, national identities in Europe. There is evidence that many Europeans do in fact already see themselves simultaneously as Europeans, members of their own nation, and members of an ethno-national subgroup. Some analysts have suggested that "the viability of the nation-state as the dominant

TABLE 15.2 Foreign Residents as a Percentage of the Population and Asylum Applications in EU Member States

Nation-State	Foreign residents % of population, 1997	Asylum applications, 1999–2001 (1000)
Austria	9	68.5
Belgium	9	103.0
Denmark	7	29.4
Finland	2	7.9
France	7	116.8
Germany	9	262.1
Greece	1	10.0
Ireland	3	29.0
Italy	2	58.7
Luxembourg	34	4.2
Netherlands	4	120.8
Portugal	2	0.7
Spain	2	24.7
Sweden	6	51.0
United Kingdom	3	260.1

Source: On foreign residents, *Eurostat*, 1999; percentages calculated by the author from *Eurostat* and *World Almanac* data. On asylum applications, UNHCR, 2002; three-year totals compiled by the author.

political actor in Europe appears to be eroding, both from above and from below,"[5] conjuring up an image of nation-states under attack from subnational governments and identities (below) and from the European Union and European identities (above). However, others, such as Alan Milward, have argued that European integration after World War II actually "rescued" the small and medium-sized nation-states of Europe by allowing them to focus on such functions as providing a welfare state that they could perform with relative effectiveness while pooling a number of regulatory functions that have enabled them to cope more adequately with globalization than would otherwise have been the case. Still others, such as Thomas Risse, have argued that "Europeanness" has been quite compatible with German national identity, increasingly so for French national identity, but less so for British national identity.[6] There are elements of truth in all of these assessments.

"...the viability of the nation-state as the dominant political actor in Europe appears to be eroding, both from above and from below."

B. Guy Peters and Christian Hunold, *European Politics Reconsidered (1999), 29.*

Democratic Development Patterns

Although ideas and practices of democracy in the broad sense of "government by the people" have a number of ancient and medieval roots in Europe, as Chapter Two has noted, modern constitutional democracy based upon mass citizen voting, elections between or among competitive political parties, representation through parliamentary bodies, guarantees of individual rights, and checks on executive authority has emerged largely within the framework of the modern nation-state. Samuel Huntington's conception of three historical "waves" of constitutional democratic development in response to social and economic pressures for greater participation and protections of individual rights provides a useful framework within which to analyze European nation-state similarities and differences. So, too, do his emphases on economic and social development and Protestant cultural values as two important stimuli to the "first wave" of democratization before 1918. This wave occurred earliest in relatively wealthy and predominantly Protestant northwestern Europe (and the United States) and gradually spread across the European continent before receding in the years between World War I and World War II (1918–1939). By 1940, the receding of the wave had left only Britain, Ireland, Finland, Sweden, and Switzerland as democra-

cies in Europe. After World War II, in the "second wave" of democratization, West Germany, Italy, and the countries that had had their constitutional democracies overthrown by internal upheaval and/or Nazi or Fascist invasion moved to reestablish democracy. American and British efforts were important in spurring the return of European democracy, both through direct pressures in zones occupied by their armed forces and through American Marshall Plan economic assistance to nascent democracies. Though much of Central and Eastern Europe established authoritarian or even totalitarian regimes linked to the Soviet Union, and Greece during 1967–1974 had a conservative authoritarian military regime, only Spain and Portugal in Western Europe remained bastions of conservative authoritarian government after World War II.

In Huntington's model, it was Greece, Spain, and Portugal that launched the "third wave" of democratization that swept across Central and Eastern Europe and around much of the globe after the mid-1970s. By this time, the Roman Catholic Church dominant in Spain and Portugal (and Latin America, which also democratized extensively) had embraced constitutional democracy, as it had not done in the past. Moreover, while Spain, Portugal, and Greece lagged behind most of Western Europe, they were more prosperous by the mid-1970s than in the past and certainly were wealthier than most nation-states in the rest of the world. Therefore, constitutional democracy grew in Europe in the wake of nation-state development and, to a considerable degree, as an accompaniment to relative economic prosperity and capitalist or mixed economies. Reflecting the importance of economics, the major receding of democracy in Europe was linked in part to the Great Depression of 1929–1939.[7]

Figure 15.1 provides a graphic illustration of the development of constitutional democracy among the 15 EU member states since 1918. The shaded sections and the dates inside them

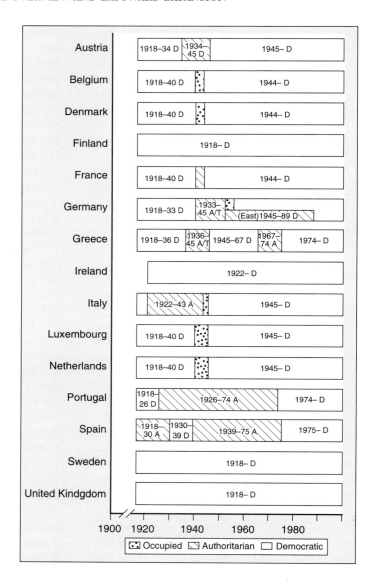

FIGURE 15.1 Democratic and Authoritarian Eras Since 1918 in EU Member States

indicate the authoritarian periods (if any) for each member state.

Development and Distribution Patterns

In broad terms, Europe moved from a predominantly feudal pattern of largely land-based, no-growth economic distribution to a largely capitalist pattern of capital-based, growth-oriented distribution between the fifteenth and nineteenth centuries. The commercial and industrial revolutions were a consequence and transformed not just economic but also social and political life in Europe. However, there were some pronounced national differences as well as similarities. Feudalism had never gained a firm foothold in most of Scandinavia and some other parts of Europe, though their economies were agriculturally based like the rest of the Continent. Moreover, some national versions of capitalism, notably in Britain and the Netherlands in the nineteenth century, involved much less state regulation and control than others, notably in France and Germany.

The European political ideologies and parties that emerged in the increasingly democratic settings of most West European nation-states during the first democratic "wave" focused heavily on distribution questions, eventually dividing in most states along left-right lines and reflecting social **cleavages,** defined by Douglas Rae as "criteria which divide the members of a community or subcommunity into groups."[8] On the left, Socialists and eventually Communists gave political voice to the new industrial working classes and demanded enhanced social and economic equality and usually a more extensive state role than in the past in owning or at least regulating the use of capital and providing social welfare. Liberals of the center or center-right generally advocated free-market capitalist distribution patterns, though some "social" liberals, especially in Britain and Scandinavia, came to advocate a mixed economy. Business and professional groups tended to rally around liberal parties. Further to the right stood traditional conservatives, who sought to slow the pace of economic modernization and block socialism but often accepted the need for some governmental regulation of capital and provision of limited social welfare, often under religious auspices. They generally drew support from defenders of the old order, based among landed aristocrats, officials of established churches, and others willing to defer to their leadership. The result was an increasing modification of capitalism in the twentieth century in favor of regulated capitalism with an extensive welfare state, often termed a mixed economy. Germany was the chief social-welfare pioneer, instituting early welfare programs in the 1880s, soon followed by

Austria, Belgium, Denmark, and Sweden. Spain, Portugal, Greece, and Ireland have generally been the slowest to expand social-welfare policies and have funded them less generously than the others.

Despite considerable similarities, three rather different types of welfare-state distribution emerged in Europe during the twentieth century, according to an influential analysis by Gösta Esping-Anderson: 1) A "liberal" welfare state emphasizing the use of means tests to restrict benefits to the poor who meet stated criteria, limited transfer payments, and modest social insurance programs. Britain and Ireland have fallen into this category, along with the United States. 2) A "corporatist-statist" welfare state, providing more resources for social security than the liberal welfare state but preserving marked status differences and promoting little equality. These, Esping-Anderson has associated with France, Germany, Italy, and Finland, though he has suggested that Austria, Belgium, and the Netherlands have tended in this direction also, despite displaying some characteristics of the third type of welfare state. 3) The social democratic–egalitarian welfare state most identified with Scandinavia: Sweden, Denmark, and non-EU member Norway, though some analysts have included Finland in this category. Of the three types, this one has placed the greatest emphasis on universal benefits and equality. Despite Europeanization, the distinctive features of these three types continue to mark the national welfare-state systems of the EU member states.[9]

Levels of social security transfer payments as a percentage of a nation-state's gross domestic product (GDP) vary considerably also in Europe, as Table 15.3 illustrates. Germany, Sweden, France, and Austria spent the highest percentages of their GDPs on social security transfers in 1999, while Ireland, Portugal, Spain, and the Netherlands ranked as the bottom four EU member states in this category. Figures on overall governmental spending as a percentage of GDP also appear in Table 15.3. On this measure of government intervention in the economy, Sweden ranked first, followed by Denmark, France, and Greece. In the lowest ranks on this measure were Ireland, Portugal, Luxembourg, and the United Kingdom.

What are the explanations for these important differences within the EU? The major factors that have been associated most positively with high social-services spending among EU member states have been high per capita wealth, large and influential labor unions, dominance of government by political parties of the Left, mobilization of women, extensive dependence on international trade, and relatively old and well-established social-welfare programs. Relative affluence has meant enhanced ability and

willingness to pay the high taxes needed to support a large welfare state. Strong unions and parties of the Left have been the greatest advocates of expanded social services spending, especially that which redistributes wealth to increase economic equality. Christian Democratic parties, especially when faced with strong social democratic competition, have been significant backers of social insurance and child benefits. Mobilization of women, particularly in conjunction with social democratic and labor union strength, has had additional effects in expanding social services and directing them toward increased gender equality. High dependence on international trade has tended to spur a desire to cushion the blows of changing trade patterns with an extensive social safety net. Finally, programs that are old and established have often generated bureaucratic momentum to expand. In the era of heightened pressures for welfare-state retrenchment since the mid-1970s, the European states having the longest periods of governments led by parties of the Left have shown the greatest resistance to reductions in social-welfare rights.[10]

Several factors since the 1970s have operated to restrain the continued growth of most European welfare states and in some instances have even imposed spending cuts and erosion of previously guaranteed social rights. Global and European competition from nation-states where welfare spending and labor costs are relatively low, aging of most European states' populations (due to lowered birth rates) that have reduced the ratios in most states of contributing workers to elderly pension and health-care recipients, revitalization of neoliberal or even economic libertarian ideology among many European elites, and the budgetary austerity promoted by the convergence criteria and stability pact associated with the Economic and Monetary Union have all contributed to a general atmosphere of restraint concerning European welfare states. Simultaneously, the member states have been shifting the "regula-

TABLE 15.3	Social Security Transfers and Total Governmental Expenditures as Percentages of GDP in EU Member States, 1999	
Nation-state	Soc. Sec. transfers as % of GDP	Govt. expend. as % of GDP
Austria	18.6	47.3
Belgium	15.7	48.0
Denmark	17.5	52.4
Finland	17.9	46.4
France	18.4	48.5
Germany	18.9	44.8
Greece	15.8	48.3
Ireland	10.2	29.3
Italy	17.3	44.6
Luxembourg	15.1	38.0
Netherlands	12.6	43.2
Portugal	11.7	38.3
Spain	12.4	36.9
Sweden	18.9	56.1
United Kingdom	13.5	37.8

Source: OECD National Accounts, 2001.

tory" aspect of regulated welfare capitalism increasingly to the EC/EU level, as has been evident regarding agriculture, trade, competition, and environmental regulation.

* * *

Political development is a continuing process. The 15 EU member states prior to 2004 possess distinctive traditions that have shaped and continue to influence their own developmental patterns even as they have come to share basic nation-state institutions and norms, constitutional democratic participatory practices, and mixed economies, as well as to pool some of their sovereignty in the European Union.

COMPARATIVE GOVERNMENTAL INSTITUTIONS AMONG THE MEMBER STATES

While sharing the broad feature of constitutional democratic polities, the member states of the EU display some national distinctions concerning the structures, powers, and roles of their contemporary governmental institutions. This section focuses on three in particular: legislative-executive relations, constitutional judicial review, and national-subnational governmental relations.

Legislative-Executive Relations

None of the pre-2004 EU member states employs a presidential model of legislative-executive relations such as the United States uses, though the French hybrid system has some distinct presidential characteristics. As has previously been discussed, Germany, Italy, Spain, and the United Kingdom employ a cabinet-parliamentary system of legislative-executive relations, in which a prime minister or her/his equivalent (i.e., chancellor in Germany) heads a cabinet of leading executive officials that is accountable to the lower chamber

of parliament (both chambers in Italy). In contrast, France has a system that mixes cabinet-parliamentary institutional structures with a strong presidency elected independently of the legislature and sometimes of a different party affiliation from the majority of its members. Among the other ten pre-2004 EU member states, all except Finland and Portugal have established cabinet-parliamentary structures and relations between their executives and legislatures. Finland has long had a hybrid pattern broadly similar to France's, though the Finnish prime minister has recently gained powers vis-à-vis the president. Between 1976 and 1982, Portugal, too, employed a hybrid model but significantly reduced presidential power in a major 1982 revision of its constitution.[11]

Among the 14 predominantly cabinet-parliamentary systems, there exist numerous variations. For example, Denmark, Finland, Sweden, and Portugal have **unicameral** parliaments of only one chamber, while all of the others have bicameral (two chamber) legislatures. Of the latter, however, Germany and Italy assign far greater constitutional powers to their second chambers than do any of the other nine bicameral states.

Another difference concerns the head of state, a largely ceremonial position except in France (and to some extent Finland and Portugal). A king or queen serves as head of state in Belgium, Denmark, the Netherlands, Spain, Sweden, and the United Kingdom, while the Grand Duke holds this position in Luxembourg. In the other eight member states, a president fills this role. Table 15.4 offers a summary, illustrating the legislative-executive structures, the number of legislative chambers, and the occupant of the head of state position in each of the 15 EU member states prior to 2004.

The actual operations of cabinets and the nature of their relations with parliaments depend on a variety of factors, including the leadership skills and orientations of the prime

TABLE 15.4 Legislative-Executive Structures, Number of Legislative Chambers, and Head of State in EU Member States

Nation-state	Legislative-Executive structure	Chambers	Head of state
Austria	Cabinet-Parliamentary	2	President
Belgium	Cabinet-Parliamentary	2	King
Denmark	Cabinet-Parliamentary	1	King
Finland	Hybrid/Cabinet-Parliamentary (a)	1	President
France	Hybrid (a)	2	President
Germany	Cabinet-Parliamentary	2 (b)	President
Greece	Cabinet-Parliamentary	2	President
Ireland	Cabinet-Parliamentary	2	President
Italy	Cabinet-Parliamentary	2 (b)	President
Luxembourg	Cabinet-Parliamentary	2	Grand Duke
Netherlands	Cabinet-Parliamentary	2	Queen
Portugal	Hybrid/Cabinet-Parliamentary (a)	1	President
Spain	Cabinet-Parliamentary	2	King
Sweden	Cabinet-Parliamentary	1	King
United Kingdom	Cabinet-Parliamentary	2	Queen

(a) Hybrid is a mix of Presidential and Cabinet-Parliamentary systems. Finland and Portugal possess a mix that most analysts now view as more Cabinet-Parliamentary than Hybrid in nature.
(b) Germany and Italy possess stronger upper chambers than the other bicameral systems. Italy's is the strongest in terms of constitutional powers.

minister, the features of the party system, and the level of trust and cooperation among the parties and between the legislature and the executive. For example, Italy has experienced frequent cabinet overthrows through no-confidence votes and threatened no-confidence votes, in contrast to Britain and Sweden, where such occurrences are rare. Party system differences are discussed further later in this chapter, but it should be noted here that the systems characterized by multiple parties (and/or factions) and pronounced ideological differences usually produce turnovers in top executive positions much more frequently than those in which one party normally wins a legislative majority and can govern alone (Britain, Spain, Greece) or in multiparty systems in which there is a fairly high degree of consensus among likely coalition partners (Germany, Sweden).

Constitutional Judicial Review

Six of the EU member states have constitutional courts that provide judicial review of laws to determine whether the laws are in accord with the national constitution. In addition to Germany, Italy, and Spain, which have been discussed at length previously in this text, Austria, Belgium, and Portugal have established such courts for these purposes. France has set up a Constitutional Council, technically not a judicial institution, which rules on the constitutionality of legislation before it has been formally enacted. Therefore, 7 of the 15 pre-2004 EU member states have constitutional judicial review by a constitutional court or similar institution. Such courts are relatively new in Europe, unlike the United States, where the Supreme Court claimed effective constitutional judicial review powers back in 1803 and has used them fairly extensively since the 1850s. In most cases, these courts in Europe reflect reactions to national experiences with authoritarian governments in the twentieth century. Table 15.5 illustrates the presence or absence of constitutional courts or similar institutions in EU member states today.

Even in the eight EU member states that lack constitutional courts with judicial review powers, the judiciary has gained powers of legal review in recent years, in a process that some analysts have termed the "juridification of the policy process," due in large part to the roles of the European Court of Justice in interpreting the EU treaties and its engagement of the courts of the member states in the process. This text has previously discussed the British example in particular as an illustration of this juridification. Old notions of parliamentary supremacy in Britain and the other member states lacking

TABLE 15.5 Constitutional Courts in EU Member States

Nation-state	Constitutional court
Austria	Yes
Belgium	Yes
Denmark	No
Finland	No
France	Yes*
Germany	Yes
Greece	No
Ireland	No
Italy	Yes
Luxembourg	No
Netherlands	No
Portugal	Yes
Spain	Yes
Sweden	No
United Kingdom	No

* Constitutional Council in France

constitutional courts have been partially modified as a result, sometimes arousing considerable controversy, as in the *Factortame* cases, which challenged British merchant shipping legislation. Regardless of whether their own nation-states have constitutional courts, lawyers in EU member states have increasingly brought suits challenging national laws on grounds that they violate EC/EU treaties on matters ranging from Belgian pension laws to British Sunday closing laws. To illustrate, a Belgian lawyer brought suit on behalf of Mrs. Defrenne, a Belgian air hostess who had been forced to retire at age 40 and therefore received a pension lower than her male colleagues, alleging that Belgian law was in violation of EC gender-equality requirements. British retail businesses that wished to open on Sundays and had failed to change restrictive British legislation on the subject challenged British law on grounds that it restricted imports and therefore violated EC requirements. Most such cases have been adjudicated by national courts, adding to the courts' enhanced roles in policy-making. Therefore, the juridification of the policy process has become a widespread phenomenon in the politics of EU member states.[12]

National-Subnational Governmental Relations

National-subnational governmental relations have most often been classified in constitutional-legal terms as either unitary, vesting supreme authority in the national government alone (though it may opt to decentralize some of that authority to subnational units), or federal, dividing that authority between the national and subnational governments (usually those at the regional level). Of the 15 pre-2004 EU member states, only three have federal systems prescribed by their constitutions: Austria, Belgium, and Germany. Both Austria and Germany have employed federalism officially for most of their histories as nation-states, though in both cases the state governments have increased their powers as a result of post–World War II efforts to use decentralization of authority as a means to diminish the likelihood of an authoritarian central government in the future. In contrast, Belgium historically had a unitary system. However, in response to sharp conflicts between the Flemings (Flemish/Dutch-speakers mainly in northern Belgium) and the Walloons (French-speakers mainly in Southern Belgium) in the 1960s and 1970s, Belgium has decentralized its system since 1980 and formally adopted a federal form of government in constitutional-legal terms in 1993.[13] Table 15.6 indicates the EU member states having federal and unitary systems.

Among the 12 nation-states of the EU that are officially unitary, there has been a pronounced trend toward decentralization in many since the late 1970s. This movement has been carried furthest in Spain, where the pressures from the Catalans and Basques for autonomy of their regional governments (autonomous communities) has been especially intense. As discussed in more depth in Chapter Thirteen, the result has been the de facto transformation of Spain into a "quasi-federal" system, but one in which some autonomous communities possess more autonomy than others—an asymmetric pattern. Similar pressures from Scotland and Wales in the United Kingdom have led to asymmetric devolution there, too, with Scotland receiving more autonomy than Wales, and the turbulent Northern Ireland remaining a question mark for the future. Unlike Spain, however, the United Kingdom has not devolved authority to regions in the rest of the country (England), where more than 80 percent of the population lives. Italy and France have also devolved considerable authority to subnational levels in recent years. Five regions possessing distinctive cultural features received some autonomy in Italy prior to the other regions, which have gained powers on a rather limited basis since the 1970s. Corsican pressures have led to offers (not yet accepted and implemented) of special territorial devolution to Corsica, a Mediterranean island off the southern coast of France. While France remains a unitary and rather centralized system, it has become more decentralized than previously, since the reforms of the 1980s. Regional ethno-national pressures, popular reactions against central governments perceived as overly remote, and the advent of regional funds and other EC/EU opportunities for expression of subnational demands and EU articulation of the subsidiarity principle of performing tasks at the lowest feasible governmental level have all played parts in stimulating a fairly general West European trend toward some devolution of authority in recent decades. Nevertheless, except for Spain, most of the unitary European nation-states remain quite centralized in comparison with their federal counterparts in Europe, Canada, and the United States.[14]

TABLE 15.6 Unitary and Federal Systems in EU Member States

Nation-state	Unitary/Federal
Austria	Federal
Belgium	Federal
Denmark	Unitary
Finland	Unitary
France	Unitary
Germany	Federal
Greece	Unitary
Ireland	Unitary
Italy	Unitary
Luxembourg	Unitary
Netherlands	Unitary
Portugal	Unitary
Spain	Unitary/"Quasi-federal"
Sweden	Unitary
United Kingdom	Unitary

COMPARATIVE PARTICIPATORY PROCESSES AMONG THE MEMBER STATES

In EU member states, as in constitutional democracies generally, elections, political parties, and interest groups have mediated between citizens and their governments. In addition, some EU member states have provided for the use of referendums as a form of direct democracy, permitting citizens to vote directly on issues, either in a nonbinding consultation or in a legally binding manner. Among pre-2004 EU members, Italy has made by far the most extensive use of referendums; Denmark, Finland, France, and Ireland have employed them with moderate frequency; the others, with the exceptions of Germany and Portugal (which have not used them at all at the national level), have employed them only on occasion. One European country, Switzerland, a non-member of the EU by choice (expressed through referendums!), has made far more use of referendums than any other European nation-state.

Arguments in favor of the wide use of the referendum are that it permits direct consultation of the citizens, enabling voters to bypass often unrepresentative political elites, and that it encourages citizens to educate themselves about issues on the ballot. Opponents point to the inherent difficulties of framing most issues in terms of clear yes or no alternatives, note the frequently low turnouts for referendums, argue that voters lack the expertise of representatives and may make unwise decisions, and suggest that referendums are unlikely to permit a careful deliberative process of the type that is (allegedly) more likely to occur in a representative parliamentary body.[15]

Some member states of the EU have provided for workplace participation in business corporate decision-making by employees, most notably Germany, Austria, and Sweden, though others have done so on a somewhat more limited basis. Arguments in favor of workplace democracy usually stress that it is a logical extension of democratic ideals and practices to the workplace, permits employees to draw upon their expertise to assist in the direction of their companies, and lays the foundation for close management-worker cooperation that may enhance productivity. Opponents of workplace democracy of the types utilized in Germany or Sweden generally argue that it threatens the private property rights of shareholders, gives too large a voice to employees who lack expertise, and introduces labor rigidity and other inefficiencies as employees use their power to give priority to job protection.[16]

Women's participation in government and in parliaments has increased in all member states of the EU in recent years but is far more widespread in the Nordic countries and the Netherlands and Belgium than elsewhere, apparently reflecting underlying cultural values as well as the strength of feminist movements in these countries. Italian and Greek women have been the least likely to win parliamentary seats, as Table 15.7 illustrates.

TABLE 15.7 Women Members as a Percentage of Total Members of Lower or Single Parliamentary Chambers, 2003

Sweden	45.3%
Denmark	38.0
Finland	37.5
Netherlands	36.7
Belgium	35.3
Austria	33.9
Germany	32.2
Spain	28.3
Portugal	19.1
United Kingdom	17.9
Luxembourg	16.7
Ireland	13.3
France	12.2
Italy	11.5
Greece	8.7

Note: The United States figure is 14.3%.

At the very least, the growing participation of women in government has provided a higher degree of descriptive representation than in the past—far more so in Northern than in Southern Europe. Beyond that, there is evidence, cited earlier in Chapter Eleven on the United Kingdom, that heightened female parliamentary involvement has also injected distinctive values into government that have advanced the broader cause of gender equality.

Election Patterns

The major variations among the EU member states in their electoral procedures involve the presence or absence of direct popular vote for a president and the distinctions between single-member districts and a first-past-the-post system of parliamentary elections and proportional representation methods of legislative elections. France, Finland, and Portugal have hybrid legislative-executive structures, as previously noted, and have direct popular elections for their presidents. Austria and Ireland, which have largely ceremonial presidents in essentially cabinet-parliamentary systems, elect their presidents in popular elections also. The other ten member states have no direct popular vote for an executive. The United Kingdom and France both use exclusively single-member districts to elect members of the House of Commons and the National Assembly, respectively. However, while the United Kingdom has a simple first-past-the-post system, France provides for a second round of voting if no candidate wins a majority in the first round. Proportional representation is used in all of the other member states except for Germany and Italy. Germany elects half of its Bundestag in single-member districts by the first-past-the-post system but allocates the other half on a proportional basis such that the overall result is fairly proportional. Italy now elects 75 percent of its national legislators in single-member districts by plurality and 25 percent by proportional representation.

There has been considerable debate in Europe over the merits of the first-past-the-post system versus proportional representation. Proponents of the former usually stress the allegedly enhanced representation that occurs through the interactions between voters and a single representative from their district and the supposed advantages in terms of governmental stability and clear-cut choices and accountability stemming from the tendency of this system to produce just two major parties in competition with one another. In contrast, supporters of proportional representation usually argue that it provides a much fairer reflection of voters' actual preferences by awarding seats among the parties in proportion to their popular voting support.[17]

Voter turnout is consistently higher in EU member states' national elections than in U.S. national elections, in part because most European governments register prospective voters so that there is no need for the prospective voters to take the initiative to register themselves as in the United States and in part because European elections are commonly scheduled on days when most citizens do not have to work. Turnout has been highest in Austria (where it is mandatory), Belgium, and Italy in most recent elections. Since the 1960s, there has been a general but not uniform decline in European voter turnouts, from an average participation rate of 85 percent in the 1965–1969 period to an average of 74 percent in the late 1990s.[18] These figures compare with the 50 percent average turnout in recent U.S. presidential elections and turnouts ranging between 35 percent and 40 percent in recent congressional elections in non-presidential election years. These figures also compare with the turnout of less than 50 percent in the European Parliamentary elections of 2004, providing one of several indicators that suggest higher levels of European interest and engagement in national elections than in Europe-wide elections. Table 15.8 summarizes the major variations among EU mem-

TABLE 15.8 EU Member State Electoral Systems and Voter Turnout

Nation-state	Presidential popular elections	Legislative electoral method	Legis. elec. voter turnout %*
Austria	Yes	Proportional	91.2
Belgium	n./a.	Proportional	92.6
Denmark	n./a.	Proportional	85.5
Finland	Yes	Proportional	76.9
France	Yes	FPP(a)/runoff	75.8
Germany	No	FPP & Proportional	86.2
Greece	No	Proportional	79.9
Ireland	Yes	Proportional	73.2
Italy	No	FPP & Proportional	90.5
Luxembourg	n./a.	Proportional	89.7
Netherlands	n./a.	Proportional	87.6
Portugal	Yes	Proportional	76.0
Spain	n./a.	Proportional	73.9
Sweden	n./a.	Proportional	86.5
United Kingdom	n./a.	FPP	76.5

* Voter turnout figures are the averages for the 1950–1997 period; from Lane and Ersson, 1999.
(a) FPP indicates use of the first-past-the-post system. In France, the second round is FPP; the first round requires a majority for election.

ber states in their election patterns with regard to the presence or absence of popular presidential elections, the type of legislative election procedures employed, and voter turnout.

Party Systems

The type of electoral system that a nation-state has used to elect its parliament has had a major impact on its party system, as Maurice Duverger, Douglas Rae, and others have illustrated.[19] The first-past-the-post system of the United Kingdom has encouraged predominantly two-party politics there and has normally yielded governments dominated by one party at a time. However, some EU member states with proportional representation, such as Spain and Greece, have also often had a single governing party at a time; and France has continued to have multiple parties despite use of a single-member system with runoffs. In practice, proportional representation systems have varied considerably in terms of how proportional they really are. Most establish a threshold that parties must achieve in their popular vote percentage in order to be eligible for proportional representation. Germany with a 5 percent threshold and Sweden with a 4 percent threshold therefore do not have as many parties as the Netherlands, which has a threshold of just 0.67 percent to gain parliamentary seats.

Despite their importance, electoral procedures are by no means the only factors influencing the number of parties in a nation-state. Moreover, the number of parties is not necessarily the most important attribute of a nation-state's political party system. On the first point, many analysts have highlighted the importance of underlying social cleavages.[20] If a nation-state has long been marked by cleavages along lines of social class, religion, regionalism, and/or ethnicity that cut across one another, it has been particularly prone to have multiple political parties. On the other hand, the presence of a dominant cleavage (social class traditionally in Britain, for example) or reinforcing cleavages (Catholicism and nonconformism with the working class, Anglican Protestantism with the upper class in Britain, for example) may reduce the potential number of parties regardless of the electoral system.

Beyond the number of parties in a national system is the key issue of ideological distance among them. This distance has often (but not always) reflected underlying cleavage patterns. When the cleavage has been sharp, it has tended to produce parties ideologically distant from one another. Several cross-cutting sharp cleavages have tended to produce ideologically fractious parties that have had difficulty compromising with one another. Giovanni Sartori has drawn a useful distinction between different types of multiparty systems. A "polarized" multiparty system is one where the ideological distances among the parties are great, and cooperation among them is fraught with difficulties. France in the Fourth Republic, Germany during the Weimar Republic, and Italy after World War I (before Mussolini) and most of the time since World War II have been polarized multiparty systems. In contrast, the Scandinavian countries have generally had multiparty systems where underlying consensus has been evident and cooperation among parties has been fairly easily achieved most of the time.[21] The Netherlands prior to the 1960s offered another possibility: fairly sharp, cross-cutting cleavages modified by what Arend Lijphart has termed a **consociational** (power-sharing) relationship among party elites in which the leaders of the parties divided along social class (working class–middle class) and religious (Protestant-Catholic) lines in society were able to work out bargains among their parties that brought considerable political stability and social peace. Austria and Belgium at

times have illustrated patterns similar to those described for the Netherlands.[22]

Descriptions of the ideological differences among political parties in most European nation-states have usually emphasized the left-right spectrum, already discussed in the chapters on the major EU nation-states. This spectrum arranges the parties from the far left Communists to the center-left Socialists, Social Democrats, and Labor parties; to the centrist Liberals or Center parties; to the center-right Conservatives and Christian Democrats; to the far right anti-immigrant parties and outright Nazis and Fascists.

Although this spectrum provides a fairly accurate guide in most European nation-states and in the European Parliament as to likely patterns of cooperation and conflict among the parties, it is only a partial guide. It has traditionally reflected a social class cleavage rather than other cleavages and is based in large part on expressed attitudes on social and economic equality (pro-equality on the left, anti-equality on the right) and state roles in the economy (relatively high on the left, relatively low on the right). This spectrum has had limited relevance to the Irish party system. It has often obscured the differences between rhetoric and actual behavior of a number of parties and their leaders. Moreover, it is difficult to place regional, populistic, nationalistic, and Green parties on the spectrum because they are expressing ideologies that primarily relate to other spectrums or dimensions of thought or underlying cleavages. Regional parties are generally taking positions near the decentralist end of a continuum running from centralism to decentralism of authority. Populistic parties are taking positions near the populistic end of a continuum running from elitism to populism. Nationalistic parties such as the French National Front, the Austrian Freedom Party, and the Danish Peoples Party are taking positions near the nationalist end of a dimension from multicultural tolerance to cultural nationalism; but these parties are also nationalistic in the sense of expressing strong skepticism or even hostility toward European integration and are usually populistic as well as nationalistic. Green parties are staking out positions near the post-materialist end of what Ronald Inglehart has described as a materialist–post-materialist continuum. Complicating matters further, some parties have mingled positions on several continuums in their party programs and appeals. For example, the Northern League in Italy has mixed Northern Italian regionalism with populism, far-right anti-immigrant appeals, and center-right neoliberalism or even economic libertarianism. Many analysts place it on the far right, but others question such placement. Figure 15.2 illustrates the mul-

tiple dimensions of European party conflict that make it difficult to describe the emergent pattern in simple left-right terms.[23]

Table 15.9 shows the partisan composition of nation-state governments in left-right terms where appropriate, the percentage of parliamentary seats held in each state by the two largest parties (a measure of two-party tendencies), and the percentage of the parliamentary seats held in each state by the far-left and far-right parties (a measure of polarization) as of June 2004. Center-left governments of one party (Spain, Sweden, United Kingdom) or two parties (Germany) ran the governments of four EU member states; center-right governments of one (Greece), two (Austria, Denmark, Ireland,

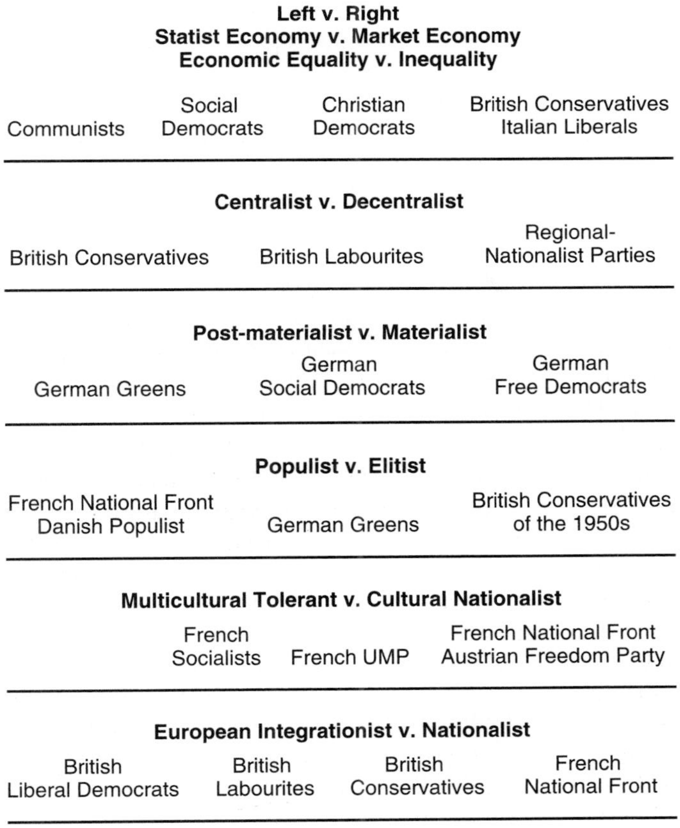

Left v. Right
Statist Economy v. Market Economy
Economic Equality v. Inequality

| Communists | Social Democrats | Christian Democrats | British Conservatives Italian Liberals |

Centralist v. Decentralist

| British Conservatives | British Labourites | Regional-Nationalist Parties |

Post-materialist v. Materialist

| German Greens | German Social Democrats | German Free Democrats |

Populist v. Elitist

| French National Front Danish Populist | German Greens | British Conservatives of the 1950s |

Multicultural Tolerant v. Cultural Nationalist

| French Socialists | French UMP | French National Front Austrian Freedom Party |

European Integrationist v. Nationalist

| British Liberal Democrats | British Labourites | British Conservatives | French National Front |

FIGURE 15.2 Dimensions of European Party Politics with Approximate Placement of Select European Parties

TABLE 15.9 Parties and Government in EU Member States, 2003

Nation-state	Governing party or coalition	Seats held by two largest parties (%)	Seats held by combined far left/far right (%)
Austria	Center-right, 2-party coalition	81	10 (a)
Belgium	Multi-party coalition	32	13
Denmark	Center-right, 2-party coalition	60	2
Finland	Multi-party coalition	54	10
France	Center-right, multi-party coalition	86	4
Germany	Center-left, 2-party coalition	81	5
Greece	Center-right, single party	94	6
Ireland	Center-right, 2-party coalition	67	0
Italy	Center-right, multi-party coalition	52	23 (b)
Luxembourg	Center-right, 2-party coalition	57	0
Netherlands	Right-left 2-party coalition	57	5 (c)
Portugal	Center-right, 2-party coalition	78	1
Spain	Center-left, single-party minority	89	1
Sweden	Center-left, single-party minority	61	12
United Kingdom	Center-left, single party	88	0

(a) Freedom Party counted as far right.
(b) National Alliance (15%), Northern League (5%), other far right (1%), Refounded Communists (2%).
(c) List Pym Fortuyn.

Sources: Percentages calculated from *Elections Around the World* (www.electionworld.org) for all nation-states except France and Italy. Percentages for Italy calculated from Fabbrini and Gilbert, "The Italian General Election of 13 May 2001." Those for France calculated from the *Financial Times,* June 18, 2002, 4.

Luxembourg, Portugal), or more (France, Italy, the Netherlands) parties ran the governments of nine EU member states; and Belgium and Finland were governed by multiparty governments of mixed ideological leanings. The pattern had been quite different just a few years previously, when the center-left had dominated almost all national governments in the EU. A surge of concerns about immigration and crime helped to fuel the rightward trend of 2001–2002, as did discontent over relatively slow economic growth in most of Western Europe. The parliaments of Greece, Spain, and the United Kingdom were more dominated by two major parties than were any of the other national legislatures. The Belgian parliament was the least dominated by two major parties, with only 30 percent of its

membership representing the two biggest Belgian parties; Finland, the Netherlands, and Italy also demonstrated strong evidence of multipartism. Italy appeared the most polarized.

One other feature of European national party systems has been the high degree of cohesion normally found within most parties in national parliaments (and to a lesser extent in the European Parliament). Compared with American political parties, almost all European parties have demonstrated a high degree of internal unity, especially with regard to legislative voting behavior. Much of this cohesion has resulted from the need by governing parties in cabinet-parliamentary systems to maintain support for the cabinet in order to avoid its downfall in a no-confidence vote. However, some of it has stemmed from party leaders' frequent control over nominations and campaign funds. Some of it has also stemmed from higher degrees of ideological coherence within most European parties than within the Democratic and Republican parties in the United States.[24]

Political parties have traditionally been more important in Europe than in the United States, not only in shaping legislative behavior but also in structuring and guiding voters' choices in elections. Although support for many European parties continues to reflect the basic societal cleavages of class and to a lesser extent religion, these cleavages no longer provide the basis for deeply entrenched loyalties to parties that they once did. Both class and religion (especially the latter) have diminished in importance to most European voters in recent years. The advent of television and other mass marketing mechanisms have also had the effect of focusing European voters' attention more on the attributes of particular party leaders than has usually been true in the past, as the heavy emphasis on Tony Blair in Britain, Silvio Berlusconi in Italy, and Gerhard Schröder in Germany has illustrated. Voter volatility in European elections, often seen as evidence of "dealignment" or detachment from old party loyalties, has been widely discussed. Despite these trends, political parties remain highly important links between voters and their national governments in most contemporary EU member states—certainly to a higher degree than in the United States.[25]

Interest Group Patterns

Because political parties are more important in European nation-states than in the United States, interest groups must often work through parties rather than both penetrating and bypassing them as they often do in American politics. Nevertheless, interest groups and large individual business corporations are important intermediaries between the public and the government across Europe. Economically based groups—including business, labor, agriculture, and professional groups—generally enjoy preeminence, as they usually do in the United States. Business groups and multinational corporations have become especially influential in all Western European political systems. On the other hand, labor unions are much stronger in Sweden and Denmark and in Northern Europe generally than they are in Italy and France, where they are internally divided and have low and declining memberships. In general, the advent of an increasingly globalized economy appears to have weakened union bargaining power by enabling corporations to shift investments (or at least to threaten to shift investments, and thus jobs) to where labor costs are lower than in highly union-organized countries. Clearly, the Nordic countries' unions have countered these trends more effectively than most labor organizations elsewhere, though even they have witnessed some loss of influence in recent years. Agricultural groups remain surprisingly influential, especially in France, despite sharp declines in the number of farmers in recent years. Nonetheless, their power has certainly waned in Europe, as has been reflected in their declining ability to shape the EU Common Agricultural Policy to their demands.

Neo-corporatist methods, whereby the government gives official or semiofficial recognition to peak associations of business and labor (and sometimes agriculture), consults them regularly, and often brokers agreements between or among them, were fairly common in much of Europe in the 1960s and 1970s and continue to a lesser degree today but have been much more widespread in some EU member states than in others. Although analysts disagree over precise measurements of neo-corporatism, there is almost universal consensus that Austria, Sweden, the Netherlands, Denmark, and Germany have employed this approach more than Southern European states or the United Kingdom. Weak, fragmented labor unions in Italy, Spain, and France have made it impractical there, while the strength of neoliberal/economic libertarian ideology in Britain since the late 1970s has made it a rarity there in recent years. It has never been used widely in the United States, both because of the weakness of organized labor and because of the strength of economic libertarian ideology. Supporters of neo-corporatism commonly argue that it promotes stable democracy by engaging the representatives of major economic sectors and especially by including organized labor as a partner with business and government. Its critics usually attack it for relying on elite bargains that inevitably exclude other interests.[26]

Table 15.10 presents recent figures on labor union membership in the EU member states and two recent indices of neo-corporatism by different authors. Though the numbers are imprecise, particularly with regard to measures of neo-corporatism, they call attention to some very real differences in interest group patterns among contemporary EU member states.

Despite broad similarities among the participatory structures and processes of the West-

TABLE 15.10   Labor Union Membership and Neo-Corporatism in EU Member States

Nation-state	Union members % of work force	Neo-corporatism EU rank*	
		Siaroff	Lijphart-Crepaz
Austria	53	1	1
Belgium	77	8	7
Denmark	80	4	4
Finland	81	6	6
France	9	10	9
Germany	29	5	5
Greece	30	15	n./a.
Ireland	55	9	8
Italy	15 (a)	13	10
Luxembourg	n./a.	7	n./a.
Netherlands	29	3	3
Portugal	42	12	n./a.
Spain	10 (b)	14	n./a.
Sweden	83	2	2
United Kingdom	34	11	11

* A rank of 1 indicates the system having the most neo-corporatist features.

(a) Many estimates are higher than 15%. Ebbinghaus and Visser give a figure of 30.9% for 1997.

(b) Most estimates are higher than 10%. The European Foundation for the Improvement of Living and Working Conditions reports a figure of 18.2% for Spain in 1997. Other estimates are generally in the 15–20% range.

Sources: Coplin and O'LearyO'Leary, eds., *Political Risk Yearbook 2000*, Vol. 6, for union membership percentages. For neo-corporatist measures, Siaroff, "Corporatism in 24 Industrial Democracies," and Lijphart and Crepaz, "Corporatism and Consensus Democracy in 18 Countries."

ern European political systems of today, this section has illustrated that there are some noteworthy distinctions in their electoral systems and in their patterns of political parties and interest groups. The nation-states also differ widely in their use or non-use of referendums and workplace democracy methods.

COMPARATIVE MEMBER STATE–EU RELATIONS

Chapters Six, Eight, Ten, Twelve, and Fourteen have examined the relationships of the major member states with the EC/EU in considerable depth, analyzing both the distinctive national approaches to and influences on the EC/EU and the effects of the EC/EU on national governmental institutions, political processes, and public policies.

Nation-State Impacts on EU Public Policies

Although the ten smaller nation-states have in general enjoyed less ability than their larger neighbors to influence the EC/EU institutions and public policies, their impact has sometimes proved significant in select areas. The Netherlands, Denmark, and Sweden have often led the way (with Germany sometimes giving their efforts a major boost) to raise EC/EU environmental standards.[27] Ireland, Portugal, and Greece have usually joined Spain in pushing successfully for expansion of structural funds for poor regions and the new Cohesion Fund of the early 1990s specifically targeted to aid these members, often termed the "poor four."[28] Belgium, the Netherlands, and Luxembourg have long been in the vanguard, often with Italy and Germany, in advocating additional powers for the European Parliament and supranational development in general.[29] In contrast, Denmark has often joined Britain in slowing European integration, perhaps most notably by

rejecting the Maastricht Treaty in a referendum in 1992 and forcing a renegotiation that gained it several special provisions. Actions by individual small member states, such as Ireland's initial rejection of the Nice Treaty in a popular referendum, Denmark's similar initial rejection of the Maastricht Treaty, and Greece's insistence on the entry of the Greek section of Cyprus to the EU in 2004, have had important consequences for the European Union as a whole from time to time. The Benelux countries (Belgium, the Netherlands, and Luxembourg) as a group have had substantial influence, for example, in the critical steps in the mid-1950s that led to the Messina Conference and the subsequent establishment of the European Communities.[30]

One way of assessing national inputs into the EU has been to examine net contributors as opposed to net beneficiaries in terms of monetary contributions from each state to the EU and payments from the EU to each state. Table 15.11 illustrates the overall patterns in a recent, largely typical year (2000). Among the major member states, Germany has long been the major net contributor, with the United Kingdom in second place. France and Italy have also often been net contributors on a smaller scale, though Italy in 2000 was a net recipient. Spain has been the major net beneficiary among the major EU states. Among the other ten members, the Netherlands and Sweden have stood out as the major net donors. Ireland, Portugal, Spain, and Greece have received substantially more than they have paid. These differences among the member states reflect not only their relative wealth (high per capita GDP positively correlated with net contribution levels) but also the complex operations of the expensive Common Agricultural Policy and the cohesion policies, different levels of non-EU imports subject to the EU import duties, and special "deals" that have been arranged on various matters at different points in time.

TABLE 15.11   Member State Contributions to and Payments from the EU, 2000

Nation-state	Net contributions to EU	Net payments from EU	Contributions/payments as % of national GDP
	(in millions of euros)		
Austria	543.5		−0.27
Belgium	327.3		−0.13
Denmark		169.1	−0.10
Finland		216.9	0.17
France	1415.3		−0.10
Germany	9273.2		−0.47
Greece		4373.9	3.61
Ireland		1674.6	1.83
Italy		713.4	0.06
Luxembourg	65.1		−0.35
Netherlands	1737.7		−0.44
Portugal		2112.0	1.93
Spain		5005.9	0.86
Sweden	1177.4		−0.50
United Kingdom	3774.7		−0.25

Source: European Commission, 2001.

State Approaches to the EU

In addition to differences between net donors and recipients, and distinctive areas of policy impact, member states have tended to vary fairly consistently over their basic approaches to the EC/EU. For example, Portugal has tended to join Britain (and sometimes Germany) in favoring Atlanticism more than most other member states. In contrast, Ireland, Sweden, Finland, and Austria have long prided themselves as neutrals—neutrality, in fact, being a major reason why Sweden, Finland, and Austria did not join the EC/EU until after the end of the Cold War. Now, of course, the meaning of neutrality has become less clear than during the Cold War.[31]

The supranational versus intergovernmental dimension has long been an important one, too, and one on which EC/EU member states have tended to take fairly consistent approaches. The Benelux countries have tended to join Germany, Italy, and Spain in giving at least rhetorical support to supranational initiatives aimed at deepening European integration. In many respects, the Benelux countries have, in fact, taken the lead since the foundation of the European integration project in the early 1950s in consistently advocating supranational development. Ireland, despite its initial choice to join Britain in the European Free Trade Association, its close trade ties to Britain, and its opting out (with Britain) of the Schengen agreements on border controls, has often taken supranational positions also, as have Austria and Finland since their admission in 1995. On the other hand, Denmark, Sweden, Greece, and Portugal have most often taken the intergovernmental approach associated with France and, even more so, Britain. However, on the supranational-intergovernmental continuum, it is important to distinguish rhetoric from reality (witness Italy's poor implementation record) and to recognize that the degree of a member state's support for one or the other approach has often varied considerably from issue to issue, depending on its leaders' perceptions of their "national interest" or their ideological goals. Thus, for instance, Britain under Margaret Thatcher was willing to accept some supranational development in 1985–1987 in order to achieve the single-market reforms that it desired; while it vehemently resisted those (such as the Social Charter and subsequent Social Chapter) that it deemed likely to have socialistic effects. As has been stressed in previous chapters, a member state's position on the intergovernmental-supranational spectrum often entails considerable complexity, reflecting the nature of the particular issues at stake, the particular government in office, and frequent gaps between rhetorical support and actual implementation. Nevertheless, Figure 15.3 provides a rough picture of the relative positions that member states have adopted over their years of membership in the EC/EU on the general issues of intergovernmentalism versus supranationalism.[32]

Popular attitudes toward the European Union also vary considerably among the EU member states. In some cases, as in the United Kingdom and Sweden, popular skepticism about national membership in the EU and the benefits of membership for their country is closely aligned with the government's cautious and intergovernmental approaches to European integration. As Table 15.12 illustrates, the British and Swedish publics demonstrated the least support for the EU among the 15 member states in the Eurobarometer survey of July 2003 (a pattern that had been duplicated quite consistently in previous opinion samplings). At the same time, the patterns of positive public views of the EU, evident in Luxembourg, the Netherlands, and Belgium in this survey and many other opinion measurements, have complemented their governments' integrationist policies. In some other cases, such as Finland and Austria, however, the "fit" between popular views and governmental approaches to the EU has been less evident.

The Impact of the EU on Nation-States

In analyzing the impact of the EC/EU on member states, it is important to stress that the impact is widely mediated through distinctive national institutions (though these may themselves undergo change in the process). As has been noted repeatedly, the European Union relies very heavily upon national administrations for implementation and national courts for adjudication of disputes. With regard to implementation, there has been considerable variation in the records of member states in transposing European directives into national law. Table 15.13 illustrates the differing records of member states with regard to the following: 1) The percentage of European directives for which the member state has sent notification of

---

Intergovernmental				Supranational
United Kingdom	Denmark	Ireland	Austria	Belgium
	France		Finland	Luxembourg
	Greece		Germany	Netherlands
	Portugal		Italy	
	Sweden		Spain	

FIGURE 15.3   Member States' Long-Term General Approaches to Issues of Intergovernmentalism and Supranationalism in the EU

TABLE 15.12   Attitudes Toward the European Union Among Populations of Member States, July 2003

Question 1: Generally speaking, do you think that (our country's) membership in the European Union is . . . ?

Question 2: Taking everything into consideration, would you say that (our country) has on balance benefited or not from being a member of the European Union?

Member state	Question 1		Question 2	
	Good (%)	Bad (%)	Benefited (%)	Not (%)
Austria	34%	19%	41%	43%
Belgium	67	7	57	23
Denmark	63	16	70	15
Finland	42	17	46	40
France	50	12	50	26
Germany	59	8	45	34
Greece	61	8	74	19
Ireland	67	5	77	10
Italy	64	6	52	22
Luxembourg	85	4	74	18
Netherlands	73	5	65	19
Portugal	61	9	68	20
Spain	62	6	62	19
Sweden	41	27	31	50
United Kingdom	30	25	32	44
EU	54	11	50	29

Source: Eurobarometer, July 2003.

transposition during 1999. The higher the percentage, the greater the rate of transposition, indicating a major step toward implementation. 2) The number of infringement proceedings brought against each member state in 1999 in the form of (a) letters of formal notice, the first infringement stage; (b) reasoned opinions by the commission, the next stage; and finally (c) referrals to the European Court of Justice. High percentages of transposition and low numbers of proceedings have generally been viewed as indicators of a high degree of implementation of Community directives. Over many years, Italy has had an especially poor implementation record, as has Greece, though Italy rose from last place (fifteenth) in 1998 to tenth place in 1999 in its notification of transposition rate and ranked fourteenth (ahead of France) rather than its once-common fifteenth place regarding infringement proceedings. In contrast, the Nordic countries, the Netherlands, and the United Kingdom have continued their long records as effective implementers of European directives.

TABLE 15.13 Implementation: Notification Rates and Infringement Records of EU Member States, 1999

Nation-state	Notification rate (rank)	Letters of formal notice	Reasoned opinions	Referrals	ECJ infringement action total (rank)
Austria	94.94 (8)	112	45	10	164 (6)
Belgium	94.88 (9)	136	67	29	232 (12)
Denmark	97.13 (1)	40	9	2	51 (1)
Finland	95.86 (4)	43	13	1	57 (2)
France	93.82 (12)	236	144	63	443 (15)
Germany	95.49 (6)	142	61	19	222 (11)
Greece	92.02 (15)	154	87	34	275 (13)
Ireland	94.13 (11)	98	54	20	172 (8)
Italy	93.62 (10)	160	94	44	298 (14)
Luxembourg	93.28 (14)	96	49	23	168 (7)
Netherlands	96.15 (3)	77	35	7	119 (4)
Portugal	93.36 (13)	114	52	18	184 (10)
Spain	96.47 (2)	112	50	12	174 (9)
Sweden	95.80 (5)	46	14	2	62 (3)
United Kingdom	95.41 (7)	83	42	9	134 (5)
EU Average	94.53	110	54	20	184

With regard to national governmental institutions, several general effects of the EC/EU are of particular note. Europeanization has almost certainly furthered the juridification of policy, strengthening national judicial roles, though the impact has been more noticeable in systems such as Britain's that previously assigned the courts only limited political roles. Other fairly widespread institutional effects of EC/EU membership have been declining roles for national parliaments and encouragement of subnational demands for increased autonomy and "fair shares" of regional development funds from the EC/EU. However, some parliaments—in Germany and Denmark, most notably—have sought with considerable success to reassert their influence within the EC/EU framework. Moreover, national-subnational governmental relations reflect a variety of domestic pressures that have often outweighed EC/EU influences. For example, in the United Kingdom, rising Scottish and Welsh nationalism predate British entry to the EC and have been fairly independent of it; while Margaret Thatcher as prime minister actually diminished the autonomy of British local governments and abolished metropolitan governments at a time when much of Western Europe was engaged in decentralization.

The general EC/EU impact on national political parties has been to bring Socialist/Social Democratic/Labor parties (and sometimes Communist and other left parties) to accept the single market and competition policies that would once have been anathema to them. In addition, it has tended to draw them to accept NATO membership also, especially when (as in Spain) this has been widely viewed as necessary for the country's integration into "Europe." Other factors partially independent of the EC/EU, such as the erosion of the traditional industrial working class in much of Western Europe, and leaders' assessments of the imperatives of an increasingly global competitive economy (illustrated in the eyes of many by the failure of Mitterrand's "socialist" Keynesian policies in the early 1980s), have also pushed the European Socialist parties toward the political center. However, there can be little doubt that Europeanization has been an important part of this process.[33]

In some member states at various points in time, EC/EU issues have split major political parties internally or formed a significant dividing line between parties. The British Labour party from the 1960s to the 1980s, the British Conservative party since the 1980s, the French Gaullist party in the late 1970s and again in the 1990s, and the Danish and Swedish Social Democratic parties in the 1990s and in the current decade have been examples of major parties divided internally in rather critical ways over key EC/EU issues. The left-right division over European issues in Italy in the 1950s and the pattern of far left and far right joint opposition to the pro-European integration positions of the center-left and center-right in many EU member states in recent years are examples of some of the different effects that the EC/EU has had on national party systems.

Still another type of influence of the EC/EU has been its drawing of individual parties into the transnational party groups that are centered in the European Parliament. The most organized and effective of these has been the Party of European Socialists (PES), which has drawn in the Socialist/Social Democratic/Labor parties of all member states and the formerly Communist party of Italy once it renamed itself and reorganized as the Left Democrats. The European People's party (EPP) and the Euro-

pean Liberal and Democratic Reformers (ELDR), while somewhat more loosely organized than the PES, have also drawn in broad arrays of Conservative and Christian Democratic national parties in the case of the EPP and Centrist and Liberal parties in the case of the ELDR. However, European Parliament elections continue to be shaped primarily by national party political issues, and voter turnout in them is uniformly lower than turnouts in national parliamentary elections. Moreover, transnational party influence on top national political party leaders has been minimal.[34]

In the realm of interest-group politics, the EC/EU has opened up new transnational arenas for them to exercise influence outside the framework of the nation-state while simultaneously pursuing lobbying and other activities in their home countries. As with political parties, it has also fostered the development of transnational interest groups, such as the Union of Industrial and Employers' Confederations of Europe (UNICE) and the European Roundtable of Industrialists (ERT) for business groups, as well as the European Trade Union Confederation (ETUC) for national labor unions. Europeanization has probably benefited multinational corporations and peak business associations and trade associations more than small business groups, labor unions, or new social movements, though in some cases (such as Britain under Thatcher) environmental groups have found that they have had more influence in Brussels than in their national government. The edge for big business has come from its extensive financial resources, organization on a transnational basis, and easy access to both EU and national officials. In a global market environment marked by increasingly high technology, executives of multinational corporations can also make persuasive arguments that they may shift substantial portions of their operations to locations where regulations are lighter and labor costs are lower if officials fail to heed their demands. Most analysts have concluded that the European Union's interest group processes have been more pluralist than neo-corporatist. But its pluralism seems to be increasingly tilted toward large business corporations and their executives. Writing of capitalism and democracy a quarter century ago, Charles Lindblom concluded, "The large private corporation fits oddly into democratic theory and vision. Indeed, it does not fit." Contemporary concerns in the European Union about the democratic deficit often reflect fears that corporate power has too often prevailed over democratic aspirations in Europe, as in the United States and the world at large. Still, European socialist parties and their allies among other parties, labor unions, and new social movements may yet impose new democratic constraints on the multinational corporations and redirect public policies toward enhanced equality. Though the likelihood does not appear great in the near future, it is greater in the European Union than in any other part of the contemporary world.[35]

"The large private corporation fits oddly into democratic theory and vision. Indeed, it does not fit."

Charles E. Lindblom, *Politics and Markets* *(1977),* 356.

---

* * *

Although the chief focus of this book as a whole is on the major nation-states in the European Union, this chapter has broadened the scope of the analysis to encompass a general comparative overview of the 15 pre-2004 member states of the European Union. It has compared and contrasted the countries regarding their patterns of political development, governmental institutions, and participatory structures and processes. It has also compared and contrasted their relations with the European Union. In the process, it has drawn upon major theories of comparative politics to enhance understanding

of broad patterns that have characterized the member states in the EU and to compare them with the United States and other countries in other parts of the world.

As the quote from Mark Mazower at the outset of this chapter suggested, the European nation-states retain distinctive identities even as Europeanization and globalization have persuaded them to pool sovereignty to an extent unimaginable half a century ago. Each member state uniquely draws upon its own historical experiences and operates through its own governmental institutions and participatory structures and processes even while engaging in the project of European integration. This chapter has not only reviewed the major nation-states in the European Union in a broader comparative context than the previous chapters have done, but it has also highlighted the most distinctive features and contributions of the smaller EU member states to provide readers with a well-rounded overview of the contemporary European Union.

The next (and final) chapter will analyze the prospective eastward enlargement of the European Union. Because the past experiences and current features of most of the prospective new EU entrant states differ markedly from those of the pre-2004 member states, this expansion is likely to pose the biggest single challenge of the next decade for the EU and its member states. In fact, expansion has already begun to alter the institutions and public policies of the current European Union as the EU prepares to confront that challenge.

SUMMARY

- Nation-state development occurred relatively early in England, France, Sweden, Denmark, and the Netherlands; in contrast, Austria, Finland, and Ireland attained nation-state status only after World War I.

- Regional language-based ethnic divisions have been particularly evident challenges to the nation-state in Spain and Belgium; religion-based cultural division in Northern Ireland has posed a major challenge to the United Kingdom; regional identity differences have challenged the Italian nation-state.

- Further complicating issues of national identity have been the perceptions of many recent foreign immigrants to European nation-states that they are not really full members of the "nation" in which they reside.

- Many Europeans see themselves simultaneously as Europeans, members of a nation, and members of an ethno-national subgroup; "Europeanness" appears to be more compatible with national identity in Germany, Italy, Spain, the Benelux countries, and increasingly even in France, than in the United Kingdom.

- The "first wave" of democratization, that which occurred prior to 1918, proved strongest and most durable in northwestern Europe; it swept over much of the rest of Europe for a time but receded in the 1920s and 1930s; the "second wave" of democratization after World War II encompassed all of the pre-2004 member states of the EU except Spain and Portugal and (for a time) Greece; Spain, Portugal, and Greece democratized for the long term only in the 1970s.

- Feudalism was the prevalent distribution system in Europe during the middle ages, though it was weaker in Britain and Scandinavia than elsewhere; free-market capitalism emerged most strongly in Britain and the Netherlands but spread eastward, usually in somewhat state-oriented forms; the modern mixed economic distribution patterns emergent in the late nineteenth and twentieth centuries have mixed socialistic concerns with social welfare with capitalistic markets and private property.

- Among the European mixed economies, Britain and Ireland best illustrate "liberal" patterns; Scandinavian countries exemplify social democratic-egalitarian welfare states; and most of the other EU member states tend toward what Esping Anderson has labeled "corporatist-statist" welfare states, providing more social security than liberal mixed economies but less equality than social democratic ones.

- The major factors associated with high social-services spending among EU member states have been high per capita wealth, large and influential labor unions, dominance of government by parties of the Left, mobilization of women, extensive dependence on international trade, and relatively old and well-established social-welfare programs.

- Global competition and shifting demographics leading to the aging of European populations have generated pressures since the 1970s to restrain the growth of European welfare states and, in some cases, even to impose spending and benefits reductions.

- No pre-2004 EU member state has a United States–style presidential form of government; cabinet-parliamentary institutions prevail in most; France has a hybrid presidential-parliamentary model, as Finland and Portugal also have had in the recent past before moving in a cabinet-parliamentary direction.

- A monarch serves as the head of state in Belgium, Denmark, the Netherlands, Spain, Sweden, and the United Kingdom, while the Grand Duke does so in Luxembourg; in the other eight pre-2004 members states, a president fills this role (with France assigning the president the most extensive constitutional powers).

- Seven of the 15 pre-2004 EU member states (Germany, Italy, Spain, France, Austria, Belgium, and Portugal) have constitutional courts or similar bodies (i.e., the French Constitutional Council) that exercise powers of constitutional judicial review; even in the other pre-2004 EU member states, the judiciary has gained powers of legal review in recent years in the course of what some analysts have termed "the juridification of the policy process."

- Of the 15 pre-2004 EU member states, only 3 have federal systems prescribed by their constitutions: Austria, Belgium, and Germany; however, there has been considerable decentralization in some of the unitary states, with Spain becoming what many analysts deem "quasi-federal" and the United Kingdom devolving some authority to Scotland and Wales; both France and Italy have introduced less dramatic decentralizing reforms in traditionally unitary systems.

- Among EU member states, Italy has made the most use of popular referendums; Denmark, Finland, France, Ireland, and Sweden have employed them with moderate frequency; the others, with the exception of Germany and Portugal (which have not used them at the national level under their current regimes) have employed them only rarely.

- Workplace participation in business corporate decision-making by employees has been most institutionalized in Germany, Austria, and Sweden.

- Women's participation in government and parliaments has increased in all EU member states in recent years but is far more widespread in the Nordic countries and the Netherlands and Belgium than elsewhere; Italian and Greek women have been the least likely to win parliamentary seats.

- The United Kingdom and France use single-member districts to elect members of the House of Commons and National Assembly, respectively, though the United Kingdom uses a simple first-past-the-post system, while France provides for runoffs; proportional representation is used in all other pre-2004 EU member states, though Germany elects half of its Bundestag members by a first-past-the-post system and Italy now elects three-fourths of its legislators by this method.

- Voter turnout is higher in EU member states' national elections than in the United States; turnout has been highest in Austria, Belgium, and Italy in recent years.

- Political parties in most pre-2004 EU member states (with Ireland the major exception) and in the European Parliament are commonly arranged along a left-right spectrum; however, regional, populistic, and green parties are often difficult to place on this spectrum.

- The parliaments of Greece, Spain, and the United Kingdom have been most dominated by two-party politics in recent years; Belgium, Finland, Italy, and the Netherlands possess the parliaments most fractured by multiple parties; coalition governments are usually necessary in multiparty systems.

- Business interest groups are powerful forces in all EU member states and in the EU itself; labor unions are generally stronger in Northern Europe (especially in Sweden and Denmark) than in Mediterranean Europe.

- Neo-corporatist methods of interest group–government relations have been more widely employed in Austria, Sweden, the Netherlands, Denmark, and Germany than in the rest of the pre-2004 EU member states.

- Major donor states to the EU have been Germany, the United Kingdom, the Netherlands, and Sweden; states consistently receiving more from the EU than they have paid to it have been Spain, Ireland, Portugal, and Greece (often termed the "poor four" before Ireland's rapid economic growth and the admission of poorer states in Central and Eastern Europe).

- The Benelux countries have given the most consistent support to supranational initiatives aimed at deepening European integration; Austria, Finland, Germany, Italy, and Spain have usually tended in a supranational direction; the United Kingdom has been the most consistently supportive of an intergovernmental EU but has often enjoyed support for this position from Denmark, France, Greece, Portugal, and Sweden; particular issues and time periods have sometimes altered the above patterns.

- Italy and Greece have had consistently poor records of implementing EU laws, and France has had a poor record in recent years; the Nordic countries, the Netherlands, and the United Kingdom have long records as effective implementers.

- Europeanization has furthered the juridification of public policies and strengthened national judicial roles, weakened national parliaments in general, encouraged subnational demands for increased autonomy, and moved most socialist and social democratic parties toward acceptance of single-market and competition policies and toward center-left rather than left ideology.

- Another influence of the EC/EU has been to draw national parties into transnational party groups that are centered in the European Parliament; however, national parties clearly retain their autonomy and distinctiveness.

- The EC/EU has fostered transnational interest groups and has probably enhanced the influence of business groups over labor unions.

- European nation-states retain distinctive features and identities despite the Europeanization associated with the EC/EU.

ENDNOTES

1. Gabriel Almond and G. Bingham Powell, *Comparative Politics: A Developmental Approach* (Boston: Little, Brown, 1966), 34–41.

2. Rogers Brubaker, *Citizenship and Nationhood in France and Germany* (Cambridge, MA: Harvard University Press, 1992); Stephen Wood, *Germany, Europe, and the Persistence of Nations* (Aldershot: Ashgate, 1998), esp. Ch. 1; Almond and Powell, *Comparative Politics*, 34–41.

3. Damian Tambini, *Nationalism in Italian Politics* (London: Routledge, 2001); Gian Enrico Rusconi, "Will Italy Remain a Nation?" in Mark Donovan, ed., *Italy*, vol. 1 (Dartmouth: Ashgate, 1998). Also see the surveys from the United Kingdom and Spain cited in Jan-Erik Lane and Svante Ersson, *Politics and Society in Western Europe*, 4th ed. (Thousand Oaks, CA: Sage, 1999), 62–65.

4. Warren Hoge, "Britain's Nonwhites Feel Un-British," *New York Times*, April 4, 2002, A6.

5. B. Guy Peters and Christian Hunold, *European Politics Reconsidered*, 2nd ed. (New York: Holmes & Meier, 1999), 29.

6. Alan Milward, *The European Rescue of the Nation-State* (London: Routledge, 1992); Thomas Risse, "A European Identity? Europeanization and the Evolution of Nation-State Identities," in Maria Green Cowles, et al., *Transforming Europe: Europeanization and Domestic Change* (Ithaca, NY: Cornell University Press, 2001), 198–216; Joachim Schild, "National v. European Identities? French and Germans in the European Multi-Level System," *Journal of Common Market Studies* 39, 2 (June 2001), 331–351.

7. Samuel P. Huntington, *The Third Wave* (Norman, OK: University of Oklahoma Press, 1991), esp. Chs. 1 and 2.

8. Douglas Rae, *The Analysis of Political Cleavages* (New Haven, CT: Yale University Press, 1970), 1. Also see Stein Rokkan, et al., *Citizens, Elections, Parties: Approaches to the Comparative Study of the Processes of Development* (New York: David McKay, 1970), esp. Chs. 2 and 3.

9. Gösta Esping-Andersen, *Three Worlds of Welfare Capitalism* (Cambridge: Polity Press, 1990).

10. Walter Korpi and Joakim Palme, "New Politics and Class Politics in the Context of Austerity and Globalization: Welfare State Regress in 18

Countries," *American Political Science Review* 97, 3 (August 2003), 425–446; Michael Hill, *Social Policy: A Comparative Analysis* (London: Prentice Hall, 1996), esp. Ch. 2; Arnold J. Heidenheimer, Hugh Heclo, and Carolyn Teich Adams, *Comparative Public Policy: The Politics of Social Choice in Europe and America*, 2nd ed. (New York: St. Martin's, 1983), 206–213.

11. Lane and Ersson, *Politics and Society in Western Europe*, 208–217; Eric Solsten, "Government and Politics," in Eric Solsten and Sandra Meditz, eds., *Finland: A Country Study*, 2nd ed. (Washington, DC: U.S. Government, 1990), esp. 229–234.

12. Dehousse, *The European Court of Justice*, Ch. 4.

13. John Fitzmaurice, *The Politics of Belgium: A Unique Federalism* (London: Hurst, 1996).

14. John Newhouse, *Europe Adrift* (New York: Pantheon, 1997), Ch. 2.

15. Thomas E. Cronin, *Direct Democracy: The Politics of Initiative, Referendum, and Recall* (Cambridge, MA: Harvard University Press, 1989); Glenn Tinder, *Political Thinking: The Perennial Questions*, 5th ed. (New York: HarperCollins, 1991), 105–109.

16. Michael Walzer, "Town Meetings and Workers' Control," in Terence Ball and Richard Dagger, eds., *Ideals and Ideologies*, 2nd ed. (New York: HarperCollins, 1995), 56–65; Jürg Steiner, *European Democracies*, 2nd ed. (New York: Longman, 1991), Ch. 8.

17. Ferdinand A. Hermens, *Democracy or Anarchy?* (Notre Dame, IN: Review of Politics, 1941); Clarence Hoag and Gerorge Hallett, *Proportional Representation* (New York: Crowell-Collier and Macmillan, 1926); Vernon Bogdanor and David Butler, eds., *Democracy and Elections: Electoral Systems and Their Political Consequences* (New York: Cambridge University Press, 1983).

18. Lane and Ersson, *Politics and Society in Western Europe*, 141.

19. Maurice Duverger, *Political Parties: Their Organization and Activity in the Modern State* (London: Methuen, 1954); Douglas Rae, *The Political Consequences of Electoral Laws*, rev. ed. (New Haven, CT: Yale University Press, 1971).

20. Rokkan, et al., *Citizens, Elections, Parties*.

21. Giovanni Sartori, *Parties and Party Systems: A Framework for Analysis* (Cambridge: Cambridge University Press, 1976).

22. Arend Lijphart, "Consociational Democracy," *World Politics* 21 (January 1969), 207–225; Kenneth MacRae, ed., *Consociational Democracy: Political Accommodation in Segmented Societies* (Toronto: McClelland and Stewart, 1974).

23. Ronald Inglehart, *The Silent Revolution: Changing Values and Political Styles Among Western Publics* (Princeton, NJ: Princeton University Press, 1977); Inglehart, *Modernization and Postmodernization: Cultural, Economic, and Political Change in 43 Societies* (Princeton, NJ: Princeton University Press, 1997); Damian Tambini, *Nationalism in Italian Politics* (London: Routledge, 2001); Anna Cento Bull, "Ethnicity, Racism, and the Northern League," in Levy, ed., *Italian Regionalism*, 171–188; Martin Schain, Aristide Zolberg, and Patrick Hossay, eds., *Shadows over Europe: The Development and Impact of the Extreme Right in Western Europe* (New York: Palgrave Macmillan, 2002).

24. See the useful collection of articles in Shaun Bowler, David Farrell, and Richard Katz, eds., *Party Discipline and Parliamentary Government* (Columbus, OH: Ohio State University Press, 1999).

25. Russell Dalton, *Citizen Politics: Public Opinion and Political Parties in Advanced Industrial Democracies*, 2nd ed. (Chatham, NJ: Chatham House, 1996).

26. Alan Siaroff, "Corporatism in 24 Industrial Democracies: Meaning and Measurement," *European Journal of Political Research* 36, 2 (October 1999), 175–205; Arend Lijphart and M. M. L. Crepaz, "Corporatism and Consensus Democracy in 18 Countries," *British Journal of Political Science* 21 (1991), 235–256.

27. Alberta Sbragia, "Environmental Policy: Economic Constraints and External Pressures," in Helen and William Wallace, eds., *Policy-Making in the European Union*, 4th ed. (Oxford: Oxford University Press, 2000), esp. 294 and 300; Leslie Eliason, "Denmark: Small State with a Big Voice," in Eleanor Zeff and Ellen Pirro, eds., *The European Union and the Member States* (Boulder, CO: Lynne Rienner, 2001), esp. 209–210; Karen Anderson, "Sweden: Retreat from Exceptionalism," in Zeff and Pirro, eds., *The EU and the Member States*, 294.

28. Michael Marks, *The Formation of European Policy in Post-Franco Spain* (Avebury, VT: Ashgate, 1997), 43–75; Richard Finnegan, "Ireland: Brussels and

the Celtic Tiger," in Zeff and Pirro, eds., *The EU and the Member States*, esp. 176, 179.

29. Jan Beyers, Bart Kerremans, and Peter Bursens, "Belgium, the Netherlands, and Luxembourg: Diversity Among the Benelux Countries," in Zeff and Pirro, eds., *The EU and the Member States*, 59; Andrew Moravcsik, *The Choice for Europe* (Ithaca, NY: Cornell University Press, 1998), 309.

30. Eliason, "Denmark," 194–199; Moravcsik, *The Choice for Europe*, 376.

31. Joaquin Roy and Aimee Kanner, "Spain and Portugal: Betting on Europe," in Zeff and Pirro, eds., *The EU and the Member States*, 238, 240, 255; Anderson, "Sweden," 287–288, 293–294.

32. Classifications of states on the supranational-intergovernmental continuum are based upon a wide variety of accounts, particularly those in Zeff and Pirro, eds., *The EU and the Member States*, and Moravcsik, *The Choice for Europe*. On Thatcher's Britain, see Stephen George, *An Awkward Partner*, 3rd ed. (Oxford: Oxford University Press, 1998), Chs. 6 and 7; and David Gowland and Arthur Turner, *Reluctant Europeans* (New York: Longman, 2000), Ch. 18.

33. Robert Ladrech, *Social Democracy and the Challenge of European Union* (Boulder, CO: Lynne Rienner, 2000); Marks, *The Formation of Euro-pean Policy*, esp. Chs. 4-6; chapters on socialist parties in John Gaffney, ed., *Political Parties and the European Union* (London: Routledge, 1996).

34. Simon Hix, "The Transnational Party Federations," in Gaffney, ed., *Political Parties and the European Union*, 308–331; Ladrech, *Social Democracy and the Challenge of European Union*, esp. 11–14.

35. The quotation is from Charles Lindblom, *Politics and Markets: The World's Political-Economic Systems* (New York: Basic Books, 1977), 356. David Coen, "The Evolution of the Large Firm as a Political Actor," *Journal of European Public Policy* 4, 1 (1997), 91–108; Franz Traxler and Philippe G. Schmitter, "The Emerging Euro-Polity and Organized Interests," *European Journal of International Relations* 1 (June 1995), 191–218; Michael Noller in collaboration with Nicola Fielder, "Lobbying for a Europe of Big Business: The European Roundtable of Industrialists," in Volker Bornschier, ed., *State-Building in Europe: The Revitalization of Western European Integration* (Cambridge: Cambridge University Press, 2000), 187–209; Andrew McLaughlin, Grant Jordan, and William Maloney, "Corporate Lobbying in the European Community," *Journal of Common Market Studies* 31, 2 (June 1993), 191–212.

Chapter 16

EASTWARD ENLARGEMENT OF THE EUROPEAN UNION

"We dreamt, whether in or out of prison, of a Europe without barbed wire, high walls, artificially divided nations and gigantic stockpiles of weapons, of a Europe free of 'blocs,' of a European policy based on respect for human rights…. We must not be afraid to dream of the seemingly impossible if we want the seemingly impossible to become a reality. Without dreaming of a better Europe we shall never build a better Europe."

—Vaclav Havel, President of Czechoslovakia, 1990.

Vaclav Havel, the Czech playwright and human rights activist, himself imprisoned for a time by the Czechoslovak Communist regime, articulated the dreams of many Central and East Europeans as he expressed his vision in 1990 of a "better Europe." Whether the reality of the expanded post-2004 European Union will fulfill the hopes of Central and East Europeans remains to be seen.

The sudden collapse of Communism and the end of the Cold War in the 1989–1991 period brought dramatic political and economic changes in Central and Eastern Europe that virtually forced the issues of eastward enlargement of the European Union onto the EU agenda just as the Treaty of European Union (Maastricht Treaty) was taking shape. Only anti-Communist NATO-member Turkey in Eastern Europe (in fact situated largely in Asia Minor, not Europe) had previously sought membership (in 1987) in the European Community. Its application had been put on hold when the European Commission had issued a negative assessment of it in December 1989. By the end of the decade of the 1990s, however, the European Union had officially listed 13 Central and Eastern European nation-states as candidates for entry, including Turkey, even though most analysts believed that Turkey (for reasons to be discussed later in this chapter) was unlikely to gain admission soon. The 13 accession states are Bulgaria, Cyprus, the Czech Republic, Estonia, Hungary, Latvia, Lithuania, Malta, Poland, Romania, Slovakia, Slovenia, and Turkey. In June 2004, the EU added Croatia as an accession state. All except Cyprus, Malta, and Turkey had been under Communist rule during the Cold War era. Beyond these 14 accession states lie a number of other European nation-states, including the giant, Russia, which has most of its population in Europe but extends across the continent of Asia as well.

This chapter first discusses the major challenges posed by a massive enlargement of the EU. It then focuses on Poland as the newest major nation-state to join the European Union

MAP 16.1   The Eastward Expansion of the European Union

and places it in a context facilitating comparisons and contrasts with the previous major nation-states in the EU. Finally, it briefly discusses Turkey and Russia and their present and likely future relations with the EU.

THE CHALLENGES OF EASTWARD ENLARGEMENT

Pressed by a growing number of Central and Eastern European states eager to enter the European Union, the European Council at its Copenhagen Summit in June 1993 adopted the so-called Copenhagen criteria by which the applications of prospective member states would be assessed. These were 1) achievement of stable constitutional democracy, including protection of minority rights; 2) achievement of a functioning market economy; and 3) adherence to the obligations of EU membership, including adoption of all of its existing laws (*acquis communitaire*). Three years later, in 1996, employing these criteria as guideposts, the European Commission made an evaluation of each applicant state's suitability for EU membership and recommended that the EU begin accession negotiations in 1998 with the Czech Republic, Cyprus, Estonia, Hungary, Poland, and Slovenia. These negotiations were endorsed by the European Council in December 1997 and began in Brussels on March 31, 1998, when the foreign ministers of each of the six nation-states held opening discussions (separately) with their EU counterparts. The substantive negotiations have proceeded between the EU and each state separately, each at its own pace and in its own way. Meanwhile, the European Council at its Luxembourg Summit in December 1997 again put Turkey's application on hold (as in 1989), arousing considerable anger among the Turks. However, the Helsinki European Council meeting of December 1999 agreed that Turkey could become an accession state and laid the groundwork for Latvia, Lithuania, Malta,

and Slovakia to move toward EU entry along with the other six prospective entrants noted previously. Bulgaria and Romania, two additional accession states, were to assume a place behind the first ten prospective EU members but likely ahead of Turkey. In December 2002, the EU leaders set 2004 as the entry date for ten of the accession states, pending each state's approval of the terms in 2003: Cyprus, the Czech Republic, Estonia, Hungary, Latvia, Lithuania, Malta, Poland, Slovakia, and Slovenia. Bulgaria and Romania were slated for likely entry in 2007. Much to the dismay of the Turkish government (and the United States government, which had pressed the EU on behalf of Turkey), the EU leaders continued to delay setting a definite timetable for accession negotiations with Turkey. As of August 2004, the deadline for EU consideration of a timetable for negotiations with Turkey was December 2004. Meanwhile, in June 2004 the EU leaders put Croatia on a fast track to enter the EU, likely to occur some time between 2007 and 2009.[1]

The likely admission of 13 (possibly 14, counting Turkey) new members to the EU presents a number of major challenges to the European Union. Though constitutional democracy now appears to have stabilized and developed a fairly strong base of support in many of the 14 applicant states, that is less clear in Slovakia, Bulgaria, Romania, and Turkey than in the other 10 nation-states. Trust in democratic institutions (including political parties, parliaments, labor unions, and private enterprises) and levels of civic engagement remain relatively low by West European standards across Central and Eastern Europe. Deep divisions between the Greek Cypriot government in Southern Cyprus and the Turkish Cypriot government claiming authority in the North create special political problems in Cyprus. Moreover, as Table 16.1 illustrates, all of the 14 except Slovenia are poorer in terms of per capita gross domestic product than even Portugal, the poorest of the pre-2004 15 member states of the EU.

TABLE 16.1 Population, GDP, and Per Capita GDP of EU Accession Candidates, Russia, and Portugal

Nation-State	Population (in millions)	GDP (in trillions)	Per capita GDP
Bulgaria	7.5	$57	$7,600
Croatia	4.5	47	10,700
Cyprus (Greek part)	0.6	9	16,000
Czech Republic	10.2	160	12,900
Estonia	1.3	17	12,300
Hungary	10.0	140	13,900
Latvia	2.3	24	10,100
Lithuania	3.6	40	11,200
Malta	0.4	7	17,700
Poland	38.6	427	11,000
Romania	22.4	154	6,900
Slovakia	5.4	72	13,300
Slovenia	2.0	37	18,300
Turkey	68.9	455	6,700
Russia	143.7	1,287	8,900
Portugal*	10.5	182	18,000

* Portugal is the poorest of the pre-2004 EU member states in per capita GDP.

Source: CIA World Fact Book, 2003. GDP and GDP per capita are calculated using the purchasing power parity method.

The economic gaps between the applicant states and the current EU members relate directly to two major public-policy challenges of eastward expansion for the EU—to the Common Agricultural Policy (CAP) and to the structural/cohesion policies. These two domains account for about 80 percent of the EU budget between them. Because about one-fourth of the GDP of the aspirant states is in agriculture, a major eastward enlargement will necessitate major revisions of the current EU agricultural policies and expenditures and relatively long transition periods for the integration of the agricultural sectors of the new members into the EU. Furthermore, the relatively low per capita GDP in all the new applicant states and the severe poverty in some of their internal regions will have major consequences for the structural funds and the Cohesion Fund. Because these have transferred wealth from the richer member states and regions within states in the EU to the poorer ones in the name of "cohesion," proposed major changes in them have aroused wide concerns, as have revisions of the CAP. The European Union has adopted a six-year budget plan for 2000–2006 that has partially addressed these problem areas. However, these issues are likely to continue to stir debate.[2]

Another major challenge to the EU posed by eastward enlargement has been the need to revamp EU institutions to accommodate the likely new member states. Obviously, the Commission would become too large and unwieldy if the 15 pre-2004 members retained their 20 Commission seats and then 13 or 14 new members gained Commission places on the same basis (two each for large nation-states, Poland and Turkey; one each for the smaller states). As a result, the Nice Summit in December 2000 agreed that the total Commission membership should not exceed a maximum of 27 (with a lower maximum perhaps to be adopted in the future), that no member should have more than one commissioner at a time, and that the nationalities of the commissioners should be determined by a system of rotation (leaving some member states without representation at some points in time) once the number of member states exceeded the number of commissioners. Commission President Romano Prodi has proposed establishment of an "inner cabinet" within the enlarged Commission, but this idea has met considerable resistance from those likely to be demoted to the "outer" ring of power among the commissioners and from small member states in general. Similarly, concerns emerged over enlarging the European Parliament to the point at which it would become unmanageable as a legislative institution. Therefore, the Nice Treaty fixed its limit at 732 and assigned each member state and prospective member state a number of representatives that would keep the total within this limit. As for the European Council, the Nice Treaty provided for expanded use of qualified majority voting, and concomitant reduction of those matters requiring unanimity, in light of the obvious difficulties of achieving unanimity among 28 or 29 member states' ministers. It also altered the weighting of the votes of the member states and, for the future, the likely accession states. Furthermore, the prospect of eastward expansion led the drafters of the Nice Treaty to seek to relieve a likely massive increase in the workload of the European Court of Justice (ECJ) by providing for the sharing of additional tasks with the Court of First Instance and the creation of specialized chambers for particular areas. The ECJ will continue to consist of one judge from each member state, thus enlarging it substantially. However, the Court may sit in a Grand Chamber of 13 judges, rather than always meeting in a plenary session of all judges. The proposed new European Union Constitution, drafted at a special convention in 2002–2003, has suggested further institutional revisions to cope with eastward enlargement. Therefore, the prospect of the eastward expansion has already necessitated a major alteration of the central institutions of the European Union and has spurred continuing debate over further revisions.[3]

Seeking to assess the destination of European integration as eastward expansion occurs, Jan Zielonka has sketched three broad structural alternatives: 1) limited enlargement in stages, admitting only a few applicant states at a time, and seeking to build a European Union federal state emphasizing cohesion, order, and a traditional border regime; 2) creation of a core group of member states able and willing to embark on further integration, and a periphery of less integrated member states; and 3) a "neo-medieval model" in which the European Union increasingly becomes more multi-layered and less state-centric, and its borders come to be more about civil rights and duties than about controlling flows of population. Though Zielonka favors the third option, and the first has been largely ruled out by the EU's addition of ten new members in 2004, some version of the second option of a "variable speed" EU may yet emerge.[4]

POLAND: THE NEWEST MAJOR NATION-STATE IN THE EUROPEAN UNION

"If Poland does not become a member of the EU, it will mean isolation, marginalization and in consequence the collapse of Polish civilization."

Former Polish Prime Minister Hanna Suchocka, May 22, 1995, *cited by Elzbieta Stadtmüller, "Polish Perceptions of the EU in the 1990s" (2000), 31.*

Among the 13 applicant states scheduled for EU entry by 2009, Poland is by far the largest. Indeed, Romania, the second-largest nation-state in the group, has a population only a little more than one-half that of Poland and a GDP of only a little more than one-third that of Poland. In comparison with the current major nation-states in the European Union, Poland has a population almost the same as that of Spain, though its GDP is less than one-half of Spain's. Therefore, Poland—the giant among the 13 most likely new members of the EU—is economically a pygmy compared with the current major EU member states, a factor likely to limit its abilities to shape the EU in the future.

This section offers an overview of Poland's political development, current governmental institutions, current political participatory processes, and relations with the European Union, in order to facilitate comparisons and contrasts with the five major nation-states of the pre-2004 European Union. Even as early as 2003, Poland was providing ample evidence that it would be an important contributor to the future course of the EU.

Political Development

During the Middle Ages, Poland at first consisted largely of Slavic tribes governed from the tenth century to the fourteenth century by the Piast dynasty. However, from 1386 to 1572, the Jagiellonian dynasty created a Polish-Lithuanian multiethnic state, composed of various Slavic groups, Lithuanians, and a large Jewish minority. The nobility played a major role during the Jagiellonian dynasty and asserted even larger roles through the Sejm (parliament) in the years after 1572. But wars, rebellions, and frequent paralysis of Polish government led to the decline of Poland by the late eighteenth century. Between 1772 and 1795, Poland was carved up by the Prussian, Austrian, and Russian empires and ceased to exist as a political entity. Nonetheless, Polish nationalism began to emerge among the general populace

even before partition and spread and intensified in the nineteenth century, fueling numerous Polish national uprisings, all of which were harshly repressed. Not until 1918, and the collapse of the German, Austrian, and Russian empires in World War I, did Poland regain its independence; and it had to fight the Red Army of the new Communist-led regime in Russia to secure that independence.[5]

The Polish nation-state created after World War I governed a population only 70 percent of whom were ethnically Polish—large minorities included Ukrainians, Jews, Belorussians, and Germans. Religion was intertwined with ethnonational identities: almost all Poles were Roman Catholics, most Ukrainians and Belorussians were Orthodox (though a large minority of the Ukrainians were Catholic), the Jews adhered to Judaism, and most Germans were Protestant. In addition to nation-building conflicts in the "new" Poland, there were difficulties over state-building, democracy, and economic-distribution issues. The initial state structure centered on a central government in a unitary system. Its cabinet-parliamentary structures were marked by unstable governments and frequent paralysis caused by multiparty conflicts in parliament. Although Poland had a medieval tradition of parliamentary checks on executive authority, its fledgling constitutional democracy did not function effectively. After just eight years, it collapsed in the face of a coup staged by forces under Josef Pilsudski, who became the dictator of Poland from 1926 until his death in 1935. Authoritarian rule became even more evident under the military regime that followed Pilsudski, until it gave way to the dual invasions of Poland by Hitler and Stalin in 1939, which again brought an end to an independent Polish nation-state. The Polish economy remained largely agricultural and mired in widespread poverty in the 1920s and 1930s, despite a land reform instituted in 1920 that led to somewhat wider distribution of land than had been the case previously.[6]

The Polish people suffered terribly during World War II. The Nazis (and in some cases their fellow Poles) exterminated more than three million Polish Jews. A similar number of other Poles perished in the war also, mostly through executions, starvation, or simply being worked to death, at the hands of both the German Nazis and the Soviet Communists. A common estimate is that more than 20 percent of the Polish population perished due to war-related causes between 1939 and 1945. Nor was Poland's ordeal to end with the termination of the war. At the Yalta Conference in 1945 among Stalin of the Soviet Union, Roosevelt of the United States, and Churchill of Britain, the Allied leadership informally agreed that Poland would be in the Soviet sphere of influence in the postwar era. A Communist regime under the Polish United Workers' party, backed by Soviet military force, imposed long-term authoritarian rule on a Poland that was moved westward to include former German territory so that the Soviet Union could retain the eastern portions that it had incorporated into its own territory.[7]

Communist rule in Poland during 1945–1989 was generally authoritarian rather than totalitarian because it faced strong resistance from the Roman Catholic Church (traditionally very strong in Poland and now a major focal point for resistance to atheistic Communism), farmers insistent on maintaining their property rights, and industrial workers. Workers' uprisings occurred repeatedly, in 1956, 1970, 1976, and (on the broadest scale) in the early 1980s. In the 1980s, they were organized by an independent, non-Communist movement calling itself Solidarity, led by shipyard electrician Lech Walesa and centered on a labor union. Although in 1981 General Wojciech Jaruzelski became prime minister with Soviet and Polish Communist backing and sought to suppress Solidarity, the Roman Catholic Church (now led by the Polish Pope, John Paul II) and many sympathizers in Western Europe and the United States helped to sustain the Solidarity move-

ment. The Communist regime in Poland had succeeded for a time in promoting economic growth and modernization of the Polish economy through a state-directed system that nonetheless permitted a larger private sector, especially in agriculture, than in the Soviet Union. It had also built a substantial welfare state. However, an economic crisis had developed by the late 1970s, helping to spark further workers' uprisings. During the 1980s, the Polish economy suffered marked decline. By 1983, analyst Andrej Korbonski was describing a combined set of crises: lack of state legitimacy and inability of state institutions to penetrate society, lack of state-linked participatory structures to articulate interests, and severe problems of economic distribution; Korbonski employed terms almost identical to those used in this text.[8]

By 1988, amid a new wave of strikes, continuing economic decline, failure of political reforms to win popular support, and lack of backing from the new Gorbachev government in the Soviet Union for a hard line, the Communist leadership in Poland was showing a willingness to compromise with Solidarity and its other opponents. Interior Minister Czeslaw Kiszczak instituted roundtable talks with Walesa and others in late summer and fall of 1988, with the backing of Prime Minister Jaruzelski. These talks led to an arrangement between the Communist government and Solidarity that brought a peaceful transition to constitutional democracy in Poland. The Sejm was to be the lower chamber of parliament, with 65 percent of the seats temporarily reserved for the Communists and their allies, and 35 percent of the seats to be elected in democratic elections in June 1989, with all seats to be chosen in democratic elections in the future. A second chamber, the Senate, would be entirely elected in a free competition along with the Sejm. The Communists hoped to maintain a considerable hold on power by this arrangement but overestimated their popular support. In the June 1989 elections, Solidarity won all of the contested seats for the Sejm and 99 of 100 seats in the Senate. Soon thereafter, Tadeusz Mazowiecki, an intellectual who was an ally of Walesa, became the prime minister, heading a "grand coalition" government of 12 Solidarity ministers, 3 from the Peasant party, 3 Communists, and 2 Democrats. The presidency of Poland, which had been abolished in 1952, was re-created; and Jaruzelski was narrowly elected by parliament as president. Thus, Poland began its peaceful transition to constitutional democracy.[9]

Since 1989, as Poland has sought to build a nation-state with legitimate state institutions, democratic participation, and an economy that can generate prosperity and overcome distribution problems, it has had some notable successes but continues to struggle and face obstacles in some areas. Poland has had three constitutional frameworks since 1989. Participatory structures appear to have had limited effectiveness. Economic reorganization has caused numerous difficulties of adjustment.

Nation-building has posed a less serious problem for post-Communist Poland than in the past or than it has for most Central and East European states. The death of most Polish Jews in the Holocaust, the expulsion of most Germans from Poland after World War II, and the redrawing of Polish boundaries in 1945 made Poland relatively homogeneous in ethno-national terms. A sense of national pride also surged in the wake of liberation from the Soviet yoke in 1989. Moreover, unlike most West European states, Poland has not attracted many immigrants from outside Europe. Despite ethno-national homogeneity, Poles have in recent years been divided over the extent to which the Polish nation should be defined in terms of Roman Catholicism. While the church hierarchy, Lech Walesa, and others have so defined it, defenders of secularism have strongly challenged them.[10]

With regard to state-building, post-Communist Poland has found it rather difficult to develop consensus on state institutions and a con-

stitutional framework. First Poland amended the 1952 Communist constitution, then it adopted the temporary "Little Constitution" of 1992, and then it ratified the Constitution of 1997—but in a referendum that drew only 43 percent of the eligible electorate and won endorsement by a narrow margin of 53–47 percent.

Despite levels of voter participation lower than in most of Western Europe in most Polish elections and referendums since 1989, high voter volatility indicating weak attachments to its new political parties, and generally low levels of citizen involvement in interest groups, Poland's elections have been consistently democratic since 1991. Moreover, there have been peaceful transitions from a grand coalition to a right coalition (1991), to a left coalition (1993), to a right coalition again (1997), and back to a left coalition (2001) and then a center-left minority government (2003). There have also been peaceful transitions between sharp antagonists in the office of president, from Jaruzelski to Walesa in 1991, and from Walesa to Kwasniewski in 1995. These orderly transfers of power indicate to almost all observers a consolidation of constitutional democracy in Poland.[11]

Successfully generating economic prosperity and resolving conflicts over economic distribution have proven perhaps the most difficult developmental challenges for post-Communist Poland. The Mazowiecki government of 1989–1990 adopted a "shock therapy" economic approach that emphasized freeing prices from the former state controls, dramatically reducing consumer subsidies, relaxing restrictions on foreign trade and investment, and taking preliminary measures to break up and privatize state-owned monopolies. Though privatization was to be a long and complex process, and though the initial effects of these changes led to a sharp decline in Poland's gross domestic product (−19 percent for 1990–1991), runaway inflation (up 554 percent in 1990), and surging unemployment (from 6 percent in 1990 to 16 percent in 1993), the general thrust of the movement toward free-market capitalism won wide support and was continued, while at a slower pace, by succeeding governments, including those led by left coalitions. Poland has enjoyed considerable economic growth since 1992, and inflation has declined markedly since 1991. However, high unemployment continues to be a problem in Poland. Furthermore, its eastern provinces remain mired in poverty, its agriculture remains inefficient, and its per capita wealth is still far below that of even the poorest pre-2004 EU member. Economic distribution problems clearly are far from resolved in Poland.[12]

Governmental Institutions

Post-Communist Poland has adopted three constitutional frameworks since 1989, the current one dating from 1997. Major issues of dispute have centered on presidential powers and national-subnational relations. The latter were deliberately left ambiguous in the 1997 Constitution and were addressed by subsequent legislation in 1998.

Since 1989, the Polish executive-legislative structure has been a hybrid of the cabinet-parliamentary and presidential systems, although the nature of the mix has varied with the constitutions and with the shifting partisan balance in parliament. Poland's current approach is broadly similar to that of France, while differing from the French model in several ways. For instance, the Polish constitution grants the president veto power over legislation (requiring a three-fifths vote of the Sejm to override) like the American constitution but in contrast to the French one. In another difference from France, Poland vests the power to declare an emergency in the hands of the prime minister and government, rather than in the hands of the president. As in France, cohabitation, involving the sharing of executive powers between a president and a prime minister of different partisan affiliations, has characterized the system at some times but not others. Though Polish presidents have been expected to give up their formal party ties (unlike French presidents, though de Gaulle rejected formal party ties), there has been no doubt of the basic allegiance of Lech Walesa to Solidarity and of Aleksandr Kwasniewski to the Democratic Left Alliance. Table 16.2 indicates the presidents and

TABLE 16.2 Polish Presidents and Prime Ministers Since 1989

Presidents		Prime ministers	
Wojciech Jaruzelski	1989–1990	*Tadeusz Mazowiecki	1989–1990
Lech Walesa	1990–1995	Jan Bielecki	1991
		Jan Olszewski	1991–1992
		Waldemar Pawlak	1992
		Hanna Suchocka	1992–1993
		*Waldemar Pawlak	1993–1995
		*Jozef Oleksy	1995
Aleksandr Kwasniewski	1995–	Jozef Oleksy	1995–1996
		Wlodzimierz Cimoszewicz	1996–1997
		*Jerzy Buzek	1997–2001
		Leszek Miller	2001–2004
		Marek Belka	2004–

*Denotes cohabitation.

prime ministers of Poland since 1989, with an asterisk denoting the prime ministers who have served in a cohabitation arrangement with presidents of another political persuasion.

Wojciech Jaruzelski, the general who had imposed martial law as the last prime minister of Communist Poland, served as the parliament-appointed president of post-Communist Poland for only one and one-half years, serving along with Solidarity-backed Tadeusz Mazowiecki, who enjoyed the backing of a grand coalition of all parties but hailed himself from Solidarity. Following Jaruzelski's early resignation in 1990, Lech Walesa, long the chief spokesman for Solidarity, won the presidency in the first direct popular vote. Although he won 74 percent of the vote in the second round of the 1990 presidential election and was a charismatic leader, Walesa soon alienated many of his colleagues and much of his base of support by demanding increased presidential powers, displaying a mercurial temperament, and proving unusually quarrelsome. The diverse forces that initially backed him and the Solidarity movement were also fractured along ideological and organizational lines. As a result, the Democratic Left Alliance (SLD), a social democratic electoral alliance with former Communists at its core, scored well enough in the 1993 parliamentary elections to become the largest party in parliament and to form governing coalitions first headed by Prime Minister Waldemar Pawlak (leader of the Peasant party) and then by Prime Minister Jozef Oleksy of the Democratic Left. During this period, cohabitation proved tense and difficult, as President Walesa battled the prime ministers and parliament repeatedly over power and policy issues. In the 1995 presidential election, Walesa met defeat at the hands of the young, dynamic former communist Aleksandr Kwasniewski, who established a cooperative relationship with the Peasant party–Democratic Left Alliance coalition government for the next two years. However, in 1997, the volatile electorate and a new determination on

much of the center-right to unite in a new Solidarity Election Action (AWS) alliance (so that they would not be penalized by failing to reach the proportional representation 5–8 percent thresholds, as they had been in 1993) led to the formation of a center-right coalition government under Prime Minister Jerzy Buzek during 1997–2001.

Thus began another cohabitation, this one between a president of the Left and a prime minister of the Right. However, this cohabitation proved less turbulent and tension-filled than the previous ones, probably owing to Kwasniewski's greater caution and better communication skills in contrast to Walesa. Morever, as its term in office progressed, the fractious center-right coalition began to disintegrate. Kwasniewski won a triumphant first-round reelection as president in 2000, with Walesa finishing in seventh place with a humiliating 1 percent of the vote this time! The following year, the Democratic Left Alliance regained first place in the parliamentary elections, again formed a coalition government with the Peasant party, and provided support for Prime Minister Leszek Miller, bringing an end to cohabitation. However, early in 2003, the Peasant party withdrew its support, leaving Miller with a minority government. In March 2004 a 30-member faction of the Democratic Left Alliance defected to form Social Democracy of Poland (SDPL), undermining Miller's minority government further and forcing Miller to step down as prime minister on May 2, to be succeeded by Marek Belka, also of the SLD and a former finance minister and economic adviser to the American-led administration in Iraq. Belka won a confidence vote in the Sejm in June 2004 after an initial failure to do so in May; but his government lacks a stable base in parliament and the country at large. Three constitutional frameworks, several changes in electoral laws, and wildly fluctuating party fortunes have made Polish legislative-executive relations considerably more subject to short-term changes than those of most nation-states. However, the conflicts have all been peacefully resolved by constitutional-legal means.[13]

In Poland's bicameral parliament, only the 460-member Sejm, elected by proportional representation, can make or break governments. Moreover, it possesses the superior lawmaking powers. However, it does share lawmaking powers with a second chamber, the Senate. The Senate is composed of 100 members elected on a first-past-the post system and serves as a check of sorts on the Sejm.

Below the prime minister and the government lies the executive bureaucracy. Previously packed by Communist appointees, it was perceived as a domain in need of cleansing by Solidarity and other anti-Communist activists. As the regime changed, many older bureaucrats opted to retire. As Poland prepared to enter the European Union, it also came under considerable pressure to move its public administration toward enhanced professionalism and efficiency. In fact, the European Union has provided both advice and funding to assist in that process, but the quality of the Polish civil service remains below most Western European standards. Similar processes have occurred at the middle and lower levels of the Polish judiciary, with similar concerns about the pace of progress there, too.[14]

The Constitutional Court of Poland possesses the power of constitutional judicial review. Under the Constitution of 1997, it gained broadened jurisdiction, Polish citizens were given the right to bring cases directly before it, and its constitutional interpretations were made final, effective in 1999. Previously they could be overridden by a two-thirds majority vote in the Sejm. There are 15 members of the Constitutional Court, elected by the Sejm, who serve staggered nine-year terms. As in the United States and Germany, abortion has been one of the most controversial matters on which the Court has ruled. In 1997, the Polish Constitutional Court, citing a constitutional "right to life," overturned legislation that the left coalition had passed in parliament easing restrictions on abortion. This decision aroused much debate, but it and other controversial rulings have been accepted as law by all parties.[15]

National-subnational governmental relations have represented another area of institutional change in post-Communist Poland. Though since 1918 Poland had been a unitary system that was highly centralized, Poland's post-Communist leaders have generally agreed on the desirability of some decentralization of authority. However, there were still so many disagreements, particularly over the number and powers of the provinces, that a new structure of 16 provinces at the regional level (with counties below them and communes at the base) did not take shape until 1998. European Union guidance and financial assistance encouraged and shaped the Polish decentralization process.[16]

Elections, Political Parties, and Interest Groups

Poland has employed both referendums and competitive presidential and parliamentary elections, it has had a multiparty system, and it has permitted a wide diversity of interest groups. However, its voter turnout has been relatively low by European standards, averaging less than 50 percent in parliamentary elections (compared with averages between 73 and 93 percent in the 15 pre-2004 member states of the EU), its party system has been highly fluid and lacking in solid roots, and its interest groups have suffered also from disorganization and lack of a strong membership base.

Since 1989, Poland has held referendums on the Constitution of 1997 (narrowly endorsed in a turnout of 43 percent) and in 1996 on a set of five questions, the most debated of which concerned dispersal of property rights to formerly state-owned corporations. The latter referendum drew only 32 percent of the eligible voters to the polls and was nonbinding because of the low turnout. In 2003, Poland held another referendum on the terms of Poland's entry to the European Union, yielding endorsement by a 78 percent majority, with a turnout of 60 percent.[17]

Presidential elections operate in Poland, as in France, on the basis of a required popular majority for the winning candidate. If there is no majority in the first round of voting, the top two vote-winners in that round face one another in a runoff. In the presidential election of 1990, Lech Walesa won 40 percent on the first ballot and went on to defeat an independent candidate, Canadian Polish expatriate Stan Tyminski, 74–26 percent in the second round. Five years later, Aleksandr Krasniewski led Walesa 35–33 percent in round one and defeated him 52–48 percent on the second ballot. The 2000 election gave Kwasniewski reelection in the first round, with 54 percent of the popular vote in a 12-candidate race. Table 16.3 gives the results for the 2000 presidential election.

Elections to the Sejm have used proportional representation. However, the raising of the threshold required for a proportional share of the parliamentary seats (now 5 percent for parties, 8 percent for electoral alliances, and 7 percent for a share of the national list) has markedly reduced the number of parties and related groups in the Sejm, from 29 after the 1991 elections to 7 following the 1993 elections in which the new, higher thresholds took effect. Senate elections have employed the Anglo-American first-past-the-post system, usually resulting in most of the seats being awarded to the two largest parties.

The Polish party system has only partially taken shape along the left-right ideological spectrum reflecting underlying class cleavages— the pattern prevalent in most of Western Europe. A major reason is that a religious (Roman Catholic)–secular cleavage has also been quite important in Poland and has cut across the class cleavage to a considerable extent. Therefore, parties have not only been arrayed on a left-right economic spectrum but also on a secular-Catholic spectrum, as Figure 16.1 illustrates. Further complicating matters in the Polish party system has been the presence at most times of "parties" that operate largely as expressions of fairly narrow interest groups, such as the Solidarity union, the Polish Peasant party, and the agrarian-based Self-Defense of the Polish Republic party. Memories of Communist Poland have also shaped party alignments and choices of allies: The old United Polish Workers' party and the Polish Peasant party worked together in the Communist era, and the Democratic Left Alliance and the Polish Peasant party continue to prefer each other as coalition partners, despite differences on religious-cultural, agrarian, and other issues.

The Democratic Left Alliance (SLD), the heirs of the old Communist party, have repositioned themselves as center-left social democrats who combine advocacy of a market-oriented social-welfare state and an emphasis on secular values (such as liberalized abortion laws and a fairly minimal role for the Catholic Church in Polish society). Their frequent allies, the Polish Peasant party, are primarily a vehicle for small farmers to defend their interests.

TABLE 16.3 The Polish Presidential Election of 2000

Candidate	Party	Popular vote %
Aleksandr Kwasniewski	SLD	53.9
Andrej Olechowski	Independent	17.3
Marian Krzaklewski	AWS	15.6
Jaroslaw Kalinowski	PSL	6.0
Andrej Lepper	Self Defense	3.1
Janusz Korwin-Mikke	UPR	1.4
Lech Walesa	ChD	1.0
Five Others		1.7
Total		100.0

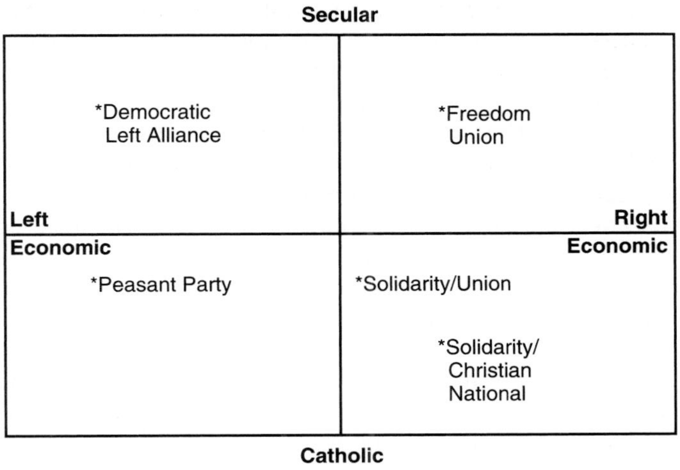

Secular

*Democratic Left Alliance	*Freedom Union

Left   **Right**
Economic   **Economic**

*Peasant Party	*Solidarity/Union *Solidarity/ Christian National

Catholic

FIGURE 16.1   Cross-Cutting Axes and Polish Political Parties

Because the majority of small farmers are Catholics and traditional in their outlook, this party tends to be more conservative than the SLD on religious-cultural matters. However, it is often more inclined to support protective state roles than the SLD on economic matters. These two parties/party groupings have been the two most stable elements in a highly turbulent Polish party arena since 1989.

The center-right and right of the political spectrum have proved to be more fractured and fluid than the center-left. Economic libertarians have battled traditional conservatives and agrarian and labor-union-based parties on economic issues. The secular right has quarreled with the Catholic right on sociocultural issues. Figure 16.1 above suggests some of the sources of conflict by its placement of the union-based section of the Solidarity Electoral Action (AWS) alliance in the Catholic but economically centrist area, the Freedom Union in the economic libertarian but secular area, and the Christian National Union part of AWS in the Catholic and traditional conservative sector. Personality differences among leaders of the Polish right have added to the difficulties of achieving unity and continuity.[18]

Interest group politics in post-Communist Poland have illustrated many of the same patterns as those seen in the party and election systems: relatively low mass involvement as well as considerable fracturing and fluidity. In fact, as noted previously, in Poland the line differentiating parties as interest-aggregating electoral

TABLE 16.4   Polish Election to the Sejm, 2001

Party	Popular vote %	Seats
Democratic Left Alliance (SLD)	41.0	216
Citizens' Platform	12.7	65
Self Defense of the Polish Republic	10.2	53
Law and Justice	9.5	44
Polish Peasant Party (PSL)	9.0	42
League of Polish Families	7.9	38
Solidarity Electoral Action (AWS)	5.6	0
Freedom Union	3.1	0
German Minority	0.4	2
Others	0.6	0
Total	100.0	460

organizations and vehicles for organizing government from interest groups as interest articulators has been poorly defined. Both the Polish Peasant party and the Self Defense of the Polish Republic party share features of agricultural interest groups and parties. The Solidarity labor union and its leader Marian Krzaklewski have played a major role in the Solidarity Electoral Action. Organized labor has been split along political-ideological lines between the National Trade Union Accord (OPZZ), associated with the Left, and Solidarity, associated with the Right. Though the two have occasionally cooperated on industrial action, they have usually appeared to be engaged in thwarting or outbidding each other. Neither has been able to mobilize most of the Polish workforce. Recent estimates are that union members now constitute only about 11 percent of the Polish labor force. Business groups, with the Confederation of Polish Employers as the largest peak organization, appear to be more fragmented and less influential than in Western Europe. On the other hand, the Roman Catholic hierarchy and an array of Catholic lay groups have played larger political roles than in most Western European countries. When parliament liberalized the abortion law in 1996, for example, the Catholic Church and related groups mobilized 50,000 protesters in the streets of Warsaw and generated 2.5 million communications of disapproval to parliament, before the Constitutional Court resolved the issue in their favor.[19]

With regard to neo-corporatist patterns of consultation, of the type widely found in Scandinavia, Austria, and some other countries of Western Europe, these have been a rarity in Poland. Polish economic-interest groups have been too fragmented and their membership rolls have been too small to make negotiations among government and major economic interest groups a regular part of wage negotiations or the policy-making process. A Tripartite Commission set up in 1994 to foster consultation among government, business, and union leaders has played relatively minor roles.[20]

Overall, the picture of political participation in Poland has been one of low turnout in elections and referendums, a fluid party system that overlaps with a rather disorganized interest group system, and weak links between government decision-makers and a large part of the Polish populace. Poland has developed all of the procedural features of constitutional democracy, but there is some question concerning the extent to which democratic participation has become effectively entrenched at this point. Perhaps it is premature to assess the long-term prospects.

Relations with the EC/EU

The development of Polish constitutional democracy and a market-oriented economy in an atmosphere suffused by an overwhelming desire to "rejoin Europe" has been comparable in some ways to the patterns seen in Spain after the end of the Franco regime. A long era of authoritarian government and a state-oriented economy characterized both countries, despite the obvious differences between a Polish Communist regime largely imposed by the Soviet Union and involving extensive state ownership and planning of the economy, and a Spanish conservative authoritarian regime mainly developed by internal forces (albeit with German Nazi and Italian Fascist aid) and gradually loosening state economic controls that it had instituted in its early years. In Poland in the 1990s, as in Spain in the 1970s, an elite consensus on the desirability of joining the EC/EU as quickly as possible extended across most of the political spectrum.

However, the gap between Poland and the EU today is considerably greater than that between Spain and the EC in the 1970s. Poland lags further behind the average EU per capita wealth today than Spain did at its time of application for EC membership. Poland's Communist economy of 1945–1989 has also required more extensive adjustment to fit EU norms than Spain's liberalizing state-oriented economy did in the 1970s and 1980s. Moreover, the Polish consensus in favor of EU membership has shown signs of dissipating, while the Spanish consensus remained firm. From the EC/EU perspective, it should also be noted, Spain was one of just three Mediterranean applicants (with Greece and Portugal) seeking entry in the 1970s. Poland is one of ten Central and East European countries that entered the EU in 2004. Therefore, the adjustment for the EU to absorb Poland and other applicant states in the years ahead will be far greater than it was for the EC to absorb Spain, Portugal, and Greece during the 1980s.

Despite the differences between the Polish and Spanish examples, Poland proved to be on a schedule to enter the European Union after only a little longer process than it took Spain to gain entry to the EC after its official application. Two years after Franco's death in 1975, Spain in 1977 made formal application to join the EC and gained admission nine years later in 1986, following arduous negotiations. A little less than five years after the June 1989 elections that marked the end of Communist Poland, and less than four years after Poland made a sharp break with its Communist past, the Polish government in 1994 made formal application to join the EU. Poland gained entry to the EU in 2004, ten years after its initial application (compared with nine years for Spain). Certainly, the negotiations were arduous—both for the EU and for Poland.

Major issues of contention included schedules for phasing in free movement of labor (with Germany and Austria particularly fearful of being overrun by Polish workers), timetables for allowing non-Polish EU citizens to purchase Polish land (a highly sensitive issue for Polish small farmers who fear that wealthy Germans and other EU citizens will swoop in to buy up fertile Polish land), methods for integrating Polish agriculture into the Common Agricultural Policy (a matter of great concern in both the EU and Poland), and formulas for distribution of cohesion and regional funds. Poland found it difficult to bring its laws into synchronicity with the *acquis communitaire* of the European Union. By 2001, it was lagging noticeably behind Hungary, the Czech Republic, Cyprus, and Slovakia in achieving synchronicity; and commentators in its fellow "first wave" entry candidate states were complaining that Poland might slow the process of entry for others. For example, the leading Slovak financial newspaper complained that Poland was "visibly becoming a brake rather than an engine in the integration process."[21] Since then, the hurdles have been overcome, though Polish-EU struggles over agricultural policy have remained intense.

Polish parties, interest groups, and public opinion showed signs of restiveness over the terms on which Poland gained entry to the EU. Opposition has been highest among rural dwellers and villagers and the poorly educated.[22] Reflecting these patterns, the Peasant party, which for a time formed part of the left coalition government, has shown increasing signs of Euroskepticism and even hostility to EU entry. Far more vehement in the rising Polish opposition to the European Union has been the Self Defense of the Polish Republic party of Andrej Lipper, a pig farmer, who led his party to a surprising third-place showing in the September 2001 parliamentary elections on a platform that included attacks on the EU as well as denunciations of corruption in the Polish elite. Typical of Polish agriculturalists' concerns were those voiced by Czeslaw Jarocki: "Farmers like me will not be able to survive May 1, 2004. The EU will eat us alive. Brussels says that out of the two million current farm holdings there should be only 700,000. Me, I do not want to be among those who will disappear."[23]

"Farmers like me will not be able to survive May 1, 2004. The EU will eat us alive. Brussels says that out of the two million current farm holdings there should be only 700,000. Me, I do not want to be among those who will disappear."

Czeslaw Jarocki, Polish farmer, *quoted by Bernard Osser, "Eastern Poland's Farmers Urge No in EU Referendum" (June 4, 2003).*

Others leading right-wing opposition to the EU have included Radio Maryja, a Catholic nationalist radio station that has gained a wide audience for its nationalistic and traditionalist appeals.[24] Despite some intense opposition, the Polish voters endorsed EU entry in a referendum on June 8, 2003, by a 78–22 percent margin, with a turnout of just less than 60 percent, thus overcoming the last hurdle to Poland's accession to the European Union in May 2004.[25]

The European Union has provided extensive guidance and funding to prepare Poland for accession. The most important sources of aid have come from the Polish-Hungarian Assistance for the Restructuring of the Economy (PHARE) program. In addition to explicitly economic assistance, PHARE has aided the development and implementation of regional-local governmental reforms and reorganization and professionalization of public administration.[26]

Polish negotiators have also succeeded in winning concessions from the European Union on some key points. For example, in March 2002, Poland gained a 12-year transition period in which it can restrict land sales to non-Polish citizens. Because the issue of land has been particularly sensitive in agricultural areas where antipathy to the EU has been building, this concession allayed some of the Polish farmers' concerns.[27]

What approaches Poland will take toward the European Union and what its impact will be are uncertain, but there are already some fairly clear indicators. Based on the record to date, it appears likely that Poland (and many other new

entrants from Central and Eastern Europe) will supplement the Atlanticist faction in the EU. Two recent analysts have stressed "intimacy in Polish-American relations is based predominantly on strategic considerations. For Poland, the US presence in Europe provides reassurance against its powerful neighbours, while for the US, Poland is a friendly state located at the strategic boundary of eastern and western Europe." The Polish government's support for American policies in Iraq has been just one of a number of illustrations of the strength of Polish Atlanticism. In addition, Poland has followed the American lead in expressing skepticism about European defense initiatives and has supported the Bush administration's missile defense program despite widespread opposition to it in the EU. Polish governmental policies have also reflected generally positive Polish popular attraction to the United States. Polls have consistently shown Poles to be fonder of Americans than respondents in any other Central and East European countries.[28]

"...intimacy in Polish-American relations is based predominantly on strategic considerations. For Poland, the US presence in Europe provides reassurance against its powerful neighbours, while for the US, Poland is a friendly state located at the strategic boundary of eastern and western Europe."

Marcin Zaborowski and Kerry Longhurst, *"America's Protégé in the East?" (2003), 1012.*

Given Poland's desires for close ties to the United States (which may block supranational efforts in the defense and foreign-policy realm in particular) and its likely inability to meet the criteria for joining the European Economic and Monetary Union and adopting the euro currency soon (both characteristics shared with most other new member states), the entry of Poland and some of the other newcomers may well impose constraints on future supranational development in the EU. The phase-in of the Common Agricultural Policy in Poland and the other new entrants is (along with the EMU) an example of at least temporarily differentiated integration of the EU as a consequence of eastward expansion. The differentiation between Poland and other newcomers on the one hand and the Western, long-term EU member states on the other hand may in turn reinforce intergovernmentalism in the EU, due to an increasing number of states at different levels of integration perceiving distinctively different national interests.

On issues of further eastward enlargement, Poland has already indicated a desire to extend EU membership beyond 25 or 29, at least to include Ukraine and Moldova and perhaps even Belarus. As *The Economist* put it in an August 2003 analysis, "It wants them as prosperous, stable and accessible neighbors, not as poor and rackety ones cut off by an EU border." Above all, Poland has already demonstrated an aggressive defense of what its leaders perceive to be the Polish national interest. For example, the Polish government's adamant refusal to accept a diminution of Poland's voting power in the EU Council of Ministers in the draft of the new EU constitution (along with a similar refusal by Spain) scuttled the effort to find a compromise at the Brussels European Summit on the constitution in December 2003, though Poland later accepted a compromise.[29]

As far as the impact of EU membership on Poland is concerned, it is quite clear that the prospect of Poland's joining the EU has played a major part in solidifying Poland's commitment to constitutional democracy and a market-oriented economy. Whether it will also bring other, less positive, changes remains to be seen. Similar patterns are evident in most of the other formerly Communist states that are joining the European Union.

TURKEY AND THE EUROPEAN UNION

Turkey offers an interesting contrast to Poland. During the Cold War, when Poland was Communist and part of the Soviet-led Warsaw Pact, Turkey aligned itself with Western Europe and the United States. It has been a member of the North Atlantic Treaty Organization (NATO) since 1952 (while Poland joined NATO only in 1998). Turkey has had association status with the EC/EU itself since 1963, made its first formal application to the EC in 1987, has had a customs union with the EU since 1995, and has been listed as a prospective accession state since 1999. Nevertheless, in contrast to Poland, which has already joined the European Union, Turkey is likely to remain outside the EU for some time to come.

Why is Turkey's accession almost certain to be delayed? One factor, largely unstated, is that many Europeans question the extent to which Turkey is genuinely "European." Article 237 of the original European Economic Community (EEC) Treaty of Rome of 1957 provided the original criterion for accession, stating that any "European state" could apply to enter the EEC. Geographically, most of Turkey is situated in Asia Minor, not in Europe. Culturally, it is predominantly Muslim rather than Christian. When the Luxembourg Summit of the European Council rejected Turkey's application in December 1997, President Süleyman Demirel of Turkey asked sarcastically, "Is it necessary for Turkey to become a Christian country before it is let into the EU? Don't you think the times for the crusades are over?"[30] Though few would admit it publicly, Turkey's location, and even more so its history and culture, fuel some of the resistance in the EU to Turkish accession.

"Is it necessary for Turkey to become a Christian country before it is let into the EU? Don't you think the times for the crusades are over?"

President Süleyman Demirel of Turkey, 1997.

Another obstacle to Turkey's membership in the EU has been its troubled relationship with EU member states Greece and Cyprus, either of which can exercise veto over accession of new members. Historically, Greece and Turkey have often been at odds. For centuries before Greece regained its independence through revolution in the 1820s, it was a part of the Ottoman Turkish Empire. The Turkish-Greek War of 1920–1923 left further bitter memories, and sharp conflicts over Greek-Turkish relations in Cyprus have continued to stir anger on both sides. In 1974, Greece attempted annexation of Cyprus, whereupon Turkey invaded Northern Cyprus (where most Turkish Cypriots live) and subsequently recognized a "Turkish Republic of Northern Cyprus" in opposition to the ethnically Greek but independent Republic of Cyprus in the South. The European Union has made resolution of the Turkish-Greek conflicts over Cyprus a condition for admission of Turkey to the EU. Progress on this matter early in 2004 improved the prospects for at least beginning serious negotiations for Turkish EU entry.[31]

The most significant "official" source of objections to Turkish entry into the European Union has been and continues to be Turkey's record with regard to constitutional democracy and human rights. Establishment of democratic criteria for EC/EU entry date back to the endorsement by the European Parliamentary Assembly of the Birkelbach report in December 1961. This report was cited to deny Spain under Franco even association status with the European Community in the 1960s and 1970s. (See Chapter Fourteen.) Nevertheless, Turkey attained EC association status in 1963, though its association agreement was "frozen" by the EC during subsequent periods of Turkish military rule. When the official opinion of the European Commission recommended against opening negotiations on EC entry with Turkey in 1989, it stressed the inadequacy of Turkey's human-rights record as a major basis for its

negative assessment (while noting economic factors also).[32] The Copenhagen criteria adopted by the European Council in June 1993 gave democracy and human rights a clear priority, stating that accession of new member states would be contingent on "stability of institutions guaranteeing democracy, the rule of law, human rights, and respect for and protection of minorities." The repeated interventions of the Turkish military in Turkish government (one in 1997), the Turkish repression of its Kurdish minority, and the general Turkish record on human rights all contributed to the European Council decision in December 1997 to put on hold Turkey's renewed application for EU membership. However, this time the Turkish government took quick steps, reportedly in collaboration with Germany, to address the EU concerns about its record. The result was that the European Council finally granted Turkey candidate status in December 1999, 12 years after Turkey's initial application. Subsequently, the EU and Turkey have finalized an Accession Partnership accord, a detailed list of guidelines to steer what promises to be a long and difficult negotiation process on Turkish EU entry.[33]

By any objective standards, Turkey's record concerning democracy and human rights has indeed set it at odds with the member states of the European Union. Most of the reasons are embodied in the means by which Turkey became a nation-state. Turkey emerged out of the ruins of the Ottoman Empire, a multiethnic empire ruled by the Turks that was defeated in World War I and subsequently disintegrated. A key role was played by military leader Mustafa Kemal Atatürk, who assumed leadership of Turkey from 1923 until his death in 1935 and sought to build a modern nation-state on a secular basis using authoritarian methods. The legacy of Atatürk in Turkey has been a political system that, in the words of analyst Hakan Yanuz, has been "superficially Western in form while remaining rigidly authoritarian and dogmatic in substance. It continues to stress republicanism over democracy, homogeneity over difference, the military over the civilian, and the state over society."[34]

Turkish military oversight of and intervention in Turkish government has been a major part of the record to which the European Union has objected. The Turkish military staged a coup in 1960, forced a revamping of Turkish civilian government by a military ultimatum in 1971, overthrew another government by a coup in 1980, and staged an effective "coup by memorandum" in 1997. The last of these interventions forced the resignation of Turkey's first Islamic fundamentalist prime minister, Necmettin Erbakan, and aimed at eradicating Islamic fundamentalist influence in Turkish government. Though the Turkish military has portrayed its interventions as rescues of "democracy" from corrupt and/or ineffective politicians (1960, 1971, 1980) or from Islamic fundamentalists (1997), most observers have seen them as attacks on constitutional democracy.[35]

Nor have the roles of the Turkish military been the sole departures from constitutional democratic norms in Turkey. Nation-building, Turkish style, has involved repeated efforts to submerge the identity of the large Kurdish minority (about 20 percent of the total population) and compel its loyalty to the Turkish "nation." Kurdish political parties, interest groups, and media of communication have been regularly repressed. Moreover, violations of human rights through torture by police, mistreatment of prisoners, and restrictions on freedom of the press and freedom of speech have been widespread in Turkey far beyond attacks on the Kurdish minority. In its 2001 progress report on Turkish movement toward meeting the EU requirements for accession, the European Commission found 9000 people in Turkish prisons for crimes associated with free expression, along with continuing torture and other mistreatment of prisoners. It also found "little sign of increased civilian control over the military." However, in August 2002, the Turkish parliament enacted an array of reforms designed to bring Turkey into compliance with requirements of the European Union. These have included repeal of the previous prohibitions on broadcasting and teaching in the Kurdish language, guarantee of the right to a retrial in civil and criminal court cases when demanded by the European Court of Human Rights, permission for non-Muslim religious foundations to buy and sell property in Turkey, and abolition of the death penalty except in times of war. If these reforms actually take effect and significantly alter Turkish governmental practices (and many EU officials remain skeptical that they will do so), then the prospects for progress on Turkey's application for EU membership should improve considerably.

Beyond these factors, of course, are the economic problems posed by Turkey's relatively low per capita gross domestic product, large agricultural sector, and persistent inflation, though these are no greater obstacles than those confronting some of the other 13 applicant states from Central and Eastern Europe. Overall, the lack of harmony between Turkish institutions, laws, and practices and the requirements of the European Union will almost certainly slow the progress of Turkey toward accession to the EU. Turkey will not soon be a major nation-state in the European Union, though its recent democratic and human-rights reforms and its moves toward a peaceful solution of the Cyprus conflict increase the likelihood of its eventual entry. Concerns about sending a negative message to the Muslim world in general may also be a factor. Analyst Thomas L. Friedman spoke for many in concluding about the European Union and Turkey: "Yes, everyone is watching, which is why the E.U. would be making a huge mistake—a hinge of history mistake—if it digs a ditch around Turkey instead of building a bridge."[36]

"Yes, everyone is watching, which is why the E.U. would be making a huge mistake—a hinge of history mistake—if it digs a ditch around Turkey instead of building a bridge."

Thomas L. Friedman, *New York Times* (January 11, 2004), IV, 15.

RUSSIA AND THE EUROPEAN UNION

Beyond the 14 accession states looms Russia. With a population of 144 million, a gross domestic product of well over one trillion dollars, and a long history as a great power, Russia would certainly be a major nation-state in the EU were it ever to seek and gain admission. However, if Turkey is on a slow path to the European Union, Russia is at present not on that path at all.

Russia was the major component of what was the Soviet Union during the days of Communism, containing about one-half the population of the former Soviet Union and three-fourths of its territory. Though its territory is located more in Asia than in Europe, 80 percent of its population lives in Europe. For many centuries, Russia has been a major player in European power politics. Its religious heritage (despite seven decades of official atheism under Communism) has been Christian, primarily Russian Orthodox. Therefore, Russia is far more "European" than is Turkey.

Since the breakup of the Soviet Union at the end of 1991, Russia has taken steps to establish both constitutional democracy and a market-oriented economy. Although some progress has been made toward democratic participation, notably through freedom to organize interest groups and political parties and to choose between competitive candidates in elections, authoritarian tendencies have continued to be evident. Under both post-Communist presidents of Russia, Boris Yeltsin (1991–1999) and

Vladimir Putin (1999–), mass media criticism has often been squelched; and the war against the Chechen rebels who have demanded autonomy or independence for Chechnya (an ethnic enclave in the South of Russia) has employed methods arousing wide European and global concerns about human-rights abuses. Moreover, Russian political parties and interest groups have been highly fragmented and fluid and have met with popular indifference and even hostility. Although the presidential and parliamentary elections have occurred peacefully, many question the fairness of the broadcast coverage. The 1996 presidential election campaign in particular was characterized by blatant media bias in favor of President Yeltsin's reelection, and similar patterns have appeared under Putin, notably during the election campaigns for parliament in 2003 and the presidency in 2004, which resulted in landslide victories for Putin's parliamentary backers and for the president himself. In the May 2004 presidential elections, Putin scored 71.2 percent of the popular vote, with Communist party candidate Nikolai Kharitonov a distant second at 13.7 percent. Furthermore, unlike Poland, Russia has not experienced peaceful transfers of power through elections from one party or alliance to another or between two antagonistic leaders—which many analysts view as an important test of whether democracy has been institutionalized successfully. Rule of law also remains far from the norm in Russia, in light of the continuing powers of the successor organizations to the Soviet-era Committee for State Security (KGB) and widespread corruption throughout the Russian state apparatus.[37]

The Russian economy declined sharply in the 1990s. While it has showed encouraging signs of recovery since 1999, the per capita gross domestic product is far below West European levels; and the distribution gap between the rich and the poor has become a chasm. Agriculture, still a significant sector of the Russian economy, has remained stagnant and inefficient. Privatization of the previously state-owned business corporations has been predominantly "insider privatization," in which the previous managers of the state firms have continued to maintain control, without open, competitive bidding. Many of the privatized firms continue to make "deals" to gain cheap loans and subsidies from the Russian state. "Crony capitalism," "capitalism of officialdom," and even "gangster capitalism" have been terms that both Russian and foreign analysts have often applied to the new Russian economic system. As of early 2004, Russia has not yet qualified for membership in the World Trade Organization, in contrast to even the People's Republic of China.[38]

Therefore, in both political and economic terms, Russia at present represents a sharp contrast to the democratic, prosperous, and market-oriented social-welfare states of the European Union. In both political and economic spheres, the gap between Russia and the EU is far greater than that between Poland and the EU. Even Turkey is probably closer than Russia to EU standards and practices, at least in the economic realm.

To date, neither Russia nor the European Union has seriously considered the possibility of Russia's becoming a major nation-state in the EU. In addition to the political and economic obstacles noted above, there is the sheer size of Russia and its background as the heartland of the Soviet "superpower" of the Cold War era. If Russia were to receive voting power in EU institutions equivalent to its population, it would dwarf the other members (even though its GDP is below that of Germany, France, Britain, and Italy). Given its recent background as a "superpower," Russia would also find it difficult to accept pooling of sovereignty and would almost certainly arouse distrust among other member states. Russian President Putin in April 2001 expressed a vision of Russia as part of a "greater Europe" and stated that integration with Europe was "becoming one of the key areas of our foreign policy."[39] A year later, in his annual address to the Russian parliament, he termed the European Union "Russia's strategic ally."[40] However, few if any analysts have suggested that he will pursue a course of seeking EU membership. There is little pressure for him to do so from Russian public opinion. A recent survey found widespread lack of knowledge of the EU among the Russian public and a dominant perception that Russia was unique. A Yaroslavl respondent in the survey summed up this view: "Russia has always followed its own path and it can't be equated or even compared with any other European country." Another typical comment was, Russia is "just too big to tuck away somewhere. It *is*, because it's Russia! Don't try to confine it to Europe, or Asia!" Instead of setting a course for Russian EU membership, Russia and the European Union have held a series of summit conferences (five during Putin's first two years in office) and have chiefly explored means of cooperation in the energy field, the fight against organized crime, and the establishment of a common economic area to enhance trade.[41]

[Russia is] "just too big to tuck away somewhere. It *is*, because it's Russia! Don't try to confine it to Europe, or Asia!"

"Russia has always followed its own path and it can't be equated or even compared with any other European country."

Comments by Russian respondents *in a survey by Stephen White, Ian McAllister, and Margot Light, "Enlargement and the New Outsiders" (2002), 140.*

CONCLUSIONS

This text began with an overview of the European Union and its member states. After describing the deepening and widening of European integration in Chapter Two, and the major institutions and public policies of the contemporary European Union in Chapters Three and Four, it has focused on the major nation-states in the European Union, analyzing their political development, governmental institutions, participatory structures and processes, and relationships with the EC/EU. Chapter Fifteen has extended the analysis to place all pre-2004 member states of the EU in a broad comparative framework. This chapter, Chapter Sixteen, has examined the eastward expansion that is already transforming the European Union and will likely continue to affect its operations and those of its member states in the future.

The European Union is not now and probably will not become a United States of Europe equivalent to the United States of America. It is a partially supranational, partially intergovernmental political system that also increasingly engages subnational governmental units. The population of the European Union plus the 14 accession states is 556 million (compared with just under 300 million in the United States). Even without including Turkey, the figure is 482 million. There can be little doubt that the European Union, and the major nation-states that are members of it, will continue to have a significant impact on global affairs in the decades ahead. However, the European Union and its member states face significant challenges before they can fulfill the dreams expressed by Czech president and former dissident Vaclav Havel in 1990 (chapter opening).

First, there is the major task of integrating the 2004 entrants: eight formerly Communist states, Cyprus and Malta, soon to be followed by formerly Communist Bulgaria, Romania, and Croatia. Never before has the EC/EU expanded so dramatically. Never before has the EC/EU sought to incorporate states possessing political, economic, and cultural heritages so divergent from those of its previous member states. Despite the magnitude of the challenge, the dreams of Havel and others still motivate and give life to the European project of expansion.

Beyond expansion and integration themselves, but related to them, stands the major task of devising a European Union constitution that will meet the needs of the expanded EU of the future. The constitutional draft unveiled in the summer of 2003 proved a disappointment to many; critics found it verbose and lacking in vision. Federalists argued that it did not push far enough toward supranational development. Defenders of national sovereignty, however, feared that it moved too far in that direction. In late 2003 the constitutional endeavor appeared to be slipping off the track to successful completion, as the Intergovernmental Conference intended to endorse the new constitution instead broke up in disarray. Though European leaders patched together a compromise constitutional document by June 2004, that document must still be ratified by all 25 member states before it can take effect—a difficult obstacle course, to be sure. Nevertheless, most analysts expected that the European Union would eventually "muddle through" to an agreement on a new, if imperfect, constitutional document.

The European Union faces other daunting challenges as well. Among these are the task of seeking to define its role in a world currently dominated by the United States and the task of engaging its citizens in an enterprise that they will recognize as genuinely democratic. These are perhaps even more complex tasks than attaining consensus on a new constitution and integrating Central and East European member states. However, even Robert Kagan, an American analyst generally quite critical of the European Union, has noted, "The difficulties of moving forward might seem insuperable were it not for the progress the project of European integration has already demonstrated."[42] That progress has indeed been remarkable: rendering war among its member states unthinkable after centuries of armed conflict, fostering a prosperous mixed economy that has brought benefits to most of its citizens in contrast to the Great Depression of the 1930s, and engaging formerly authoritarian and totalitarian states in a generally, if imperfectly, democratic enterprise, just to name a few of the most evident examples.

"The difficulties of moving forward might seem insuperable were it not for the progress the project of European integration has already demonstrated."

Robert Kagan, *Of Power and Paradise (2003), 67.*

Exactly what form the European Union will take and what sort of impact it will have in the future are not yet fully clear. These subjects will certainly continue to engage students of politics and economics. One can hope that Vaclav Havel's dreams of a "better Europe" will continue to activate the European project and capture the attention and interest of the world as they have in the past half century.

SUMMARY

- The sudden collapse of European Communism and the end of the Cold War in the 1989–1991 period brought dramatic political and economic changes in Central and Eastern Europe that virtually forced the European Union that was taking shape through the Maastricht Treaty to move toward eastward enlargement.

- The EU adopted in 1993 the Copenhagen criteria for assessing applications of prospective member states: 1) stable constitutional democracy, including protection of minority rights; 2) a functioning market economy; and 3) adherence to all existing EU laws *(acquis communitaire).*

- Ten states entered the European Union on May 1, 2004: Cyprus (Greek Cypriot section), the Czech Republic, Estonia, Hungary, Latvia, Lithuania, Malta, Poland, Slovakia, and Slovenia; Bulgaria and Romania have been slated for entry in 2007; Croatia is likely to gain entry between 2007 and 2009; as of July 2004, no date has been set for the entry of Turkey.

- Major challenges to the EU from the massive enlargement of 2004–2009 include the need to make major adjustments in agricultural and structural/cohesion policies and funds and to revamp EU institutions to accommodate the new member states; almost all of the new entrants are more agricultural and poorer than the 15 pre-2004 EU member states.

- Poland is by far the largest of the new EU entrant states.

- Poland was carved up by the Prussian, Austrian, and Russian empires between 1772 and 1795 and became a modern nation-state only in 1918; during World War II, it was dismembered by Germany and the Soviet Union; and during 1945–1989, it was a satellite of the Soviet Union; only in 1989 did it regain full status as an independent nation-state.

- Since 1989, Poland has sought to build a nation-state with legitimate state institutions, democratic participation, and a market-oriented mixed economy; it has had three constitutions since 1989 and has struggled with economic-distribution issues, but its democracy has proved resilient, if rather turbulent.

- Poland has adopted a hybrid model of legislative-executive relations, broadly similar to France's.

- The Polish president (now Alexandr Kwasniewski) is popularly elected, while the Polish prime minister (now Marek Belka) serves at the pleasure of a majority in the Sejm, the lower chamber of the Polish parliament.

- The Polish parliament is composed of the Sejm, popularly elected by proportional representation, and the Senate, elected on a first-past-the-post basis; the Sejm enjoys greater power than the Senate, including the power to remove the prime minister by a no-confidence vote.

- The Constitutional Court of Poland possesses powers of constitutional judicial review and gained broadened jurisdiction from the Constitution of 1997.

- A unitary state since 1918, Poland has moved since 1998 toward decentralization to its 16 provinces.

- Poland has employed both referendums and competitive presidential and parliamentary elections, it has a rather unstable multiparty system, and it has a diversity of interest groups.

- Polish voters endorsed EU entry in a June 8, 2003, referendum, 78 percent to 22 percent, though there remains considerable hostility to the EU on the Polish right wing and among farmers.

- Poland appears likely to support Atlanticism in the EU, to impose constraints on EU supranational development, and to favor further eastward enlargement.

- The prospect of EU membership solidified Polish constitutional democracy and the commitment of Poland to market reforms.

- Turkey is unlikely to join the European Union as soon as the other accession states enter due to questions about its European identity, its large population (which would be second only to Germany's), its human-rights record, the large political role of its military, and its economic difficulties.

- Russia, unlike Turkey, is not even a candidate for EU membership due to its large population (far greater than any current EU member), its questionable commitment to constitutional democracy and human rights, and its economic difficulties. In contrast to Turkish leaders, Russian leaders have shown little or no interest in EU membership.

ENDNOTES

1. "Croatian PM Says Accession Talks with EU to Start by March 2005," *Agence France Presse*, June 17, 2004; Philip Stephens, "Europe Would Be Foolish to Leave Turkey Out in the Cold," *Financial Times*, February 27, 2004, 13; Dexter Filkins, "Turks Look West; Will It Look Away?" *New York Times*, December 13, 2002, A12; Ian Fisher, "In a Vast Expansion of the European Union, Pluses but also Perils Lie Ahead," *New York Times*, December 13, 2002, A12; Elaine Sciolino, "European Union Turns Down Turkey's Bid for Membership," *New York Times*, December 13, 2002, A12; Jan Zielonka, "How New Enlarged Borders Will Reshape the European Union," *Journal of Common Market Studies*, 39, 3 (September 2001), 507–536; Lykke Friis and Anna Murphy, "Enlargement: A Complex Juggling Act," in Maria Green Cowles and Michael Smith, eds., *The State of the European Union: Risks, Reform, Resistance, and Revival*, vol. 5 (Oxford: Oxford University Press, 2000), esp. 192–194; Ulrich Sedelmeier, "Eastern Enlargement: Risk, Rationality, and Role-Compliance," in Cowles and Smith, eds., *The State of the EU*, 164–185.

2. Carsten Daugbjerg, "Reforming the CAP: Policy Networks and Broader Institutional Structures," *Journal of Common Market Studies* 37, 3 (September 1999), esp. 423–424.

3. European Commission, *Who's Who in the European Union? What Differences Will the Treaty of Nice Make?* (Luxembourg: European Communities Official Publications, 2001), at http://europa.eu.int/comm/igc/2000; Paul Betts, "Romano Prodi's Unlikely Allies," *Financial Times*, June 26, 2002, 10.

4. Zielonka, "How Enlarged Borders Will Reshape the European Union," 507–536.

5. Mieczyslaw Biskupski, *The History of Poland* (Westport, CT: Greenwood, 2000), Chs. 2, 3; Jerzy Lukowski, *The Partitions of Poland: 1772, 1793, 1795* (New York: Longman, 1999).

6. Biskkupski, *The History of Poland*, Chs. 7, 8. See Norman Davies, *The Heart of Europe: The Past in Poland's Present* (Oxford: Oxford University Press, 2001), esp. 219–222 and 240–244 on the early development and the spread and intensification of Polish nationalism in the eighteenth and nineteenth centuries.

7. Richard Lukas, *The Forgotten Holocaust: The Poles Under German Occupation* (New York: Hippocrene, 1997), 38–39, estimates the Polish death figure in World War II as 6,028,000, about

evenly divided between Jews and other Poles. Also see Jan Tomasz Gross, *Neighbors: The Destruction of the Jewish Community in Jedwabne, Poland* (Princeton, NJ: Princeton University Press, 2001), and Gross, *Revolution from Abroad: The Soviet Conquest of Poland's Western Ukraine and Western Belorussia* (Princeton, NJ: Princeton University Press, 1988).

8. Andrej Korbonski, "Dissent in Poland, 1956–1976," in Jane L. Curry, ed., *Dissent in Eastern Europe* (New York: Praeger, 1983), 29–39. Also see Marjorie Castle and Ray Taras, *Democracy in Poland*, 2nd ed. (Boulder, CO: Westview Press, 2002), Ch. 2.

9. Millard, *The Anatomy of the New Poland*, Ch. 3; Castle and Taras, *Democracy in Poland*, Ch. 3.

10. Frances Millard, *Polish Politics and Society* (London: Routledge, 1999), Ch. 7.

11. Millard, *Polish Politics and Society*, Chs. 2 and 6; Edmund Andrews, "Winning Party in Poland Forges Link with Farmers," *New York Times*, October 10, 2001, A12.

12. Economic figures for the 1990s are from Millard, *Polish Politics and Society*, 152. For the post-2000 problems, see "Poland: Jobs Leave," *The Economist* 358 (March 31, 2001), 99; Edmund Andrews, "Poland Opens Door to West, and Chills Blow Both Ways," *New York Times*, June 21, 1999, Al and A8.

13. Millard, *Polish Politics and Society*, Ch. 2; Charlemagne, "Jerzy Buzek, Doughty but Adrift," *The Economist* (December 9, 1999), 64; Andrews, "Winning Party in Poland Forges Link with Farmers," A12; "Poland: New Leader Wins Vote," *New York Times*, June 25, 2004, A6; Wojciech Moskwa, "Unpopular Polish Left Seeks Rebirth under New PM," Reuters News, July 4, 2004.

14. Andrej Jablonski, "The Europeanization of Government in Poland in the 1990s," in Karl Cordell, ed., *Poland in the European Union* (London: Routledge, 2000), esp. 136–138; Millard, *Polish Politics and Society*, 63–69.

15. Millard, *Polish Politics and Society*, 70–72, 132–134.

16. Jablonski, "The Europeanization of Government in Poland," 138–142; Wieslaw Bokajlo, "The Reform of Polish Local Government, and the Europe of the Regions," in Cordell, ed., *Poland in the European Union*, Ch. 9; Millard, *Polish Politics and Society*, 53–55.

17. Millard, *Polish Politics and Society*, 39 and 108–110; Aleks Szczerbiak, "Polish Public Opinion: Explaining Declining Support for EU Membership," *Journal of Common Market Studies* 39, 1 (March 2001), 105–122.; Peter S. Green, "Poles Vote Yes to Joining European Union," *New York Times*, June 9, 2003, A7.

18. This section on parties and Table 16.1 are based upon analyses in Millard, *Polish Politics and Society*, Ch. 5; Ryszard Herbut, "Parties and the Polish Party System," in Cordell, ed., *Poland and the European Union*, 86–105; Edmund Andrews, "Fuller Tally of Vote in Poland Shows Victors Need Coalition," *New York Times*, September 23, 2001, A12; Andrews, "Winning Party in Poland Forges Link with Farmers," A12; Kate Connolly, "Poles Ready to Embrace Ex-Communists," *The Guardian*, September 23, 2001; Kate Connolly, "Europe's Sleeping Giant," *The Guardian*, September 26, 2001.

19. Union membership figures are from William Coplin and Michael O'Leary, eds., *Political Risk Yearbook 2002*, vol. 7; the discussion of interest groups is based largely on Millard, *Polish Politics and Society*, Ch. 6.

20. Millard, *Polish Politics and Society*, 113–114.

21. Teresa Los-Nowak, "Contemporary Government Attitudes Towards the European Union," in Cordell, ed., *Poland and the European Union*, Ch. 2; Elzbieta Stadtmuller, "Polish Perceptions of the European Union in the 1990s," in Cordell, ed., *Poland and the European Union*, Ch. 3; Connolly, "Europe's Sleeping Giant," *The Guardian*, September 26, 2001.

22. Szczerbiak, "Polish Public Opinion," 105–122; Michael E. Smith, "EU Enlargement, Domestic Politics, and Post-Communist Transitions: The Impact of EMU on the Czech Republic, Hungary, and Poland," Paper presented at the annual meeting of the International Studies Association, New Orleans, March 2002, esp. 9–11.

23. Bernard Osser, "Eastern Poland's Farmers Urge No in EU Referendum," *Agence France Presse*, June 4, 2003. On Lipper's campaigns, see Ian Fisher, "Polish Populist, Stripped of His Post, Accuses Parliament of Corruption," *New York Times*, November 30, 2001, A12 and "Maverick Legislator in Poland Is Now Open to Slander Charge," *New York Times*, June 9, 2003, A7.

24. Millard, *Polish Politics and Society*, 120, 127, 141, 155.

25. Green, "Poles Vote Yes to Joining European Union," *New York Times*, June 9, 2003, A7; Smith, "EU Enlargement, Domestic Politics, and Post-Communist Transitions," 10.

26. Bokajlo, "The Reform of Polish Local Government, and the Europe of the Regions," 145–164.

27. "Poland: A Step Toward Europe," *New York Times*, March 22, 2002, A6.

28. Marcin Zaborowski and Kerry Longhurst, "America's Protégé in the East? The Emergence of Poland as a Regional Leader," *International Affairs* 79, 5 (October 2003), 1012. On Polish popular support for the United States, see Castle and Taras, *Democracy in Poland*, esp. 229–230.

29. "Special Report: Poland and the EU," *The Economist* (August 30, 2003), 18; Stefan Wagstyl, "Polish Political Leaders United in Approval of Miller's Stance," *Financial Times*, December 15, 2003, 5; George Parker, Judy Dempsey and Hugh Williamson, "Spain and Poland May Pay Financial Price," *Financial Times*, December 15, 2003, 4; Jacek Rostkowski, "When Should the Central Europeans Join EMU?" *International Affairs* 79, 5 (October 2003), 993–1008.

30. Friis and Murphy, "Enlargement: A Complex Juggling Act," 196.

31. Erik K. Zürcher, *Turkey: A Modern History* (London: I. B. Tauris, 1997), 33–37, 153–171, 289–291; Thomas W. Smith, "The European Union and Human Rights Reform in Turkey" (Paper presented at the International Studies Association Conference, New Orleans, March 2002), 10; Stephens, "Europe Would Be Foolish to Leave Turkey Out in the Cold," 13.

32. Timothy Bainbridge, *The Penguin Companion to European Union* (Harmondsworth: Penguin, 1998), 493.

33. Smith, "The EU and Human Rights Reform in Turkey," 7, 9–10; Ayse Isil Karakas, "The Human Rights Problematic in Turkey-European Union Relations" (Paper presented at the International Studies Association Conference, New Orleans, March 2002); Filkins, "Turks Look West; Will It Turn Away?" A12; Sciolino, "European Union Turns Down Turkey's Bid for Membership," A12.

34. M. Hakan Yanuz, "Turkey's Fault Lines and the Crisis of Kemalism," *Current History* 99 (January 2000), 34.

35. Zürcher, *Turkey*, 253–261, 271–273, 292–297; Smith, "The EU and Human Rights Reform in Turkey," 4.

36. Thomas L. Friedman, "War of Ideas, Part 2," *New York Times*, January 11, 2004, IV, 15; Smith, "The EU and Human Rights Reform in Turkey," 12; Karakas, "The Human Rights Problematic in Turkey–European Union Relations," esp. 20–25; "Turkey's Reforms: Great—If They Really Happen," *The Economist* 364 (August 10, 2002), 45–46.

37. Seth Mydans, "As Expected, Putin Easily Wins a Second Term in Russia," *New York Times*, March 15, 2004, A3; "Special Report: The Russian Elections, *The Economist* 369 (December 13, 2003), 24–28; Andrew Jack and Guy Dinmore, "Concern at 'Distorted' Result in Russia Poll," *Financial Times*, December 9, 2003, 1; William Safire, "The Russian Reversion," *New York Times*, December 10, 2003, A29; Stephen White, *Russia's New Politics: The Management of a Postcommunist Society* (Cambridge: Cambridge University Press, 2000), esp. Ch. 8; Thomas F. Remington, *Politics in Russia* (New York: Longman, 1999), 12–15, Chs. 4, 5, 7.

38. The terms in quotation marks are cited in White, *Russia's New Politics*, 141. Also see Remington, *Politics in Russia*, 15–16 and Ch. 6. For a recent account of the Russian economy in the Putin era, see Sabrina Tavernise, "Handful of Corporate Raiders Transform Russia's Economy," *New York Times*, August 13, 2002, A1, A6.

39. *Rossiiskaya gazeta*, April 4, 2001, 4, cited in Stephen White, Ian McAllister, and Margot Light, "Enlargement and the New Outsiders," *Journal of Common Market Studies* 40, 1 (2002), 140.

40. Alexander Kondrashov, "EU Pleased with Putin's Statement on Russia-EU Relations," ITAR-Tass News, April 19, 2002.

41. The quotation is from White, et al., "Enlargement," Kondrashov, "EU Pleased with Putin's Statement;" Robert Legvold, "Russia's Unformed Foreign Policy," *Foreign Affairs* 80, 5 (September/October 2001), 62–75.

42. Robert Kagan, *Of Paradise and Power* (New York: Alfred A. Knopf, 2003), 67.

Appendix

EUROPEAN UNION SIMULATIONS: ACTIVE LEARNING ABOUT THE EU

Simulations that seek to reflect real-life situations and engage students in active learning have become increasingly popular teaching devices in recent years, as a component of a broad movement in higher education toward actively involving students in participatory types of learning. By requiring students to "think on their feet," make applications of knowledge, play roles, and cope with group interaction, simulations have been found to enhance learning in various classroom environments.[1]

The author has employed simulations in a number of political science and interdisciplinary courses, including courses on European Politics and an interdisciplinary Contemporary Europe class. The following information and ideas are based on his own experiences.

PRE-SUMMIT: A SIMULATION OF PREPARATIONS FOR A EUROPEAN COUNCIL MEETING

This simulation is particularly well-suited to accompany this text on the major nation-states in the European Union. The "Pre-Summit" is designed to simulate the informal discussions through which major EU member-state leaders and the European Commission president seek to arrive at sufficient consensus to lay the ground work for a successful European Summit

(European Council) of the chief executives of all member states. This simulation works well with classes of 14–28 students, though it can certainly be utilized in larger or smaller classes.

The steps in this role-playing exercise are as follows:

1. The instructor assigns a topic or topics for the Pre-Summit negotiations. This/these may be short and clearly defined or fairly broad and open-ended, depending on the instructor's wishes. They may be drawn from past European Council sessions, some of which have been the subjects of articles, book chapters, and even books. For example, the Nice Summit of December 2000 that followed an Intergovernmental Conference and wrapped up the agreement on the Treaty of Nice might be used as the basis for a simulation on EU institutional revamping to accommodate eastward enlargement. The Luxembourg or Helsinki Summits that reached different conclusions about Turkey's application for EU membership could be other models. Or the Pre-Summit negotiations may focus on a likely agenda item or set of items from the future, such as developing new EU policies on workplace democracy or revamping EU agricultural or cohesion policies in light of eastward enlargement. (Note: http:/ue. eu.int/en/info/eurocouncil offers a nine-page description of the European Council and its

operations and presidency conclusions of all summits since the Corfu meeting in June 1994.)

2. The instructor divides the class so as to form negotiation sessions of (about) seven members each: one representing the European Commission president and one for each of the major member states. If a class has 28 students, then there will be four negotiation sessions run simultaneously, composed of 7 students in each. With 21 students in a class, there will be three such negotiation sessions. Two students can be teamed in one role, as needed, to make the numbers fit the number of students in the class: two might share the role of the Commission president, or the French role (president and prime minister), or the role of the member state chairing the negotiation session.

3. Students representing each major state and the Commission president work together, in and/or out of class, to do research on their roles and on the assigned topic or topics and to discuss these among themselves. In a class of 28 students, each national team and the Commission presidency team will be composed of 4 students. The instructor may require written reports from each student or each country team and the Commission presidency team. The author has required individual papers and has graded these.

4. The negotiation sessions occur in class meetings, preferably at round tables seating six or seven comfortably, in break-out rooms, or in well-defined sections of the classroom. Each session should be instructed to prepare a draft resolution and should be given a time period in which to reach as much agreement as possible on the draft resolution. The instructor can assign a particular member state to be president of the EU and host of

the Pre-Summit for all of the teams, or the instructor may wish to experiment with having different member states chair different negotiation sessions. If the latter approach is adopted, a subsequent topic for discussion in the debriefing after the simulation can be the impact of having different countries serve as president. After an appropriate time has elapsed (one class period, perhaps more than one, depending on the complexity of the topic or topics), the instructor collects the draft resolution from each of the sessions.

5. Subsequently (usually in the next class period), the president/host of each of the sessions gives a report on its draft resolution and/or copies of the draft resolutions are circulated to all class members. These reports or copies then serve as bases for discussion in a debriefing session, led by the instructor.

6. The instructor leads a debriefing in which she/he and the class members reflect on what the sessions accomplished or failed to accomplish, what similarities and differences appeared among the negotiation sessions (and why), how important agenda-setting is, whether and to what extent party affiliations as well as national differences affect leaders' behavior, what game theory illustrates about bargaining, and other topics that the instructor deems appropriate.

7. The instructor may opt to have each student write a paper addressing certain key points, such as those noted in number 6 above, and/or may base an examination essay question on the simulation. The author has used both approaches.

8. The time allocated for the simulation can vary as the instructor deems appropriate. The author has dedicated one to two weeks to this and other "active-learning" exercises, usually near the end of the course.

OTHER EUROPEAN UNION SIMULATIONS

The author has also employed a European Parliament Simulation, developed as part of a United States Department of Education Title VI grant, in several classes. Such a simulation can be employed even in very large classes of more than a hundred students, in which the previous simulation might prove unworkable.

In this simulation of the European Parliament, students are assigned roles as members of the European Parliament from particular nation-states and political parties. They are presented with several issues that either have come before the European Parliament or may come before it in the future and must then discuss and vote on these issues (i.e., a vote of confidence in the Jacques Santer-led Commission of 1999, or future membership for Turkey, or a resolution condemning racism by a member state, or workplace democracy—the author has used all of the above). Students interact in political party caucuses, divided proportionally as in the actual European Parliament, and with other MEPs from their nation-states, divided proportionally as in the actual European Parliament.

This simulation may be more appropriate than the previous one when time is limited or the class is large. The author has employed variations of it in university classes of varying sizes. In addition, several secondary school International Baccalaureate classes have employed it successfully.

Still another approach to European Union simulations is to join with classes at a number of different colleges and universities, following the basic method that has long been used for Model United Nations simulations. Such European Union simulations already exist in several regions of the country. For example, Peter Loedel has written about the European Union Simulation Project of the Pennsylvania/Maryland Consortium.[2] Yet another option is to participate in the transatlantic, inter-institutional EuroSim simulation sponsored by the Transatlantic Consortium for European Union Studies and Simulations. In the EuroSim process, faculty and students prepare and communicate in advance through the EuroSim and Blackboard websites and then engage in a face-to-face exercise held over four days that alternates between the United States and Europe.[3]

* * *

Active-learning role-playing exercises such as the ones described above are excellent ways to excite and engage students in learning about the European Union and its member states. The author has found that simulations have enhanced student performance on written examinations and have fostered students' interest in taking additional courses on the subject. An added benefit for the instructor is that they have also yielded very positive student responses in course/instructor evaluations and comments from university administrators at the end of the semester!

ENDNOTES

1. Elizabeth T. Smith and Mark A. Boyer, "Designing In-Class Simulations," *PS: Political Science & Politics* 29 (December 1996), 690–694; Charles C. Bonwell and James A. Eison, *Active Learning: Creating Excitement in the Classroom* (Washington, DC: George Washington University, 1991); Study Group on the Conditions of Excellence in American Higher Education, *Involvement in Learning: Realizing the Potential of American Higher Education* (Washington, DC: National Institute of Education/U. S. Department of Education, 1984).

2. Peter Loedel, "Teaching an EU Simulation," *ECSA Review* (Spring 1998), 10–11.

3. Laurie A. Buonanno, "Combining Synchronous (EU Simulation) with Asynchronous Teaching (EU On-Line)," *EUSA Review* 15, 2 (Spring 2002), 8–10.

GLOSSARY

Acquis communitaire The body of laws of the European Union.

Anarchism An ideology that views government as unnecessary and undesirable, advocating a society based on voluntary cooperation instead of governmental authority.

Atlanticism A term used to describe European desires to maintain strong ties across the Atlantic Ocean with the United States, particularly keeping the United States actively engaged in the security of Europe.

Autarky A self-sufficient economy, largely closed to the outside world by barriers to international trade and investment.

Authoritarian A form of government in which government exercises wide authority without the checks imposed by competitive democratic elections but less authority than totalitarian governments do. The German Imperial government of Otto von Bismarck and Kaiser Wilhelm I is seen by most analysts as an example of an authoritarian government.

Bicameral legislature A legislature composed of two chambers. It contrasts with a unicameral legislature consisting of only one chamber.

By-election An election held to fill a legislative vacancy at a time other than a regularly scheduled general election.

Bipolar balance of power An international power pattern in which two major power centers predominate over others, checking and balancing one another. The post–World War II pattern of the United States and the Soviet Union as two global "superpowers" is an example.

Caciques Political bosses, especially in nineteenth- and early twentieth-century Spain and Latin America, who offered favors in return for votes but often engaged in vote-stealing and intimidation that made a mockery of ostensibly democratic procedures.

Capitalism An ideology and economic system emphasizing private ownership of property, pursuit of material gain, and market exchanges of goods and services. Some variants of capitalism permit a larger governmental role than others.

Center-periphery A social, economic, and political cleavage or division between the center of a national system (usually the capital and the region surrounding it) and regions located around its territorial edges.

Checks and balances Procedures through which executives and legislatures (and often judiciaries) possess legal and political powers that limit the behavior of occupants of other institutions. The term is particularly associated with the United States government but has been applied to many other constitutional democracies also.

Cleavage A basic societal division, usually along lines of social class, religion, ethnicity, or region. Analysts such as Stein Rokkan have emphasized the extent to which social cleavages have shaped political party systems.

Clientelism A political pattern, particularly prevalent in Italy, whereby political party and factional leaders use control over the state bureaucracy to do favors for businesses, interest groups, and individuals in return for campaign contributions and other forms of political support. Often, these activities cross the boundaries of legality and are labeled as "corruption."

Coalition government A government formed by an alliance of two or more political parties that divide the ministerial posts between or among themselves. Such governments have been common in most European political systems, though relatively rare in the United Kingdom and (in recent years) in Spain.

Codetermination A system of power-sharing in German business corporations, which grants employee representatives one-third to one-half of the positions on the supervisory boards of large corporations and establishes elected works councils when employees of companies with more than five employees so request.

Common law A legal tradition, developed in England and adopted in most English-speaking countries, including the United States, that emphasizes judicial interpretations, case law, precedents, and an adversarial style in court proceedings. It stands in contrast to the Roman law, or code law, tradition prevalent on the Continent of Europe.

Comparative advantage An economic theory, first developed by David Ricardo, that stresses the benefits to individual countries of international trade and specialization, taking into account the costs (in terms of other goods given up) of producing the same commodities.

Consociational democracy A system of power-sharing, usually between or among political parties representing distinct ethnic, religious, and/or class social divisions or cleavages. Arend Lijphart is the political scientist who developed this concept. It has most frequently been applied to Belgium, the Netherlands, and Switzerland, but also sometimes to Austria.

Constitutional democracy A form of government characterized by universal suffrage, competitive elections, and constitutional protections of individual rights.

Constructivist A scholarly approach to international relations and the study of European integration that emphasizes that the "nation-state" and other units of analysis are humanly constructed units. It suggests that realism and liberal intergovernmentalism exaggerate the roles of nation-states and the rationalism of state leaders' behavior.

Corporatism An economic pattern of government, business, and labor union cooperation in running the economy. In its Italian Fascist form under Benito Mussolini, it was associated with repression of free labor unions and with political dictatorship. Since World War II, the term neo-corporatism has commonly been applied to formalized government-business corporate-labor union (and sometimes agricultural group) economic consultation in democratic political systems.

Customs union A regional trading arrangement within which there is an absence of tariffs. Its members also have a common set of tariffs and rules regarding trade from outside the customs union. The European Economic Community moved to establish a customs union by 1968.

Dealignment An election pattern indicating voters' growing detachment from political party loyalties. It contrasts with a "realignment" in which voters shift party allegiances to an unusually great degree but continue to demonstrate attachments to political parties.

Devolve To surrender powers from the central government to regional or local governments. The British central government has devolved some powers to Scotland, Wales, and Northern Ireland.

Differentiated integration A process in which some European Union members pool their sovereignty, or integrate, more fully than other members. The Economic and Monetary Union, as of 2002, is an example in that 12 EU members have adopted the common currency, while 3 have not. Some observers have argued that the future EU will pursue more differentiated integration than in the past as new members from Central and Eastern Europe enter it.

Directive A type of European Union legal instrument that obliges member nation-states to take the necessary legal steps to give it effect within their boundaries. Unlike a regulation, which is binding and directly applicable in all member states, or a decision, which is binding on those to whom it is addressed, a directive must be transposed into national law, allowing national authorities to determine the form and method.

Division A formal parliamentary vote in which members of the legislature divide into "aye" and "nay" groups to be counted.

Economic libertarianism An ideology stressing the value of an economy based on private property, pursuit of material gain, and free-market competition. It is hostile to socialism. Europeans commonly use the term neoliberalism to refer to a similar set of ideological beliefs, though the European neoliberal ideology generally tolerates more social services than American economic libertarianism does.

Euroskeptic A term used, primarily in Britain, to refer to those who express opposition to further European integration (or at least to British participation in such integration). Some Euroskeptics go so far as to advocate British withdrawal from the European Union. To the extent that Euroskeptics accept European integration, it is on an intergovernmental rather than a supranational basis.

Federal A legal relationship between a national government and state or regional governments in which the latter possess the highest authority in some policy realms. The United States and Germany possess federal systems. The term is also sometimes applied to the relations between the European Union and its member nation-states, though these are more commonly described as quasi- (partially) federal. "European federalism" commonly refers to advocacy of extensive European supranationalism.

First-past-the-post electoral system An electoral system in which each member of a legislative assembly is elected by a plurality of the vote in a district. Only one member is elected from each district and need only win more votes than any other candidates. A majority (50 percent plus one) is not required. This type of electoral system usually favors the two largest parties and tends to discourage multiparty politics.

Functionalism Theory, associated with Jean Monnet and others, that a United States of Europe could and should emerge from the spillover effects of limited economic cooperation in a few sectors.

Fusion of powers The practice in most cabinet-parliamentary systems of drawing the heads of the executive branch (prime minister and other ministers) from the legislature and making them accountable to a legislative majority, merging executive and legislative powers rather than separating them, as in the United States.

Gross Domestic Product (GDP) The total value of the goods and services produced by the economy of an entity (nation-state or regional body) in a year, excluding the income of the residents that is derived from investment abroad.

Hegemony A term referring to the dominance of one nation-state over others in international relations. A state possesses hegemonic power when it can create and enforce rules of international behavior and maintain its own dominance.

High Authority Executive body of the European Coal and Steel Community, the High Authority was the predecessor of the subsequent EC/EU Commission. Its first president was Jean Monnet.

Historical institutionalism A school of thought concerning European integration, associated with Paul Pierson in particular, that emphasizes imperfect information for political actors and unintended consequences of their actions. This approach emerged in the 1990s as a critique of liberal intergovernmentalist theory.

Intergovernmental A term referring to a decision-making process in which nation-state governments bargain with one another as distinct entities (as opposed to a supranational process that is substantially independent of nation-state control). In the European Union, the European Council of Ministers (Council of the European Union) and the European Council are primarily intergovernmental institutions.

Judicial review A practice in which a constitutional court or other judicial body may review executive or legislative actions and rule them to be either constitutionally permissible or unconstitutional and thus null and void. Long employed by the United States Supreme Court, judicial review has become increasingly widespread in Europe in recent years.

Laissez-faire capitalism A term referring to an economy emphasizing private property, unregulated pursuit of material gain, and market mechanisms. Such an economy stands in contrast to state socialism and to a mixed economy. Laissez-faire is a French term meaning "leave us alone."

Left Pertaining to ideologies and political parties that emphasize the use of government to promote increased social and economic equality. Communism and socialism are generally placed on the left of the left-right spectrum.

Liberal intergovernmentalism A school of thought associated with Andrew Moravcsik that has sought to explain European Community/European Union development by drawing upon both liberal institutionalist and realist perspectives. It emphasizes the continuing importance of European nation-state political actors in the context of post–World War II global liberalization trends.

Liberal institutionalism A school of thought among international relations scholars and practitioners that emphasizes global trends and regional patterns that often transcend the nation-state. It stands in contrast to realism and is sometimes referred to as pluralism or idealism.

Manifesto A statement of public policy pledges by a British political party, aimed at winning popular electoral support. It resembles an American party platform but is usually more specific and more likely to be a serious basis for guiding policy initiatives by the government of a victorious party than is usually the case in the United States.

Mixed economy A term referring to an economy in which there is extensive state regulation and provision of social welfare as well as a capitalist base in private property and fairly heavy reliance on market mechanisms. Such an economy represents a "middle way" between state socialism and free-market capitalism.

Multipolar balance of power An international power pattern in which three or more major power centers predominate, checking and balancing one another. Shifting alliances among these power centers are usually part of the international dynamic. Global politics from 1648 to the early twentieth century usually illustrated this pattern.

Neo-Atlanticism A term used by some analysts of Italian politics to refer to ideas, fairly widespread in the 1950s and 1960s, advocating a loosening of military ties with the United States (while retaining other ties) and orienting Italian foreign policy more towards Europe and the Mediterranean.

Neo-corporatism See corporatism.

Neofunctionalism A branch of liberal institutionalist theory, particularly associated with Ernst B. Haas, stressing how cooperation among nation-states in one policy domain would likely stimulate cooperation and joint ventures in related domains, thus moving the participating nation-states in the direction of supranational integration.

Neoliberalism A modern ideology stressing the desirability of an economy based on private property, pursuit of material gain, and market exchanges of goods and services. It is hostile to socialism. As a mainly European ideology, it resembles what many Americans term economic conservatism, though it often concedes the need for more extensive social services than most American conservatism advocates.

Pillar A term used in the European Union to refer to a set of public policy-making structures and procedures. The Treaty on European Union (Maastricht Treaty) created three pillars, two of which (Common Foreign and Security Policy and Justice and Home Affairs) were to be largely intergovernmental.

Plebiscitary A style of governing by frequent "yes-no" popular votes, particularly on constitutional matters.

Presidential A term indicating strong executive leadership by a president. Sometimes analysts suggest that prime ministers in a parliamentary system have taken on powers similar to those of the president in a presidential system.

Prime ministerial A term suggesting strong executive leadership of a cabinet by the prime minister rather than a pattern of team leadership.

Proletarians Term used, especially by socialists and communists, to refer to members of the working class.

Protocol In the European Union, a legal instrument associated with a treaty but separate from it. It is legally binding on its signatories, but these may not include all EU member states. The Social Protocol adopted by 11 European nation-states (but not Britain) at the time of the Maastricht Treaty is an example.

Qualified Majority Voting (QMV). A term used in the European Union to refer to the voting system often used in the Council of Ministers, whereby each national minister casts a "weighted" vote, based roughly on the population of her/his state. There are 15 ministers, 87 "weighted" votes, and a "qualified majority" requires at least 62 votes by at least 10 ministers, though all of these numbers are about to change as a result of further EU widening. The numbers will be altered proportionally as new members enter the EU.

Question Time A procedure in which executives must answer questions posed by members of a parliamentary body. The British Question Time is probably the best-known example.

Realism A school of thinking among international-relations scholars and practitioners that sees international relations primarily as a struggle among nation-states competing for power and pursuing distinctive national geopolitical interests.

Referendum A popular vote on an issue, in which the voting public votes "yes" or "no" concerning the proposition.

Regressive tax A tax that takes a higher proportion of the incomes or property of the poor than of the wealthy, thus creating more inequality. It is the opposite of a progressive tax.

Regulation A legal instrument of the EC/EU that has, according to European Court of Justice rulings, direct effect in member states. A **directive,** in contrast, is a legal instrument that leaves to national authorities the choice of form and methods to transpose it into national law.

Right Pertaining to ideologies and political parties that reject efforts to use government to promote enhanced social and economic equality. Ideologies and parties on the "far right" argue that government should promote appropriate inequalities (usually on an ethno-national) basis. Fascist, Nazi, and anti-immigrant ideologies and parties are generally placed on the far right, while conservative and Christian democratic ideologies and parties are usually described as center-right.

Risorgimento Italian term for the movement leading to the formation of an Italian nation-state, 1859–1861.

Roman Law A legal tradition, dating from the days of the Roman Empire and widely drawn upon in contemporary Europe, that emphasizes a detailed legal code, limited leeway for judicial interpretation, and an inquisitorial style in court proceedings. It is often contrasted to the Anglo-American common law tradition.

Separation of power The practice of separating the executive from the legislature, so that no person can serve simultaneously in both executive and legislative branches of government. This practice is usually justified as creating checks and balances to limit power. Some argue that the "separation of powers" in the United States is best described as "separate institutions sharing powers."

Socialism A political ideology that has traditionally been associated with a commitment to social and economic equality and with a large governmental role in running the economy. State socialism emphasizes the need for government ownership of business and state preeminence over market mechanisms for setting prices and wages.

Sovereignty Legal possession of supreme authority. Nation-states assert sovereignty over a particular territory.

Spillover A concept emphasized by neofunctionalist theorists who argued that cooperation among nation-states in one domain would likely instigate cooperation among them in other, related, domains, fostering increased supranationalism.

Stakeholder economy A term frequently used in modern Britain in particular to refer to a sharing of rights and responsibilities among business corporate shareholders, employees, consumers, and communities.

Subsidiarity A term used widely in the European Union to indicate that tasks should be performed at the lowest feasible level of government, implying the desirability of considerable decentralization of authority.

Supranational A term referring to a decision-making process that is substantially independent of nation-state control, in contrast to an intergovernmental process in which nation-states negotiate directly with one another. In the European Union, the European Court of Justice and the European Commission are far more supranational than is the Council of Ministers or the European Council. Advocacy of supranationalism in Europe is often referred to as European federalism. See **federal.**

Totalitarian A form of government in which the government exercises nearly total authority over all aspects of society. Prime examples include Stalin's Soviet Union and Hitler's Third Reich in Germany.

Unitary A form of government in which sovereignty (supreme authority) is vested in the central government. In contrast, a federal form of government divides supreme authority between the central government and regional or state governments. Britain and France have traditionally been unitary; Germany and the United States are federal.

Vote of confidence A parliamentary vote in which a legislative chamber indicates whether it continues to have confidence in the government (cabinet and sub-cabinet). In Britain, a simple majority can oust the government on either a vote of confidence or a vote of no confidence (the latter introduced by the Opposition). In Germany and Spain, a "constructive" vote of no confidence (by an absolute majority in favor of a new government) is required to remove the government.

BIBLIOGRAPHY

Ackrell, Robert. *The Common Agricultural Policy.* Sheffield: Sheffield Academic Press, 2000.

Adams, Ian. *Ideology and Politics in Britain Today.* Manchester: Manchester University Press, 1998.

Alden, Edward, Guy de Jonquières, and Mariko Sanchanta. "Bush Backs Down by Lifting Tariffs on Steel Imports." *Financial Times,* December 12, 2003, 1.

Allen, Christopher S., ed. *Transformation of the German Political Party System: Institutional Crisis or Democratic Renewal?* New York: Berghahn, 1999.

Allen, David. "Cohesion and the Structural Funds: Transfers and Trade-Offs." In Helen Wallace and William Wallace, *Policy-Making in the European Union,* 4th ed. (Oxford: Oxford University Press, 2000), 243–265.

Allum, Percy. *State and Society in Western Europe.* Cambridge: Polity Press, 1995.

Almarcha Barbado, Amparo, ed. *Spain and EC Membership Evaluated.* London: Pinter, 1993.

Almond, Gabriel A. "Comparing Political Systems." *Journal of Politics* 18, 2 (1956), 391–409.

Almond, Gabriel A., Russell J. Dalton, and G. Bingham Powell, eds. *European Politics Today.* 2nd ed. New York: Longman, 2001.

Almond, Gabriel A., and G. Bingham Powell. *Comparative Politics: A Developmental Approach.* Boston: Little, Brown, 1966.

Almond, Gabriel A., and Sidney Verba. *The Civic Culture: Political Attitudes and Democracy in Five Nations.* Boston: Little, Brown, 1965.

Ambler, John S., and M. Shawn Reichert. "France: Europeanism, Nationalism, and the Planned Economy." In Eleanor E. Zeff and Ellen B. Pirro, eds., *The European Union and the Member States* (Boulder, CO: Lynne Rienner, 2001), 29–58.

Anderson, Jeffrey J. *German Unification and the Union of Europe.* Cambridge: Cambridge University Press, 1999.

———. "Germany and the Structural Funds: Unification Leads to Bifurcation." In Leesbet Hooghe, ed., *Cohesion Policy and European Integration: Building Multi-Level Governance* (Oxford: Oxford University Press, 1996), 294–319.

———. "Structural Funds and the Social Dimension of EU Policy: Springboard or Stumbling Block?" In Stephan Leibfried and Paul Pierson, eds., *European Social Policy:*

Between Fragmentation and Integration (Washington, DC: Brookings, 1995), 123–158.

Anderson, Karen. "Sweden: Retreat from Exceptionalism." In Eleanor Zeff and Ellen Pirro, eds, *The EU and the Member States* (Boulder, CO: Lynne Rienner, 2001), 285–304.

Anderson, Stephanie B. "Problems and Possibilities: The Development of the CFSP From Maastricht to the 1996 IGC." In Pierre-Henri Laurent and Marc Maresceau, eds., *The State of the European Union,* vol. 4 (Boulder, CO: Lynne Rienner, 1998), 133–147.

Andrews, Edmund. "Further Tally of Vote in Poland Shows Victors Need Coalition." *New York Times,* September 23, 2001, A12.

———. "Germans Offer Plan to Remake Europe Union." *New York Times,* March 1, 2001, A1, A3.

———. "Poland Opens Door to West, and Chills Blow Both Ways." *New York Times,* June 21, 1999, A1, A8.

———. "Winning Party in Poland Forges Link with Farmers." *New York Times,* October 10, 2001, A12.

"Anger at EU Fishing Plans." *Financial Times,* June 10, 2002, 3.

Appleton, Andrew. "The New Social Movement Phenomenon: Placing France in Comparative Perspective." In Robert Elgie, ed., *The Changing French Political System* (London: Frank Cass, 2000), 57–75.

Arango, E. Rámon. *Spain: Democracy Regained.* Boulder, CO: Westview, 1995.

Ardagh, John. *France Today.* London: Penguin, 1988.

Ash, Timothy Garton, Michael Mertes, and Dominique Moïsi. "Only a Club of Three Can Bring European Unity." *Financial Times,* July 11, 2003, 8.

"Aznar Hurt, ETA Clobbered." *The Economist* 359 (May 19, 2001).

Bache, Ian. *The Politics of European Union Regional Policy: Multi-Level Governance or Flexible Gatekeeping?* Sheffield: Sheffield Academic Press/University Association for Contemporary European Studies, 1998.

Bache, Ian, Stephen George, and R. A. W. Rhodes. "The European Union Cohesion Policy and Subnational Authorities in the United Kingdom." In Liesbet Hooge, ed., *Cohesion Policy and European Integration* (Oxford: Oxford University Press, 1996), 294–319.

"Back in the Dock." *Financial Times,* January 15, 2004, 12.

"Back to Basics," *The Economist* 356 (July 22, 2000), 48–49.

Bacon, David. "Germany's New Identity." In E. Gene Frankland, ed., *Global Studies: Europe*, 7th ed. (Guilford, CT: McGraw-Hill/Dushkin, 2002), 228–229.

Bagehot, Walter. *The English Constitution*. Ithaca, NY: Cornell University Press, 1966.

Bainbridge, Timothy. *The Penguin Companion to European Union*. 2nd ed. Harmondsworth: Penguin, 1998.

Baines, Priscilla. "Parliament and the Common Agricultural Policy." In Philip Giddings and Gavin Drewry, eds., *Westminster and Europe* (New York: St. Martin's, 1996), 191–222.

Baker, David. "Britain and Europe: Treading Water or Slowly Drowning?" *Parliamentary Affairs* 56, 2 (April 2003), 237–254.

Balcells, Albert. *Catalan Nationalism*. New York: St. Martin's, 1996.

Baldwin, Richard, and Mika Widgren. "Europe's Voting Reform Will Shift Power Balance." *Financial Times*, June 23, 2003, 13.

Ball, Terence, and Richard Dagger. *Political Ideologies and the Democratic Ideal*. 3rd ed. New York: Longman, 1999.

Barber, Tony. "Berlusconi May Launch Emergency Decree to Save Media Legislation." *Financial Times*, December 17, 2003, 3.

———. "Blow for Berlusconi as Court Rules Law Is Invalid." *Financial Times*, January 14, 2004, 2.

———. "Italian Coalition Seeks Accord on Reforms." *Financial Times*, August 15, 2003, 5.

———. "Italians Get a Reminder that Their President Is More than a Figurehead." *Financial Times*, December 18, 2003, 4.

Barberis, Peter. *The Elite of the Elite: Permanent Secretaries in the British Higher Civil Service*. Aldershot: Dartmouth, 1996.

Barzini, Luigi. *The Italians*. New York: Bantam Books, 1964.

Bates, Stephen. "Signore Mortadella." *The Observer*, October 10, 1999.

Baumann, Rainer. "The Transformation of German Multilateralism: Changes in the Foreign Policy Discourse Since Unification." *German Politics and Society* 20, 4 (Winter 2002), 1–26.

Baun, Michael. *An Imperfect Union: The Maastricht Treaty and the New Politics of European Integration*. Boulder, CO: Westview, 1996.

Becker, Elizabeth. "U.S. Presses for Total Exemption from War Crimes Court." *New York Times*, October 9, 2002, A6.

Beer, Samuel H., et al. *Patterns of Government: The Major Political Systems of Europe*. 3rd ed. New York: Random House, 1973.

Beiberg, Marianne. *The Making of the Basque Nation*. Cambridge: Cambridge University Press, 1989.

Bell, David. "Western Communists and the European Union." In John Gaffney, ed., *Political Parties and the European Union* (London: Routledge, 1996), 220–234.

Bell, David A. *The Cult of the Nation in France: Inventing Nationalism, 1680–1800*. Cambridge, MA: Harvard University Press, 2001.

Beloff, Lord. "Amery on the Constitution: Britain and the European Union." *Government and Opposition* 33 (Spring 1998), 167–182.

———. *Britain and European Union*. New York: St. Martin's, 1996.

Benoit, Bertrand. "Chancellor Faces Bundesrat Battle for Agenda." *Financial Times*, August 14, 2003, 2.

———. "German Mediators Reach Eleventh Hour on Schröder Reforms." *Financial Times*, December 10, 2003, 3.

———. "Germany's Politicians Try to Trim the Constitutional Fat." *Financial Times*, August 18, 2003, 12.

———. "Schröder in Reforms Plea as Opposition Line Hardens." *Financial Times*, August 14, 2003, 2.

———. *Social-Nationalism: An Anatomy of French Euroskepticism* Aldershot: Ashgate, 1997.

———. "Surprise at Eichel's 'Emotional Response'." *Financial Times*, November 26, 2003, 4.

Berger, Suzanne. "The French Political System." In Samuel H. Beer, et al., *Patterns of Government*, 3rd ed. (New York: Random House, 1973), 333–470.

"Berlusconi Strikes Out." *The Economist* 362 (January 12, 2002), 14–15.

Betts, Paul. "Romano Prodi's Unlikely Allies." *Financial Times*, June 26, 2002, 10.

Beyers, Jan, Bart Kerremans, and Peter Bursens. "Belgium, the Netherlands, and Luxembourg: Diversity Among the Benelux Countries." In Eleanor Zeff and Ellen Pirro, eds., *The EU and the Member States* (Boulder, CO: Lynne Rienner, 2001), 59–88.

Beyme, Klaus von. *The Legislator: German Parliament as a Centre of Political Decision-Making*. Aldershot: Ashgate, 1998.

Biskupski, Mieczyslaw. *The History of Poland*. Westport, CT: Greenwood Press, 2000.

Black, Ian. "EU Calls Truce in 'Axis of Evil' Row." *The Guardian*, February 20, 2002.

———. "Two Men, One Goal, and Lots of Bickering." *The Guardian*, April 19, 2001.

Bocher, Jörg. "Franco-German Economic Relations." In Patrick McCarthy, ed., *France–Germany 1983–1993* (New York: St. Martin's, 1993), 73–92.

Bodin, Jean. *Six Books of the Commonwealth*. Abridged and translated by M. J. Tooley. New York: Barnes and Noble, 1967.

Bogdanor, Vernon. "Constitutional Reform." In Anthony Seldon, ed., *The Blair Effect*. (London: Little, Brown, 2001), 138–156.

Bogdanor, Vernon, and David Butler, eds. *Democracy and Elections: Electoral Systems and Their Political Consequences*. New York: Cambridge University Press, 1983.

Bokajlo, Wieslaw. "The Reform of Polish Local Government, and the Europe of the Regions." In Karl Cordell, ed., *Poland in the European Union* (London: Routledge, 2000), Ch. 9.

Bonwell, Charles C., and James A. Eison. *Active Learning: Creating Excitement in the Classroom.* Washington, DC: George Washington University, 1991.

Bornschier, Volker, ed. *State-Building in Europe: The Revitalization of Western European Integration.* Cambridge: Cambridge University Press, 2000.

Borrás, Susanna, et al. "The Europeanization of National Policies in Comparison: Spain as a Case Study." *South European Society & Politics* 3, 2 (Autumn 1998), 24–33.

Börzel, Tanja. "Europeanization and Territorial Institutional Change: Towards a 'Third Level' in Europe?" In Maria Green Cowles, et al., eds., *Transforming Europe: Europeanization and Domestic Change* (Ithaca, NY: Cornell University Press, 2001), 137–158.

———. "The Greening of a Polity? The Europeanization of Environmental Policy-Making in Spain." *South European Society & Politics* 3, 1 (Summer 1998), 65–92.

Bowler, Shaun, David Farrell, and Richard Katz, eds. *Party Discipline and Parliamentary Government* (Columbus: Ohio State University Press, 1999.

Bracher, Karl Dietrich. *The German Dictatorship.* New York: Praeger, 1970.

Bracken, Mike. "Who Is Romano Prodi?" *The Guardian,* March 24, 1999.

Bradbier, John. "UK Environmental Policy Under Blair." In Stephen P. Savage and Rob Adkinson, eds., *Public Policy Under Blair* (Basingstoke: Palgrave, 2001), 86–109.

Bradley, Kieran St. Clair. "The European Court of Justice." In John Peterson and Michael Shackleton, *The Institutions of the European Union* (Oxford: Oxford University Press, 2002), 118–138.

Braunthal, Gerald. "Codetermination in West Germany." In James B. Christoph and Bernard E. Brown, eds., *Cases in Comparative Politics* (Boston: Little, Brown, 1976), 215–247.

———. *Parties and Politics in Modern Germany.* Boulder, CO: HarperCollins-Westview, 1996.

———. "The SPD: From Opposition to Governing Party." In David P. Conradt, et al., eds., *Power Shift in Germany* (New York: Berghahn, 2000), 18–37.

Bremner, Charles. "Jospin Offers Devolution Plan to Corsicans." *The Times,* July 11, 2000.

Brittan, Leon. *European Competition Policy: Keeping the Playing Field Level.* London: Brassey, 1992.

Brubaker, Rogers. *Citizenship and Nationhood in France and Germany.* Cambridge, MA: Harvard University Press, 1992.

Bruni, Frank. "Leaders Broadly Back a Draft Charter for the European Union." *Financial Times,* June 21, 2003, A2.

Buck, Tobias. "Fischler to Stand Firm on Proposals for Overhaul of EU Farm Subsidies." *Financial Times,* June 3, 2003, 6.

———. "Patience Runs Low as Farm Talks Resume." *Financial Times,* June 26, 2003, 4.

Buck, Tobias, Guy de Jonquières, and Frances Williams. "Fischler's Surprise for Europe's Farmers: Now the Argument over Agriculture Moves to the WTO." *Financial Times,* June 27, 2003, 11.

Bull, Anna Cento. "Ethnicity, Racism, and the Northern League." In Carl Levy, ed., *Italian Regionalism: History, Identity, and Politics* (Oxford: Berg, 1996), 171–188.

Bull, Martin J. "The Democratic Party of the Left in Italy's Transition." In Stephen Gundle and Simon Parker, *The New Italian Republic* (London: Routledge, 1996), Ch. 10.

———. "The Italian Christian Democrats." In John Gaffney, ed., *Political Parties and the EU* (London: Routledge, 1996), 139-54.

Buller, Jim. *National Statecraft and European Integration: The Conservative Government and the European Union, 1979-1997.* London: Pinter, 2000.

Bullock, Alan. *Hitler: A Study in Tyranny.* New York: Harper & Row, 1964.

Bulmer, Simon, Charlie Jeffery, and William Paterson. *Germany's European Diplomacy: Shaping the Regional Milieu.* Manchester: Manchester University Press, 1999.

Bulmer, Simon, Andreas Maurer, and William Paterson. "The European Policy-Making Machinery in the Berlin Republic: Hindrance or Handmaiden?" *German Politics* 10, 1 (April 2001), 177-206.

Bulmer, Simon, and William Paterson. *The Federal Republic of Germany and the European Community.* London: Allen & Unwin, 1987.

———. "Germany in the European Union: Gentle Giant or Emergent Leader?" *International Affairs* 72, 1 (January 1996), 9-32.

Bulmer, Simon, and Wolfgang Wessels, *The European Council: Decision-Making in European Politics.* London: Macmillan, 1987.

Buonanno, Laurie. "Combining Synchronous (EU Simulation) with Asynchronous Teaching (EU On-line)." *EUSA Review* 15, 2 (Spring 2002), 8–10.

Calleo, David P., and Eric Staal, eds. *Europe's Franco-German Engine.* Washington, DC: Brookings, 1998.

Cameron, David R. "The 1992 Initiative: Causes and Consequences." In Alberta Sbragia, ed., *Euro-Politics: Institutions and Policymaking in the "New" European Community* (Washington, DC: Brookings, 1992), 23–74.

———. "National Interest, the Dilemmas of European Integration, and Malaise." In John T. S. Keeler and Martin A Schain, eds., *Chirac's Challenge: Liberalization, Europeanization, and Malaise in France* (New York: St. Martin's, 1996).

Campbell, Colin, et al. *Politics and Government in Europe Today.* 2nd ed. Boston: Houghton Mifflin, 1995.

Camps, Miriam. *Britain and the European Community, 1955–1963*. Princeton, NJ: Princeton University Press, 1964.

Caporaso, James, and Joseph Jupille. "The Europeanization of Gender Equality Policy and Domestic Structural Change." In Maria Green Cowles, et al., eds., *Transforming Europe* (Ithaca, NY: Cornell University Press, 2001), 21–43.

Carillo, Elisa A. *Alcide De Gasperi: The Long Apprenticeship*. Notre Dame, IN: Notre Dame University Press, 1965.

Carnoy, Martin, and Derek Shearer. *Economic Democracy*. Armonk, NY: M. E. Sharpe, 1980.

Carr, Raymond. *Spain, 1908–1939*. Oxford: Oxford University Press, 1970.

———. *The Spanish Tragedy: The Civil War in Perspective*. London: Weidenfeld and Nicolson, 1977.

Carr, Raymond, and Juan Pablo Fusi Aizpurua. *Spain: Dictatorship to Democracy*. 2nd ed. London: George Allen & Unwin, 1981.

Carrieri, Mimmo. "Industrial Relations and the Labour Movement." In Stephen Gundle and Simon Parker, eds., *The New Italian Republic: From the Fall of the Berlin Wall to Berlusconi* (London: Routledge, 1996), 294–307.

Carter, Ralph. "Leadership at Risk: The Perils of Unilateralism." *PS: Political Science and Politics* 36, 1 (January 2003), 17–22.

Castle, Marjorie, and Ray Taras. *Democracy in Poland*. 2nd ed. Boulder, CO: Westview, 2002.

Castle, Stephen. "The Deal—Big Four Emerge Triumphant After Diplomatic 'Coup'." *The Independent*, December 12, 2000.

Cesarini, Paolo. "Competition Policy." In Francesco Francioni, ed., *Italy and EC Membership Evaluated* (New York: St. Martin's, 1992), 51–70.

Chalmers, Damian. "The Positioning of EU Judicial Politics Within the United Kingdom." *West European Politics* 23, 4 (October 2000).

Charlemagne. "Jerzy Buzek, Doughty but Adrift." *The Economist* (December 9, 1999), 64.

———. "José Luis Zapatero, Spain's New Socialist." *The Economist* 359 (January 27, 2001), 54.

———. "Philadelphia or Frankfurt?" *The Economist* 366 (March 8, 2003), 52.

Christoph, James B., and Bernard E. Brown, eds. *Cases in Comparative Politics*. Boston: Little, Brown, 1976.

Chryssochoou, Dimitris N. *Democracy in the European Union*. New York: St. Martin's, 1998.

Cini, Michelle. *The European Commission: Leadership, Organisation, and Culture in the EU Administration*. Manchester: Manchester University Press, 1996.

Cini, Michelle, and Lee McGowan. *Competition Policy in the European Union*. London: Macmillan, 1998.

Clark, Martin. *Modern Italy, 1871–1995*. 2nd ed. New York: Longman, 1996.

Clemens, Clay. "Crisis or Catharsis? Germany's CDU After the Party Finance Affair." *German Politics and Society* 18, 2 (Summer 2000), 66–90.

———. "Introduction: The Kohl Legacy." In Clay Clemens and William Paterson, eds., *The Kohl Chancellorship* (Portland, OR: Frank Cass, 1998), 1–5.

———. "The Last Hurrah: Helmut Kohl's CDU/CSU and the 1998 Election." In David P. Conradt, et al., *Power Shift in Germany* (New York: Berghahn, 2000), 38–58.

Clemens, Clay, and William Paterson, eds. *The Kohl Chancellorship*. Portland, OR: Frank Cass, 1998.

Clift, Ben. "The Jospin Way." *The Political Quarterly* 72, 2 (April–June 2001), 170–179.

Closa, Carlos. "Spain: The Cortes and the EU—A Growing Together." In Philip Norton, ed., *National Parliaments and the European Union* (Portland, OR: Frank Cass, 1996).

Coates, David. "Placing New Labour." In Bill Jones, ed., *Political Issues in Britain Today*, 5th ed. (Manchester: Manchester University Press, 1999), 346–366.

Coen, David. "The Evolution of the Large Firm as a Political Actor." *Journal of European Public Policy* 4, 1 (1997), 91–108.

Cohen, J. M., and M. J. Cohen. *The Penguin Dictionary of Twentieth-Century Quotations*. Harmondsworth: Penguin, 1993.

Cohen-Tanugi, Laurent. *Alliance at Risk: The United States and Europe Since September 11*. Translated by George A. Holoch. Baltimore, MD: Johns Hopkins, 2003.

Cole, Alistair. *Franco-German Relations*. Harlow: Longman, 2001.

———. "The French Socialists." In John Gaffney, ed., *Political Parties and the European Union* (London: Routledge, 1996), 71–85.

———. "National and Partisan Contexts of Europeanization: The Case of the French Socialists." *Journal of Common Market Studies* 39, 1 (March 2001), 15–36.

———. "The *Service Public* Under Stress." In Robert Elgie, ed., *The Changing French Political System* (London: Frank Cass, 2000), 166–184.

Coleman, W. D. "From Protected Development to Market Liberalism: Paradigm Change in Agriculture." *Journal of European Public Policy* 5 (1998), 632–651.

Colley, Linda. *Britons: Forging the Nation 1707–1837*. New Haven, CT: Yale University Press, 1992.

Conant, Lisa. "Europeanization and the Courts: Variable Patterns of Adaptation Among National Judiciaries." In Maria Green Cowles, et al., ed., *Transforming Europe: Europeanization and Domestic Change* (Ithaca, NY: Cornell University Press, 2001).

Connolly, Kate. "Europe's Sleeping Giant." *The Guardian*, September 26, 2001.

———. "Poles Ready to Embrace Ex-Communists." *The Guardian*, September 23, 2001.

Conradt, David P. *The German Polity.* 7th ed. New York: Longman, 2001.

———. "Political Culture in Unified Germany: The First Ten Years." *German Politics and Society* 20, 2 (Summer 2002), 43–74.

Conradt, David P., Gerald R. Kleinfeld, and Christian Søe, eds. *Power Shift in Germany: The 1998 Election and the End of the Kohl Era.* New York: Berghahn, 2000.

Converse, Philip E., and Roy Pierce. *Political Representation in France.* Cambridge, MA: Harvard University Press, 1986.

Conversi, Daniele. *The Basques, the Catalans, and Spain: Alternative Routes to Nationalist Mobilisation.* Reno, NV: University of Nevada Press, 1997.

Coplin, William D., and Michael K. O'Leary. *Political Risk Yearbook 2002.* East Syracuse, NY: The PRS Group, Inc., 2002.

Cordell, Karl, ed. *Poland in the European Union.* London: Routledge, 2000.

Cornish, Paul, and Geoffrey Edwards. "Beyond the EU/NATO Dichotomy: The Beginnings of a European Strategic Culture." *International Affairs* 77, 3 (July 2001), 587–603.

"Could the Euro's Nuclear Option Ever Be Used?" *The Economist* 362 (February 2, 2002), 47–48.

Cowles, Maria Green. "The Politics of Big Business in the European Community: Setting the Agenda for a New Europe." American University Ph.D. Dissertation, 1994.

———. "The Transatlantic Business Dialogue and Domestic Business-Government Relations." In Cowles, et al., *Transforming Europe: Europeanization and Domestic Change* (Ithaca, NY: Cornell University Press, 2001), 159–179.

Cowles, Maria Green, James Caporaso, and Thomas Risse, eds. *Transforming Europe: Europeanization and Domestic Change.* Ithaca, NY: Cornell University Press, 2001.

Cowles, Maria Green, and Michael Smith, eds. *The State of the European Union.* Vol. 5. Oxford: Oxford University Press, 2000.

Crane, Philip, and Charles Rangel. "Unity Against Sanctions." *Financial Times*, September 16, 2002, 10.

Crawford, Leslie. "Divided by Violence." *Financial Times*, August 24, 2002, 8.

———. "Spanish Court Bars Basque Coalition from Local Elections." *Financial Times*, May 10, 2003, 8.

"Croatian PM Says Accession Talks with EU to Start by May 2005." *Agence France Presse*, June 17, 2004.

Crockatt, Richard. *The Fifty Years War.* New York: Routledge, 1996.

Cronin, Thomas E. *Direct Democracy: The Politics of Initiative, Referendum, and Recall.* Cambridge, MA: Harvard University Press, 1989.

Crooks, Ed. "EU May Yet Pay the Price of not Playing by the Rules." *Financial Times*, November 26, 2003, 4.

Crossman, Richard. "Introduction." In Walter Bagehot, *The English Constitution* (Ithaca, NY: Cornell University Press, 1966).

Curry, Jane L., ed. *Dissent in Eastern Europe.* New York: Praeger, 1983.

Cyr, Arthur J. "The Euro: Faith, Hope, and Parity." *International Affairs* 79, 5 (October 2003), 979–992.

Dahl, Robert A., ed. *Political Opposition in Western Democracies.* New Haven, CT: Yale University Press, 1966.

Daley, Suzanne. "Europe Agrees to a Review of Changes for Its Union." *New York Times*, December 8, 2001, A4.

———. "Extreme Rightist Eclipses Socialist to Qualify for Runoff in France." *New York Times*, April 22, 2002, A1, A6.

———. "French Premier Opposes German Plan for Europe." *New York Times*, May 29, 2001, A6.

Dalton, Russell. *Citizen Politics: Public Opinion and Political Parties in Advanced Industrial Democracies.* 2nd ed. Chatham, NJ: Chatham House, 1996.

Daly, Emma. "Amnesty Says Spain Is Racist in Its Treatment of Immigrants." *New York Times*, April 19, 2002, A11.

———. "Spanish Court Outlaws a Basque Party, Seeing Terrorism Links." *New York Times*, March 18, 2003, A7.

D'Amore, Ciro. "Studying Italian Politics Since the 1990s." *South European Society & Politics* 7, 1 (Summer 2002), 103–112.

Daugbjerg, Carsten. "Reforming the CAP: Policy Networks and Broader Institutional Structures." *Journal of Common Market Studies* 37, 3 (September 1999).

Davies, Alan. *British Politics and Europe.* London: Hodder & Stoughton, 1998.

Davies, Norman. *The Heart of Europe: The Past in Poland's Present.* Oxford: Oxford University Press, 2001.

Davies, Peter. *The National Front in France: Ideology, Discourse, and Power.* London: Routledge, 1999.

De Búrca, Gráinne. "The EU Charter of Fundamental Rights." *ECSA Review* 14, 2 (Spring 2001), 9–10.

Declair, Edward G. *Politics on the Fringe: The People, Policies, and Organization of the French National Front.* Durham, NC: Duke University Press, 1999.

De Esteban Alonso, Alfonso, and Alejandro López López. "Environmental Policy." In Amparo Almarcha Barbado, ed., *Spain and EC Membership Evaluated* (London: Pinter, 1993), 60–68.

Dehousse, Renaud. *The European Court of Justice: The Politics of Judicial Integration.* Basingstoke: Macmillan, 1998.

Deighton, Anne. "European Union Policy." In Anthony Seldon, ed., *The Blair Effect* (London: Little, Brown, 2001), 307–330.

———. "The Military Security Pool: Towards a New Security Regime for Europe?" *The International Spectator* 35, 4 (October–December 2000), 19–32.

Della Sala, Vincent. "Hollowing Out and Hardening the State: European Integration and the Italian Economy." *West European Politics* 20 (1997), 14–35.

———. "Italy: A Bridge Too Far?" *Parliamentary Affairs* 50, 3 (July 1997), 396–409.

———. "Parliament and Citizens in Italy: A Distant Relationship." In Philip Norton, ed., *Parliament and Citizens in Western Europe* (London: Frank Cass, 2002), 66–88.

Delzell, Charles F. *The Unification of Italy, 1859–1861: Cavour, Mazzini, or Garibaldi?* New York: Holt, Rinehart, and Winston, 1965.

Dempsey, Judy. "Europe's Divided Self." *Financial Times*, July 10, 2002.

Den Boer, Monica, and William Wallace. "Justice and Home Affairs: Integration Through Incrementalism?" In Helen Wallace and William Wallace, eds., *Policy-Making in the European Union* (Oxford: Oxford University Press, 2000), 493–519.

Deutsch, Karl, and Lewis Edinger. *Germany Rejoins the Powers.* Stanford, CA: Stanford University Press, 1959.

De Witte, Bruno. "Après Nice: Time for a European Constitution?" *ECSA Review* 14, 2 (Spring 2001), 10–11.

Diamanti, Ilvo. "The Northern League: From Regional Party to Party of Government." In Stephen Gundle and Simon Parker, eds., *The New Italian Republic* (London: Routledge, 1996), Ch. 7.

Dicey, A. V. *An Introduction to the Study of the Law of the Constitution.* 10th ed. London: Macmillan, 1959.

Díez Medrano, Juan. *Divided National: Class, Politics, and Nationalism in the Basque Country and Catalonia.* Ithaca, NY: Cornell University Press, 1995.

"A Difficult Birth." *The Economist* 371 (June 27, 2004), 53–54.

Dinan, Desmond. *Ever Closer Union.* 2nd ed. Boulder, CO: Lynne Rienner, 1999.

"Divorce After All These Years?" *The Economist* 358 (January 27, 2001), 49–50.

Donnelly, Shawn. "Public Interest Politics, Corporate Governance, and Company Regulation in Germany and Britain." *German Politics* 9, 2 (August 2000), 171–194.

Donovan, Mark. "A New Republic in Italy? The May 2001 Election." *West European Politics* 24, 4 (October 2001), 193–205.

———. "The 1994 Election in Italy: Normalisation or Continuing Exceptionalism?" *West European Politics* 17, 4 (December 1994).

Donovan, Mark, ed. *Italy.* Vol. 1. Dartmouth: Ashgate, 1998.

"Don't Go There." *Financial Times*, April 3, 2003, 12.

Dragnich, Alex N., Jorgen Rasmussen, and Joel C. Moses. *Major European Governments.* 8th ed. Pacific Grove, CA: Brooks/Cole, 1991.

Driver, Stephen, and Luke Martell. *Blair's Britain.* London: Polity Press, 2002.

Duchêne, François. "French Motives for European Integration." In Robert Bideleux and Richard Taylor, eds., *European Integration and Disintegration* (London: Routledge, 1996), 22–35.

———. *Jean Monnet: The First Statesman of Interdependence.* New York: Norton, 1994.

Duggan, Christopher, and Christopher Wagstaff, eds. *Italy in the Cold War: Politics, Culture, and Society, 1948–58.* Oxford: Berg, 1995.

Dunleavy, Patrick, Andrew Gamble, Ian Holliday, and Gillian Peele, eds. *Developments in British Politics.* Vol. 5. Basingstoke: Macmillan, 1997.

Dunn, Susan. *Sister Revolutions: French Lightning, American Light.* New York: Faber and Faber, 1999.

Duverger, Maurice. *Political Parties: Their Organization and Activity in the Modern State.* London: Methuen, 1954.

Dyson, Kenneth. "EMU as Europeanization: Convergence, Diversity, and Contingency." *Journal of Common Market Studies* 38 (November 2000), 645–666.

Dyson, Kenneth, and Kevin Featherstone. "Italy and EMU as a '*Vincolo Esterno*': Empowering the Technocrats, Transforming the State." *South European Society & Politics* 1, 2 (Autumn 1996), 272–299.

Easton, David. "An Approach to the Study of Political Systems." *World Politics* 9, 5 (1957), 383–400.

Ebbinghaus, Bernhard. "Germany." In Bernhard Ebbinghaus and Jelle Visser, eds., *The Societies of Europe: Trade Unions Since 1945* (Basingstoke: Macmillan, 2000), 279–337.

Ebbinghaus, Bernhard, and Jeremy Waddington. "United Kingdom/Great Britain." In Bernhard Ebbinghaus and Jelle Visser, eds., *The Societies of Europe: Trade Unions Since 1945* (Basingstoke: Macmillan, 2000), 705–756.

Ebbinghaus, Bernhard, and Jelle Visser, eds. *The Societies of Europe: Trade Unions Since 1945.* Basingstoke: Macmillan, 2000.

Edinger, Lewis J., and Brigitte L. Nacos. *From Bonn to Berlin: German Politics in Transition.* New York: Columbia University Press, 1998.

Edwards, John. *The Spain of the Catholic Monarchs, 1474–1520.* Malden, MA: Blackwell, 2000.

Ehrmann, Henry W., and Martin A. Schain. *Politics in France.* 5th ed. New York: HarperCollins, 1992.

Elgie, Robert, ed. *The Changing French Political System.* London: Frank Cass, 2000.

Eliasson, Leslie. "Denmark: Small State with a Big Voice." In Eleanor Zeff and Ellen Pirro, eds., *The EU and the Member States* (Boulder, CO: Lynne Rienner, 2001), 191–216.

Elliott, John Huxtable. *Imperial Spain, 1469–1716.* New York: St. Martin's, 1963.

Ellwood, D. H. "Italy, Europe, and the Cold War: The Politics and Economics of Limited Sovereignty." In Christopher Duggan and Christopher Wagstaff, eds., *Italy in the Cold War: Politics, Culture, and Society* (Oxford: Berg, 1995), 25–46.

Endo, Ken. *The Presidency of the European Commission Under Jacques Delors*. New York: St. Martin's Press, 1998.

Eriksen, Erik Oddvar, and John Erik Fossum, eds. *Democracy in the European Union: Integration Through Deliberation?* London: Routledge, 2000.

Erlanger, Steven. "Conservatives in Germany in Battle for Top Job." *New York Times*, January 10, 2002, A5.

———. "European Summit Talks Open Today; Focus Is Immigration Control." *New York Times*, June 21, 2001, A8.

———. "Europe's Military Gap." *New York Times*, March 16, 2002, A1, A4.

———. "German Right Backs Bavarian to Run Against Schröder." *New York Times*, January 12, 2002, A3.

Esenwein, George, and Adrian Shubert. *Spain at War: The Spanish Civil War in Context, 1931–1939*. New York: Longman, 1995.

Esping-Anderson, Gösta. *The Three Worlds of Welfare Capitalism*. Cambridge: Polity Press, 1990.

European Commission. "EU Fundamentally Reforms Its Farm Policy to Accomplish Sustainable Farming in Europe." IP/03/898. Luxembourg, June 26, 2003.

———. *Who's Who in the European Union? What Differences Will the Treaty of Nice Make?* Luxembourg: European Communities Official Publications, 2001.

The European Convention. *Draft Treaty Establishing a Constitution for Europe*. CONV 820/03. Brussels, June 20, 2003.

"EU Fisheries Policy: Too Much Vigour in Vigo." *The Economist* 362 (March 30, 2002), 44.

"EU Parliament Gives Prodi Vote of Approval." *The Guardian*, May 5, 1999.

"Europe's Foreign Policy: Guess Who Wasn't Coming to Dinner?" *The Economist* 361 (November 19, 2001), 47–48.

"Europe's Torment." *Financial Times*, March 20, 2003, 14.

Evans, Geoffrey. "Britain and Europe: Separate Worlds of Welfare?" *Government and Opposition* 33 (Spring 1998), 183–198.

Evans, Mark. "Political Participation." In Patrick Dunleavy, et al., eds., *Developments in British Politics*, vol. 5 (Basingstoke: Macmillan, 1997), 110–128.

"Ever Closer in All But Name." *The Economist* 366 (February 15, 2003), 47–48.

Fabbrini, Sergio, and Mark Gilbert. "The Italian General Election of 13 May 2001: Democratic Alternation or False Step?" *Government and Opposition* 36, 4 (Autumn 2001), 519–536.

Farrell, Mary. *Spain in the EU: The Road to Economic Convergence*. Basingstoke: Palgrave, 2001.

Featherstone, Kevin. *Socialist Parties and European Integration: A Comparative History*. Manchester: Manchester University Press, 1988.

Featherstone, Kevin, and Roy H. Ginsberg. *The United States and the European Union in the 1990s: Partners in Transition*. 2nd ed. New York: St. Martin's, 1996.

Fenby, Jonathan. *France on the Brink*. New York: Arcade, 1999.

Fennell, Rosemary. *The Common Agricultural Policy: Continuity and Change*. Oxford: Clarendon Press, 1997.

Ferraris, Luigi Vittorio. "Italian-European Foreign Policy." In Francesco Francioni, ed., *Italy and EC Membership Evaluated* (New York: St. Martin's, 1992).

Ferren, Sean, and Robert Mulvihill. *Paths to a Settlement in Northern Ireland*. New York: Oxford University Press, 2000.

Ferrera, Maurizio, and Elizabetta Gualmini. "Reforms Guided by Consensus: The Welfare State in the Italian Transition." *West European Politics* 23, 2 (April 2000), 187–208.

Filkins, Dexter. "Turks Look West; Will It Look Away?" *New York Times*, December 13, 2002, A12.

Finnegan, Richard. "Ireland: Brussels and the Celtic Tiger." In Eleanor Zeff and Ellen Pirro, eds., *The EU and the Member States* (Boulder, CO: Lynne Rienner, 2001), 175–190.

Fisher, Ian. "In a Vast Expansion of the European Union, Pluses but also Perils Lie Ahead." *New York Times*, December 13, 2002, A12.

———. "Maverick Legislator in Poland Is Now Open to Slander Charge." *New York Times*, January 26, 2002, A4.

———. "Polish Populist, Stripped of His Post, Accuses Parliament of Corruption." *New York Times*, November 30, 2001, A12.

Fisher, Justin. "Third and Minor Party Breakthrough?" In Andrew Geddes and Jonathan Tonge, eds., *Labour's Landslide* (Manchester: Manchester University Press, 1997), 53–69.

Fitzmaurice, John. *The Politics of Belgium: A Unique Federalism*. London: Hurst, 1996.

Fleming, Charles, and Marina Rozenman. "Victory by Far-Right Candidate Shocks France." *Wall Street Journal*, April 22, 2002, A14.

Flynn, M. K. *Ideology, Mobilization, and the Nation: The Rise of Irish, Basque, and Carlist Nationalist Movements in the Nineteenth and Early Twentieth Centuries*. New York: St. Martin's, 2000.

Foley, Michael. *The British Presidency: Tony Blair and the Politics of Public Leadership*. Manchester: Manchester University Press, 2000.

Føllesdal, Andreas, and Peter Koslowski, eds. *Democracy and the European Union*. Berlin: Springer, 1998.

"A Foreign Minister Goes, but Does a Foreign Policy?" *The Economist* 362 (January 12, 2002), 45–46.

Forster, Anthony. "Britain and the Negotiation of the Maastricht Treaty: A Critique of Liberal Intergovernmentalism." *Journal of Common Market Studies* 36, 3 (September 1998), 347–368.

Forster, Anthony, and William Wallace. "Common Foreign and Security Policy: From Shadow to Substance?" In

Helen Wallace and William Wallace, eds., *Policy-Making in the European Union*, 4th ed. (Oxford: Oxford University Press, 2000), 461–491.

——. "The IGCs and the Renegotiation of European Order After the Cold War." In Paul-Henri Laurent and Marc Maresceau, eds., *The State of the European Union*, vol. 4 (Boulder, CO: Lynne Rienner, 1998), 339–356.

"France Survey." *The Economist*, June 5, 1999.

Francioni, Francesco, ed. *Italy and EC Membership Evaluated*. New York: St. Martin's, 1992.

Frankland, E. Gene. "Bündnis '90/Die Grünen: From Opposition to Power." In David P. Conradt, et al., eds., *Power Shift in Germany* (New York: Berghahn, 2000), 80–97.

Frankland, E. Gene, ed. *Global Studies: Europe*. 7th ed. Guilford, CT: McGraw-Hill/Dushkin, 2001.

Freschi, Catherine, James Shields, and Roger Woods. "Extreme Right-Wing Parties and the European Union." In John Gaffney, ed., *Political Parties and the European Union* (London: Routledge, 1996), 235–253.

Friedman, Alan. "The Economic Elites and the Political System." In Stephen Gundle and Simon Parker, eds., *The New Italian Republic* (London: Routledge, 1996), Ch. 17.

Friedman, Thomas L. "War of Ideas, Part 2." *New York Times*, January 11, 2004, IV, 15.

Friend, Julius W. *The Linchpin: French-German Relations 1950–1990*. New York: Praeger, 1991.

Friis, Lykke, and Anna Murphy. "Enlargement: A Complex Juggling Act." In Maria Green Cowles and Michael Smith, ed., *The State of the European Union*, vol. 5 (Oxford: Oxford University Press, 2000), 186–206.

Fuller, Thomas. "European Union Votes 14–1 to Reform Agricultural Policy." *New York Times*, June 27, 2003, A9.

Furlong, Paul. "The Italian Parliament and European Integration—Responsibilities, Failures, and Successes." In Philip Norton, ed., *National Parliaments and the European Union* (Portland, OR: Frank Cass, 1996), 35–45.

Fursdon, Edward. *The European Defense Community: A History*. New York: St. Martin's, 1980.

Gaffney, John, ed. *Political Parties and the European Union*. London: Routledge, 1996.

Garcia, Caterina. "The Autonomous Communities and External Relations." In Richard Gillespie, et al., eds., *Democratic Spain* (London: Routledge, 1993), 123–140.

Gardner, Brian. "Enlargement Farm Costs—Risks for the EU Budget." The European Policy Centre, November 6, 2002. http://www.theepc.net/challenge/

Garten, Jeffrey. "The Global Economy Is in Harm's Way." *Financial Times*, April 14, 2003.

"GE/Honeywell: Engine Failure." *The Economist* 360 (July 7, 2001), 58–59.

Geddes, Andrew. "Europe: Major's Nemesis?" In Andrew Geddes and Jonathan Tonge, eds., *Labour's Landslide* (Manchester: Manchester University Press, 1997), 85–99.

Geddes, Andrew, and Jonathan Tonge, eds. *Labour's Landslide: The British General Election 1997*. Manchester: Manchester University Press, 1997.

George, Stephen. *An Awkward Partner: Britain in the European Community*. 3rd ed. Oxford: Oxford University Press, 1998.

George, Stephen, and Deborah Haythorne. "The British Labour Party." In John Gaffney, ed., *Political Parties and the European Union* (London: Routledge, 1996), 110–121.

"German Immigration Law: Here Come the Lawyers." *The Economist* 362 (March 30, 2002), 43.

"Germany's Centre-Right Opposition: Who Will Lead It into Battle?" *The Economist* 362 (January 12, 2002), 46.

Gibbons, John. "Spain: A Semi Federal State." In D. McIver, ed., *The Multinational State* (London: Macmillan, 1999).

——. *Spanish Politics Today*. Manchester: Manchester University Press, 1999.

Giddings, Philip, and Gavin Drewry, eds. *Westminster and Europe: The Impact of the European Union on the Westminster Parliament*. New York: St. Martin's, 1996.

Gillespie, Richard. "The Break-Up of the 'Socialist Family': Party-Union Relations in Spain, 1982–89." *West European Politics* 13, 1 (January 1990), 47–62.

——. "The Spanish Socialists." In John Gaffney, ed., *Political Parties and the EU* (London: Routledge, 1996), 155–169.

Gillespie, Richard, Fernando Rodrigo, and Jonathan Story, eds. *Democratic Spain: Reshaping External Relations in a Changing World*. London: Routledge, 1993.

Gillingham, John. *European Integration, 1950–2003: Superstate or New Market Economy?* Cambridge: Cambridge University Press, 2003.

Gilmour, David. *The Transformation of Spain: From Franco to the Constitutional Monarchy*. New York: Quartet Books, 1985.

Giulani, Marco. "Italy." In Dietrich Rometsch and Wolfgang Wessels, eds., *The European Union and Member States* (Manchester: Manchester University Press, 1996), 119–131.

Giulani, Mario, and Simona Piattoni. "Italy: Both Leader and Laggard." In Eleanor E. Zeff and Ellen B. Pirro, eds., *The EU and the Member States* (Boulder, CO: Lynne Rienner, 2001), 115–144.

Goetz, Klaus. "National Government and European Integration: Intergovernmental Relations in Germany." *Journal of Common Market Studies* 33, 1 (March 1995), 91–112.

Goguel, François. "Six Authors in Search of a National Character." In Stanley Hoffman, ed., *In Search of France* (New York: Harper & Row, 1963), 359–405.

Goldhagen, Daniel J. *Hitler's Willing Executioners.* New York: Alfred A. Knopf, 1996.

Gooch, George P. *English Democratic Ideas in the Seventeenth Century.* 2nd ed. New York: Harper, 1959.

Gould, James A., and Willis H. Truitt, eds. *Political Ideologies.* New York: Macmillan, 1973.

Gowers, Andrew, and Bernard Benoit. "Chancellor Says Germany Will Attempt to Ratify the New EU Constitution this Year." *Financial Times,* July 16, 2004, 2.

Gowland, David, and Arthur Turner. *Reluctant Europeans: Britain and European Integration, 1945–1998.* Harlow: Longman, 2000.

Grabbe, Heather. "The Siren Song of a Two-Speed Europe." *Financial Times,* December 16, 2003, 13.

Grant, Charles. *Delors: Inside the House that Jacques Built.* London: Nicholas Brealey, 1994.

Grant, Wyn. *Pressure Groups and British Politics.* New York: St. Martin's, 2000.

Green, Peter S. "Poles Vote Yes to Joining European Union." *New York Times,* June 9, 2003, A7.

Green, Simon. "Beyond Ethnoculturalism? German Citizenship in the New Millennium." *German Politics* 9, 3 (December 2000), 105–124.

Greenwood, Justin. *Representing Interests in the European Union.* Basingstoke: Macmillan, 1997.

Grieco, J. M. "The Maastricht Treaty, Economic and Monetary Union and the Neo-realist Research Programme." *Review of International Studies* 21, 1 (1995), 21–40.

Gros, Daniel, and Niels Thygesen. *European Monetary Integration: From the European Monetary System to European Monetary Union.* 2nd ed. London: Longman, 1997.

Gross, Jan Tomasz. *Neighbors: The Destruction of the Jewish Community in Jedwabne, Poland.* Princeton, NJ: Princeton University Press, 2001.

——. *Revolution from Abroad: The Soviet Conquest of Poland's Western Ukraine and Western Belorussia.* Princeton, NJ: Princeton University Press, 1988.

Grote, Jürgen. "Cohesion in Italy: A View on Non-Economic Disparities." In Liesbet Hooge, ed., *Cohesion Policy and European Integration* (Oxford: Oxford University Press, 1996).

Grottanelli de Santi, Giovanni. "The Impact of EC Integration on the Italian Form of Government." In Francesco Francioni, ed., *Italy and EC Membership Evaluated* (New York: St. Martin's, 1992), 179–190.

Grugel, Jean. "Spain and Latin America." In Richard Gillespie, et al., eds., *Democratic Spain* (London: Routledge, 1993).

Gueldry, Michel. *France and European Integration: Toward a Transnational Polity?* Westport, CT: Praeger, 2001.

Gundle, Stephen, and Simon Parker, eds. *The New Italian Republic: From the Fall of the Berlin Wall to Berlusconi.* London: Routledge, 1996.

Gunther, Richard. "Electoral Laws, Party Systems, and Elites: The Case of Spain." *American Political Science Review* 83, 3 (September 1989), 835–858.

Guyomarch, Alain, Howard Machin, and Ella Ritchie. *France in the European Union.* New York: St. Martin's, 1998.

Haas, Ernst. *The Uniting of Europe: Political, Social, and Economic Forces, 1950–57.* Stanford, CA: Stanford University Press, 1958.

——. "Turbulent Fields and the Theory of Regional Integration." *International Organization* 30 (Spring 1976), 173–212.

Haine, W. Scott. *The History of France.* Westport, CT: Greenwood Press, 2000.

Hainsworth, Paul. "The Right: Divisions and Cleavages in *fin de siècle* France." In Robert Elgie, ed., *The Changing French Political System* (London: Frank Cass, 2000), 38–56.

Hale, David. "Great Britain: The Reluctant European." In Ronald Tiersky, ed., *Europe Today* (Lanham, MD: Rowman and Littlefield, 1999), 95–126.

Hames, Tim. "Election Round-Up." *The Times,* June 9, 2001, E10–E11.

Hancock, M. Donald. *West Germany: The Politics of Democratic Corporatism.* Chatham, NJ: Chatham House, 1989.

Harrop, Martin. "An Apathetic Landslide: The British General Election of 2001," *Government and Opposition* 36, 3 (Summer 2001), 295–313.

Harvie, Christopher T., and Peter Jones. *The Road to Home Rule: Images of Scotland's Cause.* Edinburgh: Polygon, 2000.

Hayes-Renshaw, Fiona, and Helen Wallace. *The Council of Ministers.* London: Macmillan, 1997.

Hazell, Robert. "Reforming the Constitution." *The Political Quarterly* 72, 1 (January–March 2001).

Hearder, Harry. *Italy: A Short History.* Cambridge: Cambridge University Press, 1990.

Heffernan, Richard. *New Labour and Thatcherism: Political Change in Britain.* New York: St. Martin's, 2000.

Heidenheimer, Arnold J., Hugh Heclo, and Carolyn Teich Adams. *Comparative Public Policy: The Politics of Social Choice in Europe and America.* 3rd ed. New York: St. Martin's, 1990.

Heilbroner, Robert. *The Worldly Philosophers: The Lives, Times, and Ideas of the Great Economic Thinkers.* 4th ed. New York: Simon and Schuster, 1972.

Heinelt, Hubert, et al. *European Union Environmental Policy and New Forms of Governance.* Aldershot: Ashgate, 2001.

Helm, Jutta. "Co-Determination in West Germany: What Difference Does It Make?" *West European Politics* 9, 1 (January 1986), 32–53.

Henning, C. Randall, and Pier Carlo Padoan. *Transatlantic Perspectives on the Euro.* Washington, DC: Brookings, 2000.

Hermens, Ferdinand A. *Democracy or Anarchy?* Notre Dame, IN: Review of Politics, 1941.

Heurlin, Bertel, ed. *Germany in Europe in the Nineties.* London: Macmillan, 1996.

Heywood, Andrew. *Political Ideologies: An Introduction.* New York: St. Martin's, 1992.

Heywood, Paul. "Governing a New Democracy: The Power of the Prime Minister in Spain." *West European Politics* 14, 2 (April 1991).

Hill, Michael. *Social Policy: A Comparative Analysis.* London: Prentice Hall, 1996.

Hine, David. "Federalism, Regionalism, and the Unitary State: Contemporary Regional Pressures in Historical Perspective." In Carl Levy, ed., *Italian Regionalism* (Oxford: Berg, 1996), 109–130.

Hinsliff, Gaby, and Ian Traynor. "Europe's Grand Folly." *The Observer,* December 14, 2003.

Hix, Simon. *The Political System of the European Union.* New York: St. Martin's, 1999.

———. "The Transnational Party Federations." In John Gaffney, ed., *Political Parties and the European Union* (London: Routledge, 1996), 308–331.

Hoag, Clarence, and George Hallett. *Proportional Representation.* New York: Crowell-Collier and Macmillan, 1926.

Hoffman, Stanley. "The French Political Community." In Stanley Hoffman, ed., *In Search of France* (New York: Harper & Row, 1963), 1–117.

Hoffman, Stanley, ed. *In Search of France.* New York: Harper & Row, 1963.

Hoge, Warren. "Blair Seeks a Supreme Court Modeled on the U.S. Version." *New York Times,* June 15, 2003, 11.

———. "Britain's Nonwhites Feel Un-British, Report Says." *New York Times,* April 4, 2002, A6.

———. "British Conservatives Choose 'Euroskeptic' Leader." *New York Times,* September 14, 2001, B1.

Hollifield, James F. "The Migration Challenge: Europe's Crisis in Historical Perspective." In Henri Warmenhoven, ed., *Global Studies: Western Europe,* 6th ed. (Guilford, CT: Dushkin/McGraw-Hill, 1999), 185–191.

Holmes, Martin. "The Conservative Party and Europe: From Major to Hague." *The Political Quarterly* 69 (April–June 1998), 133–140.

Hooge, Liesbet. *The European Commission and the Integration of Europe: Images of Governance.* Cambridge: Cambridge University Press, 2001.

Hooge, Liesbet, ed. *Cohesion Policy and European Integration: Building Multi-Level Governance.* Oxford: Oxford University Press, 1996.

Hooge, Liesbet, and Gary Marks. *Multi-Level Governance and European Integration.* Lanham, MD: Rowman and Littlefield, 2001.

Hooper, John. "New CDU Chief Takes Brussels by Surprise." *The Guardian,* April 11, 2000.

Hopkin, Jonathan. "A 'Southern' Model of Electoral Mobilization? Clientelism and Electoral Politics in Spain." *West European Politics* 24, 1 (January 2001), 115–136.

Hopkin, Jonathan, and Alfio Mastropaolo. "From Patronage to Clientelism: Comparing the Italian and Spanish Experiences." In Simona Piattoni, ed., *Clientelism, Interests, and Democratic Representation* (Cambridge: Cambridge University Press, 2001), 152–171.

Hoskyns, Catherine, and Michael Newman, eds. *Democratizing the European Union: Issues for the Twenty-First Century.* Manchester: Manchester University Press, 2000.

Howarth, David. "The French State in the Euro Zone: Modernization and Legitimizing Dirigisme in the 'Semi-Sovereignty' Game." Paper presented at the ECSA Conference, Madison, WI, June 2001.

Huber, Evelyne, and John D. Stephens. *Development and Crisis of the Welfare State: Parties and Policies in Global Markets.* Chicago: University of Chicago Press, 2001.

Huber, John. "Restrictive Legislative Procedures in France and the United States." *American Political Science Review* 86, 3 (September 1992), 675–687.

Hughes, H. Stuart. *The United States and Italy.* 3rd ed. Cambridge, MA: Harvard University Press, 1979.

Hughes, Kirsty, and Edward Smith. "New Labour—New Europe?" *International Affairs* 74 (January 1998), 93–103.

Huntington, Samuel P. *The Third Wave: Democratization in the Late Twentieth Century.* Norman: University of Oklahoma Press, 1991.

Hutton, Will. *The State We're In.* London: Cape, 1994.

Hyde-Price, Adrian. *Germany and European Order: Enlarging NATO and the EU.* Manchester: Manchester University Press, 2000.

Ieraci, Giuseppi. "Who Won? Italy at the Polls and Italian Election Reform (1994–2001)." *South European Society & Politics* 7, 1 (Summer 2002), 103–112.

Inglehart, Ronald. *Modernization and Postmodernization: Cultural, Economic, and Political Change in 43 Societies.* Princeton, NJ: Princeton University Press, 1999.

———. *The Silent Revolution: Changing Values and Political Styles Among Western Publics.* Princeton: Princeton University Press, 1977.

Jablonski, Andrej. "The Europeanisation of Government in Poland in the 1990s." In Karl Cordell, ed., *Poland in the European Union* (London: Routledge, 2000).

Jack, Andrew, and Guy Dinmore. "Concern at 'Distorted' Result in Russia Poll." *Financial Times,* December 9, 2003, 1.

Jacobs, Francis, Richard Corbett, and Michael Shackleton. *The European Parliament.* 3rd ed. London: Cartermill, 1995.

Jeffery, Charlie. "Towards a 'Third Level' in Europe? The German Länder in the European Union." *Political Studies* 44, 2 (June 1996), 253–266.

Jenkins, Peter. *Mrs. Thatcher's Revolution: The Ending of the Socialist Era.* Cambridge, MA: Harvard University Press, 1988.

Joffe, Josef. "No Threats, No Temptations: German Grand Strategy after the Cold War." In Bertel Heurlin, ed., *Germany in Europe in the Nineties* (London: Macmillan, 1996), 259–272.

Johnson, Loch K., and Kiki Caruson. "The Seven Sins of American Foreign Policy." *PS: Political Science and Politics* 36, 1 (January, 2003), 5–10.

Johnson, Nevil. "The Judicial Dimension in British Politics." *West European Politics* 21, 1 (January 1998), 148–166.

———. "Taking Stock of Constitutional Reform." *Government and Opposition* 36, 3 (Summer 2001), 331–354.

Jones, Bill. "Reforming the Electoral System." In Bill Jones, ed., *Political Issues in Britain Today*, 5th ed. (Manchester: Manchester University Press, 1999), 42–61.

Jones, Bill, ed. *Political Issues in Britain Today.* 5th ed. Manchester: Manchester University Press, 1999.

Jones, Gavin. "The Trouble with a Long Coastline." *Financial Times Survey: Italy*, July 22, 2002, 3, 4.

Jones, Rachel. *Beyond the Spanish State: Central Government, Domestic Actors, and The EU.* Basingstoke: Palgrave, 2000.

Jordan, Andrew. "EU Environmental Policy at 25." In Henri Warmenhoven, ed., *Global Studies: Western Europe*, 6th ed. (Guilford, CT: Dushkin/McGraw-Hill, 1999), 195–207.

Kagan, Robert. *Of Paradise and Power: America and Europe in the New World Order.* New York: Knopf, 2003.

Kamen, Henry. *Spain, 1469–1714: A Society of Conflict.* 2nd ed. New York: Longman, 1991.

Karakas, Ayse Isil. "The Human Rights Problematic in Turkey-European Union Relations." Paper presented at the annual conference of the International Studies Association, New Orleans, LA, March 2002.

Katz, Alan, ed. *Legal Traditions and Systems.* New York: Greenwood Press, 1986.

Katzenstein, Peter. "United Germany in an Integrating Germany." In Peter Katzenstein, ed., *Tamed Power: Germany in Europe* (Ithaca, NY: Cornell University Press, 1997).

Katzenstein, Peter, ed. *Tamed Power: Germany in Europe.* Ithaca, NY: Cornell University Press, 1997.

Kavanagh, Dennis. "New Labour, New Millennium, New Premiership." In Anthony Seldon, ed., *The Blair Effect: The Blair Government 1997–2001* (London: Little, Brown, 2001), 3–20.

———. *Thatcherism and British Politics: The End of Consensus?* Oxford: Oxford University Press, 1990.

Kearney, Richard. *Postnationalist Ireland: Politics, Culture, Philosophy.* New York: Routledge, 1997.

Keeler, John T. S., and Martin A. Schain, eds. *Chirac's Challenge: Liberalization, Europeanization, and Malaise in France.* New York: St. Martin's, 1996.

Kennedy, Paul. *The Rise and Fall of the Great Powers.* New York: Random House, 1987.

Keohane, Robert, and Stanley Hoffman, eds. *The New European Community: Decisionmaking and Institutional Change.* Boulder, CO: Westview, 1991.

King, Anthony. *Britain Says Yes: The 1975 Referendum on the Common Market.* Washington, DC: American Enterprise Institute, 1977.

———. "Margaret Thatcher as a Political Leader." In Robert Skidelsky, *Thatcherism* (Oxford: Basil Blackwell, 1988), 51–64.

———. "Why Labour Won—At Last." In Anthony King, ed., *New Labour Triumphs* (Chatham, NJ: Chatham House, 1998), Ch. 7.

King, Anthony, ed., *Britain at the Polls, 2001.* New York: Chatham House, 2002.

———. *New Labour Triumphs: Britain at the Polls, 1997.* Chatham, NJ: Chatham House, 1998.

Kirchheimer, Otto. "Germany: The Vanishing Opposition." In Robert A. Dahl, ed., *Political Opposition in Western Democracies* (New Haven: Yale University Press, 1966), 237–259.

Kitschelt, Herbert. "The German Political Economy and the 1998 Election." In David P. Conradt, et al., ed., *Power Shift in Germany* (New York: Berghahn, 2000), 200–220.

Kleinfeld, Gerald R. "The Party of Democratic Socialism: Victory Across the East and on to Berlin!" In David P. Conradt, et al., eds., *Power Shift in Germany* (New York: Berghahn, 2000), 98–113.

Knowles, Elizabeth, ed. *Twentieth Century Quotations.* Oxford: Oxford University Press, 1998.

Koff, Sondra Z., and Stephen B. Koff. *Italy: From the First to the Second Republic.* London: Routledge, 2000.

Kolb, Eberhard. *The Weimar Republic.* London: Hutchinson, 1988.

Kolodziej, Edward. *French International Policy Under de Gaulle and Pompidou: The Politics of Grandeur.* Ithaca, NY: Cornell University Press, 1974.

Kommers, Donald. *Constitutional Jurisprudence in the Federal Republic of Germany.* Durham, NC: Duke University Press, 1989.

Kondrashov, Alexander. "EU Pleased with Putin's Statement on Russia-EU Relations." ITAR-Tass News, April 19, 2002.

Korbonski, Andrej. "Dissent in Poland, 1956–76." In Jane L. Curry, ed., *Dissent in Eastern Europe* (New York: Praeger, 1983), 29–39.

Korpi, Walter, and Joakim Palme. "New Politics and Class Politics in the Context of Austerity and Globalization." *American Political Science Review* 97, 3 (August 2003), 425–446.

Koslowski, Rey. "A Constructivist Approach to Understanding the European Union as a Federal Polity." *Journal of European Public Policy* 6, 4 (1999), 561–578.

Kuisel, Richard. *Seducing the French: The Dilemma of Americanization.* Berkeley: University of California Press, 1993.

Ladrech, Robert. "Europeanization of Domestic Politics and Institutions: The Case of France." *Journal of Common Market Studies* 32, 1 (March 1994), 69–88.

———. "The Left and the European Union." *Parliamentary Affairs* 56, 1 (January 2003), 112–124.

———. *Social Democracy and the Challenge of the European Union.* Boulder, CO: Lynne Rienner, 2000.

Lafontaine, Oskar. *The Heart Beats on the Left.* Translated by Ronald Taylor. Malden, MA: Blackwell, 2000.

Lancaster, Thomas, and Michael Gates. "Spain." In Alan Katz, ed., *Legal Traditions and Systems* (New York: Greenwood Press, 1986), 360–380.

Landler, Mark. "Schröder's Economic Plan Is Aided by a Union and His Party." *New York Times*, July 1, 2003, A4.

Lane, Jan-Erik, and Svante Ersson. *Politics and Society in Western Europe.* 4th ed. Thousand Oaks, CA: Sage, 1999.

Lankowski, Carl. "Germany: A Major Player." In Eleanor E. Zeff and Ellen B. Pirro, eds., *The EU and the Member States* (Boulder, CO: Lynne Rienner, 2001), 89–114.

La Palombara, Joseph. *Democracy: Italian Style.* New Haven: Yale University Press, 1987.

———. *Interest Groups in Italian Politics.* Princeton, NJ: Princeton University Press, 1964.

Larres, Klaus, ed. *Germany Since Reunification: The Development of the Berlin Republic.* 2nd ed. Basingstoke: Palgrave, 2001.

"The Latest Battle for the Continent's New Shape." *The Economist* 361 (December 8, 2001), 47–48.

Laurent, Piere-Henri, and Marc Maresceau, eds. *The State of the European Union: Deepening and Widening.* Vol. 4. Boulder, CO: Lynne Rienner, 1998.

Lees, Charles. *The Red-Green Coalition in Germany: Politics, Personalities, and Power.* Manchester: Manchester University Press, 2000.

Legvold, Robert. "Russia's Unformed Foreign Policy." *Foreign Affairs* 80, 5 (September/October 2001), 62–75.

Leibfried, Stephan, and Paul Pierson. "Social Policy: Left to Courts and Markets?" In Helen Wallace and William Wallace, eds., *Policy-Making in the European Union*, 4th ed. (Oxford: Oxford University Press, 2000), 267–292.

———. "Semisovereign Welfare States: Social Policy in a Multitiered Europe." In Stephan Leibfried and Paul Pierson, eds., *European Social Policy* (Washington, DC: Brookings, 1995), 43–77.

Leibfried, Stephan, and Paul Pierson, eds. *European Social Policy: Between Fragmentation and Integration.* Washington, DC: Brookings, 1995.

Leppert, Barbara, et al. *British and German Interests in EU Enlargement: Conflict and Cooperation.* London: Continuum, 2001.

Lequesne, Christian. "French Central Government and the European Political System." In Yves Mény, et al., eds., *Adjusting to Europe: The Impact of the European Union on National Institutions and Policies* (London: Routledge, 1996).

Levitt, Joshua. "A Cigar, a Deck of Cards, and a Sense of Humor." *Financial Times*, September 1, 2003, 4.

———. "Party Confirms Rajoy as Candidate for PM," *Financial Times*, September 3, 2003, 6.

———. "Spanish Premier to Anoint Rajoy as His Successor." *Financial Times*, September 1, 2003, 4.

Levy, Carl. "Introduction: Italian Regionalism in Context." In Carl Levy, ed., *Italian Regionalism: History, Identity, and Politics* (Oxford: Berg, 1996).

Levy, Carl, ed. *Italian Regionalism: History, Identity, and Politics.* Oxford: Berg, 1996.

Lewanski, Rodolfo. "Italian Administration in Transition." *South European Society & Politics* 4, 1 (Summer 1999), 97–131.

Lewis, Jeffrey, "National Interests: Coreper." In John Peterson and Michael Shackleton, eds., *The Institutions of the European Union* (Oxford: Oxford University Press, 2002.)

Lijphart, Arend. "Consociational Democracy." *World Politics* 21 (January 1969), 207–225.

Lijphart, Arend, and M. M. L. Crepaz. "Corporatism and Consensus Democracy in 18 Countries." *British Journal of Political Science* 21 (1991), 235–256.

Lindberg, Leon. *The Political Dynamics of European Integration.* Stanford, CA: Stanford University Press, 1963.

Lindberg, Leon, and Stuart Scheingold. *Europe's Would-Be Polity.* Englewood Cliffs, NJ: Prentice Hall, 1970.

Lindblom, Charles E. *Politics and Markets: The World's Political-Economic Systems.* New York: Basic Books, 1977.

Lindsay, Lawrence B. *Economic Puppetmasters: Lessons from the Halls of Power.* Washington, DC: AEI Press, 1999.

Linz, Juan J. "An Authoritarian Regime: Spain." In Stanley G. Payne, ed., *Politics and Society in Twentieth-Century Spain* (New York: Franklin Watts, 1976), 160–207.

Lippert, Barbara, et al. *British and German Interests in EU Enlargement: Conflict and Cooperation.* London: Continuum, 2001.

Lister, David. "Europol Prepares to Enter a Wider Arena." *The Times*, January 19, 2001.

Loedel, Peter. "Teaching an EU Simulation." *ECSA Review* (Spring 1998), 10–11.

Los-Nowak, Teresa. "Contemporary Government Attitudes Towards the European Union." In Karl Cordell, ed.,

Poland and the European Union (London: Routledge, 2000), Ch. 2.

Lovecy, Jill. "The End of French Exceptionalism." In Robert Elgie, ed., *The Changing French Political System* (London: Frank Cass, 2000), 205–224.

Lovenduski, Joni. "Women and Politics: Minority Representation or Critical Mass?" In Pippa Norris, *Britain Votes 2001* (Oxford: Oxford University Press, 2001), 179–194.

Lovenduski, Joni, and Pippa Norris. "Westminster Women: The Politics of Presence." *Political Studies* 51, 1 (March 2003), 84–102.

Ludlow, Peter. "The Treaty of Nice: Neither Triumph nor Disaster." *ECSA Review* 14, 2 (Spring 2001), 9–10.

Lukas, Richard. *The Forgotten Holocaust: The Poles Under German Occupation.* New York: Hippocrene, 1997.

Lukowski, Jerzy. *The Partitions of Poland: 1772, 1793, 1795.* New York: Longman, 1999.

Lyell, Sarah. "Britain Raises Barriers High Against the Asylum Seekers." *New York Times,* April 3, 2000, A1, A10.

Lynch, Philip. *The Politics of Nationhood: Sovereignty, Britishness, and Conservative Politics.* New York: St. Martin's, 1999.

MacIver, Don, ed. *The Liberal Democrats.* Hemel Hempstead: Prentice Hall, 1996.

MacLennan, Julio Crespo. *Spain and the Process of European Integration, 1957–85.* Basingstoke: Palgrave, 2000.

MacRae, Kenneth, ed. *Consociational Democracy: Political Accommodation in Segmented Societies.* Toronto: McClelland and Stewart, 1974.

McCarthy, Patrick. *The Crisis of the Italian State: From the Origins of the Cold War to the Fall of Berlusconi.* New York: St. Martin's, 1995.

———. "Forza Italia: The New Politics and Old Values of a Changing Italy." In Stephen Gundle and Simon Parker, eds., *The New Italian Republic* (London: Routledge, 1996), Ch. 8.

McCarthy, Patrick, ed. *France-Germany 1983–1993.* New York: St. Martin's, 1993.

McGowan, Francis. "Competition Policy: The Limits of the European Regulatory State." In Helen Wallace and William Wallace, eds., *Policy-Making in the European Union,* 4th ed. (Oxford: Oxford University Press, 2000), 115–147.

McLaughlin, Andrew W., Grant Jordan, and William A. Maloney. "Corporate Lobbying in the European Community." *Journal of Common Market Studies* 31, 2 (June 1993), 191–212.

McNeil, Donald, Jr. "At Least for a Moment, Euphoria on the Right." *New York Times,* April 22, 2002, A6.

———. "French Never-Say-Die Rightist Grasps at Top Spot a 5th Time." *New York Times,* April 19, 2002, A10.

McRoberts, Kenneth. *Catalonia: Nation-Building Without a State.* Oxford: Oxford University Press, 2001.

Maddox, Bronwen. "Jospin Is Not Rewarding Terrorism." *The Times,* August 30, 2000.

Mann, Michael. "EU Farm Policy: France to Voice Protest Against Reforms." *Financial Times,* June 27, 2002, 7.

Marcussen, Martin. "The Power of EMU-Ideas: Reforming Central Banks in Great Britain, France, and Sweden." Paper given at the ECSA Conference, Pittsburgh, PA, June 1999.

Marks, Gary, Liesbet Hooge, and Karen Blank. "European Integration from the 1980s: State-Centric v. Multi-Level Governance." *Journal of Common Market Studies* 34, 4 (1996), 341–378.

Marks, Michael. *The Formation of European Policy in Post-Franco Spain: The Role of Ideas, Interests, and Knowledge.* Avebury, VT: Ashgate, 1997.

Marquis, Christopher. "U.N. Begins Choosing the Judges for New Court." *New York Times,* February 6, 2003, A5.

Mather, Janet. *The European Union and British Democracy: Towards Convergence.* New York: St. Martin's, 2000.

May, Alex. *Britain and Europe Since 1945.* New York: Longman, 1997.

Mazower, Mark. *Dark Continent: Europe's Twentieth Century.* New York: Random House, Vintage, 2000.

Meesen, Karl. "Hedging European Integration: The Maastricht Judgment and the Federal Constitutional Court of Germany." *Fordham International Law Review* 17 (1994), 511–530.

Meller, Paul. "France Confirms Plan to Help Rescue Alstom." *New York Times,* August 7, 2003, W1 and W7.

Mény, Yves, and Andrew Knapp. *Government and Politics in Western Europe.* Oxford: Oxford University Press, 1998.

Mény, Yves, Pier Muller, and Jean-Louis Quermonne, eds. *Adjusting to Europe: The Impact of the European Union on National Institutions and Policies.* London: Routledge, 1996.

"Merger Muddle." *The Economist* 359 (June 23, 2001), 22–23.

Mezey, Michael. *Comparative Legislatures.* Durham, NC: Duke University Press, 1979.

Middlemas, Keith. *Orchestrating Europe.* London: Fontana, 1995.

Mignone, Mario B. *Italy Today: A Country in Transition.* New York: Peter Lang, 1995.

———. "The Battle for Britain? Constitutional Reform and the Election." In Andrew Geddes and Jonathan Tonge, eds., *Labour's Landslide* (Manchester: Manchester University Press, 1997), Ch. 9.

Millard, Frances. *The Anatomy of the New Poland: Post-Communist Politics in Its First Phase.* Brookfield, VT: Edwin Elgar, 1994.

———. *Polish Politics and Society.* London: Routledge, 1999.

Milward, Alan. *The European Rescue of the Nation-State.* Berkeley: University of California Press, 1992.

Minder, Ralph. "Most EU Members Failing to Meet Kyoto Protocol Pledges." *Financial Times*, December 3, 2003, 3.

Mitchell, James. "Devolution." In Bill Jones, ed., *Political Issues in Britain Today*, 5th ed. (Manchester: Manchester University Press, 1999), Ch. 7.

Moeller, Richard. "The German Social Democrats." In John Gaffney, ed., *Political Parties and the European Union* (London: Routledge, 1996), 33–52.

Moïsi, Dominique. "An Awkward Time for France to Take Over." *Financial Times*, November 20, 1995.

———. "Jospin, Too, Wants to Lead Europe." *New Statesman* (January 2, 1998), 17.

———. "The Trouble with France." *Foreign Affairs* 77, 3 (May/June 1998), 94–104.

Molins, J. M., and A. Casademunt. "Pressure Groups and the Articulation of Interests." *West European Politics* 21, 4 (October 1998), 124–146.

Mommsen, Wolfgang J. *Imperial Germany, 1867–1918: Politics, Culture and Society in an Authoritarian State*. London: Edward Arnold, 1995.

Monnet, Jean. *Memoirs*. Translated by Richard Mayne. Garden City, NY: Doubleday, 1978.

Montero, Alfred P. "Decentralizing Democracy: Spain and Brazil in Comparative Perspective." *Comparative Politics* 33, 2 (January 2001), 149–170.

Morata, Francesc. "Spain." In Dietrich Rometsch and Wolfgang Wessels, eds., *The EU and the Member States* (Manchester: Manchester University Press, 1996).

Moravcsik, Andrew. *The Choice for Europe: Social Purpose and State Power from Messina to Maastricht*. Ithaca, NY: Cornell University Press, 1998.

———. "The Death Penalty: Getting Beyond 'Exceptionalism'." *European Studies Newsletter* (January, 2002).

Morgan, Roger, and Caroline Bray, eds. *Partners and Rivals in Western Europe: Britain, France, and Germany*. Aldershot: Gower, 1986.

Morgenthau, Hans. *Politics Among Nations: The Struggle for Power and Peace*. 3rd ed. New York: Alfred A. Knopf, 1964.

Morse, Edward. *Foreign Policy and Interdependence in Gaullist France*. Princeton, NJ: Princeton University Press, 1973.

Moskwa, Wojciech. "Unpopular Polish Left Seeks Rebirth under New PM." Reuters News, July 4, 2004.

Mydans, Seth. "As Expected, Putin Easily Wins a Second Term in Russia." *New York Times*, March 15, 2004, A3.

Nair, Sami. "France: A Crisis of Integration." In Henri Warmenhoven, ed., *Global Studies: Western Europe*, 5th ed. (Guilford, CT: Dushkin/McGraw-Hill, 1997), 219–221.

Negriér, Emmanuel. "The Changing Role of French Local Government." In Robert Elgie, ed., *The Changing French Political System* (London: Frank Cass, 2000), 120–140.

Nelkin, David. "A Legal Revolution? The Judges and Tangentopoli." In Stephen Gundle and Simon Parker, *The New Italian Republic* (London: Routledge, 1996), 191–205.

Newell, James. *Parties and Democracy in Italy*. Aldershot: Ashgate, 2000.

Newell, James, ed. *The Italian General Election of 2001*. Manchester: Manchester University Press, 2002.

Newell, James, and Hilary Partridge. "Conclusion." In James Newell, ed., *The Italian General Election of 2001* (Manchester: Manchester University Press, 2002), 238–244.

Newhouse, John. *Europe Adrift*. New York: Pantheon, 1997.

———. *Imperial America: The Bush Assault on the World Order*. New York: Alfred A. Knopf, 2003.

"Nice Uncle Gerhard and the Little 'Uns." *The Economist* 358 (February 3, 2001), 50.

Nollert, Michael, in collaboration with Nicola Fielder. "Lobbying for a Europe of Big Business: The European Roundtable of Industrialists." In Volker Bornschier, ed., *State-Building in Europe: The Revitalization of Western European Integration* (Cambridge: Cambridge University Press, 2000), 187–209.

Norman, Peter. "Defiant in Defending His Views on Europe." *Financial Times*, March 10, 2002.

Norris, Pippa, ed. *Britain Votes 2001*. Oxford: Oxford University Press, 2001.

Northcutt, Wayne. *Mitterrand: A Political Biography*. New York: Holmes & Meier, 1996.

Norton, Philip. *The British Polity*. 3rd ed. New York: Longman, 1994.

———. "The Conservative Party: Is There Anyone Out There?" In Anthony King, ed., *Britain at the Polls, 2001* (New York: Chatham House, 2002), 68–94.

Norton, Philip, ed. *National Parliaments and the European Union*. Portland, OR: Frank Cass, 1996.

———. *Parliaments and Citizens in Western Europe*. London: Frank Cass, 2002.

Nugent, Neill, ed. *At the Heart of the Union: Studies of the European Commission*. Basingstoke: Macmillan, 2000.

Nugent, Neill. *The European Commission*. Basingstoke: Palgrave, 2001.

Nye, Joseph S. *The Paradox of American Power: Why the World's Only Superpower Can't Go It Alone*. Oxford: Oxford University Press, 2002.

"An Open Letter to Silvio Berlusconi." *The Economist* 368 (August 2, 2003), 23–27.

Osser, Bernard. "Eastern Poland's Farmers Urge No in EU Referendum." *Agence France Presse*, June 4, 2003.

Padgett, Stephen, ed. *Adenauer to Kohl: The Development of the German Chancellorship*. Washington, DC: Georgetown University Press, 1994.

———. "Chancellors and the Chancellorship." In Stephen Padgett, ed. *Adenauer to Kohl: The Development of the German Chancellorship*. (Washington, DC: Georgetown University Press, 1994), 1–19.

Palacio, Ana. "EU Divisions over Iraq Can Be Mended." *Financial Times*, February 17, 2003, 13.

———. "Why Batasuna Must Be Banned." *Financial Times*, September 3, 2002, 15.

Panayi, Panikos. "Racial Exclusionism in the New Germany." In Klaus Larres, ed., *Germany Since Reunification: The Development of the Berlin Republic*, 2nd ed. (Basingstoke: Palgrave, 2001), 129–148.

Paniagua Soto, Juan L. "Spain: A Fledgling Parliament, 1977–97." *Parliamentary Affairs* 50, 3 (July 1997), 410–422.

Parker, George. "Atmosphere of Resignation as Leaders Walk Away." *Financial Times*, December 15, 2003, 4.

———. "Candidates Start Lobbying for Europe's Toughest Job." *Financial Times*, November 4, 2003, 14.

———. "Leaders to Insist on EU Treaty Deadline." *Financial Times*, March 25, 2003, 8.

———. "Ministers Conduct Late-Night Burial for EU Fiscal Framework." *Financial Times*, November 26, 2003, 4.

Parker, George, and Tony Barber. "Prodi Prepared to Stay as EU President If EU Leaders Ask." *Financial Times*, April 3, 2003, 6.

Parker, George, and Judy Dempsey. "After Iraq." *Financial Times*, April 16, 2003, 13.

Parker, George, Judy Dempsey, and Hugh Williamson. "Spain and Poland May Pay Financial Price." *Financial Times*, December 15, 2003, 4.

Parker, George, and Daniel Dombey. "'Not Perfect but More than We Could Have Hoped For': Europe's Draft Constitution." *Financial Times*, June 20, 2003, 13.

Parker, Simon. "Electoral Reform and Political Change in Italy." In Stephen Gundle and Simon Parker, eds., *The New Italian Republic* (London: Routledge, 1996), 40–56.

"Parliament in Italy Passes Immunity Law for Berlusconi." *New York Times*, June 19, 2003, A11.

Partridge, Hillary. *Italian Politics Today*. Manchester: Manchester University Press, 1995.

Pasquino, Gianfranco. "Berlusconi's Victory: The Italian General Elections of 2001." *South European Society & Politics* 6, 1 (Summer 2001), 125–137.

Paterson, William. "From the Bonn to the Berlin Republic." In *German Politics* 9, 1 (January 2000).

———. "The German Christian Democrats." In John Gaffney, ed., *Political Parties and the European Union* (London: Routledge, 1996), 53–70.

Pazzi, Roberto. "Germans Are from Mars, Italians Are from Venus." *New York Times*, July 13, 2003, IV, 13.

Pederson, Thomas. *Germany, France, and the Integration of Europe: A Realist Interpretation*. London: Pinter, 1998.

Pederzoli, Patrizia, and Carlo Guarnieri. "Italy: A Case of Judicial Democracy?" *International Social Science Journal* 152 (June 1997), 253–270.

Peel, Quentin. "Bavaria's PM Exposes Split on European Union." *Financial Times*, November 3, 1993, 1.

———. "An Empire in Denial Opts Out." *Financial Times*, August 19, 2002, 11.

———. "Europe's Constitution Misses Its Moment." *Financial Times*, June 17, 2003, 15.

Perkins, Anne. "Eurosceptics Take Charge." *The Guardian*, September 15, 2001.

Peters, B. Guy, and Christian Hunold. *European Politics Reconsidered*. 2nd ed. New York: Holmes & Meier, 1999.

Peterson, John, and Michael Shackleton, eds. *The Institutions of the European Union*. Oxford: Oxford University Press, 2002.

Pfaff, William. "Europe's Unification Debate Needs the Sound of Fresh Voices." *International Herald Tribune*, January 11, 2001, 6.

Piattoni, Simona, ed. *Clientelism, Interests, and Democratic Representation*. Cambridge: Cambridge University Press, 2001.

Pierson, Paul. "The Path to European Integration: A Historical Institutionalist Analysis." *Comparative Political Studies* 29 (April 1996), 123–163.

Pilkington, Colin. *Devolution in Britain Today*. Manchester: Manchester University Press, 2003.

Pinder, John. *The Building of the European Union*. 3rd ed. Oxford: Oxford University Press, 1998.

———. *The European Union: A Very Short Introduction*. Oxford: Oxford University Press, 2001.

"Poland: Jobs Leave." *The Economist* 358 (March 31, 2001), 99.

"Poland: New Leader Wins Vote." *New York Times*, June 25, 2004, A6.

"Poland: A Step Toward Europe." *New York Times*, March 22, 2002, A6.

Pond, Elizabeth. *Friendly Fire: The Near-Death of the Transatlantic Alliance*. Pittsburgh, PA: European Union Studies Association, 2003.

Preston, Paul. *Franco: A Biography*. New York: HarperCollins, 1994.

"Proving the Case for a Constitution." *Financial Times*, December 15, 2003.

Pryce, Sue. *Presidentializing the Premiership*. New York: St. Martin's, 1997.

Pulzer, Peter. "The Devil They Know: The German Federal Election of 2002." *West European Politics* 26, 2 (April 2003), 153–164.

Putnam, Robert D., with Robert Leonardi and Raffaella Y. Nanetti. *Making Democracy Work: Civic Traditions in Modern Italy*. Princeton, NJ: Princeton University Press, 1993.

"Race and Poverty: Down and Out Up North." *The Economist* 361 (December 15, 2001), 47–48.

Rae, Douglas. *The Analysis of Political Cleavages*. New Haven, CT: Yale University Press, 1970.

———. *The Political Consequences of Electoral Laws*. Rev. ed. New Haven, CT: Yale University Press, 1971.

Rasmussen, Jorgen. "Britain: Aloof and Skeptical." In Eleanor E. Zeff and Ellen B. Pirro, eds., *The EU and the Member States* (Boulder, CO: Lynne Rienner, 2001), 145–174.

Raunio, Tapio. "Political Interests: The EP's Party Groups." In John Peterson and Michael Shackleton, eds., *The Institutions of the European Union* (Oxford: Oxford University Press, 2002), 257–276.

Rawnsley, Andrew. "A Caretaker, Not a Saviour." *The Observer*, November 2, 2003.

———. "How to Deal with the American Goliath." *The Observer*, February 24, 2002.

Rebérioux, Antoine. "European Style of Corporate Governance at the Crossroads: The Role of Worker Involvement." *Journal of Common Market Studies* 40, 1 (March 2001), 111–134.

Reitan, Earl A. *Tory Radicalism: Margaret Thatcher, John Major, and the Transformation of Modern Britain 1970–1997.* Lanham, MD: Rowman and Littlefield, 1997.

Remington, Thomas F. *Politics in Russia.* New York: Longman, 1999.

Rentoul, John. *Tony Blair.* London: Warner Books, 1996.

Rhodes, Martin. "An Awkward Alliance: France, Germany, and Social Policy." In Douglas Webber, ed., *The Franco-German Relationship in the European Union* (London: Routledge, 1999), 130–147.

———. "Populism Will Pull Italy's Coalition Apart." *Financial Times*, July 4, 2003, 13.

Rhodes, Rod. "The Civil Service." In Anthony Seldon, ed., *The Blair Effect* (London: Little, Brown, 2001), 95–115.

Richter, Michaela W. "The German Party State: A Reassessment." In Christopher Allen, ed., *Transformation of the German Political Party System: Institutional Crisis or Democratic Renewal?* (New York: Berghahn, 1999), 62–98.

Riddell, Peter. "Blair as Prime Minister." In Anthony Seldon, ed., *The Blair Effect* (London: Little, Brown, 2001), 21–42.

Riding, Alan. "Jospin's Loss Reveals a Left That Is Losing Its Platform." *New York Times*, April 22, 2002, A6.

Rieger, Elmar. "The Common Agricultural Policy: Politics Against Markets." In Helen Wallace and William Wallace, eds., *Policy-Making in the European Union*, 4th ed. (Oxford: Oxford University Press, 2000), 179–210.

Risse, Thomas. "A European Identity? Europeanization and the Evolution of Nation-State Identities." In Maria Green Cowles, et al., eds, *Transforming Europe* (Ithaca, NY: Cornell University Press, 2001), 198–216.

Rizzuto, Franco. "France: Something of a Rehabilitation." *Parliamentary Affairs* 50, 3 (July 1997), 373–339.

———. "The French Parliament and the EU: Loosening the Constitutional Straitjacket." In Philip Norton, ed., *National Parliaments and the European Union* (Portland, OR: Frank Cass, 1996), 46–59.

Robbins, Keith. "Britain and Europe: Devolution and Foreign Policy." *International Affairs* 74 (January 1998), 105–118.

Roberts, Geoffrey K. *German Politics Today.* Manchester: Manchester University Press, 2000.

———. "'Taken at the Flood'? The German General Election 2002." *Government and Opposition* 38, 1 (Winter 2003), 53–72.

Rodrigo, Fernando. "Western Alignment: Spain's Security Policy." In Richard Gillespie, et al., eds., *Democratic Spain* (London: Routledge, 1993), Ch. 4.

Rohrschneider, Robert. *Learning Democracy: Democratic and Economic Values in Unified Germany.* Oxford: Oxford University Press, 1999.

Rokkan, Stein, et al., eds., *Citizens, Elections, Parties: Approaches to the Comparative Study of the Processes of Development.* New York: David McKay, 1970.

Rometsch, Dietrich, and Wolfgang Wessels, eds. *The European Union and Member States: Towards Institutional Fusion?* Manchester: Manchester University Press, 1996.

Rosamond, Ben. *Theories of European Integration.* New York: St. Martin's, 2000.

Rose, Richard. *Do Parties Make a Difference?* 2nd ed. Chatham, NJ: Chatham House, 1984.

———. *The Problem of Party Government.* London: Penguin, 1976.

Ross, George. *Jacques Delors and European Integration.* Oxford: Oxford University Press, 1995.

Rostowski, Jacek. "When Should the Central Europeans Join EMU?" *International Affairs* 79, 5 (October 2003), 993–1008.

Rothstein, Edward. "Europe's Constitution: All Hail the Bureaucracy." *New York Times*, July 5, 2003, A17.

Roy, Joaquín and Aimee Kanner. "Spain and Portugal: Betting on Europe." In Eleanor E. Zeff and Ellen B. Pirro, eds., *The EU and the Member States* (Boulder, CO: Westview, 2001), 235–266.

Rusconi, Gian Enrico. "Will Italy Remain a Nation?" In Mark Donovan, ed., *Italy*, vol. 1 (Dartmouth: Ashgate, 1998), 477–490.

Ruzza, Carlo, and Oliver Schmidtke. "Toward a Modern Right." In Stephen Gundle and Simon Parker, *The New Italian Republic* (London: Routledge, 1996), Ch. 9.

Sa'adah, Anne. *Contemporary France: A Democratic Education.* Lanham, MD: Rowman and Littlefield, 2003.

Sabetti, Filippo. *The Search for Good Government: Understanding the Paradox of Italian Democracy.* Montreal and Kingston: McGill-Queens University Press, 2000.

Sabine, George H. *A History of Political Theory.* 4th ed. Hinsdale, IL: Dryden, 1973.

Safran, William. *The French Polity.* 5th ed. New York: Longman, 1998.

———. "The Socialists, Jospin, and the Mitterrand Legacy." In Michael Lewis-Beck, ed., *How France Votes* (New York: Chatham House, 2000), 14–41.

Safire, William. "The Russian Reversion." *New York Times*, December 10, 2003, A29.

Sage, Adam. "Bombing Follows Corsica Initiative." *The Times*, August 18, 2000.

Sains, Ariane. "Seeing Green: Forecasting Europe's Environmental Future." In E. Gene Frankland, ed., *Global Studies: Europe*, 7th ed. (Guilford, CT: McGraw-Hill/Dushkin, 2001), 204–210.

Sánchez de Dios, Manuel. "Executive Parliamentary Control." In Amparo Almacha Barbado, ed., *Spain and EC Membership Evaluated* (London: Pinter, 1993).

Sandholtz, Wayne, and John Zysman. "1992: Recasting the European Bargain." *World Politics* 42, 1 (1992), 95–128.

Sanger, David E. "Blow to Bush: Ally Rejected." *New York Times*, March 15, 2004, A1 and A11.

Sarkar, Saral. *Green-Alternative Politics in West Germany, Volume 1: The New Social Movements*. New York: United Nations University Press, 1993.

Sartori, Giovanni. *Parties and Party Systems: A Framework for Analysis*. Cambridge: Cambridge University Press, 1976.

Sassoon, Donald. *Contemporary Italy: Economy, Society, and Politics Since 1945*. 2nd ed. New York: Longman, 1997.

Savage, Stephen P., and Rob Adkinson, eds. *Public Policy Under Blair*. Basingstoke: Palgrave, 2001.

Sbragia, Alberta. "Environmental Policy: Economic Constraints and External Pressures." In Helen Wallace and William Wallace, eds., *Policy-Making in the European Union*, 4th ed. (Oxford: Oxford University Press, 2000), 293–316.

———. "Italy Pays for Europe: Political Leadership, Political Choice, and Institutional Adaptation." In Maria Green Cowles, et al., ed., *Transforming Europe* (Ithaca, NY: Cornell University Press, 2001), 79–96.

Sbragia, Alberta, ed. *Euro-Politics: Institutions and Policymaking in the "New" European Community*. Washington, DC: Brookings, 1992.

Schain, Martin A. "The Impact of the French National Front on the French Political System." In Martin Schain, Aristide Zolberg, and Patrick Hossay, eds., *Shadows over Europe: The Development and Impact of the Extreme Right in Western Europe* (New York: Palgrave Macmillan, 2002), 223–244.

Schain, Martin, Aristide Zolberg, and Patrick Hossay, eds. *Shadows over Europe: The Development and Impact of the Extreme Right in Western Europe*. New York: Palgrave Macmillan, 2002.

Schild, Joachim. "National v. European Identities? French and Germans in the European Multi-Level System." *Journal of Common Market Studies* 39, 2 (June 2001), 331–351.

Schmidt, Vivien A. "The Changing Dynamics of State-Society Relations in the Fifth Republic." In Robert Elgie, ed., *The Changing French Political System* (London: Frank Cass, 2000), 141–165.

———. *Democratizing France: The Political and Administrative History of Decentralization*. Cambridge: Cambridge University Press, 1991.

———. *From State to Market? The Transformation of French Business and Government*. New York: Columbia University Press, 1996.

———. "Loosening the Ties that Bind: The Impact of European Integration on French Government and Its Relationship to Business." *Journal of Common Market Studies* 34, 2 (June 1996), 223–252.

Schofield, Hugh. "Key Points of the EU's Historic Agreement at Nice." Agence France Presse, December 11, 2000.

Sciolino, Elaine. "Ban Religious Attire in School, French Panel Says." *New York Times*, December 12, 3002, A1.

———. "Debate Begins in France on Religion in the Schools." *New York Times*, February 4, 2004, A8.

———. "European Union Turns Down Turkey's Bid for Membership." *New York Times*, December 13, 2002, A12.

———. "Following Attacks, Spain's Governing Party Is Beaten." *New York Times*, March 15, 2004, A1 and A10.

Seaford, Helen. "The Future of Multi-Ethnic Britain: An Opportunity Missed." *The Political Quarterly* 72, 1 (January–March 2001), 107–113.

Sedelmeier, Ulrich. "Eastern Enlargement: Risk, Rationality, and Role-Compliance." In Maria Green Cowles and Michael Smith, eds., *The State of the European Union*, vol. 5 (Oxford: Oxford University Press, 2000), 164–185.

Seldon, Anthony, ed. *The Blair Effect: The Blair Government 1997–2001*. London: Little, Brown, 2001.

Seyd, Patrick. "Tony Blair and New Labour." In Anthony King, ed., *New Labour Triumphs* (Chatham, NJ: Chatham House, 1998), 49–74.

Shackleton, Michael. "The European Parliament." In John Peterson and Michael Shackleton, eds., *The Institutions of the European Union* (Oxford: Oxford University Press, 2002), 95–117.

Share, Donald. "Politics in Spain." In Gabriel A. Almond, Russell J. Dalton, and G. Bingham Powell, eds. *European Politics Today*, 2nd ed. (New York: Longman, 2001), 253–306.

Shepherd, Geoffrey. "A Comparison of the Three Economies." In Roger Morgan and Caroline Bray, eds., *Partners and Rivals in Western Europe: Britain, France, and Germany* (Aldershot: Gower, 1986).

Shepherd, Mark, and Roger Scully. "The European Parliament: Of Barriers and Removed Citizens." In Philip Norton, ed., *Parliament and Citizens in Western Europe* (London: Frank Cass, 2002), 153–177.

Sherrington, Philippa. *The Council of Ministers: Political Authority in the European Union*. London: Pinter, 2000.

Shields, James. "The French Gaullists." In John Gaffney, ed., *Political Parties and The European Union* (London: Routledge, 1996), 86–109.

Shull, Tad. *Redefining Red and Green: Ideology and Strategy in European Political Ecology*. Albany, NY: SUNY Press, 1999.

Siaroff, Alan. "Corporatism in 24 Industrial Democracies: Meaning and Measurement." *European Journal of Political Research* 36, 2 (October 1999), 175–205.

Silvia, Stephen J. "Reform Gridlock and the Role of the Bundesrat in German Politics." *West European Politics* 22, 2 (April 1999), 62–81.

Silvia, Stephen J., and Aaron Beers Sampson. "The New Abolitionism: American or European Exceptionalism Regarding the Death Penalty." *European Studies Newsletter* (January, 2002).

Simonian, Haig. *The Privileged Partnership: Franco-German Relationships in the European Community, 1969–1984*. Oxford: Oxford University Press, 1985.

Skidelsky, Robert. *Thatcherism*. Cambridge: Basil Blackwell, 1988.

Skocpol, Theda. *States and Social Revolutions*. Cambridge: Cambridge University Press, 1979.

Sloam, James. "'Responsibility for Europe': The EU Policy of the German Social Democrats Since Unification." *German Politics* 12, 1 (April 2003), 59–78.

Smith, Adam. *The Wealth of Nations*. New York: Dutton, 1957.

Smith, Dennis Mack. *Italy: A Modern History*. Ann Arbor: University of Michigan Press, 1969.

Smith, Elizabeth T., and Mark A. Boyer. "Designing In-Class Simulations." *PS: Political Science & Politics* 29 (December 1996), 690–694.

Smith, Julie. "How European Are European Elections?" In John Gaffney, ed., *Political Parties and the EU* (London: Routledge, 1996), 275–290.

Smith, Michael E. "EU Enlargement, Domestic Politics, and Post-Communist Transitions: The Impact of EMU on the Czech Republic, Hungary, and Poland." Paper presented at the annual meeting of the International Studies Association, New Orleans, LA, March 2002.

Smith, Rhea Marsh. *Spain: A Modern History*. Ann Arbor: University of Michigan Press, 1965.

Smith, Thomas W. "The European Union and Human Rights Reform in Turkey." Paper presented at the annual conference of the International Studies Association, New Orleans, LA, March 2002.

Søe, Christian. "Neoliberal Stirrings: The 'New' FDP and Some Old Habits." In Conradt, et al., eds., *Power Shift in Germany* (New York: Berghahn, 2000), 59–79.

Solsten, Eric. "Government and Politics." In Eric Solsten and Sandra Meditz, eds., *Finland: A Country Study*, 2nd ed. (Washington, DC: U. S. Government, 1990).

Solsten, Eric, and Sandra Meditz, eds. *Finland: A Country Study*. 2nd ed. Washington, DC: U. S. Government, 1990.

Sontheimer, Kurt. *The Government and Politics of West Germany*. New York: Praeger, 1973.

Sorkin, Andrew Ross. "Failure to Acquire Honeywell Is Sour Finish for G.E. Chief." *New York Times*, July 3, 2001, A1 and C4.

"Special Report: Europe's Constitution." *The Economist* (June 21, 2003), 51–54.

"Special Report: Poland and the EU." *The Economist* (August 30, 2003), 16–18.

"Special Report: The Russian Elections." *The Economist* (December 13, 2003, 24–28.

Spinelli, Altiero. *Towards the European Union*. Florence: European University Institute, 1983.

Stadtmuller, Elzbieta. "Polish Perceptions of the European Union in the 1990s." In Karl Cordell, ed., *Poland and the European Union* (London: Routledge, 2000), Ch. 3.

Staunton, Dennis. "The Mrs. Merkel Show." *The Observer*, April 30, 2000.

Steiner, Jürg. *European Democracies*. 3rd ed. New York: Longman, 1995.

Stephens, Philip. "Europe Would Be Foolish to Leave Turkey Out in the Cold." *Financial Times*, February 27, 2004, 13.

———. "The Treasury Under Labour." In Anthony Seldon, ed., *The Blair Effect* (London: Little, Brown, 2001).

Stevens, Christopher. "EU Policy for the Banana Market." In Helen Wallace and William Wallace, eds., *Policy-Making in the European Union*, 3rd ed. (Oxford: Oxford University Press, 1996), 325–352.

Stirk, Peter, and David Willis, eds. *Shaping Postwar Europe: European Unity and Disunity 1945–1957*. New York: St. Martin's, 1991.

Stone, Alec. *The Birth of Judicial Politics in France: The Constitutional Council in Comparative Perspective*. Oxford: Oxford University Press, 1992.

Story, Jonathan. "Spain's External Relations Redefined: 1975–89." In Richard Gillespie, Fernando Rodrigo, and Jonathan Story, eds., *Democratic Spain: Reshaping External Relations in a Changing World* (London: Routledge, 1993), 31–44.

Study Group on the Conditions of Excellence in American Higher Education. *Involvement in Learning: Realizing the Potential of American Higher Education*. Washington, DC: National Institute of Education/U. S. Department of Education, 1984.

Stürmer, Michael. *The German Empire, 1870–1918*. New York: Modern Library, 2000.

Sullivan, Andrew. "There Will Always Be an England." *New York Times Magazine*, February 21, 1999, 38–45+.

"A Survey of Spain." *The Economist* 357 (November 25, 2000).

Szarka, Joseph. "The Parties of the French 'Plural Left': An Uneasy Complementarity." In Robert Elgie, ed., *The*

Changing French Political System (London: Frank Cass, 2000), 20–37.

Szczerbiak, Aleks. "Polish Public Opinion: Explaining Declining Support for EU Membership." *Journal of Common Market Studies* 39, 1 (March 2001), 105–122.

Tambini, Damian. *Nationalism in Italian Politics.* London: Routledge, 2001.

Tarrow, Sidney. *Power in Movement: Social Movements and Contentious Politics.* Cambridge: Cambridge University Press, 1994.

Tavernise, Sabrina. "Handful of Corporate Raiders Transform Russia's Economy." *New York Times,* August 13, 2002, A1, A6.

Taylor, Robert. "Employment Relations Policy." In Anthony Selden, ed., *The Blair Effect* (London: Little, Brown, 2001), 244–269.

Tewes, Henning. "Between Deepening and Widening: Role Conflict in Germany's Enlargement Policy." *West European Politics* 21, 2 (April 1998), 117–133.

Thatcher, Margaret. *The Downing Street Years.* New York: HarperCollins, 1993.

Thaysen, Uwe. *The Bundesrat, the Länder, and German Federalism.* Washington, DC: American Institute for Contemporary German Studies, Johns Hopkins, 1994.

Theakston, Kevin. *The Civil Service Since 1945.* Oxford: Blackwell, 1995.

Thomas, Hugh. *The Spanish Civil War.* Rev. ed. New York: Harper & Row, 1977.

Thomson, David. *Democracy in France Since 1870.* New York: Oxford University Press, 1964.

Thorpe, Andrew. *A History of the British Labour Party.* 2nd ed. Basingstoke: Palgrave, 2001.

Tiersky, Ronald. "France, the CFSP, and NATO." In Pierre-Henri Laurent and Marc Maresceau, eds., *The State of the European Union: Deepening and Widening,* vol. 4 (Boulder, CO: Lynne Rienner, 1998), 177–190.

Tilly, Charles. *The Contentious French: Four Centuries of Popular Struggle.* Cambridge: Cambridge University Press, 1986.

Tinder, Glenn. *Political Thinking: The Perennial Questions.* 5th ed. New York: HarperCollins, 1991.

Toland, John. *Adolf Hitler.* New York: Doubleday, 1976.

"Toughening Up." *The Economist* (September 20, 2003).

Traxler, Franz, and Philippe G. Schmitter. "The Emerging Euro-Polity and Organized Interests." *European Journal of International Relations* 1 (June 1995), 191–218.

Traynor, Ian, and Martin Walker. "Solana to Run Joint Security Policy for Bickering EU." *The Guardian,* June 5, 1999.

Tsoukalis, Loukas. "Economic and Monetary Union: Political Conviction and Economic Uncertainty." In Helen Wallace and William Wallace, eds., *Policy-Making in the European Union,* 4th ed. (Oxford: Oxford University Press, 2000), 149–178.

——. *What Kind of Europe?* Oxford: Oxford University Press, 2003.

"Turkish Reforms: Great—If They Really Happen." *The Economist* 364 (August 10, 2002), 45–46.

Uçarer, Emek. "Justice and Home Affairs in the Aftermath of September 11: Opportunities and Challenges." *EUSA Review* 15, 2 (Spring 2002), 1–4.

"Undoing Britain." *The Economist* (November 6, 1999), 6–7.

Urwin, Derek W. *The Community of Europe: A History of European Integration Since 1945.* New York: Longman, 1991.

Van der Meer, Marc. "Spain." In Bernard Ebbinghaus and Jelle Visser, eds., *The Societies of Europe: Trade Unions in Western Europe Since 1945* (Basingstoke: Macmillan, 2000), 573–603.

Van Oudenaren, John. *Uniting Europe: European Integration and the Post-Cold War World.* Lanham, MD: Rowman and Littlefield, 2000.

Vanaclocha Bellver, Francisco J., and Miguel Angel Ruiz de Azúaa Antón. "The Impact of the Electoral System of the European Parliament on Spain." In Amparo Almarcha Barbado, *Spain and EC Membership Evaluated* (London: Pinter, 1992), 233–245.

Vannicelli, Primo. *Italy, NATO, and the European Community.* Cambridge, MA: Harvard University Center for International Affairs, 1974.

Varsori, Antonio. "Italy and the European Defence Community." In Peter Stirk and David Willis, eds., *Shaping Postwar Europe: European Unity and Disunity 1947–1957* (New York: St. Martin's, 1991), 100–111.

——. "Italy's Policy Towards European Integration (1947–58)." In Christopher Duggan and Christopher Wagstaff, eds., *Italy in the Cold War* (Oxford: Berg, 1995), 47–64.

Verdun, Amy. "Monetary Integration in Europe: Ideas and Evolution." In Maria Green Cowles and Michael Smith, eds., *The State of the European Union,* vol. 5 (Oxford: Oxford University Press, 2000), 91–109.

Verzichelli, Luca, and Francesco Zucchini. "The New Parliament and the Start of a Decisive Legislature." In James Newell, ed., *The Italian General Election of 2001* (Manchester: Manchester University Press), 217–237.

Visser, Jelle. "Italy." In Bernhard Ebbinghaus and Jelle Visser, eds., *The Societies of Europe: Trade Unions in Western Europe Since 1945* (Basingstoke: Macmillan, 2000), 371–428.

Visser, Jelle, Patrick Dufour, René Mouriaux, and Françoise Subileau. "France." In Bernhard Ebbinghaus and Jelle Visser, eds., *The Societies of Europe: Trade Unions in Western Europe Since 1945* (Basingstoke: Macmillan, 2000), 237–277.

Voigt, Karsten D. "Common Roots—a Common Future? Transatlantic Partnership in the Twenty-first Century."

Address at the University of Tampa, Tampa, FL, March 24, 2003.

Volcansek, Mary L. "Political Power and Judicial Review in Italy." *Comparative Political Studies* 26, 4 (January 1994), 492–509.

Wagstyl, Stefan. "Failure May Have Impact on EU's Long-Term Future." *Financial Times,* December 15, 2003, 4.

———. "Polish Political Leaders United in Approval of Miller's Stance." *Financial Times,* December 15, 2003, 5.

Walker, Martin. "Rome-Bonn Deal Puts Prodi on Course for EC Presidency." *The Guardian,* March 23, 1999.

Walker, Martin, and Ian Traynor. "Leaders Unite to Pick Italy's Prodi." *The Guardian,* March 25, 1999.

Wallace, Helen. "At Odds with Europe." *Political Studies* 45 (September 1997), 677–686.

———. "The Institutional Setting." In Helen Wallace and William Wallace, eds., *Policy-Making in the European Union,* 4th ed. (Oxford: Oxford University Press, 2000), 28–35.

———. "Relations Between the European Union and British Administration." In Yves Mény, et al., eds., *Adjusting to Europe* (London: Routledge, 1996).

Wallace, Helen, and William Wallace, eds. *Policy-Making in the European Union,* 3rd ed. Oxford: Oxford University Press, 1996.

———, eds. *Policy-Making in the European Union.* 4th ed. Oxford: Oxford University Press, 2000.

Walsh, James. *European Monetary Integration & Domestic Politics: Britain, France, and Italy.* Boulder, CO: Lynne Rienner, 2000.

Walzer, Michael. "Town Meetings and Workers' Control." In Terence Ball and Richard Dagger, eds. *Ideals and Ideologies,* 2nd ed. (New York HarperCollins, 1995), 56–65.

Warmenhoven, Henri, ed. *Global Studies: Western Europe.* 6th ed. Guilford, CT: Dushkin/McGraw-Hill, 1999.

———, ed. *Global Studies: Western Europe.* 5th ed. Guilford, CT: Dushkin/McGraw-Hill, 1997.

Watt, Nicholas, and Kevin Maguire. "A Leap in the Dark." *The Guardian,* September 14, 2001.

Webber, Douglas. "Agricultural Policy: The Hard Core." In Douglas Webber, ed., *The Franco-German Relationship in the European Union* (London: Routledge, 1999), 111–129.

Webber, Douglas, ed. *The Franco-German Relationship in the European Union.* London: Routledge, 1999.

Weiler, J. H. H. "Does Europe Need a Constitution? Reflections on Demos, Telos, and the German Maastricht Decision." *European Law Journal* (1995), 219–258.

Wessels, Wolfgang. "The EC Council: The Community's Decision-Making Center." In Robert Keohane and Stanley Hoffman, eds., *The New European Community: Decisionmaking and Institutional Change* (Boulder, CO: Westview, 1991), 133–154.

White, Stephen. *Russia's New Politics: The Management of a Postcommunist Society.* Cambridge: Cambridge University Press, 2000.

White, Stephen, Ian McAllister, and Margot Light. "Enlargement and the New Outsiders." *Journal of Common Market Studies* 40, 1 (March 2002).

Whittam, John. *Fascist Italy.* Manchester: Manchester University Press, 1995.

Williams, Charles. *Adenauer: The Father of the New Germany.* New York: Wiley, 2000.

Williams, Philip M. *Crisis and Compromise: Politics in the Fourth Republic.* Garden City, NY: Doubleday, 1966.

Willis, F. Roy. *France, Germany, and the New Europe.* Rev. ed. Stanford, CA: Stanford University Press, 1968.

———. *Italy Chooses Europe.* New York: Oxford University Press, 1971.

Wintour, Patrick. "Howard Wins Over Tory Fundraisers." *The Observer,* December 12, 2003.

Wintour, Patrick, and Clare Dyer. "Cabinet Reshuffle; Ministers Shun U.S. Model for Supreme Court." *The Guardian,* June 16, 2003, 4.

Wolf, Martin. "The Trouble with Living a Longer, More Fulfilled Life." *Financial Times,* January 7, 2004, 13.

Wollheim, Richard. "Democracy: Its History." In James A. Gould and Willis H. Truitt, eds., *Political Ideologies* (New York: Macmillan, 1973), 30–37.

Wood, D. M., and Philip Norton. "Do Candidates Matter? Constituency-Specific Vote Changes for Incumbent MPs, 1983–1987." *Political Studies* 40 (May 1992), 227–238.

Wood, Stephen. *Germany, Europe, and the Persistence of Nations.* Aldershot: Ashgate, 1998.

Woodhouse, C. M. *British Foreign Policy Since the Second World War.* London: Hutchinson, 1961.

Wright, Vincent. "The Fifth Republic: From the *Droit de l'état* to the *état de droit.*" In Robert Elgie, ed., *The Changing French Political System* (London: Frank Cass, 2000), 96–119.

Wurzel, Rüdiger. "Flying into Unexpected Turbulence: The German EU Presidency In the Environmental Field." *German Politics* 9, 3 (December 2000), 23–42.

Yanuz, M. Hakan. "Turkey's Fault Lines and the Crisis of Kemalism." *Current History* 99 (January 2000), 34.

Young, Alisdair, and Helen Wallace. "The Single Market: A New Approach to Policy." In Helen Wallace and William Wallace, eds., *Policy-Making in the European Union,* 4th ed. (Oxford: Oxford University Press, 2000), 85–114.

Young, Hugo. *One of Us.* London: Macmillan, 1989.

Young, John W. *Britain and European Unity, 1945–1992.* New York: Longman, 1997.

Zaborowski, Marcin, and Kerry Longhurst. "America's Protégé in the East? The Emergence of Poland as a

Regional Leader." *International Affairs* 79, 5 (October 2003), 1009–1028.

"Zapatero Formará Gobierno en Solitario con Acuerdos Puntuales." *El Pais*, March 15, 2004.

Zaretsky, Robert D. "Neither Left nor Right nor Straight Ahead: Recent Books on Fascism in France." *The Journal of Modern History* 73, 1 (March 2001), 118–132.

Zeff, Eleanor E., and Ellen B. Pirro, eds. *The European Union and the Member States*. Boulder, CO: Lynne Rienner, 2001.

Zielonka, Jan. "How New Enlarged Borders Will Reshape the European Union." *Journal of Common Market Studies* 39, 3 (September 2001), 507–536.

Zürcher, Erik. *Turkey: A Modern History*. London: I. B. Tauris, 1997.

INDEX